T0142355

Lecture Notes in Computer Science 12063

More information about this series at http://www.springer.com/series/7410

Matthew Bernhard · Andrea Bracciali ·
L. Jean Camp · Shin'ichiro Matsuo ·
Alana Maurushat · Peter B. Rønne ·
Massimiliano Sala (Eds.)

Financial Cryptography and Data Security

FC 2020 International Workshops, AsiaUSEC, CoDeFi, VOTING, and WTSC
Kota Kinabalu, Malaysia, February 14, 2020
Revised Selected Papers

 Springer

Editors
Matthew Bernhard
University of Michigan–Ann Arbor
Ann Arbor, USA

L. Jean Camp
Computer Science Department
Indiana University
Bloomington, USA

Alana Maurushat
Western Sydney University
Parramatta, Australia

Massimiliano Sala ⓘ
Dipartimento di Matematica
University of Trento
Trento, Trento, Italy

Andrea Bracciali ⓘ
Computing Science and Mathematics
University of Stirling
Stirling, UK

Shin'ichiro Matsuo
Department of Computer Science
Georgetown University
Washington, WA, USA

Peter B. Rønne ⓘ
Maison du Nombre
University of Luxembourg
Esch-sur-Alzette, Luxembourg

ISSN 0302-9743   ISSN 1611-3349 (electronic)
Lecture Notes in Computer Science
ISBN 978-3-030-54454-6   ISBN 978-3-030-54455-3 (eBook)
https://doi.org/10.1007/978-3-030-54455-3

LNCS Sublibrary: SL4 – Security and Cryptology

This Springer imprint is published by the registered company Springer Nature Switzerland AG
The registered company address is: Gewerbestrasse 11, 6330 Cham, Switzerland

AsiaUSEC 2020 Preface

USEC has always been targeted to be the global platform for usable security since its inception in 2012 at Financial Cryptography in Bonaire. Financial Cryptography has always been open to novel approaches, to incentives, and evaluations of the costs as well as benefits of new technologies. Ensuring effective security and privacy in real-world technology requires considering not only technical but also human aspects, as well as the complex way in which these combine. The simple fact is that if a highly secure system is unusable, users will move their data to less secure but more usable systems. Security avoidance and workarounds have been major contributors to catastrophic as well as chronic security failures. Given all this, Financial Cryptography was an excellent place for USEC to begin, and to return.

USEC moved to the Internet Society's annual Network and Distributed Systems event in 2014 for ease of travel and outreach to a broader community. Because of the reliable quality of the work in NDSS, USEC expanded in 2014 to include an annual European event. In 2020, the main USEC workshop moved back to Financial Cryptography in order to evaluate the potential for a semi-annual USEC event focusing on, and more accessible to, the Asian usable security research communities. The conference attendance was decreased by (what we now recognize as) the COVID-19 pandemic, yet the final keynote by Peter Gutmann had at least 50 people.

It is the aim of USEC to contribute to an increase of the scientific quality of research in human factors in security and privacy. To this end, we encouraged comparative studies on different populations, including replication studies to validate previous research findings.

The research included documentation of human behaviors: an exploration of privacy versus sharing behavior and perception, and a comparison of browser choices in South Korea. And in the workplace, an explanation of how the behaviors of out-sourced employees create risks is only more applicable with social distancing.

In terms of human performance one study examined how users leverage cues to differentiate phishing emails from legitimate ones, and how people deal with various types of auditory stimuli when solving CAPTCHAs. An operational browser extension that leverages usability and entertainment showed that focusing on the person rather than the threat can greatly increase human efficacy in the face of masquerade attacks. At a higher level, one author returned to the topic of how insights from psychology research can help educate people about cyber security bringing these from the field into the classroom.

Two investigations of mental models of email were complemented by a study of the mental models of workers with respect to privacy at work. A stand-alone qualitative inquiry into the perceptions of smart devices provided glimpses into the minds of how non-experts deal with the risks of always-on always-listening in-home computing. A comparative study of privacy and security perceptions illustrated that culture and jurisdiction can play a role in these.

In terms of improving efficacy of secure systems, the research included an extension of graphical password authentication and an innovative work examining empathy as opposed to fear as a motivator. A comparative study of SpotBugs, SonarQube, Cryptoguard, and CogniCrypt identified strengths in each and refined the need for improvements in security testing tools.

At every USEC event we hope to bring together researchers already engaged in this inherently interdisciplinary effort with other computer science domains. Financial Cryptography, with its history of scholarship on technical trust combined with social events that include all workshop and conference attendees, is an exemplar of how to bring the different areas of computing research together in a collegial environment.

March 2020   L. Jean Camp
                                                                      Alana Maurushat

AsiaUSEC 2020 Organization

Chairs

L. Jean Camp   Indiana University, USA
Alana Maurushat   Western Sydney University, Australia

Program Committee

Abdulmajeed Alqhatani   UNC Charlotte, USA
Ada Lerner   Wellesley College, USA
Alisa Frik   ICSI, University of California at Berkeley, USA
Andrew A. Adams   Meiji University, Japan
Hamza Sellak   CSIRO, Australia
Heather Crawford   Florida Institute of Technology, USA
Julian Jang-Jaccard   Massey University, New Zealand
Julian Williams   Durham University, UK
Julie Haney   National Institute of Standards and Technology, USA
Karen Renaud   Rhodes University, South Africa, and University of
                            Glasgow, UK
Mahdi Nasrullah Al-Ameen   Utah State University, USA
Maija Poikela   Fraunhofer AISEC, Germany
Marthie Grobler   CSIRO, Australia
Matt Bishop   University of California at Davis, USA
Mohan Baruwal Chhetri   CSIRO, Australia
Nicholas Weaver   ISCI, USA
Pam Briggs   Northumbria University, UK
Patrick Traynor   University of Florida, USA
Paul Watters   La Trobe University, Australia
Peter Gutmann   The University of Auckland, New Zealand
Sanchari Das   American Express, USA
Shigeng Zhang   Central South University, China
Shrirang Mare   University of Washington, USA
Sid Stamm   Rose-Hulman Institute of Technology, USA
Sven Dietrich   City University of New York, USA
Ruth Shillair   Michigan State University, USA
Tim Kelley   Naval Surface Warfare Center Crane Division, USA
Vaibhav Garg   Comcast Cable, USA
Wendy Seltzer   MIT, USA
Zinaida Benenson   University of Erlangen-Nuremberg, Germany

CoDeFi 2020 Preface

The workshop on Coordination of Decentralized Finance (CoDeFi) is a newly organized workshop associated with Financial Cryptography 2020. The goal of CoDeFi is to discuss multidisciplinary issues regarding technologies and operations of decentralized finance based on permissionless blockchain. From an academic point of view, security and privacy protection are some of the leading research streams. The Financial Cryptography conference discusses these research challenges. On the other hand, other stakeholders than cryptographers and blockchain engineers have different interests in these characteristics of blockchain technology. For example, regulators face difficulty to trace transactions in terms of anti-money laundering (AML) against privacy-enhancing crypto-asset.

Another example is consumer protection in the case of cyberattacks on crypto-asset custodians. Blockchain business entities sometimes start their business before maturing technology, but the technology and operations are not transparent to regulators and consumers. The main problem is a lack of communication among stakeholders of the decentralized finance ecosystem. G20 discussed the issue of insufficient communication among stakeholders in 2019. It concluded that there is an essential need to have a multi-stakeholder discussion among engineers, regulators, business entities, and operators based on the neutrality of academia.

CoDeFi aims to have common understandings of technology and regulatory goals and discussions on essential issues of blockchain technology by all stakeholders mentioned above. CoDeFI 2020 was a historical workshop because we could involve regulators and engineers in the discussion at the venue of the Financial Cryptography conference.

The workshop consisted of two parts; presentations by all stakeholders and unconference style discussions. The presentations were selected by a peer-review process, and each stakeholder presented needs for multi-stakeholder discussions and pain points. This part was an excellent opportunity to share common understandings of goals and pain points. In the second part, we discussed two topics; a suitable style for multi-stakeholder discussion and balancing privacy protection. Presentations and discussions are included as papers in these proceedings.

May 2020   Shin'ichiro Matsuo

CoDeFi 2020 Organization

Workshop Chair

Shin'ichiro Matsuo   Georgetown University and BSafe.network, USA

Program Committee

Byron Gibson   Stanford Center for Blockchain Research, USA
Shin'ichiro Matsuo   Georgetown University and BSafe.network, USA
  (Workshop Chair)
Robert Schwentker   DLT Education and BSafe.network, USA
Yonatan Sompolinsky   The Hebrew University of Jerusalem, DAGlabs, Israel
Shigeya Suzuki   BSafe.network, BASE Alliance, WIDE Project,
                             Keio University, Japan
Yuta Takanashi   JFSA, Japan
Pindar Wong   BSafe.network, USA
Anton Yemelyanov   Base58 Association, Canada
Aviv Zohar   The Hebrew University of Jerusalem, Israel

VOTING 2020 Preface

VOTING 2020 marks the 5th Workshop on Advances in Secure Electronic Voting associated with the Financial Cryptography and Data Security 2020 (FC 2020) conference held in Kota Kinabalu, Malaysia, during February 14, 2020.

This year's workshop received 17 papers with 8 being accepted for publication. Two papers presented new methods for Risk-Limiting Audits (RLAs). Stark's SHANGRLA scheme shows that RLAs for many social choice functions can be reduced to testing sets of null hypotheses of the form "the average of this list is not greater than 1/2" for a collection of finite lists of non-negative numbers. This reframing results in RLAs that can be applied to a wide range of social choice functions and can perform more efficiently than prior work. The short paper "A Note on Risk-Limiting Bayesian Polling Audits" by Morin, McClearn, McBurnett, Vora, and Zagorski provides a general form for a polling audit that is both Bayesian and risk-limiting: the Bayesian Risk-Limiting (Polling) Audit, which enables the use of a Bayesian approach to explore more efficient RLAs.

Haenni and Locher found new methods to increase the efficiency of mixnets thereby improving their work presented in last year's VOTING workshop. In another paper on mixnets Haines, Pereira, and Rønne revisited the Marked Mix-nets presented at VOTING 2017 finding an attack on the system, but also suggesting two different ways of fixing this attack, as well as considering post-quantum realizations of this mixnet construction. Verification of security of voting schemes were also considered by Zollinger, Rønne, and Ryan who used Tamarin to make a formal model and give mechanized proofs of verifiability and privacy for the Electryo paper-based scheme. Kulyk, Volkamer, Müller, and Renaud investigated the socio-technical security of code-based verification in e-voting schemes, especially testing the efficacy of the verification process in practice. Finally, two new schemes were presented. Boyd, Haines, and Rønne presented a new way of preventing vote-selling by de-incentivizing this via smart contracts. Whereas Blanchard and Selker used folding of paper ballots to create novel non-cryptographic secure voting schemes: "Origami voting."

We joined the AsiaUSEC keynote by Peter Gutmann on "Availability and Security: Choose any One" which contained many interesting observations and insights also relevant for secure voting.

We are grateful to our Program Committee for their time and effort, and especially their flexibility when we introduced a second late submission deadline. We also thank the authors of all submitted papers, and especially the presenters for joining the workshop in Malaysia despite the emerging COVID-19 crisis. We are also grateful to Ray Hirschfeld, Patrick McCorry, and IFCA for organizing all the logistics of the event, and the FC workshop chairs for their continued support of VOTING. For VOTING 2021 the tradition of staggered chairs is continued with Matt Bernhard and Thomas Haines serving as program chairs.

June 2020

Peter B. Rønne
Matthew Bernhard

VOTING 2020 Organization

Program Chairs

Peter B. Rønne   University of Luxembourg, Luxembourg
Matthew Bernhard   University of Michigan, USA

Program Committee

Roberto Araujo   Universidade Federal do Pará, Brazil
Josh Benaloh   Microsoft Research, USA
Véronique Cortier   CNRS, Loria, France
Chris Culnane   The University of Melbourne, Australia
Jeremy Epstein   SRI, USA
Aleksander Essex   Western University, Canada
Josh Franklin   OutStack Technologies, USA
Kristian Gjøsteen   Norwegian University of Science and Technology, Norway
Rajeev Gore   The Australian National University, Australia
Rolf Haenni   Bern University of Applied Sciences, Switzerland
Reto Koenig   Bern University of Applied Sciences, Switzerland
Steve Kremer   Inria Nancy, France
Robert Krimmer   Tallinn University of Technology, Estonia
Oksana Kulyk   IT University of Copenhagen, Denmark
Olivier Pereira   Université catholique de Louvain, Belgium
Mark Ryan   University of Birmingham, UK
Peter Y. A. Ryan   University of Luxembourg, Luxembourg
Steve Schneider   University of Surrey, UK
Carsten Schuermann   IT University of Copenhagen, Denmark
Philip Stark   University of California, Berkeley, USA
Vanessa Teague   The University of Melbourne, Australia
Poorvi Vora   The George Washington University, USA
Dan Wallach   Rice University, USA

WTSC 2020 Preface

These proceedings collect the papers accepted at the 4th Workshop on Trusted Smart Contracts (WTSC 2020 – http://fc20.ifca.ai/wtsc/) associated with the Financial Cryptography and Data Security 2020 (FC 2020) conference held Kota Kinabalu, Malaysia, during February 10–14, 2020.

The WTSC series focus on smart contracts, i.e. self-enforcing agreements in the form of executable programs, and other decentralized applications that are deployed to and run on top of (specialized) blockchains. These technologies introduce a novel programming framework and execution environment, which, together with the supporting blockchain technologies, carry unanswered and challenging research questions. Multidisciplinary and multifactorial aspects affect correctness, safety, privacy, authentication, efficiency, sustainability, resilience, and trust in smart contracts and decentralized applications.

WTSC aims to address the scientific foundations of Trusted Smart Contract engineering, i.e. the development of contracts that enjoy some verifiable "correctness" properties, and to discuss open problems, proposed solutions, and the vision on future developments among a research community that is growing around these themes and brings together users, practitioners, industry, institutions, and academia. This was reflected in the multidisciplinary Program Committee (PC) of this 4th edition of WTSC, comprising members from companies, universities, and research institutions from several countries worldwide, who kindly accepted to support the event. The association to FC 2020 provided, once again, an ideal context for our workshop to be run in. WTSC 2020 was partially supported by the University of Stirling, UK; the University of Trento, Italy; and FC 2020 IFCA-ICRA.

This year's edition of WTSC received 27 submissions by about 80 authors, confirming a growing trend and increased interest. Given the high quality of submission, 15 papers were accepted after double-blind peer review. Thanks to the generous effort by the PC, each paper received an average of four reviews, providing constructive feedback to authors. Revised papers after the discussion at the workshop are collected in the present volume. These analyzed the current state of the art of smart contracts and their development; addressed aspects of security and scalability, relationships of smart contracts and consensus; proposed voting protocols and incentives to security, payment protocols, payment channels, and financial languages for smart contracts; investigated the use of sharding, resource sharing, and new UTX models; and proposed the use of mainstream and intermediated programming languages for smart contract development and their formal verification. Presentations made for a full day of interesting talks and discussion. Following our tradition of excellent invited speakers (Buterin, Breitman, Mishra, Artamonov, and Grigg), the day was concluded by an invited talk by Peter Gutmann shared with the other FC 2020 workshops (AsiaUSEC, which invited him; CoDeFi; and Voting).

This year's edition was run on the verge of the COVID-19 pandemic, which disrupted the normal running of the conference, making traveling and organizing more complex and requiring some talks to be held remotely. We monitored the situation in accordance with the WHO and national guidelines, together with the FC organization.

The WTSC 2020 chairs would like to thank everyone for their usual, and this year extra, effort and valuable contributions: authors, Program Committee members and reviewers, participants, as well as the support by IFCA and FC 2020 committees, and Ray Hirschfeld for the usual exceptional organization of the event.

March 2020   Andrea Bracciali
                                                                          Massimiliano Sala

WTSC 2020 Organization

WTSC 2020 Chairs

Andrea Bracciali
Massimiliano Sala

Program Committee

Monika di Angelo	Vienna University of Technology, Austria
Igor Artamonov	Ethereum Classic Dev, UK
Daniel Augot	Inria, France
Surya Bakshi	University of Illinois, USA
Fadi Barbara	University of Turin, Italy
Massimo Bartoletti	University of Cagliari, Italy
Stefano Bistarelli	University of Perugia, Italy
Christina Boura	Versailles SQT Université, France
Andrea Bracciali	University of Stirling, UK
Daniel Broby	Strathclyde University, UK
James Chapman	IOHK, UK
Martin Chapman	King's College London, UK
Alexander Denzler	University of Lucerne, Switzerland
Nicola Dimitri	University of Siena, Italy
Nadia Fabrizio	Cefriel, Italy
Murdoch Gabbay	Heriot-Watt University, UK
Oliver Giudice	Banca d'Italia, Italy
Davide Grossi	University of Groningen, The Netherlands
Yoichi Hirai	Brainbot Technologies AG, Germany
Lars R. Knudsen	Technical University of Denmark, Denmark
Ioannis Kounelis	Joint Research Centre, European Commission, Italy
Pascal Lafourcade	University Clermont Auvergne, France
Andrew Lewis-Pye	London School of Economics, UK
Carsten Maple	Warwick University, UK
Michele Marchesi	University of Cagliari, Italy
Fabio Martinelli	IIT-CNR, Italy
Luca Mazzola	University of Lucerne, Switzerland
Sihem Mesnager	University of Paris VIII, France
Philippe Meyer	Avaloq, Switzerland
Bud Mishra	NYU, USA
Carlos Molina-Jimenez	University of Cambridge, UK
Massimo Morini	Banca IMI, Italy

Contents

CoDeFi: First Workshop on Coordination of Decentralized Finance

VOTING 2020: Fifth Workshop on Advances in Secure Electronic Voting

AsiaUSEC: First Asian Workshop on Usable Security

Tale of Two Browsers: Understanding Users' Web Browser Choices in South Korea

Jihye Woo[1], Ji Won Choi[1], Soyoon Jeon[1], Joon Kuy Han[1], Hyoungshick Kim[2], and Simon S. Woo[2(✉)]

[1] Stony Brook University, Stony Brook, NY, USA
{jihye.woo,jiwon.choi.2,soyoon.jeon,joonkyu.han}@stonybrook.edu
[2] Sungkyunkwan University, Suwon, South Korea
{hyoung,swoo}@skku.edu

Abstract. Internet users in South Korea seem to have clearly different web browser choices and usage patterns compared to the rest of the world, heavily using Internet Explorer (IE) or multiple browsers. Our work is primarily motivated to investigate the reasons for such differences in web browser usage, relating with the use of government mandated security technology, digital certificate. We conducted an IRB-approved semi-structured online user study to examine internet users' browser choices in South Korea and analyze their usage patterns. Our user study results reveal that there are clearly different users' browser preferences across different web services, and they are in turn closely related with the security policy enforced by the government 20 years ago. In our study, while younger age group tends to prefer two browsers (Chrome and IE), older age group prefers to use IE browser Also, all age groups commonly prefer the IE browser for the services requiring digital certificates issued from Korean government agencies such as finance and e-commerce sites. Our user study is quantitative to show how the standardization of technologies in a country could affect users' web browsing activities. Also, despite of the abolishment of the mandatory security technology, we still observe that people are not aware of such abolishment and habitually use technology locked-in IE browser.

Keywords: Web browser · Digital certificate · Public key infrastructure

1 Introduction

South Korea is one of the countries with the highest number of internet users in the world (with over 47 million). Interestingly, however, internet users in South Korea seem to make different choices when using web browsers compared to the rest of countries. According to the report by Korea Internet and Security Agency (KISA) [6] in 2017, 93% of internet users in South Korea strongly prefer to use

M. Bernhard et al. (Eds.): FC 2020 Workshops, LNCS 12063, pp. 3–17, 2020.
https://doi.org/10.1007/978-3-030-54455-3_1

Internet Explorer (IE). On the other hand, people in other countries strongly prefer other browsers such as Chrome (53.9%) and Safari (8.1%) in 2019 [10].

Our study is motivated by the observations on this unique trend in South Korea. Specifically, we aim to understand why South Korean internet users' choices and preferences significantly differ. We surmise that the use of digital certificates for user authentication mandated by Korean government has influenced users' web browser choices – the Korean government introduced the 'Digital Signature Act (DSA)' [8] was mandated in 1999. The goal of DSA was to support a regulated Public Key Infrastructure (PKI) to guarantee the interoperability of digital signature and encryption algorithms for all electronic transactions processed in Korean government and banking web services. As the IE was the dominant browser in South Korea at that time, the banks and security companies implemented these plugins as ActiveX controls only. This may cause the technology lock-in on IE, even after abolishment of DSA policy in 2015. More specifically, we aim to understand how mandatory security technologies enforced by the government 20 years ago still influence users' browser choices today. To better understand this phenomenon, we conducted an IRB-approved quantitative user study to investigate the browser choices preferred by users and analyze the specific browsers preferred for specific web services. Next, we correlated web services with respect to services used to require digital certificates. Our contributions are summarized below:

- We conducted a user study to understand different browser choices by users in South Korea over different services across varying age groups. The user study results show that South Koreans strongly prefer to use IE over other browsers (54% of 105 participants).
- In spite of the significant inconvenience, 20–29 age group uses two browsers for different services: IE for banking and government sites, and Chrome for entertainments, online shopping, and web searching, while older age group are not.

2   Background and Related Work

In 1999, the Korean government passed Digital Signature Act (DSA), enforcing the use of digital signature with a proprietary encryption algorithm called (SEED) [11] to use online Korean government, online banking and shopping websites. Because SEED was not supported by all commercial web browsers such as IE and Netscape, SEED had to be implemented as external plugins; ActiveX was chosen to implement them [9]. However, ActiveX only runs under Microsoft IE, resulting in the heavy use of IE (and/or Windows operating systems). To address this interoperability issue, South Korean government abolished the mandatory use of digital certificates in 2015 so that users are no longer forced to use ActiveX running on IE. Kim et al. [6] investigated which services require the use of digital certificates. According to their user survey results, the services in which digital certificates were most frequently used are 'internet banking (98.1%)' and 'government services (91.6%).' Also, they reported that 93% of the survey participants use IE, and the second most used browser was Chrome (53.9%). Kim et al. [5] studied the correlation between compatibility of the Korean banks' proprietary mechanisms and usability for bank service in Korea. They found out that usability of banking service was significantly influenced by the use of IE. Park [9] studied the low web accessibility in Korean government websites and concluded that the use of digital certificates is a main reason of the low accessibility because users should be forced to use IE when they visit Korean government websites. In this research, we conduct user studies to investigate how mandated proprietary security technologies (abolished in 2015) affect users' browser choices.

For browser usage, Weinberger and Felt [12] studied the effect of security warning with Chrome browser. They specifically evaluated the usability of different storage policies for browser warnings. Mathur et al. [7] investigated the usability of browser-based blocking extensions. They found that ill-designed blockers can significantly lower user adoption. On the other hand, Garg and Camp [3] showed that current policy and enforcement may lead to worse security outcomes, as they underestimate the market forces of supply and demand, reduce competition, and user needs. Therefore, their work shows similar conclusion as ours on risk from a government intervention on security policy. Also, Asgharpour et al. [1] researched the mental models between self-identified security experts and non-experts and showed the importance of designing the effective risk communication methods. We believe understanding mental models are also important when a national-level policy for the adoption of security technologies has been chosen.

3   Survey Methodology

We construct 17 survey questions as shown in Appendix A.1. Each question is categorized into one of the following five high level survey question (SQ) categories in Table 2 in Appendix. SQ1 and SQ2 are constructed to assess users' browser usage and preference over different web service access. SQ3 and SQ4 are designed to ask users about their experience and reasons about digital certificate usage related to habits. SQ5 is to determine whether users still use the digital certificates, after knowing the abolishment of the mandatory use of certificates to investigate the technology lock-in phenomenon. All of the user studies were reviewed and approved by our Institutional Review Board (IRB). We recruited 112 volunteers via social medias such as Facebook and KakaoTalk [4], which are popular social networking services widely used in South Korea. We posted the survey link on Facebook and also sent it to acquaintances through KakaoTalk to recruit volunteers who were older than 18 years old. We asked participants about their gender, age, occupation, current degree, nationality, and major, and We conducted the survey for 3 months.

Our survey was composed of 6 demographic questions, 3 open-ended questions, 1 Likert scale question, 5 multiple choice questions, and 2 Yes/No questions as shown in Appendix. All open-ended questions were independently coded by two different researchers in our research group and the agreement between two coders were around 90%. Cohen's kappa was used to calculate inter-rater reliability. Also, we used the Likert scale from 0 to 10 (0: Strongly disagree, 5: Neutral, 10: Strongly agree) to measure responses from participants. Specifically, we use a 10 point Likert-scale o understand more variance than a smaller Likert scale provides. With a 10 point Likert-scale, we can obtain a higher degree of measurement precision and more power to explain an agreement.

For the statistical analysis, we constructed contingency tables to test the correlation between various user responses across different age groups. We used Fisher's exact test (FET) for categorical variables with small sample size (expected values less than 5) and Chi-square (χ^2) test for categorical variables with large sample size. In addition, we used the Wilcoxon rank-sum test to compare two independent samples of the Likert scale data. For all statistical tests, we use a significance level of $p = 0.05$. We further conducted pairwise tests and compared a subset of possible pairs of conditions. If pairwise tests showed a significance, then we performed a Bonferroni correction.

Our study had the following limitations, where many of which are common for semi structured online user studies. Although we have more than 100 participants, the number of participants who were recruited for our online survey may not accurately represent the real internet user population in South Korea. We did try to mitigate this issue by recruiting from diverse age groups as shown in demographic section. Also, because of the nature of self-report surveys, users' actual behavior might be different from their responses.

4   User Study Results

Among participants, 52.2% of them are identified as female and 47.3% as male. We broke down the age group into 5 groups based on the participants' age (18–19, 20–29, 30–39, 40–49, and 50–59), where, 50% were between 20 and 29 years old (20–29), 17.9% between 40 and 49 (40–49), and 25.9% between 50 and 59 (50–59). Because of small number of participants in other groups, we proceeded our analysis with 3 groups (20–29, 40–49, and 50–59), where 20–29 age group can capture the behavior of younger internet users, and both 40–49 and 50–59 age groups can characterize older internet user population.

4.1   Analysis of Browser Usage

First, we asked each age group about a browser that they most frequently use (SQ1). As shown in Fig. 1, Chrome was the most frequently used browser in 20–29 age group with 70%. On the other hand, IE was the highest in both 40–49 and 50–59 with 100% and 79%, respectively. However, percentage of "Other" browser (Safari, Firefox, Microsoft Edge, Opera, Whale, Swing) was only 11%, 0%, and 7% for 20–29, 40–49, and 50–59 age groups, respectively. Therefore, we can observe the differences in browser preferences vs. age groups.

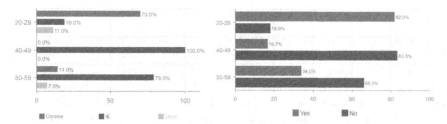

(a) SQ1. Most frequently used browser (Other: Safari, Firefox, Microsoft Edge, Opera, Whale, Swing)

(b) SQ2. Multiple browsers usage showing user response to "Question. Do you use multiple browsers?"

Fig. 1. Survey Question Responses for SQ1 and SQ2.

To find the statistical differences between different age groups, we analyzed them with the Fisher's exact test and additionally performed Bonferroni correction for pairwise-tests. The statistical test result between 20–29 vs. 40–49 age group (p-value $\approx 2.33 \times 10^{-10} \ll 0.05$), and 20–29 vs. 50–59 age group (p-value $\approx 3.50 \times 10^{-7} \ll 0.05$) show significant statistical differences. On the other hand, the result of 40–49 and 50–59 age groups (p-value $\approx 0.299 > 0.05$) does not. These results are also summarized in Table 4 in Appendix.

4.2 Analysis of Multiple Browsers Usage

Next, we determine whether users prefer to use a single browser vs. multiple browsers for specific web applications (SQ2). We analyze if there are any different browser usages with respect to the number of browsers (singe or multiple browsers) for specific application types (e.g., internet banking). We further quantify, if there are any differing behaviors across different age groups. We first asked the following question: "Do you use multiple browsers?" and participants are responded with "Yes/No." 82% of participants in age group of 20–29 responded they use multiple browsers group, while 75% of 40–49 and 66% of 50–59 said they do not use multiple browsers, which clearly demonstrate the differences.

In order to further examine, we performed the statistical testing on the use of the multiple browsers using the Fisher's exact test (FET) with additionally conducting Bonferroni correction for pairwise tests. The result between 20–29 vs. 40–49 age groups (p-value $\approx 2.33 \times 10^{-10} \ll 0.05$), and 20–29 vs. 50–59 ($p$-value $\approx 3.50 \times 10^{-7} \ll 0.05$) were statistically significant. However, the result between 40–49 vs. 50–59 (p-value $\approx 0.2999 > 0.05$) did not show significant difference. Therefore, we confirm the differences between younger group (20–29) vs. older age groups (40–49 and 50–59), where younger age group prefers to use multiple browsers and older age groups prefer single browser. To find out why there were differences in multiple browsers usage for different age groups, we asked participants about the specific browsers they use for different types of web services in the next section.

4.3   Browser Usage for Different Services

We examine the browser usage for the following 5 different web service categories: 1) online shopping, 2) government sites, 3) internet banking, 4) web searching, and 5) entertainment, where both government and internet banking sites used to require digital certificates and IE by DSA. Figure 2 shows the aggregated percentage of browser usage per each specific service across different age groups. For all services, IE has the highest percentage, compared to other browsers. In particular, government sites, internet banking, and online shopping have the highest percentage of using IE with 74.7%, 69%, and 58.9%, respectively. The second highest browser is Chrome with 44%, 40%, and 31.1%, respectively. Other browsers such as Safari, Firefox, Microsoft Edge, Opera, Whale, Swing, etc. are rarely used as shown in Fig. 2. Next, we specifically investigate how different age groups have distinctive or similar browser choices for each service.

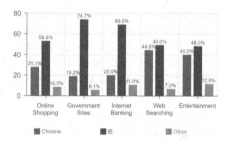

Fig. 2. Overall browser usage for each service (Other: Safari, Firefox, Microsoft Edge, Opera, Whale, Swing)

Table 1 shows the actual number of participants who use specific browsers along with the percentage of those in parentheses. For example, in online shopping case, the number of participants who prefer IE is 18 (3rd row and 3rd col) with 90% in Table 1 and the number of participants who specify to use Chrome for internet banking is 2 (4th row and 8th col) with 7%. Overall, we find that most participants in 40–49 and 50–59 age groups prefer IE, regardless of service types. However, 20–29 age group shows an interesting result. When 20–29 age group uses online shopping, web searching, and entertainment service, Chrome was the highest with 38 (60%), 42 (71%), and 39 (64%), respectively.

On the other hand, in government sites and internet banking which require Korean National Digital Certificates, the IE usage in 20–29 age group is 36 (60%), and 32 (51%), which are higher than usage of Chrome (30% and 32%). Therefore, this result also confirms that 20–29 age group tends to use 2 or more browsers. These results are also summarized as histograms in Fig. 3, where the percentage of browser usage for each service vs. each age group are presented. For example, 50–59 age group uses IE for government sites with 90%, whereas 20–29 age group uses IE with 60%. While 20–29 age group uses Chrome for web searching with 71%. Hence, we can clearly observe the differing browser

Table 1. Number of participants use specific browser for each service across different age groups (Other: Safari, Firefox, Microsoft Edge, Opera, Whale, Swing).

Age Group	Online Shopping			Government Sites			Internet Banking			Web Searching			Entertainment		
	Chrome	IE	Other	Chrome	IE	Other	Chrome	IE	Other	Chrome	IE	Other	Chrome	IE	Other
20–29	38 (60%)	16 (26%)	9 (14%)	18 (30%)	36 (60%)	6 (10%)	20 (32%)	32 (51%)	11 (17%)	42 (71%)	11 (19%)	6 (10%)	39 (64%)	10 (16%)	12 (20%)
40–49	2 (10%)	18 (90%)	0 (0%)	1 (5%)	19 (95%)	0 (0%)	1 (5%)	19 (95%)	0 (0%)	2 (10%)	19 (90%)	0 (0%)	1 (5%)	19 (95%)	0 (0%)
50–59	3 (10%)	26 (87%)	1 (3%)	2 (7%)	26 (90%)	1 (3%)	2 (7%)	26 (90%)	1 (3%)	5 (16%)	25 (78%)	2 (6%)	5 (17%)	24 (80%)	1 (3%)

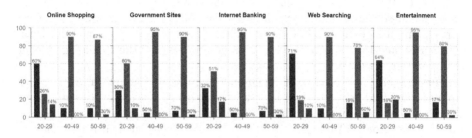

Fig. 3. Browser choice for different services (Other: Safari, Firefox, Microsoft Edge, Opera, Whale, Swing).

preference for each group vs. specific service, which also results in the use for single vs. two browsers for specific service.

Despite of inconvenience of using multiple browsers and abolishment of mandatory use of digital certificate, encryption and browser standard, it is interesting to observe that IE is the still most dominant browser across all age groups for Internet banking and government websites. To statistically analyze different characteristics per each age group, we further analyzed user's browser usage patterns by using the Fisher's exact test. As shown in Table 5, in all services, results of comparing browser choice of different age groups (20–29, 40–49, and 50–59) were statistically significant. However, it is notable that for two services such as government sites and internet banking, which require digital certificates, show relatively high p-values (2.54×10^{-2} and 7.50×10^{-4}) than other services. This shows that the differences between the user's browser usage patterns are relatively smaller compared to the usage patterns of the other services. To analyze further, we conducted an additional survey to find correlations between the use of digital certificates and the specific browser participants use by asking users' perception and usage behaviors on the use of digital certificates.

4.4 Usability of Korean National Digital Certificates

We conducted a survey to find out the usability of digital certificates by asking the following statement: "It is easy to use the Korean National Digital Certificates." And participants' responses were measured in the Likert-scale in Fig. 5 in Appendix. We calculate "Agree" as the total number of responses greater than neutral (5) and "Disagree" as the total number of responses less than neutral. As shown in Fig. 5, across different age groups, "Disagree" was much higher than "Agree", meaning *more participants felt that it is not easy to use digital certificates*. More participants in 20–29 age group (64%) felt inconvenient ("Disagree") than 40–49 (45%) and 50–59 (54%) age groups.

In Fig. 5, the proportion of "Agree" was also slightly different across different age groups. 22% of 50–59 age group perceived that it is convenient to use Korean National Digital Certificates, which was higher than the percentages from 20–29 (16%) and 40–49 (15%). We believe that this is due to the fact that 50–59 age group has used digital certificates longer than the other age groups. Therefore, participants in age group of 50–59 are much aware of and familiar with digital certificates, and they appear to have been habitually used the technology longer than younger group.

Furthermore, we conducted open-ended question survey in SQ3. Q in Appendix to find out why participants think using Korean National Digital Certificates was inconvenient. Interestingly, participants' open-ended responses varied by age groups. A user, P2, in 20–29 age group mentioned "it is very complicated to install software", showing their distaste of the Korean National Digital Certificates. In addition, both P5 (40–49 age group) and P6 (50–59 age group) commonly mentioned the complicated procedure which requires obtaining certificates issued from Korean government. Also, P7 (40–49 age group) mentioned that they are "frustrated because they have to renew and obtain new certificates within 1 or 2 years after certificates expiration".

4.5 Common Reasons for Using Digital Certificates

We asked the participants their reasons for using Korean National Digital Certificates. In particular, we tried to determine whether participants used Korean National Digital Certificates on their own will or it was required. This question is composed of multiple choices, where we provided the following choices for participants to choose: Required by services (banking (RQ1), government sites (RQ2)), personal reasons (P), and security reason (S). In particular, we divided the required reasons (RQ) to internet banking (RQ1) and government sites (RQ2) to identify specific services which users are more commonly required to use. Also, we also provide personal (P) and security (S) reasons.

Our result shows that, interestingly, security was the least common reason (0%–3.5%) to use Korean National Digital Certificates as shown in Fig. 4 in Appendix. On the other hand, most participants (20–29: 86%, 40–49: 85%, and 50–59: 93%) said they use Korean National Digital Certificates because it is required by banks as well as government sites. In particular, we find that the percentage on required by banks (RQ1) was much higher than government sites (RQ2) as shown in Fig. 4. We believe participants more frequently use internet banking over government sites. Therefore, RQ1 is much higher than RQ2. On the other hand, personal reason (P) was the third highest but it is much less than RQ1 or RQ2. Therefore, it is surprising to observe that most of participants passively use digital certificates, since it is required by service providers and not because of higher usability or added security. Therefore, this result shows that it is important to educate users about security benefits of technology than merely enforcing those.

4.6 Knowledge on the Abolishment of the Mandatory Use of National Digital Certificates

We also asked participants whether they knew about the recent abolishment of the mandatory use of Korean National Digital Certificates [9]. This question was asked to find out what percentage of the people were awaref of the change and determine whether participants would still use digital certificates in spite of new recent changes. Surprisingly, our results show that 61% of 20–29 age group and 54% of 50–59 age group did not know about the changed policy. Although 60% of 40–49 age group knew about the revised changes as shown in Fig. 6, there was no statistical difference. Overall, most of participants were not aware of recent changes and they still continue to use digital certificates.

5 Discussion and Limitations

In this study, we found significant differences in browser choices across different age groups for accessing certain types of web services. Even though mandatory DSA was abolished, IE is still strongly preferred by "Government Sites" and "Internet Banking" websites that are used to require mandatory digital certificates and legacy encryption technology. Although our study appears to be specific and focused on South Korea, our work provides a valuable lesson on how the mandatory use of a proprietary security technology can affect the users' technology choice through a practical case study at large scale. We observed that "Government Sites" and "Internet Banking" no longer require the use of Korean National Digital Certificate anymore after 2015. However, older generation who are more accustomed to old digital certificate technology appears to habitually use IE for all services. Also, the majority of the users in the 20–29 age group use IE to access these services instead of using Chrome as shown in Fig. 3. This shows that today internet users still perceive that they are required to use a web browser that is compatible for the use of older security technology and users are subsequently locked onto IE, even though this security technology is no longer required. While younger generations appear to move away from IE by using Chrome for entertainment and search services, they could not get completely away from IE, still using IE for banking and government sites. This results in young generation users to use two different browsers simultaneously, tolerating inconvenience. In addition, in contrast to widely known *technology acceptance model (TAM) theory* [2], where users choose technology based on perceived usefulness and ease of use, we observe that users tend to use mandated technology despite inconvenience. Therefore, government needs to more proactively put an effort to educate and increase the awareness of the new change so that users can explore other alternative technology options that they can choose for usability, convenience, and security. Our work clearly shows that users are habitually use older technology than exploring and adopting different options.

Along the same lines, we think it is important to provide more diverse and usable authentication alternatives to users in the future, which are compatible with all browsers. Most participants responded that they had to use digital certificates because it is required, in the presence of low usability and vulnerability. Therefore, we believe it is crucial to provide more usable, secure, and diverse authentication choices that consider needs of users' needs. In particular, when government designs a cybersecurity policy, it should be designed with caution, and government policy must consider the usability and compatibility costs they impose on users, which are not likely to be trivial, in addition to the technology values. Also, sometimes, we believe it would be better to for industries to lead the cybersecurity policies development, which they are good at and taking into account users' needs. Our study recommends, instead for government directly intervenes and regulates specific, government can have a supporting and over-seeing role, and also provide several options for users/industry to choose, instead of enforcing a single proprietary technology (e.g., IE/ActiveX).

Current limitation of this research is that our participants may not represent the real internet population in South Korea and our sample size is small (112 participants). We did not collect participants' expertise in using digital certificates. Future research is to recruit more participants and their detailed demographics information to validate our findings. A simple Likert scale was only used to measure the usability of Korean National Digital Certificate. However, our current questionnaire is not sufficient to derive conclusive results on the usability of Korean system. Although we included open-ended questions in our survey to discuss users' perceptions, it would be desirable to include more qualitative questions to more deeply understand users' reasoning. Our work provides the partial evidence on security technology adoption vs. users' habit; however more qualitative study is needed to find users' perceptions and reasoning. Lastly, we only compare the browser usage across different age groups within South Korea. However, it would be interesting to extend our user study to include and compare populations in other countries that do not enforce national digital certificate-based authentication. This will allow us to compare users' browser choices, patterns, and perceptions in the same age groups in different countries.

6   Conclusion

We shows that the external factors of the establishment of Digital Signature Act and its real-world software implementations led to a behavioral change in the population. Our results indicate one of the underlying causes of different web browser preference patterns are closely related to the use of a proprietary system (called Korean National Digital Certificate system) by cross-examining different web services that require digital certificate-based authentication. Therefore, significant differences were observed between age groups in their browser choices. Moreover, an unique coping strategy by employing two different browsers was notable. Our work sheds light on this issue by analyzing the interplay between the use of browsers and digital certificate through the lens of a user study. We also bring up the opportunity and needs, where more diverse authentication choices should be available to users and the government should enhance the awareness of new policy changes.

Acknowledgements. This research was supported by Energy Cloud R&D Program through the National Research Foundation of Korea (NRF) funded by the Ministry of Science, ICT (No. 2019M3F2A1072217), and the NRF of Korea funded by the Ministry of Science, ICT (No. 2017R1C1B5076474 and No. 2020R1C1C1006004).

A   Appendix

A.1   Survey Questions

Table 2. Five categorized survey questions.

Survey question category
SQ.1. (Preference) Users' browser preference
SQ.2. (Usage) Users' browser usage for different services
SQ.3. (Usability and habit) Usability of Korean National Digital Certificates
SQ.4. (Reasons) Common reasons of using Korean National Digital Certificates among other authentication methods
SQ.5. (Lock-in) Knowledge of the abolishment of the mandatory use of Korean National Digital Certificates

Demographic information
A. Gender
    () Male () Female () Do not wish to disclose

B. Age
    () 18–19   () 20–29   () 30–39   () 40–49   () 50–59   () 60 or above
C. Occupation
    () Student   () Office worker   () Inoccupation
    () Do not wish to disclose   () Other
D. Current degree
    () High school   () Undergraduate   () College   () Graduate
    () Doctor   () Do not wish to disclose   () Other
E. Major
F. Nationality
    () Korea   () USA   () China
    () Do not wish to disclose   () Other

SQ1. Users' browser preference
    G. Browser use in Laptop/Desktop
       - Most effective browser to use?
       () Chrome   () Safari   () Internet Explorer   () Firefox
       () Microsoft Edge   () Opera   () Whale   () Swing   () Other
    H. Browser use in Laptop/Desktop
       - Most frequently used browser?
       () Chrome   () Safari   () Internet Explorer   () Firefox
       () Microsoft Edge   () Opera   () Whale   () Swing   () Other
    I. Have you used Internet Explorer within the past two years?
       If so, why?
    J. Do you use more than 2 browsers?
       () Yes   () No
    K. Why do you use more than 2 browsers/or why not?

SQ2. Users' Browser usage for different services
    L. Which browser do you use for each service?
       - Online Shopping, Internet Banking, Government Sites,
       Web Searching, and Entertainment
       () Chrome   () Safari   () Internet Explorer   () Firefox
       () Microsoft Edge   () Opera   () Whale   () Swing   () Other
    M. Which operating system do you use?
       () Window OS   () Mac OS   () Linux OS
       () Ubuntu OS   () Do not know   () Other

SQ3. Usability of Korean National Digital Certificates

    P. (Likert-Scale) I think it is easy to use Korean National Digital Certificates.
() 0 (Strongly Disagree) () 1 () 2 () 3 () 4 () 5 (Neutral) () 6 () 7 () 8 () 9 () 10 (Strongly Agree)

    Q. (Open-ended question) If you think Korean National Digital Certificates are inconvenient, why/what are the inconveniences?

SQ4. Common reasons of using Korean National Digital Certificates among other authentication methods

    O. There are many different authentication methods. Is there any reason   for choosing Korean National Digital Certificates?
       () It is required to use in banks   () It is required to use in government sites
       () Ease to use   () As a habit   () Do not know   () Other

SQ5. Knowledge of the abolishment of the mandatory use of Korean National Digital Certificates
    N. The government policy in Korea has changed from mandatory to   personal preference on using digital certificates. Did you know this fact?
       () Yes   () No

A.2   Demographics information

See Table 3.

Table 3. Demographics of participants

Category	Number	Percentage
Female	59	52.2%
Male	53	47.3%
18–19	4	3.5%
20–29	**56**	**50%**
30–39	3	2.7%
40–49	**20**	**17.9%**
50–59	**29**	**25.9%**
Student	59	52.7%
Employed	40	35.7%
Unemployed	11	9.8%
NA	2	1.8%

Table 4. Statistically significant results for most frequently used browser

Testing method	Age group	p-value
FET	20–29 vs. 40–49	2.33×10^{-10}
FET	20–29 vs. 50–59	3.50×10^{-7}
FET	40–49 vs. 50–59	$0.299 > 0.05$

Note: Bonferroni correction is performed for the pairwise tests, where FET was used for pairwise tests.

A.3   User Responses

Table 5. Statistically significant results for browser use for each service across different age groups using Fisher's exact test (FET) (Note: Bonferroni correction is performed for the pairwise tests)

Service type	Age group	p-value
Online shopping	20–29, 40–49, and 50–59	3.10×10^{-9}
Government sites	20–29, 40–49, and 50–59	$\mathbf{2.54 \times 10^{-2}}$
Internet banking	20–29, 40–49, and 50–59	$\mathbf{7.50 \times 10^{-4}}$
Web searching	20–29, 40–49, and 50–59	2.10×10^{-10}
Entertainment	20–29, 40–49, and 50–59	6.36×10^{-12}

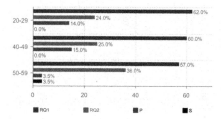

Fig. 4. Common reasons of using Korean National Digital Certificates: RQ1. Required by Banks, RQ2. Required by Government Sites, P: Personal reason, and S: Security reason.

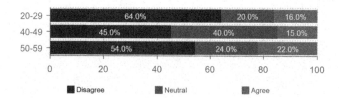

Fig. 5. User responses on usability question "Q. It is easy to use the Korean National Digital Certificates"

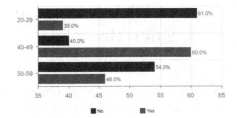

Fig. 6. Percentage of participants who are aware of policy changes

References

1. Asgharpour, F., Liu, D., Camp, L.J.: Mental models of security risks. In: Dietrich, S., Dhamija, R. (eds.) FC 2007. LNCS, vol. 4886, pp. 367–377. Springer, Heidelberg (2007). https://doi.org/10.1007/978-3-540-77366-5_34
2. Davis, F.D.: Perceived usefulness, perceived ease of use, and user acceptance of information technology. MIS Q. **13**, 319–340 (1989)
3. Garg, V., Camp, L.J.: Ex ante vs. ex post: economically efficient sanctioning regimes for online risks. In: TPRC (2013)
4. KakaoCorp. Kakaotalk. https://www.kakaocorp.com/service/kakaotalk?lang=en. Accessed 11 Mar 2019
5. Kim, H., Huh, J.H., Anderson, R.: On the security of internet banking in South Korea. Technical Report RR-10-01, March 2010
6. Kim, S., Lim, S., Kim, J., Lee, S., Lee, G.: Research on the actual condition of electronic signature system usage in electronic signature user. Technical report, KISA (2017)
7. Mathur, A., Vitak, J., Narayanan, A., Chetty, M.: Characterizing the use of browser-based blocking extensions to prevent online tracking. In: Fourteenth Symposium on Usable Privacy and Security ({SOUPS} 2018), pp. 103–116 (2018)
8. Ministry of Justice in Korea. Digital signature act, February 1999
9. Park, H.M.: The web accessibility crisis of the Korea's electronic government: fatal consequences of the digital signature law and public key certificate. In: Proceedings of the 45th Hawaii International Conference on System Sciences, pp. 2319–2328. IEEE (2012)
10. statCounter: Browser market share republic of worldwide. http://gs.statcounter.com/. Accessed 11 Mar 2019
11. Sung, J.: Differential cryptanalysis of eight-round seed. Inf. Process. Lett. **111**(10), 474–478 (2011)
12. Weinberger, J., Felt, A.P.: A week to remember: the impact of browser warning storage policies. In: Twelfth Symposium on Usable Privacy and Security ({SOUPS} 2016), pp. 15–25 (2016)

User-Centered Risk Communication
for Safer Browsing

Sanchari Das[1,2(✉)], Jacob Abbott[1], Shakthidhar Gopavaram[1], Jim Blythe[3],
and L. Jean Camp[1]

[1] Indiana University Bloomington, Bloomington, USA
`sancdas@iu.edu`
[2] University of Denver, Denver, USA
[3] USC Information Sciences Institute, Los Angeles, USA

Abstract. Solutions to phishing have included training users, stand-alone warnings, and automatic blocking. We integrated personalized blocking, filtering, and alerts into a single holistic risk-management tool, which leverages simple metaphorical cartoons that function both as risk communication and controls for browser settings. We tested the tool in two experiments. The first experiment was a four-week naturalistic study where we examined the acceptability and usability of the tool. The experimental group was exposed to fewer risks in that they chose to run fewer scripts, disabled most iFrames, blocked Flash, decreased tracking, and quickly identified each newly encountered website as unfamiliar. Each week participants increased their tool use. Conversely, those in the control group expressed perceptions of lower risk, while enabling more potentially malicious processes. We then tested phishing resilience in the laboratory with newly recruited participants. The results showed that the tool significantly improved participants' ability to distinguish between legitimate and phishing sites.

Keywords: Phishing · Risk-communication · Mental models

1 Introduction

Phishing attacks are one of the most well-known cyber attacks. In 2017 alone, there was a loss of $678 million in the US due to phishing attacks [52]. In 2015, McAfee implemented an (admittedly commercial) study of 19,000 consumers and found that 97% of participants were unable to detect phishing emails [1]. Phishing also plays a critical role in the broader e-crime ecosystem, allowing for technically simple and low-cost intrusions [36]. Thus, defeating phishing remains a significant challenge for human-security interactions [14]. To assist people requiring protection, we created a browser extension that centered the human experience to help internet users incorrectly identifying phishing attacks. We constructed the front-end as an extension using cartoons, as shown in Fig. 1. The design was built on three core components. First, our tool design we assumed

© Springer Nature Switzerland AG 2020
M. Bernhard et al. (Eds.): FC 2020 Workshops, LNCS 12063, pp. 18–35, 2020.
https://doi.org/10.1007/978-3-030-54455-3_2

that participants do not care about the technical source of risk: the site, the ads, or the route. The second component is the recognition that there are trusted web sites for social, professional, and personal reasons that vary between individuals. The third component is that we integrated secure communication as a possible way forward, as a complement to stand-alone indicators. We integrated warnings and controls so that people had to actively and knowingly choose risk-taking. To report on the implications of the toolbar mentioned above, we report on two experiments that used the interaction. For the first experiment, we conducted a naturalistic in-situ study with 44 participants to evaluate the usability and acceptability of the tool. For the second experiment, we conducted an in-lab study with 45 participants to assess efficacy of the tool. Our research questions were:

RQ1: Is the toolbar understandable? Using interviews and qualitative analysis, we evaluated whether individuals accurately describe the implications of the interaction. If it was understood, would it be used? To answer this, we conducted a naturalistic study and interviewed participants about their perceptions of the toolbar.

RQ2: Is the holistic risk management tool acceptable? In the naturalistic setup, we observed how usage and perception of the tool improved during the study.

RQ3: Do participants who were completely unfamiliar with the tool illustrate greater efficacy in detecting phishing sites? We inspected efficacy in mitigating phishing. For this, we conducted a laboratory experiment where participants were interacting with the toolbar for the first time. We evaluated the participants in the experimental group to the same mock phishing sites as a control group.

RQ4: How do stress conditions impact the risk behavior of an individual while interacting with risk-mitigation tools? The final test, of efficacy under stress, was part of the same experiment. Specifically, we evaluated in a real-time in-lab experiment under two stress conditions to better align with the cognitive experience of actual phishing [29].

Our contributions are the use of risk communication to identify and mitigate aggregate risks in a single tool. The tool includes script blocking, embeds phishing indicators, certificate warnings, and provides notification of unencrypted communication. The second contribution is personalized web risk settings based on individual choices and browsing history. In other words, we let each person easily select their own unique set of favorite or most-used websites, deciding to take the risk but knowingly. We complement that by trivially distinguishing the familiar from the unfamiliar through targeted blocking. The third contribution is a design intended to provide security without information sharing, i.e., potential loss of privacy.

Fig. 1. Toolbar showing the low, medium, and high risk tolerance buttons

2 Related Work

In 1996 Zurko [56] coined the phrase "user-centered security". This work was informed by research in user-centered security specifically studies on warnings, usability studies of security tools, and research into user perspectives on security. Cranor and Garfinkle's classic text on usable security, for example, included evaluations on browser warnings [12]. In 2006, a study of five simple commercial toolbars found that none of them had any statistically significant impact [51]. Shortly after this high impact study, the focus moved away from this type of interaction as conventional wisdom began to focus on browser indicators and warnings. A comparison of six indicators across nine browsers resulted in a redesign of security indicators for Chrome [22]. However, despite noting the importance of trust-based risk communication tools and interactive [30] and trust ensuring tools [53], comparatively little work has been done in risk communication with few exceptions [32,39].

2.1 Security as Risk Communication

Risk communication depends on estimates of the underlying risk as well as subjects' mental models of the risks [10,15]. Asgharpour et al. [4] and Wash et al. [48] showed distinct differences in the mental models between experts and non-experts by analyzing simple mental models [9,31]. Mental models and risk perception differ between individuals, and the differences between experts and non-experts is a challenge addressed by security researchers who have collaborated with cognitive science researchers in implementing mental models [6,8,47]. Applying these models requires identifying the model of the specific user, which requires observing user choices and behaviors [43,50] or the inherent natures of the risks [25]. Perceived risk offline is driven by nine characteristics of the hazard [23]: 1) voluntariness, 2) immediacy, 3) knowledge to the exposed, 4) knowledge to experts, 5) control, 6) newness, 7) common-dread, 8) chronic-catastrophic, and 9) severity. Offline, this framework informed four decades of research in risk perception and public policy in a variety of risk domains, e.g., environmental risk [24], health risk [28]. Online, this framework has been used to explain perceptions of technical security risks [25] and insider threats [21]. Mental model research not only focuses on security and privacy but also implements user perception of environmental hazards by incorporating Human-Computer Interaction (HCI) methods [10].

2.2   Browser Warnings and Toolbars

Wu et al. [51] investigated the impact of the three toolbars [11,27,37] and concluded that toolbars do not work. However, it provided no generalized findings for the design of interactions. Felt and Weinberger examined how often a person should be alerted with a warning after the dismissal of an initial warning [49]. Patil et al. [38] recommended providing delayed feedback for non-privacy critical situations. Instead we endeavored to implement real time feedback through risk indicators with the assumption that only the user knows what is privacy critical to them.

2.3   Graphical Usage in Risk Communication

Visual differences including personalized security indicators [33,40] have been proven effective in detecting Phishing websites [34]. Zhang et al. used text, infographics, and a comic to educate participants on why updating anti-virus software is important [55], users expressed that they understood why it was important and while making decisions after the study, referenced the comic example for guidance [54]. Garg et al. explored the difference between the same script when presented as a video and presented as text in educating individuals on how to avoid being victimized by phishing [26]. They used the metaphor of a solicitor impersonating a banking investigator to leverage story-telling to educate older users. Wash found individual stories told by someone users could identify with to be a highly effective form of risk communication [48].

2.4   Usability and Adaptability

Building the tool is not enough, it must also be usable and acceptable [5,16,17, 35]. Das et al. found that even technical experts do not adapt simple security tools if risk mitigation techniques are not communicated properly and if the benefits are unclear [13]. Thus, our goal was not only to build a usable and factually useful tool, but also one that communicated the risk mitigated by its use.

3   Prototype Design

Our tool focuses equally on ease of use and effective risk communication. The goal is to allow users to take a security risk only by making informed decisions with proper knowledge of the risk. The toolbar not only works on a local system but also remembers the user's choices and the context in which risks are acceptable, and minimizes risk in other contexts without storing it in the cloud. Our toolbar extension uses very simple metaphorical cartoons to indicate low, medium, and high-risk options. Figure 1 shows how the toolbar's buttons look. We instantiated the illustrations as buttons that control the browser settings while communicating the level of risk for a given connection with the selected parameters. We had three high-level contexts in the architecture (Web, Network, and User). The details of operation are described necessarily in other publications. Here the focus is on the user experiment and results. To evaluate certificates and generate custom certificate warnings, we used a machine learning approach described by Dong et al. [19], which later expanded with Microsoft [18].

The risk of the network connection was evaluated by reading the network policy and assessing the use of encryption during transmission. Our assessment also included the evaluation of familiarity of Service Set Identifier (SSIDs) and familiarity of the IDs of devices connected to the same SSID for wireless. The assessment of risk above the network level was a combination of the domain name, certificate, and page elements, mainly scripts. Domain names were evaluated based on personal history with an initial default of the top million trusted. The domain name reputation system was grounded in the initial anti-phishing reputation system described in IBM Systems Journal [45]. These visited domains became trusted one week after the first visit or upon explicit user action. That one week window is grounded in reported take-down times from private conversations in the Anti-Phishing Working Group. We evaluated the Certificates using machine learning as detailed in the specific publication on that module [19]. We evaluated the running scripts on familiarity and source. Some familiar scripts were white-listed or grey-listed based on source (e.g., Google Analytics was enabled on Google). Other indicators in our prototype included personal history, checks for common vectors for malware (i.e., Flash, iFrames), and any script that indicated cross-site scripting. This analysis was too burdensome for real-time, and we substituted a lightweight version for the actual experiment reported here. The likelihood of warnings was grounded in the risk setting chosen by the user. The default was a medium risk. The interaction was chosen based on previous work on risk perception, to align user mental model and construct on previous work on cartoons, videos, and images as online risk communication [7,26,44,54].

4   Method: Naturalistic Study

For our experiment, we recruited 82 participants by posting flyers at the university and various places of worship. The outreach to places of worship was grounded in team social connections and could arguably be considered snowball sampling. The goal of this outreach was to have a diverse sample. All stages and work were reviewed and approved by the Institutional Review Board. The first step for participants was completing an initial interview and survey that consisted of basic demographics and expertise questions. Qualitative team members from the College of Arts & Sciences conducted the interviews. We specifically sought non-technical users for this study, so 53 participants were invited to participate in the second portion of the study; the remaining 29 participants were deemed to have too much computer and security knowledge to continue the experiment. We measured the participant's expertise by a combination of knowledge skills and behavior questions from Rajivan et al.'s work [41].

Out of the invited participants, 44 decided to partake in the month-long second phase and were randomly divided into two groups: experimental and control. Both the control and experimental groups brought their personal laptops to our research house. They were assisted in the installation of Mozilla Firefox if they did not already have it installed, and the experimental extension from our technical team. No use instructions were initially given, excluding a brief installation video. The control group received a version of the extension that was designed not to interfere with their normal browsing and would only run in the background to perform risk calculation and logging usage data. The extension for the control group existed only as a data compilation tool for comparison with the experimental group. We gave the full extention to the experimental group. The default setting for each website, excluding those blacklisted, was set at medium for the experimental group on start. Participants could adjust their default ratings on the menu. Still, each new website visited would load at the selected default level until a participant changed the security rating by clicking on one of the three illustrations. After applying a new security level, the extension remembers the level given for each site and will load that on future visits.

We instructed the participants in both groups to use Firefox for their daily internet browsing. We also asked the participants not to use any other extensions during the experiment. Each participant returned once a week for four weeks for an hour session. They were paid $20 for each session. These sessions consisted of the participant being interviewed in one room while the technical team extracted their log data in another room. At the end of the four weeks, there was an exit interview and survey. We had 44 total participants complete the entire experiment, 23 in control, and 21 in the experimental group. We based the duration of the experiment in part on Anderson et al.'s work on habituation to security warnings [2]. The four week period was more extended than work by Vance et al., which combined recovery periods with functional magnetic resonance imaging (fMRI) examination of responses to warnings [46]. Their work indicated that habituation was evident within a week. Thus, our four-week experimental period should have been sufficient for any habituation effects to be apparent in the results.

5   Results: Naturalistic Study

In this section, we report on a four-week naturalistic study, which includes the interviews and the modifications of the secure browsing behavior of 44 participants. In a four week experiment, we monitored participants' practices as well as self-reported perceptions of their actions. Participants in the experimental group chose fewer online risks than those in the control group.

Interview data and computer logs were collected every week for four weeks from all participants. Crowd workers transcribed the audio files at TranscribeMe![1]. We used the online qualitative data analysis service Dedoose[2] to code the data and provide a first pass at the analysis. A team of researchers developed the original codes by examining the transcribed responses to the most relevant questions for this study. Two researchers coded small sections of transcripts until

---

[1] https://transcribeme.com/.
[2] http://www.dedoose.com/.

they achieved an inter-rater reliability score above 0.80 and then proceeded to code the remaining 200 transcripts. We asked the participants to use Firefox with the tool enabled for at least six hours per week. Users reported time with the tool fluctuated throughout the study, with 35% reporting that they used the tool for 0–9 h in the first week. By the third week, 33% reported minimal tool use, i.e., 0–9 h. By week 4, 26% reported using the tool 0–9 h; 44% used it 10–14 h, and 22% used it more. Our data collection validated these reports, which proves the tool use increased over time rather than decreasing.

Recall that, the tool accepts the settings for a second-level domain and applies that setting. The result is that there is less interaction with the toolbar over time, as an increasing number of sites will be set according to the user's preference because the websites the user visits will have been increasingly configured. The extension's most visible activity was blocking scripts that could contain malicious content. If participants clicked on the image of the pigs in the brick house, then the tool blocked large sections of advertisements, images, and videos (Low risk, high-security settings). If they clicked on the icon of the pigs in the straw house, then the tool blocked only items on the blacklist (High risk, low-security settings). In practice, this meant that the high risk, straw house, rating blocked almost nothing. Individual participants' answers to "Based on your interaction with the tool last week, what do you think the tool does?" ranged from accurate to erroneous, even in a single session. At some point in the four weeks, 88% of all participants reported accurately that the "tool blocks (removes/hides) things based on the security settings". Over half of this group also incorrectly stated that the tool provided anti-virus protection. Participants expressed their perceptions of convenience versus security and efficiency versus security, as well as wanting particular content and realizing there was a security issue. "I felt like the piggy in the brick wall. My computer was safer thanks to the tool, but there's a battle going on between security and convenience" stated one participant. The same participant then said about the high-risk setting, "The one it's currently on is its easiest setting and allows the website to work very efficiently". It is hard to judge perceptions on 'efficiency' except that the page would appear reasonable to them. Two users did report switching to the lowest security setting to speed up their computer. No participant singled out security versus privacy.

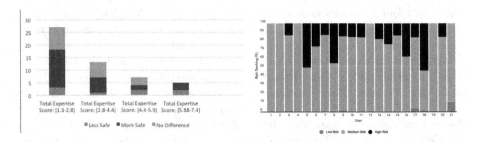

Fig. 2. Increased security perception for participants (left). Level of risk that each user chose during their fourth week of use (right).

Overall, 83% of participant responses indicated that they felt the pictures were effective as a tool for communicating computer security. Only two people said that they would have preferred words to pictures. One of those two felt it was too simple indicated, but that it would work for others: "I think it's good. I think I'm a pretty savvy internet user, it's a big part of my job and so... um, it's very easy, and it makes it very quick to notice, and I kept thinking this would probably be really good for like, my mom, who doesn't know as much". We show a more detailed breakdown of the participants'responses in Fig. 2. This comment may reflect not only ease of use, but also the fact that individuals are better at identifying rational responses to risk for others than to themselves [42]. The primary objection to the tool was that it included warnings, particularly password reuse warnings. The password warning for unsafe use was the only warning difficult to disable and triggered when a password was being sent over an unencrypted link or unprotected wireless connection. There would not be a technical solution at the browser to mitigate such a problem unless Tor or a VPN were integrated into the extension. Every other warning allowed individuals to reset their risk setting before moving forward and indicated that the person could go forward. We also inquired with the control group about the functionality of the tool. For the control group, the extension only logged their browsing activity and calculated the degree of risk for a given page. It was natural for the majority of the control group to respond that the tool gathers/tracks Internet browsing data. Only five people said otherwise, either believing that the tool was designed to track advertisements or that the tool was some form of anti-virus or malware protection. Three people reported that the tool was designed to change the computer speed, as some people reported issues with their computer operating noticeably slower.

5.1   Understanding the Tool

Participants largely understood the meaning of the pictures that conveyed their level of exposure to potential threats on webpages as a function of their own manipulated tool settings. There was some confusion between risk and protection as the lower security level represented a higher risk. The example below portrays a typical response where the confusion is evident; however, the participant's perception is on-point:

Interviewer: "This is Picture B. Can you tell me what this means?"

Participant: "Big bad wolf. This is the medium setting. Again, with what I originally thought the software would do, and these pictures... what they are, what they represent don't really line up to me. Cuz, it's not like anti-virus software. These pictures, to me, make me think, it's going to moderately protect my computer against certain websites that could be dangerous. But that's not really what it does. It just tells me whether it's safe or not, and it blocks some pictures. From what I can discern, ascertain. I don't know".

5.2   Changing Tool Risk Levels

10 of 25 experimental participants reported keeping the security setting on the lowest level the entire time. As the control group, the experimental group perceived their risk as more moderate than it was, as the graph of time spent at each level illustrates in Fig. 2b. 20 of the 25 experimental users reported reducing the settings at some point during the study period. Five said it only once, two in the first week, and three in the third. Reports of reducing the settings were consistent throughout the study. Participants generally wanted to see all of the content on the website or needed to reduce the settings to get the functionality from the site that they desired. There were more changes in risk levels than reported. By the final week, some participants reported not having to change the setting. The design goal was to make the tool highly usable. Therefore part of the customization was storing the participant's choice for a site, so it was not necessary to change the settings on return visits. Participants offered various reasons for changing the risk setting. One decreased security when the default was placed on medium for trusted sites, expressing this as, "Uh, I turned it on no security whenever it automatically bumped itself up to medium". A second participant also explained that decreasing security was needed to access content, "Most of the time, I would keep it on medium setting. That's always good. But if there's something like, if I needed to watch a video, I was like – I would go to Sports Center, and if I wanted to watch a video, I would have to put it on the low setting to watch some of the videos". A third participant explained, "On a site, like Reddit or a news – any site where if I click something and it takes me somewhere else - a site that redirects you - I would tend to put it on medium maybe more because I don't think I'm staying in the same place that I know is safe".

Eight people reported changing the setting to decrease risk, sometimes to hide advertisements (two participants), but the primary reason was playful exploration. Only three participants reported wanting to increase their security with the tool. Two of these three were in the lowest expertise score range. A total of 13 people reported simply playing with the tool. The most often mentioned benefit was ad-blocking functionality. In addition to the perceptions of changes, we examined how often there were changes. We evaluated how often a participant's browsing switched between high, medium, low-risk settings across different websites. We show the results for the last week in Fig. 2. This graph is only for the participants that continued the experiment through the fourth week. While some users chose to be at high risk, most users spent the majority of the time at medium risk. We also noticed that users chose higher risk settings when surfing social media sites; note that the tool at the lowest risk setting blocks almost all functionality of such sites. The extension defaulted to the medium level of risk whenever a user visited a new website, thus introducing protection from potentially malicious scripts and allowing the user to opt for increased or decreased protection. Not shockingly, defaults are powerful even when easy to change. One way of evaluating the graph above is that participants embraced the default setting most of the time.

5.3 Warnings

The following quotes represent how one user felt about password notifications. These findings point to the fact that people not only would not change their passwords but found the notifications about password security to be an annoyance.

Participant Week 1: "With the warnings about the passwords, there's no option to shut those notifications off. As it is with almost every security thing, it's like, 'Well, if you want to keep being reminded of this every time then"'.

The other warnings were click-through and allowed risk level changes. The warning which was explicitly mentioned as problematic was the password warning.

Participant Week 2: "So, when it gives you the, 'You've used this password before,' there's got to be a checkbox for, 'Stop reminding of this.' So, that made it worse. That's pretty much it".

None of the warnings could be disabled, but the other warnings were not subject to complaints.

6 Method: In-Lab Experiment

For the follow-up study, we conducted an in-lab experiment with 45 participants. The second phase of the study was reviewed and approved by the Institutional Review Board as well. For this phase of the study, we partially implemented the study design implemented in an eye-tracking survey for security indicators by Majid et al., where the secure browsing indicators were added to the browsing experience of the users [3]. Out of the 45 participants, nine were female, and 36 were male. Ten participants were within 18–21 (inclusive) years old, 30 were between 22–25 years old, and five were between 26–30. Twenty-four participants were undergraduate students, and 21 participants were graduate students recruited from a non-technical security course at the university. We mainly chose a younger crowd to test the usability, acceptability, and efficacy of the tool. We provided the participants with a verbal recruitment script, which explained the in-lab experiment.

We experimented in the university's computer lab, where the participants used either their personal laptop or the lab's computer where Mozilla Firefox was installed, and it was mandatory for the participants to use Mozilla Firefox for the integration of the experimental toolbar. After providing the verbal recruitment script, we informed the participants that their participation would yield an accepted payment of $2.00. After that, we randomly assigned them to a group that decided their bonus pay, which could be anywhere between $0–$8.00. We provided the students with a link which placed them in a randomly assigned group. The experiment included eight different conditions across two penalty stress conditions and four experimental presentation groups. We based the two different stress conditions by showing a time penalty for incorrect selections or a deduction in payment. The remaining presentation conditions included the control group which showed sites without our experimental toolbar, the low-risk tolerance group which presented sites through the lens of the low-risk high-security setting, the medium risk tolerance which showed places with the medium risk medium security setting, and finally the high-risk tolerance group that presented sites with the toolbar on the high-risk, low-security environment.

After the assignment of the random conditions, the participants went through the pre-screening questions, where we asked them about their age, nationality, and native language. The experiment included only participants who were more than 18 years old, lived in the US to remove cultural biases, and also to facilitate the location restriction of the in-lab study, and could read and write in English. The experimental setup provided each participant with 26 individual website images, which were randomly sorted into spoofed and non-spoofed versions of the website. If the participants trusted the site, they clicked the login or the sign-in button. If the participants didn't trust the website, then they could click the back button. If the participants clicked login for a bad site, then the error message "Clicked on a Bad Site" popped up. If the participants clicked the back button on a legitimate website, then the error message "Did not click on a good site" popped up. For a successful click, the experiment setup directed the participant to the next website. The participants in the time penalty, for every incorrect click, got a sentence of 15 seconds and could not proceed further until the penalty period ended. The timer was on during their selection of the website. Thus, we ensured the timer created the required stress condition. We penalized the other group with the bonus deduction with $0.67 from the $8.00 allotted for the max bonus pay on incorrect selections. Thus, though the time was not a stress condition here, the wrong choice still yielded them the loss of the bonus pay. After explaining the entire procedure, we also asked the participants questions to check their understanding to ensure that they correctly understood the process as the whole. After they correctly answered the whole question set, we directed the participants to their respective set of websites. After they went through the experiment, the participants answered some computer knowledge, expertise, and behavioral questions.

7   Results: In-Lab Experiment

We also report on the in-lab study, with a different set of 45 participants on the usability, acceptability, and efficacy of the implementation of the toolbar extension. We calculated how participants behaved between the toolbar and control groups and found significant improvement ($W = 18$, $p = 0.005$) in detecting Phishing websites when we compared the Toolbar Low-Risk High-Security Option with that of the control group. We also tested the stress conditions (Money versus Time) in our experiment to analyze how stress creates risk behavior changes. However, we were unable to find any significant differences between the two sets of participants while evaluating their accuracy ratings ($p = 0.8$). Thus we cannot conclude that the difference in stress conditions created much

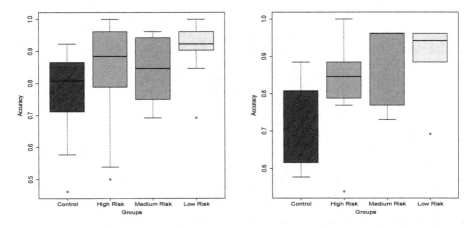

Fig. 3. Box plot of distribution of accuracy (left) and time as stress condition (right).

difference. However, we found significant results when we compared the control with the stress condition as Time and the participants who received toolbar set as low-risk tolerance with the Time condition ($p = 0.04$). Figure 3 shows the significant improvement in the accuracy of the participants who used the toolbar as compared to the participants in the control group. The participants' familiarity with the websites impacts the how the toolbar behaves. The tool modifies the interface based on whether the users are interacting with the toolbar for the first time. Therefore, to evaluate the efficacy of such a mechanism, it was critical to capture the website familiarty score for the participants. We ran a regression where the accuracy was the dependent variable, and the familiarity score was the independent value. We found a positive correlation of the accuracy of the participants with the familiarity ($r = 0.45$), and the correlation of the accuracy with the familiarity was statistically significant ($p = 0.02$). Figure 4 shows the scatter plot of the accuracy of predicting the websites correctly based on their familiarity with the website.

8   Discussion

The results of the four-week test showed that people would change their risk exposure if it is simple to do so. Significant changes in risk exposure online at the individual level, aggregated over users, creates a decrease in exposure. It also illustrated that people did not necessarily feel that they were changing their behaviors. Although the changes in risk level continued over four weeks, the reported changes in risk level decreased. Our optimistic perspective is that this implied that changing the risk level became significantly relaxed as not to be remembered. The result of the in-lab phishing study is that the tool easily distinguished between familiar and unfamiliar sites. Currently, it is trivially easy to implement a phishing site by copying the code and functionality of a legitimate website. The extensive blocking would make such attacks much more difficult.

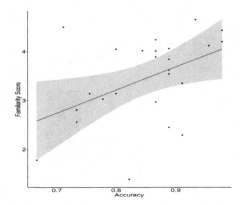

Fig. 4. Scatter plot showing accuracy of the participants in correspondence to their familiarity level with the website

The ease of overriding the blocking makes the defense acceptable. The control group expressed high levels of confidence in their safety and practices. This is not uncommon in computer security and privacy risks. Wash found that vulnerable participants whose mental models of computer security were aligned with unsafe behaviors felt quite safe online [48]. In a study of two-factor authentication, individuals rejected additional security on the basis that they thought their own passwords were secure [20]. Our instrumentation could only measure when Firefox was in use; therefore, if the participants changed browsers, then the data would not be included. If this experimental prototype were to be used in production, the measures of risk would need to be more exacting. The domain names and certificate results were consistently reliable, as shown by the previous studies where the website certificates and domain names were studied [19,45]. The use of PhishTank as a source of blacklisting was feasible only because the use of the toolbar was limited; a dedicated site would be needed in production. Instead of the rough identification for scripts, advanced collaborative script detection should be used. The computational complexity of measuring the risks of scripts is the reason we used white lists and blacklists, despite the relevant preexisting research on that topic.

9   Limitations and Future Work

To preserve the privacy of participants, we did not record the specific addresses of visited sites by a particular person or group. They were used solely on the back-end of the system in the naturalistic study. As a result, specific traffic data by group or person was intentionally not compiled. The in-lab study had a limited number of people tested under two stress conditions; given the lab setting, the generalizability of observed phishing resilience may be restricted. The components of phishing resilience are an area where additional cross-cultural studies would inform our results. This research builds on decades of findings surrounding risk perception, particularly the perception of online risks. Previous studies reported our work on understanding, estimation, and interaction with privacy risk. The default selected for the naturalistic testing of the prototype was a medium risk. The uncertainty in calculations of the security and privacy risks reifies the importance of defaults. Future work could also include bundling the toolbar with anti-virus programs, mainly as many participants believed this was already the case. Ideally, such an interaction could be bundled with other privacy-protecting systems; Tor could be an ideal candidate. A larger-scale phishing identification experiment with a more diverse population is an additional possibility for future work.

10   Conclusion

As threat detection and information technology become more complex, non-technical people who are already overwhelmed cannot be expected to manage this complexity. These two trends, increasingly sophisticated threats and increasing technical heterogeneity in the user population, have been treated as if they exist in opposition. Through our toolbar implementation and user studies (naturalistic and in-lab study) have shown that these issues can be well-aligned by combining risk communication and usable interactions with a complex, personalized back-end. In the naturalistic experiment, we found that those with the toolbar extension took fewer risks and were more aware of online risk than the control group. Participants in our in-lab experiment showed that using the toolbar extension significantly increased their accuracy in detecting spoofed websites. They determined the acceptability of risk given their history and contexts. Usability, cognitive misalignment, or incentive misalignment have all been presented as underlying the vulnerability to phishing. Among security professionals beyond the usability community, it is common to hear of the "dancing pigs" problem, where *"Given a choice between dancing pigs and security, users will pick dancing pigs every time"*. The challenge to security is framed as security awareness, where users must engage in constant vigilance. Universal constant vigilance and technical excellence is not a reasonable expectation. Our work illustrates that when people are provided clear risk communication and empowered to avoid risks, they do so. Technology needs to provide the right risk communication, at the right time, in the right context, aligned with user mental models and risk perceptions.

Acknowledgement. This paper is dedicated to the memory of programming staff Tom Denning. We want to acknowledge the substantive contributions of Mike D'Arcy as well as Timothy Kelley. We acknowledge the contributions of Jill Minor in substantive editing. This research was sponsored by DHS N66001-12-C-0137, Cisco Research 591000, and Google Privacy & Security Focused Research. The views and conclusions contained in this document are those of the authors and should not be interpreted as representing the official policies or views, either expressed or implied, of the DHS, ARL, Google, Cisco, IU, or the US Government. We also want to acknowledge contributors to the experiment itself at Indiana University, including Deborah Taylor, Prashanth Rajivan, and Krishna C. Bathina.

References

1. 97% of people globally unable to correctly identify phishing emails, May 2015. https://www.businesswire.com/news/home/20150512005245/en/97-People-Globally-Unable-Correctly-Identify-Phishing

2. Anderson, B.B., Kirwan, C.B., Jenkins, J.L., Eargle, D., Howard, S., Vance, A.: How polymorphic warnings reduce habituation in the brain: insights from an FMRI study. In: Proceedings of the 33rd Annual ACM Conference on Human Factors in Computing Systems, pp. 2883–2892. ACM (2015)

3. Arianezhad, M., Camp, L.J., Kelley, T., Stebila, D.: Comparative eye tracking of experts and novices in web single sign-on. In: Proceedings of the Third ACM Conference on Data and Application Security and Privacy, pp. 105–116. ACM (2013)

4. Asgharpour, F., Liu, D., Camp, L.J.: Mental models of security risks. In: Dietrich, S., Dhamija, R. (eds.) FC 2007. LNCS, vol. 4886, pp. 367–377. Springer, Heidelberg (2007). https://doi.org/10.1007/978-3-540-77366-5_34

5. Assal, H., Chiasson, S.: Will this onion make you cry? A usability study of tor-enabled mobile apps. In: Poster presented at the 10th Symposium on Usable Privacy and Security (SOUPS) (2014)

6. Bartsch, S., Volkamer, M., Cased, T.: Effectively communicate risks for diverse users: a mental-models approach for individualized security interventions. In: GI-Jahrestagung, pp. 1971–1984 (2013)

7. Benton, K., Camp, L.J., Garg, V.: Studying the effectiveness of android application permissions requests. In: 2013 IEEE International Conference on Pervasive Computing and Communications Workshops (PERCOM Workshops), pp. 291–296. IEEE (2013)

8. Blythe, J., Camp, L.J.: Implementing mental models. In: 2012 IEEE Symposium on Security and Privacy Workshops (SPW), pp. 86–90. IEEE (2012)

9. Bravo-Lillo, C., Cranor, L.F., Downs, J., Komanduri, S.: Bridging the gap in computer security warnings: a mental model approach. IEEE Secur. Priv. **2**, 18–26 (2010)

10. Camp, L.J.: Mental models of privacy and security. Available at SSRN 922735 (2006)

11. CoreStreet: Spoofstick (2004). http://www.corestreet.com/spoofstick/

12. Cranor, L.F., Garfinkel, S.: Security and Usability: Designing Secure Systems that People can Use. O'Reilly Media, Inc., Sebastopol (2005)

13. Das, S., Dingman, A., Camp, L.J.: Why Johnny doesn't use two factor a two-phase usability study of the FIDO U2F security key. In: Meiklejohn, S., Sako, K. (eds.) FC 2018. LNCS, vol. 10957, pp. 160–179. Springer, Heidelberg (2018). https://doi.org/10.1007/978-3-662-58387-6_9

14. Das, S., Kim, A., Tingle, Z., Nippert-Eng, C.: All about phishing: exploring user research through a systematic literature review. arXiv preprint arXiv:1908.05897 (2019)

15. Das, S., Kim, D., Kelley, T., Camp, L.J.: Grifting in the digital age (2018)

16. Das, S., Wang, B., Camp, L.J.: MFA is a waste of time! understanding negative connotation towards MFA applications via user generated content. In: Proceedings of the Thriteenth International Symposium on Human Aspects of Information Security & Assurance (HAISA 2019) (2019)

17. Das, S., Wang, B., Tingle, Z., Camp, L.J.: Evaluating user perception of multi-factor authentication: a systematic review. arXiv preprint arXiv:1908.05901 (2019)

18. Dong, Z., Kane, K., Camp, L.J.: Detection of rogue certificates from trusted certificate authorities using deep neural networks. ACM Trans. Priv. Secur. (TOPS) **19**(2), 5 (2016)
19. Dong, Z., Kapadia, A., Blythe, J., Camp, L.J.: Beyond the lock icon: real-time detection of phishing websites using public key certificates. In: 2015 APWG Symposium on Electronic Crime Research (eCrime), pp. 1–12. IEEE (2015)
20. Fagan, M., Khan, M.M.H.: Why do they do what they do?: A study of what motivates users to (not) follow computer security advice. In: Twelfth Symposium on Usable Privacy and Security (SOUPS 2016), pp. 59–75 (2016)
21. Farahmand, F., Spafford, E.H.: Understanding insiders: an analysis of risk-taking behavior. Inf. Syst. Front. **15**(1), 5–15 (2013). https://doi.org/10.1007/s10796-010-9265-x
22. Felt, A.P., et al.: Rethinking connection security indicators. In: SOUPS, pp. 1–14 (2016)
23. Fischhoff, B., Slovic, P., Lichtenstein, S., Read, S., Combs, B.: How safe is safe enough? A psychometric study of attitudes towards technological risks and benefits. Policy Sci. **9**(2), 127–152 (1978). https://doi.org/10.1007/BF00143739
24. Flynn, J., Slovic, P., Mertz, C.K.: Gender, race, and perception of environmental health risks. Risk Anal. **14**(6), 1101–1108 (1994)
25. Garg, V., Camp, J.: End user perception of online risk under uncertainty. In: 2012 45th Hawaii International Conference on System Science (HICSS), pp. 3278–3287. IEEE (2012)
26. Garg, V., Camp, L.J., Connelly, K., Lorenzen-Huber, L.: Risk communication design: video vs. text. In: Fischer-Hübner, S., Wright, M. (eds.) PETS 2012. LNCS, vol. 7384, pp. 279–298. Springer, Heidelberg (2012). https://doi.org/10.1007/978-3-642-31680-7_15
27. Herzberg, A., Gbara, A.: Trustbar: protecting (Even Naive) web users from spoofing and phishing attacks. Technical report, Cryptology ePrint Archive, Report 2004/155 (2004). http://eprint.iacr.org/2004/155
28. Johnson, B.B., Slovic, P.: Presenting uncertainty in health risk assessment: initial studies of its effects on risk perception and trust. Risk Anal. **15**(4), 485–494 (1995)
29. Kelley, T., Amon, M.J., Bertenthal, B.I.: Statistical models for predicting threat detection from human behavior. Front. Psychol. **9**, 466 (2018)
30. Likarish, P., Dunbar, D.E., Hourcade, J.P., Jung, E.: Bayeshield: conversational anti-phishing user interface. In: SOUPS, vol. 9, p. 1 (2009)
31. Lin, J., Amini, S., Hong, J.I., Sadeh, N., Lindqvist, J., Zhang, J.: Expectation and purpose: understanding users' mental models of mobile app privacy through crowdsourcing. In: Proceedings of the 2012 ACM Conference on Ubiquitous Computing, pp. 501–510. ACM (2012)
32. Marchal, S., Asokan, N.: On designing and evaluating phishing webpage detection techniques for the real world. In: 11th USENIX Workshop on Cyber Security Experimentation and Test (CSET 2018). USENIX Association (2018)
33. Marforio, C., Jayaram Masti, R., Soriente, C., Kostiainen, K., Čapkun, S.: Evaluation of personalized security indicators as an anti-phishing mechanism for smartphone applications. In: Proceedings of the 2016 CHI Conference on Human Factors in Computing Systems, pp. 540–551. ACM (2016)
34. Maurer, M.E., Herzner, D.: Using visual website similarity for phishing detection and reporting. In: CHI 2012 Extended Abstracts on Human Factors in Computing Systems, pp. 1625–1630. ACM (2012)

35. McCune, J.M., Perrig, A., Reiter, M.K.: Bump in the ether: a framework for securing sensitive user input. In: Proceedings of the Annual Conference on USENIX 2006 Annual Technical Conference, p. 17. USENIX Association (2006)
36. Moore, T., Clayton, R.: The impact of public information on phishing attack and defense (2011)
37. Netcraft: Netcraft toolbar (2004). http://toolbar.netcraft.com/
38. Patil, S., Hoyle, R., Schlegel, R., Kapadia, A., Lee, A.J.: Interrupt now or inform later?: comparing immediate and delayed privacy feedback. In: Proceedings of the 33rd Annual ACM Conference on Human Factors in Computing Systems, pp. 1415–1418. ACM (2015)
39. Patrick, A.: Ecological validity in studies of security and human behaviour. In: SOUPS (2009)
40. Raja, F., Hawkey, K., Hsu, S., Wang, K.L., Beznosov, K.: Promoting a physical security mental model for personal firewall warnings. In: CHI 2011 Extended Abstracts on Human Factors in Computing Systems, pp. 1585–1590. ACM (2011)
41. Rajivan, P., Moriano, P., Kelley, T., Camp, L.J.: Factors in an end-usersecurity expertise instrument. Inf. Comput. Secur. 25(2), 190–205 (2017)
42. Slovic, P., Finucane, M.L., Peters, E., MacGregor, D.G.: Risk as analysis and risk as feelings: some thoughts about affect, reason, risk, and rationality. Risk Anal. 24(2), 311–322 (2004)
43. Stanton, J.M., Stam, K.R., Mastrangelo, P., Jolton, J.: Analysis of end user security behaviors. Comput. Secur. 24(2), 124–133 (2005)
44. Tsai, J.Y., Egelman, S., Cranor, L., Acquisti, A.: The effect of online privacy information on purchasing behavior: an experimental study. Inf. Syst. Res. 22(2), 254–268 (2011)
45. Tsow, A., Viecco, C., Camp, L.J.: Privacy-aware architecture for sharing web histories. IBM Syst. J. 3, 5–13 (2007)
46. Vance, A., Kirwan, B., Bjorn, D., Jenkins, J., Anderson, B.B.: What do we really know about how habituation to warnings occurs over time?: A longitudinal FMRI study of habituation and polymorphic warnings. In: Proceedings of the 2017 CHI Conference on Human Factors in Computing Systems, pp. 2215–2227. ACM (2017)
47. Volkamer, M., Renaud, K.: Mental Models – general introduction and review of their application to human-centred security. In: Fischlin, M., Katzenbeisser, S. (eds.) Number Theory and Cryptography. LNCS, vol. 8260, pp. 255–280. Springer, Heidelberg (2013). https://doi.org/10.1007/978-3-642-42001-6_18
48. Wash, R.: Folk models of home computer security. In: Proceedings of the Sixth Symposium on Usable Privacy and Security, p. 11. ACM (2010)
49. Weinberger, J., Felt, A.P.: A week to remember: the impact of browser warning storage policies. In: Symposium on Usable Privacy and Security (2016)
50. Workman, M., Bommer, W.H., Straub, D.: Security lapses and the omission of information security measures: a threat control model and empirical test. Comput. Hum. Behav. 24(6), 2799–2816 (2008)
51. Wu, M., Miller, R.C., Garfinkel, S.L.: Do security toolbars actually prevent phishing attacks? In: Proceedings of the SIGCHI Conference on Human Factors in Computing Systems, pp. 601–610. ACM (2006)
52. Yakowicz, W.: The 3 biggest phishing scams of 2018, July 2018. https://www.inc.com/will-yakowicz/biggest-email-phishing-scams-2018.html
53. Yee, K.P.: Designing and evaluating a petname anti-phishing tool. In: Poster presented at Symposium on usable Privacy and Security (SOUPS), pp. 6–8. Citeseer (2005)

54. Zhang-Kennedy, L., Chiasson, S.: Using comics to teach users about mobile online privacy. Technical report, Technical Report TR-14-02, School of Computer Science, Carleton University, Ottawa, Canada (2014)
55. Zhang-Kennedy, L., Chiasson, S., Biddle, R.: Stop clicking on "Update Later": persuading users they need up-to-date antivirus protection. In: Spagnolli, A., Chittaro, L., Gamberini, L. (eds.) PERSUASIVE 2014. LNCS, vol. 8462, pp. 302–322. Springer, Cham (2014). https://doi.org/10.1007/978-3-319-07127-5_27
56. Zurko, M.E., Simon, R.T.: User-centered security. In: Proceedings of the 1996 Workshop on New Security Paradigms, pp. 27–33. ACM (1996)

Secure Email - A Usability Study

Adrian Reuter[1], Karima Boudaoud[2(✉)], Marco Winckler[2], Ahmed Abdelmaksoud[2], and Wadie Lemrazzeq[2]

[1] Technische Universität München, Arcisstraße 21, 80333 Munich, Germany
[2] Université Côte d'Azur, CNRS, I3S, Sophia Antipolis, France
`karima.boudaoud@unice.fr`

Abstract. Several end-to-end encryption technologies for emails such as PGP and S/MIME exist since decades. However, end-to-end encryption is barely applied. To understand why users hesitate to secure their email communication and which usability issues they face with PGP, S/MIME as well as with pEp (Pretty Easy Privacy), a fairly new technology, we conducted an online survey and user testing. We found that more than 60% of e-mail users are unaware of the existence of such encryption technologies and never tried to use one. We observed that above all, users are overwhelmed with the management of public keys and struggle with the setup of encryption technology in their mail software. Even though users struggle to put email encryption into practice, we experienced roughly the same number of users being aware of the importance of email encryption. Particularly, we found that users are very concerned about identity theft, as 78% want to make sure that no other person is able to write email in their name.

Keywords: Mail encryption · User study · Usability · PGP · S/MIME · pEp

1 Introduction

To prevent cyber-crime and to protect user privacy, almost all services running on the Internet critically depend on cyber security measures. Most dominantly, transport layer security (TLS) is used for securing a variety of communication protocols. Particularly when browsing the World Wide Web, transport security has found wide adoption and awareness of its imperative necessity. Internet Banking, shopping on Amazon.com, accessing governmental e-services - those are just a few examples where users became more and more aware of the security risks of web applications. A huge step towards more secure Internet communication has been the integration of end-to-end cryptography in mobile internet messenger services such as Whatsapp, Signal or Telegram. In contrast, for securing one of the most commonly used communication channels, the email end-to-end encryption is only applied by a negligible faction of email users [1]. Standardized technologies for cryptographically securing email exchanges have been available for decades. Nevertheless most users rely on unencrypted and unauthenticated email communication, often without being aware that there exist mechanisms, which would mitigate the security implications that come with it. Actually, two major end-to-end encryption technologies exist since decades, namely Pretty Good Privacy (PGP) [2]

M. Bernhard et al. (Eds.): FC 2020 Workshops, LNCS 12063, pp. 36–46, 2020.
https://doi.org/10.1007/978-3-030-54455-3_3

and Secure Multipurpose Internet Mail Extensions (S/MIME) [3]. A recent initiative called Pretty Easy Privacy (pEp) [4] made efforts to simplify the usage of end-to-end cryptography in email communication for novice users. Unfortunately, those technologies are still barely deployed. According to [1] more than 95% of the overall email traffic is exchanged without end-to-end encryption. Therefore, two main research questions came to our mind: 1) why are users hesitating to use e-mail end-to-end encryption technologies and 2) which usability issues exist that hinder users from securing their daily email communication using end-to-end encryption. To address these questions we have conducted an online survey and user testing in which participants actively use encryption, in order to get a precise and authentic view on usability issues.

The rest of the paper is organized as follows. Section 2 gives an overview about the methodology used to conduct the usability study. Section 3 discusses the obtained results. Finally, Sect. 4 concludes this paper and gives an overview about future works.

2 Methodology

In this section, we present our approach for evaluating the usability of PGP, S/MIME and pEp.

Before conducting our study, we have identified the most commonly Mail User Agents (MUA) also known as email programs, that - natively or by additional plugins - support at least one of the three technologies PGP, S/MIME or pEp. We assessed the usability of the encryption features in each of these mail programs to get a personal impression as well as to anticipate the challenges that other users might face when cryptographically securing their emails. Actually, we tested the integration of PGP, S/MIME and pEp in today's most commonly used mail programs (MUA) that support end-to-end encryption to: 1) identify which encryption technology is supported by which MUA, 2) prevent participants from testing MUAs that turn out to be unusable (e.g. due to discontinued development, incompatibility of versions and operating system,...), 3) anticipate the challenges users could face when trying to use these three technologies in the context of a specific MUA to help them to overcome common pitfalls that would otherwise ultimately hinder them from sending a secure e- mail.

Table 1 represents the Mail User Agents considered in our analysis. It also depicts the plugin required to add PGP, S/MIME or pEp functionality to a MUA if not supported natively. From this collection of MUAs, we had to choose the subset of MUAs that will be used for user testing taking into account the popularity of the MUAs and considering that each encryption technology should be tested on each major platform (if supported) and should be free of costs for our participants. We assumed that even if the technology is usable, its implementation within an e-mail program might make it difficult to use and vice-versa. Therefore, we wanted our participants to test two different implementations of e-mail encryption, to have a direct comparison of their usability: a participant would either test two different technologies or she/he would test two different implementations of the same technology. Particularly, when testing two different technologies, we let participants test a pEp implementation and a PGP or S/MIME implementation, in order to see if pEp indeed meets its goal of simplifying the mail encryption process.

Table 1. Commonly used mail user agents (MUA) and their support for PGP, S/MIME and pEp

Technology	Mail user agents	Plugin	Tested
PGP	Outlook Desktop 2013/2016	Gpg4o	✓
	Thunderbird	Enigmail	✓
	Gmail (Webmail)	FlowCrypt	✓
	Other Webmail	Mailvelope	✓
	Apple iOS	iPG mail app.	x
	Android	Maildroid and Cryptoplugin	✓
	Windows Mail	Not Supported	x
	Apple Mail (MacOS)	Not Supported	x
S/MIME	Outlook Desktop 2013/2016	Native support	✓
	Thunderbird	Native support	✓
	Apple iOS	iPhone mail app	✓
	Android	Maildroid and Cryptoplugin	✓
	MacOS	Native support	✓
	Gmail (Webmail)	Not Supported	x
	Other Webmail	Not Supported	x
	Windows Mail	Native support	x
pEp	Thunderbird	Enigmail	✓
	Android	Official pEp app	✓
	Apple iOS	App coming soon	x
	Outlook Desktop 2013/2016	pEp for outlook	x
	MacOS	Not supported	x
	Gmail (Webmail)	Not Supported	x
	Other Webmail	Not Supported	x
	Windows Mail	Not supported	x

To assess the use of PGP, S/MIME and pEp, we have employed two methods: an online survey with 50 participants and conducted a user testing with 12 participants. The details about these studies and the corresponding results are given hereafter.

2.1 Online Survey

The aim of the online survey on email end-to-end encryption technologies was threefold. First, to explore users understanding and awareness of security in emails exchanges, their expectations and opinions on end-to-end encryption. Second, to learn about the propagation of PGP, S/MIME and pEp. Third, to compare the results of the online survey, which are quantitative, with the results of the user testing, that are qualitative.

The survey included closed-ended questions (multiple choice questions), open-ended questions and ranked questions with a balanced rating scale.

2.2 User Testing

The user testing was conducted adhering to a predefined testing protocol. Each user testing started with a short interview of the participant, determining some demographic data (age, nationality, profession), the preferred MUA to access her/his emails and previous knowledge the participant had about cryptography in general or email encryption in particular. When the participant was familiar with one of the MUAs, we proposed her/him the test scenario related to this MUA so that she/he could focus on configuring and using encryption features rather than struggling with an unknown mail software. For the participants who did not have any experience or knowledge on any of the MUAs proposed, we helped them to install and set up a MUA up to the point that they were able to successfully access their mail account. Each participant was then asked to enable and configure the security features of the chosen MUA to use a specific email encryption technology and send a secured email to us. When the participants were struggling for more than 10 min with a specific configuration step, we helped them. The user test was completed once we received an email sent by the participant that was successfully encrypted and signed.

3 Evaluation

3.1 Online Survey Results

The online survey was launched on 30 November 2018 and reached 50 participants on 12 December 2018 when we started the analysis of the results.

The survey began with a demographic section. The majority of the participants was under 30 years old, coming from Germany, Egypt and Morocco. Most of them were students and employees working for IT organizations.

The results concerning the participants personal experience with email exchange showed that emails constitute a remarkable portion of their daily communications, reaching at least 7 emails per day, but most of them were nor encrypted neither signed, 38% received at least 1 mail encrypted per day, and less than half of the participants were obliged to use end-to-end encryption by their organizations. Regarding the use of email software, the participant used more than one software. More than half of the participants used dedicated mobile applications, 50% used webmail, and 44% used dedicated desktop applications.

Results for PGP
The results regarding the use of PGP are:

- 60% of the participants never heard about PGP, 40% knew PGP but only 24% were also using it.
- 70% of the participants stated that they could not use PGP for all emails due to the fact that the recipient did not use PGP.

- 25% of the participants thought that it was difficult to find the recipient's public key, 20% thought that configuring PGP was time consuming and just 5% declared that PGP is not implemented on their favorite platform/email client.
- 20% of the participants were always verifying the fingerprint of the recipient key, 30% were doing it occasionally, 35% never did and 15% did not know.
- The participants conceded that PGP guaranties privacy, confidentiality, authenticity and integrity, in addition to the fact that there was no cost for using it. However, they stated that comparing fingerprints was difficult and time consuming, and required the recipient to use it as well, which was not always the case given that PGP was not widely adopted.
- Participants suggested to make PGP supported on all platforms and simplify fingerprint comparison (Fig. 1).

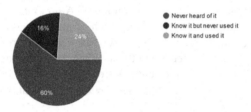

Fig. 1. Do you know a technology called Pretty Good Privacy (PGP)?

Results for S/MIME
The results regarding the use of S/MIME are:

- 64% of the participants never heard about S/MIME, 36% knew it but only 18% were also using it.
- 61% of the participants stated that the recipient was not using S/MIME.
- 28% did not trust digital certificates or its issuing entity and only 11% did not know how to obtain digital certificate.
- 17% encountered difficulties configuring their environment to use S/MIME.
- 27% admitted that they had issues with untrusted certificates and 28% indicated that having to pay for a trustworthy certificate is an obstacle.
- The participants agreed that S/MIME had the advantage of being integrated in most email clients including Apple MacOS/iOS, but they discredited it because they needed to pay to obtain a trustfully certificate.

Results for pEp
Regarding pEp, the results showed that it is not as known as PGP and S/MIME and only 10% knew it. No participant stated that she/he ever used it. Moreover, 40% of the participants hesitated to use pEp because their recipients would not use it.

Results on the Overall Impression of the Users on End-to-End Encryption

The goal of the last part of the survey was to gather the overall impression on end-to-end encryption, by scaling the degree of awareness of the participants on matter of email exchange security, especially if they had an email piracy issue.

Assessing their overall impression, the participants were mostly aware of the importance of email encryption: 66% thought that email encryption is important to very important (34% for important and 32% for very important).

Considering the scenario of non-secured email exchange, more than 60% of the participants could imagine that their emails can be passively or actively tampered with; and even larger percentage of 86% assumed that an entity other than the email recipient can read the email content (Fig. 2).

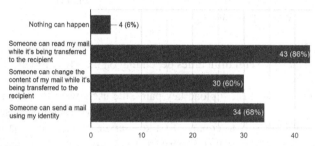

Fig. 2. Considering a scenario of using non- encrypted email communication, which of the following may occur?

Assessing the importance of specific security goals, almost all of the participants estimated the confidentiality, integrity and authenticity of their emails as important or very important. For only 6% of the participants, confidentiality does not matter and for only 2% the integrity of the sent emails does not matter (Fig. 3).

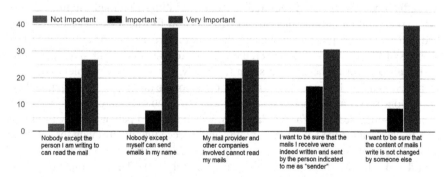

Fig. 3. Please indicate the importance that the following security goals have for you

3.2   User Testing Results

For the user testing, we have chosen a convenience sample where we have recruited 12 users mostly young people (students and IT users from Germany, Morocco and Egypt but also some family member), between 20 to 30 years old. The user testing has been done twice for each participant to test either two different implementation of the same technology or two different technologies.

The user testing allowed us to identify exactly at which steps users struggle the most. We noticed that the usability of an encryption technology largely depends on its implementation within a mail program, which leads to the fact that the same technology can be laborious to use in one MUA but convenient in another MUA.

The results presented in this part focus on the tasks that we identified as highly difficult for the participants to configure and use a specific encryption technology in the context of a specific mail program.

Results for PGP

The participants faced several difficulties depending on the MUA used:

- **Outlook 2016**: For the task "upload key pair", the users were not able to import an existing key-pair. The task "Get recipient key" was also difficult because the default configuration of Gpg4o is to connect to a key-server using an unusual port, which sometimes results in an empty response or a refused connection. The users were not able to find and download the recipient public key on this key server. Actually, is not trivial for users to identify this issue and accordingly go into the respective Outlook settings to change the port number to the one that is commonly used in combination with that key server. Moreover, when composing a new secure email and opting-in encryption and/or signature feature(s), the graphical user interface became distorted. Buttons, labels and text fields were misaligned and overlapped, making the user interface almost unusable particularly difficult to assess whether the correct option was selected.
- **Thunderbird**: Thunderbird required not only installing Enigmail plugin, but also extra configuration options that are not easy to find for the users. The participants had to activate the option "Force using PGP" in the privacy settings of Thunderbird after installing the plugin. Moreover, the option "Activate PGP" had to be applied for each mail account in the account settings. Finally, the step "Get recipient key" was identified as difficult, because Enigmail searched for the missing recipient public keys on only one server at a time. It was up to the users to manually change the key server on which Enigmail searches for missing keys, which required patience and willingness to tediously change the key server settings until succeeding in retrieving the recipient public key from one of the servers on which the recipient published her/his key.
- **Maildroid**: Maildroid (as all other mobile apps analyzed) offered no functionality to generate a PGP key-pair directly on the mobile device. The key had to be generated externally (e.g. on a PC) and then be transferred back to the mobile device. There were multiple ways to transfer the generated key pair (e.g. self-sending it via email, upload to a cloud, USB exchange), but it required intense user interaction and downgraded the user experience.

As summary, we recognize that PGP requires many configuration steps until successful usage, which was particularly the case for the task concerning the import of the public keys of recipients. This task always turned out to be difficult or tedious for all the participants, regardless of the tested platform. This is due to the design principle of PGP to let full control to the users with respect to key management – which at the same time is demanding a basic understanding of asymmetric cryptography and the technology. Following the user testing for PGP, we could conclude that the most difficult MUA to use PGP with was Thunderbird, because of the difficulties that the users faced in addition to the fact that the buttons to get configuration steps done are hidden deeply in setting menus. In contrast, FlowCrypt was the easiest tool to use PGP with, as it generates a key-pair for new user with only a few clicks and searches for the recipient key automatically on almost all commonly used key-servers. Thereby FlowCrypt solves nearly all usability issues encountered by the participants. Unfortunately it comes with two downsides: FlowCrypt uploads the generated key-pair only on its proprietary key server which is unknown to most other PGP implementations, thus making the import of public keys of FlowCrypt users harder for other users. Secondly, up to now, FlowCrypt only supports Gmail webmail.

Results for S/MIME
The difficulties encountered by the users are as follows:

- **Outlook 2016/2013**: The configuration option to let the users import their own digital certificates was not easy to find and the participants passed too much time looking for the button in the settings to import their certificate. In addition, they experienced a strange bug. The users could encrypt their outgoing emails only when replying to an encrypted email already received, but they could not encrypt a new email even though they already retrieved the certificate of the recipient.
- **iOS 12**: The users had to decompress, on a computer, the archive containing the requested certificate, received by email, from the issuing Certification Authority. Then, they had to send back the certificate (the.pfx file) as an attachment in an email to themselves. In addition, before importing the certificate, they needed to activate S/MIME manually in the settings of the iPhone. However, the respective setting option was fairly hidden in the phone settings menu.
- **Android**: The users had to decompress the received certificate file using another platform (e.g. a PC). Then, transfer back the certificate to the mobile device after decompressing it. It was the same problem as for iOS. They could only transfer it by sending an email to themselves containing the certificate (the.pfx file).

To conclude, thanks to the way S/MIME works, it can be used easily by novice users, because the users do not have to generate any keys. They receive both public and private digital certificate and they have just to import it into the MUA. Once a user receives a signed email, the sender's public certificate is integrated automatically into the MUA. So, the users do not have to do any supplementary tasks other than configuring S/MIME in the desired MUA. However, we can conclude that is very difficult to use S/MIME on Outlook, as the options to import the digital certificate are difficult to find and the user can send an encrypted email only as reply to an email that is already secured via

S/MIME (digitally signed). Also, on iOS it is very difficult to activate S/MIME on the device as the option is not easy to find and there is not any way for the users to send the pfx file back to the device than to send an email to themselves containing the pfx file. Moreover, the configuration to activate S/MIME on the iOS devices varies from one iOS version to another.

Results for pEp
pEp required only few tasks in order to configure it and use it compared to PGP and S/MIME. Thanks to automated key management, non-technical wording in its user inter-faces and abstraction of security features, pEp did not show any major usability issues that would hinder (novice) users from using it. The comparison of trustwords through the so-called pEp handshake, in order to establish trust in the recipient key, was considered as convenient and rather an easy task to do by most of the participants. Nevertheless, some of the participants did not understand why the handshake was necessary and what to do with the trustwords shown during the handshake graphical user interface. pEp showed to be the easiest technology to use, but unfortunately being not (yet) compatible with all major platforms. As a consequence, we could not test it on Apple MacOS or Apple iOS platforms, which was used by a large fraction of email users.

4 Related Work

In this section, we will give a brief overview on related work. In 2012, Moecke and Volkamer analyzed all different email services, defining security, usability and interop-erability criteria and applied them to existing approaches. Based on the results, closed and web-based systems like Hushmail were more usable, contrarily to PGP and SMIME that require add-ons to carry the key in a secure way [17]. In 2017, Lerner, Zeng and Roes-ner from University of Washington, presented a case study with people who frequently conduct sensitive business. They estimated the confidence put on encrypted emails using a prototype they developed based on Keybase for automatic key management [18]. In 2018, Clark et al. conducted a study focused on: 1) systematization of secure email approaches taken by industry, academia, and independent developers; 2) evaluation for proposed or deployed email security enhancements and measurement of their security, deployment, and usability. Through their study, they concluded that deployment and adoption of end-to-end encrypted email continues to face many challenges: usability on a day-to-day scale; key management which remains very unpractical [19]. In 2018, a group of researchers from Brigham Young University and University of Tennessee conducted a comparative usability study on key management in secure emails tools, in which they oversaw a comparative based study between passwords, public key directory (PKD), and identity-based encryption (IBE). The result of the study demonstrated that each key management has its potential to be successfully used in secure email [20].

5 Conclusion

In this paper, we identified the most frequent usability issues that users face when protecting their email communication using PGP, S/MIME or pEp. Using both online survey and user testing, we had an overall view on the awareness of the users on email encryption as well as a detailed view on the difficulties they can encounter. These difficulties have certainly an impact on the fact that they hesitate to use PGP, S/MIME or pEp.

Thanks to the online survey, we were able to identify the usability issues of each technology and assess the general impression of our audience towards the importance of email encryption. The results of the online survey showed us that the users were aware of the importance of email encryption with 32% saying it is very important. Additionally, users were very concerned about identity theft, as 78% of the participants wanted to make sure that no other person is able to write an email using their name and 80% of the participants wanted to be sure that the content of their mail is not changed by someone else, while being transferred to the recipient. This result shows that for many users, signing emails is more important than encrypting them.

Currently, we are finalizing the correlation of the online survey answers with the results of the user testing, to validate if the participants of the online survey have the same usability issues as the participants of the user testing while using a certain technology. For future work, we plan to conduct more user testing with different kinds of people (people with different age categories). In addition, thanks to the results obtained regarding identity theft and to some feedback we had on our study, we will set up another online survey to know the measures (if any) taken by the users to protect their identity.

References

1. Green, M.: The daunting challenge of secure e-mail. https://www.newyorker.com/tech/ann als-of-technology/the-daunting-challenge-of-secure-e-mail. Accessed 13 Feb 2019
2. Atkins, D., Stallings, W., Zimmermann, P.: PGP Message Exchange Formats. RFC 1991 (Informational), August 1996. Obsoleted by RFC 4880
3. Ramsdell, B.: S/MIME Version 3 Message Specification. RFC 2633 (Proposed Standard), June 1999. Obsoleted by RFC 3851
4. pEp Security: Pretty Easy Privacy. https://www.pep.security/. Accessed 13 Feb 2019
5. Elkins, M., Torto, D.D., Levien, R., Roessler, T.: MIME security with OpenPGP. RFC 3156 (Proposed Standard), August 2001
6. Callas, J., Donnerhacke, L., Finney, H., Shaw, D., Thayer, R.: OpenPGP message format. RFC 4880 (Proposed Standard), November 2007. Updated by RFC 5581
7. Wikipedia: Pretty good privacy. https://en.wikipedia.org/wiki/Pretty_Good_Privacy/. Accessed 13 Feb 2019
8. Lake, J.: What is PGP encryption and how does it work? https://en.wikipedia.org/wiki/Pre tty_Good_Privacy/. Accessed 13 Feb 2019
9. Protonmail: What are PGP/MIME and PGP/Inline? https://protonmail.com/support/knowle dge-base/pgp-mime-pgp-inline/. Accessed 13 Feb 2019
10. Borenstein, N., Freed, N.: MIME (Multipurpose Internet Mail Extensions) part one: mechanisms for specifying and describing the format of internet message bodies. RFC 1521 (Draft Standard), September 1993. Obsoleted by RFCs 2045, 2046, 2047, 2048, 2049, updated by RFC 1590

11. R. Laboratories: Cryptographic message syntax standard (1993). https://ipsec.pl/files/ipsec/Archiwum/pkcs-7.pdf
12. pEp foundation council: Pretty easy privacy whitepaper, 18 July 2018. https://pep.foundation/docs/pEp-whitepaper.pdf. Accessed 13 Feb 2019
13. Marques, H.: Pretty easy privacy: email formats and protocols, 18 July 2016. https://tools.ietf.org/html/draft-marques-pep-email-02. Accessed 13 Feb 2019
14. Marques, H., Hoeneisen, B.: Iana registration of trustword lists: guide, template and iana considerations, 26 June 2018. https://tools.ietf.org/html/draft-marques-pep-email-02. Accessed 13 Feb 2019
15. Marques, H., Hoeneisen, B.: Pretty easy privacy: contact and channel authentication through handshake. https://tools.ietf.org/html/draft-marques-pep-handshake-00. Accessed 13 Feb 2019
16. pEp security AG: pep official documentation - general information. https://www.pep.security/docs/general_information.html. Accessed 13 Feb 2019
17. Furnell, S.M., Clarke, N., Moecke, C.T., Volkamer, M.: Usable secure email communications - criteria and evaluation of existing approaches (2012)
18. Lerner, A., Zeng, E., Roesner, F.: Confidante: usable encrypted email a case study with lawyers and journalists (2017)
19. Clark, J., van Oorschot, P., Ruoti, S., Seamons, K., Zappala, D.: Securing email (2018)
20. Ruoti, S., Andersen, J., Monson, T., Zappala, D., Seamons, K.: A comparative usability study of key management in secure email (2018)

The Effects of Cue Utilization and Cognitive Load in the Detection of Phishing Emails

George Nasser[1] (ID), Ben W. Morrison[1,2(✉)] (ID), Piers Bayl-Smith[2] (ID), Ronnie Taib[3],
Michael Gayed[2], and Mark W. Wiggins[2] (ID)

[1] Charles Sturt University, Bathurst, NSW, Australia
ben.morrison@mq.edu.au
[2] Macquarie University, Sydney, NSW, Australia
[3] Data 61 CSIRO, Sydney, Australia

Abstract. Phishing emails represent a major threat to online information security. While the prevailing research is focused on users' susceptibility, few studies have considered the decision making strategies that account for skilled detection. One relevant facet of decision making is cue utilization, where users retrieve feature-event associations stored in long-term memory. High degrees of cue utilization help reduce the demands placed on working memory (i.e., cognitive load), and invariably improve decision performance (i.e., the information-reduction hypothesis in expert performance). The current study explored the effect of cue utilization and cognitive load when detecting phishing emails. A total of 50 undergraduate students completed: (1) a rail control task and; (2) a phishing detection task. A cue utilization assessment battery (EXPERTise 2.0) then classified participants with either higher or lower cue utilization. As expected, higher cue utilization was associated with a greater likelihood of detecting phishing emails. However, variation in cognitive load had no effect on phishing detection, nor was there an interaction between cue utilization and cognitive load. These findings have implications for our understanding of cognitive mechanisms that underpin the detection of phishing emails and the role of factors beyond the information-reduction hypothesis.

Keywords: Phishing emails · Cue utilization · Decision making · Cognitive load

1 Introduction

1.1 The Phishing Problem

Despite the best efforts of cybersecurity companies, the average email user must still respond to approximately sixteen phishing emails a month (Symantec 2018). In large organizations, this can amount to thousands of such emails arriving in employees' inbox each year, each with the potential to seriously disrupt productivity and damage reputation (Vergelis et al. 2018).

Over the last decade, a broad range of approaches have explored the reasons why certain users are more susceptible than others to cyberattacks (Williams et al. 2018). However, little research has explored the strategies that users adopt when making successful

© Springer Nature Switzerland AG 2020
M. Bernhard et al. (Eds.): FC 2020 Workshops, LNCS 12063, pp. 47–55, 2020.
https://doi.org/10.1007/978-3-030-54455-3_4

decisions about an email's legitimacy, such as the skilled use of cue-based associations in memory (Johnston and Morrison 2016; Morrison and Morrison 2015; Morrison et al. 2013a, 2013b; Wiggins 2015; Wiggins and O'Hare 2006). In the context of phishing detection, cue utilization is presumed to involve an individual's capacity to recognize features within an email that signal (often rapidly and unconsciously) an attempt to deceive.

When faced with a complex diagnostic task, expert decision makers automatically recognize features that cue patterns from memory, and which 'trigger' the rapid retrieval of a plausible response (e.g., a process of recognition-primed decision-making; Klein 1993). The timely recognition of these patterns will invariably reduce the demands placed on working memory, with attentional resources being deployed selectively to task-relevant features in the environment (Haider and Frensch 1999). Thus, when decision-makers possess a greater capacity for cue utilization, they have additional cognitive resources to respond to incoming demands (Brouwers et al. 2017; Ericsson and Lehmann 1996). This implies that greater levels of cue utilization may 'buffer' against the usually deleterious impacts of increased cognitive load by reducing the amount of information in the environment that needs to be processed. Such a strategy may be particularly useful in the context of phishing detection, since it is a process often engaged in tandem with other complex, resource-demanding tasks. Consistent with an information-reduction hypothesis (Haider and Frensch 1999), behavior associated with relatively higher cue utilization is likely to be associated with higher levels of task performance under increasing cognitive load (e.g., that arising from an increase in task complexity).

1.2 Study Aims

The current study was designed to test the impact of cue utilization and cognitive load on email users' ability to detect phishing emails under conditions of low, moderate, and high cognitive load. Cognitive load was manipulated using a simplified, simulated rail control task as part of a dual-task paradigm, during which participants were categorizing emails as 'trustworthy' or 'suspicious'. Behavior associated with the utilization of cues was assessed using the Expert Intensive Skills Evaluation (EXPERTise 2.0) assessment tool (Wiggins et al. 2015).

EXPERTise 2.0 comprises five tasks, each of which is designed to evaluate behavior associated with the application of cue-based associations in memory. Since cues are task-specific, an edition of the tool was developed that incorporated features associated with phishing emails. EXPERTise 2.0 has been used previously to delineate behavior associated with higher and lower cue utilization in fields as diverse a pediatric intensive care (Loveday et al. 2013b), software engineering (Loveday et al. 2014), and football coaching (Yee et al. 2019).

1.3 Hypotheses

Hypothesis one. Email users' performance on the phishing detection task would decline with increasing levels of cognitive load (low, moderate, and high).

Hypothesis two. Higher cue utilization, as determined by participants' performance on EXPERTise 2.0, would be associated with greater accuracy in detecting phishing emails.

Hypothesis three. An interaction would be evident between cue utilization and cognitive load where higher cue utilization would be associated with relatively smaller reductions in performance as cognitive increased.

2 Method

2.1 Participants

Fifty adult students (35 females, 15 males) were recruited as a sample of convenience from Macquarie University's SONA research recruitment system. The participants ranged in age from 18 to 45 years ($M_{age} = 20.44$, $SD_{age} = 4.38$). The mean age for males was 21.07 ($SD = 4.21$) and the mean age for females was 20.17 ($SD = 4.48$). All participants were naïve to the context of professional cybersecurity.

2.2 Materials

Expert Intensive Skills Evaluation (EXPERTise) Program Version 2.0.
EXPERTise is an online platform that consists of a battery of tests, each based on empirical investigations of cue utilization. The different tasks have been individually and collectively associated with differences in performance at an operational level (Loveday et al. 2013a, 2013b). Test–retest reliability ($\kappa = .59$, $p < .05$) has been demonstrated with power control operators at six month intervals (Loveday et al. 2014) and with audiologists at 18 month intervals (Watkinson et al. 2018).

Successful cue utilization is measured by individuals' ability to identify critical features quickly from an array (Feature Identification Task; FIT), categorize accurately, situations based on key features (Feature Recognition Task; FRT), quickly associate features and events in memory (Feature Association Task; FAT), discriminate between relevant features (Feature Discrimination Task; FDT), and prioritize the acquisition of information during problem resolution (Feature Prioritization Task; FPT) (Wiggins 2014).

As cue-based associations are highly contextualized, domain-specific phishing stimuli were created for each of the EXPERTise tasks. For instance, most tasks presented users with images of emails, some of which held features that may be predictive of phishing threats (e.g., sender's address, typographical errors, prompt for action, etc.). The stimuli were reviewed by a subject-matter expert in the field of cyber-security.

Rail Control Task. In the rail control task, participants manage the movement of trains using a simplified simulation (example screenshot seen in Fig. 1; Brouwers et al. 2017). The task consisted of four green horizontal lines that represent the railway track. Various intersections occur between these lines (depicted by white portions displayed on the tracks), with the option to change the track onto a new line. Trains are depicted as red lines and assigned either an odd or even three-digit code (e.g., 555, 888). The first and third train line run from right to left, while the second and fourth train line run from left to right. The goal is to ensure that even-numbered trains terminate on even terminals and odd-numbered trains terminate at odd terminals. To correct the programmed route of the train, participants must select the 'Change' icon located above each train line. The direction of the track also appears under this icon. All trains progressed at the same speed with participants having seven seconds to decide whether or not to re-route the train. Participants engaged three separate conditions (each comprising 21 trains), which varied in the number of train tracks being controlled at any one time. The ordering was linear, whereby cognitive load progressively increased throughout the task, which commenced with the top two train lines (low condition), then the top three train lines (moderate condition), and finally all four train lines (high condition).

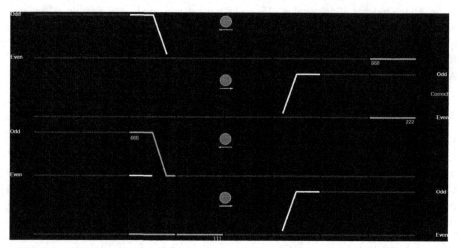

Fig. 1. The simulated rail control task display for the high load condition. (Color figure online)

Phishing Detection Task. Phishing emails were taken from Berkeley PhishTank and modified to an Australian context. The emails included 45 phishing emails and 45 legitimate emails. Participants responded to the emails at their own pace, and the task finished when all three conditions of the rail control task had been completed. The participants were required to respond to the emails, which varied in legitimacy as either: Trustworthy or Suspicious. After participants made a decision, they selected the Next button at the bottom of the screen, which opened a new email. This task was administered through a web-based email client simulator that was programmed to randomize the presentation of emails for each participant.

2.3 Apparatus

Two LG® IPSTM EA53s Desktop Monitors (24″ display size; LG Display, Yeongdeungpo District, Seoul, South Korea) were used in this experiment. The monitors connected to two Lenovo® IdeacentreTM 310S-07F (Lenovo, Quarry Bay, Hong Kong) workstations each equipped with 8 GB of RAM and running a Windows 10 operating system. Each computer connected to a Microsoft® Optical wired mouse (Redmond,

Washington, USA) that enabled participants to complete the tasks. The screen on the left of the participant operated the rail control task and the computer on the right of the participant operated the phishing detection task. EXPERTise operated through the same computer as the phishing detection task.

2.4 Procedure

The participants completed the study in individual sessions of one hour. The monitor positioned on the left of participants operated the rail control task. Participants were taken through a practice simulation of the low load condition. Participants were then informed that the task would progressively increase in complexity, starting with two active train lines, then increasing to three active train lines and finishing with all four train lines active.

The computer screen positioned to the right of the participant operated the phishing email detection task. Participants were instructed that they were to correctly identify the incoming emails as either 'Trustworthy' or 'Suspicious'. Once they had indicated a response, a 'Next' button would appear at the bottom of the screen. Participants were instructed not to attend to the rail control task at the expense of the phishing detection task, and that equal attention levels should be directed to both tasks. After completing this task, participants were instructed to complete EXPERTise on the same computer. Each of the five tasks (FIT, FAT, FDT, FPT and FAT) were accompanied by a detailed description of the task requirements on the initial screen.

3 Results

3.1 Data Reduction

Consistent with the process outlined by Wiggins et al. (2019), EXPERTise raw scores were standardized to z-scores and aggregated together to create a total EXPERTise score for each participant. In preparation for a comparison of performance, a median split categorized participants as demonstrating either relatively higher or lower levels of cue utilization (Wiggins et al. 2019).

3.2 Cue Utilization, Cognitive Load, and Phishing Detection

A 2×3 mixed-repeated ANOVA, incorporating two categories of cue utilization (high and low) as a between-groups variable, and three levels of cognitive load (low, moderate, and high) as a within-groups variable examined whether any significant difference existed in performance on the phishing detection task. The decision performance values on the phishing detection task were taken from the efficiency scores, which considered the number of correctly identified phishing emails as a proportion of the total number of emails to which participants responded.

The ANOVA results revealed no main effect for cognitive load on the phishing detection task, $F(2, 48) = 2.84$, $p = .06$ (two-tailed), $\eta p^2 = .06$. As the result was in the opposite direction to our hypothesis, a decision was made not to correct the p-value for one-tail. This means that increases in cognitive load had no adverse impact on participants' performance during the phishing detection task and hypothesis one was not supported.

The results revealed a statistically significant main effect for cue utilization, $F(1, 48)$ = 4.15, p = .02 (one-tailed), ηp^2 = .08 (medium effect), with higher cue utilization (M = .54, SE = .03) associated with greater accuracy on the phishing detection task in comparison to participants with lower cue utilization (M = .46, SE = .03) (see Fig. 2). This result supported hypothesis two.

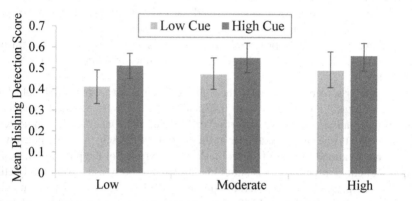

Fig. 2. The mean performance on the phishing detection task for high and low cue utilization groups across the three levels of cognitive load (error bars are 95% CI).

As participant could respond to the emails at their own pace (and therefore, potentially manage their cognitive load via their rate of response on the phishing email task), an independent t-test was used to test for a difference in the number of emails reviewed between the higher and lower cue utilization groups. The results did not reveal a statistically significant difference, $t(48)$ = −.31, p = .761. The higher cue utilization group responded to a mean of 40.80 (SD = 14.60) emails and the low cue group responded to a mean of 39.50 (SD = 15.87) emails.

Hypothesis three explored whether an interaction existed between cue utilization and cognitive load, and performance on the phishing detection task. However, the results failed to reveal any statistically significant interaction between cue utilization and cognitive load, $F(2, 48)$ = 0.25, p = .391, η_p2 = .005. Therefore, there were no differences in accuracy based on cue utilization and accounting for differences in cognitive load (see Fig. 2).

4   Discussion

The current study tested the effects of cue utilization and cognitive load on the detection of phishing emails. The purpose was to investigate the decision making strategies of skilled email users when formulating accurate assessments as to the legitimacy of an email.

4.1 Cognitive Load

Contrary to the hypothesis, email users' performance on the phishing detection task was not adversely impacted by increasing levels of cognitive load (low, moderate, and high). Instead, the results indicated a trend whereby performance on the phishing task increased with each additional level of cognitive load. The observed trend may be due to a practice effect on the rail control task (Falleti et al. 2006). All participants began the task with the low load condition and progressively increased to the high condition. The initial exposure to the low load condition is likely to have familiarized participants with the task and naturally improved their performance on the subsequent conditions, despite increases in task demands. Furthermore, the improved performance suggests that the cognitive load task might not have been sufficiently challenging to disrupt participants' cognitive resources. Instead, the task may have increased participants arousal to a level that improved decision performance (Jackson et al. 2014).

4.2 Cue Utilization

Consistent with the hypothesis, higher cue utilization was associated with greater accuracy in discriminating phishing from non-phishing emails. This suggests that behavior associated with the utilization of cue-based associations in memory is associated with an increased likelihood in detecting phishing emails while undertaking a concurrent task.

These results are broadly consistent with previous research where the detection of phishing emails is presumed to be dependent upon the capacity to identify key features, such as spelling and email addresses that signify the possibility that an email is untrustworthy (Williams et al. 2018).

4.3 Cue Utilization, Cognitive Load, and Phishing Detection

Hypothesis three was not supported insofar as no interaction was evident between cue utilization and cognitive load. The result suggests that performance on the phishing email task was not due to differences in the capacity of participants with higher cue utilization to better manage the cognitive load associated with the rail control task, but was due possibly to an inherent capability to either recognize or maintain an awareness that enabled the discrimination of phishing from non-phishing emails (Brouwers et al. 2017; Loveday et al. 2014).

These results, in particular, have implications for an explanation of phishing email detection based on an information-reduction hypothesis (Haider and Frensch 1999). Indeed, it suggests that alternative theoretical perspectives may be involved, including the possibility that respondents are making judgements based on a template or prototype of trustworthy emails, and/or the detection of phishing emails is dependent upon a heightened level of awareness for features that characterize emails that are untrustworthy.

4.4 Limitations

A notable limitation of the current work was the use of an equal number of phishing and legitimate emails in the Phishing Detection Task. In reality, most users will receive far fewer phishing emails than legitimate ones. As such, the ratio adopted may be problematic when considering a truth-default theory in human communication (Levine 2014). However, achieving realistic base-rates in an experimental design is challenging, as it would require participants to assess a significantly greater number of emails overall. Future studies may wish to address this limitation, as well as other experimental artefacts that may impact the generalizability of the findings to real-world environments.

4.5 Conclusion

The current study provides an exploration of the cognitive processes associated with decision making in cybersecurity. We found an improvement in discrimination based on participants' utilization of cues associated with the detection of phishing emails. These results provide support for the proposition that the detection of phishing emails is based on the recognition of specific features that reflect untrustworthy emails. The use of cue-based training interventions has proven effective in other domains (e.g., Morrison et al. 2018), and these findings imply potential value in their adoption in the cyber-security domain.

References

Brouwers, S., Wiggins, M.W., Griffin, B., Helton, W.S., O'Hare, D.: The role of cue utilisation in reducing the workload in a train control task. Ergonomics **60**(11), 1500–1515 (2017)

Ericsson, K.A., Lehmann, A.C.: Expert and exceptional performance: evidence of maximal adaptation to task constraints. Annu. Rev. Psychol. **47**(1), 273–305 (1996). https://doi.org/10.1146/annurev.psych.47.1.273

Falleti, M.G., Maruff, P., Collie, A., Darby, D.G.: Practice effects associated with the repeated assessment of cognitive function using the CogState battery at 10-minute, one week and one month test-retest intervals. J. Clin. Exp. Neuropsychol. **28**(7), 1095–1112 (2006). https://doi.org/10.1080/13803390500205718

Haider, H., Frensch, P.A.: Information reduction during skill acquisition: the influence of task instruction. J. Exp. Psychol.: Appl. **5**(2), 129–151 (1999). https://doi.org/10.1037/1076-898X.5.2.129

Jackson, S.A., Kleitman, S., Aidman, E.: Low cognitive load and reduced arousal impede practice effects on executive functioning, metacognitive confidence and decision making. Public Libr. Sci. One **9**(12), e115689–e115689 (2014). https://doi.org/10.1371/journal.pone.0115689

Johnston, D., Morrison, B.W.: The application of naturalistic decision-making techniques to explore cue use in rugby league playmakers. J. Cogn. Eng. Decision Making **10**(4), 391–410 (2016). https://doi.org/10.1177/1555343416662181

Klein, G.: A Recognition-Primed Decision (RPD) Model of Rapid Decision Making Decision Making in Action: Models and Methods, pp. 138–147. Ablex, Westport (1993)

Levine, T.R.: Truth-default theory: a theory of human deception and deception detection. J. Lang. Soc. Psychol. **33**(4), 378–392 (2014). https://doi.org/10.1177/0261927X14535916

Loveday, T., Wiggins, M.W., Harris, J.M., O'Hare, D., Smith, N.: An objective approach to identifying diagnostic expertise among power system controllers. Hum. Factors: J. Hum. Factors Ergon. Soc. **55**(1), 90–107 (2013a). https://doi.org/10.1177/0018720812450911

Loveday, T., Wiggins, M.W., Searle, B.: Cue utilization and broad indicators of workplace expertise. J. Cognitive Eng. Decis. Making **8**(1), 98–113 (2014). https://doi.org/10.1177/1555343413497019

Loveday, T., Wiggins, M.W., Searle, B.J., Festa, M., Schell, D.: The capability of static and dynamic features to distinguish competent from genuinely expert practitioners in pediatric diagnosis. Hum. Factors **55**(1), 125–137 (2013b). https://doi.org/10.1177/0018720812448475

Morrison, B.W., Morrison, N.M.V.: Diagnostic cues in major crime investigation. In: Wiggins, M.W., Loveday, T. (eds.) Diagnostic Expertise in Organizational Environments, pp. 91–98. Ashgate Publishing, Surrey (2015)

Morrison, B.W., Morrison, N.M.V., Morton, J., Harris, J.: Using critical-cue inventories to advance virtual patient technologies in psychological assessment. In: Shen, H., Smith, R., Paay, J., Calder, P., Wyeld, T. (eds.) Proceedings of the 25th Australian Computer-Human Interaction Conference: Augmentation, Application, Innovation, Collaboration (OzCHI 2013), pp. 531–534. ACM, New York (2013). http://dx.doi.org/10.1145/2541016.2541085

Morrison, B.W., Wiggins, M.W., Bond, N.W., Tyler, M.D.: Measuring relative cue strength as a means of validating an inventory of expert offender profiling cues. J. Cogn. Eng. Decis. Making **7**(2), 211–226 (2013). https://doi.org/10.1177/1555343412459192

Morrison, B.W., Wiggins, M.W., Morrison, N.: Utility of expert cue exposure as a mechanism to improve decision-making performance among novice criminal investigators. J. Cogn. Eng. Decis. Making **12**(2), 99–111 (2018). https://doi.org/10.1177/1555343417746570

Symantec. Internet Security Threat Report (2018). https://www.symantec.com/content/dam/sym antec/docs/reports/istr-23-2018-en.pdf

Vergelis, M., Shcherbakova, T., Sidorina, T.: Spam and phishing in 2018 (2019). https://secure lisst.com/spam-and-phishing-in-2018/89701/

Watkinson, J., Bristow, G., Auton, J., McMahon, C.M., Wiggins, M.W.: Postgraduate training in audiology improves clinicians' audiology-related cue utilisation. Int. J. Audiol. **57**(9), 681–687 (2018)

Wiggins, M.: The role of cue utilisation and adaptive interface design in the management of skilled performance in operations control. Theor. Issues Ergon. Sci. **15**(3), 282–292 (2014). https://doi.org/10.1080/1463922X.2012.724725

Wiggins, M.W.: Cues in diagnostic reasoning. In: Wiggins, M.W., Loveday, T. (eds.) Diagnostic Expertise in Organizational Environments, pp. 1–11. Ashgate Publishing, Surrey (2015)

Wiggins, M.W., Griffin, B., Brouwers, S.: The potential role of context-related exposure in explaining differences in water safety cue utilization. Hum. Factors **61**(5), 825–838 (2019). https://doi.org/10.1177/0018720818814299

Wiggins, M.W., Loveday, T., Auton, J.: EXPERT Intensive Skills Evaluation (EXPERTise 2.0) Test. Macquarie University, Sydney, Australia (2015)

Wiggins, M., O'Hare, D.: Applications of micro-simulation in cognitive skills development. In: Karwowski, W. (ed.) International Encyclopedia of Ergonomics and Human Factors, 2nd edn, pp. 3262–3267. Taylor & Francis, United Kingdom (2006)

Williams, E.J., Hinds, J., Joinson, A.N.: Exploring susceptibility to phishing in the workplace. Int. J. Hum.-Comput. Stud. **120**, 1–13 (2018). https://doi.org/10.1016/j.ijhcs.2018.06.004

Yee, D.J., Wiggins, M.W., Auton, J.C., Warry, G., Cklamovski, P.: Technical and social cue utilization in expert football coaches, Sport Exerc. Perform. Psychol. (2019). https://doi.org/10.1037/spy0000170

Cue Utilization, Phishing Feature and Phishing Email Detection

Piers Bayl-Smith$^{(\boxtimes)}$ (ID), Daniel Sturman (ID), and Mark Wiggins (ID)

Macquarie University, Sydney, NSW, Australia
piers.bayl-smith@mq.edu.au

Abstract. Cognitive processes are broadly considered to be of vital importance to understanding phishing email feature detection or misidentification. This research extends the current literature by introducing the concept of cue utilization as a unique predictor of phishing feature detection. First year psychology students (*n = 127*) undertook three tasks measuring cue utilization, phishing feature detection and phishing email detection. A multiple linear regression model provided evidence that those in a higher cue utilization typology ($n = 55$) performed better at identifying phishing features than those in a lower cue utilization typology ($n = 72$). Furthermore, as predicted by the Elaboration Likelihood Model (ELM) and Heuristic-Systematic Model (HSM), those who deliberated longer per email demonstrated an increased ability to correctly identify phishing features. However, these results did not translate into improved performance in the phishing email detection task. Possible explanations for these results are discussed, including possible limitations and areas of future research.

Keywords: Phishing · Cue utilization · Feature identification · Elaboration likelihood model · Heuristic-systematic model

1 Introduction

1.1 Study Aims

Despite significant investment in cyber security solutions, employees remain the most significant risk to maintaining a protected information environment. Specifically, phishing emails are a major attack vector through which an organization's information security can be compromised. Recent research has suggested that for businesses, 74% of all cyber threats originate via email sources [1], whereas in Australia, phishing was the top registered scam category reported to the Australian Competition and Consumer Commission [2]. Costs to businesses and individuals have steadily been on the rise at a global level, occasioning in business disruption, information and intellectual property loss, and revenue loss, with damages reported in the hundreds of millions of dollars [2, 3].

Given the importance of human factors and phishing, this study investigates what cognitive factors may influence phishing detection. In particular, whether cognitive processing impact an individual's ability to detect suspicious features characteristic of a phishing email, as well as their ability to correctly distinguish between legitimate and non-legitimate email communications. Unique to this study, we examine the role of cue-based processing when assessing phishing emails.

© Springer Nature Switzerland AG 2020
M. Bernhard et al. (Eds.): FC 2020 Workshops, LNCS 12063, pp. 56–70, 2020.
https://doi.org/10.1007/978-3-030-54455-3_5

1.2 Phishing Features and Cognitive Processing

Phishing emails are deceptive forms of communication that endeavor to appear legitimate, but are in fact attempts to obtain personal credentials or sensitive information [4]. By promising some form of false utility, they aim to convince targets to either reply, click on an embedded URL link, or download an attachment. Researchers have identified common features inherent in phishing emails that may be used by recipients to identify that an email is malicious [5–7]. These can include poor visual presentation, spelling and grammatical errors, a sender's address that does not match the expected domain name, and questionable URL links. By identifying such features, individuals can increase their likelihood of recognizing an email as a phishing attempt, and can take appropriate protective actions [4, 8]. In contrast, when such features are either misidentified or neglected, the recipient is at increased risk of complying to the phishing email. In support of this contention, several studies, both qualitative and quantitative, have demonstrated a link between the identification of suspicious features and phishing detection performance [e.g., 4, 9, 10].

Avoiding phishing scams however does not merely require an ability to identify the relevant features of an email, but also relies on applying appropriate levels of cognitive resources to assess the entirety of an email message [4]. To encourage limited processing, phishing emails will often resort to social engineering techniques, such as appeals to authority or urgency [6, 11]. By utilizing these forms of persuasion, an email recipient may be inspired to respond quickly and without deliberation – only later realizing that they have become a victim to a phishing scam [12]. Researchers have also posited that individual factors may lead to less cognitive processing of emails including personality [13], habitual use of emails [14], threat perceptions [15] and self-efficacy [16].

From a theoretical perspective, phishing research has utilized dual-process cognitive models that differentiate between easy and rapid processes from those that are more effortful, time intensive and deliberate [17–20]. Utilizing theoretical frameworks such as the Heuristic-Systematic Model (HSM) [21] and Elaboration Likelihood Model (ELM) [22], researchers have proposed that recipients fail to identify phishing emails due to quick-fire heuristic processes rather than being systematically attentive to the content of the message [14]. That is, rather than examining the broad range of features within an email, such as sender's address, URL hyperlinks and formatting issues, people respond to emails only with a cursory appraisal. Social engineering strategies, individual factors and context can play an important role in whether people are motivated to engage in more systematic or elaborative processes when analyzing an email. However, utilization of more deliberative processes, whilst effortful and taking longer, will improve detection of the salient features of an email that indicate it to be suspicious [14, 23].

Previous phishing research has typically measured systematic or elaborative processing via survey, asked after exposure to a phishing email [4, 17, 19]. Results have generally been supportive of the notion that deeper processing of emails leads to more accurate levels of phishing detection. However, given the debate on whether cognitive processes can be explicitly understood and reported [24], survey items may not provide an accurate gauge of systematic or elaborative cognitive processing. Harrison et al. [23] utilized an alternative method to assess elaboration, where participants were asked an open ended question on why they did or did not respond to a phishing email. Here, word count was used as an indicator of cognitive processing. Although this method overcomes the potential shortcomings of survey questions, this measure is indirect, open to possible confounds and occurs post-exposure to the phishing email. In contrast to these approaches, by using evaluation time, this study provides a more direct indication of cognitive processing whilst the participant is assessing an email. Therefore, in line with these considerations, we hypothesize the following:

Hypothesis 1: The more time taken to assess an email will be associated with an increased correct identification of suspicious features characteristic of a phishing email.

Hypothesis 2: The more time taken to assess an email will be associated with an increased detection of phishing emails (hit rate) and lower incidence of incorrectly identifying a genuine email (false alarm).

Although there is much to commend using the existing theoretical paradigm, we will also investigate an alternative theoretical framework drawing from research on cue utilization and expertise [25].

1.3   Cue Utilization

Cues comprise associations between situation specific environmental features and task-related events or objects. Through repeated exposure to feature-event relationships, cues are acquired and retained in long-term memory. These cues can later be activated rapidly and non-consciously when key features are identified, enabling fast and accurate responses [26–28]. As cues are acquired through repeated exposure, cue-based processing is often associated with expert performance [29, 30].

Experts appear to have the facility of being able to innately identify an appropriate response to a problem based on limited information [31, 32]. They are also faster at generating situation assessments with greater accuracy than novices [33, 34]. According to the Recognition-Primed Decision (RPD) model [29], experienced decision makers base their judgements upon satisfying rather than a deliberate analytical assessment of all available options. Through the acquisition of cues based in memory, experts recognize patterns in the situation, what to expect, what further cues need to be attended to, and what goals need to be realized [35]. These patterns in turn actuate scripts that are then implemented into action. In contrast, non-experts or those who are inexperienced, are unlikely to know which cues to attend to, and do not know how to utilize cues in a meaningful way.

Cue utilization refers to an individual difference in the capacity to acquire, recognize and apply cues [36, 37]. Effective cue utilization allows individuals to attend to features of greater relevance, reducing the overall number of features to which they attend, and thereby increasing speed and performance [38–41]. To measure cue utilization, this study uses the online assessment tool, EXPERT Intensive Skills Evaluation (EXPERTise 2.0) [42]. This tool is designed to assess behaviors that are consistent with the utilization of cues, distinguishing relative participant performance in the operation of cues. EXPERTise 2.0 has demonstrated construct validity [43, 44], predictive validity [45], and test-retest reliability [46]. In the context of phishing, individuals with relatively higher cue utilization, as measured by EXPERTise 2.0, should be able to more rapidly identify features which are indicative of phishing emails, in turn enabling more accurate classifications of phishing emails. Therefore, we hypothesize:

Hypothesis 3: Participants in the higher cue utilization typology, as determined by performance in EXPERTise 2.0, will be associated with an increased identification of suspicious features characteristic of a phishing email, compared to participants in the lower cue utilization typology.

Hypothesis 4: Participants in the higher cue utilization typology, as determined by performance in EXPERTise 2.0, will be associated with an increased detection of phishing emails (hit rate) and lower incidence of incorrectly identifying a genuine email (false alarm), compared to participants in the lower cue utilization typology.

2 Method

2.1 Participants

Students enrolled in a first-year psychology program at Macquarie University, Australia, were invited to participate in an online study investigating the impact of cue utilization on phishing detection tasks. In total, 127 students participated in the study. Of these, 65.4% were female with an average age of 22.7 years (SD = 8.3 years), ranging from 18 to 54 years. The majority (81.9%) were in some form of paid employment, with 12.5% having managerial responsibilities. Only 14 respondents (11.0%) had received formal cyber security training by their organization. Students who completed the study were provided with course credit. The ethical considerations of this study were reviewed and approved by the Macquarie University Human Research Ethics Committee.

2.2 Materials

Expertise 2.0 – Phishing Edition
The present study employed the phishing edition of EXPERTise 2.0, which comprises a battery of four tasks: The Feature Identification Task (FIT); the Feature Recognition Task (FRT); the Feature Association Task (FAT); and the Feature Discrimination Task (FDT).

During the FIT, participants are required to identify, as quickly as possible, key features of concern in a series of domain related stimuli. In the phishing edition of EXPERTise, participants were presented with 10 scenarios, each consisting of a single phishing email. For each email that was presented, participants were required to click on the area of the email that aroused the most suspicion, or to click on an icon titled "Trustworthy Email". For this task, response latency for each scenario was recorded. Higher cue utilization is generally associated with a lower mean response latency [25, 47].

In the FRT, participants are presented with domain related stimuli for short periods, and then required to categorize the stimuli. The phishing edition of EXPERTise consists of 20 email stimuli, 10 which contain a genuine email and 10 which contain a phishing email. Each email is presented for only 1000 ms, after which participants are asked to classify the email as "Trustworthy", "Untrustworthy", or "Impossible to tell". The FRT assesses the capacity to rapidly extract key information, therefore the short display time was chosen to reflect the nature of this task. Higher cue utilization is typically associated with a greater number of correct classifications [48].

For the FAT, participants are presented with two phrases used in a given domain and are required to rate the perceived relatedness of each phrase. In the phishing edition of EXPERTise participants are presented with 14 pairs of phrases which are related to the computing environment and phishing (e.g., 'Email', 'Malware'). Each pair of stimuli are presented side by side for 2000 ms, after which participants were asked to rate the perceived relatedness of the words on a scale ranging from 1 (Extremely unrelated) to 6 (Extremely related). For the FAT, higher cue utilization is typically associated with a greater mean variance in ratings, being selected within a shorter period of time [49].

In the FDT, participants are presented with the details of a problem-oriented scenario and are required to select an appropriate response. Participants are then provided with a list of features from the scenario and are asked to rate the perceived importance of each feature in determining their chosen response, ranging from 1 (Not important at all) to 10 (Extremely important). The phishing edition of EXPERTise consists of a spear phishing email, claiming that an unpaid invoice is going to result in legal and financial costs. The 11 features being rated contain factors related to the work environment and email (e.g., "your bosses anger", "the senders email address"). Higher cue utilization is typically associated with a greater variance in feature ratings [41, 50].

Phishing Feature Task

The phishing feature task was setup on Qualtrics [51], an online survey platform. This task involved participants viewing a genuine email that had one of four features manipulated by the researchers; the senders email address with an incongruent domain name, introduction of poor spelling, insertion of a URL with an incongruent domain name, or changes to the look of the email to make it appear more rudimentary (see Appendix for an example stimuli). Participants were informed that each image was legitimate but had one feature changed. Each email image was displayed for a maximum of 20 s, but they could proceed forward at any time. After the image was displayed, respondents were asked which feature most aroused their suspicion. Nine features of an email were then listed as options, including a tenth option of "I don't know". The time spent evaluating each email and the feature selected was collected for each participant.

Phishing Detection Task

The phishing detection task was also setup within Qualtrics [51]. In this task, an image of an email was displayed for a maximum of 20 s, after which participants were asked to judge whether the email was trustworthy or suspicious. Respondents were able to move forward to the question of trustworthiness before the 20 s had elapsed. All emails were either genuine or examples of real phishing attempts that had been collected overtime by the researchers (see Appendix for an example stimuli). In total, there were ten emails that needed to be assessed by each respondent; five genuine and five phish. The time each email was attended to and trustworthiness responses were collected for each participant.

Demographic and Cyber-security Expertise
To control for possible confounds, we have included age, gender and self-reported cyber-security expertise. Previous research has suggested younger adults (18-25 years) are more susceptible to phishing attacks [52]. This may be associated with less exposure to phishing emails, lower internet use across one's lifetime, lack of cyber education, or the use of specific types of attack strategies within a phishing email [52–54]. Gender has also been identified as being an important consideration when examining phishing susceptibility, with females potentially at more risk of responding to phishing emails [52, 55]. This may be explained by differences in personality, self-efficacy and lack of technical training [16, 52, 55]. However, it should be noted that the effects for gender have not been consistently found significant across all research [56]. Cyber-security proficiency was assessed by a single item, "What is your proficiency in cyber security." For this study, the five-point Likert-type response has been converted into a categorical variable, where the options "Very Good" and "Expert" have been labelled "High proficiency", and "None", "Poor" and "Average" are categorized as "Low proficiency". Overall, 27.6% of participants considered cyber security proficiency to be high. Self-efficacy and cyber security knowledge has been implicated as a protective factor against phishing attacks [16].

2.3 Procedure

Participants were sent a link to the Qualtrics survey platform where they were first asked a series of demographic questions along with items pertaining to their cyber security history and knowledge. Respondents then completed the phishing detection task and phishing feature task before being automatically forwarded to the EXPERTise 2.0 platform. Within EXPERTise 2.0, participants completed the four tasks associated with cue-utilization (FIT, FRT, FAT, FDT), with detailed instructions being provided for each task. The total time to complete the online study was approximately 30 min.

3   Results

3.1   Cue Utilization Typologies

Using a standard approach for classifying participants into cue utilization typologies [57], scores for each EXPERTISE task were converted to standardized z-scores, and a cluster analysis was performed to identify two cue utilization typologies. Fifty-five participants were classified as having relatively higher cue utilization and 72 participants were classified as having relatively lower cue utilization. The higher cue utilization typology consisted of participants with shorter mean response latencies on the FIT, greater mean accuracy on the FRT, a higher mean ratio of variance to reaction time on the FAT, and a greater mean variance in ratings on the FDT. There were significant differences in FIT, FAT, FRT, and FDT mean scores between the higher and lower cue utilization typologies (see Table 1). Additional clustering solutions were examined post-hoc but were not found to be suitable due to low participant numbers in additional clusters (n < 5).

Table 1. Raw and standardized EXPERTise task scores by cue utilization typology

	Higher cue utilization ($n = 55$)			Lower cue utilization ($n = 72$)			
	Mean	SD	z-score	Mean	SD	z-score	t
FIT	3749	2708	−0.35	9423	5895	0.27	−3.58**
FRT	11.0	2.62	0.44	10.25	2.94	−0.33	4.64**
FAT	1.60	0.88	0.50	0.87	0.60	−0.39	5.53**
FDT	10.0	3.65	0.77	3.93	2.59	−0.59	10.33**

* Significant at the 0.05 level (two-tailed); **Significant at the 0.01 level (two-tailed)

$$x + y = z \qquad (1)$$

3.2 Performance on the Phishing Feature Task

Across the 16 emails used in the phishing feature task, participants were on average able to detect the suspicious feature 6.5 times. A multiple linear regression was conducted to determine the effects of cue utilization typology and average email deliberation time upon phishing feature task performance. Age, gender and subjective cyber security proficiency were included as control variables. A summary of results is displayed in Table 2. Overall, the combined predictors had a significant effect in explaining the variance of feature detection performance ($r2 = .21$, $F(5,126) = 6.40$, $p < .01$). In support of Hypothesis 1, the mean review time for each email was associated with a significant positive effect, such that on average for every 4.4 s of additional viewing time (1 SD increase in time), an additional 1.12 features were correctly detected. Hypothesis 3 was also supported, where those in the high cue utilization typology were significantly more likely to detect an additional 1.42 features than those grouped in the low cue utilization typology. No significant effects for age, gender or subjective cyber security proficiency were found.

3.3 Performance on the Phishing Detection Task

Performance on the phishing detection task indicated that on average, 3.2 emails were correctly identified as phish (hit rate), ranging from 0 correct to 5 correct. For emails that were genuine, on average 1.1 emails were incorrectly identified as being suspicious (false alarm), ranging from 0 false alarms to 4 false alarms. Calculating for potential bias [58], no significant differences were found contingent upon cue utilization typology.

Table 2. Multiple linear regression for the phishing feature task

Predictor	DV = Phishing feature detection performance			
	b	SE	β	t
Age	−0.04	0.03	−0.11	−1.25
Gender	−0.25	0.45	−0.46	−0.56
Cyber proficiency	0.56	0.48	0.10	1.16
Phishing feature review time	0.25	0.52	0.43	4.58**
Cue utilization typology	1.42	0.45	0.27	3.17**

** Significant at the 0.01 level (two-tailed)

To examine the effects of cue utilization typology and average email deliberation time upon phishing detection performance, two separate multiple linear regression models were tested. The first model included phishing detection hit rate as the dependent variable, with average email review time, cue utilization, age, gender and subjective cyber security proficiency included as predictor variables. Results indicated that the predictor variables accounted for 10.3% of total variance ($F(5,126) = 2.79$, $p = .02$), with only gender significantly related to phishing detection hit-rate ($\beta = 0.19$, $p = .03$), where on average, males were more likely to correctly identify phishing emails when compared to females. The second model utilized the same independent variables, but included phishing detection false alarms as the variable of interest. Overall, this model was not significant ($F(5,126) = 1.94$, $p = .09$), with no predictors demonstrating a significant relationship with the dependent variable. Therefore, both models lack evidence to support Hypotheses 2 and 4.

4 Discussion

This study examined the influence of processing time and cue utilization upon the identification of suspicious phishing features and phishing detection. Overall, the results suggest that both the time processing emails and a high cue utilization typology have a positive impact upon being able to perceive features that may indicate that an email is suspicious. However, these factors did not translate into an enhanced proficiency to discriminate phishing emails nor a lower incidence of incorrectly identifying a phishing email.

According to dual-process cognitive theories such as HSM [21] and ELM [22], increased systematic processing or elaboration of an incoming communication should improve the detection of suspicious features that may identify the message as fraudulent [14]. The current study provides additional support for this contention. Participants who on average assessed email images for longer periods of time, demonstrated a greater ability to identify the suspicious feature that had been changed in an otherwise genuine email. A similar result was found for cue utilization. That is, those in the high cue utilization typology exhibited an improved ability in detecting suspicious features within an email. This supports the notion that those with higher cue utilization are more able to generate accurate situational assessments, thereby identifying features that do not fit with the expected patterns of the situation. Practically, these results suggest that users do not approach emails with similar cognitive processes or capabilities. According to Downs et al. [8], phishing succeeds when attackers are able to manipulate recipients into generating inaccurate mental models. Therefore, it is incumbent upon organizations to adequately train users on phishing feature identification to minimize differences in cognitive processing and cue-utilization. Furthermore, email clients should allow individuals to easily identify features that indicate that an email may be suspicious, thereby maximize the opportunity to create accurate mental models.

Although longer deliberation time and higher cue utilization was associated with increased ability to identify suspicious features in an email, this did not translate into improved phishing detection or lower rates of genuine email misidentification. This supports the contention made by Vishwanath et al. [4] that phishing is more than just the ability to detect phishing features. Research has indicated that phishing detection can be influenced by a large variety of factors, including personality, threat perceptions and self-efficacy [13–16]. As an alternative explanation, there may be some methodological considerations that may account for the null results. First, with only five phishing emails and five genuine emails, there may not have been enough variability in the task. Even if participants had chosen randomly, on average they would have correctly identified 2.5 emails correctly. Future research should include a larger section of phishing emails, including the possibility of changing the base-rate of phishing to genuine emails. Second, the task may have been too easy. The phishing examples used in this study were not overly sophisticated, nor were they personally addressed to the participant. That is, they may contain multiple features that indicate their fraudulent nature and therefore be too easy to detect. Furthermore, any persuasion strategies used by the phishing emails will be mollified by not being of personal import to the participant (e.g., they were under no threat or open to the utility being offered). Future research should then try to increase the fidelity of the experiment by simulating the work environment or use actual phishing simulations upon employees naïve to the study.

Of some interest, phishing detection was significantly related to gender. This supports previous research that suggests females may be more vulnerable to phishing than males [52, 55]. However, no such effect was not found with the phishing feature detection task. Explanations for our results then must be explained by factors not examined in this study, including self-efficacy, differences in personality or less online experience or knowledge [13, 52].

4.1 Limitations and Future Research

Apart from the limitations noted in the previous section as they relate to the phishing detection task, as an introductory study examining the role of cue utilization in phishing detection, this study has several limitations which also provide future avenues for further research. First, cue utilization as measured by EXPERTise 2.0 only gauges individual differences in the ability to detect and discriminate domain relevant features. What aspects of an email communication are actually being examined when discriminating between genuine from phishing emails was not able to be determined using EXPERTise 2.0.

Future research should engage eye-tracking technologies to determine which features are attended to when reviewing an email message. This, in conjunction with cue utilization performance, should provide a more comprehensive understanding of what security features of an email are important and which features may need to be highlighted to ensure a secure email environment.

Second, this study had participants assess images of phishing emails rather than respond to actual emails. Therefore, the results may not be applicable in actual work or personal settings. The images used were displayed within an email application shell, but they were not able to be operated as a real email message would (e.g., hovering over hyperlinks to reveal additional information). Future studies would benefit from the use of more sophisticated simulations allowing researchers to draw more meaningful real-world inferences.

Third, drawing from a sample of first year psychology students, the sample for this study was broadly homogenous. In organizations and personal contexts, a wide range of people of different ages, experiences, knowledge and network privileges have access to email. Therefore, future research needs to continue to investigate additional individual and contextual factors to understand why individuals may fall for phishing scams. This study suggests that cue utilization may be a key feature, although more research is needed with a broader demographic sample.

5   Conclusion

Phishing scams are on the rise globally, costing millions in damages. This study again reinforced the notion that more deliberative or systematic processing of incoming communications reduce the risk posed by phishing scams. Furthermore, this was the first study to investigate the potential role of cue utilization in phishing feature and email detection. It was found that a more deliberative processing of emails and higher cue utilization resulted in an improved ability to detect suspicious features in an otherwise genuine email but did not necessarily improve overall phishing detection. Linking these cognitive processes to phishing detection may provide additional capacities to understanding the threat posed by phishing, and thereby improve possible protective interventions, usability initiatives and training programs.

Appendix

See Figs. 1 and 2.

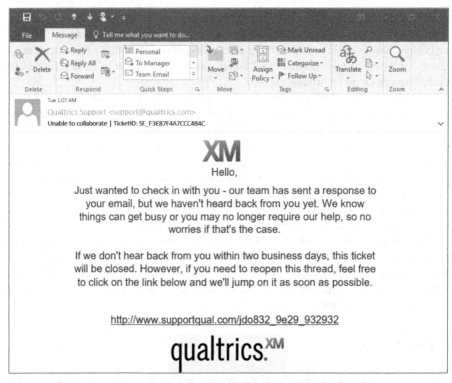

Fig. 1. Example stimuli for Phishing Feature Task – URL was changed

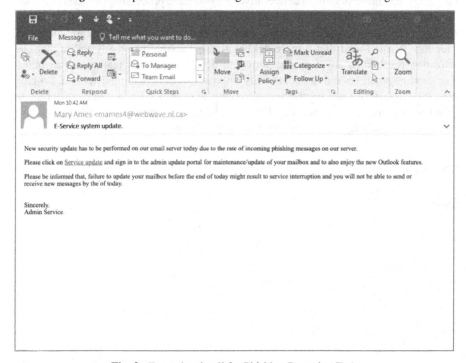

Fig. 2. Example stimuli for Phishing Detection Task

References

1. Neely, L.: 2017 Threat Landscape Survey: Users on the Front Line (2017)
2. Australian Competition & Consumer Commission: Targeting scams: Report of the ACCC on scams activity 2018. Canberra (2019)
3. Bissell, K., LaSalle, R., Dal Cin, P.: The cost of cybercrime (2019)
4. Vishwanath, A., Herath, T., Chen, R., Wang, J., Rao, H.R.: Why do people get phished? Testing individual differences in phishing vulnerability within an integrated, information processing model. Decis. Support Syst. **51**, 576–586 (2011). https://doi.org/10.1016/j.dss.2011.03.002
5. Parsons, K., Butavicius, M., Pattinson, M., Calic, D., Mccormac, A., Jerram, C.: Do users focus on the correct cues to differentiate between phishing and genuine emails? In: Australasian Conference on Information Systems, pp. 1–10. Adelaide (2015)
6. Zielinska, O.A., Welk, A.K., Mayhorn, C.B., Murphy-Hill, E.: A temporal analysis of persuasion principles in phishing emails. Proc. Hum. Factors Ergon. Soc. Annu. Meet. **60**, 765–769 (2016). https://doi.org/10.1177/1541931213601175
7. Furnell, S.: Phishing: can we spot the signs? Comput. Fraud Secur. **2007**, 10–15 (2007). https://doi.org/10.1016/S1361-3723(07)70035-0
8. Downs, J.S., Holbrook, M.B., Cranor, L.F.: Decision strategies and susceptibility to phishing. In: Proceedings of the Second Symposium on Usable Privacy and Security - SOUPS 2006, p. 79. ACM Press, New York (2006). https://doi.org/10.1145/1143120.1143131
9. Molinaro, K.A., Bolton, M.L.: Evaluating the applicability of the double system lens model to the analysis of phishing email judgments. Comput. Secur. **77**, 128–137 (2018). https://doi.org/10.1016/j.cose.2018.03.012
10. Williams, E.J., Hinds, J., Joinson, A.N.: Exploring susceptibility to phishing in the workplace. Int. J. Hum Comput Stud. **120**, 1–13 (2018). https://doi.org/10.1016/j.ijhcs.2018.06.004
11. Parsons, K., Butavicius, M., Delfabbro, P., Lillie, M.: Predicting susceptibility to social influence in phishing emails. Int. J. Hum Comput Stud. **128**, 17–26 (2019). https://doi.org/10.1016/j.ijhcs.2019.02.007
12. Hadnagy, C., Fincher, M.: Phishing Dark Waters: The Offensive and Defensive Sides of Malicious E-mails. Willey, Indianapolis (2015)
13. Halevi, T., Memon, N., Nov, O.: Spear-phishing in the wild: a real-world study of personality, phishing self-efficacy and vulnerability to spear-phishing attacks. SSRN Electron. J. (2015). https://doi.org/10.2139/ssrn.2544742
14. Vishwanath, A., Harrison, B., Ng, Y.J.: Suspicion, cognition, and automaticity model of phishing susceptibility. Commun. Res. 1–21 (2016). https://doi.org/10.1177/0093650215627483
15. Jansen, J., van Schaik, P.: Persuading end users to act cautiously online: a fear appeals study on phishing. Inf. Comput. Secur. **26**, 264–276 (2018). https://doi.org/10.1108/ICS-03-2018-0038
16. Sun, J.C.-Y., Yu, S.-J., Lin, S.S.J., Tseng, S.-S.: The mediating effect of anti-phishing self-efficacy between college students' internet self-efficacy and anti-phishing behavior and gender difference. Comput. Human Behav. **59**, 249–257 (2016). https://doi.org/10.1016/j.chb.2016.02.004
17. Musuva, P.M.W., Getao, K.W., Chepken, C.K.: A new approach to modelling the effects of cognitive processing and threat detection on phishing susceptibility. Comput. Human Behav. **94**, 154–175 (2019). https://doi.org/10.1016/j.chb.2018.12.036
18. Workman, M.: Wisecrackers: A theory-grounded investigation of phishing and pretext social engineering threats to information security. J. Am. Soc. Inf. Sci. Technol. **59**, 662–674 (2008). https://doi.org/10.1002/asi.20779

19. Vishwanath, A.: Examining the distinct antecedents of e-mail habits and its influence on the outcomes of a phishing attack. J. Comput. Commun. **20**, 570–584 (2015). https://doi.org/10.1111/jcc4.12126

20. Luo, X., Zhang, W., Burd, S., Seazzu, A.: Investigating phishing victimization with the heuristic-systematic model: a theoretical framework and an exploration. Comput. Secur. **38**, 28–38 (2013). https://doi.org/10.1016/j.cose.2012.12.003

21. Chaiken, S.: Heuristic versus systematic information processing and the use of source versus message cues in persuasion. J. Pers. Soc. Psychol. **39**, 752–766 (1980). https://doi.org/10.1037/0022-3514.39.5.752

22. Petty, R.E., Cacioppo, J.T.: The elaboration likelihood model of persuasion. Commun. Persuas. **19**, 1–24 (1986). https://doi.org/10.1007/978-1-4612-4964-1_1

23. Harrison, B., Svetieva, E., Vishwanath, A.: Individual processing of phishing emails. Online Inf. Rev. **40**, 265–281 (2016). https://doi.org/10.1108/OIR-04-2015-0106

24. Nisbett, R.E., Wilson, T.D.: Telling more than we can know: Verbal reports on mental processes. Psychol. Rev. **84**, 231–259 (1977). https://doi.org/10.1037/0033-295X.84.3.231

25. Loveday, T., Wiggins, M.W., Searle, B.J.: Cue utilization and broad indicators of workplace expertise. J. Cogn. Eng. Decis. Mak. **8**, 98–113 (2014). https://doi.org/10.1177/1555343413497019

26. Brunswik, E.: Representative design and probabilistic theory in a functional psychology. Psychol. Rev. **62**, 193–217 (1955). https://doi.org/10.1037/h0047470

27. Ericsson, K.A., Lehmann, A.C.: Expert and exceptional performance: evidence of maximal adaptation to task constraints. Annu. Rev. Psychol. **47**, 273–305 (1996). https://doi.org/10.1146/annurev.psych.47.1.273

28. Salthouse, T.: Expertise as the circumvention of human processing limitations. In: Toward a General Theory of Expertise: Prospects and Limits, pp. 286–300. Cambridge University Press, Cambridge (1991). https://doi.org/10.1037/e578082012-006

29. Klein, G.A.: A recognition-primed decision (RPD) model of rapid decision making. In: Decision Making in Action: Models and Methods, pp. 139–147 (1993). https://doi.org/10.1002/bdm.3960080307

30. Anderson, J.R.: Rules of the Mind. Lawrence Erlbaum, Hillsdale (1993)

31. Abernethy, B.: Anticipation in squash: Differences in advance cue utilization between expert and novice players. J. Sports Sci. **8**, 17–34 (1990). https://doi.org/10.1080/02640419008732128

32. De Groot, A.D.: Thought and Choice in Chess. The Hague, Mouton

33. Calderwood, R., Klein, G.A., Crandall, B.W.: Time pressure, skill, and move quality in chess. Am. J. Psychol. **101**, 481 (1988). https://doi.org/10.2307/1423226

34. Müller, S., Abernethy, B., Farrow, D.: How do world-class cricket batsmen anticipate a bowler's intention? Q. J. Exp. Psychol. **59**, 2162–2186 (2006). https://doi.org/10.1080/02643290600576595

35. Klein, G.A.: The recognition-primed decision (RPD) model: looking back, looking forward. In: Zsambok, C.E., Klein, G.A. (eds.) Naturalistic Decision Making, pp. 285–292. Lawrence Erlbaum Associates, Mahwah (1997)

36. Wiggins, M.W., Loveday, T., Auton, J.C.: EXPERT Intensive Skills Evaluation (EXPERTise) Test. Macquarie University, Sydney (2015)

37. Lansdale, M., Underwood, G., Davies, C.: Something Overlooked? How experts in change detection use visual saliency. Appl. Cogn. Psychol. **24**, 213–225 (2010). https://doi.org/10.1002/acp.1552

38. Brouwers, S., Wiggins, M.W., Helton, W., O'Hare, D., Griffin, B.: Cue utilization and cognitive load in novel task performance. Front. Psychol. **7**, 1–12 (2016). https://doi.org/10.3389/fpsyg.2016.00435

39. Sturman, D., Wiggins, M.W., Auton, J.C., Loft, S.: Cue utilization differentiates resource allocation during sustained attention simulated rail control tasks. J. Exp. Psychol. Appl. (2019). https://doi.org/10.1037/xap0000204
40. Williams, A.M., Ward, P., Knowles, J.M., Smeeton, N.J.: Anticipation skill in a real-world task: measurement, training, and transfer in tennis. J. Exp. Psychol. Appl. **8**, 259–270 (2002). https://doi.org/10.1037/1076-898X.8.4.259
41. Weiss, D.J., Shanteau, J.: Empirical assessment of expertise. Hum. Factors J. Hum. Factors Ergon. Soc. **45**, 104–116 (2003). https://doi.org/10.1518/hfes.45.1.104.27233
42. EXPERTise 2.0 [Computer Software] (2019). https://expertise.mq.edu.au/
43. Wiggins, M.W., Azar, D., Hawken, J., Loveday, T., Newman, D.: Cue-utilisation typologies and pilots' pre-flight and in-flight weather decision-making. Saf. Sci. **65**, 118–124 (2014). https://doi.org/10.1016/j.ssci.2014.01.006
44. Small, A.J., Wiggins, M.W., Loveday, T.: Cue-based processing capacity, cognitive load and the completion of simulated short-duration vigilance tasks in power transmission control. Appl. Cogn. Psychol. **28**, 481–487 (2014). https://doi.org/10.1002/acp.3016
45. Watkinson, J., Bristow, G., Auton, J., McMahon, C.M., Wiggins, M.W.: Postgraduate training in audiology improves clinicians' audiology-related cue utilisation. Int. J. Audiol. **57**, 681–687 (2018). https://doi.org/10.1080/14992027.2018.1476782
46. Loveday, T., Wiggins, M.W., Festa, M., Schell, D., Twigg, D.: Pattern recognition as an indicator of diagnostic expertise. In: Latorre Carmona, P., Sánchez, J., Fred, A. (eds.) Pattern Recognition - Applications and Methods. Advances in Intelligent Systems and Computing, vol. 204. Springer, Berlin (2013). https://doi.org/10.1007/978-3-642-36530-0_1
47. Schriver, A.T., Morrow, D.G., Wickens, C.D., Talleur, D.A.: Expertise differences in attentional strategies related to pilot decision making. Hum. Factors J. Hum. Factors Ergon. Soc. **50**, 864–878 (2008). https://doi.org/10.1518/001872008X374974
48. Wiggins, M.W., O'Hare, D.: Expert and novice pilot perceptions of static in-flight images of weather. Int. J. Aviat. Psychol. **13**, 173–187 (2003). https://doi.org/10.1207/S15327108IJA P1302_05
49. Morrison, B.W., Wiggins, M.W., Bond, N.W., Tyler, M.D.: Measuring relative cue strength as a means of validating an inventory of expert offender profiling cues. J. Cogn. Eng. Decis. Mak. **7**, 211–226 (2013). https://doi.org/10.1177/1555343412459192
50. Pauley, K., O'Hare, D., Wiggins, M.: Measuring expertise in weather-related aeronautical risk perception: the validity of the Cochran–Weiss–Shanteau (CWS) index. Int. J. Aviat. Psychol. **19**, 201–216 (2009). https://doi.org/10.1080/10508410902979993
51. Qualtrics core-XM [Computer Software] (2019). https://www.qualtrics.com/au/core-xm/sur vey-software/
52. Sheng, S., Holbrook, M., Kumaraguru, P., Cranor, L.F., Downs, J.: Who falls for phish? A demographic analysis of phishing susceptibility and effectiveness of interventions. In: Proceedings of the 28th International Conference on Human Factors in Computing Systems - CHI 2010, p. 373. ACM Press, New York (2010). https://doi.org/10.1145/1753326.1753383
53. Gavett, B.E., Zhao, R., John, S.E., Bussell, C.A., Roberts, J.R., Yue, C.: Phishing suspiciousness in older and younger adults: the role of executive functioning. PLoS One. **12** (2017). https://doi.org/10.1371/journal.pone.0171620
54. Oliveira, D., et al.: Dissecting spear phishing emails for older vs young adults. In: Proceedings of the 2017 CHI Conference on Human Factors in Computing Systems - CHI 2017, pp. 6412–6424. ACM Press, New York (2017). https://doi.org/10.1145/3025453.3025831
55. Halevi, T., Lewis, J., Memon, N.: A pilot study of cyber security and privacy related behavior and personality traits. In: WWW 2013 Companion - Proceedings of 22nd International Conference World Wide Web, pp. 737–744 (2013). https://doi.org/10.1145/2487788.2488034
56. Bullee, J., Montoya, L., Junger, M., Hartel, P.: Spear phishing in organisations explained. Inf. Comput. Secur. **25**, 593–613 (2017). https://doi.org/10.1108/ICS-03-2017-0009

57. Wiggins, M.W., Brouwers, S., Davies, J., Loveday, T.: Trait-based cue utilization and initial skill acquisition: implications for models of the progression to expertise. Front. Psychol. **5**, 1–8 (2014). https://doi.org/10.3389/fpsyg.2014.00541

58. Stanislaw, H., Todorov, N.: Calculation of signal detection theory measures. Behav. Res. Methods Instrum. Comput. **31**, 137–149 (1999). https://doi.org/10.3758/BF03207704

Dis-Empowerment Online: An Investigation of Privacy-Sharing Perceptions and Method Preferences

Kovila P. L. Coopamootoo$^{(\boxtimes)}$

Newcastle University, Newcastle upon Tyne, UK
kovila.coopamootoo@newcastle.ac.uk

Abstract. While it is often claimed that users are empowered via online technologies, there is also a general feeling of privacy dis-empowerment. We investigate the perception of privacy and sharing empowerment online, as well as the use of privacy technologies, via a cross-national online study with N = 907 participants. We find that perception of privacy empowerment differs from that of sharing across dimensions of meaningfulness, competence and choice. We find similarities and differences in privacy method preference between the US, UK and Germany. We also find that non-technology methods of privacy protection are among the most preferred methods, while more advanced and standalone privacy technologies are least preferred. By mapping the perception of privacy dis-empowerment into patterns of privacy behavior online, and clarifying the similarities and distinctions in privacy technology use, this paper provides an important foundation for future research and the design of privacy technologies. The findings may be used across disciplines to develop more user-centric privacy technologies, that support and enable the user.

Keywords: Privacy · Sharing · User · Empowerment · Privacy-technology · Quantitative

1 Introduction

Although the internet is often seen as an empowering environment for consumers, the indiscriminate amount of information collected in today's data-intensive web, characterized with mass sharing, collection, aggregation, mining and selling of individuals' data, is also seen to come with privacy-, identity- and empowerment-related issues [15].

Internet users often express discomfort with the data collection that enables personalization, and a large portion takes some kind of action such as clearing cookies and browsing history [18]. However, the methods employed by individuals may not be enough to protect one's privacy, because, as example, a particular web browser on a specific machine comprises a unique fingerprint that can be traced by web servers across the web, and this information in conveyed through

© Springer Nature Switzerland AG 2020
M. Bernhard et al. (Eds.): FC 2020 Workshops, LNCS 12063, pp. 71–83, 2020.
https://doi.org/10.1007/978-3-030-54455-3_6

headers that are automatically exchanged by every web browser and web server behind the scenes [14].

In general, privacy experts perceive an overall sense of privacy dis-empowerment online [6]. The perception of privacy *dis*-empowerment has mainly been attributed to business models and the social web that favour sharing and data analytics, to privacy of personal content [12,17]. Other reasons include human challenges to the adoption of privacy technologies, and human-computer mismatches. We posit that privacy dis-empowerment is evidenced in the failure to use privacy technologies [1,10].

Use of privacy technologies is thought to be moderated by user perception of technology. In particular, perceived usefulness and effectiveness do not match the technology's offering, and users exhibit poor trust in the technology [1,3,10], and in-correct mental models [1]. However, individuals are likely impacted by their own self-perception, in addition to their perception of the technology. As a result, they likely engage with some privacy technologies more than others, employ privacy technologies in a certain way, or develop non-technology methods of protection.

Contributions: In this paper, we seek to better understand how the perception of privacy (dis)-empowerment is mapped out into patterns of privacy behavior online. We employ a quantitative method as we investigate how individuals protect their privacy from others - whether individual others or organisations - in particular what privacy methods they use. We investigate the link between perception of dis-empowerment and behavior across 40+ privacy methods elicited from users themselves. The paper makes the following contributions: (1) We provide a cross-national report of users' perception of empowerment. (2) We find that individuals use 22 privacy methods on average, where 40 to 50% of the 10 topmost preferred methods are non-technology methods that are reported to be used by 71% to 85% of the surveyed participants. (3) We identify similarities and differences in privacy and sharing method preferences between the three countries.

This paper therefore provides valuable insights into individuals' methods of protecting their privacy online, that includes both non-technology methods and the use of privacy technologies. This helps to ground the perceptions of privacy dis-empowerment into behavior patterns. The paper also helps to identify privacy technologies that appear to be more accessible to users.

Outline: In the rest of the paper, provide the aim and method of our study, followed by the results and a discussion, and conclusion.

2   Aim

Our research aim is to compare privacy and sharing empowerment perceptions and to map perceptions of privacy *dis*-empowerment onto usage of privacy and sharing methods. We do so via the research questions below.

2.1   Privacy vs Sharing Empowerment

Thomas & Velthouse [21] defined *Psychological Empowerment* as increased intrinsic task motivation and proposed a theoretical model with four perceptions or cognitions, namely *perception of impact, competence, meaningfulness,* and *choice* [21]. The model captures individuals' interpretive processes via which they assess the actions they engage in. Compared to other psychological empowerment models, Thomas & Velthouse's model focuses on intrinsic motivation and involves positively valued experiences that individuals derive directly from a task, and impact behavior.

With the power imbalance between online users and others (including more able other individuals perceived as threatening and organisations), individuals likely perceive privacy and sharing empowerment differently online. We investigate as **RQ1**, "How do individuals' perception of privacy and sharing empowerment differ?" via the hypotheses:

$H_{1,0}$: There is no difference in individuals' perception of privacy and sharing empowerment.
$H_{1,1}$: There is a significant difference in individuals' perception of privacy and sharing empowerment.

2.2   Privacy and Sharing Methods, Similarties and Differences

We investigate as **RQ2**, "What methods are mostly used to protect one's privacy and to share information online?" and **RQ3**, "How similar are individuals' [privacy/sharing] methods usage and preference? What patterns of use emerge? Are there similarities or differences between countries?"

3   Method

We conduct two survey studies online via an evidence-based method [7,8]. The first study is mainly aimed at identifying a preferred list of privacy methods. The second and main study employs the compiled list of methods to query a representative sample of participants about their use of the range of privacy methods identified.

The studies have a within subject design, where participants answered both the privacy and sharing empowerment questions. We compared privacy and sharing empowerment for each participant. However, we compared preferred privacy and sharing methods between countries, thereby including a between-subject analysis. We randomly assigned participants to answer either the privacy or sharing empowerment questions first.

3.1   Participants

Recruitment. For the first study, we sampled $N = 180$ participants, comprising $N = 58$ US participants, $N = 62$ UK participants and $N = 60$ German (DE) participants. The US sample was recruited from population of Amazon Mechanical Turk workers, while the UK and DE sample were from Prolific Academic. The data quality of Prolific Academic is comparable to Amazon Mechanical Turk's, with good reproducibility [16].

For the second study, we recruited an $N = 907$ sample from the US, UK and DE via Prolific Academic. The sample was representative of age, gender and ethnicity demographics of the UK and US countries, as provided by Prolific Academic. For the DE sample, we did not achieve a representative sample in terms of gender and age. While we use that sample to investigate our research questions, we foresee extending to representative samples of other countries in the future.

The studies lasted between 10 to 20 min. Participants were compensated at a rate of £7.5 per hour, slightly above the minimum rate of £5 per hour suggested by Prolific Academic.

Demographics. Table 1 provides a summary of the demographic details for the two studies, with sample size N, mean age, gender, education level and ethnicity. 5% of the German sample had an education level lower than high school for the first study and 1% for the second study. For the second study, 6 UK participants reported to have a PhD, 4 for the US and 9 for DE.

Table 1. Participant characteristics

	Country	N	Mean Age	Gender		%Education Level				% Ethnicity				
				#Female	#Male	HighSchool	College	Undergrad	Masters/PhD	White	Black	Asian	Mixed	Other
First Study	US	58	35.53	29	29	24.1	31.0	36.2	8.6	82.8	5.2	5.1	5.2	1.7
	UK	62	30.65	43	19	22.6	19.4	41.9	16.1	88.7	3.2	3.2	4.8	-
	DE	60	30.68	27	33	30.0	13.3	28.3	21.7	96.7	-	-	3.3	-
Second Study	US	303	43.72	155	148	39.9	22.1	20.1	14.2	69.3	14.9	8.9	4.3	2.6
	UK	303	44.21	154	149	26.7	17.5	32.0	18.5	77.6	5.3	10.9	4.3	2.0
	DE	301	28.91	115	186	31.2	15.6	28.6	23.6	93.0	0.7	1.9	3.7	0.7

3.2 Procedure

The aim of the first study was to identify and compile a list of privacy and sharing methods preference. We did so via an open-ended question and across three countries. The first study consisted of (a) a questionnaire on demographics, (b) a description of privacy online, and the four psychological empowerment questions, (c) an open-ended query to list three to five tools most often employed to achieve the purpose of privacy online, (d) a description of sharing online, and the four psychological empowerment questions, (e) an open-ended query to list three to five tools most often employed to achieve the purpose of sharing online.

The second study followed the same format of the first study, except that we changed the open-ended queries of the first study to close-ended privacy and sharing methods questions, for participants to select the methods they mostly use from the whole list provided. We also shifted to a larger sample for the three countries.

We defined privacy and sharing for the two studies, thereby focusing participants to a specific meaning. We developed the definition of [privacy/sharing] online with inputs from Coopamootoo & Groß's findings of the cognitive content of individuals' [privacy/sharing] attitude [9]. In particular, privacy attitude has contents of 'others as individuals or organisations who pose a threat, while sharing attitude includes 'others as connections including friends, family'.

We defined privacy online as *"to control access to information that are sensitive or personal, to be informed of other individual and business practices such as collection, processing and use of personal information disclosed, and to have the choice on disclosure and how one's information is dealt with"*. We defined Sharing online as . *"to create content and share with other web users (such as sharing one's opinion or expertise) and also to share personal information or life events with close connections, friends and family"*.

3.3   Measurement Apparatus

Perception of Psychological Empowerment. Measures of psychological empowerment have mainly been employed within management and social science research [13,20]. In particular, Spreitzer proposed a four-factor scale based on Thomas & Velthouse's conceptualization [21]. The scale has been widely applied in the context of organizational management [20]. It has also been evaluated for construct validity [11]. In addition, Spreitzer's formulation was observed as seminal to research on psychological empowerment [19]. However, so far, sparse application appear in relation to technology, such as Van Dyke et al.'s measure of consumer privacy empowerment in E-Commerce [22].

The Psychological Empowerment Scale consists of 12-items focused on the four dimensions of empowerment defined by Thomas & Velthouse [21], in particular areas of (1) meaning, (2) competence, (3) self-determination/choice, and (4) impact. Whereas Van Dyke et al. apply these four dimensions to the notice, choice and access concepts to then develop four perceived privacy empowerment items [22], we directly adapted Spreitzer's scale [20] for online [privacy/sharing] activities. We used the four cognitions of the model to create a task assessment questionnaire directed towards the purpose of either privacy or sharing online.

We set the [privacy/sharing] questions as follows:
'Purpose' refers to that of achieving [privacy/sharing] online as detailed above.
'Actions' are those that one would take with the aim to accomplish that purpose, that is [privacy/sharing] online.
Please provide your responses on the scale from 1 to 100.

(1) *How do you perceive the impact of the actions you have taken online in the past to accomplish the purpose detailed above?*

(2) *How do you perceive your skills to successfully achieve the purpose detailed above?*

(3) *To what extent is the purpose detailed above meaningful to you?*

(4) *How do you perceive your choice to determine what actions to take to successfully accomplish the purpose detailed above?*

We used a Visual Analogue Scale (VAS) [23] with boundaries from 1 to 100. The 1 minimum value was set to 'no impact at all', 'not skilled at all', 'not meaningful at all' or 'I have no choice at all', pertainig to the four questions above. The 100 maximum value was set to very 'big impact', 'very skillful', 'very meaningful" or 'I have lots of choices.

Compared to Likert-type scales which have coarse-grained discrete measurement data produced by only three to seven categories, the line continuum of a VAS enables the rater to make more fine-grained responses [4]. This aspect of VAS helps to avoid the systematic bias of values resulting from scale coarseness [2] and facilitates collection of measurement data with higher variability, which theoretically enhances their reliability [5].

Privacy and Sharing Behavior. We queried participants on the individual privacy and sharing methods they most often use, eliciting participants' own methods via open-ended question in the first study and requesting preference report from the compiled list in the second study. In the second study, we asked participants to rate the list of privacy and sharing methods provided with whether they use them 'very often' or 'very rarely/not at all'.

4 Results

4.1 Empowerment Perception

We investigate RQ1 with respect to the US, UK and DE samples in the second study, "How do individuals' perception of privacy versus sharing empowerment differ?" We conduct a paired-samples t-test for privacy and sharing for each of the four cognitions for the three countries. We summarize the differences in perception of privacy and sharing empowerment cognitions in Table 2 below.

4.2 Privacy and Sharing Methods

We provide the full list of privacy methods compiled in the first study in Table 3, with the $N = 180$ sample. This list of 43 privacy methods was then used to query participants in the second study. We loosely categorise the privacy methods into four possible protection categories, namely (1) anonymity (ANO), (2) browsing history and tracking prevention (BHP), (3) communication privacy & filtering (COP), and (4) preventing leaking and stealing of data (PLS).

We also compile participants' responses of 3 to 5 most used sharing methods in the first study. We end up with 39 sharing methods coded across the three countries. We categorize the sharing methods across five themes, as shown in Table 4. The 'Community' theme includes social networks or community sharing. With respect to Facebook, some participants referred to Facebook in general, while others specified updates or photos. The 'Messaging' theme includes

Table 2. Task assessment differences between privacy activities & sharing activities

Assessment component	Privacy		Sharing		$t(df)$	p	Difference		95% CI	
	M	SD	M	SD			ΔM	SE	LL	UL
United States					$t(302)$					
Meaningfulness	76.36	21.739	63.94	30.823	8.489	$< .000^{***}$	15.419	1.816	11.845	18.993
Competency	58.81	23.508	66.05	24.380	−5.087	$< .000^{***}$	−7.238	1.423	−10.037	−4.438
Choice	61.78	22.397	72.49	22.532	−7.331	$< .000^{***}$	−10.706	1.460	−13.580	−7.832
Impact	58.16	22.489	58.65	25.862	−.287	.774	−.498	1.734	−3.911	2.914
United Kingdom					$t(302)$					
Meaningfulness	70.06	24.786	59.84	26.875	5.862	$< .000^{***}$	10.211	1.742	6.783	13.639
Competence	56.87	22.714	62.20	23.084	−4.013	$< .000^{***}$	−5.330	1.328	−7.944	−2.716
Choice	59.10	21.562	66.81	21.907	−5.747	$< .000^{***}$	−7.716	1.343	−10.358	−5.047
Impact	54.79	21.885	57.42	24.265	−1.604	.110	−2.637	1.644	−5.872	.598
Germany					$t(300)$					
Meaningfulness	69.63	22.998	48.59	29.984	9.947	$< .000^{***}$	21.040	2.115	16.877	25.202
Competence	58.73	23.280	62.85	24.678	−2.662	.008**	−4.123	1.549	−7.171	−1.075
Choice	55.57	19.782	68.94	23.202	−8.870	$< .000^{***}$	−13.365	1.507	−16.331	−10.400
Impact	53.26	21.793	49.03	24.558	2.550	.011*	4.223	1.656	.964	7.481

CI refers to the Confidence Interval, LL to the Lower Limit, UL to the Upper Limit.

email and instant messaging methods, referring to a particular tool or instant messaging in general. The other sharing themes are 'Photos', 'File-Sharing' and 'Streaming'.

The rest of the results section pertains to the second and main study.

We investigate RQ2 "What methods are mostly used to protect one's privacy and to share information online?" How similar are individuals' [privacy/sharing] methods usage and preference? What patterns of use emerge? Are there similarities or differences between countries?"

Table 5 shows a depiction of the top 10 privacy methods preferences across the three countries, where we observe that 4 of the privacy methods appear in the top 10 most reported methods in all three countries. These methods are (1) privacy settings, (2) limit sharing, (3) website care, and (4) no newsletter.

In addition, we find 8 privacy methods similarities in the top 10 most reported methods for both the UK and US, 6 methods similarities between the UK and DE, and 5 methods similarities between the US and DE.

Table 6 shows a depiction of the top 10 sharing methods preferences across the three countries, where we observe that 5 of the sharing methods appear in the top 10 of all three countries, and 8 appear in the top 10 most reported methods for both the US and the UK.

We investigate whether there is a difference in privacy method preference between countries. On average, participants reported to protect their privacy with 22 different ways ($m = 21.86$, $sd = 7.11$). DE and US participants reported

Table 3. Privacy methods categorised by design type and privacy protection.

Privacy Protection	Built-in	Standalone	User-Defined
Anonymity	Encryption	Erasery	Not Store Info
	Clear/Delete info/history	TOR	Anonymous profile names
	Pseudonyms/Onion	Proxy	NotGivePI/LimitSharing/MinimalInfo
		IPHider	Several/Bogus/LimitedUse Emails
		Virtual machine	Fake Info
			Limit Use of SNS Accounts
			SwitchOffCamera/Devices/PortableHD
			No Access Acc In Public Place/Networks
			Not use FB
			Not Engaging Online/Careful/Not Signing Up
Browsing History & Tracking Prevention	Private Browsing/incognito	DuckDuckGo	
	Anti-tracking addon	Ghostery	
	No location tracking	NoScript	
	Clear/Limit cookies		
Communication & Filtering	Adblock	Firewall	
	HTTPS	VPN	
Prevent Leaking & Stealing of Data	Privacy settings	Password manager	Not save or reuse password
	Opt out	Paypal	Read terms of service
	Private profiles	Anti-spyware	Request data collected, GDPR
		Anti-malware	no newsletter, think twice
		Kapersky	Website care/No suspicious sites

using 3 and 2 more privacy methods on average than UK participants respectively

We compute a Chi Square test on each of the 43 privacy methods. We find that for 23 privacy methods, there is a statistically significant association between privacy method employed and country of residence, after multiple comparisons correction, as detailed in Table 7 in the Appendix. The table shows both the percentage of participants within each country who listed the privacy method, as well as the percentage taken by each country for each listed method. It also shows the privacy protection category of the method.

In addition, the table provides a measure of association in privacy method preference across country of residence, with effect size Cramer V depicting the magnitude of association between the privacy method and the country, where $V < .20$ corresponds to a weak association, $.20 < V < .40$ corresponds to a moderate association and $V > .40$ corresponds to a strong association.

Table 4. Sharing methods categorised by theme.

Community	Photos	Messaging	File-Sharing	Streaming
Discord	Facebook photos	Email	box.com	Twitch
Facebook	Flickr	Facebook messenger	cloud	Vimeo
Facebook updates	Google photos	Instant messaging	dropbox	YouTube
Forums	iCloud photos	Telegram	FTP	
Google hangouts	Instagram	WhatsApp	Google Drive	
LinkedIn	Social network photos		Microsoft OneDrive	
News site comments	Pinterest			
Personal blog	Photo blog			
Reddit	Snapchat			
Skype				
Slack				
Social networks				
Social network updates				
Teamviewer				
Tumblr				
Twitter				

5   Discussion

Privacy vs Sharing Empowerment: That participants perceive privacy to be more meaningful than sharing across the three countries, yet perceive lower competency and choice with regards to privacy can be expected given the looming sense of privacy dis-empowerment online users are habituated to. However by providing statistical evidence from a relatively large representative sample, we demonstrate that privacy dis-empowerment is not just a passing or one-time feeling but is perceived across countries and demographics. This finding can contribute to explaining the privacy paradox, that although individuals are concerned about their privacy, their observed behavior differ, as they have poor perceptions of competency and choice.

In addition, although the internet is thought to empower individuals, we do not observe a positive difference in perceived sharing impact versus perceived privacy impact. This aspect requires further investigation in eliciting users' understanding of the results of their sharing. Only DE shows a higher perceived impact for privacy.

Table 5. Top 10 privacy methods by country starting with most frequently mentioned

United States			United Kingdom			Germany		
Method	Design	CAT	Method	Design	CAT	Method	Design	CAT
1 Website care	UD	PLS	1 Website care	UD	PLS	1 AdBlock	BI	COP
2 Privacy settings	BI	PLS	2 Limit Sharing	UD	ANO	2 Bogus Emails	UD	ANO
3 Limit Sharing	UD	ANO	3 Privacy settings	BI	PLS	3 Privacy settings	BI	PLS
4 Research before engaging	UD	ANO	4 Clear Info/History	BI	ANO	4 Limit Sharing	UD	ANO
5 Anti-Malware	ST	PLS	5 Paypal	ST	PLS	5 No Newsletter	UD	PLS
6 No Newsletter	UD	PLS	6 Research before engaging	UD	ANO	5 Paypal	ST	PLS
7 AdBlock	BI	COP	7 No Newsletter	UD	PLS	5 Website care	UD	PLS
8 Clear Info/History	BI	ANO	8 Firewall	ST	COP	5 Firewall	ST	COP
9 Clear/Limit Cookies	BI	BHP	9 Anti-Malware	ST	PLS	9 HTTPS	BI	COP
10 Not Access Accts in Public Place	UD	ANO	10 Not Access Accts in Public Place	UD	ANO	10 Pseudonyms	BI	ANO

BI, ST & UD refer to design type of built-in, standalone and user-defined respectively.
ANO, BHP, COP & PLS refer to privacy protection categories of anonymity, browsing history and tracking prevention, communication privacy & filtering, and preventing leaking & stealing of data respectively.

Table 6. Top 10 sharing methods by country starting with most frequently mentioned

United States		United Kingdom		Germany	
1	Email	1	Email	1	Email
2	Youtube	2	WhatsApp	2	WhatsApp
3	Google Drive	3	Facebook Messenger	3	YouTube
4	Facebook Messenger	4	YouTube	4	Reddit
5	Reddit	5	Instant Messaging	5	Instagram
6	Instant Messaging	6	Facebook updates & newsfeed	6	Google Drive
7	Forums	7	Google Drive	7	DropBox
8	Instagram	8	Instagram	8	Instant Messaging
9	Facebook updates & newsfeed	9	Twitter	9	Discord
10	Facebook photos	10	Facebook photos	10	Forums
10	Social network sites (exclu. FB)				
10	Twitter				

5.1 Methods Preference and Behavior

DE and US participants reported using 3 and 2 more privacy methods on average than UK participants respectively, where although there are similarities in that 4 items are among the top 10 most used privacy methods in countries, they differ across 23 methods. DE shows a higher use of 19 methods, a higher portion of which are more technologically advanced PETs rather than simpler builtin PETs. This may indicate higher awareness of and skill to use PETs, as well as an outcome of privacy culture and regulation.

Among the similarities, we find that user-defined or non-technology methods (1) of being careful of websites, (2) to limit sharing, (3) research before engaging (2 out of 3 countries), (4) not subscribe to newsletters, and (5) not access accounts in public places appear in the most used methods in both countries. For the three countries, these non-technology methods made up 40% to 50% of the top 10 most preferred privacy methods, while advanced, dedicated and standalone PETs such as Tor, Ghostery or NoScript are among the least used privacy methods. This demonstrates that users rely more on their own non-technology means to protect themselves than privacy technologies.

Questions can be raised for future research following these usage patterns. In particular, "what are reasons for reliance on non-technology methods rather than advanced PETs?", "are users concerned enough and aware of PETs to use them?", "how were their previous experience with PETs?", "how can we encourage users to adopt more advanced and dedicated PETs?"

6   Conclusion

This paper provides an initial investigation of a mapping between perceived privacy dis-empowerment online and preferences for privacy and sharing methods, as well as offers a cross-national investigation. We identify a few non-technology privacy methods that are preferred over more advanced and standalone privacy-enhancing technologies. This raises questions for future research, in particular why individuals prefer methods that seem more accessible and integrated within non-privacy focused environments and non-technology methods, rather than more advanced and more technical privacy technologies.

Table 7. Privacy method differences across countries with chi square test, sorted by effect size V

Privacy Method	CAT	% Participants	% in Country			% in Method			$X^2(2)$	p	Cramer V
			US	UK	DE	US	UK	DE			
1 Pseudonyms	ANO	53.1	47.2	36.6	76.1	29.6	23.0	47.4	101.087	.000***	.334
2 Anonymous Profiles	ANO	59.2	57.8	44.2	75.7	32.6	25.0	42.5	65.522	.000***	.263
3 Have several emails	ANO	72.5	70.6	60.4	86.7	32.5	27.8	39.7	53.343	.000***	.243
4 NoScript	BHP	15.9	12.9	6.9	27.9	27.1	14.6	58.3	52.823	.000***	.241
5 Give fake info	ANO	45.3	42.2	33.7	60.1	31.1	24.8	44.0	44.234	.000***	.221
6 Adblock	COP	76.5	77.6	65.0	87.0	33.9	28.4	37.8	41.045	.000***	.213
7 VPN	COP	37.7	32.7	28.4	52.2	28.9	25.1	45.9	41.250	.000***	.213
8 HTTPS	COP	68.1	69.0	56.8	78.7	33.8	27.8	38.3	33.724	.000***	.193
9 TOR	ANO	13.5	10.6	7.6	22.3	26.2	18.9	54.9	31.172	.000***	.185
10 Virtual Machines	ANO	13.8	12.2	6.9	22.3	29.6	16.8	53.6	30.803	.000***	.184
11 Anti-tracking extension	BHP	31.2	30.7	21.1	41.9	32.9	22.6	44.5	30.308	.000***	.183
12 Not use Facebook	ANO	43.0	43.2	32.7	53.2	33.6	25.4	41.0	25.857	.000***	.169
13 Paypal instead of online banking	PLS	74.6	66.3	74.6	83.1	29.7	33.4	36.9	22.302	.000***	.157
14 Proxy	ANO	26.7	22.1	21.5	36.5	27.7	26.9	45.5	22.438	.000***	.157
15 Read terms of service	PLS	44.2	50.8	48.5	33.2	38.4	36.7	24.9	22.385	.000***	.157
16 Not access accts in public place	ANO	66.7	73.9	69.3	56.8	37.0	34.7	28.3	21.308	.000***	.153
17 Request data collected	PLS	19.1	17.8	12.5	26.9	31.2	22.0	46.8	20.660	.000***	.151
18 DuckDuckGo	BHP	21.5	26.1	12.9	25.6	40.5	20.0	39.5	20.092	.000***	.149
19 Ghostery	BHP	11.8	10.2	6.9	18.3	29.0	19.6	51.4	19.739	.000***	.148
20 Kapersky	PLS	14.1	9.9	11.6	20.9	23.4	27.3	49.2	17.617	.000***	.139
21 Firewall	COP	74.9	69.6	71.9	83.1	31.1	32.1	36.8	16.504	.000***	.135
22 Switch off camera	ANO	34.7	68.0	56.8	69.4	35.1	29.3	35.6	12.743	.002**	.119
23 Anti-spyware	PLS	65.3	72.9	62.7	60.1	37.3	32.1	30.6	12.241	.002**	.116

These differences are statistically significant under Bonferroni correction.
Effect size *Cramer V* $< .20$ corresponds to a weak effect, $.20 < V < .40$ corresponds to a moderate effect.

7   Appendix

References

1. Abu-Salma, R., Sasse, M.A., Bonneau, J., Danilova, A., Naiakshina, A., Smith, M.: Obstacles to the adoption of secure communication tools. In: 2017 IEEE Symposium on Security and Privacy (SP), pp. 137–153. IEEE (2017)
2. Aguinis, H., Pierce, C.A., Culpepper, S.A.: Scale coarseness as a methodological artifact: correcting correlation coefficients attenuated from using coarse scales. Organ. Res. Methods **12**(4), 623–652 (2009)
3. Benenson, Z., Girard, A., Krontiris, I.: User acceptance factors for anonymous credentials: an empirical investigation. In: WEIS (2015)
4. Chimi, C.J., Russell, D.L.: The likert scale: a proposal for improvement using quasi-continuous variables. In: Information Systems Education Conference, Washington, DC, pp. 1–10 (2009)

5. Cook, C., Heath, F., Thompson, R.L., Thompson, B.: Score reliability in webor internet-based surveys: unnumbered graphic rating scales versus likert-type scales. Educ. Psychol. Measur. **61**(4), 697–706 (2001)
6. Coopamootoo, K.P.L.: Towards empowering the human for privacy online. In: Kosta, E., Pierson, J., Slamanig, D., Fischer-Hübner, S., Krenn, S. (eds.) Privacy and Identity 2018. IAICT, vol. 547, pp. 67–80. Springer, Cham (2019). https://doi.org/10.1007/978-3-030-16744-8_5
7. Coopamootoo, K.P.L., Groß, T.: Evidence-based methods for privacy and identity management. In: Lehmann, A., Whitehouse, D., Fischer-Hübner, S., Fritsch, L., Raab, C. (eds.) Privacy and Identity 2016. IAICT, vol. 498, pp. 105–121. Springer, Cham (2016). https://doi.org/10.1007/978-3-319-55783-0_9
8. Coopamootoo, K.P.L., Groß, T.: Cyber security and privacy experiments: a design and reporting toolkit. In: Hansen, M., Kosta, E., Nai-Fovino, I., Fischer-Hübner, S. (eds.) Privacy and Identity 2017. IAICT, vol. 526, pp. 243–262. Springer, Cham (2018). https://doi.org/10.1007/978-3-319-92925-5_17
9. Coopamootoo, K.P., Groß, T.: Why privacy is all but forgotten - an empirical study of privacy and sharing attitude. In: Proceedings on Privacy Enhancing Technologies, vol. 4, pp. 39–60 (2017)
10. Harborth, D., Pape, S.: Examining technology use factors of privacy-enhancing technologies: the role of perceived anonymity and trust (2018)
11. Kraimer, M.L., Seibert, S.E., Liden, R.C.: Psychological empowerment as a multi-dimensional construct: A test of construct validity. Educ. Psychol. Measur. **59**(1), 127–142 (1999)
12. Mansell, R.: Empowerment and/or disempowerment: the politics of digital media. Popul. Commun. **12**(4), 223–236 (2014)
13. Menon, S.T.: Psychological empowerment: definition, measurement, and validation. Can. J. Behav. Sci./Revue canadienne des sciences du comportement **31**(3), 161 (1999)
14. Nikiforakis, N., Kapravelos, A., Joosen, W., Kruegel, C., Piessens, F., Vigna, G.: Cookieless monster: exploring the ecosystem of web-based device fingerprinting. In: 2013 IEEE Symposium on Security and Privacy, pp. 541–555. IEEE (2013)
15. O'Hara, K., Tuffield, M.M., Shadbolt, N.: Lifelogging: privacy and empowerment with memories for life. Identity Inf. Soc. **1**(1), 155–172 (2008). https://doi.org/10.1007/s12394-009-0008-4
16. Peer, E., Brandimarte, L., Samat, S., Acquisti, A.: Beyond the turk: alternative platforms for crowdsourcing behavioral research. J. Exp. Soc. Psychol. **70**, 153–163 (2017)
17. Pierson, J.: Online privacy in social media: a conceptual exploration of empowerment and vulnerability. Commun. Strat. **88**, 99–120 (2012)
18. Rainie, L., et al.: Anonymity, privacy, and security online. Pew Res. Center **5** (2013)
19. Seibert, S.E., Wang, G., Courtright, S.H.: Antecedents and consequences of psychological and team empowerment in organizations: a meta-analytic review (2011)
20. Spreitzer, G.M.: Psychological empowerment in the workplace: dimensions, measurement, and validation. Acad. Manag. J. **38**(5), 1442–1465 (1995)
21. Thomas, K.W., Velthouse, B.A.: Cognitive elements of empowerment: an interpretive model of intrinsic task motivation. Acad. Manag. Rev. **15**(4), 666–681 (1990)
22. Van Dyke, T.P., Midha, V., Nemati, H.: The effect of consumer privacy empowerment on trust and privacy concerns in e-commerce. Electron. Mark. **17**(1), 68–81 (2007)
23. Wewers, M.E., Lowe, N.K.: A critical review of visual analogue scales in the measurement of clinical phenomena. Res. Nurs. Health **13**(4), 227–236 (1990)

Security and Privacy Awareness in Smart Environments – A Cross-Country Investigation

Oksana Kulyk[1,2(✉)], Benjamin Reinheimer[2], Lukas Aldag[2], Peter Mayer[2],
Nina Gerber[3], and Melanie Volkamer[2]

[1] IT University of Copenhagen, Copenhagen, Denmark
okku@itu.dk
[2] Karlsruhe Institute of Technology, Karlsruhe, Germany
{oksana.kulyk,benjamin.reinheimer,lukas.aldag,
peter.mayer,melanie.volkamer}@kit.edu
[3] Technische Universität Darmstadt, Darmstadt, Germany
n.gerber@psychologie.tu-darmstadt.de

Abstract. Smart environments are becoming ubiquitous despite many potential security and privacy issues. But, do people understand what consequences could arise from using smart environments? To answer this research question, we conducted a survey with 575 participants from three different countries (Germany, Spain, Romania) considering smart home and health environments. Less than half of all participants mentioned at least one security and privacy issue, with significantly more German participants mentioning issues than the Spanish ones and the Spanish participants in turn mentioning significantly more security and privacy issues than the Romanian participants. Using open coding, we find that among the 275 participants mentioning security and privacy issues, 111 only expressed abstract concerns such as "security issues" and only 34 mentioned concrete harms such as "Burglaries (physical and privacy)", caused by security and privacy violations. The remaining 130 participants who mentioned security and privacy issues named only threats (i.e. their responses were more concrete than just abstract concerns but they did not mention concrete harming scenarios).

1 Introduction

Smart environments are becoming increasingly popular for end users, with smart homes reaching a household penetration of 9.5% worldwide in 2019 and an expected increase to 22.1% by 2023 [21]. Smart environments offer a multitude of possible applications, one of them being the assistance of elderly people or those suffering from a health impairment by equipping their households with connected health devices (e.g., blood pressure monitors) and sensors (e.g., drop sensors) - often referred to as smart health environments. However, such smart environments of home and health applications also introduce potential security

© Springer Nature Switzerland AG 2020
M. Bernhard et al. (Eds.): FC 2020 Workshops, LNCS 12063, pp. 84–101, 2020.
https://doi.org/10.1007/978-3-030-54455-3_7

and privacy issues [5,7,10,11,18]. While there is an increasing body of research on the security and privacy vulnerabilities of smart environments (and how to address these vulnerabilities), it remains an open question, to which extent end users are aware of these issues. A number of studies investigating user perception of security and privacy risks in smart environments have been conducted in the US, however, less is known about users' awareness in other countries. In this work we aim to gain broader insights into this topic by conducting a large-scale qualitative survey with 596 participants from three different countries (Germany, Romania, Spain). These countries were chosen based on previous research conducted in Europe, which showed different security and privacy conceptions for the southern, northern, eastern, and western parts of Europe [6,15].

We considered two examples of smart environments (smart home and smart health). Smart homes as a smart environment which has been around for some years already, have a larger user base and have been more present in the media compared to smart health environments. On the other hand, smart health environments could be considered as handling even more sensitive data than smart homes. Moreover, we included both owners and non-owners of these environments in our sample.

We find that less than half of the participants mentioned any security and privacy issues in smart environments, and that most participants focused on threats (e.g., data collection, monitoring, and data theft) or expressed abstract concerns about their security and privacy. Only 34 out of 596 participants described a potential harm caused by security and privacy violations that could result from living in smart environments, such as being burgled, being influenced in one's behavior, or getting increased insurance rates. This suggests that most participants lack a thorough understanding of how living in smart environments could affect their lives. At the same time, our study has demonstrated significant differences between the countries in terms of awareness about security and privacy issues. As such, the German participants seem to be more aware of security and privacy issues associated with smart environments than the Spanish and Romanian participants, with 74% of them naming at least one security and privacy issue compared to 44% of Spanish participants and 22% of Romanian participants. Furthermore, the participants named more security and privacy issues associated with smart homes than with smart health. This is alarming, as particularly smart devices that are connected to the users' body have the potential to severely harm their health if these devices are compromised in a cyber-attack. We discuss the implication of our findings, concluding the need for taking the cultural context into account when designing measures for data protection such as general awareness campaigns or services providing information to the end users relevant for data protection.

2 Background and Related Work

Although there are several studies on *users' awareness and perception of security and privacy threats*, in most of these studies participants were shown lists with different threats and asked to evaluate these. Few researchers, however, asked users to provide security and privacy threats on their own. Some studies e.g., Harbach et al. [9] or Stadion et al. [20] had a slightly different context in their study and asked the participants about the dangers of the primary use of the Internet. The participants could name only very few consequences and were not aware of most of the possible ones. Similar studies e.g., Bellekens et al. [4], Oomen and Leenes [17] or Aktypi et al. [1] with lists of various security and/or privacy risks found that people are unaware of concrete privacy and security risks and mainly worried about general privacy issues. In their study, Zeng et al. [23] focused on the group of smart home users and their knowledge of security and privacy threats. Unfortunately, the study comprises only very few participants, and therefore the significance of the dissemination of the knowledge of consequences is only limited here. Therefore, we have chosen the approach of questioning both users and non-users within the framework of a large-scale online study. Karwatzki et al. [12] had in their study 22 focus groups in which they asked the participants about possible privacy consequences. Whereas this is probably the most extensive study that has been conducted so far on people's awareness of privacy issues, Karwatzki et al. do not report how many participants referred to a particular issue. Moreover, their participants mostly referred to consequences that could arise from using online social networks, a well-established technology, while we focus on two emerging technologies, i.e., smart home and smart health environments. Garg [8] conducted a survey with 834 US-American IoT users, of which 115 reported to no longer use IoT devices due to privacy concerns. Another survey with experts and lay users [19] shows that if people care about concrete security and privacy issues, these are often of a financial or social nature, identifying identity theft, account breach, and job loss as the top rated tech-related risk scenarios.

Further studies focused on *influence of culture* on security and privacy risk perception. As such, Lancelot Miltgen et al. [15] conducted focus groups with participants from seven EU countries. The countries were chosen based on cultural differences and internet usage. Europe was divided into four major blocks: Northern, Eastern, Western, and Southern Europe. The findings suggest a difference between North and South with respect to responsibility versus trust. Also, people in the Southern countries perceive data disclosure as a personal choice, whereas people from Eastern countries feel forced to disclose personal data. A study by Cecere et al. [6] relying on a data set collected in 2009 by the EU Commission in 27 different European countries showed comparable outcomes to Lancelot Miltgen et al. [15]. Northern and Eastern European countries seem to be less concerned by potential misuse of personal data. People living in Southern and Central Europe, at the same time, tend to be more worried about their personal data. They explain their findings by the institutional legacy of former collectivistic countries. Eastern countries are seen as more collectivistic, therefore are accustomed to government control, which reflects fewer privacy concerns.

3   Methodology

We conducted a qualitative survey with open answer questions to investigate people's understanding of potential security and privacy issues associated with the use of two different instances of smart environments – namely smart home and smart health environments – while considering people from different cultural backgrounds (i.e., from Germany, Spain, and Romania).

3.1   Smart Environments

Smart environments are a rather broad area as this can be any environment with any types of interconnected devices and sensors. We consider the transformation of people's homes into smart environments most relevant and thus decided to focus on our research on these smart environments in people's homes. Firstly, this includes all classical smart home devices (ranging from smart TVs to other smart household appliances, to various sensors e.g., for light and temperature) which have been around for several years. Secondly, this also includes smart health environments, i.e., equipping households with connected health devices (e.g., blood pressure monitors) and sensors (e.g., fall detectors) which are connected to the attending physician and/or various health services. We consider it worthwhile to study both of these smart environments, as (1) smart homes are likely to be more frequently used, but also more discussed in the media compared to smart health households; and (2) smart health data may be considered more sensitive than smart home data, but also might bring more advantages as it helps saving lives while smart homes are mainly for one's convenience. All these different characteristics might make a difference with respect to people's awareness of security and privacy issues.

We used the following definition of smart home and smart health devices for our study considering descriptions from other researchers such as used in [2, 14] while providing examples for the various types of connected devices:

A smart home is an environment in which household appliances (e.g., refrigerator, washing machine, vacuum cleaner), integrated devices (e.g., lights, windows, heating) and entertainment electronics (e.g., TV, game consoles) are networked and can be controlled via the Internet.

Smart health comprises health care devices (e.g., blood pressure monitors, scales, thermometers) and special sensors (e.g., drop-sensors, sensors in the toilet, heat sensors) which are connected to the Internet.

The actual descriptions used in the survey are provided in the Supplementary materials A. These texts were pre-tested regarding their understandability and iteratively improved. One of our aims with the texts was to clearly emphasise the unique selling proposition for smart homes in the one case and smart health devices in the other.

3.2   Country Selection

The participants of our study were inhabitants of Spain, Romania, and Germany. The original concept included participants from Norway, which had to be abandoned due to a lack of participants (see supplementary materials for more details). Various factors led to the decision for the countries mentioned above. First of all, most studies referring to privacy and security are conducted in the US. In combination with the findings that national culture influences privacy and security concerns studying European countries seemed as an obvious extension of existing research. Studies concerning Internet privacy tend to split Europe into four major parts – namely northern, central/western, eastern, and southern Europe [6,15]. This separation is based on cultural differences and equalities as well as Internet usage. Therefore, we decided to include participants from each of these major parts of Europe. Spain representing the Southern European states, Romania representing the Eastern states, and Germany representing Central/Western states. Norway would have been the representative for the Northern part of Europe.

3.3   Study Procedure

We used a between-subject design, randomly assigning participants to one of the considered technologies. All questionnaires were presented in participants' native language (i.e., German, Romanian, and Spanish) and implemented in SoSciSurvey [13]. The study procedure is:

Welcome and Informed Consent. We first thanked participants and provided them with information about our study (i.e., length, purpose, compensation, anonymity of their data, opportunity to withdraw from participation at any time). Participants were asked to provide their consent for participation and processing of their data by clicking on a button which was labeled with "I agree".

Introduction of Smart Environment. Participants were randomly assigned to one of the smart environments which was introduced to them in a brief descriptive text (see Appendix A).

Open Question on Consequences of Smart Environment Usage. We used an open answer format inspired by Harbach et al. [9] to ask participants about possible consequences. In order to encourage the participants to list as many consequences as they are aware of, the questionnaire included ten text boxes and participants were instructed to enter one consequence per box, beginning with the most severe one: "Please enter all the consequences that may arise when using [smart home/health]. Please begin with the most severe possible consequence and leave the additional boxes empty if you do not know any further consequences." Participants also had the opportunity to provide as many additional consequences as they wanted in an extra text box at the end of the site.

Demographics and Thanks. At the end of the study, we asked the participants for demographic information. On the last page, we thanked the participants and provided contact details in case any questions would occur as well as the code they needed to receive their compensation from the panel.

3.4   Recruitment and Participants

We recruited our participants using the European panel "clickworker"[1], which is similar to Amazon Mechanical Turk (MTurk), but focuses on European users.

Participants received a compensation which corresponds to minimum wage in the respective country at the time the survey [2] was conducted, i.e., 1.50€ in Germany and 0.80€ in Spain. In Romania, we started with minimum wage, but since we had trouble finding Romanian participants with this low payment, we raised the compensation from 0.30 to 1€).

All relevant ethical preconditions given for research with personal data by our universities' ethics committee were met. On the start page, all participants were informed about the purpose and procedure of the present study. Participants had the option to withdraw at any point during the study without providing any reason and we informed them that in this case all data collected so far would be deleted. Participants were assured that their data would not be linked to their identity and that the responses would only be used for study purposes. Furthermore, we used SoSciSurvey [13] for the survey implementation, which stores all data in Germany and is thus subject to strict EU data protection law.

3.5   Data Analysis

First, as the questionnaires were presented in the main language of each country, the responses were cross translated, i.e., the responses were translated to English and then back to the original language to ensure the quality of the translation. Both translation processes were done by researchers who are used to work in a bilingual environment. The translated responses were then analysed using three rounds of coding.

In a first coding round, we used a closed coding approach, to identify those responses related to privacy and/or security. To that end, two researchers independently coded the responses. Differences in the codings were resolved using codings from a third independent researcher with a majority decision. Responses that were not clearly related to security and privacy were sorted out in this round as well.

In a second coding round, we then further analysed the responses clearly related to privacy and/or security. To that end, two researchers independently reviewed a subset of the responses using an open coding methodology to create a code book of security- and/or privacy-related themes from the responses. Open coding is a bottom-up method to structure qualitative data, based on participants' responses, rather than using pre-selected categories to code the responses. The codes were then discussed between the two original and an additional researcher, resulting in a final code book.

Using this process, a hierarchical code book arose, distinguishing between *abstract concerns* (i.e. responses such as "security issues" that do not specify a

---

[1] https://www.clickworker.com/, visited March 01, 2019.
[2] Which took, according to our pretests, about 10 min to complete.

concrete result of a security and privacy violation), *threats* (i.e. responses such as "data theft" that specify a security and privacy violation but not necessarily mention a concrete harm resulting from it) and *harms* (i.e. responses that specify the concrete effect on one's well-being as a result of security and privacy violation, e.g. "home burglary"). The complete code book including codes in these three categories is provided in the supplementary materials (Appendix A.1). This code book was then used in a third round of coding by the two original researchers to perform selective coding of the responses.

All statistical analyses based on these three rounds of coding were conducted using the R statistics software environment.

4   Results

A total of 596 participants completed our study. Of them, 21 were excluded from further analysis because they provided at least one obvious nonsense-answer, e.g., "ahdjhdg". Out of the remaining 575 participants, 196 were from Germany, 185 from Romania and 196 from Spain. 206 participants reported to use their assigned smart environment (i.e., smart home or smart health) often or sometimes. Participants from age groups "<20" to "66–75" were represented in the sample, with the majority of the participants being from the age group "26–35". Further details on the demographics of the sample are provided in the supplementary materials.

4.1   Total Responses

Overall, we analysed 1117 responses (excluding two duplicate responses)[3]. Of them, 38 stated that the respective participants do not know any consequences that could result from using smart environments. 387 responses (stated by 275 participants) described negative aspects of smart environment usage that clearly referred to privacy and/or security issues (e.g, hacking or increased insurance rates due to access to medical information). Out of the participants mentioning at least one security and privacy issue, 147 were from Germany, 86 from Spain and 42 from Romania; 164 of them were assigned the smart home scenario, and 111 the smart health scenario.

4.2   Security and Privacy Issues

We categorized the security and privacy issues named by the participants on the three axes introduced in Sect. 3.5, namely, whether the response describes abstract concerns, threats, or the harm on themselves (see Sect. 4.2). Of all the participants mentioning at least one security and privacy issue, 111 mentioned

---

[3] Note that as described in Sect. 3.3, each participant was encouraged to list as many consequences as they could think of, having a total of 11 open questions which they could fill in.

only abstract concerns (of them, 43 participants from Germany, 46 from Spain and 22 from Romania; 72 assigned to smart home and 39 to smart health scenario), 34 mentioned at least one concrete harm (19 from Germany, 11 from Spain, 4 from Romania; 22 assigned to smart home and 12 to smart health scenario) and 130 mentioned at least one threat but no concrete harm (85 from Germany, 29 from Spain, 16 from Romania; 70 assigned to smart home and 60 to smart health scenario) (Table 1).

Table 1. Number of participants mentioning "only abstract concerns", "at least one concrete harm", "at least one threat but no concrete harm" (from left to right - Germany, Romania, Spain, smart home, smart health).

	▬	▮▮	▬	🏠	😊	Total
Only abstract concerns	43	46	22	72	39	111
At least one concrete harm	19	11	4	22	12	34
At least one threat but no concrete harm	85	29	16	70	60	130

Overall, more German participants named security and privacy issues than Spanish or Romanian ones. The German participants also named threats more often and were more likely to describe the harm on themselves than participants from other countries. Moreover, German participants not only mentioned somewhat more security issues than Spanish participants, but also more of the German participants mentioned more threats and described the harm on themselves. In contrast, more of the Spanish answers described abstract concerns. Romanian participants provided the least responses referring to each category of security and privacy issues (Table 2).

The most responses in the abstract concerns category described the possibility of a cyber-attack, while at the same time the most of the concerns mentioned by the German participants referred to privacy and data protection. The general privacy concerns were also mentioned more prominently in the smart health context than in relation to smart homes. Most of the responses mentioning a threat referred to privacy-related issues as well, such as the possibility of being monitored or spied on in one's own home, one's data being collected, or information about oneself getting disclosed or passed on to somebody else. The responses in the smart health context furthermore focused more on data being shared with third parties or stolen via unauthorised access, compared to the smart home context that focused on data collection or overall surveillance. Although only very few participants described the harm from the consequences that could result from living in smart environments on themselves, those who did, mostly named financial loss as both direct (e.g. via unauthorised access to one's financial accounts) and indirect (e.g. as increased insurance rates due to leakage of personal data), burglary due to both access to one's security system as well as to private information about when one is (not) at home and the possibility of being influenced in one's opinion or behavior.

Table 2. Number of participants mentioning each of the detailed security and privacy issues (from left to right - Germany, Romania, Spain, smart home, smart health).

	▬	❚❚	⊒	🏠	⊟	Total
Abstract concerns						
Concerns about attacks	27	31	23	59	22	81
Concerns related to data abuse	17	3	0	7	13	20
General privacy concerns	33	22	4	38	21	59
General security concerns	11	9	3	17	6	23
Other	1	0	0	0	1	1
Threats						
Being spied on	44	4	3	34	17	51
Manipulation of functionality	0	2	1	3	0	3
Data being shared	25	5	1	12	19	31
Data collection	27	6	4	24	13	37
Data theft	20	14	9	20	23	43
Profiling	9	3	0	7	5	12
Transparency	11	2	0	8	5	13
Other	0	1	0	1	0	1
Harms						
Being blackmailed	2	0	1	2	1	3
Being influenced	3	4	0	4	3	7
Burglary	4	2	1	5	2	7
Financial loss	5	3	1	6	3	9
Health impairment	2	1	1	1	3	4
Identity theft	2	0	1	3	0	3
Other	2	1	0	1	2	3
Personalised ads	2	0	0	2	0	2

4.3   Statistical Analysis

In order to investigate the differences in security and privacy risk perception among the participants in our sample, we looked at the awareness of security- and privacy risks, which we measured as a binary outcome, whether a participant mentioned at least one security- or privacy-related issue. In addition to looking at country of the participant and the smart environment to which they were assigned, we included age, gender and their smart environment usage (as actual users, potential users or non-users) as predictor variables. The logistic regression analysis has shown the country of the participant, the smart environment (either smart home or smart health) to be a significant factor ($p < .001$), as well as, to a lesser extent, smart environment usage ($p = .003$) and age ($p = .036$) (see the ouput of the analysis in the supplementary materials). The gender of the participant was not shown to be significant ($p > .05$). The post-hoc tests furthermore have shown significant differences between all the three countries ($p < .001$), with participants from Germany naming security and privacy issues most frequently, followed by Spain and Romania. Significantly more participants mentioned security and privacy issues for smart homes than for smart health devices, and significantly more potential than actual smart home and smart health users named security and privacy issues ($p = .002$).

5   Discussion

Several limitations apply to our study. Firstly, we chose a survey design, which prevented us from asking participants to further explain their answers if the meaning was unclear to us. Thus, some responses may have been related to security and privacy issues but were not considered in our final analysis. However, this study design allows us to compare the responses from a large sample of participants from three different countries, which would not have been possible with an interview study design. Furthermore, as we used a panel for recruitment, our sample might be biased in terms of age, academic background and technical expertise. However, if even younger, well-educated and tech-savvy people lack awareness of security and privacy issues associated with living in smart environments, the problems faced by the rest of the population might be even bigger.

Less than a half of the participants in our study mentioned at least one security or privacy-related issue of smart home usage, indicating that while there is some degree of awareness of these issues, for many users this awareness is still lacking. Our study furthermore shows that there are indeed differences between countries in terms of awareness about security and privacy risks. This might have an impact on data protection regulations and the success of their implementation and enforcement, especially if one aims to implement these on a global level given the cross-border nature of Internet-based services. Furthermore, as social factors are commonly recognized to play a role in the security and privacy behaviour of end users (e.g. resulting in reluctance to use security- and privacy-enhancing tools due to the fear of appearing overly paranoid, see e.g. [22]), it is worth investigating, how the different degree of awareness of security and privacy risks in various countries should be considered in developing security and privacy protection support methods.

The participants furthermore named security and privacy consequences of using smart health devices less often. When it comes to the differences in specific consequences, several differences between the two smart environments occur. As such, codes that imply transferring the data into the hands of third parties are mentioned more frequently in the context of smart homes than smart health. On the other hand, the issues mentioning data collection without referring to further sharing of the data are more prominently featured in the smart home context. A possible explanation is that while the participants understand the sensitivity of data collected by smart health devices, they are more likely to perceive the entity collecting the data as trustworthy (e.g., when consulting a physician) and therefore be more concerned about repurposing the data by other entities. As researchers stress the importance of context in determining privacy issues (see e. g. [3,16]), our findings provide a further confirmation for this approach, indicating the need to consider both cultural factors and context of a specific system or data exchange in order to support the end users with their security and privacy protection.

Acknowledgements. This work was partially funded by the European Unions Horizon 2020 Research and Innovation Programme through the GHOST project (https://www.ghost-iot.eu/) under Grant Agreement No. 740923. We specifically want to thank the project partners, Spanish Red Cross (https://www.cruzroja.es), TECSOS Foundation (https://www.fundaciontecsos.es), Televes (https://www.televes.com) and Kalos (https://kalosis.com/) for supporting our study with Spanish and Romanian translations. The research reported in this paper has furthermore been supported by the German Federal Ministry of Education and Research within the framework of the project KASTEL_SKI in the Competence Center for Applied Security Technology (KASTEL).

A   Supplementary Materials

A.1   Code Book

The following code book was used to analyse the responses in the survey. The responses could be assigned multiple codes as follows. If multiple abstract concerns, but no concrete issues (that is, no threats or harms) were named in a response, the respective codes were simply assigned to the responses. However, if codes from both, the concrete and the abstract categories would have been coded in a response, only the concrete codes were assigned, since the response specifies either the threat or the harm related to the concern, hence, it is no longer seen as abstract.

Abstract Concerns. The response mentions an abstract concern, without specifying either the threat that the adversary poses or the concrete harm that can result from the threat.

- General security concerns
    - Description: The response explicitly mentions security
    - Example: "security issues"
- General privacy concerns
    - Description: The response explicitly mentions privacy or data protection
    - Example: "Lack of privacy"
- Concerns related to data abuse
    - Description: The response explicitly mentions misuse or abuse of data
    - Example: "Possible misuse of personal data"
- Concerns about attacks
    - Description: The response explicitly mentions hackers or cyber-attacks.
    - Example: "They could hack into my data"

Threats. The response a specific way one's security and privacy might be violated, without also necessarily mentioning the concrete harm a violation might cause.

- Data theft
  - Description: The response explicitly mentions data theft or someone stealing the data, or otherwise makes clear that the issue is with non-legal means of getting access to the data
  - Example: "If my data is stolen"
- Manipulation of functionality
  - Description: The response describes how unauthorised access or control to the system interferes with the functioning of the system.
  - Example: "Deactivation of the burglar alarm"
- Data collection
  - Description: The response mentions data being collected and stored
  - Example: "Smart home appliances collect information"
- Being spied on
  - Description: The response explicitly mentions spying, surveillance, monitoring or eavesdropping, or otherwise makes clear that the issue is about external observation of some kind
  - Example: "increased risk of monitoring in the personal environment"
- Being transparent
  - Description: The response explicitly mentions transparency (in a sense of users of smart environment being transparent to observation) or otherwise makes clear that the issue is about being totally exposed (as opposed to the codes "Data collection" or "Being spied on" where there is no such focus on total character of the exposure)
  - Example: "My way of life would not be private, but would be almost anytime x-rayed"
- Profiling
  - Description: The response explicitly mentions profiling or analysis or otherwise makese clear that the collected data is further processed
  - Example: "A profile is created which allows conclusions about my person"
- Data being shared
  - Description: The response makes clear that the collected data is shared with others, also referring to legal transfer to third parties.
  - Example: "Transmission of my data not only to the doctor, but also to the health insurance company"

Harms. The response mentions an impact on one's well-being that is the result of a security and privacy violation.

- Burglary
  - Description: The response mentions being robbed as either the result of manipulating the smart system or by learning the habits of the household members (i.e. times when no one is at home)

- Example: "Being connected to the internet, intelligent devices can be hacked and can indicate whether they are at home or not, then causing a break"
  - Financial loss
    - Description: The response mentions financial loss, either direct (e.g. someone hacking into one's financial accounts) or indirect (e.g. insurance companies raising rates as the result of access to one's health data)
    - Example: "Automated internet-connected systems can be remotely accessed by unauthorized people who could steal any amount from the user's account"
  - Being blackmailed
    - Description: The response mentions blackmail, either via controlling the smart home or threatening to expose sensitive information leaked from the smart system.
    - Example: "Takeover of the flat/the house by hackers for the purpose of extortion"
  - Personalised ads
    - Description: The response mentions being targetted with personalised ads
    - Example: "My personal data is recorded in detail. As a consequence I will be targeted with 'tailored' advertisements"
  - Being influenced
    - Description: The response mentions decision or opinion manipulation as the result of access to data
    - Example: "That companies get too much information about my preferences and use it to try to modify my opinions or habits, as has happened with Facebook and Trump"
  - Health impairment
    - Description: The response mentions using smart health devices to harm one's health
    - Example: "Someone hack into your service and cause you a serious health problem by sending false information"
  - Identity theft
    - Description: The response mentions identity theft or fraud as the result of access to personal data
    - Example: "Theft of identity"

A.2 Description of Smart Environments as Stated in the Questionnaire

Smart Home. Smart home refers to a household in which household appliances (e.g., refrigerator, washing machine, vacuum cleaner), integrated devices (e.g. lights, windows, heating), and entertainment electronics (e.g., TV, voice assist, game consoles) are networked and can be controlled via the Internet.

This new technology delivers several conveniences:

- Increased quality of life e.g. concerning the refrigerator by detecting low supplies of important products and automatic ordering of these

- Building protection e.g. concerning lights by individual profiles for switching on and off
- Simplified ordering processes e.g instructing voice assistants such as Alexa via simple verbal orders

Smart Health. Smart health describes a household in which health equipment (e.g. blood pressure monitor, scales, thermometer), special sensors (e.g., drop sensors, sensors in the toilette, heat sensors), and wearables (e.g. smartwatches, fitness trackers or smartphones) are connected.

This new technology delivers several conveniences:

- Improved information for doctors, e.g., blood pressure measuring instruments reporting and transmitting regular measurements
- Improved emergency response, e.g., drop detectors sending a direct emergency message to the rescue service
- Improved health, e.g., fitness trackers analyzing your sleep patterns

A.3 Questionnaire

Do you use smart home devices (e.g. refrigerator, automated light, voice assistants like alexa connected to the internet)/smart health devices (e.g. blood pressure measuring devices, case sensors, fitness tracker connected to the internet)?
Yes, I often use use smart home devices/smart health devices.
Yes, I sometimes use use smart home devices/smart health devices.
I do not use smart home devices/smart health devices, but I would like to use them in the future.
I do not use use smart home devices/smart health devices and I do not want to use them in the future.

Please enter all the consequences that may arise from using [smart home/health]. Please begin with the most severe possible consequence and leave the additional boxes empty if you do not know any further consequences.

Gender: *m/f/other*
Age:
$< 20, 20 - 25, 26 - 35, 36 - 45, 46 - 55, 56 - 65, 66 - 75, 76 - 85, > 85$

A.4 Demographics of the Sample

The following tables describe the demographics of our sample (excluding the participants who provided nonsense answers) in terms of age, gender and smart environment usage distributed between the three countries and the two smart environments (Tables 3 and 4).

We also aimed to include Norwegian participants in our study, but had trouble recruiting them. Initially, we chose the clickworker panel since they assured

Table 3. Demographics from left to right - Germany, Romania, Spain, smart home/health.

	▬	▐▐	▨	🏠	🩺	Total
Female	88	61	97	123	123	246
Male	108	124	97	182	147	329
<20	11	50	14	43	32	75
20–25	28	56	56	77	63	140
26–35	65	59	55	98	81	179
36–45	33	14	57	49	55	104
46–55	36	5	9	26	24	50
56–65	20	1	2	11	12	23
66–75	3	-	1	1	3	4

Table 4. Usage frequency of smart environments from left to right - Germany, Romania, Spain, smart home/health.

	▬	▐▐	▨	🏠	🩺	Total
Often		27	24	31	48	34	82
Sometimes		32	34	58	55	69	124
Never, but I would like to in the future		88	109	89	169	117	288
Never, and I would not like to in the future	49	18	16	33	50	83

us to have a large enough user base in all four countries considered in our study. We started to recruit with minimum wage (3€) in Norway, but after a month only 17 participants had completed the questionnaire, compared to less than one week in Germany and Spain. We thus raised the compensation to 4.50€, which lead to another 73 completed questionnaires after 2,5 month. Since the Norwegian sample was still too small compared to the other samples, we asked several Scandinavian researchers for their advice. Unfortunately, none of them was aware of a platform like MTurk reaching Norwegians; also searching in Norwegian it was not possible to find an alternative Scandinavian panel (via internet and by asking other research colleagues). The contacted researchers further told us that finding Scandinavian participants for studies is a well-known problem, as most Scandinavians are not interested in participating in research studies for a small or moderate compensation, and Scandinavian researchers thus often rely on students or use foreign panels like MTurk. Finally, we decided not to include the 90 Scandinavian participants in our analysis, due to the small sample size, the long recruiting period and the Scandinavian researchers' experience with recruitment, all of which lead us to worry about the 90 participants in our sample being hardly representative for the Norwegian population.

A.5   Output of the Statistical Analysis

The following tables (Tables 5, 6 and 7) describe the results of the statistical analysis, investigating the effect of country of the participant, the smart environment they were assigned to, their usage habits of smart environment and their age and gender on security and privacy awareness, measured as naming at least one security and privacy issue.

Table 5. Analysis of deviance output for whether a participant named at least one security or privacy issue (factors ordered by p-value)

	LR Chisq	Df	Pr(>Chisq)
Country	108.54	2	0.0000
Environment	12.63	1	0.0004
User	11.50	2	0.0032
Age	13.43	6	0.0367
Gender	0.49	1	0.4828

Table 6. Post-hoc tests for comparison between the countries

Contrast	Estimate	SE	df	z.ratio	p.value
DE - RO	2.7108	0.2903	Inf	9.336	<.0001
DE - ESP	1.4535	0.2528	Inf	5.749	<.0001
RO - ESP	−1.2573	0.2574	Inf	−4.884	<.0001

Results are given on the log odds ratio (not the response) scale.

Table 7. Post-hoc tests for comparison between the usage habits

Contrast	Estimate	SE	df	z.ratio	p.value
Non-user - potential user	−0.2432	0.3033	Inf	−0.802	0.4225
Non-user - user	0.4853	0.3181	Inf	1.526	0.1271
Potential user - user	0.7286	0.2179	Inf	3.343	0.0008

Results are given on the log odds ratio (not the response) scale.

References

1. Aktypi, A., Nurse, J.R.C., Goldsmith, M.: Unwinding Ariadne's identity thread: privacy risks with fitness trackers and online social networks. In: Workshop on Multimedia Privacy and Security (MPS), pp. 1–11. ACM (2017)
2. Baig, M.M., Gholamhosseini, H.: Smart health monitoring systems: an overview of design and modeling. J. Med. Syst. **37**(2), 9898 (2013). https://doi.org/10.1007/s10916-012-9898-z
3. Barkhuus, L.: The mismeasurement of privacy: using contextual integrity to reconsider privacy in HCI. In: Proceedings of the SIGCHI Conference on Human Factors in Computing Systems, pp. 367–376. ACM (2012)
4. Bellekens, X., Hamilton, A., Seeam, P., Nieradzinska, K., Franssen, Q., Seeam, A.: Pervasive ehealth services a security and privacy risk awareness survey. In: Conference On Cyber Situational Awareness, Data Analytics And Assessment (CyberSA), pp. 1–4. IEEE (2016)
5. Buescher, N., Boukoros, S., Bauregger, S., Katzenbeisser, S.: Two is not enough: privacy assessment of aggregation schemes in smart metering. In: Proceedings on Privacy Enhancing Technologies (PoPETs), vol. 2017, no. 4, pp. 198–214 (2017)
6. Cecere, G., Le Guel, F., Soulié, N.: Perceived internet privacy concerns on social networks in Europe. Technol. Forecast. Soc. Chang. **96**, 277–287 (2015)
7. Fernandes, E., Jung, J., Prakash, A.: Security analysis of emerging smart home applications. In: Symposium on Security and Privacy (SP), pp. 636–654. IEEE (2016)
8. Garg, R.: An analysis of (non-)use practices and decisions of internet of things. In: Lamas, D., Loizides, F., Nacke, L., Petrie, H., Winckler, M., Zaphiris, P. (eds.) INTERACT 2019. LNCS, vol. 11749, pp. 3–24. Springer, Cham (2019). https://doi.org/10.1007/978-3-030-29390-1_1
9. Harbach, M., Fahl, S., Smith, M.: Who's afraid of which bad wolf? A survey of IT security risk awareness. In: Computer Security Foundations Symposium (CSF), pp. 97–110. IEEE (2014)
10. He, W., et al.: Rethinking access control and authentication for the home internet of things (IoT). In: Symposium on Usable Privacy and Security (SOUPS), pp. 255–272. USENIX (2018)
11. Ho, G., Leung, D., Mishra, P., Hosseini, A., Song, D., Wagner, D.: Smart locks: lessons for securing commodity internet of things devices. In: Asia Conference on Computer and Communications Security (ASIACCS), pp. 461–472. ACM (2016)
12. Karwatzki, S., Trenz, M., Tuunainen, V.K., Veit, D.: Adverse consequences of access to individuals' information: an analysis of perceptions and the scope of organisational influence. Eur. J. Inf. Syst. **26**, 688–715 (2017)
13. Leiner, D.J.: Sosci survey (version 2.5.00-i) (2017). https://www.soscisurvey.de/. Accessed 01 Mar 2019
14. Lymberis, A.: Smart wearable systems for personalised health management: current r&d and future challenges. In: Engineering in Medicine and Biology Society, vol. 4, pp. 3716–3719. IEEE (2003)
15. Miltgen, C.L., Peyrat-Guillard, D.: Cultural and generational influences on privacy concerns: a qualitative study in seven European countries. Eur. J. Inf. Syst. **23**(2), 103–125 (2014)
16. Nissenbaum, H.: Privacy as contextual integrity. Wash. L. Rev. **79**, 119 (2004)

17. Oomen, I., Leenes, R.: Privacy risk perceptions and privacy protection strategies. In: de Leeuw, E., Fischer-Hübner, S., Tseng, J., Borking, J. (eds.) IDMAN 2007. TIFIP, vol. 261, pp. 121–138. Springer, Boston, MA (2008). https://doi.org/10. 1007/978-0-387-77996-6_10
18. Ronen, E., Shamir, A.: Extended functionality attacks on IoT devices: the case of smart lights. In: Symposium on Security and Privacy (SOUPS), pp. 3–12. IEEE (2016)
19. Skirpan, M.W., Yeh, T., Fiesler, C.: What's at stake: characterizing risk perceptions of emerging technologies. In: Conference on Human Factors in Computing Systems (CHI), p. 70. ACM (2018)
20. Staddon, J., Huffaker, D., Brown, L., Sedley, A.: Are privacy concerns a turn-off?: engagement and privacy in social networks. In: Symposium on Usable Privacy and Security (SOUPS), p. 10. ACM (2012)
21. Statista: Smart home worldwide (2018). https://www.statista.com/outlook/279/ 100/smart-home/worldwide. Accessed 01 Mar 2019
22. Volkamer, M., Renaud, K., Kulyk, O., Emeröz, S.: A socio-technical investigation into smartphone security. In: Foresti, S. (ed.) STM 2015. LNCS, vol. 9331, pp. 265–273. Springer, Cham (2015). https://doi.org/10.1007/978-3-319-24858-5_17
23. Zeng, E., Mare, S., Roesner, F.: End user security and privacy concerns with smart homes. In: Symposium on Usable Privacy and Security (SOUPS), pp. 65–80. USENIX (2017)

Understanding Perceptions of Smart Devices

Hilda Hadan and Sameer Patil[(✉)]

Luddy School of Informatics, Computing, and Engineering,
Indiana University Bloomington, Bloomington, IN 47408, USA
{hhadan,patil}@indiana.edu

Abstract. We explored perceptions regarding the value and sensitivity of the data collected by a variety of everyday smart devices. Via semi-structured interviews, we found that people's conceptualizations of operational details and privacy and security threats of "smart" functions are greatly limited. Our findings point to the need for designs that readily enable users to separate the physical and digital aspects of device operation and call for further exploration of the design space of privacy and security controls and indicators for smart devices.

Keywords: Smart devices · Smart objects · Privacy preferences · Privacy practices · Data value · Data sensitivity · Usable privacy

1 Introduction

Increasingly, common household devices and objects are made "smart" by augmenting their functions with technical capabilities and Internet connectivity, often referred to as the Internet of Things (IoT). Although such smart capabilities offer a range of personal benefits, the corresponding data handling operations can raise significant concerns due to the potential for impacting personal privacy and enabling surveillance.

Data collection and use by smart devices is often not apparent to users. Therefore, a proliferation of smart devices in everyday environments can exacerbate the problem of understanding and controlling data capture and disclosure by these technologies, thus underscoring the importance and urgency of ensuring that smart devices provide usable privacy. In this regard, researchers have attempted to uncover people's understanding of device operation and data handling, typically focusing on a single device, such as a smart speaker. We build on these efforts via semi-structured interviews that examined these aspects across

H. Hadan and S. Patil—Understanding Perceptions of Smart Devices, Proceedings of AsiaUSEC '20, Financial Cryptography and Data Security 2019 (FC). February 14, 2020 Kota Kinabalu, Sabah, Malaysia Springer, 2020.

M. Bernhard et al. (Eds.): FC 2020 Workshops, LNCS 12063, pp. 102–121, 2020.
https://doi.org/10.1007/978-3-030-54455-3_8

a variety of smart devices. Specifically, we tackled the following research questions: (i) What are people's understandings of smart device[1] operation and data handling? (ii) How do people perceive the value and sensitivity of the data collected by smart devices? (iii) What rights and controls do people expect over data collected by smart devices? and (iv) What actions, if any, do people take to control the data collection and manage privacy?

Our findings confirm several aspects pertaining to people's privacy knowledge, preferences, and practices identified in past studies of online privacy and individual smart devices. Additionally, we identify significant gaps in understanding regarding device operation, data handling, and privacy threats and corresponding impact on judgments of data value and sensitivity, expectations regarding rights and controls, and actions pertaining to privacy management.

2 Related Work

Literature related to our research falls under two broad themes: privacy and security of smart devices and data value and sensitivity.

2.1 Privacy and Security of Smart Devices

There has been a substantial amount of work on people's perception of smart technologies such as smart homes [19, 22–26], smart speakers/voice assistants [1, 5, 15, 17], smart TVs [8, 9, 16], smart thermostats [13], and so on [20]. In general, such studies found that people's concerns regarding privacy and security aspects of smart devices are limited [1, 15, 19] due to their superficial knowledge regarding the operational aspects of smart technologies [1, 5, 25, 26], limited understanding of data handling [14, 18], and incomplete consideration of risks [1, 15]. Even those aware of the risks and wishing to prevent third party sharing or secondary use of their data are often willing to trade privacy for the benefits and conveniences of smart devices [16, 25].

2.2 Data Value and Sensitivity

Several studies have attempted to study data valuations in monetary terms, finding that people generally prefer money in exchange for data, even when the monetary benefit is small [2, 11, 12]. However, recent research suggests that individuals are willing to pay for privacy [3]. Yet, when people are not explicitly prompted to consider privacy and security, they rarely do so prior to purchase and tend to become aware of these issues only afterward via media reports and/or unexpected device operation [6]. Moreover, people's limited understanding of how their data is collected and used [14, 18] makes it difficult for them to ascribe appropriate monetary valuations to their data.

---

[1] In the rest of the paper, we use the term smart devices to refer to any typical household device or object with augmented capabilities and/or Internet connectivity.

In contrast, people may find it easier to express valuations in qualitative terms and in relation to sensitivity that is often associated with privacy-related matters. Several studies indicate that smart device users would prefer to take data sensitivity into account, especially when prompted to consider privacy choices and actions [3,17]. While numerous studies of smart devices indicate that people are willing to trade privacy for convenience and benefits [9,25], the relationship to data sensitivity has received less research attention.

2.3   Relationship to Research Objectives

Our objective was to uncover perspectives on smart devices without a narrow focus on specific devices or usage contexts typical of previous studies. To that end, our research covered a wide variety of smart devices with the goal of studying the extent to which findings of device-specific studies apply across devices and noting salient commonalities and differences that affect people's operational understanding, privacy preferences, and usage practices related to smart devices in general. Additionally, we investigated whether qualitative descriptions of data value and sensitivity can be useful for bridging the gap between smart device operation and people's privacy expectations.

Unlike most studies that include *users* of a device, we asked people about devices they own and use, as well as those they do not. We believe that it is important to include those who do not currently use a device. First, users of a device are a biased sample and, as such, may not surface the full spectrum of issues, especially about privacy/security concerns (which may presumably be lower for them). Second, smart devices are still in infancy, and their design and features can still be shaped before they become entrenched. To that end, it is important to understand the needs and expectations of non-users/non-adopters so that these could be addressed. Third, novel design ideas often start by gathering requirements from *prospective* users (since the system does not exist yet) and can proceed with their participation (e.g., via participatory design).

3   Method

We conducted semi-structured interviews with 15 individuals (5 Men, 9 Women, and 1 Other) during the spring and summer of 2019 (see Appendix for the interview protocol). Participants were selected based on an online screening questionnaire (see Appendix) advertised locally. All participants were 18 years of age or older (Range: 18–31, Mean = 24) with some experience of using smart devices (see Appendix: Tables 1 and 2). All participants had lived in the United States for at least five years. Participants were compensated $10 cash. We continued collecting data until we reached theoretical saturation, encountering similar responses compared to earlier participants. Overall, our interviews captured perceptions and expectations based on actual as well as imagined usage scenarios regarding a variety of smart devices. All study materials and procedures were reviewed and approved by our university's Institutional Review Board (IRB).

Based on the devices mentioned in the screening questionnaire responses, participants were asked about reasons for purchase, user experience, understanding of operations and data handling. In particular, we inquired about data value, sensitivity, control, and rights. Since the smart devices mentioned by the participants varied, we asked the same set of questions for a list of commonly used smart devices including Smart TV, Smart Speaker, Smart Toy, Smart Thermostat, Smart Weighing Scale, and Smart Refrigerator. Based on the experience of the first 8 interviews, we slightly modified the interview protocol to ask participants to rank perceived benefits and data sensitivity of 10 smart devices: Smart Speaker, Smart TV, Smart Thermostat, Smart Doorbell, Smart Toy, Smart Refrigerator, Smart Security Camera, Smart Light Bulb, Smart Household Appliance (e.g., Coffee Maker, Toaster), and Smart Car.

Interview transcripts were coded with an iterative inductive approach inspired by grounded theory [10], involving open coding, identification of categories, and aggregation into themes connected to our research objectives.

4 Findings

We organized participant views regarding data and privacy into the various themes that emerged from the interviews.

4.1 Perceptions Regarding Data

Data Types: Participants mentioned a wide variety of data that they think is collected by various smart devices. We categorized the responses into 9 categories: Location (e.g., device location, owner location), Account Information (e.g., demographics, billing information), Voice, Visuals (e.g., video, images), Histories (e.g., browsing history), Health Information, Device Usage Logs, Power Usage, Environmental Data, and Data from Other Devices.

All 15 participants believed that a smart device needs to collect its location for its operation. Three of the participants expressed the belief that a smart thermostat needs to collect the owner's location to adjust the temperature at the perfect time before the owner comes home. Eleven participants further believed that a smart thermostat has the capability of capturing environmental data to adjust temperature accordingly. If a smart device involved logging into accounts, four participants believed that their account information, such as credit card information and basic demographics, is collected by the device. Participants generally expected that only those smart devices that operate via voice, such as smart speakers, smart toys, and smart TVs, would collect their voice. Similarly, six participants believed that only devices with visual functions, such as smart refrigerators, security cameras, smart doorbells, and smart toys, have the capability of capturing visuals, and eight participants thought that only devices with health- or food-related functions, such as smart weighing scales, smart mattresses, and smart refrigerators, could collect information related to health. One participant expected only devices with energy-saving functions, such as smart thermostats and smart cars, to collect power usage. All participants believed that smart TV companies could access the history of their online activities, such as web browsing and purchases, and a smart speaker could grab data from other devices due to its ability to connect to other devices: *"So pretty much anytime that I'm logging in somewhere that is giving them [smart speakers] access [...] they're pulling information."* (P6, Female, 25). Only one participant thought that a smart car would communicate with other devices and systems. All participants suspected that smart devices could log usage information, such as frequency and duration of use. Regarding frequency, participants tended to expect smart speakers, smart TVs, smart refrigerators, smart thermostats, and smart toys to collect data continuously when switched on. On the other hand, smart weighing scales, smart cars, security cameras, smart mattresses, smart doorbells, and smart door locks were expected to collect data only when people interacted with them. Some participants suspected that smart speakers "listen" even when switched off.

Data Flow and Storage: Most participants were aware that their data is sent to the companies which provide them services, such as Google, Amazon, Apple, Samsung, etc. These companies included device manufacturers as well as app developers. Two participants believed that the data collected by smart refrigerators and smart thermostats is sent to third-party contractors because the device makers are too small to maintain databases. Another two participants believed that their data is stored locally within the devices or within the mobile apps, if the devices connected to their phones.

Data Access and Control: Possible parties identified by participants as being able to access the data collected by smart devices included: companies that provide the service (e.g., device manufacturers, app developers), third-parties (e.g., data buyers, advertisers, device retailers), hackers and technical support personnel, and the government. Besides these specific parties, four participants thought that "everyone" could access their information: *"probably the world, the company, whoever they agreed to sell or share the information with"* (P15, Male, 21). P2 believed that her various accounts are somehow all connected online.

Participants expressed mixed opinions about the ability to access and control their own data. For smart devices with no user interfaces (e.g., controlled via mobile apps, web sites, etc.), most participants did not know how to control or access their data because *"there's not really an interface"* (P7, Male, 31). In contrast, P5 assumed she would be able to access the data if she has a login. For smart devices with a user interface on the device, participants generally thought that they have only partial access to the data local to the device but no access to the data sent to the server. Three participants said that they could gain access to server-side data by requesting it from the respective companies. They also believed that the companies are legally obligated to provide the data upon request.

Five participants expected the companies to take responsibility for protecting their data but two of them simultaneously expressed a lack of trust that the companies would do so diligently: *"it's probably encrypted and there's probably network protections going on. I feel like they [the companies] don't do very much. But they do some stuff."* (P1 Male, 24).

Data Value: Participants were aware that their data is used to infer their preferences, facilitate device operation, generate recommendations and advertisements, and improve the devices and future products. Most participants mentioned that their data was sold for a low price online but could not identify the parties to whom the data was sold. Participants generally tended to deem their data as valuable for device manufacturers, service providers, third-party buyers, advertisers, and the government but not for their friends because *"they [friends] already know me pretty well."* (P10, Female, 22). Three participants recognized that their data could potentially be used for malicious purposes such as blackmail. One participant thought that his data does not have monetary value because it is already traded for free services online. Another three participants believed that their smart devices could not possibly hold any valuable data because of limited and infrequent use of the device.

Two participants desired monetary returns for their data: *"If I spent $200 on a TV and they are collecting my data, shouldn't they give me the TV for free?"* (P5, Female, 24). In contrast, another two participants derived value from the customization enabled by the use of their data: *"When things pop up that are so heavily personalized, I can see the value in it."* (P2, Female, 21).

Data Sensitivity: Participants offered mixed opinions about the sensitivity of the data collected by smart devices. Three participants considered the data sensitive because many of these devices are mainly used in private places, such as homes, cars, etc., but with only a vague characterization of the extent of that sensitivity. Two of the three participants mentioned that they enjoyed the benefits of the devices even though that required their data to be visible to other parties. On the contrary, three participants felt that the data collected by their smart devices is not sensitive because they did not provide confidential or personally identifiable information to these devices. For instance, a participant perceived that the data collected by her smart lock is neither sensitive nor valuable: *"Anyone who enters has a passcode that we gave them. So that means they're allowed to enter."* (P10, Female, 22). The possibility of the passcode being stolen did not occur to her.

Surprisingly, some participants showed little concern for privacy because they figured that machines are not "clever" enough to know everything about them: *"I'm not worried that it uses my data, I just use it carefree. What they [the companies] probably want to see is just how normal people live, but that's something that machines can't quantify easily."* (P2, Female, 21). In contrast, others were unconcerned because of the belief that their data is already everywhere and they have little control over its spread: *"I'm personally at the point where I don't care anymore as long as they don't have access to my social security number. Everyone has my cell phone number. I know a few websites have my credit card information, my banking info, and my PayPal account."* (P3, Female, 22).

Data Sensitivity in Relation to Benefit: We asked participants P9 to P15 to rank 10 common smart devices based on 1) benefits of using the devices and 2) the sensitivity of the data collected by these devices (see Appendix: Fig. 1). We compared their rankings with their perceptions of data operation to see if their perceived threats corresponded with their reported behavior.

Smart speakers were ranked as the most beneficial. This matched purchasing choices: 10 out of 15 participants either owned or considered getting a smart speaker. Among the devices we covered in the interviews, smart toys and smart thermostats were ranked the lowest on benefit. Again, these rankings align with purchasing decisions: no participants were willing to get a smart toy, and only four out of 15 owned or considered getting a smart thermostat.

Despite ranking the highest on benefits, smart speakers were ranked the highest in terms of sensitivity as well because they *"can hear every single one of your conversations."* (P14, Female, 22). Participants worried about continuous surveillance. Similarly, smart security cameras were ranked as the second most sensitive due to the capability for continuous video monitoring.

Surprisingly, participants ranked smart toys ninth in terms of sensitivity. Five of the seven participants who did the ranking activity did not imagine that smart toys could collect much sensitive information, contradicting the qualitative responses of the first eight participants. A potential reason for the lack of concern could be no prior exposure to such toys and/or no experience with children. Only one of the seven participants ranked a smart toy as highly sensitive: *"I feel like those are pretty interactive and possibly would collect a lot more than you can imagine."* (P14, Female, 22).

Data Rights: At a high level, all participants expressed similar views regarding data rights. They believed that the company that collects the data owns it, not themselves: *"If I bought the device, that's basically granting the company the right to learn all information about me."* (P2, female, 21). However, when it came to specific smart devices, participants' expectations of rights were driven largely by perceptions of data collection and usage, resulting in different opinions regarding different smart devices. For smart devices that could collect visual, voice, demographic, billing, and health-related data, such as smart speakers, smart TVs, smart doorbells, smart security cameras, smart refrigerators, and smart toys, the majority of participants expected significantly more data rights and control. They wanted details, such as what is being collected and who can see it, and desired the ability to stop data collection and minimize secondary use. Two participants expressed hopes of stopping *"unnecessary data collection"* even though *"there is a blurred line between what information is necessary and what isn't"* (P15, Male, 21). In addition, participants wanted the ability to delete their data permanently from servers, with a mechanism to verify the deletion.

A small number of participants were uncertain about data rights because they *"don't know what's being collected and what it's to be used for"* (P5, female, 24). P6 indicated that she would like to have more control over data only if a device collected her personal information. P5 specifically mentioned California Consumer Privacy Act [4] and the European Union's General Data Protection

Regulation (GDPR) [7] and believed that she has full rights to her data even though she felt that it is owned by the device manufacturer. For smart toys that could be used by children under the age of 13, P5 asserted that the children and their parents or guardians would have full rights to their data due to Children's Online Privacy Protection Act (COPPA) [21].

4.2   Perceptions Regarding Privacy

Privacy Concerns: Participant responses showed significantly more concerns regarding smart toys and demanded that smart toys include obvious indicators to show when they are on. P4 wanted smart toys to use his own server for data storage instead of relying on the manufacturer's servers. In the case of smart toys, participants specifically highlighted the importance of data transparency and wanted data collection and transmission processes to be *"crystal clear"*: *"The toy around children should be visibly clear on when it's actually collecting information."* (P7, Male, 31).

On the contrary, most participants were less concerned about the data collected by smart devices they deemed comparatively benign, such as smart thermostats, smart door locks, and smart cars. None of the participants were eager to assert rights over this data. Five participants felt that the data collected by these devices is *"not very important"* because these devices do not collect confidential information. Therefore, they did not see the necessity to have control or access for this data. Alternatively, two participants felt that controlling a few devices would not help minimize data exposure because their data is already everywhere.

Privacy Protecting Actions: When asked about specific actions for managing privacy, participants mentioned several crude techniques (with the exception of one technically savvy participant who tinkered with the Domain Name System (DNS) configuration). In the order of most frequent mentions, these included:

(1) Turning the device off (7 participants)
(2) Not caring because no confidential information is involved (4 participants)
(3) Self-regulating (e.g., using the device only for limited purpose, not providing sensitive information, etc.) (3 participants)
(4) Re-configuring home DNS (1 participant)
(5) Going through device privacy settings (1 participant)
(6) Disconnecting from the Internet (1 participant)
(7) Using 'old-style' (i.e., non-smart) devices (1 participant)

Simply turning the device off was the most common strategy to avoid being monitored. While this is a feasible option for devices such as smart speakers and smart TVs, it is not really possible to turn off others, such as smart refrigerators and smart thermostats, as their basic (non-smart) functions require constant operation. Participants reported self-regulating the exposure of sensitive information to smart devices and associated apps and services, especially those used less frequently. As long as participants deemed that sensitive information was not involved, they were unconcerned about privacy and security. Only one participant interacted with privacy settings, and another mentioned temporarily disconnecting the device from the Internet or using a non-smart analog of the smart device. In general, participants claimed ignorance of privacy management options available for smart devices.

5   Discussion

Our findings serve as replication and validation of several past investigations focused on specific smart devices (see Sect. 2). In light of the rapidly changing technological landscape (especially in technologies such as smart devices), it is important to verify that past results continue to apply. Moreover, there is increasing recognition of the importance of efforts to replicate and validate prior work and results. Unlike most device-specific prior work mentioned in Sect. 2, our findings cover a large variety of devices, thus indicating which of the insight gained from single-device studies is generalizable across smart devices. Further, our findings offer a number of major takeaways regarding smart device privacy.

Understanding of Data Collection and Use is Limited. Our broad investigation echoes the findings of past studies of privacy in technological contexts, including specific smart devices, in terms of the limited understanding exhibited by participants regarding operational details and policies for data collection, use, and storage. The variety of data types in participant responses suggest that participants had an idea that smart devices use diverse types of data and are likely to send it to the device manufacturer and/or service provider(s) associated with the device. However, specific operational details, such as granularity, collection frequency, storage location, retention periods, etc., were largely unknown. Similarly, it was widely recognized that the data holds value for those who collect it. Yet, participants were not able to ascribe concrete valuations to the data. Moreover, a notable proportion of participants underestimated the inferential powers of large-scale computational data fusion and analyses that can often reveal a surprising amount of private traits.

Threat Models are Simplistic. Although participants had heard in the media about privacy issues with specific smart devices, they typically did not consider those when evaluating potential risks of smart device capabilities. For instance, the threat of computational inference of private information was ignored. Participants did not take into account that Internet connectivity makes smart devices vulnerable to hacking. In general, malicious acts, such as stolen passcodes, unauthorized access, etc., were overlooked when considering threats posed by smart capabilities of devices, as were security vulnerabilities created by bugs, unpatched software, etc. Limited operational understanding contributed to the simplicity of the threat models and evaluations of the sensitivity of the data captured by smart devices. A lack of full awareness of the threat landscape sometimes led to a false sense of privacy whereby participants did not feel the need to manage data privacy and were even careless when they deemed that no private information was involved.

Expectations are Shaped by the Primary Device Function. Notably, participant expectations regarding smart device data collection were driven by the *primary*, i.e., *non-smart*, use for the device. For instance, participants expected a thermostat to collect only the environmental data necessary to achieve its function of regulating the home temperature and not include unrelated sensors, such as a microphone. As a result, when considering privacy implications, participants often failed to note unexpected sensors, such as cameras in smart toys, microphones in smart TVs, etc. Not taking into account the full spectrum of sensors present within smart devices further contributed to the lack of appreciation for the power of data fusion and computational inferences enabled by smart device data collection.

Privacy Practices are Rudimentary. The various aspects noted above contributed to lowering privacy concerns which in turn led to rudimentary privacy protection practices, if any. A couple of reasons further contributed to the limited attention to privacy management. First, participants, especially those who owned smart devices, valued the benefits of the devices highly enough to tolerate their data practices even for sensitive data. Second, the physical nature of the devices made it challenging to adjust privacy settings without access to a traditional user interface, especially for devices not associated with apps and/or online services.

6   Limitations

Our sample is composed mostly of young students from the United States. Therefore, applicability to the general population requires verification via studies of samples covering diverse age and cultural ranges. That said, younger individuals are typically more likely to own and use smart devices owing to greater familiarity and comfort with technology. Our findings are derived from self-reports. Complementary studies that examine real-world interaction with smart devices can help ascertain the degree to which self-reports match behavior.

7   Conclusion

Our investigation shows that data practices and privacy threats of smart devices are opaque to users which can lead a false sense of privacy and/or a perceived lack of control. By taking a broad perspective we could surface insight applicable across devices, such as separation of smart and non-smart aspects. Our study covered users as well as non-users. As such, many of the findings are applicable regardless of device ownership and use. Based on our findings, we call for augmenting smart devices with transparent indicators of data handling, enhancing physical interfaces for privacy management, and compartmentalizing smart capabilities and remote data transfer. There is also a need for public policy to catch up with these developments and update and enforce privacy regulations in this rapidly developing domain.

Acknowledgments. We thank the study participants. We are grateful to anonymous reviewers for feedback that helped improve the paper.

Appendix

Participant Demographics and Smart Device Ownership

Table 1. Demographics of the sample

ID	Age	Gender	Affiliation	School/Department/Major
1	24	Male	Undergraduate Student	Liberal Studies
2	21	Female	Undergraduate Student	Marketing
3	22	Female	Undergraduate Student	English
4	27	Male	Graduate Student	Computational Linguistics
5	24	Female	Graduate Student	Cybersecurity
6	25	Female	Staff	Psychological & Brain Sciences
7	31	Male	Graduate Student	Communication & Culture
8	23	Female	Undergraduate Student	Law & Public Policy
9	21	Female	Undergraduate Student	Art Management
10	22	Female	Undergraduate Student	Neuroscience, Spanish
11	29	Male	Graduate Student	Religious Studies
12	22	Other	Undergraduate Student	Psychology
13	21	Female	Undergraduate Student	Game Design
14	22	Female	Undergraduate Student	Management
15	21	Male	Undergraduate Student & Staff	English

Table 2. Smart device ownership or willingness to purchase

Device	P1	P2	P3	P4	P5	P6	P7	P8	P9	P10	P11	P12	P13	P14	P15
Smart TV*	O	✔	O	O	✘	✔	✔	O	O	O	O	✔	O	✘	O
Smart Speaker*	O	O	✘	O	✘	✔	✘	✘	O	O	O	✘	O	O	O
Smart Thermostat	✘	✔	✘	✘	✘	✔	✘	✘	–	O	–	✔	✘	–	–
Smart Toy*	✘	✘	✘	✘	✘	✘	✘	✘	–	–	–	–	–	–	–
Smart Weighing Scale*	–	–	–	–	–	–	–	–	✘	✘	✘	✘	O	✘	✘
Smart Refrigerator*	–	–	✔	–	✘	✔	–	O	✘	✘	✔	✘	✘	✘	✘
Smart Car	✘	–	–	✘	O	–	✔	–	–	–	–	–	–	–	–

*: Included in the interview protocol
O: Own the device
✔: Considered getting the device
✘: Not considered getting the device
–: Not mentioned by the participant

Results of the Ranking Exercises

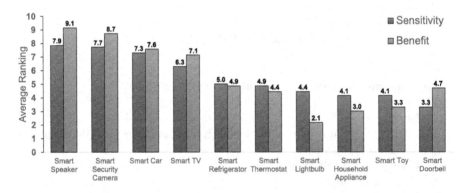

Fig. 1. Ranking of data sensitivity and device benefit

Screening Questionnaire

Thank you for your interest in participating in our study on Understanding People's Use and Perceptions of Internet-Connected Everyday Objects.

Please fill out this brief 1-minute questionnaire regarding yourself and your experience of using Internet-connected devices. We will use your answers to determine if you are eligible to participate in the study.

If you qualify, we will contact you via email for a 45–60 minute in-person/video conference/telephone interview for which you will receive $10 cash/cash equivalent (for in-person interview) or $10 Amazon gift certificate (for video interview) as a token of our appreciation for your participation. If you do not qualify for participation, your responses will be safely discarded.

1. What is your Year of Birth?
2. What is your Gender?
   (a) Male
   (b) Female
   (c) Something else. Please specify:
   (d) Do not wish to answer
3. How long have you been living in the United States?
   (a) All my life
   (b) Less than a year
   (c) 1 year
   (d) 2 years
   (e) 3 years
   (f) 4 years
   (g) 5 years
   (h) 6 years
   (i) 7 years
   (j) 8 years
   (k) 9 years
   (l) 10 years
   (m) More than 10 years
4. Are you a resident of Bloomington, Indiana?
   (a) Yes
   (b) No
5. Are you affiliated with Indiana University Bloomington?
   (a) Yes
   (b) No
6. [If YES to Q5] What is your affiliation with Indiana University Bloomington? (*Check all that apply.*)
   (a) Undergraduate Student
   (b) Graduate Student
   (c) Faculty
   (d) Staff
   (e) Retired
   (f) Something else. Please specify:
7. [If Q6 is answered as Faculty, Staff, Retired] What department or school are you affiliated with?
8. [If Q6 is answered as Undergraduate Student, Graduate Student] What is your major/field of study?
9. Which of the following Internet-connected device(s) do you own?
   (a) TV
   (b) Thermostat
   (c) Speaker (e.g., Amazon Echo, Google Home, etc.)
   (d) Refrigerator
   (e) Light bulb
   (f) Doorbell
   (g) Door lock

(h) Burglar alarm

(i) Toy

(j) Small household appliance (e.g., Coffee maker, Toaster, Crock pot, etc.)

(k) Garage door opener

(l) Car

(m) Other. Please specify:

10. How would you rate your familiarity with the following concepts or tools?

	I've never heard of this	I've heard of this but I don't know what it is	I know what this is but I don't know how it works	I know generally how this works	I know very well how this works
IP address	O	O	O	O	O
Cookie	O	O	O	O	O
Incognito mode/private browsing	O	O	O	O	O
Encryption	O	O	O	O	O
Proxy server	O	O	O	O	O
Secure Sockets Layer (SSL)	O	O	O	O	O
Tor	O	O	O	O	O
Virtual Private Network (VPN)	O	O	O	O	O
Privacy settings	O	O	O	O	O

11. Please indicate whether you think each statement is true or false. Please select "I'm not sure" if you don't know the answer.

	True	False	I'm not sure
Incognito mode/private browsing mode in browsers prevents websites from collecting information about you.	O	O	O
Tor can be used to hide the source of a network request from the destination.	O	O	O
A VPN is the same as a proxy server.	O	O	O
IP addresses can always uniquely identify your computer.	O	O	O
HTTPS is standard HTTP with SSL to preserve the confidentiality of network traffic.	O	O	O
A request coming from a proxy server cannot be tracked to the original source.	O	O	O

12. How would you prefer to be interviewed? (*Check all that apply.*)
    (a) In-person
    (b) Telephone
    (c) Video Conference (e.g., Zoom)
13. If you qualify for the study, which email address should we use to contact you for scheduling a study session?

Semi-structured Interview Protocol

The interview should take around 45–60 minutes. I would like to ask you some questions about Internet-connected objects and devices you commonly use. It could be any object that connects to the Internet in some way. Some examples are security cameras, thermostats, TVs, etc. I would like to ask about your experiences of using such objects and devices and your thoughts on how they operate.

Before we start, do you have any questions?

1. Tell me a little bit about yourself.
2. Tell me your experience with technology.
3. Tell me some Internet-connected objects or devices you commonly use.

For participants who do not own a smart device, ask the following questions:

4. Have you ever considered getting one? Could you give me some examples?
5. [If No to Q4] What has prevented you from getting one?
6. [If Yes to Q4] Imagine that you have a (the item mentioned in Q4 or each of the following devices: Smart Speaker, Smart TV, Smart Weighing Scale, Smart Refrigerator, Smart Toy, Smart Thermostat, Anything else the participant thinks could be Internet-connected): How would you set it up?
7. How would you use it? What would be the process?
8. What data do you think it would use?
9. How do you think it would use this data?
10. What is your opinion about the data being collected and used?
11. What is the benefit or value you perceive in this data?
12. How do you perceive the sensitivity of the data?
13. How often do you think it would use this data?
14. How often do you think you would interact with it?
15. How or where do you think it would store this data?
    (a) What do you mean by cloud/local/etc.?
    (b) Who will provide the storage service?
    (c) Where is the storage located?
    (d) What kind of storage is it?
    (e) How will the storage protect your data from unauthorized access?
16. Who do you think owns this data?
    (a) How do you think they would access it?
    (b) Why do you think they own the data?

(c) Why would they want to own the data?

(d) What could they do with the data?

17. Who do you believe can see this data? How do you think they access it?

18. What benefit or value do you perceive other parties can get from this data (e.g., anyone else besides yourself, such as your friends, colleagues, other companies, device manufacturers, government, etc.)? Why?

19. Do you think you would be able to control or access this data? Why or why not?

   (a) What rights do you think you would have over the data?

   (b) What rights would you like to have over the data?

   (c) Why do you believe so?

   (d) Would you like to have control and access? If yes, how would you want to view/access/control the data? If no, why not?

20. What do you think the data collected by this device is worth? Why?

21. Who would pay for this data? (May need to inform the participant that different parties could have different valuations.)

22. How do you handle or manage the data collected about you by this device?

   (a) If the person does not manage or handle data: Why not?

   (b) If the person does manage or handle data: Why do you do it this way?

   (c) If the person wishes to manage or handle data but cannot do it or cannot do it well: What would make it easier or more convenient for you to manage the data?

For smart device owned by the participant, ask following questions:

23. When did you buy it?

24. Why did you buy it?

25. How did you set it up?

26. Could you please describe your experience? How do you use it? What is the process?

27. How do you think it operates?

28. What data do you think it uses?

29. Why do you think it uses this data?

30. How do you think this data is used?

31. What is your opinion about the data being collected and used?

32. What is the benefit or value you perceive in this data?

33. How do you perceive the sensitivity of the data?

34. How often do you think it uses this data?

35. How often do you interact with it?

36. How or where do you think it stores these data?

   (a) What do you mean by cloud/local/etc.?

   (b) Who do you think provides the storage service?

   (c) Where is the storage located?

   (d) What kind of storage is it?

   (e) How will the storage protect your data from unauthorized access?

37. Who do you think owns this data?
    (a) How do you think they access it?
    (b) Why do you think they own the data?
    (c) Why would they want to own the data?
    (d) What could they do with the data?
38. Who do you believe can see this data? How do you think they access it?
39. What benefit or value do you perceive other parties can get from this data (e.g., anyone else besides yourself, such as your friends, colleagues, other companies, device manufacturers, government, etc.)? Why?
40. Do you think you can control or access this data? Why or why not?
    (a) What rights do you think you have over the data?
    (b) What rights would you like to have over the data?
    (c) Why do you believe so?
    (d) Would you like to have control and access? If yes, how would you want to view/access/control the data? If no, why not?
41. What do you think the data collected by this device is worth? Why?
42. Who would pay for this data? (May need to inform the participant that different parties could have different valuations.)
43. How do you handle or manage the data collected about you by this device?
    (a) If the person does not manage or handle: Why not?
    (b) If the person does manage or handle: Why do you do it this way?
    (c) If the person wishes to manage or handle but cannot do it or cannot do it well: What would make it easier or more convenient for you to manage the data?

Give participants handouts and ask the following questions:

44. Here is a sheet of paper that has various common objects that are augmented with smart Internet-connected capabilities. Could you please write down your ranking of these devices in terms of the benefit or value you expect from them? Please rank in order starting from the most beneficial and ending with the least beneficial.

Device	Rank
Smart Speaker (e.g., Echo, Alexa, Google Home)	
Smart TV	
Smart thermostat	
Smart doorbell	
Smart toy	
Smart refrigerator	
Internet connected home security camera	
Smart light bulb	
Smart household appliance (e.g., Coffee maker, Toaster, Crock pot, etc.)	
Smart car	

(a) Could you elaborate why you ranked the devices the way you did?
(b) Why do you think [device] is the most beneficial one?
(c) Why do you think [device] is the least beneficial one?

45. Here is another sheet of paper that has the same common objects that are augmented with smart Internet-connected capabilities. This time could you please write down your ranking of these devices in terms of your opinion regarding the sensitivity of the data they collect and process? Please rank in order starting from the most sensitive and ending with the least sensitive.

Device	Rank
Smart Speaker (e.g., Echo, Alexa, Google Home)	
Smart TV	
Smart thermostat	
Smart doorbell	
Smart toy	
Smart refrigerator	
Internet connected home security camera	
Smart light bulb	
Smart household appliance (e.g., Coffee maker, Toaster, Crock pot, etc.)	
Smart car	

(a) Could do you elaborate why you ranked the devices the way you did?
(b) Why do you think [device] is the most sensitive one?
(c) Why do you think [device] is the least sensitive one?

Wrap-up:

46. Is there anything you want to add?
47. Is there any other question I should have asked?

References

1. Abdi, N., Ramokapane, K.M., Such, J.M.: More than smart speakers: security and privacy perceptions of smart home personal assistants. In: Fifteenth Symposium on Usable Privacy and Security (SOUPS 2019). USENIX Association, Santa Clara, August 2019. https://www.usenix.org/conference/soups2019/presentation/abdi
2. Acquisti, A., John, L.K., Loewenstein, G.: What is privacy worth? J. Legal Stud. **42**(2), 249–274 (2013). https://doi.org/10.1086/671754
3. Barbosa, N.M., Park, J.S., Yao, Y., Wang, Y.: "What if?" Predicting individual users' smart home privacy preferences and their changes. In: Proceedings on Privacy Enhancing Technologies, vol. 2019, no. 4, pp. 211–231 (2019). https://doi.org/10.2478/popets-2019-0066

4. California State Legislature: California consumer privacy act of 2018 (2018). https://leginfo.legislature.ca.gov/faces/billTextClient.xhtml?bill_id=201720180AB375
5. Chandrasekaran, V., Fawaz, K., Mutlu, B., Banerjee, S.: Characterizing privacy perceptions of voice assistants: a technology probe study. CoRR abs/1812.00263 (2018). http://arxiv.org/abs/1812.00263
6. Emami-Naeini, P., Dixon, H., Agarwal, Y., Cranor, L.F.: Exploring how privacy and security factor into IoT device purchase behavior. In: Proceedings of the 2019 CHI Conference on Human Factors in Computing Systems. CHI 2019. Association for Computing Machinery, New York (2019). https://doi.org/10.1145/3290605.3300764
7. European Parliament and Council of the European Union: Regulation (EU) 2016/679 of the European parliament and of the Council of 27 April 2016 on the protection of natural persons with regard to the processing of personal data and on the free movement of such data, and repealing Directive 95/46/EC (General Data Protection Regulation) (2016). http://data.europa.eu/eli/reg/2016/679/oj
8. Ghiglieri, M., Waidner, M.: HbbTV security and privacy: issues and challenges. IEEE Secur. Priv. 14(3), 61–67 (2016). https://doi.org/10.1109/MSP.2016.54
9. Ghiglieri, M., Volkamer, M., Renaud, K.: Exploring consumers' attitudes of smart TV related privacy risks. In: Tryfonas, T. (ed.) HAS 2017. LNCS, vol. 10292, pp. 656–674. Springer, Cham (2017). https://doi.org/10.1007/978-3-319-58460-7_45
10. Glaser, B.G., Strauss, A.L.: Discovery of Grounded Theory: Strategies for Qualitative Research. Routledge, Abingdon (2017)
11. Grossklags, J., Acquisti, A.: When 25 cents is too much: an experiment on willingness-to-sell and willingness-to-protect personal information. In: Proceedings of the Sixth Workshop on Economics of Information Security, WEIS 2007 (2007)
12. Hann, I.H., Hui, K.L., Lee, S.Y.T., Png, I.P.: Overcoming online information privacy concerns: an information-processing theory approach. J. Manag. Inf. Syst. 24(2), 13–42 (2007). https://doi.org/10.2753/MIS0742-1222240202
13. Hernandez, G., Arias, O., Buentello, D., Jin, Y.: Smart Nest thermostat: a smart spy in your home. In: Blackhat USA (2014). https://blackhat.com/docs/us-14/materials/us-14-Jin-Smart-Nest-Thermostat-A-Smart-Spy-In-Your-Home-WP.pdf
14. Kang, R., Dabbish, L., Fruchter, N., Kiesler, S.: "My data just goes everywhere:" user mental models of the Internet and implications for privacy and security. In: Eleventh Symposium On Usable Privacy and Security (SOUPS 2015), pp. 39–52. USENIX Association, Ottawa, July 2015. https://www.usenix.org/conference/soups2015/proceedings/presentation/kang
15. Lau, J., Zimmerman, B., Schaub, F.: Alexa, are you listening? Privacy perceptions, concerns and privacy-seeking behaviors with smart speakers. Proc. ACM Hum.-Comput. Interact. 2(CSCW), 1–31 (2018). https://doi.org/10.1145/3274371
16. Malkin, N., Bernd, J., Johnson, M., Egelman, S.: "What can't data be used for?" Privacy expectations about smart TVs in the US. In: European Workshop on Usable Security (Euro USEC) (2018)
17. Malkin, N., Deatrick, J., Tong, A., Wijesekera, P., Egelman, S., Wagner, D.: Privacy attitudes of smart speaker users. Proc. Priv. Enhanc. Technol. 2019(4), 250–271 (2019). https://doi.org/10.2478/popets-2019-0068
18. Matsakis, L.: We're all just starting to realize the power of personal data, December 2018. https://www.wired.com/story/2018-power-of-personal-data/

19. Oulasvirta, A., et al.: Long-term effects of ubiquitous surveillance in the home. In: Proceedings of the 2012 ACM Conference on Ubiquitous Computing, UbiComp 2012, pp. 41–50. Association for Computing Machinery, New York (2012). https:// doi.org/10.1145/2370216.2370224

20. Pierce, J.: Smart home security cameras and shifting lines of creepiness: a design-led inquiry. In: Proceedings of the 2019 CHI Conference on Human Factors in Computing Systems. CHI 2019. Association for Computing Machinery, New York (2019). https://doi.org/10.1145/3290605.3300275

21. United States Congress: Children's online privacy protection act of 1998. 15 U. S. C. 6501–6505. https://uscode.house.gov/view.xhtml?req=granuleid%3AUSC-prelim-title15-section6501&edition=prelim

22. Worthy, P., Matthews, B., Viller, S.: Trust me: doubts and concerns living with the Internet of Things. In: Proceedings of the 2016 ACM Conference on Designing Interactive Systems, DIS 2016, pp. 427–434. Association for Computing Machinery, New York (2016). https://doi.org/10.1145/2901790.2901890

23. Yao, Y., Basdeo, J.R., Kaushik, S., Wang, Y.: Defending my castle: a co-design study of privacy mechanisms for smart homes. In: Proceedings of the 2019 CHI Conference on Human Factors in Computing Systems, CHI 2019. Association for Computing Machinery, New York (2019). https://doi.org/10.1145/3290605. 3300428

24. Zeng, E., Mare, S., Roesner, F.: End user security and privacy concerns with smart homes. In: Thirteenth Symposium on Usable Privacy and Security (SOUPS 2017), pp. 65–80. USENIX Association, Santa Clara, July 2017. https://www.usenix.org/ conference/soups2017/technical-sessions/presentation/zeng

25. Zheng, S., Apthorpe, N., Chetty, M., Feamster, N.: User perceptions of smart home IoT privacy. Proc. ACM Hum.-Comput. Interact. 2(CSCW), 1–20 (2018). https:// doi.org/10.1145/3274469

26. Zimmermann, V., Bennighof, M., Edel, M., Hofmann, O., Jung, J., von Wick, M.: 'Home, smart home' - Exploring end users' mental models of smart homes. In: Dachselt, R., Weber, G. (eds.) Mensch und Computer 2018 - Workshopband. Gesellschaft für Informatik e.V., Bonn (2018). https://doi.org/10.18420/muc2018-ws08-0539

In Our Employer We Trust: Mental Models of Office Workers' Privacy Perceptions

Jan Tolsdorf[(✉)][ID] and Florian Dehling[ID]

Data and Application Security Group, TH Köln - University of Applied Sciences,
Cologne, Germany
{jan.tolsdorf,florian.dehling}@th-koeln.de
https://das.th-koeln.de

*Jan Tolsdorf, Florian Dehling, In Our
Employer We Trust: Mental Models of
Office Workers' Privacy Perceptions,
Proceedings of AsiaUSEC'20, Financial
Cryptography and Data Security 2020
(FC). February 14, 2020
Kota Kinabalu, Sabah, Malaysia Springer,
2020*

Abstract. The increasing digitization of the workplace poses new threats to the right to privacy for employees. Previous work on this matter was rather quantitative and with a strong focus on monitoring and surveillance. Yet, there is a lack of comprehensive explanations for employees' privacy perceptions and what drives their risk and trust perceptions.

We conducted an interview study with 22 German employees to qualitatively examine (1) issues and themes related to the expectations of privacy of office workers and (2) their beliefs and understandings of how their data is handled by their employers.

We present the mental model of the *believing employee*, which is characterized by a high level of trust in the lawful processing of personal data by the employer and little fear of invasions of privacy. The mental model is strongly influenced by the uncertainty regarding the processing of personal data by employers and compensates missing experiences regarding privacy at work with analogies from private online use.

Keywords: Privacy in the workplace · Privacy perceptions ·
Informational self-determination · Mental models

Supported by the German Federal Ministry of Education and Research (BMBF) under the research project "TrUSD - Transparente und selbstbestimmte Ausgestaltung der Datennutzung im Unternehmen" (transparent and self-determined design of data use in organizations) (16KIS0899).

1   Introduction

The workplace undergoes major changes in times of digitization. In particular, it leads to an increase of companies processing personal data of their employees. Therewith associated threats to the preservation and assurance of the individual right to privacy have been disregarded lately. While employees demand for more transparency and control over their personal data [29], existing Privacy Enhancing Technologies (PETs) [32] and Transparency Enhancing Technologies (TETs) [25] are only available for the business-customer relationship. Their adoption to the working sphere is likely to fail when not fulfilling employees' mental models and actual privacy demands [14]. We contribute to this matter by presenting German office workers' mental models of privacy perceptions, in order to lay a basis for future tool developments. Our approach differs from that of a large stream of research that adapts the US-American definition of privacy as the *right to freedom from intrusion* [19]. Instead, we refer to a more holistic definition of privacy as the *right to informational self-determination* that warrants each individual transparency and personal control over the collection, use and disclosure of their personal data by others. This concept is very present in European and Canadian societies [19] and was also incorporated into the General Data Protection Regulation (GDPR) in the European Union. It has further paved the way for our modern understanding of information privacy, manifesting itself in the Privacy by Design (PbD) paradigm [12].

2   Related Work

Mental Models Mental Models Mental models (MMs) are simplified internal representations of external reality that enable individuals to make sense of their environment, including simple actions, systems or even complex phenomena [18]. MMs are generally considered to be incomplete, incorrect and highly context-dependent, making them unstable or rather inconsistent [27]. Irrespective of their correctness towards representing a phenomena, MMs are incredibly helpful in given or unfamiliar situations by guiding the decision making process to behave in a certain way [10]. In the context of HCI and privacy, previous work has primarily considered MMs of privacy in general [28] and in the context of private technology use [14,15]. The latter with a strong reference to online services [7,20,30,31]. Individuals were found to rely on several incomplete and poorly formed submodels [30] or use highly simplified models, even against better knowledge [2].

Privacy Perceptions in the Workplace. Information privacy in the work context was found to be (at least) a tripartite concept comprising of employees' beliefs in having control over the (1) gathering (e.g. collection and storage) and (2) handling (e.g. processing) of personal information as well as the (3) perceived legitimacy of the employer to process data (e.g. expected usage) [3,9].

Investigations on privacy perceptions in the workplace are strongly marked by theoretical considerations or empirical findings of quantitative studies based on "privacy as intrusion" [34,35,37] and the overall topic of employee monitoring and workplace surveillance [4]. While many employees agree that it is mostly used for coercive control reasons instead of caring reasons, only few employees reported it to be an invasion of their privacy [36]. Besides, employees are aware that disclosure of certain personal information is unavoidable in the course of their employment and are aware of possible privacy invasions [5]. Though, they may deliberately withhold data if they expect benefits [5] or fear adverse consequences [33]. Employees were also found to weigh up constraints over affordances [23], substantiating the validity of the privacy calculus [11] in the workplace: employees are generally willing to disclose information if they receive adequate gratification in return. High levels of concern and anxiety regarding the misuse of information by the employer are reasons that hinder disclosure.

3 Methodology

To elicit MMs of employees' privacy perceptions in digitized workplaces, we conducted semi-structured interviews with 22 employees from small to large sized organizations in Germany during the period July until September 2019.

Participants and Recruiting. We aimed at recruiting a heterogeneous sample in terms of people with different professional and socio-demographic backgrounds in order not to limit privacy perceptions by demographic characteristics [21]. Participants were invited using organizations' internal mailing lists or direct invitation. Employees participated voluntarily and without payment, though some employees were exempted from normal duties for participation during working hours. Participants' demographics are available in Appendix A.

Interview Guideline Design. We adopted an *expert model* approach to design an appropriated interview guideline, as it proved itself valuable in eliciting mental models before [7,24]. We executed an iterative development process: we derived an initial version of the expert model by capturing and sorting all relevant aspects from selected themes on data protection law, general privacy literature, as well as technical and organizational circumstances of workplace environments. The model was then repeatedly reviewed and discussed in expert groups, with participants from the various fields of law, psychology, ergonomics, IT systems engineering, security and privacy, followed by subsequent adjustments of the model. We further conducted three pilot interviews to check the validity of the interview guideline's questions and structure. A copy is available in Appendix B.

Evaluation. We conducted a qualitative analysis by carrying out a deductive coding approach by converting the expert model to a code-book. We followed established guidelines [22] and common practices for semi-structured interviews [8]. First, transcribed audio recordings were segmented into thematic sections based on our interview guideline. Then, a randomly selected 50%-subset of the interviews was independently coded by two researchers. In a subsequent revision step, a *negotiated agreement* approach was used to discuss disagreements and resolve coding differences by revising the categories and coding scheme in order to avoid interpretation bias. Afterwards, the same two coders coded all interviews. Gwet's gamma (AC2) [16] was used as a measure of the quality of the inter-rater agreement (IRA) as it takes into account the kappa-paradox, a problem where low kappas occur despite a high percentage of agreement [13].

Limitations. As participation was voluntary, sampling is affected by self-selection bias and limited to the population of people being employed at the organizations we contacted. Despite individual demographic differences, our sample contains only participants with a German cultural background. The results might not be the same in different cultures or organizations. Since a qualitative approach was chosen, we do not claim to provide generalization on the topic of employee privacy perceptions, but aim at elaborating and exploring reasoning and views.

Ethics. Our study complies with the strict German and European privacy regulations. The data was either collected anonymously or converted to anonymous data after the interview. Any contact information was stored separately. Participants were informed about their right to withdraw their data during or after the study. We emphasized that leaving the interview will not have any negative consequences and assured that neither the fact of their participation nor the interview's content will be reported back to their employer.

4   Findings

In the following section, we present our findings based on our coding. Only codes with at least moderate agreement ($IRA_{AC2} > 0.74$) are respected.

4.1   Self-disclosure and Consent

We asked interviewees about their abilities and liberties to take control over data disclosure and how they agreed to its use by the employer.

Employees as Data Providers. The vast majority of participants responded that they actively disclose data to their employers *"systematically within the scope of data entry forms"*. Participants were particularly conscious about the data they provided during the recruitment process. Participant P06 noted that disclosure then rather happens in the course of *"personal conversation or even written exchange"*. In this regard, one participant indicated that it is generally hard to tell who had access to documents (i.e. CV) and is in possession of which kind of information. Participant P14 did not consider his employer to *"actively obtain data from me, instead I rather believe that I provide data"* and compared himself to a kind of data provider who is in control over what data will be disclosed. Another employee commented *"I have no qualms in that case. If I believe that my employer is allowed to be interested in gathering my data and that's what he needs, he gets the data - anything else that goes beyond that, I refuse."* Two senior executives claimed to even have some control over the use of disclosed data. While one of them manifested his control beliefs by being responsible for performing certain data processing operations, the other linked the freedom and ability to actively input data into systems he has access to as control capabilities.

Concern. We found that employees reported to be generally unconcerned when disclosing personal information, justifying their attitudes with strong trust beliefs. Participant P06 expressed that *"in the course of digitization and Facebook and no idea what else there is [...] I can already imagine that more can happen with the data [...] But I would say that my employer doesn't do that"*. In line with this view, various participants justified their lack of concern by referring to law, claiming that their employer *"will of course adhere to the applicable data protection regulations"* as *"this is top priority"* to the organization and its employees. A manager put emphasis on the appropriateness of the types of data that is elicited: *"employers do not record eye color, nose length or shoe size, but record the data necessary for the contractual relationship and payroll accounting"*, concluding that there is no reason to be concerned or worried about. Only one participant showed concerns and directed attention to a loss of control and uncertainty going along with the disclosure of sensible personal data to employers: *"in the worst case, it could even be used against me at some point."*

Giving Consent. When being asked how they agreed to the use of their data by their employer, participant P08 responded: *"Not at all. Or simply by providing it - it was tacit consent."* The majority of respondents gave similar explanations and characterized their consent therefore as *implicit*. Participant P16 explained that the consent *"is not stated in my employment contract, [instead] this is done here on a basis of trust"*. Participants emphasized that implicit consent is not necessarily a loss of control. Instead, active data disclosure was seen as a form of *"indirect approval"* because one is *"still conscious of [disclosing] it"*. However, there were also participants who admitted not to *"remember if there was a consent form back then"* (P05). In such cases, employees stated that they really do not mind their data being processed anyway.

Half of the participants declared that they *explicitly consent* and claimed to have actually signed a corresponding data protection statement at the beginning of their employment which is ultimately valid. Moreover, implicit and explicit consent are by no means dichotomous, but the type of consent *"depends on the type of data, [...] for many [data] there do exist privacy declarations stating that the data can be used"* (P11) and that one usually signs at the beginning of an employment. Consent for subsequent data disclosures, however, occurs implicitly: *"but then there is also a lot of data, which is naturally produced as you work. Which means, of course, that there is no need for separate approval"*.

4.2 Data Processors

When we asked who collects and processes personal information in the course of their professional activities, all except one participant mentioned entities both inside and outside their respective organizations. The one who disagreed claimed that her personal data is *"certainly not!"* processed nor collected by external entities outside her organization because she is *"very, very careful"*.

Legally Mandatory Entities. Two-thirds of the respondents named external data processors who are legally mandatory for an employment relationship. Thereby, registration with the social security agency at the beginning of the employment and paying income tax to the tax authority were most frequently mentioned, followed by health insurance companies and the statutory pension insurance.

Service Providers and Customers. Regardless of employer or occupation, employees named service providers, customers and business partners as external data processors who receive and process at least partial extracts of their personal data. Yet there was a tendency to not know which kind of information this involves. For example, while one employee assumed that data is shared anonymously, the senior manager clearly stated that the data *"contains the first name and surname and the professional e-mail address"*. Similarly, other participants reported they are unaware of the exact data but expect their employer to abide the law, act most carefully and to only share little information.

Human Processors. Our results suggest that office workers think of human-like data processors, since any processing was associated with some form of human interaction. We did not find any evidence for autonomous or purely algorithmic processing being part of the participants' explanations. Unlike participants from medium and large organizations, employees from the small sized enterprise generally only referred to a specific person when explaining business processes and giving examples. They were also very aware of the fact which person has access to what kind of data. While employees were generally familiar with information systems at the workplace, they only attributed data storage purposes to it.

Communication and Internet Services. Solely participants with an IT background mentioned communication service providers and intermediary systems when being asked about external processors. Participant P10 pointed out that there are no differences between private and work related internet use as *"every moment you are on the internet data is collected"*. In this context, participant P21 noted that popular service providers *"now also know that I work here"* as he uses his private accounts for work as well. A senior employee showed awareness of the fact that he possesses an account for the manufacturer of their business software, but added *"I'm actually not sure what data [the manufacturer] has about me, ... there is obviously somehow also an account which was set up there for me, so probably data also flowed, but I don't know which data"*. Participant P04 explained that with modern software it is difficult to know whether and if so which data the manufacturers may collect *"unintentionally"* and explained that *"there is also a lack of transparency for the most part - even if you choose that no data should be sent"* it might still happen. For instant messaging apps and email, participant P14 also claimed that *"providers get at least the message and then my name, they know where I work"*. Participant P12 pointed out that even the simplest processes involve several different and often unknown intermediaries.

4.3 Purposes of Data Processing

We asked about the purposes for which their employers process personal data. Respondents broadly agreed that the data would be processed primarily in the context of normal employment processes and considered it as justified and fully legitimate, although it may leads to very undesirable consequences for employees.

Administration Tasks. The overwhelming majority of participants agreed that their data would be used primarily *"for all correspondence and salary payments"*. Certain data were thereby assigned to specific purposes. For example, participant P04 explained that *"the bank account is used for the salary transfer, the date of birth to register me at the competent authority, my social security number because of the salary"*. Though, further purposes other than administration tasks were mentioned; an employee from the public sector explained that her employer requires certain personal information related to skills and education in order to determine *"what to do with [her]"* and assign her suitable activities.

Acquisition. Employees from the private sector replied that their employers disclose information on their skills to potential customers to acquire new orders. Participant P16 stated: *"[my employer uses it] for economic purposes - to sell me!"*. Another employee pointed out that this kind of personal information is *"also data I publish privately on [an employment-oriented social networking site]"* and therefore, the data that his employer discloses to potential customers is *"publicly available anyway"*. Yet, he remarks that *"some of my colleagues may not have done that - in this regard it is only okay for me personally"*.

Employee Assessment. Participants from the private sector discussed the topic of employee assessment, considering *performance evaluation* and *suitability determination*. Evaluation could either have positive or negative results for the respective employee. Yet, negative consequences were not linked to their own employment, but to hypothetical scenarios with either other or fictitious employers. Participant P08 summarized these topics stating that he can *"well imagine that some employers collect information about their employees to be able to get rid of them if necessary, or when it comes to announcing dismissals, in order to be able to react accordingly, or when salary demands or additional requests come in, to have something available to compare employees. When it comes to promotion to know who is best suited or is not well suited, i.e. is not able to work under pressure, is often ill, is irascible, has any convictions which stand in the way of promotion"*. Monitoring activities such as working time tracking were also particularly present in this context.

Duty of Care. However, working time tracking was not exclusively linked to employee surveillance activities. In fact, a small group of participants noticed that employers have a duty of care to their employees and considered this as a valid and important purpose to process individual-related data. Most present was the issue of overworking and inadequate rest or vacation periods in this context. A team manager elaborated on this topic and referred to situations where employees carry out various activities alongside their job. He explained that for employees in his team, he expects them to disclose certain information about their private lives in order for him to both, verify that employees meet their obligations and secondly, in order to fulfill his duty of care.

4.4 Invasion of Privacy

To better understand employees' perceptions of privacy violations, we asked participants to discuss aspects and situations that would violate their privacy.

Processing Without Knowledge. We asked participants about their thoughts and judgment on their data being processed without their knowledge - two distinct positions emerged: Some of the subjects stated that they would perceive such processing as a restriction of their privacy. They considered the linkage of working times and ticket systems or the interpretation of financial and health data. For example, participant P15 expressed concerns about the handling of sick notes that must be sent to the employer, but may contain hidden clues about the illness. She justified her uneasiness with the resulting uncertainty as to what conclusions would be drawn from it: *"then it goes on to the headquarters and then you just don't know what conclusions they draw from it"*.

Contrary, a much larger group of participants did not express any concern with unwitting use. They either doubted the need to be notified about the forwarding: *"I'm gonna say no, otherwise [the employer] would have done it."* (P20); emphasized its legitimacy: *"I think if the data is used then I already assume that this is appropriate"* (P14); or pointed out that they *"don't have any big problems with that, they are also no particularly precarious data"*.

Abusive Data Usage. We asked participants for what purposes their employer may use their data and also asked for practical examples of data misuse. Thereby, interviewees raised concerns about the transfer of their data to third parties - two models got identified in this thematic area: one describes the sale of employee data with vague intentions. Participant P03 claimed that an illegal usage of data has to be bound to a somehow *"commercial interest"*. Even more prevalent was the idea of employers passing on personal data to advertisers: *"the employer could also pass the data on to companies that collect e-mail addresses, postal addresses, for advertising, for calls, for any subscription sales, surveys, etc."* (P08). The second model identified is closer related to the work environment and aims at targeted advertisements based on data which gets transmitted to insurance providers by employers: *"I know that health insurance policies for privately insured persons or civil servants are always opened at the right time in order to obtain their deals"* (P01). One participant thought of an even more explicit use of advertisement in the workplace, describing that employers could be *"passing on data to advertising agencies in order to place targeted advertisements to enforce certain behavior at work the employer benefits from."*

5 Discussion

Contrary to our expectations, we generally did not identify groups based on participants' demographic backgrounds that can be linked to a particular set of attributes on privacy beliefs and perceptions. Instead we identified recurring statements and justifications among all of our participants. We refer tho this overarching mental model as *the believing employee:* First of all, our participants were largely satisfied with the ways in which they regulated disclosure and how they disclosed the data. Almost all participants uttered to at least partially give implicit consent to data processing and considered it as sufficient for disclosure in daily business. Also, participants hardly expressed concerns and demonstrated to have strong trust beliefs in the lawful processing by employers. Yet, respondents were often unaware of what data was actually available to their employer or third parties, even though they themselves claimed to have actively provided it. This applies to both data made available during the application process and also to data from the normal working routine. Still, all subjects showed awareness for their employers' reasons behind the processing and disclosure of certain personal data. This finding entails that employees assumably possess a certain baseline set of associations between actual data and purposes and thus only require additional support in cases of unexpected data usage or data flows. Concerning abusive data usage, the kind of possible misuse scenarios that our participants expressed indicate that they made use of analogies from their private lives. The majority of participants stated that their data could be misused for advertising purposes. Some respondents made comparisons with services such as Facebook or Google, which indicates that they mapped the risks and consequences they experienced in their private sphere to the work context.

Apart from these commonalities in the vast majority of the participants' answers, we also found nuances in the consideration of *knowledge* and *uncertainty*; considering *knowledge*, participants' explanations were naturally biased by additional knowledge they possessed either due to their position or their profession. That is, managers superior knowledge on data flows influenced their beliefs on control. Similarly, only IT professionals identified intermediary services as hidden data processors, whereas non-IT professionals were particularly ignorant about these entities. We refer to this nuanced model as *the knowing & informed employee*; with regards to *uncertainty*, we found that some participants expressed concern due to a lack of transparency about which data were available to their employers. In particular, permanent data storage is regarded as a threat because employers are believed to be able to use it against workers at any time. Similar to previous findings [5,33], these participants perceived unwitting processing of personal data as a violation if they feared negative effects for their careers. We refer to this theme as *the fearing employee.*

5.1 Implications for Transparency and Control

From our findings we deduce that transparency rather than control over personal data is required by office workers. There are two reasons for this: first, employees are seemingly happy with the control abilities they currently have; second, the overall high level of uncertainty holds risks for employees' privacy at work as it is known to lead to adverse effects and paradoxical observations [1]. The general lack of knowledge about who has access to personal data stands in contradiction to the fundamentals of informational self-determination. In this regard, *privacy dashboards* have proven themselves useful in improving awareness and transparency of users in online services [6,38] and are currently reviewed in the scope of organizations as well [29]. But also the implementation of *privacy notifications* in the workplace have the potential to contribute to more awareness. While this measure is known to be effective for making informed privacy decisions [17,26], its implementation is often challenging to not annoy users. However, our results indicate that their use can well be limited to certain processes. The use of analogies from private lives for data misuse scenarios demonstrates that the complexity of the subject exceeded the cognitive abilities of our participants. We assume that they have not been confronted with data abuse by employers before. However, a clear understanding of risks is indispensable to make informed privacy decisions. Further research is needed to raise awareness in this topic without unnecessarily burdening the relationship between employee and employer.

6 Conclusion

Our findings show that privacy perceptions at work are largely uniform among employees of different professions and organizations. We identified three mental models of privacy perceptions with tiny but distinct differences:

(1) The *believing employee* is characterized by a very high level of faith in employers to comply with legal requirements when processing personal data and is heavily influenced by an uncertainty bias which compensates for missing factual knowledge. They are aware of active data disclosure and are thus comfortable with using implicit consent by either disclosing or withholding data. Unwitting data usage does not constitute a violation of privacy while unlawful data processing is attributed exclusively to other employers. Any violations of privacy are heavily primed by the use of analogies from the private sphere.

(2) The *knowing & informed employee* represents a nuance of the *believing employee* that justifies in additional knowledge on a topic on data processing activities in the organization. Knowledge may come from the position in the company or the professional background. The employee falls back into the believing model in situations where additional information is unavailable.

(3) The *fearing employee* also represents a nuance of the *believing employee*, which is reflected in the fact that uncertainty is expressed in concern about possible negative consequences of employers' data processing. Ignorance of

what information employers have available contributes to a high degree of uncertainty in the disclosure of data. Unwitting data usage that results in unintended consequences for employees is perceived an invasion of privacy.

The main challenges for the future are to close gaps and deal with misunderstandings regarding the access of individuals and organizations to employees' personal data, and to provide transparency on data processing so that employees can act in a self-determined manner and not under uncertainty and belief.

Acknowledgments. The authors would like to thank Hartmut Schmitt and Svenja Polst for their support in conducting interviews, the involved organizations for their support in recruiting participants and last but not least all employees for their participation and valuable insights on privacy perceptions in the workplace.

Appendix A   Participants

See Table 1.

Table 1. Participants demographics

ID	Age	Sex	Education	Employment (years)		Profession	Organization Size
				Total	Current Employer		
P01	46–55	m	academic degree	21–25	6–10	Administration Employee	L
P02	56–65	f	academic degree	26–30	0–5	Administration Employee	L
P03	46–55	m	academic degree	16–20	6–10	Administration Employee	L
P04	26–35	m	apprenticeship	6–10	0–5	Software Developer	M
P05	46–55	f	higher education entrance qualification	26–30	6–10	Administration Employee	L
P06	46–55	f	secondary school or higher	31–35	31–35	Administration Employee	L
P07	36–45	m	higher education entrance qualification	21–25	11–15	IT Administrator	S
P08	46–55	f	apprenticeship	31–35	11–15	Sales	S
P09	46–55	m	apprenticeship	36–40	11–15	Supporter	S
P10	26–35	m	apprenticeship	6–10	0–5	Software Developer	S
P11	46–55	m	academic degree	21–25	6–10	Administration Employee	L
P12	36–45	m	academic degree	11–15	6–10	Research Assistant IT	L
P13	26–35	f	academic degree	11–15	11–15	Software Developer	M
P14	26–35	m	academic degree	6–10	6–10	Software Developer	M
P15	36–45	f	academic degree	16–20	11–15	Research Assistant IT	L
P16	18–25	m	academic degree	0–5	0–5	Software Developer	M
P17	56–65	f	academic degree	26–30	0–5	Administration Employee	L
P18	46–55	m	academic degree	16–20	0–5	Software Developer	M
P19	46–55	m	academic degree	16–20	6–10	Administration Employee	L
P20	44–45	f	academic degree	21–25	11–15	Software Developer	M
P21	18–25	m	academic degree	0–5	0–5	Research Assistant IT	L
P22	26–35	f	secondary school or higher	16–20	16–20	Administration Employee	L

Appendix B   Interview Outline (Translated)

1. Welcome and general instructions: At the start of the interview, participants were welcomed and briefed about the study procedure, the study conditions and asked for their consent to elicit data (drawings, hand writings, answers to questionnaire, voice recording).
2. Use of technical tools during everyday work: In the first part of each interview, participants were asked to summarize their job profile and to explain the kind of technical tools (hardware and software) they use for their ordinary working activities. All tools were written down on moderation cards and displayed on the table.
   - Please describe to me with which tasks you mainly deal with in your daily work.
   - Which technical aids or tools do you use in your daily work?
3. Data gathering and processing by employers: The next part of the interview consisted of questions related to how employers gather data from their employees, for what purposes employees believe their employers require and process data about them and on employers' abilities and liberties to take control over data disclosure. We further elaborated on these topics by asking whether third parties are involved in any of these activities and asked them to draw or rather sketch data flows if they answered yes.
   - How does your employer obtain such data from and about you?
   - For what purposes can this data be used?
   - How do you consent to the use of this data?
   - What freedoms do you have when it comes to your company data?
   - Are there any third parties besides your employer who use or collect such data about you within the scope of your activities?
4. Privacy expectations: We asked participants about their awareness of data processing and possible data misuse scenarios.
   - Do you think it is possible for your employer to use data about you without your knowledge?
   - Suppose an employer collects or uses data without the consent of its employees: What consequences could data misuse have for employees?
5. Debriefing and questionnaire on demographics: At the end of the survey, participants were asked whether they want to add anything to the previous discussion and to fill out a post-questionnaire on demographics.

References

1. Acquisti, A., Brandimarte, L., Loewenstein, G.: Privacy and human behavior in the age of information. Science **347**(6221), 509–514 (2015). https://doi.org/10.1126/science.aaa1465
2. Acquisti, A., Grossklags, J.: Privacy and rationality in individual decision making. IEEE Secur. Privacy Mag. **3**(1), 26–33 (2005). https://doi.org/10.1109/MSP.2005.22

3. Alge, B.J., Ballinger, G.A., Tangirala, S., Oakley, J.L.: Information privacy in organizations: empowering creative and extrarole performance. J. Appl. Psychol. **91**(1), 221–232 (2006). https://doi.org/10.1037/0021-9010.91.1.221
4. Backhaus, N.: Context sensitive technologies and electronic employee monitoring: a meta-analytic review. In: 2019 IEEE/SICE International Symposium on System Integration (SII), pp. 548–553 (2019). https://doi.org/10.1109/SII.2019.8700354
5. Ball, K., Daniel, E.M., Stride, C.: Dimensions of employee privacy: an empirical study. Inf. Technol. People **25**(4), 376–394 (2012). https://doi.org/10.1108/09593841211278785
6. Buchmann, J., Nebel, M., Roßnagel, A., Shirazi, F., Simo, H., Waidner, M.: Personal information dashboard: putting the individual back in control. In: Hildebrandt, M., O'Hara, K., Waidner, M. (eds.) Digital Enlightenment Yearbook 2013, pp. 139–164. Iso Press, Amsterdam (2013)
7. Camp, L.J.: Mental models of privacy and security. IEEE Technol. Soc. Mag. **28**(3), 37–46 (2009). https://doi.org/10.1109/MTS.2009.934142
8. Campbell, J.L., Quincy, C., Osserman, J., Pedersen, O.K.: Coding in-depth semistructured interviews: problems of unitization and intercoder reliability and agreement. Sociol. Methods Res. **42**(3), 294–320 (2013). https://doi.org/10.1177/0049124113500475
9. Chen, X., Ma, J., Jin, J., Fosh, P.: Information privacy, gender differences, and intrinsic motivation in the workplace. Int. J. Inf. Manag. **33**(6), 917–926 (2013). https://doi.org/10.1016/j.ijinfomgt.2013.08.010
10. Craik, K.J.W.: The Nature of Explanation. Cambridge University Press, Cambridge (1943)
11. Dinev, T., Hart, P.: An extended privacy calculus model for E-commerce transactions. Inf. Syst. Res. **17**(1), 61–80 (2006). https://doi.org/10.1287/isre.1060.0080
12. Domingo-Ferrer, J., et al.: European Union, European Network and Information Security Agency: Privacy and data protection by design - from policy to engineering. ENISA, Heraklion (2014)
13. Feinstein, A.R., Cicchetti, D.V.: High agreement but low Kappa: I. The problems of two paradoxes. J. Clin. Epidemiol. **43**(6), 543–549 (1990). https://doi.org/10.1016/0895-4356(90)90158-L
14. Fischer-Hübner, S., Pettersson, J.S., Angulo, J.: HCI requirements for transparency and accountability tools for cloud service chains. In: Felici, M., Fernández-Gago, C. (eds.) A4Cloud 2014. LNCS, vol. 8937, pp. 81–113. Springer, Cham (2015). https://doi.org/10.1007/978-3-319-17199-9_4
15. Gerber, N., Zimmermann, V., Volkamer, M.: Why johnny fails to protect his privacy. In: 2019 IEEE European Symposium on Security and Privacy Workshops (EuroSPW), pp. 109–118 (2019). https://doi.org/10.1109/EuroSPW.2019.00019
16. Gwet, K.L.: Computing inter-rater reliability and its variance in the presence of high agreement. Br. J. Math. Stat. Psychol. **61**(1), 29–48 (2008). https://doi.org/10.1348/000711006X126600
17. Jackson, C.B., Wang, Y.: Addressing the privacy paradox through personalized privacy notifications. Proc. ACM Interact. Mob. Wearable Ubiquitous Technol. **2**(2), 68:1–68:25 (2018). https://doi.org/10.1145/3214271
18. Jones, N., Ross, H., Lynam, T., Perez, P., Leitch, A.: Mental models: an interdisciplinary synthesis of theory and methods. Ecol. Soc. **16**(1) (2011). https://doi.org/10.5751/ES-03802-160146
19. Krebs, D., Doctor, J.: "Privacy by design": nice-to-have or a necessary principle of data protection law? JIPITEC - J. Intellect. Prop. Inf. Technol. E-Commerce Law **4**(1), 2–20 (2013)

20. Kumar, P., Naik, S.M., Devkar, U.R., Chetty, M., Clegg, T.L., Vitak, J.: 'No telling passcodes out because they're private': understanding children's mental models of privacy and security online. Proc. ACM Hum.-Comput. Interact. 1(CSCW), 64:1–64:21 (2017). https://doi.org/10.1145/3134699
21. Kwasny, M., Caine, K., Rogers, W.A., Fisk, A.D.: Privacy and technology: folk definitions and perspectives. Technical HFA-TR-0804, Atlanta, GA: Georgia Institute of Technology School of Psychology - Human Factors and Aging Laboratory, Florence, Italy (2008)
22. Mayring, P.: Qualitative content analysis [28 paragraphs]. Forum Qual. Sozialforschung/Forum: Qual. Soc. Res. 1(2), Art. 20 (2000). https://doi.org/10.17169/fqs-1.2.1089
23. Mettler, T., Wulf, J.: Physiolytics at the workplace: affordances and constraints of wearables use from an employee's perspective. Inf. Syst. J. 29(1), 245–273 (2019). https://doi.org/10.1111/isj.12205
24. Morgan, M.G., Fischhoff, B., Bostrom, A., Atman, C.J. (eds.): Risk Communication: A Mental Models Approach. Cambridge University Press, Cambridge (2002)
25. Murmann, P., Fischer-Hübner, S.: Tools for achieving usable ex post transparency: a survey. IEEE Access 5, 22965–22991 (2017). https://doi.org/10.1109/ACCESS.2017.2765539
26. Murmann, P., Reinhardt, D., Fischer-Hübner, S.: To be, or not to be notified: eliciting privacy notification preferences for online mHealth services. In: Proceedings of the 34th IFIP International Information Security and Privacy Conference (IFIP SEC), Lisbon, Portugal (2019)
27. Norman, D.A.: Some observations on mental models. In: Gentner, D., Stevens, A.L. (eds.) Mental Models, pp. 7–14. Lawrence Erlbaum Associates Inc. (1983)
28. Oates, M., Ahmadullah, Y., Marsh, A., Swoopes, C., Zhang, S., Balebako, R., Cranor, L.F.: Turtles, locks, and bathrooms: understanding mental models of privacy through illustration. Proc. Privacy Enhanc. Technol. 2018(4), 5–32 (2018). https://doi.org/10.1515/popets-2018-0029
29. Polst, S., Kelbert, P., Feth, D.: Company privacy dashboards: employee needs and requirements. In: Moallem, A. (ed.) HCII 2019. LNCS, vol. 11594, pp. 429–440. Springer, Cham (2019). https://doi.org/10.1007/978-3-030-22351-9_29
30. Prettyman, S.S., Furman, S., Theofanos, M., Stanton, B.: Privacy and security in the brave new world: the use of multiple mental models. In: Tryfonas, T., Askoxylakis, I. (eds.) HAS 2015. LNCS, vol. 9190, pp. 260–270. Springer, Cham (2015). https://doi.org/10.1007/978-3-319-20376-8_24
31. Schomakers, E.M., Lidynia, C., Ziefle, M.: Hidden within a group of people - mental models of privacy protection. In: Proceedings of the 3rd International Conference on Internet of Things, Big Data and Security, pp. 85–94. SCITEPRESS - Science and Technology Publications, Funchal, Madeira, Portugal (2018). https://doi.org/10.5220/0006678700850094
32. Shen, Y., Pearson, S.: Privacy enhancing technologies: a review. Technical HPL-2011-113, HP Laboratories, UK (2011)
33. Smith, S.A., Brunner, S.R.: To reveal or conceal: using communication privacy management theory to understand disclosures in the workplace. Manag. Commun. Q. 31(3), 429–446 (2017). https://doi.org/10.1177/0893318917692896
34. Stone, E.F., Gueutal, H.G., Gardner, D.G., McClure, S.: A field experiment comparing information-privacy values, beliefs, and attitudes across several types of organizations. J. Appl. Psychol. 68(3), 459–468 (1983). https://doi.org/10.1037/0021-9010.68.3.459

35. Tolchinsky, P.D., McCuddy, M.K., Adams, J., Ganster, D.C., Woodman, R.W., Fromkin, H.L.: Employee perceptions of invasion of privacy: a field simulation experiment. J. Appl. Psychol. **66**(3), 308–313 (1981). https://doi.org/10.1037/0021-9010.66.3.308
36. Watkins Allen, M., Coopman, S.J., Hart, J.L., Walker, K.L.: Workplace surveillance and managing privacy boundaries. Manag. Commun. Q. **21**(2), 172–200 (2007). https://doi.org/10.1177/0893318907306033
37. Woodman, R.W., Ganster, D.C., Adams, J., McCuddy, M.K., Tolchinsky, P.D., Fromkin, H.: A survey of employee perceptions of information privacy in organizations. Acad. Manag. J. **25**(3), 647–663 (1982). https://doi.org/10.5465/256087
38. Zimmermann, C., Accorsi, R., Müller, G.: Privacy dashboards: reconciling data-driven business models and privacy. In: 2014 Ninth International Conference on Availability, Reliability and Security, pp. 152–157 (2014). https://doi.org/10.1109/ARES.2014.27

Behaviour of Outsourced Employees as Sources of Information System Security Threats

David Oyebisi[1]([⊠]) and Kennedy Njenga[2]

[1] School of Computing, Engineering and Mathematics, Western Sydney University, Sydney, Australia
decool123@gmail.com
[2] Department of Applied Information Systems, University of Johannesburg, Johannesburg, South Africa

Abstract. There is an increased need for information systems to be protected against unauthorized access and retrieval, particularly from legitimate 'insider' outsourced employees. While most studies have focused on organisations' employees as threats, only a few have focused on the role the outsourced employees' play as a potential threat. The study seeks to investigate the insider threat behaviour of an outsourced employee in developing countries as security threats to information systems by virtue of their privileged access. The study is quantitative and adopts social bond and involvement theories for this purpose. The research sample was chosen from organisations in Nigeria and South Africa which are the largest two national economies in Africa. Close-ended questionnaires were used and the data were analysed using factor analysis. The study found that outsourced employees exploit information systems vulnerabilities because they are not actively involved in the organisation and lack moral values and beliefs. The findings of this study will assist organisations in developing countries to mitigate the information security threats posed by outsourced employees.

Keywords: Digital data · Insider threat · Outsourced employee

1 Background

The advent of the internet and recent developments in electronic and mobile commerce have seen the increase of digital assets and digital data which can be shared among millions of users once it is created. Laws and regulations to protect organisations' digital assets are not uniformly defined, protected and regulated across boundaries. Considerable measures have been taken to prevent data breaches but most efforts have proven to be unsuccessful. A often under-appreciated vulnerability is when a trusted permanent and outsourced employee that have legitimate access to sensitive information of their organisation perpetrate cybercrime. Although malicious attacks can be initiated by both

D. Oyebisi and K. Njenga—Behaviour of Outsourced Employees as Sources of Information System Security Threats: Proceedings of AsiaUSEC'20, Financial Cryptography and Data Security 2020 (FC). February 14, 2020 Kota Kinabalu, Sabah, Malaysia Springer, 2020.

M. Bernhard et al. (Eds.): FC 2020 Workshops, LNCS 12063, pp. 137–148, 2020.
https://doi.org/10.1007/978-3-030-54455-3_10

insiders and outsiders, disguised former or malicious employees can be potentially disastrous since they can use the knowledge and skills acquired legitimately during work process for illicit gain (Schaefer et al. 2017).

Many organisations have taken measures to instil good cybersecurity protection, ideas, and perception into their employees. Despite all these measures, Aldawood and Skinner (2019) findings have shown that with state-of-the-art cybersecurity awareness and policies, a malicious employee can still steal sensitive information from their organisation. They suggest the need to profile at-risk employees and newly hired staff and tailored an adequate cybersecurity training program for them. However, newly employed workers may not necessarily be a malicious attacker.

Australia's largest bank (Commonwealth Bank of Australia) recently recorded a glitch in the banking app that was recently launched. The banking app erroneously activated multiple payments due to an error screen (Bajkowski 2019). This error may have been averted if an effective penetration test has been conducted before the banking app is launched. Many Australian organisations are witnessing a decline in outsourcing penetration testing with contractual clauses where only Australian citizens are eligible employees to work on many projects. There is this untested assumption that there are more risks involved with outsourcing cybersecurity.

Researchers in the area of cybercrime and behaviour have traditionally emphasised permanent employees within the corporate structure as insider threats. Insider threat research has downplayed or ignored the role of outsourced employees. Since there is no national law and regulatory framework that specifically regulate outsourcing, there has been a considerable increase in outsourcing due to low operating costs abroad, and the abundance of highly skilled offshore workers (Borgese and Pascoe 2019; Wallbank 2019). Such an increase in outsourcing necessitates the importance of examining the cybercrime threats and risks posed by outsourced employees. This study seeks to fill the gap by focusing on the outsourced employees of organisations as a potential cybersecurity threat and their motive behind cybercrime.

2 Research Objective

The goal of this study is to explain the extent to which an outsourced employee could be a potential information security threat and how an organisation can discourage insider threats. To achieve this goal, the following objective is formulated:

To examine the major reasons why outsourced employees exploit the vulnerability of an organisation's secured information system.

3 Literature Review

A significant level of access and trust are given to an employee to work effectively in the organisation (Bamforth 2015). The privileged access that enables an employee to perform their legitimate functions also allows them to abuse the system which makes it necessary to find a middle ground where adequate privileges are granted while malevolent usage is mitigated (Dini and Lopriore 2015; Kim et al. 2016). Analysing such middle ground may reduce insider abuse (Kim et al. 2016). All organisations should endeavour to track all their employee's access to confidential information, ensuring that adequate mechanisms are available to detect and prevent any unauthorized access to sensitive data and information. Even with adequate technology to monitor employees' access to computer systems, intruding into the privacy of employees through electronic monitoring technology is a growing concern (Eivazi 2011).

Research has shown that it is very difficult to determine and predict the motives behind insider attacks although it is believed that employees often do so to perpetrate fraud and for financial gain or revenge (Breeden 2017). And insider threat attacks may also be motivated by overzealousness on the part of employees to get the job done, because of stress, espionage and some exacerbated factors outside the work environment such as family issues (Roy Sarkar 2010). Malice is often associated with acts of revenge while espionage may result from a request from competitors. Once an insider has been motivated by one or more of the above-mentioned factors, s/he will scan for any vulnerability in the organisation's system to exploit but then it can also be the case that such attacks are actually made possible by the vulnerability of organisation's system such as poor access control policies (Huang et al. 2016).

To profile insider threat attacks, Baracaldo and Joshi (2013) have suggested a framework that expands the role based access control (RBAC) model by integrating risk evaluation processes, and the trust that an information system has for its users. The framework helps to adapt doubtful changes in insiders' behaviour by deleting privileges when the trust of insiders' falls below predefined levels. In this way, insider threat attacks could be avoided if access control systems can automatically generate exemptions in real-time when a user is embarking on actions that are inappropriate for their roles and responsibilities.

Babu and Bhanu (2015) also suggest that insider threats may be reduced by proper management of privileges in the information system environment. They propose a privilege management mechanism that integrates risk and trust to develop an efficient prevention mechanism against any forms of insider threats. Their approach successfully identified the malicious behaviour of insiders and any unauthorized requests by splitting user behaviours based on keystroke contents. However, none of the models is yet to identify potential insider attackers in advance. To identify the likelihood of insider attacks and to avert any possible internal threats, Roy Sarkar (2010) recommends a three-pronged approach where technological behavioural and organisational assessments are taken into consideration.

Employees' attitude towards insider threats is influenced by their cultures and belief systems. According to Liu (2014), when individuals move from one location to another, their cultural beliefs and values move with them while their institutional and external economic is abandoned. The culture and value they portray will also influence people around them. The workplace is not an exemption. Employees cultural beliefs and values also influence their attitudes and behaviours concerning information security. An organisation can cultivate an information security culture through effective policies that will enhance employees' information security awareness (Von Solms and Von Solms 2004; AlHogail 2015; Dhillon et al. 2016).

4   Theoretical Framework

This study adopts social bond theory and involvement theory on the relationship between two entities to explore the insider threat behaviour of an outsourced employee. According to Hirschi's (1969) social bonding opinion an individual is less likely to commit delinquent acts when such an individual has a considerable level of social bonding in a particular society. The theory describes a unbreakable link that exists between individuals within a group and is suitable to understand a social problem that exists among entities. In corporate settings, employees with a greater level of social bonding with his/her organisation are less likely to commit a malicious act (Thompson 2014). Hirschi (1969) categorised social bond into four components – attachment, commitment, involvement and personal norms.

Involvement theory identifies the degree of contribution in terms of energy and time given to a specific activity (Lee et al. 2004). In other words, the degree of time and energy sacrificed for any task determines the level of commitment and involvement of the individual. As in the case of information security awareness program, Rocha Flores et al. (2014) claim that lack of information security awareness and knowledge can be attributed to low levels of employee's involvement. There is no doubt that involvement influences the attitudes and behaviour of employees.

4.1   Conceptual Model

Figure 1 represents the conceptual model adopted in this study. Involvement is the antecedent variable while social bond and insider threat behaviours are the independent variable and dependent variable respectively.

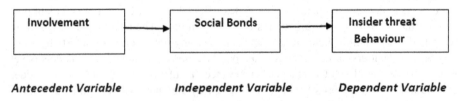

Antecedent Variable   *Independent Variable*   *Dependent Variable*

Fig. 1.   General conceptual model

Involvement (perception) of employees has a direct impact on their social bonds to the organisation. Attachment, commitment, involvement, and belief as collective components of the social bond, in turn, shape the insider threat behaviour of employees. The interdependence of these research constructs is illustrated in the model below.

4.2   Hypotheses

Research has shown that collaboration and teamwork in the workplace have a positive impact on the productivity of an organisation (Flores-Fillol et al. 2017). According to Hamilton et al. (2003) collaboration and teamwork result in between 6 and 18 per cent higher productivity. Not only will collaboration and teamwork ensure effective

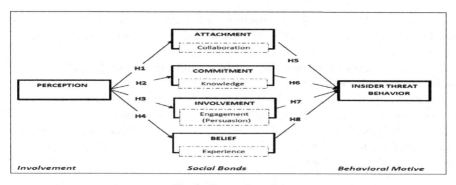

Fig. 2. Research model

communication between employees management, but they also improve the attachment of employees to the organisation (Velez and Neves 2017). Based on the above claims the following hypothesis is proposed:

H1: There is a positive relationship between employees' perception and attachment
Employees' commitment can be understood as psychological attachment to the organisation and it is crucial in determining whether an employee will remain with the organisation for a foreseeable future and at the same time work with other employees to achieve the organization's goals (Devece et al. 2016; Wombacher and Felfe 2017). Based on the perceived commitment of the employee to the organisation, the following hypothesis is proposed:

H2: There is a positive relationship between employees' perception and commitment
Employees' involvement is the opportunity given to employees to participate in the decisions that affect their organisation. This may be based on employees' task discretion and/or organizational participation (Markey and Townsend 2013). It enhances productivity and job satisfaction, encourages employees to provide private information to further the interest of their organisation, generates trust and a sense of control among the employees, and minimizes the resources required to monitor and implement policy compliance among employees. Based on these benefits, the following hypothesis is proposed:

H3: There is a positive relationship between employees' perception and involvement
Many factors shape an employee perception of belief. According to Javanmard (Javanmard 2012), religiosity is associated with unconcealed behaviours that employees may exercise and it is formally linked to institutions such as churches and temples. It is important also to note that employee beliefs and value systems are reflections of their different cultures (Buchtel 2014). Based on the above, the following hypothesis is proposed:

H4: There is a positive relationship between employees' perception and Belief
The attachment of employees to their organisations result in loyalty and loyal employees do their best to safeguard the interests of the organisation (Esmaeilpour and Ranjbar

2017). Given that employee that is attached to her supervisor, job, and organisation is less likely to display inside threat behaviours, the following hypothesis is proposed:

H5: There is a negative relationship between employees' level of attachment and insider threat behaviour

Committed employees are most likely to dedicate their energy and time to their career development and advancement and are unlikely to break rules and regulations that will ridicule and jeopardize their status. Therefore, employees that are more committed to their organisation are unlikely to commit insider threat attacks. Based on this, the following hypothesis is proposed:

H6: There is a negative relationship between employees' level of commitment and the insider threat behaviour

According to Hirschi (1969), an engaged employee that spent considerable energy and time in conventional activities will be occupied and have fewer times to spend on deviant acts. Thus, an individual that is actively involved in the organisation is less likely to commit insider threat attack. Therefore:

H7: There is a negative relationship between employees' level of involvement and the insider threat behaviour

Employees' beliefs, values and norms shape the way they perceive organisational issues and have a direct influence on their behaviour in the organisation including how they will comply with information security policies (Van der Werff and Science Steg 2016). According to Lee et al. (2004), employees with reasonable personal norms tend to conform to organisational information security behaviour. Therefore, the following hypothesis is proposed:

H8: There is a negative relationship between employees' level of belief and the insider threat behaviour

5   Research Methodology

Quantitative research method was identified as a suitable approach to collect data and to test hypotheses. A structured questionnaire was used and was considered as the ideal instrument that enabled a large amount of data to be collected from respondents' within a short period (Saris and Gallhofer 2014). Respondents were identified from the corporate sector through judgmental, non-probability sampling technique. Only outsourced employees were considered. This technique provides a reliable representative sample that presents an accurate result. This study follows Daniel's (2012) steps in selecting a sample. Firstly, a target population was identified. Secondly, the inclusion and exclusion criteria were used to select the sample. Thirdly, a plan was created to recruit and select the population elements. Fourthly, sample size was determined. Based on the recommendations of Daniel (2012), this study adopts a fixed approach where 155 questionnaires were administered. The questionnaire was designed to have an introduction section where respondents were made to understand the purpose and benefits of the study.

The approximate time of completion, ethical and privacy issues were also addressed in this section. The questionnaire consists of two major parts. The first part represented the biological information of respondents while the other part consisted of the main questions.

5.1 Data Collection

Data was collected from identified outsourced employees mostly in the field of banking, e-commerce, audit, and insurance. An appointment was booked with those employees that are interested to partake in the survey. To minimise the numbers of incomplete questionnaires, responses from each participant were reviewed as soon as a questionnaire is completed. Respondents were asked to respond to any omitted questions.

5.2 Demography

Demographic information of respondents as shown by Table 1 and shows that male participants account for 53% while female participants account for 47%. Over half the respondents were aged between 30 to 39 years with most having a bachelor or masters degree. A majority has less than 3 years' work experience. This suggested that their level of commitment was not strongly nurtured.

5.3 Analysis

Exploratory Factor analysis helps reduce measurable variables to a smaller latent variable that has a common variance (Pallant 2016). Exploratory factor analysis was used to determine the relationship between the subset of the study variables. Tabachnick and Fidell (2014) suggest a minimum sample size of 150 cases provided that the dataset has a high factor loading score above .08. A reverse scoring was checked collectively for all questions (items) to ensure that similar questions were asked. All components in the Component Matrix table (table excluded) were positive. In addition to correlation matric, Bartlett's test of Sphericity and Kaisers-Meyer- Olkin (KMO) also confirm the factorability of a dataset. The results have shown a Significant of ($p < .05$) for Bartlett's test of Sphericity and KMO index of .6 for all items.

The internal consistency indicator adopted in this study was the Cronbach alpha coefficient. The decision to use the Cronbach alpha coefficient was because it is suitable for multiple Likert scale questions (questionnaire) which were the research instrument favoured in this study (Pallant 2016). The researcher also ensures that Cronbach alpha coefficients is used to measure each construct. Pallant (2016) recommends a Cronbach alpha coefficient of .7 and above for a reliable scale. Cronbach alpha coefficients were calculated and reported for each construct separately. The Cronbach's Alpha values of .7 and above for each construct in this study suggest a good internal consistency of all the items that constitute the research instrument (questionnaire). Table 2 depicts the Cronbach Alpha coefficient of the study constructs.

Table 1. Participants' demography

Participants' demography

Measure	Items	Frequency	Percent
Gender distribution	Male	79	53%
	Female	71	47%
Age distribution	Younger than 20	1	1%
	20–29	45	30%
	30–39	78	52%
	40–49	23	15%
	50 and older	1	1%
Highest qualification level	Grade 12/O level or lower	10	7%
	Diploma or Certificate	24	16%
	Bachelor Degree(s)	72	48%
	Master's degree	42	28%
	Doctorate degree	2	1%
IT certification	Yes	74	49%
	No	76	51%
Years of IT experience	Less than 1 year	45	31%
	1–2 years	23	16%
	2–5 years	21	14%
	5–10 years	38	26%
	10–15 years	9	6%
	More than 15 years	9	6%

Table 2. Reliability test

Reliability test

Construct	Number of items	Cronbach's alpha
Perception of Organisation (POO)	5	.835
Attachment to Organisation (ATO)	5	.791
Commitment to Organisation (CTO)	5	.673
Involvement In Organisation (IIO)	5	.809
Belief (B)	5	.714
Insider Threat Behaviour (ITB)	10	.822

6   Testing the Model

Standard multiple regression was used to test the research hypotheses. The Correlation between outsourced employees' perception and outsourced employees' attachment, commitment, involvement, and belief were accessed. In the same vein, the correlation between insider threat behaviour and outsourced employees' attachment, commitment, involvement, and belief were assessed simultaneously using Pearson Correlation. All the p-values are less than .05 and suggest a correlation among the variables. Employees' attachment, employees' commitment, employees' involvement, and belief are jointly significant and explained.

50.3% of the variance in the employees' attachment is explained by employees' perception. Employees' perception was statistically significant to predict employees' attachment (beta = 709, Sig Value < 0.5). Therefore, the higher the perception of an employee, the higher the attachment to the organisation and vice versa. Therefore, hypothesis 1 is accepted. The contribution of Employees' perception to the prediction of Employees' commitment was also assessed. The beta coefficient of .453 and a sig value (less than .05) indicate that employees' perception makes a significant contribution to the prediction of employees' commitment. Based on the regression analysis test result for hypothesis 2, a positive perception of employees will result in reasonable commitment to the organisation. Therefore, hypothesis 2 is accepted.

The beta coefficient (.409) and the sig value (<.05) indicates that the employees' perception makes a significant contribution to the prediction of employees' involvement. The regression analysis for hypothesis 3 confirms a positive relationship between employees' perception and employees' involvement. Employees' are more involved in the organisation when their perception of the organisation is positive. Therefore, hypothesis 3 is accepted. The Pearson coefficient of .177 explains the weak correlation between employees' perception and employees' belief. Additionally, the r-square value (.031) indicates that 3% of the variance in the employees' belief is explained by the employees' perception while the p-value (sig. = .031). Henceforth hypothesis 4 is rejected. A positive or negative perception of employees' does not have any significant influence on their belief.

The contribution of attachment, commitment, involvement, and belief, individually to the prediction of insider threat behaviour suggests that belief makes the strongest contribution with a beta coefficient of .405. This was followed by employees' involvement with a beta coefficient of .182. However, employees' attachment and employees' commitment seemed to contribute insignificantly to explaining the threat behaviour with a Beta Coefficients of .136 and −.087 respectively. The significant value of belief and employees' involvement are less than .05 while the significant value of employees' attachment and commitment are greater than .05. Figure 2 below illustrates the result of the hypotheses test (Fig. 3).

If we have to make a prediction of threat behaviour and take into account employees' attachment, employees' commitment, employees' involvement and belief, employees' attachment and commitment are insignificant because they contribute little to the model. The most important factors of predicting threat behaviour are the level of employees' involvement in the organisation and their belief. Hypotheses 7 and 8 are accepted and hypotheses 5 and 6 are therefore rejected.

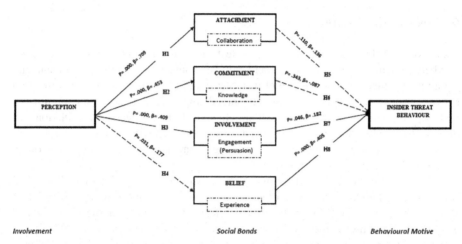

Fig. 3. Revisited model based on correlation and regression test and hypothesis

7   Contribution and Implication

Our findings have shown that the most important factors for predicting insider threat behaviour would include employees' involvement in the organization and their belief. This is important since involvement and belief as to be seen as a management and leadership philosophy and not necessarily a goal. Without enabling people, chances are that they will act contrary to the desired success of the organisation. Indeed some could act contrary to policy and to be deviant. In the discipline of Information Systems, this is crucial due to the need to protect these systems from threats of deviant acts. Organisations should try to engage outsourced employees by giving a sense of ownership and commitment for them to be positive co-contributors to organizational success. These findings have huge potential implications for management and business models as we have a global shortage of cybersecurity workers there is a lot of pressure to outsource this function- how do we fill the gap and yet provide security and reduce insider threats?

8   Conclusion

This study considered the potential threat that an outsourced employee could be to an organisation. The study focused on deviant behaviour as a potential source of this threat. Involvement theory and four elements of Social Bond Theory were examined. I demonstrate how the perception of employee shaped their attachment, commitment, involvement and belief to their organization. I further used these four elements to explain the bonds the employees would have with the organisation. I explained that the predisposition to be deviant will be determined by how strong these elements are present and how they shape the ties an outsourced employee has to an organisation. A theoretical model was developed to test this and the quantitative research methodology adopted. The work presents useful insights as to the outsourced employees' involvement and belief being strong determinants to predict deviance and therefore risk to information systems. I believe the work carried out would be useful in helping management foster an environment whereby properly motivated, involved, committed employees are they insourced or outsourced will help contribute to organisational goals.

9   Declaration of Replication Studies

The author declares that part of this paper has previously been published in a conference proceeding.

Acknowledgements. The author thanks Professor Alana Maurushat who provided valuable feedback during the preparation of this paper. Professor Alana Maurushat is Professor of Cybersecurity and Behaviour at Western Sydney University.

References

Aldawood, H., Skinner, G.: Reviewing cyber security social engineering training and awareness programs—pitfalls and ongoing issues. Future Internet **11**(3), 73 (2019)

AlHogail, A.: Design and validation of information security culture framework. Comput. Hum. Behav. **49**, 567–575 (2015)

Babu, B.M., Bhanu, M.S.: Prevention of insider attacks by integrating behaviour analysis with risk based access control model to protect cloud. Procedia Comput. Sci. **54**, 157–166 (2015)

Bamforth, R.: How to free your business and staff with self-service, computer weekly, pp. 16–19 (2015)

Bajkowski, J.: CBA Netbank app error causes mistaken multiple payments, iTnews (2019). https://www.itnews.com.au/news/cba-netbank-app-error-causes-mistaken-multiple-payments-530665. Accessed 6 Sept 2019

Baracaldo, N., Joshi, J.: An adaptive risk management and access control framework to mitigate insider threats. Comput. Secur. **39**, 237–254 (2013)

Borgese, A., Pascoe, N.: Outsourcing 2019—Laws and Regulations—Australia—ICLG. International Comparative Legal Guides International Business Reports. https://iclg.com/practice-areas/outsourcing-laws-and-regulations/australia. Accessed 1 Sept 2019

Breeden, J.: Are Careless Insiders the Biggest Federal Cyber Threat?. NextGov.com, USA (2017)

Buchtel, E.E.: Cultural sensitivity or cultural stereotyping? Positive and negative effects of a cultural psychology class. Int. J. Intercult. Relat. **39**, 40–52 (2014)

Daniel, J.: Sampling Essentials: Practical Guidelines for Making Sampling Choices. Sage, Los Angeles (2012)

Devece, C., Palacios-Marqués, D., Pilar Alguacil, M.: Organizational commitment and its effects on organizational citizenship behavior in a high-unemployment environment. J. Bus. Res. **69**(5), 1857–1861 (2016)

Dhillon, G., Syed, R., Pedron, C.: Interpreting information security culture: an organizational transformation case study. Comput. Secur. **56**, 63–69 (2016)

Dini, G., Lopriore, L.: Password systems: design and implementation. Comput. Electr. Eng. **47**, 318–326 (2015)

Eivazi, K.: Computer use monitoring and privacy at work. Comput. Law Secur. Rev. **27**(5), 516–523 (2011)

Esmaeilpour, M., Ranjbar, M.: Investigating the impact of commitment, satisfaction, and loyalty of employees on providing high-quality service to customer. Rom. Econ. Bus. Rev. **12**(1), 82–98 (2017)

Flores-Fillol, R., Iranzo, S., Mane, F.: Teamwork and delegation of decisions within the firm. Int. J. Ind. Organ. **52**, 1–29 (2017)

Hamilton, C., Coates, R., Heffernan, T.: What develops in visuo-spatial working memory development? Eur. J. Cogn. Psychol. **15**(1), 43–69 (2003)

HirschI, T.: Causes of Delinquency. University of California Press, Berkeley (1969)

Huang, C., Liu, J., Fang, Y., Zuo, Z.: A study on web security incidents in China by analyzing vulnerability disclosure platforms. Comput. Secur. **58**, 47–62 (2016)

Javanmard, H.: The impact of spirituality on work performance. Psychol. Relig. Spiritual. **6**(3), 175–187 (2012)

Kim, J., Park, E.H., Baskerville, R.L.: A model of emotion and computer abuse. Inf. Manag. **53**(1), 91–108 (2016)

Lee, S.M., Lee, S., Yoo, S.: An integrative model of computer abuse based on social control and general deterrence theories. Inf. Manag. **41**(6), 707–718 (2004)

Liu, C.: Feature: the enemy within: the inherent security risks of temporary staff. Comput. Fraud Secur. **2014**(5), 5–7 (2014)

Markey, R., Townsend, K.: Contemporary trends in employee involvement and participation. J. Ind. Relat. **55**(4), 475–487 (2013)

Pallant, J.: SPSS survival manual: a step by step guide to data analysis using IBM SPSS, 6th edn. Allen & Unwin, Sydney (2016)

Rocha Flores, W., Antonsen, E., Ekstedt, M.: Information security knowledge sharing in organizations: investigating the effect of behavioural information security governance and national culture. Comput. Secur. **43**, 90–110 (2014)

Roy Sarkar, K.: Assessing insider threats to information security using technical, behavioural and organisational measures. Inf. Secur. Tech. Rep. **15**(3), 112–133 (2010)

Saris, W.E., Gallhofer, I.N.: Design, Evaluation, and Analysis of Questionnaires for Survey Research, 2nd edn. Wiley, Hoboken (2014)

Schaefer, T., Brown, B., Graessle, F., Salzsieder, L.: Cybersecurity: common risks: a dynamic set of internal and external threats includes loss of data and revenue, sabotage at the hands of current or former employees, and a PR nightmare. Strateg. Finan. **99**(5), 54–61 (2017)

Tabachnick, B.G., Fidell, L.S.: Using Multivariate Statistics, 6th edn. Pearson Education, Harlow (2014)

Thompson, N.: What is Travis Hirschi's Social Control Theory? Enotes (2014). http://www.eno tes.com/homework-help/what-travis-hirschis-social-control-theory-196501. Accessed 16 June 2016

Van der werff, E., Science Steg, L.: The psychology of participation and interest in smart energy systems: comparing the value-belief-norm theory and the value-identity-personal norm model. Energy Res. Soc. **22**, 107–114 (2016)

Velez, M.J., Neves, P.: The relationship between abusive supervision, distributive justice and job satisfaction: a substitutes for leadership approach. Revue Europeenne de Psychologie Appliquee **67**(4), 187 (2017)

Von Solms, R., Von Solms, B.: From policies to culture. Comput. Secur. **23**(4), 275–279 (2004)

Wallbank, P.: The future of outsourcing. Theaustralian.com.au (2019). https://www.theaustralian.com.au/business/business-spectator/news-story/the-future-of-outsourcing/22a80aea41b2700fc209173dbc6d20d4. Accessed 1 Sept 2019

Exploring Effects of Auditory Stimuli on CAPTCHA Performance

Bruce Berg, Tyler Kaczmarek, Alfred Kobsa, and Gene Tsudik[✉]

UC Irvine, Irvine, USA
{bgberg,tkaczmar,kobsa,gtsudik}@uci.edu

Abstract. CAPTCHAs have been widely used as an anti-bot means for well over a decade. Unfortunately, they are often hard and annoying to use, and human errors have been blamed mainly on overly complex challenges, or poor challenge design. However, errors can also occur because of ambient sensory distractions, and performance impact of these distractions has not been thoroughly examined.

The goal of our work is to explore the impact of auditory distractions on CAPTCHA performance. To this end, we conducted a comprehensive user study. Its results, discussed in this paper, show that various types of auditory stimuli impact performance differently. Generally, simple and less dynamic stimuli sometimes improve subject performance, while highly dynamic stimuli have a negative impact. This is troublesome since CAPTCHAs are often used to protect web sites offering tickets for limited-quantity events, that sell out very quickly, i.e., within seconds. In such settings, introduction of even a small delay can make the difference between obtaining tickets from the primary source, and being forced to use a secondary market. Our study was conducted in a fully automated experimental environment to foster uniform and scalable experiments. We discuss both benefits and limitations of unattended automated experiment paradigm.

1 Introduction

Completely Automated Public Turing tests to tell Computers and Humans Apart (aka CAPTCHAs) are programs that generate and evaluate challenges that are easy solvable by a human, while hard to solve by software. CAPTCHAs have been used to prevent bot-based abuse of services for well over a decade [22]. They have become a fairly routine hurdle for users seeking to access online resources, such as: discussion forums, ticket sales, banking, and email account creation. Because of their widespread adoption, successful attacks, and pervasive dislike by users, most recent efforts in development have been invested into creating CAPTCHAs that are [3]: (1) usable: where humans are successful at least 90% of the time, (2) secure/robust: a state-of-the-art bot should not be successful more than 0.01% of the time, and (3) scalable: challenge are either automatically generated, or drawn a space that is too large to hard-code responses for each challenge. Consequently, CAPTCHA developers focused on text-based CAPTCHAs,

© Springer Nature Switzerland AG 2020
M. Bernhard et al. (Eds.): FC 2020 Workshops, LNCS 12063, pp. 149–165, 2020.
https://doi.org/10.1007/978-3-030-54455-3_11

i.e., those that present a jumbled alphanumeric code. This approach is popular since human users are quite good at identifying these alphanumeric codes in a distorted image, thus satisfying the usability requirement. Also, image segmentation and recovery known to be a hard problem for AI, satisfying the security requirement. Finally, such challenges can be randomly generated, satisfying the scalability requirement [8].

However, not much attention has been paid to user's physical context while solving CAPTCHAs. Security-critical tasks, such as CAPTCHAs, are often performed in noisy environments. In many real-world settings users are exposed to various sensory stimuli. Impact of such stimuli on performance and completion of security-critical tasks is not well understood. Any specific stimulus (e.g. police siren or fire alarm) can be incidental or malicious, i.e., introduced by the adversary that controls the environment. This threat is exacerbated and accentuated by the growth in popularity of Internet of Things (IoT) devices, particularly in contexts of "smart" homes or offices. As IoT devices become more common and more diverse, their eventual compromise becomes more realistic. One prominent example is the Mirai botnet [13] which used a huge number of infected smart cameras as zombies in a massive coordinated DDoS attack. A typical IoT-instrumented home environment, with "smart" lighting, sound and alarm systems (as well as appliances) represents a rich and attractive attack target for the adversary that aims to interfere with a user's physical environment in particular in order to inhibit successful CAPTCHA solving. We believe that this is especially relevant to some time-critical scenarios, such as web sites that sell limited numbers of coveted tickets for concerts, festivals, promotional airfares, etc. In these settings, a delay of just a few seconds can make a very big monetary difference.

In order to explore effects of attacks emanating from the user's physical environment we experimented with numerous subjects attempting to solve text-based CAPTCHAs in the presence of unexpected audio stimuli. We tested a total of 51 subjects in a fully unattended experimental setting. We initially hypothesized that introduction of audio stimuli would negatively impact subject task completion. While this was mostly confirmed, certain types of stimuli surprisingly demonstrated positive effects.

This paper is organized as follows: The next section describes the design and setup of our experiments are, followed by experimental results in Sect. 3. Next, we discuss the implications of the results and advantages of the unattended experimental environment. The paper concludes with directions for future work. Due to size limitations, we placed the following sections into the Appendix: (**A**) overview of related work and background material, (**B**) limitations of our study, and (**C**) ethical considerations.

2   Methodology

This section describes our experimental setup, procedures and subject parameters.

Apparatus: Our experimental setting was designed to allow for fully automated experiments with a wide range of sensory inputs. To accommodate this, we located the experiment in a dedicated office in the Psychology Department building of a large public university. The setup is comprised entirely of the following popular commercial-off-the-shelf (COTS) components: (1) Commodity Windows desktop computer with keyboard and mouse. (2) 19" Dell 1907FPc monitor, (3) Logitech C920 HD Webcam, and (4) Logitech Z200 Stereo Speaker System[1]. This experimental setup is supposed to mimic the typical environment where an average user might be presented with a CAPTCHA, i.e., an office.

Procedures: As mentioned earlier, the experimental environment was entirely unattended. An instructional PowerPoint presentation was used for subject instruction, instead of a live experimenter. This presentation was each subject's only source of information about the experiment. Actual experimenter involvement was limited to off-line activities: (1) periodic re-calibration of auditory stimuli, and (2) occasional repair or repositioning of some components that suffered minor damage or were moved throughout the study's lifetime. This unattended setup allowed the experiment to run without interruption 24/7/365. It was conducted over a 3-month period. The central goal was to measure performance of subjects attempting to solve as many CAPTCHAs as possible within a fixed timeframe. Subjects were expected to solve them continuously for 54 min. During this period, a subject was exposed to 4 rounds of 6 auditory stimuli. The control and stimuli were presented in a random order within each round, to mitigate any ordering effects on subject performance.

Why CAPTCHAs? We picked CAPTCHAs as the security-critical task for several reasons. First, CAPTCHAs do not require the subjects to enter any personally identifying information (PII) or secrets in order to solve them, and can be dynamically generated on the fly, allowing for the study of subject behavior across many different solution attempts. This is in contrast with other security-critical tasks, such as password entry. Second, solving CAPTCHAs is a fairly common task and it is reasonable to assume that all potential subjects are familiar with them, unlike infrequent tasks, e.g., Bluetooth pairing. Finally, the cognitive effort needed to solve CAPTCHAs (recognize-and-type) is higher than the simple comparison task in Bluetooth pairing, and is similar to recall-and-type tasks, such as password entry [20].

Phases: The experiment runs in four phases:

1. **Initial:** subject enters the office, sits down at a desktop computer and starts the instructional PowerPoint presentation. Duration: Negligible.
2. **Instruction:** subject is instructed in the nature of CAPTCHAs and the experimental procedure. Duration: 2–4 min
3. **CAPTCHA:** subject is presented with a random CAPTCHA. Upon submitting a solution, a new CAPTCHA is presented, regardless of the accuracy of the response. Subjects are exposed to the stimulus conditions for 24 rounds, each round lasting 2:15. Duration: 54 min.

---

[1] With the volume knob physically disabled.

4. Final: subject is taken to a survey page and asked to enter basic demographic information. Duration: 2–3 min

The entire experiment lasts between 58 and 61 min. Each subject's participation is recorded by the webcam and by screen-capturing software, to ensure compliance with the procedure. Since our objective is to assess overall impact of auditory stimuli on subject performance (and not performance degradation due to a surprise), the first 15 s of each stimulus condition were not used in data collection. This should accurately capture the enduring effect of the auditory stimuli, and ignore the spiking effect (i.e., surprise) on the attentional system due to the introduction of an unexpected stimulus [20].

2.1 CAPTCHA Generation

Since the study was concerned primarily with usability and less with robustness, we used text-based CAPTCHAs that follows the guidelines of [4] to create challenges that are highly usable, and can be quickly solved in bulk. To facilitate this, a challenge generation algorithm was selected that created 5-character alphanumeric codes with thin occluding global lines, a small amount of global distortion and minimal local distortion of the characters. This yielded challenges that our subjects could easily and quickly solve in the baseline, i.e., Control case.

2.2 Stimuli Selection

The experiment consisted of two categories of auditory stimuli: (1) static with single volume level, and (2) dynamic, that changed volume throughout presentation.

Static sound stimuli were the sounds of: (1) crying baby, (2) babbling brook, and (3) human voice reading individual letters and digits in random order at a rate of two per second. (1) and (2) were chosen for their ecological significance as a source that needs attention, and a relaxing sound, respectively. The human voice stimulus was chosen to interfere with the task-specific cognitive processes used to solve CAPTCHAs. This is analogous to the Stroop effect, a phenomenon where subjects who attempt to read the written name of a color that is rendered in a different color (e.g., the word "red" written in blue ink) do so slower and in a more error-prone way than reading the same words in plain black ink [15]. Specific volumes of the three static stimuli were:

(1) Crying baby: 78 dB, (2) Babbling brook: 70 dB, and (3) Human voice: 75 dB

The two dynamic stimuli included: (1) randomly generated looming sounds, and (2) randomly ordered menagerie of natural, aversive sounds. The looming stimulus was an amplitude modulated tone that increased from nearly silent to 85 dB over 5 s. Its intensity curve is shown in Fig. 1. Once the looming sound completed, it repeats at a different Left/Right speaker balance, selected randomly. This repeats continuously for the entire 2:15 min stimulus window. The natural stimulus consisted of a randomly generated sequence of aversive sounds, which included: circular saw cutting wood, blaring vuvuzela, nails on a chalkboard, and spinning helicopter rotors. These sounds were played at a randomly selected volume from 75 to 88 dB. Each lasted for up to 2 s before changing to the next random sound.

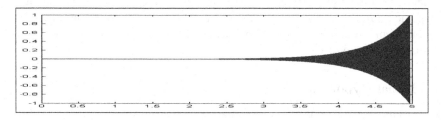

Fig. 1. Looming sound intensity function

Even the highest stimuli volume (88 dB) is well within the *safe range*, as defined by US Occupational Safety & Health Administration (OSHA) guidelines.[2]. Clearly, an adversary that controls the victim's environment would not be subjected to any such ethical guidelines, and could thus use much louder stimuli.

2.3 Psychophysical Description of Stimuli

The chosen stimuli have the potential to produce different effects. Except for the babbling brook, selection of the sounds was guided by the intent to elicit a negative emotional response and increased level of general arousal. It is reasonable to expect a negative impact of these sounds on task performance. However, any capture of an individual's attention by an aversive stimulus is likely to be momentary, occurring primarily when the stimulus is first introduced. In cognitive science, attention is conceptualized as a limited resource. Probably for good reason, the greatest demand on attention is in response to a change in the environment. Once an assessment is made that a stimulus does not require a response, adaptation to the stimulus from a foreground target into a background context proceeds relatively rapidly as attention is redistributed to other demands. Although an aversive sound may remain aversive throughout its presentation, its capacity to disrupt performance on a complex task might rapidly fade after onset. This could serve to sharpen an individual's focus for the task at hand [21].

However, the auditory attentional system is not nearly as adept at dealing with many rapid changes in the environment that occur in quick succession [1].

---

[2] OSHA requires all employers to implement a Hearing Conservation Program where workers are exposed to a time-weighted average noise level of 90 dB or higher over an 8 h work shift. Our noise levels were for a much lower duration, and only the very loudest was within the regulated range. See: https://www.osha.gov/SLTC/noisehearingconservation/.

Dynamic synthetic sounds can be designed to attract attention resources without being aversive. To the human auditory attention system, a looming sound is not easily classified as a single, non-threatening change in the environment. Instead, it embodies a context of continuous, approaching and potentially threatening change. This unclassifiable context "tricks" the system into a state of sustained engagement, and can deplete the subject's attentional resources. Because of this phenomenon, we suspect that highly dynamic sounds have the greatest impact on subject performance.

2.4   Initial Hypotheses

Our initial intuitive hypothesis was that introduction of unexpected auditory stimuli while solving CAPTCHAs would have negatively impact subject performance. We expected two outcomes, as compared to a distraction-free (Control) setting:

[H1]: Higher error rates, and
[H2]: Longer completion times in successful cases

We hypothesized this because, although mixed results were observed in [2] for Bluetooth pairing, solving CAPTCHAs is a more difficult cognitive task (requires more attention) even in the distraction-free (Control) case [21].

2.5   Recruitment

Recruitment was handled through the human subjects lab pool of Psychology Department at a large public university. A brief description of the study was posted on an online bulletin, and undergraduate students were allowed to sign up for the experiment and were compensated with course credit. Not surprisingly, the subject pool was dominated by college-age (18–25) individuals and the gender split was somewhat uneven: 35 female (69%) and 16 male subjects (31%).

3   Results

This section discusses the results, starting with data cleaning and proceeding to subject task completion effects.

Data Cleaning: A total of 58 subjects took part in the study. However, 7 of them were non-compliant with the experimental procedure, and prematurely quit the experiment. Since this behavior was captured by the recording software, all data from these subjects was discarded.

Task Failure Rate: As Table 1 shows, every audio stimulus – except for brook – had a substantial, statistically significant impact on subject failure rates. Furthermore, each of these was shown by their Odds ratios to have a large effect

Table 1. Subject failure rates

Stimulus	#Successful entries	#Unsuccessful entries	Failure rate	Odds ratio wrt control	p
None (Control)	6413	616	0.088	-	-
Baby	6074	1544	0.203	2.31	< 0.001
Brook	6332	574	0.083	0.901	0.090
Looming	5039	719	0.125	1.483	< 0.001
Natural	5787	723	0.111	1.299	< 0.001
Voice	4582	697	0.132	1.581	< 0.001
Total	34227	4873	0.125	-	-

Table 2. Avg times (sec) for successful solutions

Stimulus	Mean time	Standard deviation	DF wrt control	t-value wrt control	p	Cohen's D
None (Control)	4.621	3.771	-	-	-	-
Baby	4.520	5.267	12485	0.016	0.986	0.022
Brook	3.472	5.100	11743	15.026	< 0.001	0.400
Looming	6.092	2.212	11450	17.373	< 0.001	0.323
Natural	5.909	4.751	12198	18.505	< 0.001	0.300
Voice	6.480	6.985	10993	18.07	< 0.001	0.331

size. Thus, the impact on failure rates, though seemingly small, is a large proportional increase in failures when subjects are exposed to any stimulus, with the most impactful stimulus (crying baby) more than **doubling** subject failure rates. Interestingly, there was no direct correlation between dynamicity of the stimulus and its impact on failure rates, as the Brain Arousal Model would suggest [21]. This opens up a potential attack vector for the adversary that controls the auditory environment, as discussed in Sect. 4.

Task Completion Times: Table 2 shows average completion times for successful CAPTCHA completions under each stimulus. Results illustrate that all stimuli (except crying baby) have a statistically significant departure from the mean ($p < 0.001$) after applying a conservative Bonferroni correction to account for 5 pairwise comparisons to Control. However, while the looming, natural and voice stimuli have a negative effect on subject performance and slow down subject task completion, brook has a positive effect and lower average task completion times. Also, although these effects appear to be highly pronounced due to their significance, their effect size is small, with Cohen's D values ranging from 0.300 to 0.400. Implications of these impacts on task completion times are discussed in Sect. 4.

Table 3 shows a one-way analysis of variance (ANOVA) evaluation of differences in means of each stimulus, excluding Control. There is a significant difference ($p < 0.0001$) in completion times across different stimuli. Furthermore, Bartlett' test for homogeneity of variances was performed over each stimulus, again excluding Control. Bartlett's test rejected the null hypothesis that all distributions of completion times have the same variance ($\chi^2 = 5521.543$, $p < 0.0001$). These results assert that different stimuli influence subject task performance differently. This suggests that there are different aspects to the specific stimulus that can be altered to impact performance differently. Implications are discussed in the next section.

Figure 2 shows frequency distributions of response times by stimulus. They are similar to exponentially modified Gaussian distributions, consistent with reaction time distributions [24]. This is not unexpected, since subjects were

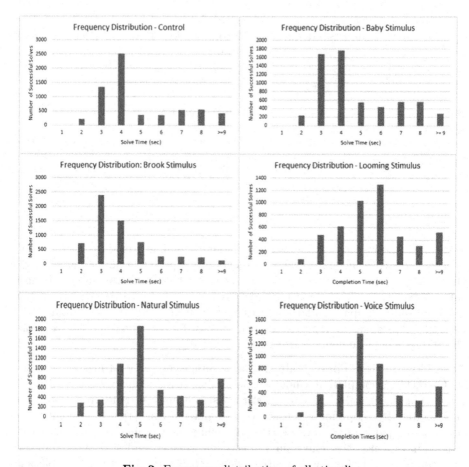

Fig. 2. Frequency distribution of all stimuli

instructed to solve CAPTCHAs as quickly and as accurately as they could. Although this correlation can help future studies into the cognitive task of completing text-based CAPTCHAs, it is out of the scope of this paper.

We note that the stimuli with the greatest impact on subject completion times have much heavier tails than other distributions. These correspond to the highly dynamic stimuli which also negatively impact subject failure rates. In particular, voice stands out because it is a task-specific stimulus; its exaggerated effect on subject performance is discussed below.

4   Discussion of Observed Effects

As results show, subjects solving CAPTCHAs are not uniformly impacted by different stimuli. We observed both positive and negative effects. More dynamic or task-specific stimuli (such as looming, voice and natural) negatively impact

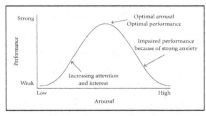

Fig. 3. Yerkes-Dodson relationship between sensory arousal levels & performance

Table 3. One-Way ANOVA between stimulus completion time distributions

Source of variation	Sum of squares	Degrees of freedom	Variance	F	p
Between groups	41601.39	4	10400.349	412.340	<0.0001
Within groups	676183.75	26809	25.22		
Total	717785.15	26813			

subject performance, while the simplest static stimulus (brook) had a positive effect. Interestingly, crying baby had a substantial negative effect on subject failure rates, though it did not significantly influence subject completion times.

The above is mostly consistent with the Yerkes-Dodson Law, which, states that a subject's overall level of sensory arousal is a determining factor in their performance at any task. At a low level of arousal, a subject is uninterested, and unengaged with the task at hand, and thus does not perform optimally. Similarly, an overstimulated subject is likely to have attention split between the arousing stimuli and the task at hand; thus performance suffers. However, there is a middle ground where a subject's overall arousal level allows being engaged with, yet not overwhelmed by, the task, thus yielding optimal performance. This relationship between sensory arousal and performance generally follows an upside-down U-shaped curve, as shown in Table 3 [7]. We now consider the implications of beneficial and negative observed effects.

Beneficial Effects: Only the babbling brook stimulus had a positive impact on subject failure rates and completion times.

Intuitively, our subjects were not highly engaged with the assigned task. Their general level of sensory arousal was similar to that of performing any boring/routine security-critical task. Because of this low level of initial engagement, the Yerkes-Dodson Law implies that introduction of additional stimulation can improve task performance. In our case, this resulted in increased speed of correct CAPTCHA completion under the babbling brook stimulus. This simple and static (yet relaxing) stimulus served to pique subject arousal without overwhelming their attentional resources.

The above illustrates the fine line between optimal sensory arousal and overstimulation. While our subjects might not have been sufficiently engaged with the task at hand, results imply that cognitive resources required to successfully solve CAPTCHAs as quickly as possible left little additional room for stimulation before the subject became overstimulated. However, this beneficial effect suggests that there must be a range of stimulation that can reliably improve performance. Thus, there could be a way for benign actors to incorporate sensory stimulation into security-critical tasks (such as CAPTCHAs) to push subjects along the Yerkes-Dodson curve towards a more beneficial level of sensory arousal, yielding better performance.

Negative Effects: Several types of auditory stimuli negatively impacted subjects' successful completion. However, collected data shows that this impact is not consistent across all stimuli. The negative effect may be tied to certain features of a particular stimulus. Instances of significant degradation in subject success rates were linked to dynamic sound stimuli, more than static ones. However, this comes with the noted exception of crying baby. While static, it had by far the greatest negative impact on subject failure rates. This could be related to the ecological significance of the sound of a crying baby. In turn, it might be that highly dynamic or aversive stimuli (e.g., Natural or Looming) are not necessarily the most effective adversarial stimuli, despite what the Yerkes-Dodson model asserts. Instead, ecologically-significant stimuli such as crying baby could be crafted for a specific victim population.

Negative impact on subject task completion rates under these conditions could pave the way for the adversary who controls the ambient soundscape. Through the use of specifically-crafted sounds with shifting intensity levels (or high ecological significance), the adversary could force a user into failing CAPTCHAs as a denial-of-service (DoS) attack. Moreover, not being limited by any ethical boundaries, the adversary can increase the volume far beyond OSHA-recommended safe levels. This would allow creation of even more dynamic stimuli and could push performance degradation beyond the doubling of errors we observed with the crying baby stimulus. Also, more dynamic stimuli impacted completion speed of successful subjects, slowing them down. The one-way ANOVA analysis we performed on stimuli distributions implies that different stimuli impact completion speeds differently. Furthermore, voice was the stimulus with the greatest impact on subject completion times. This is noteworthy because the task itself revolves around visual interpretation of letters and numbers.

It is reasonable to assume that subjects are confounded by the sensory crossfire of listening to random letters and numbers being read aloud while they try to read and write random letters and numbers. This is analogous to the Stroop effect, and implies that some features of the specific stimuli impact completion speeds differently [15]. The adversary can use the knowledge of the specific task to construct an optimal interfering stimulus.

The real threat of negative effects occurs when they are combined. CAPTCHAs are often used as a defense against the abuse of bots at point-of-sale of limited-quantity time-sensitive services, such as event tickets or travel flash sales. These limited commodities typically sell out completely, within seconds of availability [11]. Therefore, even a single CAPTCHA failure or a second-long delay, can cause a victim to totally miss out on a potentially important (to them) opportunity.

5   Unattended Setup Analysis

Advantages: The primary goal of our study was **not** to assess accuracy of the unattended experimental setup. However, results from the Control case are analogous to the attended experiment in [4] which used short alphanumeric CAPTCHAs with 1-px. global lines. Results obtained in the Control case for our experiment: mean solving time of 4.62 s and accuracy of 0.912 for a 5 character code are consistent with predictions in [4] for the same type of CAPTCHAs. This reinforces equivalence between unattended and attended experimental paradigms.

In general, unattended setups are very well-suited for completing rote, repetitive tasks, such as solving numerous CAPTCHAs. Since subject performance appears to be in-line in both paradigms, an unattended setup saves person-hours that are otherwise spent on logistics of scheduling and physically attending experiments. Moreover, there is no burden on the subject to adhere to a particular schedule, or a limited time-window, since the experiment can run 24/7/365. Furthermore, although it was not done in this case, the unattended paradigm allows for seamless, identical replication in multiple locations simultaneously, which is impossible in an attended manner. Finally, this paradigm entirely avoids experimenter bias: since no one is present during the experiment, there is no way to taint data collection by experimenter's actions.

Limitations: As mentioned earlier, some subjects were non-compliant and their data was discarded. This occurred despite clear instructions (during the initial phase) that CAPTCHAs had to be solved continuously for 54 min. Non-compliance is a basic limitation of the unattended setup: no one can enforce the rules in real-time[3].

Our setup did not capture fine-grained data about subjects' awareness of the stimuli. In the video recordings of some subjects, there is some evidence of them noticing the stimuli in obvious ways, such as making verbal remarks, or turning their heads towards the speakers. However, there is no firm evidence that shows any subject's failure to notice a given stimulus. Such information would be crucial for development of a realistic adversarial model.

The nattended setup might be both appropriate and useful for assessment of task performance, completion of questionnaires or any study that has subjects act in a fixed manner. However, it is not well-suited for adaptive data collection, e.g., what may be obtained in a loosely-structured interview. Also, since there is no on-site real-time interaction, every subject has an identical experience, which can cause the loss of corner-case data.

6   Conclusions and Future Work

As IoT-enabled sensory environments become more common, the threat of having to complete security-critical tasks in an adversary-controlled environment

---

[3] Although it would have been possible to detect non-compliance automatically, e.g., via an inactivity timeout, non-compliant subject data would still be discarded.

increases. This trend motivates studying the impact of external stimuli on performance of such tasks. Research described in this paper sheds some light on the impact of sensory stimulation on performance of security-critical tasks. However, there remain numerous outstanding issues and directions for future work:

- Our results highlight the threat of realistic distributed adversary that aims to induce extra errors and/or longer task completion. While this may not be seen as dire, due to the nature of CAPTCHAs, it opens up a worrisome attack vector for cognitively similar tasks. Notably, many systems implementing two-factor authentication use a similar challenge format to CAPTCHAs, with the distinction that challenges are sent to the user in plain text, instead of a distorted image. Replication of a similar experiment using more security-sensitive task (e.g., two-factor authentication) would point to a more obvious security threat. This would outline practical security concerns for emergent IoT-rich environments where the auditory environment could become adversary-owned.
- It is unclear whether our results can be generalized to non-text CAPTCHAs. Many popular CAPTCHA implementations utilize photographic images, such as Google's ReCAPTCHA, which asks users to identify numbers in pictures of address signs, or objects within regions of a picture (e.g. all regions of a large image that contain a car) [23]. Since recognition of objects within images is a different cognitive task than "deciphering" distorted text, it would be worthwhile to see if effects of unexpected auditory stimuli could be replicated with other CAPTCHA types.
- Finally, we intend to further explore the space of sensory stimuli's impact on performance of security-critical tasks. We aim to create a general framework of the Yerkes-Dodson relationship between sensory stimulation and user performance of arbitrary security-critical tasks. This framework would be instrumental in both detailing the potential threats of a hostile "smart" sensory environment and describing a set of best-practice for service providers that want to optimize usability for required security challenges.

A   A: Background and Related Work

This section overviews related work in automated experiments, and human-assisted security methods. We also provide psychological background theory related to effects of sensory arousal on subject task performance.

A.1   Automated Experiments

There has been a prior study focusing on effects of visual and auditory stimuli on completion of a specific security-critical task – Bluetooth pairing [2]. It showed that introduction of unexpected stimuli has a spectrum of beneficial and detrimental effects on subject performance. That initial result motivates a more thorough examination of the space of security-critical tasks, since Bluetooth pairing is a very simple (and infrequent) cognitive task that only requires a single button press to confirm matching codes [5].

Some prior work focused on evaluating virtually-attended remote experiments and unattended online surveys. in comparison with those conducted in the traditional lab setting. Ollesch et al. [16] collected psychometric data in a physically attended experimental lab setting and its virtually attended remote counterpart. No significant differences were found. This is further reinforced by Riva et al. [19] who compared data collected from unattended online, and attended offline, questionnaires. Finally, Lazem and Gracanin [14] replicated two classical social psychology experiments where both the participants and the experimenter were represented by avatars in Second Life[4], instead of being physically co-present. Here too, no significant differences were observed.

A.2   User Studies of Text-Based CAPTCHAs

Given ubiquity of CAPTCHAs, it is surprising that only a few usability studies have been conducted.

Chellapilla et al. [6] performed the first usability evaluation of CAPTCHAs, by examining character-based CAPTCHAs and evaluating Robustness/Usability tradeoffs. Results showed that sophisticated segmentation algorithms can violate robustness goals of popular, currently deployed text-based CAPTCHAs. However, service providers are hesitant to switch to more difficult CAPTCHAs for fear of low user acceptability.

Bursztein et al. [3] conducted a large-scale evaluation of user performance with several CAPTCHA schemes. Performance varied widely from scheme to scheme, with user's success rates ranging from 91% to 70%. This contradicted self-reported statistics, e.g., from Ebay, which claimed a 98% successful completion rate. Audio-only CAPTCHAs were found to be extremely difficult for most users, with success rates as low as 35%. This motivates guidelines for user-friendly text-based, and the need for further study of audio-only, CAPTCHAs.

Yan and El Ahmed [8] examine what makes CAPTCHAs usable, and nonintrusive. Color is identified as the primary culprit in intrusiveness, as clashing schema can interfere with presentation of the site itself. Furthermore, coloring a CAPTCHA lowers robustness, since it gives an easy target for segmentation, i.e., separating the image by color. Surprisingly, inclusion of color in a CAPTCHA is clamed to be a benefit for both usability and robustness if done correctly. However, what constitutes correct color usage is left as an open problem.

Khalil et al. examine the impact of alphabet familiarity on CAPTCHA performance using different character sets [12]. Familiarity with the alphabet used to construct a text-based CAPTCHA does not impact error rates. However, users' satisfaction is positively correlated with their familiarity level with the alphabet being used.

---

[4] See `secondlife.com`.

Burszstein et al. [4] paramaterized CAPTCHA features to find the most usable combination. This was done with particular focus on low-security CAPTCHAs that could sacrifice robustness and allow bots to achieve > 0.01% success rate. Subjects were found to prefer CAPTCHAs composed of English-language words with positive connotations (such as "cutest") with simple global distortions, and very few intersection or occluding lines. The study concluded with a candidate CAPTCHA design that showed a 95.4% success rate.

To date, there has been no evaluation of user performance with CAPTCHAs in a noisy environment.

A.3   Effects of Sensory Stimulation

Sensory stimulation has variable impact on task performance. This is due to many factors, including the subject's current level of arousal. The Yerkes-Dodson Law stipulates an inverse quadratic relationship between arousal and task performance [7]. It implies that, across all contributing stimulants, subjects who are either at a very low – or very high – level of arousal are unlikely to perform well, and there exists an optimal level of arousal for correct task completion.

An extension to this law is the notion that completion of less complex tasks that produce lower levels of initial arousal in subjects benefits from inclusion of external stimuli with low to medium arousal. At the same time, completion of complex tasks that produce a high level of initial arousal suffers from inclusion of external stimuli. Hockey [10] and Benignus et al. [1] classified this causal relationship by defining task complexity as a function of the task's event rate (i.e., how many subtasks must be completed in a given time-frame) and the number of sources that originate these subtasks. External stimulation can serve to sharpen the focus of a subject at a low arousal level, improving task performance [17]. Conversely, it can overload subjects that are already at a high level of arousal, and induce errors in task completion [9].

O'Malley and Poplawsky [18] argued that sensory noise affects behavioral selectivity. Specifically, while a consistent positive or negative effect on task completion may not occur, a consistent negative effect was observed for tasks that require subjects to react to signals on their periphery. Meanwhile, a consistent positive effect on task completion was observed for tasks that require subjects to react to signals in the center of their field of attention. This leads the authors to claim that sensory stimulation has the effect of narrowing the subject's area of attention.

B   B: Study Shortcomings

This section discusses some shortcomings of the study.

Homogeneous Subjects: Our subject group was comprised of young and tech-savvy college students. This is a consequence of the experiment's location and recruitment methods. Replication of this experiment in a non-academic setting would be useful. However, recruiting an appropriately diverse set of subjects is still difficult, even in a public setting. Ideal venues might be stadiums, concert halls, fairgrounds or shopping malls. Unfortunately, deployment of the unattended setup in such public locations is logistically infeasible. Since such public areas are already full of other sensory stimuli, reliable adjustment of subjects' arousal level in a consistent manner would be very hard. Furthermore, it would be very difficult to secure expensive experimental equipment.

Synthetic Environment: Even though we attempted to provide a realistic environment for CAPTCHAs, our setup was obviously a contrived, artificial and controlled space. Typically, people encounter CAPTCHAs while using their own devices from their own homes or offices. As such, it would be intuitive to conduct a study remotely over the Internet. However, this would introduce many compounding and potentially dangerous variables. First, there would be no way of knowing ahead of time the exact nature of the potential subjects' auditory environment. This could lead to complications ranging from the trivial nullification of collected data (e.g., if subject's audio-out is muted) all the way to potential hurting subject's auditory faculties (e.g., in-ear headphones turned to a dangerously high volume).

This further complicates measurement of any effects of auditory stimuli, as it becomes unclear if any two subjects encounter the stimuli the same way. For example, a subject using headphones at a high volume is going to have a drastically different experience than a subject using speakers at a low volume. These differences will confound the actual impact of the stimuli, making it extremely difficult to quantify any meaningful effect on task performance. Because of the need of homogeneity in presentation of the stimuli, it is easy to see how such an online experiment would be ineffective in practice.

C   C: Ethical Consideration

Experiments described in this paper were fully authorized by the Institutional Review Board (IRB) of the university, well before the study. The level of review was: Exempt, Category II. Further IRB-related details are available upon request. No sensitive data was harvested during the experiments and minimal identifying information was retained. In particular:

1. No names, addresses, phone numbers or other identifying information was collected from the participants.
2. Although email addresses were solicited in order to confirm participation, they were erased very soon thereafter.
3. Video recordings of the experiments were kept for study integrity purposes. However, they were erased before the IRB expiration time.

Finally, with regard to safety, sound levels were maintained at between 70 and 88 dB, which is (especially, for only 2:15 min) generally considered safe.

References

1. Benignus, V.A., Otto, D.A., Knelson, J.H.: Effect of low-frequency random noises on performance of a numeric monitoring task. Percept. Motor Skills **40**(1), 231–239 (1975)
2. Berg, B.G., Kaczmarek, T., Kobsa, A., Tsudik, G.: An exploration of the effects of sensory stimuli on the completion of security tasks. IEEE Secur. Privacy **15**(6), 52–60 (2017)
3. Bursztein, E., Bethard, S., Fabry, C., Mitchell, J.C., Jurafsky, D.: How good are humans at solving captchas? A large scale evaluation. In: 2010 IEEE Symposium on Security and Privacy (SP), pp. 399–413. IEEE (2010)
4. Bursztein, E., Moscicki, A., Fabry, C., Bethard, S., Mitchell, J.C., Jurafsky, D.: Easy does it: more usable captchas. In: Proceedings of the 32nd Annual ACM Conference on Human Factors in Computing Systems, pp. 2637–2646. ACM (2014)
5. Chang, R., Shmatikov, V.: Formal analysis of authentication in Bluetooth device pairing. In: FCS-ARSPA 2007, p. 45 (2007)
6. Chellapilla, K., Larson, K., Simard, P., Czerwinski, M.: Designing human friendly human interaction proofs (HIPS). In: Proceedings of the SIGCHI Conference on Human Factors in Computing Systems, pp. 711–720. ACM (2005)
7. Cohen, R.A.: Yerkes-Dodson law. In: Kreutzer, J.S., DeLuca, J., Caplan, B. (eds.) Encyclopedia of Clinical Neuropsychology, pp. 2737–2738. Springer, Heidelberg (2011)
8. El Ahmad, A.S., Yan, J., Ng, W.-Y.: Captcha design: color, usability, and security. IEEE Internet Comput. **16**(2), 44–51 (2012)
9. Harris, W.: Stress and perception: the effects of intense noise stimulation and noxious stimulation upon perceptual performance. Ph.D. thesis, University of Southern California (1960)
10. Hockey, G.R.J.: Effect of loud noise on attentional selectivity. Q. J. Exp. Psychol. **22**(1), 28–36 (1970)
11. Kaiser, E., Feng, W.-C.: Helping ticketmaster: changing the economics of ticket robots with geographic proof-of-work. In: INFOCOM IEEE Conference on Computer Communications Workshops, pp. 1–6. IEEE (2010)
12. Khalil, A., Abdallah, S., Ahmed, S., Hajjdiab, H.: Script familiarity and its effect on CAPTCHA usability: an experiment with Arab participants. Int. J. Web Portals (IJWP) **4**(2), 74–87 (2012)
13. Kolias, C., Kambourakis, G., Stavrou, A., Voas, J.: DDoS in the IoT: Mirai and other botnets. Computer **50**(7), 80–84 (2017)
14. Lazem, S., Gracanin, D.: Social traps in second life. In: 2010 Second International Conference on Games and Virtual Worlds for Serious Applications (VS-GAMES), pp. 133–140, March 2010
15. MacLeod, C.M.: Half a century of research on the stroop effect: an integrative review. Psychol. Bull. **109**(2), 163 (1991)
16. Ollesch, H., Heineken, E., Schulte, F.P.: Physical or virtual presence of the experimenter: psychological online-experiments in different settings. Int. J. Internet Sci. **1**(1), 71–81 (2006)
17. Olmedo, E.L., Kirk, R.E.: Maintenance of vigilance by non-task-related stimulation in the monitoring environment. Percept. Motor Skills **44**(3), 715–723 (1977)
18. O'Malley, J.J., Poplawsky, A.: Noise-induced arousal and breadth of attention. Percept. Motor Skills **33**(3), 887–890 (1971)

19. Riva, G., Teruzzi, T., Anolli, L.: The use of the internet in psychological research: comparison of online and offline questionnaires. CyberPsychol. Behav. **6**(1), 73–80 (2003)
20. Rogers, R.D., Monsell, S.: Costs of a predictible switch between simple cognitive tasks. J. Exp. Psychol.: General **124**(2), 207 (1995)
21. Söderlund, G., et al.: Positive effects of noise on cognitive performance: explaining the moderate brain arousal model. In: The 9th Congress of the International Commisssion on the Biological Effects of Noise, Leibniz Gemeinschaft, pp. 378–386 (2008)
22. Von Ahn, L., Blum, M., Hopper, N.J., Langford, J.: Captcha: using hard AI problems for security. In: International Conference on the Theory and Applications of Cryptographic Techniques, pp. 294–311. Springer, Heidelberg (2003)
23. Von Ahn, L., Maurer, B., McMillen, C., Abraham, D., Blum, M.: reCAPTCHA: human-based character recognition via web security measures. Science **321**(5895), 1465–1468 (2008)
24. Whelan, R.: Effective analysis of reaction time data. Psychol. Rec. **58**(3), 475–482 (2008)

PassPage: Graphical Password Authentication Scheme Based on Web Browsing Records

Xian Chu, Huiping Sun[✉], and Zhong Chen

School of Software and Microelectronics, Peking University, Beijing, China
xavierchu@pku.edu.cn, {sunhp,chen}@ss.pku.edu.cn

Abstract. This paper proposes a two-factor graphical password authentication scheme, PassPage, which is suitable for website authentication with enhanced security. It leverages the implicit memory based on the user's web browsing records. Whenever the user tries to log in, the server returns 9 small pages as a challenge, and asks the user to select all the pages the user has browsed besides inputting a text password. We performed user experiments on 12 volunteers. The experiment results showed that the average login success rate on a news website is steadily over 80% when the users are familiar with the login process, and the login success rate does not decrease sharply in 6 days.

Keywords: PassPage · Authentication · Two-factor authentication · Graphical password · Implicit memory

1 Introduction

Currently, most websites still use username and text password as a basic user authentication. Using only a text password is not safe, since the length and strength of text passwords that users can remember are limited, and they could be obtained by hackers using guessing attacks, shoulder surfing attacks, dictionary cracking attacks, or other attacks. Some websites use dynamic codes via phone messages or emails as a supplementary authentication. This kind of two-factor authentication is most successful, but it relies much on other devices or accounts, and it takes much time for users to receive the codes and input them. Graphical password authentication can be another alternative authentication factor which is more user-friendly. However, most existing graphical password authentication schemes cannot get rid of setting and remembering secrets. They put much memory burden on users if used on multiple websites.

We aim to propose a new authentication scheme which does not put more operation burden or memory burden on users. Our idea is to utilize the user's knowledge related to the website. It should be remembered naturally by the user when the user browses web pages. It should have a high entropy too. On many websites, including news sites, social networking sites, video sites, forums and blogs, the pages the user browses meet our needs.

In this scheme, the website leverages page scripts to record the user's browsing history automatically and the website server saves it for a period of time. Whenever the

© Springer Nature Switzerland AG 2020
M. Bernhard et al. (Eds.): FC 2020 Workshops, LNCS 12063, pp. 166–176, 2020.
https://doi.org/10.1007/978-3-030-54455-3_12

user tries to log in, the server returns 9 small pages as a challenge, and the user needs to select all the pages he or she has visited. Besides, the user needs to input a text password, which is served as another factor. This kind of two-factor authentication scheme is more secure than traditional text password authentication scheme while not increasing much memory burden. We call this scheme PassPage because the graphical passwords are taken from web pages and displayed as web pages.

In order to test the usage performance of PassPage, we developed an experimental authentication system and conducted user experiments on 12 volunteers. We developed the Chrome browser extension to record users' browsing history automatically, and wrote simulated sign-up page, login page and reset password page, so that all experimental data is sent to our experimental server, without bringing any change to the source codes of actual websites. The results showed that the average login success rate on a news website is steadily over 80% when the users are familiar with the authentication process, and the login success rate does not decrease sharply in 6 days.

2   Related Work

Our work mainly deals with two-factor authentication, combining text password authentication with graphical password authentication. There have been numerous researches working on graphical password authentication [1–13], including recall-based mode and recognition-based mode. Some researchers proposed novel graphical authentication schemes [2, 3, 6, 8, 10]. Some researchers worked on enhancing security of graphical authentication [7–9, 12, 13], especially resisting shoulder surfing attacks.

In order to enhance the security of graphical password authentication, users have to remember high-entropy secrets. But we do not intend to put more burdens on users' memorability. Thus, the proposed graphical authentication scheme is based on implicit memory. There have been some researches talking about authentication based on implicit memories [14–18].

Tamara Denning et al. first proposed the idea of implicit memory for authentication [14]. The author believes that a good implicit memory authentication scheme needs to meet the following conditions: the secret can remain in the brain for a long time; the registration process and authentication process do not require the user to remember something purposely; the secret is random and has a high entropy; the process of forming the memory and the process of authentication are different. The authors proposed an implementation, but the experiment did not perform very well: the correct rate of users who have seen the complete graphics is only 7% higher than those of users who have not seen the complete graphics. Also, this scheme consumes much time for users to study it.

Sauvik Das et al. conducted a detailed investigation and analysis of people's daily memory [15]. Among the 2,167 daily problems coming from mobile phone data, only 1381 problems (about 64%) were answered correctly by the experimental users, most of which are recognition problems, and the correct rate is not affected by time. According to the survey, users' answers to social-related issues (such as calls and text messages) are much more accurate than those related to mobile phones usage (such as usage time and duration). The downside is that the authentication takes too long, on average more than one minute, so it only works when password authentication is not working properly.

The PassApp proposed by Huiping Sun et al. built a mobile phone unlocking system based on users' familiarity with the applications installed on their mobile phones [16]. The system randomly selects 4 apps installed on the phone and 12 apps not installed, and puts the icons of these 16 apps together in a random order. Users need to select the icons of all 4 installed apps to unlock the phone. This system works well for ease of use and security. On average, testers can remember 89% of their applications on their phones, with a success rate of 95%. However, this scheme can only be used on mobile phone unlocking.

The PassFrame proposed by Ngu Nguyen et al. uses a wearable miniature camera to record anything the users see in their daily lives [17]. When user authentication is required, some images are taken from the video for the user to select or sort. It is a flexible authentication scheme using implicit memory, which confirms the possibility that what users have seen can be used as passwords. But it is not practical as it is extremely privacy invasive.

The LEPs proposed by Simon Woo et al. is a textual password for asking questions about life experiences [18]. Users need to pre-set some facts about life experience, including birth, party, graduation, wedding, travelling and other aspects, and enter the answer to the question in text when logging in. The system authenticates the user through fuzzy matching. LEPs are 30–47 bits stronger than traditional 8-character passwords. Force attacks and dictionary attacks are almost ineffective, and the possibility of being guessed by friends are only 0.7%.

All these schemes utilizing implicit memory do not utilize the user's knowledge related to the website. Unlike these schemes, PassPage is suitable to be used for website authentication, and the secret pool keeps growing when the user is browsing.

3   Design of PassPage

PassPage mainly consists of four system modules: the sign-up module, the browsing history recording module, the decoy web pages maintenance module, and the login module. The order relation of them is shown in Fig. 1.

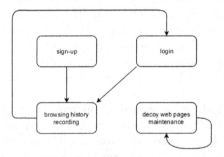

Fig. 1. Order relation of system modules

3.1 Sign-up Module

The user submits the email address, username and password to sign up an account. The email address is necessary in case the user forgets the secrets. The information is sent to the server. If the information is legitimate, the server saves it into the database and returns a session to the client. Then the client automatically logs in to the website.

3.2 Browsing History Recording Module

Once the user logs in to the website, the browsing history recording module starts to work. There is a client script automatically running when the page is open. The script identifies the user by checking the session, and then records the user's browsing history. Some pages with high click rates and low recognition rates (such as the homepage and website information pages) are not recorded. If the page needs to be recorded, the script uploads its HTML content as well as the username to the server. The server saves the HTML content in a file with a random file name, and then stores the username and the file name in the user page database. After that, the file name is returned to the client.

Besides, if the page needs to be recorded, the script keeps recording the time of the user staying between scrollings in the page. When the user closes the page, the script sends the file name and the time array to the server. The server saves the total browsing time, the total scrolling count and the time array in the user page database.

3.3 Decoy Web Pages Maintenance Module

Since the server should return a challenge consisting of correct pages and decoy pages when the user logs in, the server must maintain a decoy web page database. The server should have access to all the pages on the website. It must request web pages once every day and save them in the decoy page database. The topics of pages should be as diverse as possible, but pages with high click rate and low recognition rate should not be saved. The server saves the pages in HTML files and stores file name, title, and adding time of each web page in the database.

If the number of decoy pages increases too fast, old decoy pages can be deleted at regular time. Assuming that 500 new decoy pages are added every day, then the server find out the pages added 3 days ago but no longer than 10 days ago from the database, and randomly delete half of them. In this way, the number of old decoy pages will gradually decrease, but will not reach zero. There is a high possibility that several pages will retain permanently. The reason why the long-lasting web pages are not removed completely is that the server should return decoy pages with adding times close to those of correct pages when the user attempts to log in, so the long-time non-login user can see decoy web pages added long time ago. The page selection algorithm is described in the next section.

3.4 Login Module

The user inputs the registered username and password, and then clicks 'next step' button. The lower layer will display 9 small pages in 3*3 format. The user can scroll the lower

Fig. 2. One implement of login page (after clicking 'next step')

layer up and down. Figure 2 is one implement of login page. The small pages might be transformed beforehand.

The user must select all the visited pages from the 9 pages by clicking on them. After selecting all the visited pages, the user can log in. If the graphical authentication is passed and the password is correct, the login is successful. If the login fails, the user can select the pages again or change them by clicking the 'change' button. Each user is given only three chances to log in. If the user still attempts to log in after failing three times, the server refuses it and the user has to reset the password through email authentication.

After the user clicks 'next step' button, the client first sends the username and the password to the server. Only if the password authentication is passed, the graphical authentication could start. The client sends the username to the server. The server returns the file names of 9 web pages (see Page Selection Algorithm), and then the client requests 9 HTML files from the server according to the file names. These 9 web pages consist of pages which have been visited by the user (called real pages) and pages which have never been visited by the user (called decoy pages), and the client will display them. When the user clicks 'login', the client sends the username and the file names of all selected pages to the server. If the authentication is passed, the server returns a session to the client.

Page Selection Algorithm. First, the server selects all the pages the user visited and puts them into the *allRealPages* set, including the file names, the titles, browsing logs and adding time, and gets the size of the set. If $size = 0$, the graphical authentication is invalid and the email authentication has to be used. If $1 <= size <= 5$, the server randomly selects 1–2 page(s) from *allRealPages* as the real pages. If $size >= 6$, it randomly selects

3 pages from *allRealPages* as the real pages. The server should select real pages which are more likely to be remembered and recognized by the user. After that, the server takes out decoy pages from the decoy page database, ensuring that the titles of selected decoy pages are different from those in *allRealPages*, and the adding times of selected decoy pages are close to those of real pages. The server takes out 9 pages in total. All the pages are loaded from HTML files, which means the size of each page is only about 1 KB and all 9 pages can be loaded in a moment.

In order to prevent the adversary from constantly changing pages to find out the recurring real web pages, the server requires each user to log in before changing pages again. Based on this, the number of consecutive login failures of the user is limited. If the user fails for 3 times consecutively, the account will be locked and can only be restored by resetting the graphical password.

4   User Experiments

4.1   Experiment Procedure

In order to test the usage performance of PassPage, we developed an experimental authentication system. We developed the server using Java and wrote pages and Chrome browser extension using HTML, CSS and JS. The pages are simulated sign-up page, login page and reset password page. The Chrome browser extension is used to record users' browsing history. We chose the news website www.sohu.com for test. All the experimental data is sent to our experimental server, without bringing any change to the source code of the actual website.

We sent a recruitment invitation in online chatting groups. Everyone could join our experiments regardless of age, sex, major or computer skill as long as he or she would have 10 min of free time in successive 6 days. Anyone interested is invited to sign on an experiment agreement. Finally, we received agreements from 23 volunteers. Their ages are between 19 and 29. About half of them major in computer science or software engineering.

We wrote a detailed experiment guide on a web page, so that volunteers could follow it and do the experiment by themselves. On the first day, they downloaded and installed our extension in their Chrome browsers. Then they opened the simulated sign-up page, and registered test accounts. After that, they browsed the pages in www.sohu.com for several minutes. From the second day to the sixth day, they opened the simulated login pages and tried to log in with their test accounts. Everyone was asked to log in for 5 times every day. After that, they browsed the pages in www.sohu.com for several minutes. All the login processes were recorded by the system.

After completing the whole experiment, every volunteer filled in a feedback table, which contains seven statements about user experience. Every statement is followed by five levels of consent. Every volunteer chose one level of consent as a score for every statement.

Finally, nine volunteers completed their experiments. Each of them was paid 50 Chinese yuan as a reward. Three volunteers only completed part of their experiments. Each of them was paid 10 Chinese yuan.

4.2 Experiment Results

The volunteers performed 277 login trials in total. We first calculated the accuracy rates of text passwords and the success rates of logins for volunteers with more than 5 logins. The success of the two-factor authentication, requiring both the accuracy of text password and the success of graphical authentication, is regarded as the success of login.

As is shown in Table 1, the login success rates varied a lot on different volunteers. The login success rates of 4 volunteers are over 90% while those of 2 volunteers are not more than 50%. Through our investigation, User 6 did not notice that the number of real pages was always 3 and he chose 1 or 2 page(s) for several times, so his login success rate is only 50%. User 11 was so careless that he forgot his text password and inputted wrong password for many times, so his login success rate is only 29.2%.

Table 1. Password accuracy rates and login success rates

User ID	Total login count	Password accuracy rate	Login success rate
1	27	100.0%	63.0%
2	30	100.0%	93.3%
3	33	100.0%	93.9%
4	26	100.0%	96.2%
5	27	100.0%	77.8%
6	10	100.0%	50.0%
9	20	100.0%	85.0%
10	33	100.0%	93.9%
11	24	41.7%	29.2%
12	35	82.9%	68.6%

We also calculated the average used time of inputting usernames and passwords as well as the average total used time of logins.

As is shown in Table 2, the average total used time of logins is about four times than that of inputting usernames and passwords. The average time consumed for graphical authentication is 20 s. Compared with other graphical authentication schemes and the dynamic code authentication scheme, it is a reasonable value, though.

Table 2. Comparison between average used time of two authentication schemes

Average used time of inputting usernames and passwords	Average total used time of logins
7.519 s	27.120 s

Then we calculated the success rates of graphical authentication as the interval between sign-up and login increasing. We grouped the login records by the interval between sign-up and login (called login interval), setting 24 h as one day, and got the results in Table 3.

Table 3. Graphical authentication success rates by login interval

Login interval (day)	Password accuracy count	Login success count	Graphical authentication success rate
1	39	25	64.10%
2	47	37	78.72%
3	45	38	84.44%
4	44	40	90.91%
5	51	46	90.20%
6	31	27	87.10%

As we can see in Table 3, the success rate of the first day was abnormally low. It might be caused by the volunteers' unacquaintance with this scheme. From the third day to the sixth day, the graphical authentication success rate was steadily above 80%. We can infer that users can remember most of the web pages they visited in 6 days. We also calculated the success rates of graphical authentication as the number of real pages increasing. The result is that the success rate is still 88.89% when the number of real pages grows to 35–40.

In addition, we calculated the average staying time and the average scrolling count of recalled real pages and missed real pages. The staying time of a real page is the total time during which the page keeps open on the foreground. The scrolling count of a real page is the total count of the user scrolling the page. The results are shown in Table 4. We can conclude that it's easier for users to recall pages on which they stayed for longer time and scrolled for more times.

Table 4. Average staying time and scrolling count of recalled real pages and missed real pages

Page type	Staying time	Scrolling count
Recalled pages	23.178 s	5.56
Missed pages	14.842 s	4.97

At last, we collected the answers of feedback tables. The average score of every statement is shown in Table 5.

We find that our volunteers hold positive views in general. Most volunteers think the login success rate of this scheme is acceptable, and it is not hard to use it.

Table 5. Average score of every statement

Index	Statement	Average score
1	I'd like to use this scheme	3.4
2	I think this scheme takes up lots of memory	3.4
3	I think this scheme is very annoying	2.6
4	I think this scheme is hard to use	2.3
5	I think the login success rate of this scheme is acceptable	4.1
6	I think there are big problems with this scheme	3.0
7	I think this scheme can be used widely	3.5

5   Widespread Use of PassPage

We developed the experiment system only for the news site www.sohu.com on PC browser. There remains much to do for widespread use on multiple websites and multiple platforms.

5.1   PassPage on Multiple Websites

PassPage can be used on multiple websites, but it should be modified for specific web-sites. The most important matter is to find out high-entropy knowledge for every user on every website. For instance, on a shopping website, it may be the goods the user bought or watched in detail. On a social networking website, it may be the posted photos or videos the user watched. On a job website, it may be the jobs the user applied for. On a bank website, it may be the financing products the user bought. These kinds of information are implicit memories that can be transformed to passwords in pages.

In fact, PassPage cannot be used on all websites, and will be less effective or success-ful in certain websites. But it is still an optional authentication factor on most websites if the difficulty of authentication is reduced.

5.2   PassPass on Multiple Platforms

PassPage can be used on multiple platforms too. Since the browsing records are bound with username and stored in the server, the user can log in on any platform such as PC browser, tablet software or phone APP. The website developers need to enable their software or APP to record users' browsing history on these platforms. They also need to develop suitable login interfaces for different platforms.

6   Security and Privacy

Our scheme enhances the security of password authentication. Let's just focus on the security of the graphical password authentication. Assume that an adversary already knows a username and the corresponding password, and he tries to log in to the user's account through graphical authentication. The adversary only knows the number of real pages is among 1–3. There is no other clue for the adversary to pass the graphical authentication easily. So he randomly selects 1–3 pages with $C(9, 1) + C(9, 2) + C(9, 3) = 129$ choices, but only one choice is correct, so the possibility he makes a correct choice is only $1/129 \approx 0.775\%$.

For the sake of privacy, the website must come to an agreement with users in advance so that the browsing records can be collected legally. It should be ensured that only the website server has access to these records. Furthermore, users' browsing records should be encrypted or partly encrypted in the server database.

7   Conclusion and Future Work

This paper proposes a two-factor graphical password authentication scheme, PassPage, which is suitable to be used on website accounts. It leverages users' implicit memories of browsing web pages. The experiment results showed that the average login success rate on a news website is steadily over 80% when the users are familiar with the login process, while an adversary with a random selection only has 0.775% possibility to pass the graphical authentication, not to mention that the adversary has to input an accurate password. Our experiments also showed the login success rate does not decrease sharply in 6 days. It can be concluded that this scheme integrates usability, efficiency and security.

In future work, we will study more about user behaviors of browsing web pages so that the graphical authentication challenge can be more favorable for users. For example, the server should find out pages which are more likely to be remembered and recognized by the user. Besides, the login process still needs to be optimized to increase the login success rate.

References

1. Robert, B., Chiasson, S., Van Oorschot, P.C.: Graphical passwords: learning from the first twelve years. ACM Comput. Surv. (CSUR) **44**(4), 19 (2012)
2. Brostoff, S., Sasse, M.A.: Are passfaces more usable than passwords? A field trial investigation. In: McDonald, S., Waern, Y., Cockton, G. (eds.) People and Computers XIV—Usability or Else!, pp. 405–424. Springer, London (2000). https://doi.org/10.1007/978-1-4471-0515-2_27
3. Bianchi, A., Oakley, I., Kim, H.: PassBYOP: bring your own picture for securing graphical passwords. IEEE Trans. Hum.-Mach. Syst. **46**(3), 380–389 (2015)
4. Uellenbeck, S., et al.: Quantifying the security of graphical passwords: the case of Android unlock patterns. In: Proceedings of the 2013 ACM SIGSAC Conference on Computer & Communications Security. ACM (2013)
5. Stobert, E., Biddle, R.: Memory retrieval and graphical passwords. In: Proceedings of the Ninth Symposium on Usable Privacy and Security. ACM (2013)
6. Zhu, B.B., et al.: CAPTCHA as graphical passwords—a new security primitive based on hard AI problems. IEEE Trans. Inf. Forensics Secur. **9**(6), 891–904 (2014)
7. Gao, H., et al.: A survey on the use of graphical passwords in security. JSW **8**(7), 1678–1698 (2013)

8. Rao, K., Yalamanchili, S.: Novel shoulder-surfing resistant authentication schemes using text-graphical passwords. Int. J. Inf. Netw. Secur. **1**(3), 163 (2012)
9. Renaud, K., et al.: Are graphical authentication mechanisms as strong as passwords?. In: 2013 Federated Conference on Computer Science and Information Systems. IEEE (2013)
10. Khan, M.A., et al.: g-RAT—a novel graphical randomized authentication technique for consumer smart devices. IEEE Trans. Consum. Electron. **65**(2), 215–223 (2019)
11. Mackie, I., Yıldırım, M.: A novel hybrid password authentication scheme based on text and image. In: Kerschbaum, F., Paraboschi, S. (eds.) DBSec 2018. LNCS, vol. 10980, pp. 182–197. Springer, Cham (2018). https://doi.org/10.1007/978-3-319-95729-6_12
12. Mokal, P.H., Devikar, R.N.: A survey on shoulder surfing resistant text based graphical password schemes. Int. J. Sci. Res. (IJSR) **3**(4), 747–750 (2014)
13. Gaikwad, A.: A survey in shoulder surfing resistant graphical authentication system. Int. J. Emerg. Technol. Comput. Sci. **2**(3) (2017)
14. Denning, T., et al.: Exploring implicit memory for painless password recovery. In: Proceedings of the SIGCHI Conference on Human Factors in Computing Systems (2011)
15. Das, S., Hayashi, E., Hong, J.I: Exploring capturable everyday memory for autobiographical authentication. In: Proceedings of the 2013 ACM International Joint Conference on Pervasive and Ubiquitous Computing (2013)
16. Sun, H., et al.: PassApp: my app is my password!. In: Proceedings of the 17th International Conference on Human-Computer Interaction with Mobile Devices and Services (2015)
17. Nguyen, N., Sigg, S.: PassFrame: generating image-based passwords from egocentric videos. In: 2017 IEEE International Conference on Pervasive Computing and Communications Workshops (PerCom Workshops). IEEE (2017)
18. Woo, S., et al.: Life-experience passwords (LEPS). In: Proceedings of the 32nd Annual Conference on Computer Security Applications (2016)

Empathy as a Response to Frustration in Password Choice

Kovila P. L. Coopamootoo[(✉)]

Newcastle University, Newcastle upon Tyne, UK
kovila.coopamootoo@newcastle.ac.uk

Abstract. Previous research often reports that password-based security is frustrating, irritating or annoying, and as a result it often leads to weak password choices. We investigated the impact of empathy as a countermeasure to the anger-related states. We designed an online study with N = 194 participants. The experimental group received an empathic message while the control group did not. Participants presented with the empathic message created significantly stronger passwords than those who did not receive the message. Our finding differs from previous research because it shows participants creating stronger passwords with an empathic response to anger arousal. This antidote to frustrated states with regards to password choice provides an initial step towards more supportive and emotionally intelligent security designs.

Keywords: Password · Security · Emotion · User · Choice · Frustration · Anger · Empathy

1 Introduction

Frustration is an emotional state resulting from "the occurence of an obstacle that prevent[s] the satisfaction of a need" [3]. Frustration is the most common precursor and often an elicitor of anger [29]. Frustration, annoyance and irritation are emotional states of anger emotion.

User experience of frustration with information security is nowadays well known. For example, Furnell & Thompson discussed security controls that 'annoy', 'frustrate', 'perturb', 'irritate' users as well providing an effort overhead [13]. Stanton et al. observed that users feel weary of being bombarded by warning, feel bothered of being locked out for mistyped passwords, and describing security as 'irritating', 'annoying', and 'frustrating', together with being cumbersome, overwhelming [34].

With regards to password security, user discontent has been observed when forced to adhere to password policies [17,21], and annoyance by the shift to

Kovila P.L. Coopamootoo, Empathy as a Response to Frustration in Password Choice: Proceedings of AsiaUSEC'20, Financial Cryptography and Data Security 2020 (FC). February 14, 2020 Kota Kinabalu, Sabah, Malaysia Springer, 2020.

M. Bernhard et al. (Eds.): FC 2020 Workshops, LNCS 12063, pp. 177–191, 2020.
https://doi.org/10.1007/978-3-030-54455-3_13

stricter password policies [27,32]. Passwords chosen following annoyance due to stricter policies were 46% more likely to be guessed [27].

We posit that user frustration and annoyance with password security are here to stay because (1) passwords as a simple method of authentication is both widely used and is easy to implement, and (2) frustration triggered with password security is mainly due to complexity requirements that contributes to strong passwords.

However, security research has yet to respond to the challenges posed by the emotions induced during interaction, as well as their consequences. Meanwhile, the HCI community has proposed lines of research that address the impact of emotions while interacting with computers, such as affective computing [31] and empathic designs [40].

On the user side, individuals have the skills to manage and regulate emotional states and employ coping strategies [14], including passive methods that do not address the emotion themselves such as interacting with the media, consuming food or alcohol, and active methods where people discuss or address their emotions directly as a means of managing them, such as active listening and empathy.

As a way to respond to anger-related states in security, we propose empathy as an affective response and investigate the main RQ "How does empathizing with users impact security behavior, in particular, password choice?" via an online study reported in this paper.

We observe stronger password choices in the empathy condition, with reported anger acting as a positive confounder to password strength. We also report in detail how password characteristics impact emotions, where the odds of inducing a higher level of anger with a unit increase in password length, number of digits and lowercase letters, and password strength, range from 12% to 31%. We therefore offer a first step towards more supportive and emotion-intelligent security designs, as well as provide a deeper understanding of the emotions involved with password choice.

In the rest of the paper, we first present background literature followed with the aim, research questions, procedure and methods of the study, followed by the results and discussion sections. We end the paper with a limitation and a conclusion section.

2   Background

2.1   User Password

Text passwords are created by users as an authentication token that only they know. To combat the inherent and user-induced weaknesses of text passwords, administrators and organisations typically set a series of rules - via a password policy - to which users must adhere when choosing a password. Users develop strategies to cope with password policies. For example, users do not create entirely new passwords, as shown by a study where only 30% of respondents did create an entirely new password when presented with a stronger password requirements [32]. Most users also reuse passwords across sites, where reuse by a student population is 100% [1] and in the general population ranging from 34.6 to 82%) [1,23]. Users are thought to maintain between 3 (32%) to 5 (24%) distinct passwords only [4]. Another coping strategy involves transformation rules, such as to always pick the same number, or always place a number in the same location in their passwords [32].

Individuals cope with negative emotions via different strategies, where coping is conceptualized as cognitive and behavioral efforts to manage specific external and/or internal demands that are appraised as taxing or exceeding the resources of the person [24]. Two broad classes of coping methods are usually identified, that is either emotion or problem-focused coping. The problem-focused strategy consists of efforts to maintain concentration on the steps needed to fulfill task requirements. Therefore, when individuals remain focused on the task rather than on the damage done by a negative event, they are likely to buffer the adverse effect of negative emotion on their behavior and performance [7].

2.2 Empathy

Baron-Cohen & Wheelwright defined empathy as, 'the drive to identify another person's emotions and thoughts, and to respond to these with an appropriate emotion' (p. 361) [5]. In short, empathy is the ability to feel for someone else. It differs from sympathy. While sympathy refers to an understanding of what another is going through, empathy is an emotional response, that is how someone feels in response to others' situations [19].

Researchers distinguish between dispositional and situational empathy [35]. Dispositional empathy, also known as trait empathy, is the tendency for people to imagine and experience the feelings and experiences of others. In contrast, state or situational empathy, is an immediate response to a specific eliciting situation.

2.3 Frustration Regulation

Computer interaction often has unpleasant side effects including strong, negative emotional states such as frustration, confusion, anxiety, that not only affect the interaction itself, but may also impact productivity, learning, social relationships, and overall well-being. In consequence, computing research have designed meaningful ways to respond to negative emotions such as frustration, thereby supporting users to manage and regulate their emotions. As example, Klein et al. [22] investigated the impact of ignoring emotions, enabling individuals to vent their feelings versus providing an active affect-support agent with components of active listening, empathy and sympathy, where continued interaction resulted with the agent.

3   Aim

We provide the research questions and hypotheses under investigation.

3.1 Impact of Empathy on Password Choice

Empathy has been used as a response to user frustration, or the negative feelings that arise from interacting with computers before [22]. These are in the form of text dialogue and empathic agents that supports emotion regulation of frustration states [18].

We investigate the influence of empathizing with users on password choice via RQ-E *"How does empathizing with users impact password strength?"* We define the hypotheses $H_{E,0}$: "Empathizing with users does not impact password strength". $H_{E,1}$: "Empathizing with users impacts password strength".

3.2 Impact of Password Characteristics on Emotions

While password security is often thought to involve negative emotions, we are yet to determine the fine-grained details of how password characteristics (such as strength, length and number of characters) evoke anger and other emotions.

We investigate how password characteristics are linked with the extent of emotions induced via RQ-D *"How does password characteristics influence reports of emotions?"* We define the hypotheses $H_{D,0}$: "Password characteristics do not influence reports of emotions". $H_{D,1}$: "Password characteristics influence reports of emotions".

4 Methodology

We designed a between-subject online experiment, where participants were assigned to either of the two conditions, namely the empathy experimental condition or the control condition. We measure password strength as the main dependent variable.

We diligently follow the good practice guidelines for empirical research in security and privacy [8,9,25,30], themselves founded on scientific hallmarks. *First* we replicated validated methods using the standard questionnaires described later in Sect. 4.5. *Second*, we define research questions and hypotheses at the fore in Sect. 3 and discuss limitations in Sect. 6. *Third*, we follow the standard APA Guidelines [2] to report statistical analyses, and we report on effect sizes, assumptions and test constraints.

4.1 Sample Participants

We recruited participants from the Amazon Mechanical Turk (MTurk) crowdsourcing service. MTurk has extensively contributed to user studies before, including that for password research [23]. Passwords created via MTurk in previous studies have been found to be comparable to those of controlled lab studies [27] and in general 70% of study passwords are at least somewhat comparable with real world passwords [12].

With the study lasting on average 20 min and no more than 40 min, participants were remunerated with \$1.5 for their time. This is well within the payment frame for MTurk workers, where \$2 per hour has been suggested [16].

The sample $N = 194$ participants consisted of 99 male and 95 female. The mean age $= 37.43$, $sd = 10.922$. 36.3% of the participants had at least an undergraduate education level, 29.3% graduated from college while 32.3% graduated from high school and 2% either did not graduate from high school or did not attend school. 13.6% of the participants reported a computer science related education background.

We aimed for 50% of the participants to be randomly assigned to the empathy condition and 50% to the control condition. However, 6 participants were excluded due to not fully completing the questionnaires. We consequently ended up with $N = 99$ assigned to the empathy condition and $N = 95$ to the control condition.

4.2 Procedure

The procedure consisted of (1) a pre-task questionnaire for demographics, (2) introduction to the email scenario, (3) either the empathy manipulation or the control (4) a task to enter the chosen password, (5) the password reuse, the brief mood inventory and the empathy quotient questionnaires, Fig. 1 depicts the experiment design. We discuss the ecological validity in the Discussion, Sect. 6.

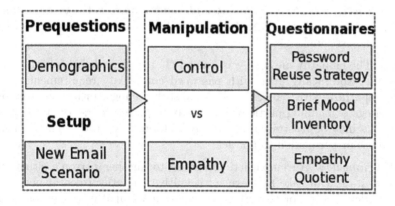

Fig. 1. Experiment design.

4.3 Scenario

Setting: We designed a scenario to choose a password similar to Das et al. [4] where participants were asked to assume they are creating a new account on a new email system where they would also create a password. Instead of asking participants to only think about the password as in Das et al. we adapted the scenario to typing the password into the survey. In particular we ask participants:

"For the following questions, imagine that you are creating a new account on a new email system".

Password Policy: Compared to Das et al. who set the new email system to www. bestmail.com with no password policy suggested, our scenario did not focus on a particular email system. We however focused on a password policy suggestion set to the password complexity of mail.google.com, that is, eight or more characters long including digits, uppercase letters and symbols [20]. In both conditions, participants were then presented with the message *"Our questions will focus on the password you choose for this new account, where you can use 8 or more characters with a mix of letters, numbers & symbols for security"*.

We chose GMail's password policy because it is the most widely used email account and we assumed that most participants would have heard of such a password policy before. The GMail password policy suggestion also fits that of other email system requirements, where passwords created following the suggested policy may also comply with policies for shopping and financial websites [4].

Password ReUse: Similar to Das et al.'s study, we query participants about reuse of an existing password. We asked participants to select from three options for reuse strategy. We used the same items as Das et al. [4].

4.4 Manipulation

We designed a static text message as the empathy manipulation. The empathy message said *"We empathize with you that choosing a complex password can sometimes feel frustrating, annoying and cumbersome, yet take your time to create your password"*. In contrast, the control message said *"Take your time to create your password"*.

Framing: The empathy message was framed (1) to acknowledge feelings of frustration that specifically arise with password complexity requirements; (2) to clearly empathize with participants about such feelings, rather than ignoring these feelings or blaming participants; (3) to propose a course of action even if participants may be frustrated, thus to avoid them using the empathy message as an excuse or permission to not act.

Cognitive Empathy: An empathetic response to another person's situation or emotional state, can take the form of cognitive empathy (mental perspective taking, understanding of the other) or emotional empathy (vicarious sharing of emotions) [33]. As a first and simple step towards investigating the impact of empathy with regards to security, we chose to employ a cognitive empathy response rather than an emotional one.

Empathic Accuracy: In providing a verbal response to individuals' emotions, it is important to communicate empathy within the context as accurately as possible to avoid negative consequences [10,19]. As a result, we focused the empathy message to 'complex passwords', as feelings of frustration from strict policies have previously been reported in research [27], rather than leaving it open to *"choosing a password"* or security in general.

Priming: We ensured that both conditions were similarly primed towards security with the same password policy suggestion via the phrase *"for security"*.

4.5 Measurements

Emotion: To measure moods and emotions, previous security and privacy research [15, 28] have employed the short form of the Brief Mood Introspection Scale (BMIS) [6, 26] or PANAS-X [37]. We set the time boundary of the elicitation to "How do you feel right now?" We use the short form of the BMIS, the brief mood inventory (BMI) in this study, including the 8 dimensions, "I feel" ... (a) excited, (b) thoughtful, (c) tired, (d) happy, (e) worn out, (f) sad, (g) angry, and (h) calm. We used *bmi_angry* as elicitation of the anger-related emotional states of frustration, annoyance, or irritation, that have previously been mentioned with respect to security. We added three items as manipulation check for the empathy condition. These were (a) that I am understood, (b) that my condition is received, and (c) that I am cared for. These are to measure participants' receiving of the empathic message. We adapted the 5-point Likert-type items to that used within the 60-item PANAS-X anchored on 1 - "very slightly or not at all", 2 - "a little", 3 - "moderately", 4 - "quite a bit" and 5 - "extremely".

Password Strength: We measured password strength via $\log_{10}$ number of password guesses and an ordinal value from 0 to 4 of password strength via zxcvbn [39]. zxcvbn is a client-side password strength checker developed by Dropbox and is open-sourced. We chose zxcvbn as it employs advanced heuristics [36], and it considers the composition of a password more thoroughly than other checkers, providing a realistic evaluation of the complexity of the password [11].

Empathy: In addition to demographics information, we measured dispositional empathy via the Empathy Quotient (EQ) questionnaire [5]. Dispositional empathy is related to personality trait, and refers to an individual's propensity to empathize with others, that is to give empathy. The EQ has been used across a variety of populations including people with asperger's syndrome. The EQ was designed to be a short, easy to use scale that measures both cognitive and affective components of empathy. It is a 60-item questionnaire with a 4-point Likert items anchored on 1 - "strongly agree", 2 - "slightly agree", 3 - "slightly disagree", and 4 - "strongly disagree". The EQ consists of 40 empathy related items that are scored and summed up and 20 filler items that are not scored.

4.6 Ethics

The study received ethics approval from the institution and followed its ethics guidelines. Although we requested participants' text password, we computed password strength via zxcvbn offline and anonymised and stored participant data on an encrypted hard disk. After computing password strength and characteristics, we remove the actual passwords from the database used for analysis by the research team.

5 Results

We describe the password characteristics across the two conditions in Table 2 and password reuse strategy in Table 3 in the Appendix.

5.1 Manipulation Check

We investigate how participants' responses (1) to feeling understood, (2) that their condition is received and, (3) feeling cared for differs between the two conditions. We observe a significant difference in feeling understood, with $p = .045$, as well as feeling that one's condition is received, with $p = .038$, between the two conditions, with a Mann-Whitney U test.

5.2 Password Strength Between Conditions

We compute an independent samples t-test between the empathy versus control conditions with the zxcvbn $\log_{10}$ guesses as dependent variable. There was a statistically significant difference in password strength between the empathy ($M = 9.349$, $SD = 2.989$) and control ($M = 8.366$, $SD = 2.567$) conditions, $t(192) = 2.451$, $p = .015$, CI[.191, 1.773], effect size $Hedges\ g = .351$, CI[.067, .635] (which is between a small and medium effect).

In addition, we compute a Mann-Whitney test on the ordinal values of zxcvbn password strength score across the two conditions. There was a statistically significant difference in password strength score, where participants in the control condition chose weaker password strength ($Mdn = 2.0$) than participants in the empathy condition ($Mdn = 3.0$), $U = 3959.5$, $z = -1.981$, $p = .048$.

We therefore reject the null hypothesis $H_{E,0}$ that "Empathizing with users does not impact password strength".

5.3 Impact of Password Characteristics on Emotions

We investigate how password choice (strength and characteristics) discriminate between reported emotion levels, via RQ-D "How do password characteristics influence reports of emotions?" Table 1 summarizes the models' regression coefficients.

We compute ordinal regressions with password strength, password length, number of digits and characters as predictors variable and bmi_angry as target variable. The ordinal regression model with password strength as predictor, was statistically significant with $X^2(194, 1) = 7.307$, $p = .007$. In particular, a one unit increase in password strength was associated with a 14% increase in the odds of reporting a higher level of anger, Wald $X^2(1) = 6.891$, $p = .009$, odds ratio 1.14. The model has a correct classification rate of 64.4%.

However, the proportion of variance in anger level explained by password strength is quite small with pseudo $R^2 = 2.0\%$ (McFadden), 3.7% (Cox & Snell) and 4.3% (Nagelkerke). We reject the null hypothesis $H_{D,0}$ that "Password characteristics do not influence reports of emotions".

Table 1 shows the regression results for different password characteristic predictors while we provide detailed explanation in the Appendix.

Table 1. Coefficients of the ordinal regressions with password characteristics as predictors and bmi_angry as target variable.

Models	Predictors	B	SE	Wald χ^2	df	p	Odds Ratio	95% CI LL	UL
1	password strength	.135	0.052	6.891	1	**.009****	**1.14**	1.03	1.27
2	password length	.117	.044	6.947	1	**.008****	**1.12**	1.03	1.23
3	#digits	.269	.099	7.454	1	**.006****	**1.31**	1.08	1.59
	#lower case letters	.134	.046	8.317	1	**.004****	**1.14**	1.04	1.25
	#upper case letters	−.040	.128	.097	1	.755	.96	.75	1.24
	#symbols	.056	.178	.098	1	.754	1.06	.75	1.50

CI refers to the Confidence Interval, LL to the Lower Limit, UL to the Upper Limit.

6   Discussion

Impact of Empathy: The theme of a more supportive and humane alternative to traditional security designs is inline with not making the users the enemy or merely blaming them as the weakest link in security. Our approach contributes to this theme and can ease the burden of compliance.

While we demonstrate a small to medium effect of empathy via the static message, the effect is a positive impact on password choice. This is a first step towards regulating frustrated states during security interaction, and an antidote to user frustration with security. Our research therefore paves the way for empathy to be included as a design choice within security interactions, where affective agents may be further developed. Such agents may detect user emotion in real time and/or engage in a dialogue with users via a text-agent or an embodied agent, as demonstrated previously by Klein et al. [22] and Hone [18].

In addition, by using a static message, we aimed to only validate emotions rather than change them, as observed by the lack of difference in emotions between the conditions.

Ecological Validity: We employed a similar scenario as Das et al. [4] where participants imagine creating a password for an email account. The characteristics of the passwords in Das et al. were compared to leaked datasets. In addition, imagination of a scenario is a valid mood induction protocol [38].

With regards to using an online sample for a password study, Fahl et al found that 70-80% MTurk passwords are at least somewhat comparable to actual user passwords [12] whereas Mazurek et al. reported that MTurk passwords are similar in strength to genuine passwords, and have similar characteristics in terms of structure and composition [27]. Our MTurk study passwords were also not dissimilar to leaked passwords (CSDNcomp8 and SFcomp8 from [27]).

Limitations: Our manipulation was limited to a simple, static, empathy text message. However, our empathy message design is only a first step towards more supportive (and humane) security systems, where different framing of the stimulus and more interactive versions may further be researched.

Although we did not control participants' emotions at the start of the study, we perceive any incidental emotions would balance out in the two conditions. Also, anger may be one of those emotions that people do not openly acknowledge or know they are feeling. We will therefore complement self-reported emotions in future studies with emotion recognition sensors for comparison and more in-depth evaluation.

7   Conclusion

While previous research have associated frustration with security, in particular in inducing weak security choices, with a simple text empathy stimulus, we were able to demonstrate how anger emotion can act as a positive confounder to password strength, rather than cause weaker passwords. These findings provide a first step towards an antidote to user frustration with cyber security.

We also provide a first study demonstrating in detail how password strength, length and type of characters impact emotional states associated with anger. We show that the odds of inducing higher levels of anger with each unit increase in these password characteristics range from 12% to 31%. This deeper understanding of the emotions involved in password choice can trigger further research into better supporting users to comply to security requirements.

8   Appendix

8.1   Password Characteristics

Table 2. Password descriptives

Characteristics	Empathy condition (N = 99)			Control condition (N = 95)		
	mean	median	sd	mean	median	sd
strength	9.35	8.67	3.00	8.37	8.00	2.57
length	11.57	11.00	3.39	10.54	9.00	2.90
# digits	3.04	3.00	1.82	3.00	3.00	1.54
# lwrcase	6.29	6.00	3.89	5.42	5.00	3.33
# uprcase	1.33	1.00	1.25	1.25	1.00	1.39
# symbols	0.90	1.00	0.86	0.86	1.00	0.86

8.2   Password ReUse Strategy

Table 3. Password choice strategy (in %)

Strategy	%
Reuse an existing password as is	6.7
Modify an existing password	16.0
Create an entirely new password	77.3

8.3   Empathy Quotient

We measured dispositional empathy via the Empathy Quotient (EQ) question-naire [5]. The sample had a mean EQ of 40.361, $sd = 12.778$.

We do not observe a difference between conditions. However we observe a difference between gender, where women scored a higher dispositional empathy (mean $= 42.305$, $sd = 12.637$), EQ, than men (mean $= 38.495$, $sd = 12.697$). The difference was statistically significant with the independent samples t-test, with $t(192) = 2.094$, $p = .038$, CI$[.222, 7.399]$, effect size $Hedges\ g = .300$, CI$[.017, .583]$, which is between a small and medium effect.

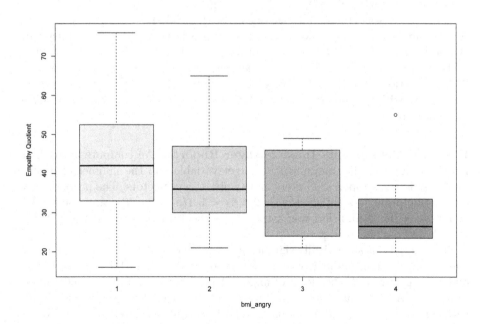

Fig. 2. Plot of empathy quotient vs reported anger.

We compare the mean EQ across the different levels of bmi_anger with an ANOVA. We find a significant difference in EQ across levels of reported anger, where participants with a low EQ expressed more anger, $F(3, 190) = 6.28$, $p < .000$. The boxplot in Fig. 2 depicts the decreasing mean EQ as bmi_anger increases from 1 to 4.

However, we did not find a correlation between EQ and receiving empathy through bmi_understood, bmi_received or bmi_cared-for.

8.4   Impact of Password Characteristics on Emotions

Password Strength Impacts Anger Reports Model Assumptions. There is no difference in the coefficients between models, with $X^2(2) = 2.324$, $p = .313$. This means that the proportional odds assumption is satisfied, that is the coefficients that describe the relationship between, the lowest versus all higher levels of bmi_anger are the same as those that describe the relationship between the next lowest level and all higher level. The model goodness of fit assumption was also satisfied via the Pearson Chi-Square statistic with $X^2(443) = 471.605$, $p = .168$.

Password Length Impacts Anger Reports. We compute an ordinal regression model, with bmi_anger as target variable and password length as predictor. The proportional odds assumption was satisfied with $X^2(2) = 1.523$, $p = .467$, and the model goodness of fit assumption was satisfied via the Pearson Chi-Square statistic with $X^2(47) = 52.562$, $p = .267$.

The model was statistically significant with $X^2(194, 1) = 7.323$, $p = .007$. A one unit increase in password length was associated with a 12% increase in the odds of reporting a higher level of anger, Wald $X^2(1) = 6.947$, $p = .008$, odds ratio 1.12. The model has a correct classification rate of 63.4%. However, The proportion of variance in anger level explained by password strength is quite small with pseudo $R^2 = 2.0\%$ (McFadden), 3.7% (Cox & Snell) and 4.4% (Nagelkerke).

Password Components Impact Anger Reports. We compute an ordinal regression model, with bmi_anger as target variable and the number of digits, lowercase letters, uppercase letters and symbols as predictors. The proportional odds assumption was satisfied with $X^2(8) = 3.478$, $p = .901$, and the model goodness of fit assumption was satisfied via the Pearson Chi-Square statistic with $X^2(425) = 467.062$, $p = .078$.

The model was statistically significant with $X^2(198, 4) = 12.838$, $p = .012$. A one unit increase in number of digits was associated with a 31% increase in the odds of reporting a higher level of anger, Wald $X^2(1) = 7.454$, $p = .006$, odds ratio 1.31. A one unit increase in number of lowercase letters was associated with an 14% increase in the odds of reporting a higher level of anger, Wald $X^2(1) = 8.317$, $p = .004$, odds ratio 1.14. The model has a correct classification rate of 64.4%. However, The proportion of variance in anger level explained by password strength is quite small with pseudo $R^2 = 3.5\%$ (McFadden), 6.4% (Cox & Snell) and 7.5% (Nagelkerke).

Password Strength Impacts Reports of Excitement. We compute an ordinal regression model, with bmi_excitement as target variable and password strength as predictor. The proportional odds assumption was satisfied with $X^2(3) = 1.871$, $p = .600$, and the model goodness of fit assumption was satisfied via the Pearson Chi-Square statistic with $X^2(591) = 594.171$, $p = .456$.

The model was statistically significant with $X^2(194,1) = 4.086$, $p = .043$. A one unit increase in password length was associated with a 9% decrease in the odds of reporting a higher level of excitement, Wald $X^2(1) = 4.000$, $p = .045$, odds ratio .910. However, The proportion of variance in excitement level explained by password strength is quite small with pseudo $R^2 = .07\%$ (McFadden), 2.1% (Cox & Snell) and 2.2% (Nagelkerke).

References

1. Alomari, R., Thorpe, J.: On password behaviours and attitudes in different populations. J. Inf. Secur. Appl. **45**, 79–89 (2019)
2. American Psychological Association (APA): Publication manual. American Psychological Association, 6th revised edn. (2009)
3. Amsel, A.: Frustration theory: many years later. Psychol. Bull. **112**(3), 396 (1992)
4. Das, A., Bonneau, J., Caesar, M., Borisov, N., Wang, X.: The tangled web of password reuse. In: NDSS, pp. 23–26 (2014)
5. Baron-Cohen, S., Wheelwright, S.: The empathy quotient: an investigation of adults with asperger syndrome or high functioning autism, and normal sex differences. J. Autism Dev. Disorders **34**(2), 163–175 (2004)
6. Baumeister, R., Bratslavsky, E., Muraven, E., Tice, D.: Ego depletion: is the active self a limited resource? Pers. Soc. Psychol. **74**, 1252–1265 (1998)
7. Carver, C.S.: Cognitive interference and the structure of behavior. In: Cognitive Interference: Theories, Methods, and Findings, pp. 25–45 (1996)
8. Coopamootoo, K.P.L., Groß, T.: Evidence-based methods for privacy and identity management. In: Lehmann, A., Whitehouse, D., Fischer-Hübner, S., Fritsch, L., Raab, C. (eds.) Privacy and Identity 2016. IAICT, vol. 498, pp. 105–121. Springer, Cham (2016). https://doi.org/10.1007/978-3-319-55783-0_9
9. Coopamootoo, K.P.L., Groß, T.: Cyber security and privacy experiments: a design and reporting toolkit. In: Hansen, M., Kosta, E., Nai-Fovino, I., Fischer-Hübner, S. (eds.) Privacy and Identity 2017. IAICT, vol. 526, pp. 243–262. Springer, Cham (2018). https://doi.org/10.1007/978-3-319-92925-5_17
10. Cramer, H., Goddijn, J., Wielinga, B., Evers, V.: Effects of (in) accurate empathy and situational valence on attitudes towards robots. In: 2010 5th ACM/IEEE International Conference on Human-Robot Interaction (HRI), pp. 141–142. IEEE (2010)
11. De Carnavalet, X.D.C., Mannan, M., et al.: From very weak to very strong: analyzing password-strength meters. In: NDSS, vol. 14, pp. 23–26 (2014)
12. Fahl, S., Harbach, M., Acar, Y., Smith, M.: On the ecological validity of a password study. In: Proceedings of the Ninth Symposium on Usable Privacy and Security, p. 13. ACM (2013)

13. Furnell, S., Thomson, K.L.: Recognising and addressing 'security fatigue'. Comput. Fraud Secur. **2009**(11), 7–11 (2009)
14. Gross, J.J., Thompson, R.A.: Emotion regulation: Conceptual foundations (2007)
15. Groß, T., Coopamootoo, K., Al-Jabri, A.: Effect of cognitive depletion on password choice. In: The LASER Workshop: Learning from Authoritative Security Experiment Results (LASER 2016), pp. 55–66. USENIX Association (2016)
16. Hara, K., Adams, A., Milland, K., Savage, S., Callison-Burch, C., Bigham, J.P.: A data-driven analysis of workers' earnings on Amazon mechanical turk. In: Proceedings of the 2018 CHI Conference on Human Factors in Computing Systems, p. 449. ACM (2018)
17. Herley, C.: So long, and no thanks for the externalities: the rational rejection of security advice by users. In: Proceedings of the 2009 Workshop on New Security Paradigms Workshop, pp. 133–144. ACM (2009)
18. Hone, K.: Empathic agents to reduce user frustration: the effects of varying agent characteristics. Interact. Comput. **18**(2), 227–245 (2006)
19. Ickes, W.J.: Empathic Accuracy. Guilford Press, New York (1997)
20. Inc', G.: Google mail account page, August 2019. https://accounts.google.com/
21. Inglesant, P.G., Sasse, M.A.: The true cost of unusable password policies: password use in the wild. In: Proceedings of the SIGCHI Conference on Human Factors in Computing Systems, pp. 383–392. ACM (2010)
22. Klein, J., Moon, Y., Picard, R.W.: This computer responds to user frustration: theory, design, and results. Interact. Comput. **14**(2), 119–140 (2002)
23. Komanduri, S., et al.: Of passwords and people: measuring the effect of password-composition policies. In: Proceedings of the SIGCHI Conference on Human Factors in Computing Systems, pp. 2595–2604. ACM (2011)
24. Lazarus, R.S., Folkman, S.: Stress. Appraisal, and Coping, p. 725 (1984)
25. Maxion, R.: Making experiments dependable. In: Jones, C.B., Lloyd, J.L. (eds.) Dependable and Historic Computing. LNCS, vol. 6875, pp. 344–357. Springer, Heidelberg (2011). https://doi.org/10.1007/978-3-642-24541-1_26
26. Mayer, J.D., Gaschke, Y.N.: The experience and meta-experience of mood. J. Pers. Soc. Psychol. **55**(1), 102 (1988)
27. Mazurek, M.L., et al.: Measuring password guessability for an entire university. In: Proceedings of the 2013 ACM SIGSAC Conference on Computer & Communications Security, pp. 173–186. ACM (2013)
28. Nwadike, U., Groß, T., Coopamootoo, K.P.L.: Evaluating users' affect states: towards a study on privacy concerns. In: Lehmann, A., Whitehouse, D., Fischer-Hübner, S., Fritsch, L., Raab, C. (eds.) Privacy and Identity 2016. IAICT, vol. 498, pp. 248–262. Springer, Cham (2016). https://doi.org/10.1007/978-3-319-55783-0_17
29. Oatley, K., Duncan, E.: The experience of emotions in everyday life. Cogn. Emotion **8**(4), 369–381 (1994)
30. Peisert, S., Bishop, M.: How to design computer security experiments. In: Futcher, L., Dodge, R. (eds.) WISE 2007. IAICT, vol. 237, pp. 141–148. Springer, New York (2007). https://doi.org/10.1007/978-0-387-73269-5_19
31. Picard, R.W.: Affective Computing. MIT Press, Cambridge (2000)
32. Shay, R., et al.: Encountering stronger password requirements: user attitudes and behaviors. In: Proceedings of the Sixth Symposium on Usable Privacy and Security, p. 2. ACM (2010)
33. Smith, A.: Cognitive empathy and emotional empathy in human behavior and evolution. Psychol. Rec. **56**(1), 3–21 (2006)

34. Stanton, B., Theofanos, M.F., Prettyman, S.S., Furman, S.: Security fatigue. IT Prof. **18**(5), 26–32 (2016)
35. Stueber, K.: Empathy. In: Zalta, E.N. (ed.) The Stanford Encyclopedia of Philosophy. Metaphysics Research Lab, Stanford University, fall 2019 edn. (2019)
36. Ur, B., et al.: Design and evaluation of a data-driven password meter. In: Proceedings of the 2017 CHI Conference on Human Factors in Computing Systems, pp. 3775–3786. ACM (2017)
37. Watson, D., Clark, L.A., Tellegen, A.: Development and validation of brief measures of positive and negative affect: the PANAS scales. J. Pers. Soc. Psychol. **54**(6), 1063 (1988)
38. Westermann, R., Spies, K., Stahl, G., Hesse, F.W.: Relative effectiveness and validity of mood induction procedures: a meta-analysis. Eur. J. Soc. Psychol. **26**(4), 557–580 (1996)
39. Wheeler, D.L.: zxcvbn: Low-budget password strength estimation. In: Proceedings of USENIX Security (2016)
40. Wright, P., McCarthy, J.: Empathy and experience in HCI. In: Proceedings of the SIGCHI Conference on Human Factors in Computing Systems, pp. 637–646. ACM (2008)

Fixing the Fixes: Assessing the Solutions of SAST Tools for Securing Password Storage

Harshal Tupsamudre$^{(\boxtimes)}$, Monika Sahu, Kumar Vidhani, and Sachin Lodha

TCS Research, Tata Consultancy Services, Pune, India
{harshal.tupsamudre,monika.sahu1,kumar.vidhani,sachin.lodha}@tcs.com

Abstract. Text passwords are one of the most widely used authentication mechanisms on the internet. While users are responsible for creating secure passwords, application developers are responsible for writing code to store passwords securely. Despite continued reports of password database breaches, recent research studies reveal that developers continue to employ insecure password storage practices and have several misconceptions regarding secure password storage. Therefore, it is important to detect security issues relating to password storage and fix them in a timely manner before the application is deployed.

In this paper, we survey several open-source (SpotBugs, SonarQube, CryptoGuard, CogniCrypt) Static Application Security Testing (SAST) tools to understand their detection capabilities with respect to password storage vulnerabilities and determine if the remediation fixes suggested by these tools are consistent with the OWASP or NIST recommended password storage guidelines. We found that none of the surveyed tools covers all potential vulnerabilities related to password storage. Further, we found that solutions suggested by the tools are either imprecise or they are not in accordance with the latest password storage guidelines. We conduct a study with 8 developers where each of them attempted to replace insecure SHA-1 based password storage implementation with PBKDF2 solution recommended by the surveyed tools. The study results show that, in the absence of specific examples, developers choose insecure values for PBKDF2 parameters (salt, iteration count, key length). Thus, although the use of PBKDF2 is in adherence with the tool requirements, the resulting password storage code may not be secure in practice.

Keywords: Secure password storage · Security testing tools

1 Introduction

Text based passwords are the most common way of authenticating users on the internet. Plenty of research studies have been conducted to investigate the

Harshal Tupsamudre, Monika Sahu, Kumar Vidhani, Sachin Lodha, Fixing the Fixes: Assessing the Solutions of SAST Tools for Securing Password Storage, Proceedings of AsiaUSEC'20, Financial Cryptography and Data Security 2019 (FC). February 14, 2020 Kota Kinabalu, Sabah, Malaysia Springer, 2020.

M. Bernhard et al. (Eds.): FC 2020 Workshops, LNCS 12063, pp. 192–206, 2020.
https://doi.org/10.1007/978-3-030-54455-3_14

password creation and password management strategies (storage, reuse etc.) of end-users [22,29,33,39,43]. Recently, some efforts have been made to understand the steps taken by developers to protect users' passwords on the server [18, 30–32]. The use of a weak password could jeopardize the security of the user, but a weaker server-side password implementation could put the security of all application users at risk (including the ones who have put great efforts to create a stronger password). In two recent studies, one involving GitHub developers [18] and the other involving freelance developers [30], researchers found that many developers do not store passwords securely unless prompted to do so. Further, most of the developers who attempt to store passwords securely, use either insecure methods (e.g., base64 encoding, encryption or hashing without using a proper salt) or outdated methods (e.g., MD5 or SHA-1). These results are not surprising, since various password database breaches [12] reveal that even developers from reputed companies are guilty of adopting insecure password storage practices. For instance, a data breach at LinkedIn in 2012 revealed that user passwords were stored using insecure SHA-1 hash function and without salt [27]. A data breach at Adobe in 2013 revealed that user passwords were encrypted instead of hashed [16]. These insecure coding practices by developers are often attributed to usability issues within existing cryptography APIs (e.g., poor documentation and insufficient code examples) [17,26,45], and to their lack of expertise in the security related concepts and technologies [30–32].

Several guidelines are available on how to store users' passwords securely. OWASP recommends the use of bcrypt hash function, a unique 16 character long random salt for each password and a common 32 character long random pepper for all passwords [11]. NIST recommends PBKDF2 for password hashing to be used with HMAC-SHA-256 and a work factor of at least 10,000 iterations [25]. Salting provides protection against an attacker pre-computing hashes using rainbow tables. However, for salting to work properly, it should be generated using cryptographically secure pseudo-random number generator (PRNG) [11]. Java provides two PRNGs *java.util.Random* and *java.security.SecureRandom*, of which the latter is cryptographically secure [4]. Encryption is highly discouraged since an attacker who gains access to the decryption key can recover plaintext passwords easily. Additionally, passwords protected with simple hash algorithms such as MD5 and SHA-1 are vulnerable to GPU-based cracking [38].

Security issues related to password storage are so common that they are assigned unique IDs and placed in Common Weakness Enumeration (CWE) which is a community-developed formal list of software weaknesses [3]. This list is intended to serve as a common language for describing software security weaknesses and is referenced by software security tools targeting these vulnerabilities. Further, some of these issues appear consistently in OWASP top 10 critical web application security risks [10]. The description of vulnerabilities pertaining to insecure password storage along with CWE-ID numbers and examples are shown in Table 1. The first part of the table enumerates issues specific to hashing and the second part enumerates issues specific to salting. For ease of reference, we also associate a mnemonic with each CWE-ID.

Table 1. Vulnerabilities related to password storage.

CWE	Description	Example	Mnemonic
CWE-327	Use of a broken or risky cryptographic algorithm	MD5, SHA-1	Weak hash
CWE-256	Unprotected storage of credentials	Plaintext	Plaintext
CWE-257	Storing passwords in a recoverable format	AES Encryption	Encryption
CWE-261	Weak cryptography for passwords	Base64 encoding	Base64
CWE-916	Use of password hash with insufficient computational effort	1000 PBKDF2 iterations	Fewer iterations
CWE-759	Use of a one-way hash without a salt	No salt	No salt
CWE-760	Use of a one-way hash with a predictable salt	Salt based on username	Predictable salt
CWE-330	Use of insufficiently random values	*java.util.Random*	Insufficient randomness
CWE-338	Use of cryptographically weak PRNG	*java.util.Random*	Weak PRNG

If password storage vulnerabilities are expected in the application source code, then it is important to detect and fix them in a timely manner, before the application is deployed. Several open-source and commercial source-code analysis tools are available that analyze applications for security vulnerabilities. Previous research mostly focused on understanding the insecure coding practices of developers [18,30–32] and the usability of cryptography APIs [17,45]. However, it is also important to understand the detection capabilities of the existing security testing tools and to check whether they assist developers in eliminating the detected vulnerabilities.

In this paper, we survey four Java source code analysis tools, SpotBugs [13], SonarQube [15], Cryptoguard [5] and CogniCrypt [6], and identify their capabilities in detecting security issues pertaining to password storage. We focus only on vulnerabilities shown in Table 1. Of these four tools, the first two tools are recommended by OWASP and the latter two tools are developed by security researchers [28,34]. A good testing tool not only detects and reports vulnerabilities, but also suggests remediation fixes wherever applicable. Therefore, we also analyze the recommended solutions provided by the surveyed tools and determine if they are consistent with the OWASP (or NIST) recommended password storage guidelines.

- We found that none of the surveyed tools covers all vulnerabilities related to password storage (Table 1).
- Most of the tools detect the use of weak PRNG *java.util.Random* and suggest to replace it with OWASP recommended cryptographically secure PRNG *java.security.SecureRandom* [4].
- All tools detect the use of weak hash functions MD5 and SHA-1 (CWE-327). However, we found multiple problems with the suggested solutions. CogniCrypt recommends the use of fast hash function SHA-256 whereas CryptoGuard does not recommend any solution at all.
- SpotBugs and SonarQube implement NIST recommended PBKDF2 for password hashing using HMAC-SHA-X, where X is 256 or 512, and PBEKeySpec API [2]. Both solutions use a PBEKeySpec constructor that requires user-supplied password along with three parameters, namely *salt, iterationCount* and *keyLength*. SpotBugs does not specify a value for salt and uses 4096 iterations which are not enough as per the latest NIST guidelines [25]. Whereas SonarQube does not specify values for any of the three parameters.
- We also conduct a usability study with 8 developers to further assess the recommended PBKDF2 solution of SonarQube. The study results show that since the parameters of PBEKeySpec constructor are not specified in the solution, 6 developers chose weak values for at least one parameter.

The organization of this paper is as follows. First, we describe work related to passwords. Then, we describe a sample code containing different password storage vulnerabilities. Subsequently, we describe each tool briefly and evaluate it by running on a sample code. We also assess the remediation solutions provided by each tool. Later, we conduct a study to assess the recommended PBKDF2 solution of SonarQube. Finally, we conclude and discuss the future work.

2 Related Work

Text password offers several deployment benefits compared to alternative schemes such as graphical passwords and biometrics [19], thereby making it the most dominant authentication method on the internet. However, multiple security studies reveal that passwords suffer from several security and usability issues. For instance, users choose predictable passwords and reuse their passwords across multiple accounts [20,22,29,33]. To improve the security of text passwords, researchers explored diverse composition policies [35–37] and developed various interventions [12,23,40,42,44]. Further, to prevent users from choosing leaked passwords, free online services such as haveibeenpwned [12] are available that check user-entered password against millions of passwords in breached databases.

Most of the research studies involving developers were conducted either to understand how well developers implement security-related tasks or to test the usability of the existing cryptography APIs. Storing password data is one of the most common tasks carried out by software developers, however this task is prone to security issues. Acar *et al.* [18] recruited 307 active GitHub users and requested them to implement 3 security related tasks including a credential storage task. The authors found that, of the 307 participants, only 162 (52.8%) stored user credentials in a secure manner. Of the 145 participants who stored password insecurely, 74 (51%) hashed the password without using a proper salt, 45 (31%) participants stored the password in plaintext, 19 (13.1%) participants used a static salt instead of a random salt, 7 (4.8%) participants used MD5, while 6 (4.1%) used SHA-1 family hashes. Similar results were obtained in a recent study conducted by Naiakshina *et al.* [30] involving 43 freelance developers. Of the 43 participants, 10 (23.2%) participants used MD5, 8 (18.6%) participants used Base64 encoding, 7 (16.3%) participants used Bcrypt, 7 (16.3%) participants used SHA-1 family hashes, 6 (13.9%) participants used symmetric encryption and 5 (11.6%) participants used PBKDF2. Further, only 11 participants generated salt using strong PRNG (*java.security.SecureRandom*) whereas 2 participants used static salts, 1 participant used username and 1 generated salt using weak PRNG (*java.util.Random*).

Acar *et al.* [17] conducted an online study with 256 developers to investigate the usability of Python crypto-APIs. They found that poor documentation and missing code examples caused developers to struggle with security. Wijayarathna and Arachchilage [45] conducted a study with 10 developers to evaluate the usability of scrypt password hashing functionality of Bouncycastle API. The authors identified 63 usability issues developers face while using the API for secure password storage. Again, the key factors affecting the usability of API were poor documentation, lack of examples and difficulty in identifying correct parameters to use in API method invocation. Further, if the API is not properly documented, then developers refer to unreliable third party sources and tutorials which could put security of the entire application at risk [21].

Gorski *et al.* [24] conducted a controlled online experiment with 53 participants to study the effectiveness of API-integrated security advice, which informs about an API misuse and places secure programming hints as guidance. They found that 73% of the participants, who received the security warning and advice fixed their insecure code. In this paper, we survey several SAST tools to understand their detection capabilities and analyze their remediation fixes pertaining to insecure password storage. To the best of our knowledge, there has not been any study conducted to evaluate the recommended solutions of security testing tools in the context of password storage.

3   Approach

To determine the detection capabilities of each tool in the context of insecure password storage practices, we take the following two-step approach.

1. We refer to the online documentations of SpotBugs [1], SonarQube [9] and CogniCrypt [14] list different security vulnerabilities that they attempt to address along with remediation fixes. We focus only on vulnerabilities related

to password storage listed in Table 1. The online documentation of Crypto-Guard is not available, hence we refer to its paper [34].

2. To confirm the detection of password storage vulnerabilities as listed in the tool's documentation, we run it on sample code shown in Fig. 1. The sample code consists of five methods, each demonstrating different vulnerabilities. The first four methods are derived from the CRYPTOAPI-BENCH created recently in [34]. The first method *hashPassword* returns an insecure SHA-1 hash of the password (CWE-327) and does not use salt (CWE-759). The second method *generateSalt* uses weak PRNG (CWE-330) with static seed and generates salt of insufficient size (4 bytes). The third method *getPBEParameterSpec* derives the values of salt (CWE-760) and number of iterations (CWE-916) required for PBEKeySpec from the user's password. The fourth method *encryptPassword* returns the encrypted version of the password (CWE-257). We added the fifth method *encodePassword* which returns base64 encoding of the password (CWE-261).

```
1   private static final int SALT_SIZE = 4;
2   private static byte[] hashPassword(String password) {
3       MessageDigest md = MessageDigest.getInstance("SHA-1");  //Weak Hash (CWE-327)
4       md.update(password.getBytes());  //No Salt (CWE-759)
5       return md.digest();
6   }
7   private static byte[] generateSalt() {
8       Random r = new Random(0);  //Weak PRNG (CWE-330), Constant Seed 0
9       byte[] salt = new byte[SALT_SIZE];  //Insufficient Salt Size
10      r.nextBytes(salt);
11      return salt;
12  }
13  private static PBEKeySpec getPBEParameterSpec(String password) {
14      MessageDigest md = MessageDigest.getInstance("MD5");  //Predictable Salt (CWE-760)
15      byte[] saltGen = md.digest(password.getBytes());
16      byte[] salt = new byte[SALT_SIZE];
17      System.arraycopy(saltGen, 0, salt, 0, SALT_SIZE);
18      int iteration = password.toCharArray().length + 1;  //Fewer Iterations (CWE-916)
19      return new PBEKeySpec(password.toCharArray(), salt, iteration, 256);
20  }
21  private static byte[] encryptPassword(String password, String key) {
22      Cipher cipher = Cipher.getInstance("AES/CBC/PKCS5Padding");
23      SecretKeySpec secretKey = new SecretKeySpec(key.getBytes(), "AES");
24      cipher.init(Cipher.ENCRYPT_MODE, secretKey);
25      return cipher.doFinal(password.getBytes());  //Encryption (CWE-257)
26  }
27  private static byte[] encodePassword(String password) {
28      Base64.Encoder encoder = Base64.getEncoder();
29      return encoder.encode(password.getBytes());  //Base64 (CWE-261)
30  }
```

Fig. 1. Sample code with password storage related vulnerabilities.

3.1 Tools

In this section, we describe each tool in more detail. The password storage vulnerabilities covered by each tool as per its online documentation are shown in Table 2. The vulnerabilities detected after executing each tool on sample code are summarized in Table 3. Both online documentation and execution results are in concurrence with each other. We developed sample code using Eclipse IDE

(Oxygen 4.7.1a) and JDK 1.8 on Windows 10 (64-bit) machine. Also, we used the latest versions of all security testing tools.

SpotBugs (v4.0). SpotBugs is an open source tool that uses static analysis approach to detect more than 400 vulnerabilities in Java applications. Find-SecBugs (v1.10.1) is a plugin of SpotBugs which detects 135 different security vulnerabilities using over 816 unique API signatures [1]. Both SpotBugs and FindSecBugs are available as eclipse plugins. Running FindSecBugs on sample code, revealed three vulnerabilities which are depicted in Table 3. It detects the use of weak hash functions SHA-1 and MD5 at line numbers 3 and 14 respectively. It also detects the usage of weak PRNG *java.util.Random* at line number 8. FindSecBugs displays error markers within Eclipse IDE to highlight the lines of code with vulnerabilities and provides a brief description of each detected vulnerability as shown in Table 3. To view more details about vulnerability and suggested remediation, one can open the SpotBugs explorer and click on the error marker. We note that the detailed description of vulnerabilities given by FindSecBugs eclipse plugin matches exactly with its online documentation [1].

Table 2. Detection capabilities of different tools as per their online documentation.

CWE-ID	Bug	SpotBugs	SonarQube	CryptoGuard	CogniCrypt
CWE-327	Weak hash	√	√	√	√
CWE-256	Plaintext	×	×	×	×
CWE-257	Encryption	×	×	×	×
CWE-261	Base64	×	×	×	×
CWE-916	Fewer iterations	×	×	√	×
CWE-759	No salt	×	×	×	×
CWE-760	Predictable salt	×	×	√	√
CWE-330, CWE-338	Weak PRNG	√	√	√	×

FindSecBugs recommends developers to use PBKDF2 instead of MD5 and SHA-1. It provides two different implementations of PBKDF2, one using bouncy castle API and the other using cryptography API of Java 8 or later (refer to Fig. 2). Although, both solutions employ NIST recommended HMAC-SHA-256 for password hashing, we found the following two issues in their implementation:

- They do not specify what the size of salt should be or how it should be generated. OWASP recommends at least 16 bytes unique random salt generated using cryptographically secure PRNG *java.security.SecureRandom*.
- The number of iterations used in both examples is 4096. This was sufficient according to older NIST 2010 guidelines [41], however it is not enough as per the latest NIST 2017 guidelines [25]. The current recommendation is to use at least 10,000 iterations.

Further, the PBEKeySpec solution uses 256 bytes key length when the recommendation is to use 256 bits [8]. FindSecBugs also recommends the use of

Table 3. Vulnerabilities detected by different tools in sample code.

Code line/method	Mnemonic	Description
SpotBugs		
3	Weak hash	This API SHA1 (SHA-1) is not a recommended cryptographic hash function
8	Weak PRNG	This random generator (java.util.Random) is predictable
14	Weak hash	This API MD5 (MDX) is not a recommended cryptographic hash function
SonarQube		
3	Weak hash	Make sure that hashing data is safe here
8	Weak PRNG	Make sure that using this pseudorandom number generator is safe here
14	Weak hash	Make sure that hashing data is safe here
CryptoGuard		
hashPassword	Weak hash	Violated Rule 2: Found broken hash function ***Constants: ["SHA1"]
generateSalt	Weak PRNG	Violated Rule 13: Untrused PRNG (java.util.Random)
getPBEParameterSpec	Weak hash	Violated Rule 2: Found broken hash function ***Constants: ["MD5"]
getPBEParameterSpec	Predictable salt	Violated Rule 9a: Found constant salts in code
getPBEParameterSpec	Fewer iterations	Violated Rule 8a: Used < 1000 iteration for PBE
CogniCrypt		
3	Weak hash	First parameter (with value "SHA1") should be any of SHA-256, SHA-384, SHA-512
14	Weak hash	First parameter (with value "MD5") should be any of SHA-256, SHA-384, SHA-512
19	Predictable salt	Second parameter was not properly generated as randomized

cryptographically secure PRNG instead of weak PRNG (line 8). Specifically, its detailed reports says, "A quick fix could be to replace the use of java.util.Random with something stronger, such as java.security.SecureRandom."

```
/*Solution (Using bouncy castle):*/
public static byte[] getEncryptedPassword(String password, byte[] salt) {
    PKCS5S2ParametersGenerator gen = new PKCS5S2ParametersGenerator(new SHA256Digest());
    gen.init(password.getBytes("UTF-8"), salt.getBytes(), 4096);
    return ((KeyParameter) gen.generateDerivedParameters(256)).getKey();
}
/*Solution (Java 8 and later):*/
public static byte[] getEncryptedPassword(String password, byte[] salt) {
    KeySpec spec = new PBEKeySpec(password.toCharArray(), salt, 4096, 256 * 8);
    SecretKeyFactory f = SecretKeyFactory.getInstance("PBKDF2WithHmacSHA256");
    return f.generateSecret(spec).getEncoded();
}
```

Fig. 2. Solutions by FindSecBugs to replace weak hash functions MD5 and SHA-1.

SonarQube (v8.0). SonarQube is a more comprehensive code quality and vulnerability detection tool that uses static analysis and supports 27 programming languages. It consists of 554 rules for detecting various security vulnerabilities in Java applications [9]. SonarQube is available as free community edition and three paid editions. It also comes in the form of eclipse plugin SonarLint, however we found that some of the detection rules are not available in SolarLint. Hence, we used its standalone free community edition. The results obtained after running SonarQube on sample code are shown in Table 3.

Similar to FindSecBugs, SonarQube also produces a detailed report along with remediation fixes. It suggests the replacement of weak PRNG *java.util.Random* (line 8) with cryptographically strong PRNG *java.security.SecureRandom*. It also suggests replacing MD5 and SHA-1 with PBKDF2, and provides a list of secure coding practices [7]. It uses NIST recommended HMAC-SHA-512 algorithm for implementing PBKDF2, however we found the following problem with its solution (Fig. 3). It also employs PBEKeySpec constructor, but does not specify the values for its parameters (*salt*, *iterationCount* and *keyLength*).

```
void foo(char[] password, byte[] salt, int iterationCount, int keyLength) {
    SecretKeyFactory factory = SecretKeyFactory.getInstance("PBKDF2WithHmacSHA512");
    PBEKeySpec spec = new PBEKeySpec(password, salt, iterationCount, keyLength);
    factory.generateSecret(spec).getEncoded();
}
```

Fig. 3. Solution by SonarQube to replace weak hash functions MD5 and SHA-1.

CryptoGuard. CryptoGuard is an open source high precision cryptographic vulnerabilities detection tool for Java applications [34]. It uses a set of fast and highly accurate slicing algorithms to detect 16 different cryptographic vulnerabilities such as predictable keys, constant passwords, custom trust manager, insecure random number generators, static salts, insecure cryptographic hash, and so on. It operates on source code, jar file and APK. The vulnerabilities detected after running CryptoGuard on sample code is shown in Table 3. Instead of reporting line numbers, CryptoGuard reports method names, which could be cumbersome for developers to locate the vulnerabilities exactly. Although CryptoGuard has more coverage in terms of detecting security issues pertaining to password storage, *it does not suggest any remediation fixes for them*.

CogniCrypt (v1.0.0.201905151726). CogniCrypt is an open source security vulnerabilities detection tool from the CROSSING research center of Technische Universität Darmstadt [28]. It employs static analysis and its scope is limited to the detection of inappropriate use of cryptography in Java applications. It comes with an important code generator feature to help developers in generating the right code for a given security requirement. The static analysis is based on rules developed in a domain-specific CrySL language that specify the correct use of an API [14]. The static analysis reports any deviations from the usage pattern defined within the rules. CogniCrypt is available as eclipse plugin and generates errors markers when it detects incorrect and insecure parts of code. Running CogniCrypt on sample code produced three vulnerabilities as described in Table 3. It detects the use of weak hash functions MD5 and SHA-1. However, *its remediation to use fast hash functions SHA-256, SHA-384 or SHA-512 results in insecure password storage code.* It also flags that salt is not generated randomly for PBEKeySpec, however *it does not specify how the salt should be generated.*

4   Study

CryptoGuard has comparatively good detection capabilities, however it does not provide any recommendation to implement secure password storage. CogniCrypt recommends the use of fast SHA-256 hash function, which is an insecure solution in the context of password storage. Therefore, we do not include these two tools in the study. SpotBugs recommends two PBKDF2 solutions, one using Bouncycastle API, and the other using HMAC-SHA-256 and PBEKeySpec API. Recently, researchers found several usability issues with Bouncycastle API [45], hence we do not consider it in our study. SonarQube also recommends a similar solution using HMAC-SHA-512 and PBEKeySpec API. The constructor of PBEKeySpec requires four parameters, namely user-supplied *password, salt, iterationCount* and *keyLength.* SpotBugs sets the value of *iterationCount* to 4096 and *keyLength* to 256 bytes, however it leaves the choice of salt to the developers (Fig. 2). On the other hand, SonarQube does not specify the values of any of these three parameters (Fig. 3). Therefore, we decided to evaluate whether SonarQube's detailed vulnerability report is helpful for developers to implement secure password solution. We note that study results pertaining to salt parameter are relevant to SpotBugs as well, since the salt parameter is unspecified in its recommended solutions.

Methodology. For the study, we designed a simple password storage task as described in [45]. We provided participants with a simple web application that includes functionalities for registering users and login users. The web application protected passwords using *hashPassword* function (given in Fig. 1) which employs insecure SHA-1 hash algorithm (CWE 327). We requested participants to secure passwords using the vulnerability report generated by SonarQube. The report discourages the use of SHA-1 and provides a PBKDF2 implementation using Java PBEKeySpec API (Fig. 3). The report is similar to the one available online [7]. Further, participants were allowed to access any resource on the internet in order to implement the recommended solution.

Setup. The study was setup on a dedicated Windows 10 (64-bit) machine. We created the web application project in Eclipse Oxygen (4.7.1a) using JDK 1.8. The function *hashPassword* was present in a separate source file, so that participants could focus on the task. Participants were provided the vulnerability report of SonarQube and were allowed to use Chrome browser for implementing the solution. At the end of the task, we stored the browsing history of each participant. For the implementation to work properly, participants were required to choose three parameters (*salt*, *iterationCount* and *keyLength*) of PBEKeySpec.

Result. We recruited 8 developers within our organization for the study. The information profile about each participant, their choices for three parameters *salt, iterationCount* and *keyLength* of PBEKeySpec and the time required for implementing the solution are shown in Table 4. We found that only two participants (P2, P7) chose the parameters as recommended by NIST as they had relevant experience of password storage task. These participants were aware of PBKDF2 specification and generated a unique 16 bytes salt using cryptographically secure PRNG *java.security.SecureRandom*, set *iterationCount* to 10,000 and *keyLength* to 256 bits. Of the remaining 6 participants, one participant (P5) generated a secure unique random salt for each password, four participants used a constant salt and one participant used userid as salt. Participants P4 and P8 set the value of *iterationCount* to 10,000 whereas the remaining participants 4 participants chose insufficient number of iterations.

Most of the participants chose a correct value of *keyLength* (256 bits). Analysis of browsing history of these participants reveal that they referred to the OWASP web page [8] (link was provided by SonarQube in its vulnerability report) which recommends the value of key length to be 256 bits, however it does not specify the number of iterations. Interestingly, the same page also recommends the size of salt to be 32 bytes. Four participants browsed Oracle's documentation for PBEKeySpec, however it does not recommend any values for the parameters. Three participants searched for the concept of salt (wikipedia). The concept of salt is not widely known, which was also observed in the previous study [31]. We also tested the submitted implementation of each participant using SonarQube. However, *none of the submitted solutions were flagged for vulnerabilities by SonarQube which is a serious concern.* Thus, detecting vulnerabilities just using method signatures is not enough.

Limitations. We found that developers chose incorrect parameters and implemented insecure password storage when the security testing tools do not provide specific recommendations. Our observation is based on a convenience sample of 8 developers. However, similar observations were made in a recent study [45] pertaining to usability of cryptography APIs. Their study results [45] also show that developers have difficulty in identifying correct parameters to use in Bouncycastle API method invocation.

Table 4. Participants information and their choice of parameters for PBEKeySpec.

Participant	Development Experience	Stored Pass -words Before	salt	iteration Count	keyLength	Time (in min)
P1	5.7 years	×	2 bytes (constant value)	50	256	25 min
P2	7.6 years	√	16 bytes (unique SecureRandom)	10,000	256	12 min
P3	6.8 years	√	Userid	12	256	29 min
P4	2.8 years	×	11 bytes (constant value)	10,000	256	27 min
P5	3 years	√	16 bytes (unique SecureRandom)	0	0	32 min
P6	0.6 years	×	8 bytes (constant value)	20	222	30 min
P7	15 years	√	16 bytes (unique SecureRandom)	10,000	256	9 min
P8	3 years	×	16 bytes (constant value)	10,000	256	35 min

5 Conclusion and Future Work

In this paper, we surveyed four open-source security testing tools (SpotBugs, SonarQube, CryptoGuard and CogniCrypt) to understand their detection capabilities pertaining to password storage vulnerabilities. We found that Crypto-Guard has comparatively good coverage, however it does not specify any remediation to fix the insecure password storage code. CogniCrypt detects the use of weak hash functions (MD5 and SHA-1), however it suggests SHA-256 hash function, which is insecure in the context of passwords. Both SpotBugs and SonarQube recommend the use of PBKDF2 and provide example solutions using PBEKeySpec API. However, SonarQube leaves the equally important choice of PBKDF2 parameters (*salt*, *iterationCount* and *keyLength*) to developers. Further, SpotBugs solution uses 4096 iterations which is insufficient as per the latest NIST 2017 guidelines [25] and leaves the important choice of *salt* parameter to developers. In our study involving 8 developers who were tasked with implementing SonarQube's recommended solution, we found that 6 of them chose insecure values for at least one PBKDF2 parameter. Therefore, it is crucial that security testing tools provide specific password storage solutions to developers.

We note that the insecure password storage is just one of the many implementation issues associated with the code that handles passwords. Other issues include hard-coded password (CWE-259), password in configuration file (CWE-260) and exposure of passwords in log files (CWE-200). Further, several commercial SAST tools such as Synopsys Coverity and HP Fortify are available. In future, we aim to compare the detection capabilities and remediation fixes of open-source as well as commercial tools with regard to insecure password code.

References

1. Bugs Patterns. https://find-sec-bugs.github.io/bugs.htm. Accessed 19 Dec 2019
2. Class PBEKeySpec. https://docs.oracle.com/javase/7/docs/api/javax/crypto/spec/PBEKeySpec.html. Accessed 19 Dec 2019
3. Common Weakness Enumeration. https://cwe.mitre.org/. Accessed 19 Dec 2019
4. Cryptographic Storage. https://cheatsheetseries.owasp.org/cheatsheets/Cryptographic_Storage_Cheat_Sheet.html. Accessed 19 Dec 2019
5. CryptoGuard. https://github.com/CryptoGuardOSS/cryptoguard. Accessed 19 Dec 2019
6. Eclipse CogniCrypt. https://www.eclipse.org/cognicrypt/. Accessed 19 Dec 2019
7. Hashing data is security-sensitive. https://rules.sonarsource.com/java/RSPEC-4790. Accessed 19 Dec 2019
8. Hashing Java. https://www.owasp.org/index.php/Hashing_Java. Accessed 19 Dec 2019
9. Jave 554 Rules. https://rules.sonarsource.com/java/. Accessed 19 Dec 2019
10. OWASP Top 10–2017. https://www.owasp.org/images/7/72/OWASP_Top_10-2017_%28en%29.pdf.pdf. Accessed 19 Dec 2019
11. Password Storage. https://cheatsheetseries.owasp.org/cheatsheets/Password_Storage_Cheat_Sheet.html. Accessed 19 Dec 2019
12. Pwned websites- Breached websites that have been loaded into Have I Been Pwned. https://haveibeenpwned.com/PwnedWebsites. Accessed 19 Dec 2019
13. SpotBugs. https://spotbugs.github.io/. Accessed 19 Dec 2019
14. The CrySL Language. https://www.eclipse.org/cognicrypt/documentation/crysl/. Accessed 19 Dec 2019
15. Your teammate for Code Quality and Security. https://www.sonarqube.org/. Accessed 19 Dec 2019
16. Anatomy of a password disaster - Adobe's giant-sized cryptographic blunder (2019). https://nakedsecurity.sophos.com/2013/11/04/anatomy-of-a-password-disaster-adobes-giant-sized-cryptographic-blunder/
17. Acar, Y., et al.: Comparing the usability of cryptographic APIs. In: 2017 IEEE Symposium on Security and Privacy (SP), pp. 154–171, May 2017. https://doi.org/10.1109/SP.2017.52
18. Acar, Y., Stransky, C., Wermke, D., Mazurek, M.L., Fahl, S.: Security developer studies with github users: exploring a convenience sample. In: Thirteenth Symposium on Usable Privacy and Security (SOUPS 2017), pp. 81–95. USENIX Association, Santa Clara, July 2017. https://www.usenix.org/conference/soups2017/technical-sessions/presentation/acar

19. Bonneau, J., Herley, C., van Oorschot, P.C., Stajano, F.: The quest to replace passwords: a framework for comparative evaluation of web authentication schemes. In: 2012 IEEE Symposium on Security and Privacy, pp. 553–567, May 2012. https://doi.org/10.1109/SP.2012.44

20. Das, A., Bonneau, J., Caesar, M., Borisov, N., Wang, X.: The tangled web of password reuse. In: NDSS, vol. 14, pp. 23–26 (2014)

21. Fischer, F., et al.: Stack overflow considered harmful? The impact of copy paste on Android application security. In: 2017 IEEE Symposium on Security and Privacy (SP), pp. 121–136, May 2017. https://doi.org/10.1109/SP.2017.31

22. Florencio, D., Herley, C.: A large-scale study of web password habits. In: Proceedings of the 16th International Conference on World Wide Web, WWW 2007, pp. 657–666. ACM, New York (2007). https://doi.org/10.1145/1242572.1242661

23. Forget, A., Chiasson, S., van Oorschot, P.C., Biddle, R.: Improving textpasswords through persuasion. In: Proceedings of the 4th Symposium on Usable Privacy and Security, SOUPS 2008, pp. 1–12. ACM, New York (2008). https://doi.org/10.1145/1408664.1408666

24. Gorski, P.L., et al.: Developers deserve security warnings, too: on the effect of integrated security advice on cryptographic API misuse. In: Fourteenth Symposium on Usable Privacy and Security (SOUPS 2018), pp. 265–281. USENIX Association, Baltimore, MD, August 2018. https://www.usenix.org/conference/soups2018/presentation/gorski

25. Grassi, P.A., et al.: Digital identity guidelines. NIST Spec. Publ. **800**, 63–3 (2017). https://doi.org/10.6028/NIST.SP.800-63b

26. Green, M., Smith, M.: Developers are Not the enemy!: the need for usable security APIs. IEEE Secur. Privacy **14**(5), 40–46 (2016). https://doi.org/10.1109/MSP.2016.111

27. Kamp, P.H.: LinkedIn password leak: salt their hide. Queue **10**(6), 20:20–20:22 (2012). https://doi.org/10.1145/2246036.2254400

28. Krüger, S., et al.: CogniCrypt: supporting developers in using cryptography. In: Proceedings of the 32Nd IEEE/ACM International Conference on Automated Software Engineering, ASE 2017, pp. 931–936. IEEE Press, Piscataway (2017). http://dl.acm.org/citation.cfm?id=3155562.3155681

29. Morris, R., Thompson, K.: Password security: a case history. Commun. ACM **22**(11), 594–597 (1979). https://doi.org/10.1145/359168.359172

30. Naiakshina, A., Danilova, A., Gerlitz, E., von Zezschwitz, E., Smith, M.: & #34; if you want, i can store the encrypted password: a password-storage field study with freelance developers. In: Proceedings of the 2019 CHI Conference on Human Factors in Computing Systems, CHI 2019, pp. 140:1–140:12. ACM, New York (2019). https://doi.org/10.1145/3290605.3300370

31. Naiakshina, A., Danilova, A., Tiefenau, C., Herzog, M., Dechand, S., Smith, M.: Why do developers get password storage wrong?: A qualitative usability study. In: Proceedings of the 2017 ACM SIGSAC Conference on Computer and Communications Security, CCS 2017, pp. 311–328. ACM, New York (2017). https://doi.org/10.1145/3133956.3134082

32. Naiakshina, A., Danilova, A., Tiefenau, C., Smith, M.: Deception task design in developer password studies: exploring a student sample. In: Fourteenth Symposium on Usable Privacy and Security (SOUPS 2018), pp. 297–313. USENIX Association, Baltimore, August 2018. https://www.usenix.org/conference/soups2018/presentation/naiakshina

33. Pearman, S., et al.: Let's go in for a closer look: observing passwords in their natural habitat. In: Proceedings of the 2017 ACM SIGSAC Conference on Computer and Communications Security, CCS 2017, pp. 295–310. ACM, New York (2017). https://doi.org/10.1145/3133956.3133973

34. Rahaman, S., et al.: CryptoGuard: high precision detection of cryptographic vulnerabilities in massive-sized Java projects. In: Proceedings of the 2019 ACM SIGSAC Conference on Computer and Communications Security, CCS 2019, pp. 2455–2472. ACM, New York (2019). https://doi.org/10.1145/3319535.3345659

35. Segreti, S.M., et al.: Diversify to survive: making passwords stronger with adaptive policies. In: Thirteenth Symposium on Usable Privacy and Security (SOUPS 2017), pp. 1–12. USENIX Association, Santa Clara, July 2017. https://www.usenix.org/conference/soups2017/technical-sessions/presentation/segreti

36. Shay, R., et al.: Correct horse battery staple: exploring the usability of system-assigned passphrases. In: Proceedings of the Eighth Symposium on Usable Privacy and Security, SOUPS 2012, pp. 7:1–7:20. ACM, New York (2012). https://doi.org/10.1145/2335356.2335366

37. Shay, R., et al.: Can long passwords be secure and usable? In: Proceedings of the SIGCHI Conference on Human Factors in Computing Systems, CHI 2014, pp. 2927–2936. ACM, New York (2014). https://doi.org/10.1145/2556288.2557377

38. Sprengers, M.: GPU-based password cracking. Master's thesis, Radboud University Nijmegen Faculty of Science Kerckhoffs Institute (2011)

39. Stobert, E., Biddle, R.: The password life cycle: user behaviour in managing passwords. In: 10th Symposium On Usable Privacy and Security (SOUPS 2014), pp. 243–255. USENIX Association, Menlo Park, July 2014. https://www.usenix.org/conference/soups2014/proceedings/presentation/stobert

40. Tupsamudre, H., Dixit, A., Banahatti, V., Lodha, S.: Pass-roll and pass-scroll: new graphical user interfaces for improving text passwords. In: EuroUSEC (2017)

41. Turan, M.S., Barker, E., Burr, W., Chen, L.: Recommendation for password-based key derivation. NIST Spec. Publ. **800**, 132 (2010)

42. Ur, B., et al.: Design and evaluation of a data-driven password meter. In: Proceedings of the 2017 CHI Conference on Human Factors in Computing Systems, CHI 2017, pp. 3775–3786. ACM, New York (2017). https://doi.org/10.1145/3025453.3026050

43. Ur, B., et al.: "I Added '!' at the end to make it secure": observing password creation in the lab. In: Eleventh Symposium on Usable Privacy and Security (SOUPS 2015), pp. 123–140. USENIX Association, Ottawa, July 2015. https://www.usenix.org/conference/soups2015/proceedings/presentation/ur

44. Wheeler, D.L.: zxcvbn: low-budget password strength estimation. In: 25th USENIX Security Symposium (USENIX Security 2016), pp. 157–173. USENIX Association, Austin, August 2016. https://www.usenix.org/conference/usenixsecurity16/technical-sessions/presentation/wheeler

45. Wijayarathna, C., Arachchilage, N.A.G.: Why Johnny can't store passwords securely?: A usability evaluation of bouncycastle password hashing. In: Proceedings of the 22nd International Conference on Evaluation and Assessment in Software Engineering 2018, EASE 2018, pp. 205–210. ACM, New York (2018). https://doi.org/10.1145/3210459.3210483

Incorporating Psychology into Cyber Security Education: A Pedagogical Approach

Jacqui Taylor-Jackson[1]([✉]), John McAlaney[2], Jeffrey L. Foster[1], Abubakar Bello[3], Alana Maurushat[3], and John Dale[4]

[1] School of Psychology, WSU, Sydney, NSW, Australia
{J.Taylor-Jackson,Jeff.Foster}@westernsydney.edu.au
[2] Department of Psychology, Faculty of Science and Technology, Bournemouth University, Poole, Dorset, UK
jmcalaney@bournemouth.ac.uk
[3] School of Social Sciences, WSU, Sydney, NSW, Australia
{A.Bello,A.Maurushat}@westernsydney.edu.au
[4] LiMETOOLS Ltd., Bournemouth, UK
john@limetools.biz

Abstract. The role of the human in cyber security is well acknowledged. Many cyber security incidents rely upon targets performing specific behavioural actions, such as opening a link within a phishing email. Cyber adversaries themselves are driven by psychological processes such as motivation, group dynamics and social identity. Furthermore, both intentional and unintentional insider threats are associated with a range of psychological factors, including cognitive load, mental wellbeing, trust and interpersonal relations. By incorporating psychology into cyber security education, practitioners will be better equipped with the skills they need to address cyber security issues. However, there are challenges in doing so. Psychology is a broad discipline, and many theories, approaches and methods may have little practical significance to cyber security. There is a need to sift through the literature to identify what can be applied to cyber security. There are also pedagogical differences in how psychology and cyber security are taught and also psychological differences in the types of student that may typically study psychology and cyber security. To engage with cyber security students, it is important that these differences are identified and positively addressed. Essential to this endeavor is the need to discuss and collaborate across the two disciplines. In this paper, we explore these issues and discuss our experiences as psychology and cyber security academics who work across disciplines to deliver psychology education to cyber security students, practitioners and commercial clients.

1 Introduction

Although there is a lack of empirical assessment regarding the cognitive aptitudes, communication skills and team-working needed for cyber security professions to be effective

Jacqui Taylor-Jackson, John McAlaney, Jeff Foster, Abubakar Bello, Alana Maurushat, John Dale, Incorporating Psychology into Cyber Security Education: A Pedagogical Approach, Proceedings of AsiaUSEC'20, Financial Cryptography and Data Security (FC). February 14, 2020 Kota Kinabalu, Sabah, Malaysia Springer, 2020.

© Springer Nature Switzerland AG 2020
M. Bernhard et al. (Eds.): FC 2020 Workshops, LNCS 12063, pp. 207–217, 2020.
https://doi.org/10.1007/978-3-030-54455-3_15

[1] in this paper we show how we have introduced psychology into cyber security programmes to ensure that professionals have an understanding of behavior to relate to their domain-specific knowledge and technical skills. Cyber security incidents are composed of a sequence of behavioural actions, each of which is determined by a range of psychological factors. In many cases cyber adversaries actively attempt to exploit and manipulate psychological processes of their targets, such as for example through the use of phishing emails. This reflects the view of humans as being the weakest link in cyber security [2]. However, despite the recognised importance of the human element it could be argued that cyber security education and training programs often neglect to fully address the psychological components of cyber security. This is despite the extensive research literature in psychology that is highly relevant to cyber security – understanding motivation, predicting future actions, designing human-centred policies and interfaces, and changing behaviour and organisational culture. These are topics that are taught within psychology programs in colleges and universities across the world, as well as within behaviour change and training courses in commerce and industry. As such there is existing experience pedagogical knowledge on how best to educate people about psychology across a range of settings, which could be better utilised for the education of cyber security students and practitioners.

This lack of interdisciplinary approaches to teaching psychology as part of cyber security could in part be explained by the nature and typical pedagogical approaches used in each discipline. Psychology is a very broad discipline; ranging from sub-topics that are highly reliant on quantitative, technological approaches such as neuropsychology, to those which are deeply rooted in qualitative approaches. There is a finite amount of time available to deliver any cybersecurity education or training; it would not be practical or desirable to deliver a course that includes all the different approaches to psychological research. In addition, some of the epistemological and ontological assumptions that are made in psychology differ from those used in cyber security and computing. As with other social science subjects many areas of psychology draw upon concepts such as social constructionism, which argues that humans create subjective interpretations of their social reality. In contrast subjects aligned with technology and engineering could be argued to take a more positivist approach, in which there is an assumption that there is an objectively correct explanation for any phenomena. When educating cyber security students about psychology it is important to have an appreciation of these differences.

Drawing upon our own interdisciplinary activities to deliver psychology content as part of cyber security education and training programs this paper will explore and discuss two topics. Firstly, we will identify the areas of psychology that, based on our own experiences, is likely to be the most useful and relevant to cyber security students. Secondly, we will suggest how best to address the ontological and epistemological differences in approaches that may arise in psychology and cyber security education and training activities.

2   Identifying Relevant Areas of Psychology

Psychology is a broad discipline, with many areas of research that could potentially be pertinent to a complex and multi-faceted issue such as cyber security. To identify areas which are the most important we consider the issue in terms of understanding both the cyber adversaries and their targets.

2.1 The Adversaries

A common form of psychological manipulation used by cyber attackers is social engineering, exemplified by phishing emails. Whilst the stereotypical phishing email is characterized by poor grammar and often crude attempts at manipulation it has been noted that these are becoming increasingly sophisticated and persuasive [3] with the most convincing tricking users up to 45% of the time [4]. These phishing emails exploit the decision-making heuristics – mental short cuts – humans use as a necessity to navigate their complex environments and social worlds. An example of this would be use of a company logo within a phishing email in the hope that the recipient will use the presence of this an indicator that the email is genuine. Other psychological processes relevant to phishing include Protection Motivation Theory [5] in which a fear appeal (e.g. a phishing email falsely claiming that a bank account has been hacked) is used to motivate a user into taking actions that put themselves at risk. However, not all of the processes cited by social engineers are supported by psychological research. For instance neuro-linguistic programming has been listed by some social engineers as an effective technique [6] but is largely considered a pseudo-science by psychologists [7]. This demonstrates the importance of evidence based, psychologically informed cyber security education.

Adversaries' common psychological patterns may help in recognizing threats. There are many forums and website on which individuals discuss cyber security attacks, both actual and hypothetical. It has been noted through analysis of these discussions and chat logs that cyber adversaries often appear to display cognitive dissonance over their actions. This refers to the discomfort felt by individuals when they have two contradictory beliefs or values. Regardless of how dismissive an individual cyber attacker may be of their targeted victim they are still likely to feel at least a degree of guilt over causing harm to others. Rogers [8] notes that cyber attackers engage in various strategies to reduce cognitive dissonance. This includes the use of euphemistic language; blaming their actions on social pressures whilst minimizing their own individual roles in group-based actions; minimizing the negative consequences of their actions; and vilifying and dehumanizing their targets. Awareness of these processes may help cyber security practitioners better review possible threats, and also aide them in differentiating an actual, imminent threat from idle chat.

Another important area of psychology in relation to cyber adversaries is motivation and group identity [30]. Various typologies of adversaries have been proposed, including Seebruck's circular order circumplex model [9] which divides hackers into those motivated by prestige, recreation, revenge, profit and ideology. An awareness of these varying motivations is important for cybersecurity students, as this will improve their understanding of the behavioural patterns and possible future actions on adversaries. For example, the motivations and actions of a hacktivist group using a distributed denial of service attack to make an ideological protest against an organisation are different from those who are financially motivated. This is linked to group processes. It is of course often difficult to attribute blame in the case of many cyber security incidents, but several of the more high profile cases that have been investigated in depth have contained a group element [10, 30]. It is known from social psychological research that being part of a group alters an individual's behaviour and cognition in a number of ways, although we are often unaware of the degree to which the membership of the group is influencing us [11]. This includes cognitive biases which lead them to overestimate the ability of their own group, whilst underestimating the skill level of their opponents, as well as making riskier and more extreme decisions than would be the case if the individual acted alone [12]. An awareness that cyber adversaries are acting as a group can also be used to inform how best to publicly respond to the attack. As suggested by the category differentiation model [13] an external party identifying a group as a group reinforces their sense of group cohesion, which may in turn make further actions and attacks more likely Such a processes is argued to have been evident in relation to the hacktivist collective Anonymous, where media reports of their activities emboldened the group and reinforced their sense of group identity [10]. By having an awareness of these group processes cybersecurity students may again be better placed to better predict the future behaviour of cyber adversaries.

2.2 The Targets

Cyber security attacks that involve a human element often rely upon the target performing, or failing to perform, certain behavioural actions. By examining demographic factors and individual differences it may be possible to identify which individuals are at particular risk. As has been demonstrated by such research those who are most at risk may not match popular stereotypes of vulnerable computer users. For instance, it has been observed that younger adults may be at greater risk at being tricked by phishing emails, despite their presumed greater familiarity with internet technologies than older adults [14]. This is related to the cognitive biases that individual may demonstrate in relation to their cyber security behaviors, with for instance individuals being shown to ignore warnings about risks if they are confident in their ability to minimize the consequences of a security breach [15]. In addition, there is evidence that people do not change their use of social network sites, even if they have previously been hacked [16]. Organisations have also not been found to change their security practices post breach or they make only a few modifications with the belief that these changes shield them from future attacks [31]. There is little understanding that threat vectors change and evolve often becoming more sophisticated and difficult to detect [31]. This may reflect the privacy paradox [17] in which individuals are motivated to maintain their reputation and identity online, even at the cost of taking actions to protect themselves. Further cognitive biases include exaggerating unusual risks whilst downplaying more common risks; underestimating risks that fall under the individuals remit whilst overestimating risks outside their control; perceiving personified risks to be greater than anonymous risks; believing themselves to be at less risk than their peers; and finally overestimating risks that may become a focus of public discussion [18, 19].

It is important to note that these cognitive biases do serve an evolutionary function. As discussed by Kahneman [20] cognitive biases and other forms of decision making heuristics are necessary as it would not otherwise be possible for us to process the vast amount of information that we are continually encountering. In other words, while ideally we would approach every situation with thorough, comprehensive consideration, the cognitive demands of doing so would be too great. Instead, we must make use of heuristics and biases to come to quick decisions, often based on relatively limited information. The tendency of people to do so can easily create frustrations for cyber security practitioners, who would prefer users to be approaching any situation relating to cyber security with the slower, more considered approach. Successful social engineering strategies are often based on encouraging targets to engage in the quicker form of decision making, which is why for instance many phishing emails will include a fear appeal or an element or urgency. Many attempts to promote positive cyber security behaviors in the workplace aim to encourage users to always be taking the slower, more thorough approach to cyber security related activities, rather than making quicker decisions based on a smaller number of cues. Yet psychologists would argue that this is not sustainable; and that it is important to accept that the tendency of humans to make quick decisions is an evolutionary need, not an inherent design flaw. By better understanding how humans make decisions, cyber security practitioners may be better placed to determine how to design systems that take these factors into account.

As with cyber adversaries, the individuals who are targeted in cyber-attacks are also often part of groups. These social influences need to be acknowledged when considering cyber security behaviours, that is how group processes may hinder or help when cyber security processes and policies are being implemented. For example, as based on the Theory of Planned Behaviour it has been noted that the intention someone has to perform a desired behaviour (such as updating software) is in part determined by whether they think influential others will support or condemn their actions [21]. For instance, the IT department of a company may direct all staff members to take actions to ensure that the software on their PCs is up to date, but if an individual user is concerned that their immediate manager will be unhappy about the downtime this will cause then they will be less likely to follow these actions. Social interactions and interpersonal relationships are also factors relating to insider threat, both intentional and unintentional. Band et al. [22]. identify several relevant factors, including stressful events observable in personal and work life, and stressful events in relation to the workplace, including conflicts and sanctions. These factors are of course highly psychological in nature, and making use of pre-existing psychological educational materials could help educate cyber security students on how to identify and measure key psychosocial factors.

3 Pedagogical Approaches

Successfully incorporating psychology into cyber security education relies not just on identify what information should be delivered, but also how it should be delivered. It is important to acknowledge that cyber security students and training course attendees will often have a certain perception of what psychology entails. A common perception we encounter is that psychology is only concerned with mental illness, and that the methods that are used are highly personal and subjective. It can come as a surprise to cyber security students that psychology as an academic discipline is far broader, and in many countries, will only be offered as a science degree (e.g. a Bachelor of Science in the UK, as opposed to a Bachelor of Arts). As discussed in Taylor [23] there are important differences in ontology and epistemology between psychology and computing-related disciplines, which shape how students view the world and how receptive they may or may not be to different educational approaches. In this section, we will review our experiences teaching psychological principles to cyber security students and practitioners across a range of settings. This includes undergraduate and postgraduate courses, short courses for continuing professional development and training packages for commercial and industrial partners.

3.1 Understanding Student Motivations and Expectations

Students undertaking some form of cyber security education or training can come from varied backgrounds, including those entering university or colleges course directly from school and those who are already working in industry. Differences between reasons why students chose computing and psychology degrees has been investigated by a number of psychologists. For example, it has been found [24] that computing students were primarily interested in developing problem-solving and logical thinking skills, as well as increasing future earning potential. Psychology students on the other hand placed more emphasis on understanding other people, oneself and developing greater personal independence. In addition, and perhaps not surprisingly, psychology students also expressed greater interest in understanding social relationship and interacting with people, whereas computing students were more interested in understanding and interacting with technological systems. It is important to take these differences into account when planning and delivering cyber security education and training. This relates not to just to the academic background of the individual, but also their level of maturity and life experiences. In our experience younger undergraduate students from both psychology and computing backgrounds appear to feel less equipped to discuss the moral, ethical and philosophical issues that arise in cyber security. Gibb et al. observe that undergraduates' may not have yet fully developed their understanding of how moral issues relate to societal functioning [25]. Therefore, cyber security education may need to be tailored towards the student population to whom the material is being delivered.

It is also important to recognize that students studying for cybersecurity courses are likely to have been taught in different ways and may approach studying in different ways, compared to those studying for psychology degrees. On the one hand, based on our own experience computing assignments tend to require answers that are unequivocally right or wrong, or at least where there is finite set of correct solutions. Within psychology, on the other hand, the emphasis can often be on the quality of the debate that is put forward by the student, with there often being no correct answer. This is not of course the case with all areas of psychology – in some sub-disciplines such as neuropsychology for instance there is a clearer sense of information being either right or wrong, which is in keeping with such sub-disciplines being considered more 'scientific' than other areas of psychology. Nevertheless, we would argue that there is a greater emphasis in psychology on an objective evaluation of theories, whereas assignment in computing tend to have a more problem-solving focus, which solutions or answers deemed to be either correct or incorrect. Depending on their background it has also been our experience that cybersecurity students can find the methodological approaches used in psychology to be quite different from what they have previously experienced. An experience we often have when we presented multiple (occasionally contradictory) theories to cyber security students is to be asked which theory is the correct one – they are then often surprised, and at times frustrated, when we reply there is no single, universally accepted theory which is seen as the correct one.

3.2 Perspective Shifting

It has been our experience that cyber security students tend to focus on how the actions of the target enabled or facilitated the cyber-attack. However, in our experience it seems that while students are interested in the how and the what, they are less interested in the why. Similarly, cyber adversaries tend not to be considered, beyond an analysis of what their actions were. In the sessions we have delivered with cyber security students we have attempted to promote a deeper understanding of the psychological processes displayed by both the targets and the cyber adversaries. One way we do this is by asking the students to consider the incident from the perspective of both parties. For example, students are asked to identify high risk group and to consider how advice should be tailored to that group so that it will be understood and acted upon. They are then asked to design a cyberattack that would circumnavigate their own advice, again taking into account the psychological characteristics of the target group. In doing so students are encouraged to think about the various psychological processes discussed in Sect. 2 and to develop a deeper understanding of why adversaries may have chosen a target, why they chose a particular attack methodology and why the targets may have failed to identify and mitigate the attack.

Another instance where we extended a two-way relationship between psychology and cyber security is during the teaching of digital investigations and forensics. The processes of cyber forensic analysis function in a complex problem space, due to the increased uncertainty surrounding forensics investigations in general. Since digital investigations refer to an activity related to an individual or a group of cyber criminals, an understanding of psychology plays a significant role. For example, if when deciphering the evidence files an exhaustive search becomes the final option (due to failure of all cryptanalytic attacks), the data would need to be decrypted based on constructing case-specific dictionaries according to the psychology of the suspect's behaviour. In such cases, behavioural profiling is used to identify certain traits, preferences or tastes of the suspect that can assist in constructing a collection of dictionaries of passwords. These shifts to employing psychological perspectives in the analysis of digital evidence also contributes to the understanding of the socio-psychological behaviour of cyber criminals. Moreover, it was found that integrating psychology and digital investigations and forensics on an epistemological level not only resulted in added value for the cyber security students, but also of paramount importance that cyber security involves psychology in order to compensate for the significant uncertainty that governs the analysis of cybercrime.

Finally, cyber security students—and their professional counterparts—often approach cyber security concerns with the addition of new systems; adding authentication requirements, password requirements, policies, and permissions restrictions. But these approaches often add complexity to an already complex operations ecosystem, make the work of the employees more arduous, and rarely patch the true causes of the security gaps. The types of evidence-based design principles offered by the user-design field of psychology helps cyber security students better understand the need for usable security systems—systems that improve security and reduce potential loss where employees do not feel overburdened—and how to implement them. Usually, the goal is clarity for the user, but user design can also be used to add desirable difficulties for end-users [26]. Desirable difficulties, or a marker that breaks up the flow of current activities, can be used as a tool for increasing awareness at key times [27]. Teaching cyber security students about usable design, and more specifically usable security, allows them to consider new approaches to cyber security that account for the ways in which their staff will interact with the systems they create.

4 Teaching Psychology in the Workplace

Many of the learning outcomes emerging from teaching psychology and cybersecurity are now being used as the basis for commercial tools that can be used to address cyber security practice within organization. However, there are important differences in context between a college and university course and the work place. Cyber security students may be skeptical about the role of psychology, but it is reasonable to assume that they do at least have an interest in cyber security overall. As such the main challenge is to demonstrate to them why psychology is an important topic in relation to cyber security. In organisations however, users may not have initial interest in cyber security at all. Even if they do there may be greater pressures of time and money within a workplace, that mean that cyber security education has to be delivered in a much shorter time scale. The academic authors of this paper have explored these challenges in conjunction with practitioners.

In the UK, we have worked with LiMETOOLS, a highly specialised publisher of learning tools that bring about behavioural change in areas of high commercial risk management, including cyber security. Making use of social cognitive learning theory [28] employees are prompted to consider how behavioural actions may lead to and facilitate cyber security attacks way similar to the perspective taking exercises used with students. Interactive dramas are used immerse learners in examples of realistic cyber security incidents, followed by interactive quizzes to assess knowledge. A tool targeted at graduate workers who used social networks heavily has also been created. As such rather than attempting to cover the full range of possible cyber security risks the tool focuses on a key area that is often utilized by social engineers. The tool exposes a fictional hacker at work, whilst facilitating the learner through a process creating their own action plan. On the basis that prevention is better than cure a second tool offers graduate recruiters an audit tool for new potential employees to calculate their vulnerability in the cyber domains relevant to a wide range of industrial sectors. As such the tool both educates and audits at the same time.

Further prevailing methods used by organisations in Australia involving psychology to address cyber security risks are centered on HATCH Training (Hacking and Tricking Capricious Humans) using real time scenarios to help employees learn different cyber-attack situations and the processes to tackle them. This method particularly has been found effective in reducing phishing, ransomware, physical manipulations, and spear phishing related attacks. In addition, simulation-based training using gamification tools where live examples are presented along with solutions is now commonly applied by large organisations. The gamification aspects of the training are focused on assessing the behaviour of hypothetical victims of cyber-attacks through psychological manipulations. This was observed to have a major impact on increasing the level of cyber security risks awareness among employees. Besides, some well-resourced organisations now find it crucial to apply psychology to boost cyber security by targeting specific behavioural limitations such as cultural influence, biases, and cognitive preferences to identify noncompliant security behaviour of employees, as well as employees that are overestimating their capability to mitigate security risks. This strategy creates the possibility for organisations to design role-specific interventions for any identified weak points.

The key learning outcomes of these trials so far indicate six critical requirements for this kind of workplace learning that combines psychology and cyber security factors:

i)   the immersive aspect of the approach through videos and dramatizations appear to be particularly effective with younger learners, who appear to be more easily distracted when less immersive teaching strategies are used;

ii) integrating well-executed and psychologically backed game design with intellectual challenges, and positive reinforcement techniques improves learner's engagement, thus, promoting behaviour change and knowledge retention;

iii) learners demonstrated the wish to have control over their pace of learning and also the device on which they engage with the educational materials; this is consistent with psychological research that would suggest that giving people a feeling of control over their own behaviour change process is likely to improve outcomes [29];

iv) it is important to find a balance between the activities. Users respond best when there is a combination of videos, quizzes and interactive sessions. Users who did appear to find any one particular activity too extensive were observed to attempt to cheat the system to move to the next activity;

v)   raising awareness is not by itself sufficient. Indeed, several users noted that after viewing the video materials they felt more nervous and uncertain than before about how to respond to cyber security threats. This relates to the aforementioned Protection Motivation Theory [16] in which individuals who are too afraid of a possible threat may not even attempt to avoid the threat, if they believe that such avoidance is not possible. The developer mitigates this risk by following up the input experience immediately with a module that supports the user in producing their own positive action plan to minimise the risk; and

vi) learners need to know how they are performing at regular intervals during the experience. The developer's Learning Management Software (LMS) is configured so that the learner can see their scores regularly and receive comparative data about their performance against the rest of their peer group. This can incentivise the enthusiasm for learning by itself.

5 Conclusions

We strongly believe that there is potential for the field of psychology to contribute to cyber security education and practice. To do so we need to consider which areas of psychological research are most pertinent to cyber security, whilst taking a pragmatic approach that acknowledges the time and resources available when delivering cyber security education and training. We also need to acknowledge the differences in epistemological and ontological assumptions between psychology and cyber security students, and how these translate into teaching practice. By doing so we can work in an inter-disciplinary manner to better equip cyber security students and practitioners with the skills and knowledge they need to address cyber security challenges.

References

1. Dawson, J., Thomson, R.: The future cybersecurity workforce: going beyond technical skills for successful cyber performance. Front. Psychol. **9** (2018). 1664-1078. https://www.frontiersin.org/article/10.3389/fpsyg.2018.00744
2. Kearney, W.D., Kruger, H.A.: Can perceptual differences account for enigmatic information security behaviour in an organisation? Comput. Secur. **61**, 46–58 (2016)
3. Iuga, C., Nurse, J.R.C., Erola, A.: Baiting the hook: factors impacting susceptibility to phishing attacks. Hum.-Centric Comput. Inf. Sci. **6**(1), 1–20 (2016). https://doi.org/10.1186/s13673-016-0065-2
4. Bursztein, E., et al.: Handcrafted fraud and extortion: manual account hijacking in the wild. In: Proceedings of the 2014 Conference on Internet Measurement Conference, Vancouver, BC, Canada, pp. 347–358. ACM (2014)
5. Johnston, A.C., Warkentin, M., Siponen, M.: An enhanced fear appeal rhetorical framework: leveraging threats to the human asset through sanctioning rhetoric. Mis Q. **39**(1), 113–134 (2015)
6. Hadnagy, C.: Social Engineering: The Act of Human Hacking. Wiley Publishing Inc., Indianapolis (2011)
7. Witkowski, T.: Thirty-five years of research on neuro-linguistic programming. NLP research data base. State of the art or pseudoscientific decoration? Pol. Psychol. Bull. **41**(2), 58–66 (2010)
8. Rogers, M.K.: The psyche of cybercriminals: a psycho-social perspective. In: Anal. Ghosh, G., Turrini, E. (eds.) Cybercrimes: A Multidisciplinary Analysis, pp. 217–235. Springer, Berlin (2010). https://doi.org/10.1007/978-3-642-13547-7_14
9. Seebruck, R.: A typology of hackers: classifying cyber malfeasance using a weighted arc circumplex model. Digit. Invest. **14**, 36–45 (2015)
10. Olson, P.: We Are Anonymous. Back Bay Books, New York (2012)
11. Darley, J.M.: Social organization for the production of evil. Psychol. Inq. **3**(2), 199–218 (1992)
12. Wallach, M.A., Kogan, N., Bem, D.J.: Group influence on individual risk-taking. J. Abnorm. Psychol. **65**(2), 75 (1962)
13. Doise, W.: Groups and Individuals: Explanations in Social Psychology. Cambridge University Press, Cambridge (1978)
14. Sheng, S., et al.: Who falls for phish? A demographic analysis of phishing susceptibility and effectiveness of interventions. In: Proceedings of the SIGCHI Conference on Human Factors in Computing Systems 2010, Atlanta, Georgia, USA, pp. 373–382. ACM (2010)

15. Rifon, N.J., LaRose, R., Choi, S.M.: Your privacy is sealed: effects of web privacy seals on trust and personal disclosures. J. Consum. Aff. **39**(2), 339–362 (2005)

16. Power, A., Kirwan, G.: Cyberpsychology and New Media: A Thematic Reader. Psychology Press, New York (2014)

17. Utz, S., Kramer, N.: The privacy paradox on social network sites revisited: The role of individual characteristics and group norms. Cyberpsychol.: J. Psychosoc. Res. Cyberspace **3**(2) (2009)

18. Schmidt, M.B., Arnett, K.P.: Spyware: a little knowledge is a wonderful thing. Commun. ACM **48**(8), 67–70 (2005)

19. Schneier, B.: The Psychology of Security. In: Vaudenay, S. (ed.) AFRICACRYPT 2008. LNCS, vol. 5023, pp. 50–79. Springer, Heidelberg (2008). https://doi.org/10.1007/978-3-540-68164-9_5

20. Kahneman, D.: Thinking Fast and Slow, 1st edn. 499 pp. Penguin, Westminster (2011)

21. Venkatesh, V., et al.: User acceptance of information technology: toward a unified view. Mis Q. **27**(3), 425–478 (2003)

22. Band, S.R., et al. Comparing insider it sabotage and espionage: a model-based analysis. Software Engineer Institute, Carnegie Mellon (2006)

23. Radford, J., Holdstock, L.: Gender differences in higher education aims between computing and psychology students. Res. Sci. Technol. Educ. **13**(2), 163–176 (1995)

24. Taylor, J.: Teaching psychology to computing students. Psychol. Teach. Rev. **14**(1), 21–29 (2008)

25. Gibbs, J.C.: Moral Development and Reality: Beyond the Theories of Kohlberg and Hoffman. SAGE Publications, Newcastle upon Tyne (2003)

26. Making things hard on yourself, but in a good way: creating desirable difficulties to enhance learning. In: Psychology and the Real World. Essays Illustrating Fundamental Contributions to Society, no. 2, pp. 59–68 (2011)

27. Linn, M.C., Chang, H.-Y., Chiu, J.L., Zhang, Z.H., McElhaney, K.: Can desirable difficulties overcome deceptive clarity in scientific visualizations? In: Benjamin, A.S. (ed.) Successful Remembering and Successful Forgetting: A Festschrift in honor of Robert A. Bjork (pp. 235–258). Taylor & Francis (2011). https://doi.org/10.4324/9780203842539

28. Bandura, A.: Social cognitive theory. In: Ewen, R.B. (ed.) An Introduction to the Theories of Personality, pp. 365–386. Lawrence Erlbraun Associates, Mahwa (2003)

29. Steptoe, A., Wardle, J.: Locus of control and health behaviour revisited: a multivariate analysis of young adults from 18 countries. Br. J. Psychol. **92**(Pt 4), 659–672 (2001)

30. Maurushat, A.: Ethical Hacking. University of Ottawa Press, Ottawa (2019)

31. Maurushat, A., Bello, A., Bragg, B.: Artificial intelligence enabled cyber fraud: a detailed look into payment diversion fraud and ransomware. Indian J. Law Technol. **15**(2) (2019)

CoDeFi: First Workshop on Coordination of Decentralized Finance

Effectiveness of Multi-stakeholder Discussions for Decentralized Finance: A Conference Report of CoDeFi 2020

Shin'ichiro Matsuo[✉]

Georgetown University, Washington, D.C., USA
Shinichiro.Matsuo@georgetown.edu

Abstract. After the invention of Bitcoin [1], the decentralization of the finance system became a big trend in technology, business, and regulation points of view. On the one hand, the decentralization manner of technology development is the right solution for innovation dilemma, but on the other hand, it makes for regulators to achieve regulatory goals. This is an existing problem for communication technology, especially for the global Internet, but this is a new problem for the financial industry and regulators. Lack of well-organized collaboration among stakeholders, there were many scams, and financial crimes were occurred based on blockchain technology. This article summarizes the needs of multi-stakeholder discussion, the background of the CoDeFi 2020 workshop, and unconference style discussions by all stakeholders.

Keywords: Blockchain · Governance · Decentralized finance

1 Introduction

1.1 Background

In the long history of technology development, introducing a new technology provides many benefits and, sometimes, many frictions to our life and society. The friction is usually controlled by some kind of rules and regulations which come from an agreement by a group of peoples. For example, Internet technology unbundles the communication architecture, which was monopolized by big telecommunication companies to layered and open architecture. The distributed structure of the Internet made a huge amount of permissionless innovation in terms of global communication. On the other hand, the Internet experienced many frictions with society and government. For example, cybersecurity and privacy are the new and serious issues for community and government; then, the European Union created the General Data Protection Regulation (GDPR), a regulation for personal data protection. Censorship by the government is another issue in terms of the relationship between government and citizens. This is an existing and old problem for the Internet. After the invention of Bitcoin, a global

© Springer Nature Switzerland AG 2020
M. Bernhard et al. (Eds.): FC 2020 Workshops, LNCS 12063, pp. 221–229, 2020.
https://doi.org/10.1007/978-3-030-54455-3_16

payment protocol that does not assume the existence of any trusted party, similar evolution happened among the financial industry and regulators. While it will provide a huge amount of potential innovations for the financial industry by unbundling functionalities of finance, the global space for payment may provide a way of bypass regulations. Anti-Money Laundering (AML) and Counter Financing of Terrorism (CFT) are the prime issues for international financial regulators. Hence, Financial Action Task Force (FATF) published "Travel Rule" to prevent crypto-asset transactions for money laundering and terrorist financing. The appearance of global (not international) and permissionless space is an entirely new situation for the financial industry. In general, regulations write things prohibited, but for the financial industry, regulations write only things allowed. Many governments are seeking new permissionless innovations based on permissionless blockchain as a solution to innovation dilemma, on the other hand, the need to seek a good direction to regulate crimes over the permissionless platform. New services and programming code which realize them born every day from grassroots. Thus, it is too difficult to regulate financial services over a permissionless blockchain. Regulators need help from open-source style engineers to achieve their regulatory goals.

On June 8th and 9th, 2019, Distributed Ledger Technology-related innovations have been referenced in the Communique at the G20 Finance and Central Bank Meeting in Fukuoka, Japan, referencing the report produced by the Financial Stability Board (FSB) [2]. The following is the historical sentence that G20 considers the Introduction of multi-stakeholder governance for decentralized finance.

G20 Communique - Section 13 "We welcome the FSB report on decentralized financial technologies, and the possible implications for financial stability, regulation and governance, and how regulators can enhance the dialogue with a wider group of stakeholders."

Usually, introducing a multi-stakeholder discussion may imply that the government gives up some power, which is not usually occurring. However, this is a historical moment G20 agrees with this direction.

1.2   A Series of Workshop

After the G20, BSafe.network, an academic and neutral group of 31 universities in 14 countries which operates global Blockchain testbed, held a series of the workshop as Table 1, which gather all stakeholders in one place and discuss a specific topic, in several diversified countries.

At G20 meets G-20, 24 participants, including three regulators, five engineers, four startup entrepreneurs, five researchers, six financial industry, and one attorney participated. The topics discussed were (1) Lack of consumer protections e.g., with cryptocurrency exchanges, and (2) Challenges of entrepreneurs to build businesses involving blockchain tech while facing an uncertain regulatory environment.

Table 1. A series of multi-stakeholdoer discussion workshops

Date	Title of the event	Venue
June 13, 2019	G20 meets G-20	Vancouver, Canada
September 3, 2019	Fin/sum 2019	Tokyo, Japan
September 8, 2019	Decentralized finance architecture	Tel Aviv, Israel
November 11, 2019	Security standardization research	London, UK
November 12, 2019	Multi-stakeholder workshop for financial diversity	Dublin, Ireland
February 14, 2020	CoDeFi 2020	Kota Kinabaru, Malaysia
February 18, 2020	Stanford Blockchian conference	Palo Alto, USA
Febraury 26, 2020	CoDeFi NY	New York, USA

The Decentralized Finance Architecture Workshop in Tel Aviv, was co-located with Scaling Bitcoin 2019, which is an annual conference for Bitcoin core engineers and academic researchers. There were 54 participants, including ten regulators, 17 researchers, 14 financial Services, blockchain business, nine developers, two investors, and 2 media. It discussed privacy protection, the security of custody, and the FATF Travel Rule.

The CoDeFi 2020 workshop is one of the workshops in this series. Given the nature of the Financial Cryptography conference, the workshop gathered mainly academic researchers and blockchain engineers. Furthermore, it is notable that regulators joined the workshop to provide its view. Hence, This workshop was an excellent opportunity to discuss complicated issues by all stakeholders at the place where cypherpunks were a part of the participants.

2   Issues of Blockchain Ecosystem Toward Social Foudation

2.1   Three Aspects Toward Healthy Ecosytem

As described in the Introduction, the main goal is achieving both permissionless innovation and regulatory goals. Moreover, as same as the Internet, decentralized financial systems based on permissionless blockchain technology implies global space. Here, "global" has a different meaning from "international," that is, while international means the relationship between nations, global means a matter independent from nations. The Internet is global space, and Bitcoin and other permissionless blockchain technology are creating global spaces for finance. Laurence Lessig proposed a figure to explain how orders in the era of the Internet and programming code. He claimed that social order would be composed of architecture, norm, market, and law. In this sense, decentralized finance may be outside of the governance of nations. Hence, we should take three aspects into account - permissionless innovation, global space, and achieving regulatory goals. When we create a new style of order, we should create a healthy harmonization among them.

2.2   Pain Points of Stakeholders

There are four categories of stakeholders in the blockchain ecosystem, open-source style engineer, business entity, regulators, and consumers.

Open source style engineers sometimes do not want to talk with regulators, and there are few connections and no common language with regulators. Thus, it is very hard to communicate with each other and regulate open-source style engineer. In the case of the Bitcoin core, there is no responsible corporation to maintain software code.

Business entities sometimes try to start a business before maturing technology and want to avoid friction against regulations. Regulators may not follow up on the speed of new services.

Consumers need transparency for the blockchain business they use, but in many cases, white papers and web sites are not suitable for verifying the soundness of the blockchain business and technology.

From the above, despite good collaborations are needed among all stakeholders, but due to the lack of communication channels, common language, and common incentives, such collaborations are missing now.

2.3   How Multi-stakeholder Discussions Help to Create a Better Order of Decentralized Finance

The major problem with communication among stakeholders is the lack of shared understandings. This is caused by a lack of common language and definitions of words. In many cases, open-source style engineer does not understand the regulations and regulators do not read the programming code. In reality, sometimes engineers write programming codes but do not write documents that are verifiable by the third party. Without such a document, anyone, including regulators and consumers, cannot check if the programming codes are good for society and our life. Communication by multi-stakeholder supported by neutral academia will help to have the same understanding by translating the technology to publicly verifiable documents.

The first step to solve this problem is creating common documents, and potentially common running code, for a particular issue by all stakeholders. The process facilitates such a common understanding.

The next phase of collaboration is co-creating a new technology and regulation. Usually, a new idea of technology and business comes from grassroots. It is not easy to stop such a grass-root innovation. However, regulators may contribute to polishing the new technology and business to make them regulation friendly. On the other hand, engineers may contribute to polishing regulations with documents and programming code if the regulations are open to the public for modification, for example, at the GitHub repository.

Nowadays, several standardization bodies are utilizing this type of process, that is, the draft standard documents are on the public repository, then any sort of proposal and pull request are allowed to post. Of course, the law and regulation should be decided as a result of the designated process (e.g., democracy), this type of joint work dramatically solve the problem of misunderstandings and support rapid permissionless innovations.

3   Goals and Structure of the Workshop

This workshop is designed to provide multi-stakeholders an environment for understanding, exploration, and discussion of distributed ledger technologies. As permissionless blockchain and distributed ledger technology (DLT) platforms evolve and mature, there is an urgent need for multi-stakeholders to engage in their planning, development, roll-out, and operation, in order for innovation of a wide variety of financial applications to proliferate and become mainstream. Thus far, it has been mainly developer & startup communities that are driving these protocols, platforms, and applications for this new era of computing. New standards, governance mechanisms, and design patterns are evolving and need input from a variety of perspectives. There is a growing trend towards decentralized computing systems in which distributed ledger technologies are a fundamental component. These systems are designed to be global computing systems; they will likely form the basis of new financial services and businesses, including a distributed Financial Market Infrastructure (dFMI). These new financial services and businesses could bring huge benefits to the global financial system. However, financial regulators, central banks, the BIS and IMF, while recognizing the potential of DLT systems, have also been keenly aware of the challenges in the adoption, and designing for the consumer protections required to balance usability, safety while supporting innovation. While it is likely that many G20 countries will be leading the design and development of these new infrastructures, all countries should be considered and encouraged to participate in the planning.

Basic Structure of the Workshop is as follows.

- Lecture about background of multi-stakeholder discussions for Decentralized Finance
- Selected talks from all stakeholders
- Unconference style multi-stakeholder discussions on selected discussion topics

The workshop agenda is as follows.

- Presentation by Stakeholders
  - Session 1 (9:00–10:30)
    * Opening Remarks - Shin'ichiro Matsuo, Program Chair (9–9:15)
    * Keynote by Ian Miers (9:15–9:45)
    * Shigeya Suzuki, Lecture on the Internet's Governance (9:45–10:30)
  - Session 2 (11:00–12:30)
    * Yuta Takanashi, Future of Finance - from G20 to the practical implementation of multi-stakeholder governance on decentralized finance
    * Yuji Suga, Securing Cryptocurrency Exchange: Building up Standard from Huge Failures

- Unconference style Multi-stakeholder Discussions
  - Session 3 (14:00–15:30)
    * Selection of discussion topics (14:00–14:10)
    * Multi-stakeholder discussions (14:10–15:10)
    * Report Back (15:10–15:30)
  - Session 4 (16:00–17:30)
    * Selection of discussion topics (16:00–16:10)
    * Multi-stakeholder discussions (16:10–17:10)
    * Report Back (17:10–17:30)

Program Committee members are as follows.

- Byron Gibson, Program Manager at Stanford Center for Blockchain Research
- Shin'ichiro Matsuo, Georgetown University and BSafe.network (Workshop Chair)
- Robert Schwentker, DLT Education, and BSafe.network
- Yonatan Sompolinsky, The Hebrew University of Jerusalem, DAGlabs
- Shigeya Suzuki, Keio University, BSafe.Network, BASE Alliance and WIDE Project
- Yuta Takanashi, JFSA and ex-Georgetown University
- Pindar Wong, BSafe.network
- Anton Yemelyanov, Base58 Association
- Aviv Zohar, The Hebrew University of Jerusalem

4   Main Discussions at Unconference Sessions

There are two sessions on (1) How to facilitate the multi-stakeholder discussion, and (2) Privacy and Traceability.

4.1   Facilitating Multi-stakeholder Discussion

Source of Misunderstanding. Firstly, the group started the discussion with the pain points. Many of pain points are caused by misunderstandings among stakeholders. Especially, understanding and definition of the same term are different for each stakeholder. Thus, creating a dictionary of terms is the essential starting point. Moreover, the ways of defining terms are also different. For example, a description of the law tends to be more generic. The other example is blockchain engineer and business entity use the word of "smart contract," however it is not a legal contract. From a legal point of view, a smart contract is just a procedure from the viewpoint of the lawyer. Participants agree that without common definition and understanding of terms, any collaboration is a waste of time.

Technology and Law. In the era of blockchain, programming codes may become a part of the law, and engineers may be treated as a creator of law. However, many engineers often do not know about the law, for example, on civil law and common law. The idea of decentralization and anti-censorship of permissionless blockchain comes from the philosophy of cypherpunks. However, it is a bit far from law. On the other hand, the law cannot regulate Technology itself, and the target of regulation is mainly service providers. To think about the target of regulation, design of technology and operation layers, and design of division of responsibility is essential.

Target Area of Collaboration. From the FATF and regulator point of view, AML is the essential issue. Banks are requested by the local regulator to conduct its process to prevent money laundering and terrorist financing. On the other hand, anonymous crypto-asset and layer two technology may be tools to facilitate them. Engineers generally do not want to help illegal use of blockchain. The potential direction is that regulators and engineers have a common goal of AML/CFT, then regulators check the programming code and engineers check and improve regulations. As an extreme idea, regulators will make a pull request to the GitHub repository of Bitcoin, Ethereum, and other projects. Utilizing a common repository to improve software codes and regulations is a better way to deal with rapidly growing innovation. To realize this, regulators need to have a group of experts and software engineers.

4.2   Privacy and Traceability

Introduction. One participant introduced the topic by mentioning that in many cases, discussion on privacy vs. traceability falls on the debate between complete privacy and complete traceability or just a balance between them. However, this may not be the appropriate attitude toward discussion. The right way of thinking is that they are not incompatible. Several participants supported the idea that we should design the architecture to incentivize good things and disincentivize bad things. One participant emphasized the appropriate way is to regulate processes and services on top of the protocol layer but not protocol itself. Echoing this notion, one participant insisted that if an engineer decided to change the technology for the sake of regulation, it is a kind of suicide as an engineer in this community.

Merchant Based KYC and Transaction Monitoring. One example of suggested practical way to handle issues of privacy and risk of money laundering and terrorist financing is that regulators mandate that merchants are receiving cryptocurrencies conduct customer due diligence and monitor the suspicious activities by checking where the money (cryptocurrency) comes from. One participant posed a question on how we should handle mixing and other privacy-enhancing technologies that would make it difficult for merchants to check if the money is not tainted (e.g., comes from illicit activities). Answering this question, one participant insisted that what merchants need to do is not tracing all the history of the cryptocurrency as this practice could erode the fungibility, but check if the customer successfully proves that cryptocurrency has the legitimate source. Another participant argued that if merchants adopt a rule to stop the transactions when the mixing was used in the history of the said cryptocurrency, engineers will adopt new technology to hide the fact that mixing was used in order to maintain fungibility, which would reduce the effectiveness of the rule. On the other hand, another participant shared a different view that punishment on the usage of mixing services would encourage market participants to check if the cryptocurrency comes through mixing services, which would eventually disincentivize people from using such services. However, another participant introduced the research of the technical issue, arguing that almost all the cryptocurrency would become contaminated in the longer run, which casts doubt on the effectiveness of the punishment.

Regulatory Nudge. Following the discussion, one participant suggested enhancing utilization of incentive mechanisms in order to address issues of privacy and criminal activities, citing an example that Singaporean tax authority incentivizes people to submit receipts to them in order to detect sales tax evasion by giving a ticket for a national lottery in exchange of the receipt. On the other hand, another participant pointed out that such drastic change of policy may require that authorities prove that the issue is large/serious enough; however, once the issue becomes large enough, such subtle regulatory nudge would not be effective enough.

Designing the Architecture of the System. On the design aspect, one participant pointed out that current vertically integrated protocols may not be ideal not just from engineering perspectives but also regulatory perspectives because vertically integrated protocols hinder regulators from sharpening the target of the regulation (e.g., regulate only on the payment layer but not consensus layer, etc.) Another participant argued that the ecosystem is still in the try and error phase and predicted that, at a certain point in time, ecosystem participants organically start moving toward further standardization and interoperability, as we saw in the case of the Internet.

Backdoor and Technology Neutrality of Regulation. One participant posed a question on the backdoor in the cryptography discussed in the past (e.g., Clipper chip in the US) and in some jurisdictions now. Another participant strongly insisted that a backdoor for authorities would risk the entire system as the key for the backdoor could be hacked and cause unintended data breaches. Another participant pointed out the difficulty of deciding who controls the backdoor key as the system is global and may have no home jurisdiction. One participant, on the contrary, mentioned that regulators might decide to pursue regulatory goals through regulation on a protocol, which may breach the principle of technology neutrality of regulation. To this possibility, many participants agreed on the importance of transparency in the design and implementation of the protocol.

5   Conclusion and Future Activity

The CoDeFi 2020 workshop discussed (1) the importance of multi-stakeholder discussion to achieve both benefits from permissionless innovation and regulator goals for a better society, (2) the suitable form of collaboration among stakeholders, and (3) potential collaboration topics with including all stakeholders. As a result of the workshop, all stakeholders had the same understandings of the regulatory goals and potential innovations.

Twenty-five days after the workshop, a new initiative named Blockchain Governance Initiative Network (BGIN) was established. This initiative aims to be a place of neutral place of multi-stakeholder discussion to create technology and operational standards. It is a similar goal as Internet Engineering Task Force (IETF). The first work of BGIN is discussing identity/privacy and key management issues regarding blockchain-based finance, which was discussed at the CoDeFi 2020. The discussions at the workshop will be referred to and included in the future discussion and document at BGIN.

References

1. Nakamoto, S.: Bitcoin: A Peer-to-Peer Electronic Cash System. https://bitcoin.org/bitcoin.pdf
2. Financial Stability Board: Decentralised financial technologies - Report on financial stability, regulatory and governance implications. https://www.fsb.org/wp-content/uploads/P060619.pdf

Multistakeholder Governance for the Internet

Shigeya Suzuki[✉][iD]

Graduate School of Media and Governance, Keio University,
5322 Endo, Fujisawa, Kanagawa 252-0882, Japan
shigeya@wide.ad.jp

Abstract. In this paper, we introduce how multistakeholder governance for the Internet initiated and evolved by showing key events, example disputes, and the current organization of the Internet Corporation for Assigned Names and Numbers (ICANN). The Internet has been growing for the last fifty years. Both technological and deployment efforts drove the growth of the Internet. Since internet technology initially does not impose any border between computers communicating, it effectively provides connectivity globally. Globally available borderless networks create conflicts. For example, each of the nations controls the trademark registration, which is not unique if we look beyond jurisdictional borders. Once these registered names started using on the global Internet, there may be possibilities of conflicts of use of the name. To resolve such a dispute, we need a mechanism. The Internet's multistakeholder governance born and start evolving since the so-called dot-com bubble time; finally, the movement established ICANN as a place to discuss issues among multiple stakeholders. Now ICANN is grown enough and showing how the Internet Multistakeholder model is useful for other fields.

Keywords: Internet · Governance · Multistakeholder · Multistakeholderism · ICANN

1 Introduction

The Internet evolved from a computer networking research project started in early 1970. At that time, of course, there was no intention to be used as a business, no concept of crossing borders among nations. It was a research network, which initially picked a person for managing a database of nodes for consistency. At that time, there were almost no resources that require conflict resolution mechanisms.

The commercialization of the Internet started when National Science Foundation lifts the ban on the commercial use of the Internet in 1992. The Internet is a single system that covers the whole world. The global system breaks the border between nations. All of the so-called dot-com businesses started making use of the advantage.

© Springer Nature Switzerland AG 2020
M. Bernhard et al. (Eds.): FC 2020 Workshops, LNCS 12063, pp. 230–241, 2020.
https://doi.org/10.1007/978-3-030-54455-3_17

The resources – domain names, IP addresses, and protocol numbers – were not limited resources at the age of research network. The business use of the Internet causes conflicts to get the best resources for the business. Conflict resolutions require rulings. Making decisions on problems require a mechanism for governance.

Hufty described governance [7] as: *"the processes of interaction and decision-making among the actors involved in a collective problem that lead to the creation, reinforcement, or reproduction of social norms and institutions."* For the governance of the resources for the Internet, it needs interaction among multiple-stakeholders, such as administrators who control the domain name system, operators that operate DNS servers, and end-users who use the domain names. Berejka described multistakeholder process in [4] as: *"In broad strokes, a multistakeholder process is comprised of representatives of groups or communities, both for profit and not, that aspire to develop norms that will guide those very same stakeholders' behavior."* Multistakeholderism is necessary for the globally used system like the Internet.

The governance of the Internet was not built in a day. It was initially started as resource allocation management by an individual. As the Internet started using in business, more and more issues raised. It was impossible to cope with conflicts without policies, which all of the stakeholders can agree with it. A gradual and long term discussion among stakeholders created understandable and agreeable policies. That is how the Internet Corporation for Assigned Names and Numbers (ICANN) established, or the born of multistakeholderism for the Internet.

In this paper, we will describe the Internet multistakeholderism. In Sect. 2, Domain Name System (DNS) is briefly described as a piece of background knowledge for the discussion, followed by an introduction of why multistakeholder governance is necessary for DNS. In Sect. 3, key events of the establishment of Internet multistakeholderism to understand the reason why and how. In Sect. 4, two example dispute events are described. In Sect. 5, introduces current organization of ICANN, and lastly, we wrap-up the discussion in Sect. 6.

2 The Internet Multistakeholderism

In this section, after providing a brief overview of the Internet Domain Name System, we describe the reason why multistakeholder governance is necessary for the Internet.

2.1 Brief Overview of the Internet Domain Name System

Domain Name System (DNS, onwards) [20], is a system translating from a domain name into some IP addresses or other data used for the protocols for the Internet.

Any users of the Internet see domain names day by day. The domain (organization) part of an email address, which is the part the right of the at-mark of an email address, is a domain name, i.e., the domain name of the email address "`user@example.com`" is "`example.com`". The World Wide Web's Uniform Resource Locator (URL), which shown in the location box of any browser, also contains a domain name. The domain name part in an URL is the string between double slash (`//`) to the next and first single slash (`/`), i.e., the domain name of URL "https://fc20.ifca.ai/workshops.html" is "`fc20.ifca.ai`". The label may contain language-specific characters other than English alphanumeric characters by using a particular encoding scheme [19].

A domain name consists of multiple "label" separated by periods. The domain name only consists of the right-most label is called top-level domain. It is possible to use partial (relative) domain name inside an intranet – i.e., "fc20" in the above case – but, for the brevity of paper, let us assume the domain name discussing here is "fully-qualified" (absolute) domain names, like the one used in an email address or an URL – i.e., "fc20.ifca.ai".

The domain names are organized in a tree-like hierarchy. Part of the tree's administration is delegated to an authority of the zone. The unit of delegation is called "zone." Since the administrator has full control of the delegated zone, the administrator has control of which label to be registered in the zone. By adding a label that points to name server resource records, the zone administrator may delegate the control of the zone to the administrator of the name server, which the newly added label points.

The most significant zone of the domain name system is called "root zone." The root zone administrator has control over which top-level domain name to exist, and also which zone. In the early days of the DNS, there were only seven top-level domains, namely, ".com," ".edu," ".gov," ".int," ".mil," ".net," and ".org."

2.2 Needs for Multistakeholder Governance for the Internet Domain Name

Since the so-called dot-com bubble started on and around 1995, businesses and other entities begin realizing the importance of domain name.

The user, business, or any entities, who willing to use the domain name system typically want to pick a domain name to include a string that represents the entity's name. The domain name can contain any strings – a sequence of characters – but the owners willing to use the purest form of the domain name, one of the labels exactly matches the string of the interest of the entity, like "google.com" or "amazon.com" which includes the company's titles.

Since the Internet is a global system and everyone uses the same domain name system, every user will use the single DNS namespace, which shared among all of the users. As mentioned in the previous section, no duplicates allowed in labels sharing the same parent labels.

The single namespace nature of the DNS causes conflicts between parties that want to use the same label, which shares the same parent labels. In the intellectual property context, the selection of the label may cause conflict with the owner of the trademarks of the same string. One of the ways to avoid conflicts is by expanding the namespace. One of the ways of expanding namespace is introducing new gTLDs.

While the trademarks are guaranteed to be unique within a jurisdiction, it is possibly not unique among multiple jurisdictions. Due to that, there is an international conflict resolution mechanism. Unfortunately, at the time of the dot-com bubble, there was no such mechanism existed for the DNS.

In summary, the following three reasons initiate a multistakeholder style discussion on DNS.

- Disputes on Intellectual Property.
- Pressure to add new gTLDs.
- Debates in the Internet's operational community did not resolve.

3 Key Events on Multistakeholder Governance for the Internet

Following is a summary of key events while in the evolution of the Internet development concerning gTLD and ICANN[1]. We will describe key events in three phases: Beginning of Network Resource Allocation Management (1972–1994), Discussions on gTLD towards the establishment of ICANN (1996–1998), and finally, the event on ICANN to leaving US oversight.

3.1 Beginning of Network Resource Allocation Management (1972–1994)

We can observe the beginning of network resource allocation management in 1972 initiated by Jon Postel as part of ARPANET activity. ARPANET is a research network established by the US Department of Defense's Advanced Research Project Agency (DARPA). Later, ARPANET became the basis of the Internet.

May 30, 1972 – Beginning of the Network Resource Allocation Management.   Jon Postel, a graduate student at UCLA, proposed to have a "numbering czar" to be appointed to manage various numbers in emerging ARPANET. This event is the beginning of the Internet's number authority, later will be known as Internet Assigned Numbers Authority—IANA.

January 1983 – TCP/IP Becomes the Protocol for ARPANET.

Around 1987 – ARPANET to the Internet.   National Science Foundation (NSF)'s NSFnet, which links the research community, grown and exceeded the size of ARPANET. As the growing interconnected TCP/IP network becomes the common TCP/IP backbone, people started calling the network "internet."

---

[1] This is a summary that refers to the carefully summarized information that appeared in the literature [24]. Some of the expressions are from the literature. Please refer to the literature for full and detailed references.

December, 1988 – Appearance of the name "IANA".   The term "IANA" appeared the first time in RFC1083 [18].

October, 1992 – Beginning of Commercial Use of the Internet.   NSF lifted the rule to ban commercial traffic on the Internet.

September, 1995 – Beginning of Charge for Domain Name Registration.   NSF allowed Network Solutions (which will become the part of VeriSign) to charge for domain name registration services.

March, 1994 – Clarification on IANA's Responsibility.   RFC 1951 "Domain Name System Structure and Delegation [22]" published. This document states that IANA is "responsible for overall coordination and management of the DNS."

3.2   Discussions on gTLD Towards Establishment of ICANN (1996–1998)

From 1996 through 1998, various interested parties (multistakeholder) discussed gTLD implementation. The series of events is the beginning of Internet multistakeholderism.

June, 1996 – Postel's International TLD Proposal.   Jon Postel proposed the process for the creation of new international TLDs in an Internet-Draft "New Registries and the Delegation of International Top Level Domains [23]."

November, 1996 – Establishment of the International Ad Hoc Committee (IAHC).   IAHC established to refine the above mentioned Postel's Internet-Draft. The group supported by seven organizations consists of twelve individuals [3].

December, 1996.   IAHC published a document "Draft Specifications for Administration and Management of gTLDs [17]." Name "generic Top-Level Domain (gTLD)" appeared the first time in the document.

February, 1997.   IAHC produced the final report "Generic Top Level Domain Memorandum of understanding (gTLD MoU) [2]." The document includes notable proposals which evolved and implemented in ICANN policies:

- Registry/Registrar model
- Notification mechanism on name assignments
- A resolution mechanism on trademark-related domain name disputes

July, 1997.   The US Department of Commerce published "Request for Comments on the Registration and Administration of Internet Domain Names [25]."

January 28, 1998 – Controversial DNS Root Operation.   Jon Postel sent an email to the operators of non-US government DNS root servers to replace the reference of one of the root servers with a server which set-up by Postel. This move removed the effect of the US government. On February 3rd, Postel requested to revert the change. The controversial operation demonstrated that a single individual could control the DNS. This event accelerated discussion, eventually led to the formation of ICANN.

February, 1998. The National Telecommunications and Information Administration(NTIA) of the US Department of Commerce published a proposal so-called "Green Paper [5]."

June, 1998. NTIA published a statement of policy, so-called "White Paper [6]."

September 30, 1998 – Establishment of ICANN.

3.3   ICANN Left from the US Oversight (2014–2016)

At the establishment of ICANN in 1998, it was under the US government's oversight. That means it was not a genuinely bottom-up multistakeholder forum. The events between 2014 through 2016 made ICANN leave the US government's oversight. This event is a remarkable moment for the Internet multistakeholderism.

March 14, 2014. NTIA announces a transition plan [21].

September 30, 2016. The IANA functions contract between the US Department of Commerce and ICANN expired

October 1, 2016—ICANN Left from US Government Oversight.

4   Examples of Disputes

Different stakeholders may have different purposes to use the names. The difference cause conflict in the use of names. In this section, two prominent cases of disputes on domain name will be described.

4.1   Example: madonna.com Cybersquatting Incident

An business person specialized in adult entertainment industry purchased a domain name "madonna.com," then register the name "MADONNA" as a trademark in Tunisia, and started operating an adult entertainment portal web site in 1998. Internationally well-known musician Madonna through her attorneys, objected to the use of "madonna.com" domain name in June 1999.

At the time, ICANN was working on Uniform Domain Name Dispute Resolution Policy (UDRP) [13]. UDRP became in effect on October 24, 1999. Finally, on October 12, 2000, World Intellectual Property Organization (WIPO) issued an arbitration that Madonna to win the dispute: "Therefore, we decide that the disputed domain name <madonna.com> should be transferred to the Complainant [26]."

4.2   Example: .amazon gTLD Dispute

For gTLD, conflicts get to very serious. In 2012, the US based Amazon.com, Inc. applied for three gTLDs: ".amazon" (US English), ·アマゾン (Japanese Katakana), and ·亚马逊 (Simplified Chinese).

In 2013, while three independent objectors filed objections, Amazon.com got the approval for implementation (January 2014). ICANN Government Advisory Committee (GAC) issued an advisory not to process the application. ICANN board accepted the advisory, directed the ICANN office not to proceed. In 2015, Amazon.com sent a proposal to a south American regional group Amazon Cooperation Treaty Organization (ACTO) [1]. ACTO declined. The proposal is not publicly available. In 2016, Amazon.com submitted a request [15] for ICANN's Independent Resolution Process (IRP) [9]. Amazon won in July 2017.

The dispute is still on-going at the time of the writing (April 2020). For the brevity of the paper, the author stops describing further details.

5   ICANN and Its Activities

In this section, we briefly present current organization of ICANN. The procedure and policies of ICANN described in ICANN Bylaws [16].

5.1   ICANN and Its Core Value

ICANN – The Internet Corporation for Assigned Names and Numbers – is coordinating maintenance and procedures of the namespace on the Internet, namely, Domain Name, IP addresses (IPv4 and IPv6), Autonomous System Number, Protocol identifiers. It also has a mission to facilitate the coordination of the operation of the DNS root name server system.

According to ICANN's website [14], its bottom-up, consensus-driven and, multistakeholder approach allow to achieve the following major accomplishments:

– Established market competition for generic domain name (gTLD)
– Implemented an efficient and cost-effective Uniform Domain Name Dispute Resolution Policy (UDRP)
– Adopted guidelines for the deployment of Internationalized Domain Names (IDN)
– Jointly completed deployment of Domain Name System Security Extensions (DNSSEC) for the root zone
– Created the New gTLD Program in 2013
– The world broadly accepts ICANN as the place to work out Internet governance policies.

As in the statement of the core values in ICANN Bylaws, it is focusing on broad and informed participation, reflecting the functional, geographic, and cultural diversity of the Internet at all levels of policy development and decision-making, while promoting competition. Every aspect of ICANN Bylaws, i.e., how to select the board members, or how to choose a representative of the specific group, are very carefully designed to reflect the core values.

5.2 ICANN's Multistakeholder Model

ICANN's multistakeholder model consists of the ICANN Board of Directors, three supporting organization, four advisory committees, and two governance accountability entities:

- The ICANN Board of Directors (see below)
- Supporting Organizations develop and recommend policies concerning the Internet's technical management within their areas of expertise:
  - Generic Names Supporting Organization (GNSO)
  - Address Supporting Organization (ASO)
  - Country Code Names Supporting Organization (ccNSO)
- Advisory Committees are formal advisory bodies to ICANN board:
  - At-Large Advisory Committee (ALAC)
  - Security and Stability Advisory Committee (SSAC)
  - Root Server System Advisory Committee (RSSAC)
  - Governmental Advisory Committee (GAC)
- Governance Accountability implemented with two entities assure inclusive representation and accountability:
  - Nomination Committee (NomCom)
  - Ombudsman

The ICANN board of directors consists of sixteen voting members and five non-voting members. Voting members are (the number in parenthesis are the number of seats): President and CEO (1), GNSO (2), ASO (2), ccNSO (2), Nominating Committee (8), and ALAC (1). Non-voting members are: SSAC (1), RSSAC (1), IETF (1), and GAC (1).

5.3 ICANN's Decision

ICANN's decisions are driven by a bottom-up process that involves discussions and advice among ICANN's groups, as well as participation from around the world. The board of directors, which is the final decision-making body, decides with concerning advice.

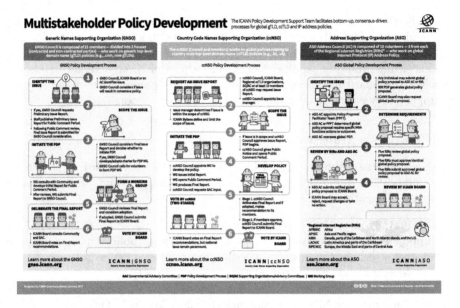

Fig. 1. ICANN's multistakeholder Policy Development at GNSO (Generic Names Supporting Organization), ccNSO (Country Code Names Supporting Organization), and ASO (Address Supporting Organization) [11]

5.4 Policy Development

ICANN develops DNS Policy, Operational Policy, and also General Practices [8]. DNS Policies are developed through formal policy development processes (PDPs) as defined in ICANN Bylaws. The operational policy defines how ICANN operates. It is not necessary to follow PDPs.

Supporting organizations (NGSO, ccNSO, and ASO) each manage different resources, also have different governance mechanisms and different policy development processes. Figure 1 depicts the process of supporting organizations.

Here is one of the examples of the steps ICANN took, on the New gTLD Program:

2005.   Issues Raised, GNSO decides to initiate PDP.

2005 through 2007.   Development of Policy Recommendations. Adopted by the GNSO Council in September 2007.

June 2008.   ICANN Board Policy Approval. Start of implementation Process.

Adoption.   After the approval of the ICANN Board, the policy takes effect, and adoption starts. Then, other related activities started. For example, ICANN began to develop materials to support to use the new gTLD program – Applicant Guidebook [12]. The development started in October 2008, finally published in May 2011.

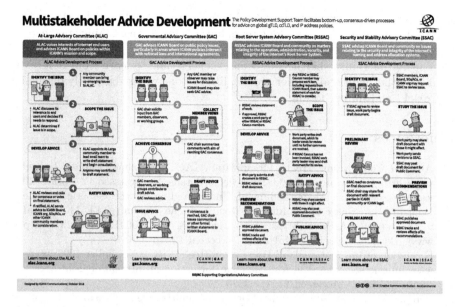

Fig. 2. ICANN's Multistakeholder Advice Development at ALAC (At-Large Advisory Committee), GAC (Governmental Advisory Committee), RSSAC (Root Server System Advisory Committee), and SSAC (Security and Stability Advisory Committee) [10]

5.5 Advice Development

At ICANN, besides policy development, various stakeholders provide advice to the board. Four of the advice committees – ALAC, GAC, RSSAC, and SSAC – have their advice development processes depicted in Fig. 2.

The purpose and source of the advice are as follows:

ALAC. Voices interest of Internet end users.

GAC. Advises on public policy issues, particularly in the area where ICANN policies intersect with national laws and international agreements.

RSSAC. Advises on the matters relating to the operation, administration, security, and integrity of the root server system of DNS.

SSAC. Advises on issues relating to the security and integrity of the Internet's naming and allocation systems.

6 Conclusion

In this paper, we discussed the multistakeholder governance for the Internet. Through the series of events, we showed how the multistakeholder style conflict resolution evolved. Also, we introduced the current organization of ICANN.

ICANN is now more than 20 years old. One of the contributors for the ICANN said to the author that it was a long road, but it is finally reasonably good enough to satisfy it's core values.

The author thinks that it is now an excellent time to learn from ICANN to establish other multistakeholder groups, like the one we are currently discussing at CoDeFi and similar forums.

References

1. Amazon Cooperation Treaty Organization (ACTO), online: English Language page: http://www.otca-oficial.info/projects/details/15. Accessed 12 April 2020
2. Establishment of a Memorandum of Understanding on the Generic Top Level Domain Name Space of the Internet Domain Name System (gTLD-MoU), Online in the Internet Archive: https://web.archive.org/web/20091205200123/, http://www.gtld-mou.org/gTLD-MoU.html. Accessed 12 April 2020
3. Formation of International Ad Hoc Committee (IAHC), November 1996. https://www.internetsociety.org/history-timeline/formation-of-international-ad-hoc-committee-iahc/. Accessed 12 Apr 2020
4. Berejka, M.: A case for government promoted multi-stake holderism. J. Telecomm. High Tech. L. **10**, 1 (2012)
5. Department of Commerce National Telecommunications and Information Administration: Improvement of Technical Management of Internet Names and Addresses (15 CFR C hapter XXIII Docket No 980212036–8036-01), Feburary 1998
6. Department of Commerce National Telecommunications and Information Administration: Management of Internet Names and Addresses (Statement of Policy). Federal Register, June 1998. https://www.gpo.gov/fdsys/pkg/FR-1998-06-10/html/98-15392.htm. Accessed 12 Apr 2020
7. Hufty, M.: Investigating policy processes: the governance analytical framework (GAF). In: Research for Sustainable Development: Foundations, Experiences, and Perspectives, pp. 403–424 (2011)
8. ICANN: Developing Policy at ICANN Online: https://www.icann.org/policy. Accessed 12 Apr 2020
9. ICANN: Independent Review Process Documents Online: https://www.icann.org/resources/pages/accountability/irp-en. Accessed 12 Apr 2020
10. ICANN: Multistakeholder Advice Development Online: https://www.icann.org/en/system/files/files/multistakeholder-advice-development-31oct18-en.pdf. Accessed 12 Apr 2020
11. ICANN: Multistakeholder Policy Development Online: https://www.icann.org/en/system/files/files/multistakeholder-policy-development-31jan17-en.pdf. Accessed 12 Apr 2020
12. ICANN: New gTLD Applicant Guidebook Online: https://newgtlds.icann.org/ja/applicants/agb. Accessed 12 Apr 2020
13. ICANN: Uniform Domain-Name Dispute-Resolution Policy Online: https://www.icann.org/resources/pages/help/dndr/udrp-en. Accessed 12 Apr 2020
14. ICANN: Welcome to ICANN!, February 2012. https://www.icann.org/resources/pages/welcome-2012-02-25-en. Accessed 12 Apr 2020
15. ICANN: Amazon EU S.àr.l. v. ICANN (.AMAZON), March 2016. https://www.icann.org/resources/pages/irp-amazon-v-icann-2016-03-04-en. Accessed 12 Apr 2020

16. ICANN: Bylaws for Internet Corporation for Assigned Names and Numbers—A California Nonprofit Public-Benefit Corporation, November 2019. https://www. icann.org/resources/pages/governance/bylaws-en. Accessed 12 Apr 2020
17. International Ad Hoc Committee: Draft Specifications for Administration and Management of gTLDs, December 1996. https://tools.ietf.org/html/draft-iahc-gtldspec-00. Accessed 12 Apr 2020
18. Internet Activities Board: RFC1083: IAB Official Protocol Standards, December 1988. (Status: Historical). https://tools.ietf.org/html/rfc1083. Accessed 12 Apr 2020
19. Klensin, J.: RFC 5890: Internationalized Domain Names for Applications (IDNA): Definitions and Document Framework, August 2010. https://tools.ietf.org/html/ rfc5890. Accessed 12 Apr 2020
20. Mockapetris, P.: RFC 1034: Domain Names - Concepts and Facilities, November 1987
21. National Telecommunications and Information Administration: NTIA Announces Intent to Transition Key Internet Domain Name Function, March 2014. https:// www.ntia.doc.gov/press-release/2014/ntia-announces-intent-transition-key-internet-domain-name-functions. Accessed 12 Apr 2020
22. Postel, J.: RFC1591: Domain name system structure and delegation, March 1994. https://tools.ietf.org/html/rfc1591. Accessed 12 Apr 2020
23. Postel, J.: New registries and the delegation of international top level domains, June 1996. https://tools.ietf.org/html/draft-postel-iana-itld-admin-01. Accessed 12 Apr 2020
24. Snyder, J., Komaitis, K., Robachevsky, A.: The History of IANA: An Extended Timeline with Citations and Commentary. Internet Society, May 2016. https:// www.internetsociety.org/ianatimeline/. Accessed 12 Apr 2020
25. US Department of Commerce: Request for Comments on the Registration and Administration of Internet Domain Names. Federal Register, July 1997. https:// www.gpo.gov/fdsys/pkg/FR-1997-07-02/pdf/97-17215.pdf. Accessed 12 Apr 2020
26. WIPO Arbitration and Mediation Center: ADMINISTRATIVE PANEL DECISION - Madonna Ciccone, p/k/a Madonna v. Dan Parisi and "Madonna.com" - Case No. D2000–0847, October 2000. https://www.wipo.int/amc/en/domains/ decisions/html/2000/d2000-0847.html. Accessed 12 Apr 2020

Future of Finance
From G20 to Practical Implementation of Multi-stakeholder Governance on Blockchain Based Finance

Yuta Takanashi[✉]

Financial Service Agency Japan, Tokyo, Japan
tkns1192@gmail.com

Abstract. Financial regulators regulate financial intermediaries and activities to achieve their regulatory goals and, in so doing, address various market failures. These objectives are needed in the social interest regardless of the technologies used by the financial system. The blockchain-based financial system, however, has characteristics that could undermine the ability of regulators to achieve regulatory goals. Thus, financial regulators must discover ways to continue to achieve regulatory goals. This situation is similar to the case of telecommunication regulators during the rise of the Internet. In the face of such difficulties in cyberspace, it was suggested to invoke not just law but also social norms, market mechanisms, and architecture to achieve a certain level of oversight. Now, G20 financial regulators recognize the need for cooperation with other stakeholders. Because code embedded in a blockchain system could determine the level of oversight within a blockchain-based financial system, regulators should consider ways to cooperate with engineering communities to develop codes that appropriately facilitate mechanisms to achieve regulatory goals and must empower society to use such codes in order to achieve regulatory goals, which requires consideration on alignment with social norms and market competitiveness. Thus, regulators must cooperate with other stakeholders, including businesses and users.

Keywords: Blockchain · Governance · Decentralized finance

1 Introduction

In this paper, we will discuss (1) financial regulatory issues raised by blockchain technology, (2) lessons from the Internet as a reference point, and (3) ways to deal with regulatory issues via a multi-stakeholder governance approach.

The main contribution of this paper is to reveal the need for regulators to play a role in establishing a multi-stakeholder governance mechanism in order to achieve their regulatory goals. Building upon analysis of implications for regulability from blockchain-based financial activities and lessons from the experience of the Internet in Sects. 2 and 3, Sect. 4 discusses why and how should regulators influence code development as well as the way businesses and users use

© Springer Nature Switzerland AG 2020
M. Bernhard et al. (Eds.): FC 2020 Workshops, LNCS 12063, pp. 242–253, 2020.
https://doi.org/10.1007/978-3-030-54455-3_18

code within the ecosystem. It concludes that regulators need to cooperate with other stakeholders, including the engineering community, businesses and users to achieve regulatory goals, and should establish a multi-stakeholder governance mechanism for a blockchain-based financial system. The final part of this paper provides some thoughts on the critical challenges for establishing such a mechanism, though some open questions remain.

2 Financial Regulatory Goals and Implication of Blockchain

Regulation and economic policy play a role when there are failures in the market such as externality, information asymmetry, imperfect competition and so on.[1] In particular, financial regulators around the world regulate financial intermediaries and activities to address such failures by achieving their regulatory goals[2] and serve social interests.[3]

2.1 Three Important Regulatory Goals for Financial Regulators

There could be various ways to describe their goals; however, in this paper, I mainly focus on the following three goals.

The first goal is to maintain financial stability.[4] As we see in the case of the global financial crisis around 2009, once the financial system loses its stability, society and the economy suffer significant disruptions, and lots of people lose their jobs because of the externality of the financial system, which the financial regulators are expected to avoid. Thus, financial regulators regulate financial institutions by, for example, imposing affirmative approval requirements as well as various prudential regulations such as capital and liquidity requirements.

The second goal is to protect investors and consumers.[5] Investors and consumers usually face difficulty in collecting all the necessary information to understand the risks associated with their interactions with financial services and businesses, which could cause insufficiently informed decisions and cause unexpected losses. Thus, financial regulators impose regulation on financial institutions as agents and disclosure requirements on market participants.

The third goal is to prevent financial crimes.[6] This means that financial regulators aim at preventing the financial system from being used for criminal purposes such as money laundering (ML) and financing terrorism (FT). Thus, financial regulators criminalize ML/CF and mandate financial institutions as a gatekeeper of the financial system to conduct customer due diligence (CDD) and

[1] JOHN ARMOUR ET AL., *PRINCIPLES OF FINANCIAL REGULATION*, 2016.

[2] *Id.*

[3] Endo, Our Future in the Digital Age, 2019, available at https://www.fsa.go.jp/common/conference/danwa/20190608/05.pdf.

[4] JOHN ARMOUR ET AL., Supra note 1.

[5] *Id.*

[6] *Id.*

monitor transactions to detect suspicious activities to stop and inform enforcement authorities including national Financial Intelligence Unit (FIU).[7, 8]

2.2   Implementation and Enforcement of Financial Regulation

In achieving financial regulatory goals, a financial regulator needs to 1) identify risks they need to address and examine if they need to establish new regulations and/or amend existing regulations, 2) establish new regulations and/or amend existing regulations with careful considerations to maximize effectiveness and minimize the cost associated with their decisions[9], and 3) implement and enforce regulations as shown in Fig. 1.

Currently, a large part of the financial regulations targets financial institutions such as banks, insurance companies, and securities broker-dealers as financial intermediaries bridging their customers[10]. Thus, financial regulators ensure effective enforcement of their regulations, relying on changes in behaviors of these financial institutions.

In this paper, I mainly focus on the third and final step in this process, considering that blockchain affects this step the most, as I discuss in the following.

Fig. 1. Life cycle of regulatory approaches

---

[7] The Financial Action Task Force recommends national authorities to take this approach. See FINANCIAL ACTION TASK FORCE, THE FATF RECOMMENDATIONS: INTERNATIONAL STANDARDS ON COMBATING MONEY LAUNDERING AND THE FINANCING OF TERRORISM & PROLIFERATION, http://www.fatfgafi.org/media/fatf/documents/recommendations/pdfs/FATF%20Recommendations%202012.pdf (updated June 2019).

[8] It should be pointed out that making use of financial systems for criminal purposes is only one method for criminals to achieve their purposes. Hence financial regulation is only one part of governmental efforts to prevent such crimes. Regulatory approaches toward nonfinancial institutions and/or police enforcement actions against individual criminals are also available. See. Takanashi et al., *Call for Multi-Stakeholder Communication to Establish a Governance Mechanism for the Emerging Blockchain-Based Financial Ecosystem, Part 1 of 2*, Vol. 3.1, 2020, available at https://stanford-jblp.pubpub.org/pub/multistakeholder-comm-governance.

[9] ARMOUR ET AL., *supra* note 1.

[10] Endo, *supra* note 3.

2.3   Blockchain Affecting Regulatory Enforceability

Blockchain could enable users to conduct financial transactions on a peer-to-peer basis without the need to rely on financial intermediaries such as banks as we see in the case of Bitcoin.[11] This means that current regulatory approaches relying on regulation and its enforcement at the financial intermediaries would mostly lose their effectiveness[12] as shown Fig. 2.

Then, financial regulators may consider to directly regulate users; however, enforcing regulations on each user level would entail difficulty given the physical limitation at the enforcement authorities and users may choose deploying anonymization technologies[13], which further increase difficulties for enforcement authorities to know who does what in the financial system[14].

Other than disintermediation and anonymization, blockchain-based financial system, depending on its technical and business design, could have several other characteristics that reduce enforceability of financial regulations.

1. Autonomous nature: when regulators find problems in operation and services of financial institutions, they usually issue a business suspension order to secure time to address issues; however, blockchain could create an autonomous system providing financial services such as payment[15], which regulators cannot stop even when they find any problems.
2. Immutability: when regulators find problems in financial transactions such as ML, they order financial institutions to modify transactional records; however, blockchain provides an immutable record of transactions on the distributed ledger[16], which regulators cannot make ex-post remedy once the transactional data is recorded.
3. Global nature: each jurisdiction has different legal frameworks and take different regulatory approaches; however, blockchain-based finance is by nature, global activity within the cyberspace, which could cause jurisdictional issues.
4. Permissionless nature: as discussed above, regulators regulate financial institutions as gatekeepers of the financial system, and unauthorized users cannot access to it; however, users may be able to access to the blockchain-based financial system without any permission, and even anyone can develop new systems and services without permission[17], which erodes the effectiveness of regulatory approaches focusing on gatekeepers.

---

[11] Takanashi et al., Supra note 8 at 13.

[12] Endo, *supra* note 3.

[13] Takanashi et al., *Supra* note 8 at 13.

[14] Endo, Introductory Remarks by Commissioner Toshihide Endo BG2C Special Online Panel Discussion, 2020, available at https://www.fsa.go.jp/common/conference/danwa/20200310_English_Introductry_remarks_Commissioner.pdf.

[15] Nakamoto, Bitcoin: A Peer-to-Peer Electronic Cash System, 2008, available at https://bitcoin.org/bitcoin.pdf.

[16] *Id.*

[17] De Filippi and Wright, Blockchain and the Law The Rule of Code. Harvard University Press, 2018, at Chapter 2.

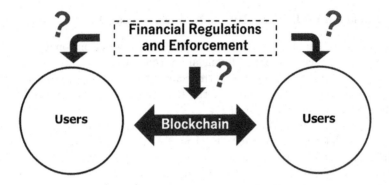

Fig. 2. Blockchain based finance and regulations

Emerging Blockchain Privacy-Enhancing Technologies. In considering the difficulties for regulators associated with the blockchain-based financial system, I shed light on the emergence of sophisticated anonymization technologies as one of the areas we should continue monitoring. As we can see in Table 1, lots of new technologies are proposed or even deployed in the actual use cases. Some of these privacy-enhancing technologies are developed not just for improving anonymity but also for other purposes such as improving scalability[18].

Anonymity has benefits and risks. When ordinary people transact with others for everyday purposes, anonymity is essential to preserve privacy with censorship resistance, better security, and fungibility of coins; however, when it comes to preventing financial crimes such as ML/FT and other cybercrimes, anonymity could cause problems to conduct an investigation and enforce regulations. Thus, determining how much anonymity should users enjoy in what circumstances would require value judgment and politics to resolve competing values.

Table 1. Emerging blockchain privacy enhancing technologies

Technology	Use cases
Mixing	Bitcoin, Bitcoin Cash, Litecoin, Ethereum Dash etc.
Stealth Address	Bitcoin (Wallet), Monero
Ring Signature	Monero
Zero-Knowledge Proof (zk-SNARKs)	Zcash, Ethereum
Lightning Network	Bitcoin, Litecoin, Ethereum
Atomic Cross-Chain Swap	Bitcoin, Litecoin, Ethereum etc.
Mimblewimble	Grin, Beam
Schnorr Signature	Grin, Beam
Dandelion	Grin, Zcoin

---

[18] For example, Lightning Network is expected to greatly improve scalability by using the second layer for transactions. See. Poon and Dryja, *The Bitcoin Lightning Network: Scalable Off-Chain Instant Payments*, 2016, available at https://lightning. network/lightning-network-paper.pdf.

2.4   Question We Need to Answer

Given the above considerations, we need to find answers to the following questions when we design and pursue the future of finance with blockchain technology.

1. How could we continue to achieve financial regulatory goals even in the blockchain-based financial system as public interest?
2. How should we resolve competing values such as anonymity and crime prevention?

3   Lessons from the Case of the Internet

Both the telecommunication industry and the financial industry before the advent of the disruptive innovations; the Internet and blockchain respectively were heavily regulated through regulation and enforcement on the intermediating entities both domestically and internationally. However, in the case of the telecommunication industry, the advent of the Internet drastically changed the regulatory landscape.

3.1   How Has the Internet Affected Regulation?

It is pointed out that the following characteristics of the Internet affected the ability of telecommunication regulators to achieve their regulatory goals, such as contents regulation[19].

1. The global scope of the communication: Because the Internet is a global network, the communication happening on the Internet is by default global. Thus, any attempt to impose regulatory oversight on activities on the Internet requires cross-jurisdictional cooperation, which is very costly and slow.
2. The large scale of communication: With the Internet's ability to facilitate a large amount of communication, the scale of the information sharing is massively enlarged. On the Internet, anyone can create content and share it globally with a little marginal cost. The huge volume of information communication and transactions could easily overwhelm the capacity of traditional regulatory processes to impose oversight.
3. Distributed control and new institutions: The decision-making processes over the operation of the Internet and the standards of the Internet technology, including Internet protocols, are all developed not through the process governed by the traditional nation-states system but through the organic process within the global network actors. Such global network actors form several new important institutions such as ICANN (the Internet Corporation for Assigned Names and Numbers) and IETF (the Internet Engineering Task Force). Thus, regulators cannot unilaterally impose oversight on either the Internet's day-to-day operation nor technical standards.

---

[19] L. Mueller, *Networks and States: The Global Politics of Internet Governance*, MIT Press, 2010.

3.2   Brief History of the Internet and the Emergence of Multi-stakeholderism

When the Internet had grown as an important social and economic infrastructure, some of the nation-states actors attempted to grab control over the Internet through the United Nations process. This attempt was eventually failed and governments, during the two World Summit on the Information Society (WSIS) sessions, accepted the concept of multistakeholderism and roles of the private sector stakeholders in managing the Internet and established a non-binding forum called Internet Governance Forum (IGF) to discuss policy issues[20].

3.3   Pathetic Dot Theory

In the case of activities within cyberspace, Lawrence Lessig discusses the concept of regulability and provides a theoretical model for oversight[21]. Lessig pointed out that "Regulability is... a function of design" and "different design reflects different values the designer embraces". Here "design" means code that shapes the system. Based on this basic understanding, he presented a general framework to govern cyberspace, which is the so-called "pathetic dot theory". Figure 3 depicts the concept of the pathetic dot theory. In the cyberspace, the dot, a target to regulate, is controlled by the four constraints, law, norm, market, and architecture. The law imposes certain constraints on the target, but it is not the only one constraint when someone does something in cyberspace. The social norm would also impose the constraints on the target's behavior by, for example, a request from others in the community on do's and don'ts. If the behavior is associated with economic activities, the market mechanism, such as cost and benefit, will affect the target's behavior. Not just law, norm, and market, the architecture will also affect the target's behavior as well by defining technological capabilities and limitations. These constraints affect each other, and the change of one constraint could change the effectiveness of others.

Among these four factors, Lessig stipulates, "a code of cyberspace, defining the freedoms and controls for cyberspace, will be built. About that, there can be no debate.", which is a compelling message. Then he asks, "What values should be protected there? What values should be built into the space to encourage what forms of life?" This is also a clear message that the development of code itself is a process to choose some values over others, which we simply call politics.

---

[20] L. Mueller, *supra* note 19 at Chapter 4.
[21] Lessig, *Code: And Other Laws Of Cyberspace*, Basic Books, 1999.

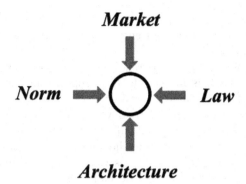

Fig. 3. Pathetic dot theory

4   Our Idea and Initiatives in the Regulatory Community

4.1   Application of Pathetic Dot Theory to Blockchain-Based Finance

De Filippi and Wright propose to apply Lessig's Pathetic Dot Theory to blockchain-based system[22]. Their argument is that each of the four constraints is still workable in the blockchain system as activities within the blockchain system is conducted in the cyberspace. For example, LAW and REGULATION still can be applied to ecosystem participants such as users, internet service providers, minors and developers/engineers. The government can still intervene in the MARKET by, for example, participating in mining and controlling the price of the crypto assets. NORMS will play a role in determining the behaviors of the ecosystem participants, and the government may be able to influence norms. The government can translate law and regulation into code (ARCHITECTURE) to automatically enforce them within a blockchain-based system.

They admit the certain limitations of each mechanism; however, they emphasize that activities within a blockchain system are not completely uncontrollable, but rather government should utilize these four mechanisms cleverly to achieve their regulatory goals[23].

4.2   Our Basic Idea

I, with fellow authors, proposed practical implementation of the above concept proposed by De Filippi and Wright in our paper[24] by applying the concept of multi-stakeholder governance grown in the Internet community. Our basic idea is that regulators should include specific codes and architecture that help

---

[22] De Filippi and Wright, *Blockchain and the Law The Rule of Code*, Harvard University Press, 2018, at Chapter 11.

[23] *Id.*

[24] Takanashi et al., *Supra* note 8.

society attain regulatory goals in the early design of protocols and applications by cooperating with developers and engineering community through enhanced mutual understanding and respect.

Establishment of a cooperative relationship between engineering community and regulators itself is no easy task as engineering community seems to embrace cypherpunk philosophy[25]; however, even when regulators and developers/engineering community successfully develop codes and architecture they are intended, they still need that codes and architecture to be used in the ecosystem in order to gain intended outcome. In other words, it is useless if the codes and architecture are ignored and no one uses them. Thus, regulators need to pay attention to the alignment of the code developed with regulations and norms as well as its competitiveness in the markets to let community participants use the code that facilitates activities addressing concerns.

As we discussed above, regulators can make an effort to influence the norm and the market; however, other stakeholders also have a strong influence on these factors, as we saw in the Internet case. Thus, the engineering community is not the only one stakeholder whom regulators should seek cooperation with.

When it comes to norms, it is essential to understand that different stakeholders naturally have very different norms around technology and social benefit, and sometimes they are competing with each other. Thus, it is not that simple in reality to align codes with norms. Whose norm should code be aligned with, and how? The answer to this question could differ case by case basis; however, if different stakeholders get together to develop certain standard norms shared among them, the tasks to align codes with norms could become much easier.

Not just norms but it are also important to understand market structures that influence the market competitiveness of the code developed. Even if the codes are aligned with norms, it may still be ignored if the code is not competitive in the market. Although code is usually developed in the engineering community, businesses play essential roles in distributing it with services in the market. In so doing, business players analyze the market competitiveness of the code and its services. Thus, regulators need to take businesses and markets into consideration as well.

Of course, the engineering community developing code is not immune to the influence of other factors. For example, it could be the case where the code that the engineering community develops is just ignored because it circumvents the regulation, is not regarded to be aligned with norms in the community, or simply is not attractive for businesses. In this scenario, efforts from the engineering community become meaningless. In fact, we discussed, there could be concerns about potential criminal usage of blockchain technology, and many incumbent businesses decided not to use blockchain technology as there is regulatory uncertainty.

All the stakeholders act with their own agendas, and their efforts to pursue different agendas without coordination could lose its meaning or, in the

---

[25] Lopp, *Bitcoin and the Rise of the Cypherpunks*, 2016, available at https://www.coindesk.com/the-rise-of-the-cypherpunks.

worst-case scenario, it causes unintended consequences including over-regulation and development of socially harmful technology. Thus, it is vital for stakeholders to work together to find common ground among them.

All in all, in order to align the codes with the norm and make it more competitive in the market, stakeholders from regulators, the engineering community, businesses, and civil society, including consumers, should seek cooperation to find an optimal solution by developing a cooperative environment. We call such activities "multi-stakeholder governance". The simplified illustration of our proposal on the healthy multi-stakeholder governance for the blockchain-based financial system is provided in Fig. 4.

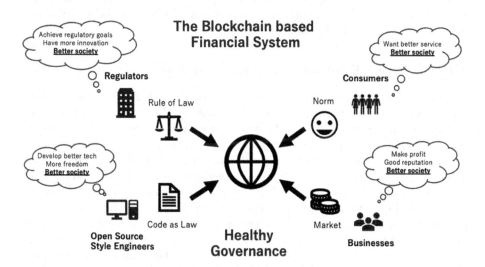

Fig. 4. Healthy governance for the blockchain based financial system

4.3   Reports from G20 and Regulatory Community

Regulators seem to understand fast-changing reality and started the discussion on the way they cope with it. The notable example would be the discussion at the G20 under the Japanese Presidency in 2019.

The Financial Stability Board (the FSB) are asked to give consideration on the financial stability, regulatory and governance implications of decentralized financial technologies by G20 Japanese Presidency and published a report in June 2019[26] that points out that "Decentralised financial technologies are likely to continue to evolve rapidly. Early liaison between regulators and a wider

---

[26] FSB, *Decentralised financial technologies Report on financial stability, regulatory and governance implications*, 2019, available at https://www.fsb.org/2019/06/decentralised-financial-technologies-report-on-financial-stability-regulatory-and-governance-implications/.

group of stakeholders might help ensure that regulatory and other public policy objectives are considered in the initial design of technical protocols and applications. This should help limit the emergence of unforeseen complications at a later stage." The report further proposes that "Authorities may, therefore, wish to enhance their dialogue and cooperation with a wider group of stakeholders, including software developers, the engineering community, as well as businesses, academia, and other relevant stakeholders such as investors, consumers, and users. This would help to assess the opportunities and risks of decentralized financial technologies."

Following the publication of the FSB's report, G20 leaders agreed with the FSB's analysis and proposal by declaring that "We also welcome the FSB's work on the possible implications of decentralized financial technologies and how regulators can engage other stakeholders[27]."

4.4 Challenges Ecosystem Participants to Overcome

It could be interpreted that regulators and authorities in G20 countries are ready for deepening cooperation with wider stakeholders, including the engineering community; however, as indicated above, the establishment of the cooperative relationship among stakeholders should not be relaxed. As Fig. 5 shows, different stakeholders pursue their own agenda and barriers that impede cooperation among them. For example, regulators and engineering communities lack a common language to discuss and have little connection among them at this moment, which could be a high hurdle for them to start work together. For another example, businesses and consumers do not necessarily have mutual trust as consumers face difficulty to understand the risks associated with services and investment opportunity due to lack of transparency provided by businesses as we see in the case of lost of Initial Coin Offering (ICO) cases[28].

I recognize that these difficulties could cause a lack of coordination, huge misunderstandings and unintended negative impacts from independent efforts pursuing their own interests. As blockchain technology and ecosystem based on this technology was first introduced in around ten years ago, and still these difficulties hamper the development of healthy ecosystem with multi-stakeholder governance, it has become more apparent that such ideal governance mechanism seems not to grow organically and someone needs to take a leading role to give impetus for its development. Taking the above difficulty and developments in the regulatory community into consideration, our paper proposes that regulators should take this role and make efforts as the first mover.

---

[27] G20 Leaders, *G20 OSAKA LEADERS' DECLARATION*, 2019, available at https://www.mofa.go.jp/policy/economy/g20_summit/osaka19/en/documents/final_g20_osaka_leaders_declaration.html.

[28] EY, *EY study: Initial Coin Offerings (ICOs)*, 2018, available at https://assets.ey.com/content/dam/ey-sites/ey-com/global/news/2018/10/ey-ico-research-web-oct-17-2018.pdf.

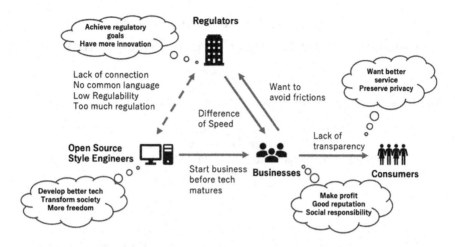

Fig. 5. Current situation and challenges

4.5   Areas for Further Considerations and Critical Attributes of the Governance Mechanisms

Our paper identified several areas that require us to give further considerations.

1. Possible agendas to deal with
2. Incentives for each stakeholder to participate in the governance mechanism
3. The way to legitimate the governance mechanism
4. Relationship with existing governance mechanism in the financial sector
5. The way to have participants to abide by the outcome from the activities

I will not give detailed explanations on each of them here, but I believe just claiming needs for multi-stakeholder governance is much easier than actually establishing it that is practically workable and develops implementable outcomes.

At this moment, I believe the governance mechanism should 1) focus on developing tangible impacts rather than just becoming a discussion forum, 2) be open and inclusive that allows anyone can join and contribute, 3) embrace the diversity and actively seek participants from various stakeholder groups, 4) provide a transparent process to develop outcome and 5) takes a bottom-up approach and deny dictatorship from any one of stakeholder groups and 6) value fairness and neutrality among participants. These key attributes are proposed as core values of the Blockchain Governance Initiative Network (BGIN), of which I am taking part as one of the initial contributors[29]. Although we need careful analysis and considerations if and how these key attributes of the governance mechanism could help us answer the above areas for further considerations, I believe it is time to start the implementation of our concept and should find answers in the trial and errors process of the endeavor to develop healthy multi-stakeholder governance.

---

[29] BGIN, *Genesis*, 2020, available at https://github.com/bgin-global/genesis-documents/commit/a1d55b2823c7e4bcde88788d57a068a26b3a1dc8.

Securing Cryptocurrency Exchange: Building up Standard from Huge Failures

Yuji Suga[1]([✉]), Masaki Shimaoka[2], Masashi Sato[2], and Hirotaka Nakajima[3]

[1] Internet Initiative Japan Inc., Tokyo, Japan
suga@iij.ad.jp
[2] Intelligent Systems Laboratory, SECOM CO., LTD., Tokyo, Japan
[3] Mercari, Inc. R4D, Tokyo, Japan

Abstract. After the original publication of the Bitcoin paper, cryptocurrency exchanges emerged to connect the fiat currency world to the cryptocurrency world. Although many users of cryptocurrency exchanges demonstrate confidence in this simple role for an exchange, recent security incidents suggest that a gap exists between the perception of users and the reality. That is, operations, informational assets to be protected, and security postures should be clarified. In this paper, we summarize the results of an investigation of 16 registered and 16 semi-registered cryptocurrency exchanges by Japanese regulators, then analyze the reality of functionalities, implementation, and operations of cryptocurrency exchanges. Then, we propose short-term directions and long term works to fix pitfalls through building technology and management standards to secure the cryptocurrency exchange and custodian, which are essential building blocks toward healthy blockchain ecosystem.

Keywords: Cryptocurrency exchange · Information security management · Key management · Governance

1 Introduction

1.1 Background

Eliminating the trusted third party in realizing network-based services is one of the biggest dreams in applied cryptography. The main reason why we seek to eliminate the trusted party is, it is too difficult to realize an expected trusted party. Such difficulties are caused by the operator's mistakes, malicious activities, and collusion with other parties. Many cryptographic techniques like secret sharing scheme, threshold cryptography, and multi-party computation protocol are well studied to realize many network-based services without trusted parties.

The sentence, "An electronic payment system based on cryptographic proof instead of trust, allowing any two willing parties to transact directly with each other without the need for a trusted third party." is the explanation of Bitcoin - one of the most attractive cryptographic protocols - described in the original

© Springer Nature Switzerland AG 2020
M. Bernhard et al. (Eds.): FC 2020 Workshops, LNCS 12063, pp. 254–270, 2020.
https://doi.org/10.1007/978-3-030-54455-3_19

paper [1]. Bitcoin is one of the most excellent cryptographic protocols which claimed to realize such a payment scheme among cryptographic protocols that try to eliminate the trusted party.

Despite this attractive claim of Bitcoin, there are fundamental assumptions in the claim. That is, it holds only when the payment is conducted by Bitcoin, and no exchange to any other payment methods exists. Its "without trusted third party" claim realized by the distributed protocol is applicable only on the ledger of payment records for Bitcoin. If we wish to exchange Bitcoin to other assets like fiat currency, the action of exchange is outside of what original paper claims. That is, we need to assume some kinds of trust at a party which exchanges so-called trustless cryptocurrency to other assets. Most people believe that cryptocurrencies are operated in the "trustless" manner, as most cryptocurrency advertisement says. However, the cryptocurrency exchanges in real life are hidden trusted parties.

Throughout the history of trustless cryptocurrency, there are many incidents have happened. In 2013, Mt. Gox lost many Bitcoin due to their careless operation and transaction malleability [2]. In 2018, CoinCheck was hacked by a targeted attack [3] and lost over 500M US dollar(USD) equivalent NEM, which 700,000 customers deposited in their account at CoinCheck, and Zaif also lost 50M USD [4]. In 2019, Binance [5] and Bitpoint [6] was hacked in a similar way. There are many other examples of cryptocurrency incidents reported from all over the world. Such incidents are caused by a misunderstanding of required trust in operating such a party associated with trust-less cryptocurrency. When considering the amount of value that such companies deal with, these companies - implicitly assumed to be trusted - should be secure enough against any kinds of attacks including cyberattacks on cryptography, key management. However, even now, such companies do not have enough expertise and human resources to secure their implementations and operations against such security concerns.

Usually, when we build an information system, we conduct the design and implements of security mechanisms and operations, with aligning information security management system (ISMS). However, at this moment there isn't any agreed unified security standard. Hence, the design and implementation of each cryptocurrency exchanges vary among operators. This situation makes operations challenging to secure the cryptocurrency exchange.

Given this situation, we first need to figure out the reality of cryptocurrency exchanges, and then we need to proceed to implement the existing ISMS process into an implicitly trusted party associated with the trust-less ecosystem.

1.2   Security Incidents and Their History

After Bitcoin was introduced in 2008, there have been many incidents happened at cryptocurrency exchanges. The following are the summaries of significant incidents that happened in Japan. Table 1 shows the past major incidents which happened at cryptocurrency exchanges. Here, we describe the abstract of three significant incidents and their source of problems.

Table 1. Major incidents at cryptocurrency exchanges

Name of exchange	Dates	Amount of lost (at that time)	Abstract of incidents
MyBitcoins	July 29, 2011	27,000 BTC (370,000 USD)	Disappear
Linode	March 2012	46,703 BTC (200,000 USD)	Web host hack
Bitcoinica	March and May 2012	61,000 BTC	Web host hack
Bitfloor	September 2012	24,000 BTC (250,000 USD)	Server attack
Mt. Gox	February 2014	850,000 BTC (473,000 USD)	Transaction malleability and server hack
Bitstamp	January 2015	19,00 BTC	Server attack
Cryptsy Exchange	July 2016	11,325 BTC	Server attack
Bitfinex	August 2016	119,756 BTC	Server attack
Gatecoin	2016	250 BTC, 185,000 ETC	Attack on hot wallet
Zaif	January 2018	65M USD	
NiceHash	December 2017	4,700 BTC	Server attack
CoinCheck	January 2018	580M USD	Targeted attack
BitHumb	June 2018	30M USD	Server attack
Monappy	September 2018	140K USD	Attack on hot wallet
Zaif	September 2018	50M USD	Attack on hot wallet
Binance	May 2019	40M USD	Attack on hot wallet
Bitpoint	July 2019	32M USD	Attack on hot wallet

Mt. Gox Incident (2014): Mt. Gox was the world's largest cryptocurrency exchange in 2014, which occupied about 70% of Bitcoin transactions. The exchange did not segregate customers' assets from the exchange's asset. The customers' assets were not recorded into Bitcoin blockchain, however, recorded into some segregated ledger. Thus, the attacker had a chance to attack the segregated ledger instead of the attack on the blockchain and cryptographic keys itself. The CEO of Mt. Gox claimed that the incident was caused by transaction malleability of Bitcoin protocol. By utilizing this vulnerability, the adversary could convince the exchange modified transaction IDs. This was one of the factors of stealing Bitcoin. Several experts pointed out that this vulnerability caused the loss, however, another significant factor of loss was internal malicious activities and attacks on the segregated ledger from outside.

CoinCheck Incident (2018): In January 2018, CoinCheck, one of the biggest cryptocurrency exchanges, but it was semi-registered to Japan Financial Service Agency (JFSA) was hacked and about 526,800,010 XEM was stolen. It was equivalent to 500M USD, and 260,000 customers of CoinCheck were victims. This incident happened with the targeted attack as the first step. Adversary sent CoinCheck several emails to inject malware. As a result, the adversary succeeds to intrude into the CoinCheck's network. The adversary could control computers remotely; then the adversary obtained a secret cryptographic key. After that, the adversary sent XEM stored inside the CoinCheck's network outside within 30 min. This indicates that all XEM are associated with one secret cryptographic key, and the amount of coins which each customer has is managed with a segregated ledger. This was the same situation as the Mt. Gox incident. The XEM stored in the hot wallet, that is the device that was connected to the internal network. Multi-signature, which is a general technique to divide signing privilege among multiple persons, was not implemented. The main reason why CoinCheck did not implement was, the cryptographic algorithm and its parameter (elliptic curve) did not fit to software/hardware of key management device. This implies, the kind of coin can affect the specification and operation of cryptocurrency exchange, but such difficulties were not disclosed at that time.

Zaif Incident (2018): In September 2018, a hot wallet in Zaif was hacked and about 50M USD equivalent Bitcoin and other cryptocurrencies were lost. The specific problems of Zaif are it is registered cryptocurrency exchange under the current regulation. Moreover, Zaif was subject to administrative sanctions twice after the investigation described in this section. However, it did not make compliant these sanctions.

Recent Incidents in 2019: In May 2019, Binance was hacked and about 40M USD equivalent Bitcoin and other cryptocurrencies were lost. Also In July 2019, BitPoint was hacked and about 32 M USD equivalent cryptocurrencies were lost.

1.3   Contributions

The aim of this paper is giving a real status on the security of cryptocurrency exchange to consider the future of uniformed security technology, management, governance, and standards. Firstly, we give a detailed analysis of what levels of security and governance are implemented and what are missing. Then we reconsider the governance and security management required to a cryptocurrency exchange. Then we show the required technology and operations from the above analysis. The construction of this paper is as follows. We discuss the desired governance and security management conclusions from the above analysis. We also discuss future direction toward the security standard of technologies and operations for cryptocurrency exchanges and explain the current status of security documents in ISO and IETF, which are also led by the authors of this paper.

2 Analysis of the Reality of "Cryptocurrency Exchanges"

2.1 Trends of the Shortage of Governance and Security Management

During JFSA, Japanese governmental regulation authority did audit and investigation, it issued administrative penalties to cryptocurrency exchanges with problems. After the CoinCheck incident, JFSA issues 20 administrative penalties to 17 cryptocurrency exchanges. Each release for the administrative penalty explained problems to be fixed. There were 22 kinds of problems are explained. Table 2 shows 6 major problems and which problems are applicable to each cryptocurrency exchange. These 6 problems were those in which over 25% of cryptocurrency exchange was requested to fix them. They are corporate management issue, system risk issue, anti-money laundering, segregation of customers' asset, customer protection and consideration to deal with new cryptocurrencies.

Table 2. Major problems which each cryptocurrency exchange was requested to fix

Problems	(1)	(2)	(3)	(4)	(5)	(6)	(7)	(8)	(9)	(10)	(11)	(12)	(13)	(14)	(15)	(16)	(17)
Management	x	x		x	x	x	x		x		x	x		x		x	x
System risk	x	x	x	x	x	x	x		x	x	x	x	x	x	x	x	x
AML	x	x		x	x	x	x		x	x	x	x	x	x	x	x	x
Segregation	x			x		x	x		x			x	x	x	x	x	x
Customer	x			x	x			x		x	x					x	
New coin	x			x		x			x			x				x	

From this table, the first significant result is that most of all cryptocurrency exchanges which were penalized did not have qualified corporate management, system risk management and systems and operations for anti-money laundering. This indicates there are no common understandings on the implementation and operations of financial services. The lack of management of system risks indicates that such cryptocurrency exchanges do not have enough number of qualified system architects, engineers, and operators. As we described in Sect. 1.2, most of the incidents were caused by attacks from outside, and the amount of assets should incentivize the attackers to mount actual attacks. Thus, each cryptocurrency exchange should hire a group of experienced security experts. However, the reality is not the case.

2.2 Functionalities Which Real Cryptocurrency Exchanges Have

As described in this section, there are many perception gaps between what users of cryptocurrency exchange think and real cryptocurrency exchange. From the word "Exchange," a general person thinks the task of the cryptocurrency exchange is matching selling orders to buying orders like a general stock exchange. However, a user has an account at the cryptocurrency exchange, then deposit some amount of money to the account. This implies the cryptocurrency exchange has similar functionality as a bank. Moreover, most cryptocurrency exchanges keep a (private) signature key of each user inside their server. This means such cryptocurrency exchanges have the functionality of custodians.

By the investigation, some cryptocurrency exchanges do not record the transfer of cryptocurrency into the original blockchain but manage another database (hopefully some blockchain system) as a ledger inside the exchange. In such a case, cryptocurrency is "sold" in exchange of customer's money, but nothing is sold and the customer buys something without the existence of the cryptocurrency. In some cases, cryptocurrency is sold by the exchange itself with some information as it seems matched with some order. However, the suggested price is shown by the exchange, and the transaction is conducted by the price asked. In this case, the customer thinks the transaction is conducted by the result of matching over the market, but the reality is simple purchasing. In this case, the "exchange" is not a true exchange, but a currency shop. There is an essential reason why an average customer deposits the signature key to the cryptocurrency exchange is, it is not easy to securely manage the signature key for such an average person.

From above all, the functionality of cryptocurrency exchange is apparently beyond the "exchange", and in some case, it is a simple shop, and in the worst case, this might be selling nothing in exchange of real money.

2.3   Shortage of Security Consideration

From the analysis of functionalities described in the previous subsection, most of the existing cryptocurrency exchanges have more functionalities than any one of the stock exchanges, banks, custodians, and shops. Thus, the cryptocurrency exchange needs to manage security risks according to all the functionality it has. Hence, the security consideration should be the sum of security management for each function and more. With considering the amount of values each cryptocurrency exchange deals with, it should be a big target of cyber attacks. Such cyber attacks cause most of the past incidents described in Sect. 1.2. Thus, each cryptocurrency exchange should be tolerant to global scale cyberattacks.

However, unfortunately, most cryptocurrency exchanges are startup companies. Thus, they do not have enough capability to hire enough experts to design, implement and operate secure cryptocurrency exchange. The number of such qualified experts is quite limited, thus attracting a sufficient number of qualified experts is not entirely a matter of money. As a result, most cryptocurrency exchanges are not designed by general security management methodology for infrastructure. They include not only cryptography but for security for the entire system . However, such system-level security consideration was omitted. For example, the early stage discussion right after the CoinCheck incident was a treatment of cold wallet, which is only a part of security management.

2.4   Issues Which Are Common to the Financial Industry and Specific to Cryptocurrency Exchanges

Most of the issues are common to the financial industry. However, the rest is specific to cryptocurrency exchanges. Among the six significant problems described in Sect. 2.1, corporate management and customer protection is common to the financial industry, and there are no specific matters to cryptocurrency exchange. Here, we describe issues specific to cryptocurrency exchange. System risk is, of course, common to the financial industry, but the design and security management of information system depends on each specific business conditions. For example, key management is one of the most significant issues in the application of cryptography. Given the real world business of cryptocurrency exchange, many customers deposit their private cryptographic keys. The key management life-cycle is different from ordinary Public Key infrastructure (PKI). Informational assets, attack surfaces, threats, and risks vary due to each business environment. We will analyze the security management of cryptocurrency exchanges in Sect. 3. AML is also a common issue for all financial business, but anonymous cryptocurrency causes many difficulties than ordinary financial services. In the case of CoinCheck incident, the stolen NEM coin could not be actually traced. Currently, cryptocurrency exchange is one of few targets of regulation, because it is the connecting point between cryptocurrency and real-world economy. With current regulation which fits FATF recommendation, most of all cryptocurrency exchange conducts verification of identity. The introduction of Decentralized Exchange (DEX) will eliminate the point of regulation. Thus it should increase this difficulty.

2.5   Drawback in Incentive Design for Key Management

Segregation of customers' assets has another discussion issue. In the case of CoinCheck incident, all assets deposited at CoinCheck are managed by using one cryptographic key pair (address), and this is the reason why the entire customer assets were stolen in a short period. In the CoinCheck incident, the stolen cryptocurrency was NEM, of which the underlying consensus mechanism is based on Proof-of-Stake (PoS). There are many reasons including transaction throughput, to manage the assets of many customers by using one key. It is not clear that this was the reason why CoinCheck managed all assets by using one address. However, in general, PoS type cryptocurrency may give cryptocurrency exchange terrible incentive to manage all assets with one key, because the cryptocurrency exchange can gain mining (or similar) reward by utilizing the vast amount of customer's cryptocurrency. As a result, cryptocurrency exchange produces a new single point of failure, and it is things that should be avoided from the security point of view. Of course, this type of operation is out of the scope of cryptocurrency, but we need to care about the possibility to happen these kinds of things. Each consensus mechanism has pros. and cons. generally. However, this is one issue of the downside of PoS type cryptocurrency, and we need to have clear operation policy for PoS type cryptocurrency.

3   Reconsidering Governance and Security Management

3.1   Threat Modeling and Security Requirements

In parallel to the investigation by JFSA, we worked on creating a document on security management of cryptocurrency exchange right after the CoinCheck incident. Even now, there is no standardized architecture and implementation of software/hardware for cryptocurrency exchange. Therefore, we cannot edit one standard document toward the secure implementation and operation of cryptocurrency exchange. We gathered information about real cryptocurrency exchanges from their engineers, then create a model of cryptocurrency exchange system. Figure 1 shows an example of system model of cryptocurrency exchange.

The model consists of Customer Interface for login and transaction, Customer Authentication Function, Customer Credential Database, Customer Assets Management Function, Blockchain Node for incoming transactions, Incoming transaction management Function, Order processing function, Assets Database, Transaction Signing Function for outgoing transactions, Exchange Operation Modules, Operator Authentication Function, and Operator Audit Database. Details are described in Sect. 5.2 on [9].

We defined each functional element to distinguish functions logically, and do not show the actual arrangement on the actual system. For example, in our actual system, the address management unit may be managed by an integrated database. Also, there are implementations with multiple functions packaged together. For example, each functional element of the transaction signature system may be integrated with the customer property management system, or the transaction signature system may be operating as another system.

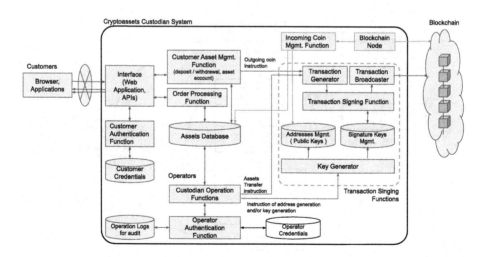

Fig. 1. System model of cryptocurrency exchange

3.2 Keys in Cryptocurrency Exchange

There are four types of keys used in cryptocurrency exchange; 1) *Signature Key* which is a private key for signing transactions, 2) *Verification Key* which is a public key for verification of transactions, 3) *Key Encryption Key (KEK)* which is a secret key to keep confidentiality of signature key, and 4) *Master Seed* which is a seed, e.g. random number, to generate a signature key in the deterministic wallet. Signature keys and verification keys are asymmetric key cryptography.

After a pair of a signature key and a verification key (hereafter "key pair") is generated, an address to receive transactions is generated from the verification key. By notifying a sender of crypto assets this address, the sender is able to transfer the asset to the address. When the recipient transfers the asset to the other address, the original recipient signs the transaction data which includes the transfer order. The inactive state of the signature key is the state such that the signature key is stored securely in the signature key management function of Fig. 2. An example of inactivation is encryption by encryption/decryption key (e.g. pass phrase), that is, the signature key is encrypted. In the contrary, activation is the process to make the key usable to sign, by decrypting the inactivated key. The activation is assumed to be executed in transaction signing function of Fig. 2. Activation and inactivation may be executed in an implementation of wallet, when the wallet has both functions. The signature key is not needed after its generation until execution of signing to transaction. Thus, there is a way to manage the signature key in offline manner with storing the verification key and address online(cold wallet).

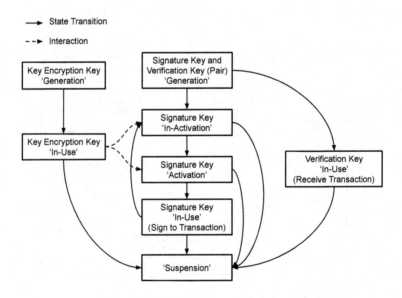

Fig. 2. Key life-cycle at cryptocurrency exchange

On the Usage of Multiple Keys: In some crypto assets system, it is recommended not to use the same key pair twice, thus it produces multiple key pairs. This feature is for preventing trace and not relevant to the business efficiency of a cryptocurrency exchange. However, a cryptocurrency exchange should manage addresses for each customer. Thus it should manage multiple key pairs for the same crypto assets.

On the Suspension of Keys: Suspension of key usage is only an operation inside a cryptocurrency exchange. By definition of blockchain based crypto assets system, any user cannot cancel transaction once it is made. As another case, it is difficult to revoke signature key even after the suspension of key. For example, a customer accidentally operates some crypto assets for suspended address. In such case, the suspended signature key is needed to make a reimbursement. Thus, suspension of keys should be conducted with considering such cases.

In the cryptocurrency exchange, the role and risk of the signature key are extremely large. This is not only to enable the transfer of coins but also to disappear due to the anonymity of the crypto assets, the property that it is impossible to revoke the signature keys against leakage/theft or roll back the transaction by. In this section, we show the risk of fraudulent use that could lead to the loss of signature keys, leakage/theft, and damage of values. It also shows supply chain risks when introducing the wallet.

3.3   Analysis Based on Governance and Security Management Standard

At cryptocurrency exchanges, it is mandatory to establish, conduct, maintain and continuously improve security management. As requirements in terms of security management, items described in [7] are sufficiently considered according to the business process of each cryptocurrency exchange. Especially, the following items should be carefully considered, because a cryptocurrency exchange retains customer's assets and should deal with issues specific to crypto assets.

On stakeholders[1], it is needed to consider protection of customer's assets, as well as division of responsibility with outsourcers including security of private key management for crypto asset, and mattes by which a cryptocurrency exchange may give social impacts like money laundering.

On security policy[2], a cryptocurrency exchange should define a security policy which includes security objectives and controls. Especially, it is recommended to disclose the security policy on the management of crypto assets to customers to facilitate self evaluation.

Continuous risk evaluation and improvement[3], a cryptocurrency exchange should watch security risks of crypto assets in addition to aligning the general security management framework, because the risks change and increase due to

---

[1] ISO 27001 [7] Clause 4.

[2] ISO 27001 [7] Clause 5.

[3] ISO 27002 [8] Clause 6, 8, 9 and 10.

rapid development of related technology. It is especially important to continuously evaluate risk and improve security objectives, policy and controls to keep effectiveness of security controls after starting their operations. A cryptocurrency exchange should decide security objectives and controls with considering viewpoint as a countermeasure to threat as lost, theft, leak and abuse of customer's assets data and private key for crypto assets, requirements for actual business, compliance to laws and rules and social responsibilities to prevent crimes in use of crypto assets like scam and money laundering.

The cryptocurrency exchange conducts threat analysis, vulnerability evaluation, risk evaluation and defining security objectives and controls according to its actual business and system. Security objectives and controls should be decided with considering threats and risks specific to crypto assets, as well as general security objectives and controls described in ISO 27002 [8]. Consideration of security objective and controls described in [8] is mandatory. The next clause describes specific items to be considered by a cryptocurrency exchange.

Risk Analysis of Signature Key. Risk analysis differs depending on the assumed threats, system configuration, threat modeling, and so on. Here, the threats concerning the signature key and the factors that can cause the threat are assumed as follows. The following as the actor giving input to the signature key based on Fig. 2.

Threats: lost, leakage, theft and fraudulent use.

Factors of Threats

- *Mis-operation*: An act that an authorized user (including an administrator) of the system accidentally operated by mistake. For example, it is incorrectly supposed that an operation to coin 100,000 yen is incorrectly dispatched for 1 million yen.
- *Legitimate users' malice*: Acts performed by a legitimate user of the example, theft or unauthorized use of the signature private key due to internal fraud. In this case, it is the purpose of identifying acts that can be factors, and the purpose and incentive of the act are not limited here.
- *Spoofing*: An act other than an authorized user of the system impersonating a legitimate user (more accurately impersonating some kind of operation). For example, an internal burglar without administrator privilege accesses the system with administrator authority.
- *Intrusions from outside*: An act of an outsider accessing the system malicious intrusion from the outside by exploiting the system's vulnerability, incorporating malware into the exchanging system via targeted e-mail to the exchanges' administrator or the like and generating a private signature private key (or transaction creation) from the outside, allows remote control, etc.
- *Unintended behaviors of implementations*: The system behaves unexpectedly by the designer or operator irrespective of the intention or malice of the operation. For example, a signature private key leaks due to a bug in the exchange management system.

Actors: Exchange operation modules, transaction signing modules, customer asset management function implementation, and incoming coin management function implementation.

Of these threat factors, theft and fraudulent use are regarded as threats that can only be caused by explicit malicious factors. As a result, the possible risks for the signature key to be assumed are figured in Table 3.

Objectives of security management at a cryptocurrency exchange contain secure protection of customer's assets, compliance to business requirements, laws and rules, and realization of social responsibility. Security policies and execution statements derived from the objectives are recommended to be publicly available for consumers, business partners, auditor and regulators to help their judge.

4   Directions to Secure Cryptocurrency Exchanges

4.1   Required Technologies

From above analysis, there are six issues where we need to consider to introduce enhanced technologies to make cryptocurrency exchange trustable.

Authenticity and Integrity of Segregated Ledger: Many cryptocurrency exchanges manage customers' assets by using the segregated ledger, and they record not all transactions on the public blockchain, because of efficiency and latency reasons. Assuring integrity and authenticity of the segregated ledger is an essential part of the security of their business. Introducing a transparent way, such as cryptographic timestamp, to assure such characteristics is needed.

Multi-signature: Multi-signature is a major technology to avoid loss of customers' assets when the loss of one or minor part of keys occurs.

Underlying Cryptographic Background and Implementation: HSM (Hardware Security Module) is the trust anchor of the cryptocurrency exchange. In general, HSM supports standard cryptographic algorithms. However, cryptocurrency may implement special algorithms or parameters such as curves of ECC. Standardization of underlying cryptographic algorithms and selecting HSMs that support more algorithms are needed.

Key Management and Wallet: Most cryptocurrency exchanges manage assets using the hot wallet for online transactions and the cold wallet to protect keys from attack from the network. For the online wallet, utilizing certification programs like CMVP and products with such certification are needed.

Audit: Internal audit and third-party audit are needed to provide transparency to customers and regulators. Technology to make audits easy such as the cryptographic timestamp is needed.

Table 3. Result of risk analysis

Risk	Attack surface	Threat by lost	Threat by leakage	Threat by theft	Threat by fraudulent use
Illegal operation (route is legitimate)	End-user's malice	x	x	x	x
	Operator's malice in custodian	x	x	x	x
	Spoofing to end users	x	x	x	x
	Internal frauds (spoofing to operators)	x	x	x	x
Intrusion from outside	Intrusion into the transaction signing modules	x	x	x	x
	Intrusion into the incoming coin management function	x	x	x	x
	Intrusion into the customer asset management function	x	x	x	x
	Intrusion into the exchange operation modules	x	x	x	x
System behaviors different from human operation	Unintended behaviors of the transaction signing modules	x	x		
	Unintended behaviors of the incoming coin management function	x	x		
	Unintended behaviors of the customer asset management function	x	x		
	Unintended behaviors of the exchange operation module	x	x		
Mis-operation	Mis-operation of end user	x	x		
	Mis-operation of operator	x	x		

External Evaluation: To clarify the security level of implementation, certification as common criteria (ISO/IEC 15048) is needed. Establishing protection profile is helpful to conduct an external evaluation.

4.2   Required Operations

Basics of Key Management. General private cryptographic keys should be isolated from other informational assets, the number of access to private keys should be limited as minimum as possible and be prepared for unintentional loss of private keys.

- They should be isolated from other informational assets. Rigorous access control is mandatory.
- Limit the number of access to private keys as minimum as possible.
- Be prepared for unintentional loss of private keys.

The followings are three basic security control to realize above. Additional security controls specific to crypto assets custodians are described in and after **Backup**. Three security controls as state management of private keys, Administrator role separation, and mutual check-and-balance and backup of private keys are needed.

1. *State management of signature key*: Unnecessary activation of the signature key increases the risk of abuse, leakage, and theft, though keeping the activation state is efficient from a business viewpoint. On the other hand, frequent activation/inactivation may give an impact on business efficiency. It is important to consider the trade-off between the risk and business efficiency and provide clear key management policy to customers.
2. *Administrator role separation and mutual check-and-balance*: It is a fundamental form of operation of a critical business process that uses the private key to perform cryptographic operations by multiple parties to prevent internal fraud and errors. Mutual oversight and limitation make internal frauds, mis-operation, digital signature by a lone adversary more difficult.
3. *Backup of private key*: Lost of the private key makes signing operations by using the key impossible any more. Thus backup of the private key is important security control. On the other hand, risks of leakage and theft of backup keys should be considered. It is needed to inactivate the backup key.

Backup. Backup is the most fundamental and useful measure against the loss of the signature key, but are also risks of leakage and loss of the backup device. These risks depend on the kind backup device. Thus security controls on such devices should be considered independently. Typical ways are cloning to the tamper-resistant cryptographic key management device, backup to storage for digital data and Backup to paper. Details are described in Sect. 7.3.6.4 on [9].

Offline Management. There is a type of offline key management (as known as "cold wallet"). It makes to prevent leakage and theft caused by the intrusion, by isolating private keys from the system network and requiring some offline operation. For preventing abuse of keys and malicious transaction, however, an explicit approval process is needed additionally.

Distributed Management. It is also a good security control to distribute the right to use the private key to multiple entities. There are two examples; division of secret key and multi-signature technique. Details are described in Sect. 7.3.6.3 on [9].

4.3 Standardization Activities and Future Direction

Current Activities. As described in Sect. 1, it is too early to define some technology and operational standards at well-recognized standardization bodies like ISO, IEC, ITU-T, etc, because blockchain technology and its architecture are currently dynamically changing. Though it is too early to define some technologies and operational standards, several standardization bodies started already their activities and study toward the future standard. On the security of cryptocurrency exchange, ISO TC307 started two projects to make a technical report on the security of blockchain and distributed ledger technology (ISO TR23245) and a technical report on security practice of digital asset custodians (ISO TR 23576 [10]). Here, "digital asset custodians" means financial institutes which store cryptographic keys associated with the crypto assets (or cryptocurrencies), hence existing cryptocurrency exchanges are included in this category of institutes. The results of the study described in Sect. 3 are now developed as an internet draft [9] in IETF. This has almost the same contents as ISO TR 23576. Despite the difficulty to create a technical standard on blockchain technology, such standard or agreed document is needed to operate any organization associated with blockchain technology because they design their security control in their own way, and they need to share common knowledge to raise the bottom level of security. These documents are useful not only for constructing a cryptocurrency exchange, but also audit, creating and operating management lifecycle, providing pieces of evidence of secure operation to the public, and earning trust to operators of trustless financial systems.

Future Direction
Considering the needs of standards for blockchain technology and standards, there are two challenges to establish workable ones. The first is, as we already mentioned, the technology is dynamically changing, thus it is too early to make "standards." The second is most of blockchain technology and implementations are made by small startups, where ISO/IEC 27000 framework is heavy to apply. To deal with these two challenges, we propose a three steps approach.

Step1: Issuing technical documents as snapshots and preliminary. Before technological architecture becomes stable, a series of technical documents as snapshots are published. The current ISO TRs and IETF internet-draft align this concept.

Step2: Design structure of standards. When layers of technology and operations become clear, the workable structure of standards will be discussed and designed. This will include 1) technology standards that assure all layers of blockchain such as cryptography, consensus algorithm, key management protocol with aligning existing standards and ISO/IEC 29128 framework. 2) Operational standards, and 3) standards for the certification process.

Step3: Create a series of standards. Based on existing technical reports published in step 1 and other existing standards/technical documents, a series of standards will be edited and published. To make the document workable, all stakeholders will be involved in this process.

5 Conclusion

In spite of the advanced regulation on the exchanges in Japan, our analysis reveals the shortage of technical, operational, and governance expertise. The analysis implies the needs of a feedback loop for continuous enhancement and needs of standardization to raise the bottom level.

We conducted modeling and risk analysis on the cryptocurrency exchange, aligning to ISO/IEC 27000, and created an example system and key management model. We found that the key lifecycle and management model is largely different from ordinary PKI. We showed typical key management model from the analysis. Establishing a concrete enhancement and new key management especially for PoS, is essential to not re-invent the wheel and to make a healthy cryptocurrency ecosystem. As a direction toward standardization, we propose three steps approach to handle this emerging technology.

References

1. Nakamoto, S.: Bitcoin: a peer-to-peer electronic cash system (2008). https://bitcoin.org/bitcoin.pdf
2. Decker, C., Wattenhofer, R.: Bitcoin transaction malleability and MtGox. In: Kutyłowski, M., Vaidya, J. (eds.) ESORICS 2014. LNCS, vol. 8713, pp. 313–326. Springer, Cham (2014). https://doi.org/10.1007/978-3-319-11212-1_18
3. Shane, D.: $530 million cryptocurrency heist may be biggest ever, CNN Tech (2018). https://money.cnn.com/2018/01/29/technology/coincheck-cryptocurrency-exchange-hack-japan/index.html
4. GURUBARAN, $60 Million Worth Cryptocurrencies Stolen Hackers From Japanese Cryptocurrency Exchange, GBHackers on security (2018). https://gbhackers.com/60-million-cryptocurrencies-zaif-exchange/
5. Binance: Binance Security Breach Update (2019). https://binance.zendesk.com/hc/en-us/articles/360028031711
6. Wolfie, Z.: Bitpoint Exchange Hacked for $32 Million in Cryptocurrency (2019). https://www.coindesk.com/japanese-exchange-bitpoint-hacked-by-32-million-worth-in-cryptocurrencies
7. International Organization for Standardization, Information Technology - Security Techniques - Information Security Management Systems - Requirements, ISO/IEC TR 27001:2013 (2013). https://www.iso.org/standard/54534.html
8. International Organization for Standardization, Information Technology - Security Techniques - Code of practice for information security controls, ISO/IEC TR 27002:2013 (2013). https://www.iso.org/standard/54533.html

9. Sato, M., Shimaoka, M., Nakajima, H.: General Security Considerations for Cryptoassets Custodians (2020). https://www.ietf.org/id/draft-vcgtf-crypto-assets-security-considerations-06.txt
10. International Organization for Standardization, Blockchain and distributed ledger technologies - Security of digital asset custodians, ISO/IEC TR 23576 (2019). https://www.iso.org/standard/76072.html

VOTING 2020: Fifth Workshop
on Advances in Secure Electronic Voting

Origami Voting: A Non-cryptographic Approach to Transparent Ballot Verification

Enka Blanchard[1]([✉]) and Ted Selker[2]

[1] Digitrust, Loria, Université de Lorraine, Paris, France
Enka.Blanchard@gmail.com
[2] UMBC, Baltimore, USA
ted.selker@gmail.com
http://www.koliaza.com, http://ted.selker.com/

Abstract. Over the past four decades, fear of election manipulation and hacking has spurred the security technology community to propose a variety of voting systems to implement verifiable voting. Most of these rely on hard to understand cryptographic protocols, which can affect whether users actually verify their selections. Three-Ballot and Vote/Anti-Vote/Vote, two related systems among the few non-cryptographic end-to-end verifiable voting systems, made improvements in security while eliminating complex protocols. They unfortunately suffered from usability issues, and although they did not require cryptographic primitives, they still relied on electronic devices. To address this, we introduce three folded-paper based systems that allow verifiable voting and resist common attacks despite not relying on any cryptography or electronic devices. The proposals are based on 1) semi-translucent ballots, 2) masking tape, or 3) folding and punching. These Origami voting methods help users understand the underlying mechanisms and give them a direct geometric approach to verification.

Keywords: Usable security · Voting systems · Verifiable voting · Low-technology

1 Introduction

Voting, whether it is on a proposal in parliament or to elect politicians, has been a driver of innovation for more than a century, from Edison's invention of the first electrical voting system in 1868 [24] to demonstrations with every manner of new technology—exemplified in recent years with blockchain voting, although its advantage over established verifiable voting systems remains to be proved, especially since the technology has not been around long enough to be thoroughly tested [5,34,50]. The introduction of new approaches for voting is often slow, as with the 40-year delay in implementing the secret ballot in the USA after its

© Springer Nature Switzerland AG 2020
M. Bernhard et al. (Eds.): FC 2020 Workshops, LNCS 12063, pp. 273–290, 2020.
https://doi.org/10.1007/978-3-030-54455-3_20

successful introduction in Australia—from which stems the name "Australian ballot" [3]. This resistance has come first from elected officials wanting to keep the ability to influence and coerce, sometimes under the guise of defending the *"manly pride that scorns concealment, and the sturdy will that refuses to bend to coercion"* [32]. Many costly or complex systems were created specifically for dealing with votes within a parliament, offering a higher level of secrecy against the higher usability of the frequently used system of voting by raising one's hand [24]. This proposed secrecy has been the source of arguments from both citizens and party leadership, sometimes aimed at keeping an elected official beholden to their promises [15], as secrecy can both ruin transparency of a representative and create the possibility for coercion.

One of the main sources of research and debate on political reform has been the use of audits, and the technological tools to make them easier. Errors with counting and re-counting ballots are well-publicised, leading to a slew of systems that produce both a mechanised or electronic tally and an auditable record ballot (that are rarely checkable or checked by voters), from lever machines to optical scan methods [6]. The design challenges of helping the voter secure voting systems though audits are evident in systems such as secret-ballot receipts [8], Scantegrity [9,10]—an end-to-end independent verification system that coexists with a normal ballot—or audio audit trails [41], which improve the usability of auditing. Others require changing the infrastructure by using electronic-only systems [17,22,27], sometimes not even requiring polling places but instead some forms of e-identification [43,49].

All the systems mentioned try to improve accuracy, integrity, and prevent coercion, miscounting, ballot box stuffing and related fraud, generally through difficult to understand means. Those problems have been central to election security since the late 19th century [33], but some of the focus has now shifted to other considerations[1] [2,16,29]. First, manipulation of voter registration lists [7], accessibility of voting [4] and turnout buying [29] can have stronger impacts than the previously mentioned problems [6,30,36]. Second, familiarity with the voting system is essential[2], and technological changes without adequate training generally come with a strong temporary increase in error rates [18,20].

With people being increasingly concerned with the threat of election hacking [31]—and legitimately so [43]—a number of experts have warned about the lack of adequate technology [37]. There is also a strong pressure to return to low-tech, non-electronic systems, as it is supposedly much harder for an external adversary to massively manipulate them [26]. Unlike the USA, some countries such as France or Switzerland did not mechanise their voting systems and still use paper ballots massively with little evolution in voting practice in more than

---

[1] Luckily today, in most major elections in western democracies the error rate is generally at least one order of magnitude lower than the margin of victory [13]. Easily identifiable boldfaced fraud is still extant in many countries such as Russia [14], Honduras [16] or Albania [12].

[2] Co-existence of redundant systems is possible, as in Estonia, but have an adverse effect on the adoption rate [48].

a century [13]. Some European countries are also considering or implementing moratoriums on using electronic devices at any point in the voting process. Avoiding electronics and cryptography altogether poses a problem for most of the newly developed end-to-end verifiable voting systems that guarantee the authenticity and anonymity of all ballots.

To address these issues as well as the mechanical and cognitive difficulties of making correct selections, we propose origami voting, a set of systems inspired by Ron Rivest and Warren Smith's two related Three-Ballot and Vote/Anti-Vote/Vote (VAV) systems[3] [39]. Three-Ballot and VAV systems both use a set of three ballots to guarantee anonymity and verifiability. Those protocols have many variants, but the simplest—which we'll briefly describe—apply to 2-candidate races. It works by making the voters use three simultaneous ballots, while enforcing that they vote at least once for each candidate, thus giving at most a 1-vote advantage to the candidate of their choice. All the ballots feature a unique identifier, and are made public after the voting period ends. After casting three ballots—two of which compensate for each other by giving votes to both candidates—the voter gets a receipt for one of them, showing who it is for and the corresponding unique identifier. As that receipt can be for any candidate, it is impossible to guess the voter's choice, but as the receipts are not public, modifying or removing ballots in the ballot box includes a high risk of discovery.

Unfortunately the initial Three-Ballot and VAV proposals had vulnerabilities. First, when voting for more than a few different races, it made unique identifying voting patterns on ballots possible, reintroducing the risk of coercion and vote-selling. This effect and its probability of happening in real races has been well studied in a variety of articles [1,19,46]. Although it poses a real risk in places with many concurrent races[4], many countries— such as Spain, Greece, France or Malawi [38]—don't have many concurrent elections, and this article will focus on this case (called the Short Ballot Assumption in the original articles).

A second weakness of Rivest and Smith's systems has been the high complexity and poor usability for the voter, not only in the practical implementation [25,45] but also because of the many steps necessary to correctly use the scheme—here requiring voters to accurately vote 3 times, once against their the candidate they favour – which is known to make it harder for voters to use correctly [44]. Finally, the system relies on the assumption that the ballots are all correctly filled and checked, which is dependent on the separate step of scanning and validating the ballots with a machine without storing them. This introduces a vulnerability coming from the use of potentially insecure hardware, and all the proposed solutions so far rely on external electronic remedies either through trusted hardware [47] or online services [28,40].

---

[3] To be precise, the design of our Origami ballots is closest in appearance to VAV, but the underlying mechanisms are closer to the original Three-Ballot proposal.

[4] Linked to the problems with many parallel races, having many different candidates on a single ballot increases confusion and proximity errors, with smaller candidates adjacent to high-ranked ones getting an additional 0.4% of the latter's vote [42].

Contributions. We propose three candidate designs that enforce that the ballots are correct (and cast as intended) through mechanical and perceptual means. They extend previous non-cryptographic end-to-end verifiable voting approaches by reducing the selections to one step and removing the need to be checked by a separate device. The first protocol relies on translucent paper, allowing a voting official to check that the ballot is correctly filled without knowing who the voter voted for. The second is similar but simpler for the voter, with the higher usability coming at the expense of increased manufacturing complexity and cost. The third protocol is based on folding and hole-punching and has multiple desirable properties, including resistance even to attacks where voters film themselves in the ballot booth, a practice sometimes authorised under the name of "ballot selfies" [21]. As with the original schemes, it is possible to use optical scanning machines to check the ballots. However, the fact that a voting official can check the ballots without gaining information means that one doesn't have to rely on such external systems. The ideal system might be to have people randomly assigned to one or the other, with discrepancies indicating probable fraud.

2   Constraints

To limit the confusion of voters, the execution of any candidate protocol should be familiar, hence close to the following:

- The voter comes into the polling station and proves that they are a registered voter (e.g. by showing the relevant ID).
- They are given instructions as to how to vote[5];
- Voters obtain some physical objects if necessary (e.g. ballots, pens, envelopes, magnifiers);
- They move into a privacy booth where they can manipulate the ballot;
- If needed, a machine or a voting official checks that their ballot (or envelope) is correct;
- They cast their ballot by inserting it into a ballot box.

Moreover, the protocols should satisfy the following constraints, in no specific order of importance (as some of these are equally necessary):

1. It should not allow multiple voting: there should be no way for a voter to give a multiple vote advantage to a single candidate. This should hold even if some but not all other agents (such as voting officials) are corrupt;
2. There must be no way for a third party to find out a particular voter's vote, and allow no way for a voter to prove that they voted a particular way;
3. As a consequence of the previous constraint, if a receipt is given that indicates a specific vote, the vote indicated on it must be either chosen by the voter or close to uniformly distributed among all possibilities;

---

[5] As has been suggested [18], in the first few public uses of the system, all users should receive detailed instructions and a test experience to show how they can use the voting system and ask for support before they mark their actual ballot.

4. If some of the ballots are modified after being cast, voters must have a constant probability of being able to find out and prove that there was a modification;
5. A voter must not be able to prove there was a modification when there wasn't, even if their initial ballot was not correctly filled;
6. Finally, the whole system must not depend on any single machine or human agent that could modify any ballot or count unnoticed[6].

The above constraints have to be supplemented by some additional concerns which are crucial to any voting system, not just the ones considered here. The voters must be comfortable with the ballot, with its use, and be reasonably confident whether they have used it correctly. They must also know how to spoil their ballot and get a replacement one if they make a mistake. Finally, they must have confidence in the fact that they voted correctly and that their vote is private and secure.

All the ballots in the protocols shown here also assume that there is a single election, and no concurrent races.

These constraints support the main goal: to optimise usability and simplicity while a voter creates an accurate verifiable ballot that requires no electronic devices.

3 Translucent Ballot

3.1 Protocol

This first protocol uses a ballot on which voters can write. The design, as indicated in Fig. 1, has three similar single ballots side by side, with one receipt under the left ballot. Each ballot has four different parts:

- A central translucent rectangle split in two cells, one of which the voter has to cover by marking over it;
- A legend over each cell, indicating which candidate it corresponds to;
- A single unique but not memorable ballot segment identification method— here a barcode—under the translucent rectangle;
- A single green dot in the top right corner of the left ballot;

The receipt has a fully transparent rectangle in the same position, but otherwise the elements are the same as in the left ballot with the vertical order reversed, with the bottom of the receipt being slightly narrower and longer. When folded over, rectangles should be aligned with each other, and the green dot should be visible, with the bottom of the receipt protruding, to be removed after the voter casts their ballots.

One important thing to note is that the barcodes are not initially present on the ballot. Instead, during a preliminary phase before going into a voting

---

[6] We can reasonably assume that some voting officials should be honest, which introduces redundancy for counting, and each of the steps should be corroborated by a group such as one representative from each party and one election official.

booth, the voter receives the ballot sheet without barcodes, and a sheet of three pairs of identical barcode stickers. They can then choose which pair goes on the first ballot and the receipt, and paste them in the appropriate places, then take one from each other pair, paste them on the ballot sheet, and shred the two remaining stickers. The whole process should happen under supervision, just to make sure that the ballots are correctly pasted in a way that does not make the ballots identifiable, and that the receipt barcode corresponds to the one above.

The instructions for the voter are as follows:

- Select a pair of identical barcode stickers from the three pairs and stick them on the leftmost ballot and the receipt in the indicated region. Then take one from each of the other two pairs and stick them on the corresponding zones on the central and right ballots.
- Choose whether you want to audit your ballot for A or B, colour the corresponding cell on the left ballot. Make an X on the corresponding cell on the receipt. Colour the cell corresponding to the other option on the right ballot.
- Choose whether you want to vote for A or for B, and colour the corresponding cell on the central ballot.
- Fold the three ballots horizontally, leaving the central ballot between the two others. Both cells will appear to be filled in.
- Fold the receipt vertically on the same side as the ballot it's attached to.
- You should end up with a single stack of ballots, with no visible barcode on the outside and a green dot visible in one corner.

The instructions can be indicated directly on the ballot in the space left (if there is enough space, which depends on ballot size), both textually and diagrammatically to avoid language issues. Alternatively, it could also be printed on the remaining space if rectangular sheets are used, but that creates security risks if one isn't careful[7].

The ballot must have the following properties:

- On both ends of the stack, there is a single cell that is entirely coloured. This cell is different on each end. Other than the cell, ballots on each end aren't marked.
- On one side, an X is superimposed on the coloured cell, and a green dot is visible in the corner.

Once this is done, the ballots are separated from each other with a paper guillotine, along the dotted lines. The ballots are all cast into a ballot box[8] and the voter keeps their receipt. The ballots are then all mixed and revealed to the public (which can be scaled by scanning them and putting them online, this electronic part being independent of the vote).

---

[7] For example, having a full rectangle and not an L-shape makes the folding more complicated, and introduces the problem of how to handle having translucent cells inside the instructions. As those cells could be coloured or not, the complexity of the ballot and the number of variables to check to prevent double-voting increases.

[8] To prevent problems between those two steps, the guillotine can be integrated with the ballot box.

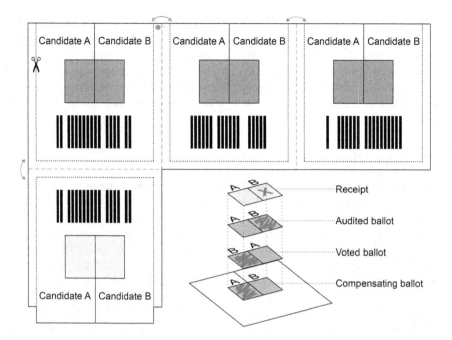

Fig. 1. The translucent ballot and on the bottom right a view of the superposition of the translucent rectangles when folded. The three ballots and the receipt are separated by solid lines which correspond to the folds. Once folded, all the cutting lines are aligned with the receipt sticking out, allowing the voter to keep a receipt that allows them to know their ballot was included. The ballots are simultaneously cut and dropped in the ballot box. The only difference between the three ballots lies in the green dot which is cut off in this process. (Color figure online)

3.2 Constraint Satisfaction

We can now check the six constraints:

1) To check the first property, the officials make sure that there is at least one ballot that is for A, and one for B. The last ballot doesn't matter, as it is either valid (a vote for one candidate), blank or entirely coloured, and the last two options make no difference. Thus, the voter can't give a 2-vote advantage to a candidate.

2) Because the rectangle is translucent and there is at least one fully coloured cell in the stack, if the correct materials are chosen, there should be no way to discern whether it is the second or the third layer that is coloured. Thus, it is not possible to determine whether the central ballot is for A or B.

4) The receipt is a copy of the chosen ballot, with the same barcode. As long as ballots with receipts aren't identifiable from other ballots, if a ballot is modified, the receipt has a 1/3 probability of being able to prove as much. The green dot, which identifies which ballot has a receipt, is discarded in the cutting process, after it is used to check the correctness of the folding.

3) and 5) The voter chooses whether they keep a receipt for A or B. However, because the green dot has to be visible, the X mark and the coloured cell right underneath have to correspond to the receipt and the left ballot.

Constraint number 6) is satisfied as there is no need for any device that could monitor or alter the vote, except potentially for the publication—which is partially independent of the vote—where it can be done in parallel to publicly accessible ballots.

3.3 Design Choices

Multiple design choices are relevant in this ballot, while some are of no importance. The first important one is the barcode, which can be considered poorly usable, as it is much harder to read and transcribe than even a long number. However, this is a feature in this context, as the barcode is there to ensure three properties. The first is that every ballot should be unique (easily done with a barcode). The second is that it should be easy to check that the one on the receipt and on the corresponding ballot are identical, which anyone can do by aligning them. Finally, it should be very hard for the voter to keep receipts for all three ballots. If the unique identifiers were easy to read, to remember or to copy, it would be much easier to coerce the voter into keeping receipts for all three, for example, by writing them down discreetly[9]. Instead of the barcode, it would be possible to use alternative identifiers, as long as they are not easily readable by a human (like a string of characters) while being easy to compare to check that two such identifiers are indeed identical.

Having the barcodes as stickers on a second sheet is costly, but it prevents attacks from someone who has access to the ballot printing process. Knowing all the barcodes on the left-side ballot gives an adversary knowledge over which barcodes are safe to modify and which aren't. As the barcodes are not easily readable, the method shown should be safe unless the process is systematically filmed with good cameras.

The green dot, could be replaced by any way to ensure that the receipt and the left ballot are on the same side (with both folds being performed correctly). Whatever this feature, it must later be absent on the ballots that are cast to prevent identifying which ballot has a receipt.

Unlike in the original schemes, the voter does not choose which ballot to keep a receipt for, but instead has an imposed ballot with a receipt on which they vote however they want (this difference is analysed at the end of this article).

One potential usability issue is that it could be possible to partially attack the privacy of the vote if the cells are not fully coloured. Considering the existing difficulties in properly marking ballots even with weaker constraints, this could be problematic. This leads us to a second design that ensures a completely filled in ballot.

---

[9] Some people have learned to read barcodes, but it is much harder to coerce and train someone into reading one, remembering the result or writing it down without error than with serial numbers.

4   Taped Ballot

4.1   Protocol

This is a variant of the previous ballot design but uses masking tape and string to help with the issue of completely filling the ballot. Instead of colouring multiple translucent cells independently, which can lead to making mistakes, guided by connected strings the voter tears off two sets of masking tape, as can be seen on Fig. 2. The strings also operate as a memory aid and physical prosthetic to understanding the system and performing the procedure reliably.

The translucent rectangles of proposal one are replaced by rectangular holes in the ballot, covered by masking tape. The receipt has a slightly larger hole, with two strips of diagonal masking tape that shows both sides of the underlying rectangle when removed.

The instructions are simpler, as the voter has to make only two actions: choose and tear off the tape of their choice on the central ballot (corresponding to their vote), and choose and tear the one they want to audit and the ones it is attached to.

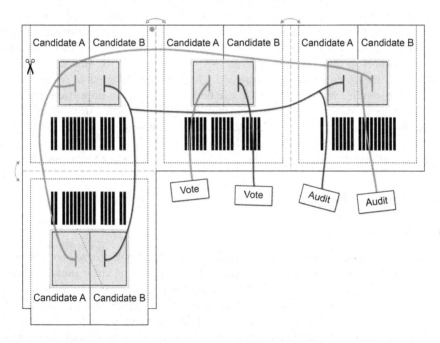

Fig. 2. The taped ballot. Four strings are visible (in different colours here for ease of understanding), attached to different pieces of tape covering holes in the ballots. The voter pulls on one of the two audit strings to remove a set of tapes. They then pull on one of the two voting strings before folding the ballot as in the previous protocol. As the holes in the receipt are bigger, it makes it easy to check that the receipt corresponds to the left ballot. (Color figure online)

4.2 Constraint Satisfaction

When it comes to constraint 1), the official just has to make sure that, beneath the hole of the receipt, the left ballot only has the corresponding piece of tape removed, which is visible thanks to the fact that the tape covering the hole is not aligned with the tape underneath, being diagonal.

Constraint 2) is satisfied because the official can check that, on both sides of the ballot, a single piece of tape has been removed.

Proposal 2, fulfils constraints 3), 4), 5) and 6) for the same reasons as proposal 1, but it also has different properties, analysed below.

4.3 Design Choices

The main goal of proposal 2 is to reduce the selection actions to two, to lower the probability of making mistakes during the several selection actions required with such a multi-ballot system. The strings (which should be of a single colour, unlike on Fig. 2) are but one method of linking together each set of masking tape. Once again, this seemingly non-optimal choice comes from the constraint of having all ballots indistinguishable when cast. Using alternatives like partially adhesive stickers or tear tape might make it simpler and more usable, but creating a tape pattern that links each set while keeping the ballots indistinguishable is a complex endeavour. Having symmetrical tape patterns on a recto-verso ballot is another option, but also decreases the usability. With this design, each ballot cast has a single piece of tape attached with a string that is cut at one end, not revealing whether it was a left ballot or not. It is important that the labels on each strings are indistinguishable (Audit or Vote, instead of Audit A/Audit B). This is to ensure that they can hang outside the ballot during the cutting/casting process, preventing the ballots inside from being distinguishable while not allowing officials near the ballot box to check what the voter chose.

5 Punched Ballot

5.1 Protocol

This third proposal stems from a different idea and seeks to reduce the user burden by making it simpler for the voter. In this case, the voter makes a single selection action to get their vote. In its simplest form, an already folded ballot (with barcode stickers pasted) is given to the voter who goes in a privacy booth. There, they can examine it—and unfold/refold it if wanted—before inserting it in a metal frame. They then come out of the booth where an official checks that the frame is correct, before punching a hole in the zone corresponding to the candidate of their choice. The ballots are then separated and cast by cutting them away as with the previous methods, while the voter keeps their receipt.

As the other two proposed candidates, the ballot has three main parts and the receipt (Fig. 3). By folding along the lines, the voter can align the three ballots in two different ways, such that two ballots are facing one way or the

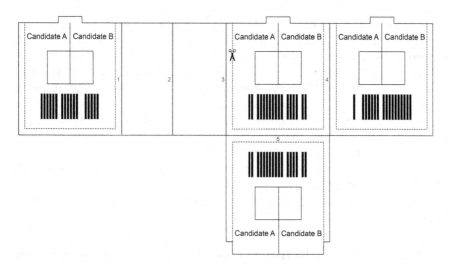

Fig. 3. The punched ballot before being folded. The voter starts by folding lines 4 and 5, in the order of their choice, leaving the central ballot on top. They can then fold either 2 behind the central ballot or 1 behind and 3 on top of the central ballot. They then end up with a stack of ballots with the central rectangles aligned, the receipt sticking up at the top, and empty white paper on either the left or the right.

other. This means that, when they punch a hole, they give two votes to one candidate or the other.

If the ballot does not come pre-folded, the voter starts by doing the folding: fold over line 5 and then line 4, each time leaving the central ballot on top. Two selection options are then possible. Either the left ballot will be facing the same direction as the central ballot, in which case punching A on this side results in two votes for A, or it will be facing the other direction, in which case, because of symmetry, punching A results in two votes for B. For the first option, the voter starts by folding line 3 over the central ballot, and then line 1 to leave the left ballot on top. For the second option, they simply need to fold line 2 below the central ballot.

Voting with a folded ballot means that there is an excess of paper on one side, which is to be hidden by the metal frame (to preserve the secrecy of on which side there is an excess of paper, which indicates which way the ballot is folded).

5.2   Constraint Satisfaction

Constraint 1) depends on the voter not having the opportunity to unfold the ballot and punch holes on the unfolded ballot inside the privacy booth. As long as this is true, a single hole is punched, which, because of the folding, creates at least one vote for A and one for B. If it is possible to unfold the ballot and fold it differently (not aligned with the folding lines for example), it becomes necessary to check alignment with the metal frame. This can easily be done through the protruding bits at the top of the ballot.

Constraint 2) is satisfied as, once the ballot is folded and set into the frame, there is no way to know how the third ballot hidden inside is oriented, and the visible holes are always one for A and the other for B.

Constraint 3) is satisfied because the voter can choose to fold one way or another, which, combined with their choice of vote, determines which hole is punched on the receipt.

Constraint 5) is satisfied as the receipt corresponds, by the necessity of the folding, to the central ballot.

Constraints 4) and 6) are satisfied in the same way as the previous two proposals.

6   Advantages and Drawbacks of the Solutions Proposed

The translucent design has multiple advantages:

- The voter can easily choose which ballot to audit, as with the masked ballot.
- It allows concurrent elections by having multiple voting rectangles aligned vertically (present on the receipt in reverse order).
- It is quite familiar to many voters—or at least more so than the masked ballot.
- The correctness of the ballot can be checked by a voting official or a machine that simply measures the intensity of light reflected through the translucent rectangle.
- It is easy to fold it correctly.

It also has a few drawbacks:

- Several steps have to be correctly followed to fold it correctly.
- It requires the officials to check for translucency.
- Both the previous drawbacks increase complexity, putting more pressure on polling stations and potentially increasing costs[10].
- Even when the voter isn't saddled with voting multiple times for a race, the folding confronts the voter with the complexity of Three-Ballot/VAV systems.
- If the rectangle is big, it might be possible to identify the vote if they are not entirely coloured.

The masked ballot has similar features, but removes most of the complexity by leaving two choices: vote A or B, and audit A or B, and pull the corresponding strings. The drawbacks are that it requires expensive and difficult to make ballots, and cannot be extended to concurrent races. Quality control in manufacturing the masked ballot could even become a source of confusion and error if the

---

[10] From the first author's experience in French polling stations, which already use paper ballots, the main choke-point generally lies with the identity verification process, so the additional time costs could be inconsequential.

adhesive or strings have any uncertainty. This approach is the most open to partially or completely unreadable ballots due to problems such as hanging chads, as it depends on adhesives to work and strings not to be snagged incorrectly.

The punched ballot is—for the voter and the officials—the simplest of the three systems, requiring only one step to set up the ballot and one step to vote. It removes the direct choice of who to audit by making it dependent on the orientation of the frame. If it comes pre-folded, all there is to do is orient it carefully and punch the correct hole. The frame can aid a blind voter as well. However, there are known problems with punched ballots [6,20], and this system also requires a bit more equipment.

7   Attacks on the Proposed Systems

The main attacks against Three-Ballot concern either multiple races on a single ballot [11,19] or small numbers of voters [1]. The first is avoided here by having a single race per ballot—as is already the case in a number of voting systems. The second is mostly a matter of choosing where to use this technology.

However, the proposals shown here make certain new attacks possible. For example, in certain cases, the receipt is easy to see for a voting official. However, even knowing which voter has what kind of receipt does not allow an adversary to arbitrarily change votes, as they still have no information on which ballot belongs to whom. It can only inform them when a very small proportion of voters kept a receipt for candidate A, making the attack shown in [1] a bit easier. This attack is especially relevant on the first two designs due to the green dot and the fact that the official is effectively checking whether the voter is auditing A or B. As they cannot simultaneously see the barcodes, it is a limited flaw.

Another attack can target all instances of Three-Ballot derivatives, as well as almost all low-tech paper-based systems. Suppose an adversary can insert some identifying mark in the paper that is not visible to the naked eye (on the fibre texture or with microdots for example). It then becomes possible to both track how someone voted, and find which are the non-tracked ballots that can be safely discarded. Of course, this requires not just the ability to make such marks, but also to check for them during the tallying or examination phases. A weaker version of this attack is also possible. It requires checking the cutting marks on the sides of the ballots to identify whether the ballot was on top or in the middle during the folding and cutting process. If this is reliably noticeable, there is an opportunity to identify tracked ballots. Rivest and Smith's article [39] already addressed this by stating that the ballot scans should be in low-definition. The exact position and orientation of the barcode stickers themselves could also facilitate this kind of attack, although the supervision makes it harder to implement this in practice.

In parallel to this, to check that the printing process happened correctly, there should be the option of taking whatever ballot sheet is given to the voter and putting it in a pile to be audited (either by voter choice or randomly assigned), before giving them another ballot sheet. This should happen after the barcode stickers are pasted onto the ballots. The discarded ballots can be checked publicly after the election to make sure that they weren't manipulated, and should of course be held securely in the meantime.

This brings us to a real vulnerability that is generally hard to address: it is possible to prove that one voted one way by filming the whole process, which is becoming increasingly relevant in the age of ballot selfies [21]. There are once again solutions, as long as the voter—or the person spying on them—can't film continuously out of the privacy booth[11]. The first is allowing users to get back to the ballot distribution table, spoiling their ballot, and start the whole process again (making what happened the first time in the privacy booth irrelevant). The second can be done with the third design, where only the folding and inserting of the ballot in the frame is done in the privacy booth. Once outside, the voter can easily flip the frame, and vote differently.

8   Discussion

Cryptographic solutions to improve security typically require additional actions by the voter, sometimes even at the cost of accuracy. They often require careful encoding and multiple confusing actions. Moreover, most of the systems based on Three-Ballot/VAV left behind the initial non-cryptographic design (which was their main advantage) to use more involved electronic devices. The systems proposed in this article sought to provide an alternative that requires no technology more complex than a hole puncher. The proposals above have different properties, but they all seek to make the inner workings of a Three-Ballot/VAV style ballot take the fewest number of steps to be visible and understandable. They give the voter a better model of the process, which increases both compliance and performance when dealing with secure systems [35].

Three main questions remain:

– How usable are the designs in practice?
– How does one accommodate races with many different candidates while keeping usable simple ballots?
– What is the simplest way to handle many concurrent races?

The designs shown here can potentially be adapted to one or two more candidates, but with more candidates they will eventually get to the geometric limits of paper folding. The simplest solution to handle many races is to make voters select for each race on separate ballots. There is also the possibility of having a long strip of ballots all attached to each other, but care has to be taken to prevent someone mixing and matching: parts of one ballot could be used to give a multiple-vote advantage on another race.

The exercise of designing such ballots is one way we propose to push opportunities for secure ballots forward, opening the possibility of further designs

---

[11] Some countries have tried to prevent such possibilities by banning cellphones in the polling stations and even—in the case of India [23]—in a small radius around them.

which explore other folding and geometrical patterns. The other is that the protocols shown here present actual ballot designs that could be deployed today to increase the actual security and integrity of secret ballots for voters, even in places that forbid electronic voting. Our three approaches use simple physical actions as verification prosthetics to guide a voter to complete an algorithmic improvement in security and verification of the candidate selection. The original authors of Three-Ballot and VAV protocols were sceptical about the protocols' practicability. This article then celebrates that protocols can be made that help voters see how they made selections, compare their selections to their goals, and verify that the ballots were counted correctly afterwards. The protocols shows that even the very difficult goal of having a voter create and verify complex selections can be tested in a transparent manner by a voter themself. Origami voting is a first demonstration of using simple paper-folding technology to allow a user to successfully fill out a complex multi-ballot, with no use of cryptography or external devices. We are hopeful that this work will encourage many new schemes in this direction.

Acknowledgements. We'd like to thank L. Gabasova, the members of the VoteVerif workshop and especially Peter Roenne for their comments. We are also extremely grateful to Josh Benaloh and Peter Roenne for their help with improving this article. This work was supported partly by the french PIA project "Lorraine Université d'Excellence", reference ANR-15-IDEX-04-LUE.

References

1. Appel, A.W.: How to defeat Rivest's Threeballot voting system (2006). http://citeseerx.ist.psu.edu/viewdoc/download?doi=10.1.1.116.5156&rep=rep1&type=pdf
2. Beaulieu, E.: From voter ID to party ID: how political parties affect perceptions of election fraud in the US. Electoral Stud. **35**, 24–32 (2014)
3. Blanchard, N.K., Selker, T.: Improving voting technology is hard: the trust-legitimacy-participation loop and related problems. In: 2018 Workshop on Socio-Technical Aspects in Security and Trust, STAST, San Juan, Puerto Rico (2018)
4. Borghesi, C., Raynal, J.C., Bouchaud, J.P.: Election turnout statistics in many countries: similarities, differences, and a diffusive field model for decision-making. PloS One **7**(5), 1–12 (2012)
5. Boucher, P.: What if blockchain technology revolutionised voting. European Parliament (2016, Unpublished manuscript)
6. Bullock III, C.S., Hood III, M.: One person - no vote; one vote; two votes: voting methods, ballot types, and undervote frequency in the 2000 presidential election. Soc. Sci. Q. **83**(4), 981–993 (2002)
7. Carreras, M., İrepoğlu, Y.: Trust in elections, vote buying, and turnout in Latin America. Electoral Stud. **32**(4), 609–619 (2013)
8. Chaum, D.: Secret-ballot receipts: true voter-verifiable elections. IEEE Secur. Priv. **2**(1), 38–47 (2004)
9. Chaum, D., et al.: Scantegrity II: end-to-end verifiability for optical scan election systems using invisible ink confirmation codes. EVT **8**, 1–13 (2008)

10. Chaum, D., Essex, A., Carback, R., Clark, J., Popoveniuc, S., Sherman, A., Vora, P.: Scantegrity: end-to-end voter-verifiable optical-scan voting. IEEE Secur. Priv. **6**(3), 40–46 (2008)

11. Cichoń, J., Kutyłowski, M., Węglorz, B.: Short ballot assumption and threeballot voting protocol. In: Geffert, V., Karhumäki, J., Bertoni, A., Preneel, B., Návrat, P., Bieliková, M. (eds.) SOFSEM 2008. LNCS, vol. 4910, pp. 585–598. Springer, Heidelberg (2008). https://doi.org/10.1007/978-3-540-77566-9_51

12. Donno, D., Roussias, N.: Does cheating pay? The effect of electoral misconduct on party systems. Comp. Polit. Stud. **45**, 575–605 (2012). https://doi.org/10.1177/0010414011427130

13. Enguehard, C., Graton, J.D.: Machines à voter et élections politiques en france: étude quantitative de la précision des bureaux de vote. Cahiers Droit Sci. Technol. **4**(4), 159–198 (2014)

14. Frye, T., Reuter, O.J., Szakonyi, D.: Hitting them with carrots: voter intimidation and vote buying in Russia. Br. J. Polit. Sci. **49**(3), 1–25 (2018)

15. Giannetti, D.: Secret voting in the Italian parliament. Secrecy and publicity in votes and debates, pp. 108–130 (2015)

16. González-Ocantos, E., Kiewiet de Jonge, C., Nickerson, D.W.: Legitimacy buying: the dynamics of clientelism in the face of legitimacy challenges. Comp. Polit. Stud. **48**(9), 1127–1158 (2015)

17. Hanifatunnisa, R., Rahardjo, B.: Blockchain based e-voting recording system design. In: 2017 11th International Conference on Telecommunication Systems Services and Applications (TSSA), pp. 1–6. IEEE (2017)

18. Hanmer, M.J., Park, W.H., Traugott, M.W., Niemi, R.G., Herrnson, P.S., Bederson, B.B., Conrad, F.C.: Losing fewer votes: the impact of changing voting systems on residual votes. Polit. Res. Q. **63**(1), 129–142 (2010)

19. Henry, K.J., Stinson, D.R., Sui, J.: The effectiveness of receipt-based attacks on threeballot. IEEE Trans. Inf. Forensics Secur. **4**(4), 699 (2009)

20. Herron, M.C., Sekhon, J.S.: Overvoting and representation: an examination of overvoted presidential ballots in Broward and Miami-Dade counties. Electoral Stud. **22**(1), 21–47 (2003)

21. Horwitz, D.A.: A picture's worth a thousand words: why ballot selfies are protected by the first amendment. SMU Sci. Tech. Law Rev. **18**, 247 (2015)

22. Huszti, A.: A secure electronic voting scheme. Period. Polytech. Electr. Eng. **51**(3–4), 141–146 (2008)

23. Indian Election Commission: Maintenance of law and order and prevention of electioneering within the prohibited area around polling stations - instructions regarding use of cellular phones (1998). https://ceo.gujarat.gov.in/Pdf/23Feb2018013934PM.pdf

24. Jones, D.W., Hall, M.: Technologists as political reformers: lessons from the early history of voting machines. In: Society for the History of Technology Annual Meeting, Las Vegas, vol. 13 (2006)

25. Jones, H., Juang, J., Belote, G.: ThreeBallot in the field (2006)

26. Ju, C.: "you can't hack a piece of paper": Jake Braun talks us election security. Chicago Policy Review (Online) (2018). http://chicagopolicyreview.org/2018/04/01/you-cant-hack-a-piece-of-paper-jake-braun-talks-u-s-election-security/

27. Juang, W.S., Lei, C.L.: A secure and practical electronic voting scheme for real world environments. IEICE Trans. Fundam. Electron. Commun. Comput. Sci. **80**, 64–71 (1997)

28. Kutyłowski, M., Zagórski, F.: Scratch, click & vote: E2E voting over the Internet. In: Chaum, D., Jakobsson, M., Rivest, R.L., Ryan, P.Y.A., Benaloh, J., Kutyłowski, M., Adida, B. (eds.) Towards Trustworthy Elections. LNCS, vol. 6000, pp. 343–356. Springer, Heidelberg (2010). https://doi.org/10.1007/978-3-642-12980-3_21

29. Larreguy, H., Marshall, J., Querubin, P.: What is the effect of turnout buying? Theory and evidence from Mexico. Harvard University, Cambridge (2014, Unpublished manuscript)

30. Levitt, J.: The truth about voter fraud (2007). https://papers.ssrn.com/sol3/papers.cfm?abstract_id=1647224

31. Maike, V.: The portrayal of Russia in US media in the aftermath of the 2016 election hacking scandal. Master's thesis (2018)

32. McKenna, M.: Building "a closet of prayer" in the new world: the story of the "Australian ballot" (2001)

33. Miller, W.R.: Harrison county methods: election fraud in late nineteenth-century Texas. Locus **7**, 111–128 (1995). http://archive.today/2019.02.18-013902/courses.missouristate.edu/bobmiller/populism/texts/harrison_county_methods.htm

34. Moura, T., Gomes, A.: Blockchain voting and its effects on election transparency and voter confidence. In: Proceedings of the 18th Annual International Conference on Digital Government Research, DG.O 2017, pp. 574–575. ACM, New York (2017). https://doi.org/10.1145/3085228.3085263

35. Mwagwabi, F., McGill, T., Dixon, M.: Improving compliance with password guidelines: how user perceptions of passwords and security threats affect compliance with guidelines. In: 2014 47th Hawaii International Conference on System Sciences (HICSS), pp. 3188–3197, January 2014. https://doi.org/10.1109/HICSS.2014.396

36. Nichter, S.: Vote buying or turnout buying? Machine politics and the secret ballot. Am. Polit. Sci. Rev. **102**(1), 19–31 (2008)

37. Orman, H.: Secure voting: a call to arms. IEEE Internet Comput. **21**(5), 67–71 (2017)

38. Reynolds, A., Steenbergen, M.: How the world votes: the political consequences of ballot design, innovation and manipulation. Electoral Stud. **25**(3), 570–598 (2006). https://doi.org/10.1016/j.electstud.2005.06.009. http://www.sciencedirect.com/science/article/pii/S0261379405000612

39. Rivest, R.L., Smith, W.D.: Three voting protocols: ThreeBallot, VAV, and twin. In: Proceedings of the USENIX Workshop on Accurate Electronic Voting Technology, EVT 2007, p. 16. USENIX Association, Berkeley (2007). http://dl.acm.org/citation.cfm?id=1323111.1323127

40. Santin, A.O., Costa, R.G., Maziero, C.A.: A three-ballot-based secure electronic voting system. IEEE Secur. Priv. **6**(3), 14–21 (2008)

41. Selker, T., Cohen, S.: An active approach to voting verification. Technical report, Caltech/MIT Voting Technology Project (2005)

42. Sled, S.M.: Vertical proximity effects in the California recall election. Technical report, Caltech/MIT Voting Technology Project (2003)

43. Springall, D., Finkenauer, T., Durumeric, Z., Kitcat, J., Hursti, H., MacAlpine, M., Halderman, A.J.: Security analysis of the Estonian internet voting system. In: Proceedings of the 2014 ACM SIGSAC Conference on Computer and Communications Security, pp. 703–715. ACM (2014)

44. Stewart, G., Lacey, D.: Death by a thousand facts: criticising the technocratic approach to information security awareness. Inf. Manag. Comput. Secur. **20**(1), 29–38 (2012). https://doi.org/10.1108/09685221211219182

45. Strauss, C.E.: A critical review of the triple ballot (3ballot) scheme, part 1 (2006). https://www.cs.princeton.edu/~appel/voting/Strauss-TroubleWithTriples.pdf

46. Strauss, C.E.: A critical review of the triple ballot voting system, part 2: cracking the triple ballot encryption (2006). https://www.cs.princeton.edu/~appel/voting/Strauss-ThreeBallotCritique2v1.5.pdf
47. Uzunay, Y., Bicakci, K.: Trusted3Ballot: improving security and usability of three ballot voting system using trusted computing. In: 2014 5th International Conference on Intelligent Systems, Modelling and Simulation (ISMS), pp. 534–539. IEEE (2014)
48. Vassil, K., Solvak, M., Vinkel, P., Trechsel, A.H., Alvarez, M.R.: The diffusion of internet voting. Usage patterns of internet voting in Estonia between 2005 and 2015. Gov. Inf. Q. **33**(3), 453–459 (2016)
49. Vinkel, P.: Remote Electronic Voting in Estonia: Legality, Impact and Confidence. TUT Press, Tallinn (2015)
50. Wang, B., Sun, J., He, Y., Pang, D., Lu, N.: Large-scale election based on blockchain. In: International Conference on Identification, Information and Knowledge in the Internet of Things, vol. 129, pp. 234–237 (2018). https://doi.org/10.1016/j.procs.2018.03.063. http://www.sciencedirect.com/science/article/pii/S1877050918302874

Towards Improving the Efficacy of Code-Based Verification in Internet Voting

Oksana Kulyk[1,2]([⊠]), Melanie Volkamer[2], Monika Müller[2], and Karen Renaud[3,4]

[1] IT University of Copenhagen, Copenhagen, Denmark
okku@itu.dk
[2] Karlsruhe Institute of Technology, Karlsruhe, Germany
{oksana.kulyk,melanie.volkamer,monika.muller}@kit.edu
[3] Abertay University, Dundee, Scotland
k.renaud@abertay.ac.uk
[4] Rhodes University, Grahamstown, South Africa

Abstract. End-to-end verifiable Internet voting enables a high level of election integrity. Cast-as-intended verification, in particular, allows voters to verify that their vote has been correctly cast, even in the presence of malicious voting devices. One cast-as-intended verification approach is code-based verification, used since 2015 in legally-binding Swiss elections. We evaluated the Swiss paper-based polling sheet and voting interface, focusing on how well it supported voters in verifying their votes. We uncovered several potential issues related to manipulation detection. We improved the paper-based polling sheet and voting interface accordingly. Then, we carried out a between-subjects lab study with 128 participants to compare the original and improved sheet and interface wrt. usability and its effectiveness in supporting manipulation detection. Our improvements significantly enhanced detection. Our study delivered insights into participants' somewhat ineffectual reactions to detected anomalies, i.e. starting over again and trying to cast the same vote again, or calling the telephone number provided by the interface. This problem is likely to manifest in any verifiable voting system and thus needs to be addressed as future work.

Keywords: e-voting · Verifiability · Usability

1 Introduction

As the world's population increases, traditional elections become more expensive and challenging [13]. The diffusion of the Internet has changed the way we vote [24]. While some of these changes have positively impacted our lives, there are negative side effects too due to the activities of malicious actors, such as dissidents seeking to disrupt Internet-enabled elections [10,12]. Attackers could

© Springer Nature Switzerland AG 2020
M. Bernhard et al. (Eds.): FC 2020 Workshops, LNCS 12063, pp. 291–309, 2020.
https://doi.org/10.1007/978-3-030-54455-3_21

replace or discard votes by manipulating vote casting devices (laptop or smart-phone) or the vote-casting software. This causes problems *first*, for the election authorities, who need to ensure the integrity of the election and *second*, for the voters themselves, who need to have confidence in the election outcome.

One way of reassuring both stakeholders, and of maximising the probability that malicious activities will be revealed, is to build verifiability into the voting system allowing voters to verify that their vote has indeed been cast as they intended. Voters can all help to reveal anomalies resulting from malicious activities.

However, for verifiability to deliver this assurance, it relies on two key assumptions: (1) that voters will indeed perform all the necessary verification steps, and (2) that they will do so correctly. These assumptions have been challenged by empirical studies into verifiable Internet voting systems [1,14,20,27]. The complexity and unfamiliarity of verification process can prevent voters from performing the necessary steps correctly, or at all.

If voters do not verify correctly, this renders the integration of verifiability into Internet voting systems fruitless, particularly as ever more sophisticated attacks emerge. If malicious actors can control what voters see, by manipulating the vote-casting device and/or vote-casting software, they can subvert the process. They could, for example, assure the voter that their vote has been cast successfully although, in reality, additional steps are mandated to finalise the process. Malicious attacks have been discussed in the literature [11,17], but we are not aware of any empirical evaluation of the efficacy of verification provision being carried out. Nor have researchers systematically addressed these issues. Both gaps are narrowed by our research.

The widely-used Swiss verifiable Internet voting system utilises code-based verification (Sect. 2) so we commenced by investigating its usability and the ease of cast-as-intended verification. We then developed and improved the verification mechanism (Sect. 3) and evaluated both the original and improved mechanisms in a between-subjects lab study with 128 participants (Sect. 4). We found that the improvements preserved usability and participants detected significantly more manipulations (Sect. 5). We discuss our findings in Sect. 6, including lessons learned related to those aspects influencing 'correct' verification. We conclude in Sect. 7.

2   Background

We describe the idea and the process of the code-based verification, including its implementation in the Swiss system, and provide further background by describing related work on the usability of cast-as-intended verification.

2.1   Code-Based Verification

Code-based verification systems issue voters with a unique *polling sheet*, delivered via snail mail. This provides the voting system's website address, instructions, and one or more codes to facilitate verification. A number of variants of code-based verification approaches exist, including the one used in Swiss elections [25]. Their code sheets provide three types of codes: (1) verification,[1] (2) confirmation *and* (3) finalisation. The system responds to a cast vote by displaying a 'verification code'. The voter compares this to the code that appears on their personalized code sheet. If they match, the voter enters the confirmation code (also provided on the sheet). Otherwise, they ought to report the anomaly to the election authorities. A finalisation code is subsequently displayed to reassure the voter that the voting system has indeed cast their vote as intended, and that the voter has confirmed that the code matching their choice was correctly displayed.

Note that the code-based verification is not sufficient to ensure the election integrity on its own; namely, one still has to ensure that the election authorities are trustworthy and perform the tallying procedure correctly. Further mechanisms, such as tallied-as-stored verifiability methods, should be employed for this purpose.

2.2 Manipulations

Achieving verifiability relies on voters assiduously and attentively going through all the verification steps. An adversary wanting to replace a vote for candidate 'A' with a vote for candidate 'B' might manipulate the voting interface and subvert the verification protocol (see [17]) via various strategies: (1) Replace the verification code with another code, or (2) Remove the verification code entirely, or Both strategies can be applied by keeping the rest of the interface as is or by (3) adding messages such as: *"thank you for your vote - you are done"* or *"the verification code for your candidate is correct"* to allay suspicions. Aside from these two manipulations, the adversary can take other steps in ensuring that the verification procedure is not followed correctly, such as withholding the confirmation code. This attack type, however, leaves a trace in the voting system, when the vote is recorded as "attempted" *but not confirmed.* A large number of these might raise alarms during auditing. Furthermore, even if the attack succeeds, the adversary only blocks the vote, but is unable to replace it. Note, however, that in order to account for all the attacks exploiting this vulnerability, a systematic investigation involving attack trees is needed. Even then, achieving comprehensiveness remains an open challenge when it comes to exploiting the human factor.

2.3 Related Work

Research into *verification-related mental models* [21,23] revealed a number of factors that could prevent voters from verifying, such as a lack of knowledge, required effort and misconceptions. Other studies focused on *usability* evaluating user experiences and voter satisfaction [9,16,18,19,22,28]. Some studies

---

[1] This type of code is also commonly referred to as a check or return code in the literature.

reported high satisfaction, while others uncovered usability issues. A study into the usability of the Norwegian Internet voting system, which relies on code-based verification, mentions a lack of understandability related to the range of different codes. None of these studies measured verification effectiveness i.e. whether their participants were able to verify their votes. This was indeed evaluated for verifiable voting systems, such as for *Prêt à Voter* and Scantegrity II in [1,2], for BingoVote in [5], for StarVote in [3], for EasyVote in [7,8], for the ballot-marking devices used in the US elections in some of the states [6] and for Helios Internet voting system in [1,14,20,27]. Some reported high rates of verification effectiveness [3,7], others reported issues [1,1,2,5,20] including verification misconceptions, which resulted in participants being unable to verify their votes successfully. Some studies evaluated the *effectiveness of code-based verification* by deliberately introducing manipulations during the process. Kulyk *et al.* [15] evaluated the effectiveness of a code-based approach and manipulated the verification code, replacing it with an incorrect code. While all participants detected the manipulation, the removal of the verification code was not tested. The study focused exclusively on verification effectiveness, without evaluating other usability aspects, such as satisfaction or efficiency. The study by Gjøsteen and Lund [11] evaluated the Norwegian Internet voting system, which provided verifiability by sending the verification codes to the voters via SMS after they had submitted their vote. In the attacks simulated in the study, no such code was sent, but only 6 of 30 participants detected this. Similar to [15], the voting interface was unaffected by the manipulations. No specific evaluation has been carried out to detect whether voters detect user interface manipulations while verifying their cast votes.

3   Improving the Swiss Voting System

In this section, we describe our initial analysis of the Swiss voting system as well as our modifications calculated to improve the usability of their cast-as-intended verification, to make it more likely that voters will detect manipulations to their device's voting interface.

3.1   Issues with the Original System's Cast-as-Intended Verification

We organized a brainstorming session between the authors and also arranged feedback sessions with other participants including a lay person, an expert in human-computer interaction, an expert in general security, and an expert in electronic voting security. Participants received background information and were instructed to think aloud while casting a vote for a specific candidate. Afterwards they were given the election information sheet, including the polling sheet providing the codes (Fig. 1). They used our laptop to interact with the voting system. Notes were taken and the session ended by eliciting responses about what would prevent them from verifying their votes.

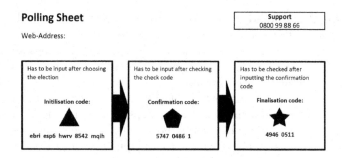

Fig. 1. The version of the polling sheet

The sessions revealed a number of issues. Here, we focus on those relevant to cast-as-intended verification steps (note: the remaining general usability issues were addressed in producing our improved version).

Lack of a Step-by-Step Process. The process of casting and verifying a vote consists of a number of steps that are new to the voters, given their familiarity with traditional paper-based voting. The polling sheet makes it look as if there are three steps (three boxes linked by arrows): entering the initialisation code, entering the confirmation code, checking for the finalisation code. This is a serious issue because the vital step of comparing the displayed code with the matching vote choice code could easily be omitted. The point at which the vote is finally stored, and the process concluded, is unclear. Voters might assume that once the confirmation code has been entered, their vote has been cast. They might not notice that the finalisation code is incorrect or missing. The voter's interaction with the system requires them to conduct more steps than those communicated on the original polling sheet and the steps do not match. This makes it even less likely that the voter will notice manipulations. It is also not clear what the voter ought to do if codes do not match. Instructions provided by the interface cannot be trusted because these can be removed. Details about who to contact for voter support is not prominent on the polling sheet (and it is not clear that support should be contacted if the voter detects a code mismatch).

Unclear Explanations. The presentation of so many codes, without explanation, is confusing. Voters could easily be left wondering why they are needed and why they ought to be verified. Moreover, no instructions are provided to tell voters what to do if the codes fail to appear on the interface. The same term is used for different concepts. For example, the initialisation code is actually an authentication code, while the others are codes used for verification. Finally, voters are not told which codes ought to be entered into the system, and which ought to be compared to codes on the sheet (but not provided to the system).

Finalisation Page Header. While the voters need to compare the displayed finalisation code with their sheet's code in order to make sure that their vote has indeed been cast, the final finalisation code display page includes a "thank you for your vote" message, which might mean that voters assume they are done, and unwittingly omit the final verification step.

These issues point to the lack of clarity. A voter who is unfamiliar with the process might miss crucial verification steps, e.g. forgetting to compare the verification codes. This requirement is not explicitly mentioned on the sheet rendering the voting system vulnerable to manipulations described in Sect. 2.2.

3.2 Proposed Improvements

Based on the aforementioned feedback, we proposed improvements to the sheet and the voting interface. We focused primarily on improving the voting materials, since, as discussed in Sect. 2, an adversary who controls the voting environment is likely also to be capable of modifying the website interface. The improvements were refined over several feedback sessions:

Polling Sheet. The layout of the text on the provided sheet was changed in order to provide a more structured overview of the steps the voter has to perform to cast and verify her vote. In the first place, we included a sequence diagram with the individual steps clearly marked, including alternative actions to be taken if verification reveals potentially malicious activities. We also rewrote the explanation texts to improve understandability, and referred to the initialisation code as a "password" in order the better to distinguish it from the codes used during the verification process. The resulting polling card is provided in Fig. 2.

Voting Interface. We rewrote the explanatory texts to improve clarity and to provide the voters with more explicit guidelines regarding the vote casting and the verification processes. An example of the resulting interface is provided in Fig. 3.

4 Evaluation Methodology

We describe the methodology we followed in evaluating our proposed improvements and their comparison with the original Swiss system (Fig. 4).[2]

4.1 Manipulations

We evaluate the voter's ability to detect two possible manipulations: *replacing* the verification code, or *removing* it from the output screen. We made the following modifications to the voting website interface:

---

[2] For screenshots of the voting website and polling sheets for both of the evaluated systems, see https://secuso.org/code-based-supplemental-material.

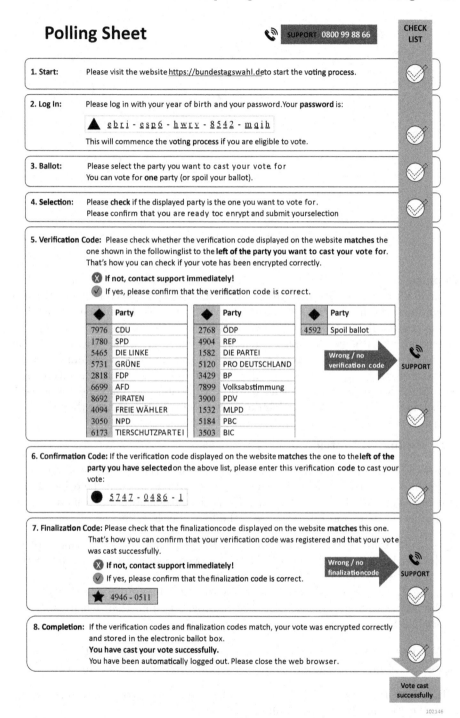

Fig. 2. The improved version of the polling sheet (translated from German). Both the website and the phone number are fictitious.

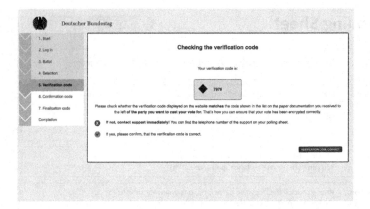

Fig. 3. The improved version of the verification web page.

Replace. We removed all the instructions in the interface that explained what to do if the verification code did not match the one on the code sheet. We also modified the instructions to verify the verification code by mentioning that the code could be found anywhere on the code sheet. We added a "Support" button, which gave the voter a number to call if they had any issues. The number was different from the one on the polling sheet, assuming that an attacker would replace it to prevent voters from reporting it to the authorities.

Remove. We replaced the output of the verification code and the verification instruction with a message congratulating the voter on casting their vote.

4.2 Evaluated Metrics and Hypotheses

The main focus of our study is to evaluate how well the participants were able to detect both *replace* and *remove* type manipulations in both the original and improved systems. Because the aim of our improvements was to increase the manipulation detection rate, we tested the following hypotheses:

$H_{replace}$ Participant voters are more likely to detect manipulations that replace the verification code when using the improved system than when using the original Swiss system (the *replace*-Manipulation).

H_{remove} Participant voters are more likely to detect manipulations that remove the verification code when using the improved system than when using the original Swiss system (the *remove*-Manipulation).

We assessed the usability of both systems under normal conditions, that is, in absence of manipulations. We therefore evaluate the following metrics:

Efficiency. How long did participants take to cast their votes and to complete verification in absence of manipulations.

Effectiveness. How many participants are able to cast their votes in absence of manipulations.

Satisfaction. Participants' satisfaction, using the SUS measurement tool (calculated on a scale from 0 to 100).

Because our improvements focused on enhancing manipulation detection, we did not expect any differences in general usability. As such, while we aimed to make the voting process clear by adding instructions, the presence of these instructions, while improving understandability, could decrease efficiency if they take longer to read. We nonetheless measure these criteria and report on descriptive statistics, in order to identify opportunities for further refinements. We furthermore conducted a qualitative evaluation of the usability of both systems, by analysing the feedback from the participants who used the unmanipulated systems.

4.3   Study Type

We conducted a between-subjects lab study, with participants randomly assigned to one of the following six groups:

Original-No-Manipulation. The group interacting with the original system interfaces, with no manipulation occurring,

Original-Replace. The group interacting with the original system interfaces and subjected to a manipulation that *replaces* the verification code,

Original-Remove. The group interacting with the original system interfaces and subjected to a manipulation that *removes* the verification code,

Improved-No-Manipulation. The group interacting with the improved system interfaces, with no manipulation occurring,

Improved-Replace. The group interacting with the improved system interfaces and subjected to a manipulation that *replaces* the verification code,

Improved-Remove. The group interacting with the improved system interfaces and subjected to a manipulation that *removes* the verification code,

The purpose of using six groups is to support evaluation of the usability of both the original system and the improved variant under two conditions: normal voting, where no manipulation occurs, and an attempted attack with the adversary either replacing or removing the verification code. The two groups without manipulation *Original-No-Manipulation* and *Improved-No-Manipulation* are used to study the system under normal conditions. We evaluate user satisfaction and effectiveness in terms of being able to cast and verify votes in the absence of manipulations. The four groups with manipulations (*Original-Remove, Original-Replace, Improved-Remove* and *Improved-Replace*) allow us to evaluate the effectiveness of the system under the attempted attack scenario, namely, the ability of participants to detect different kinds of manipulations with either the original system (hypothesis $H_{replace}$) or the improved system (hypothesis H_{remove}).

4.4   Study Procedure

The participants in each group are told that the evaluation goal was to study the usability of an Internet voting system, to be used in forthcoming German Parliament elections. Before the study, the participants were asked to read and sign a consent form, detailing the study procedure (not mentioning the manipulations), explaining that data collected during the study was anonymised and would be analysed by the research group which the paper authors are a part of. They were told that they could abort the study at any time, in which case all the data collected so far would be deleted. The participants were told about the reimbursement of 10 Euros that they could claim for participating.

After signing the consent form, the participants were presented with a role card telling them to assume a role of Mr. or Ms. Müller, born in 1970, opting to cast their election vote over the Internet. The role card informed them that they would receive the election materials to be used to cast a vote for the SPD[3] party.[4] The participants were provided with a mock-up welcome letter from the election authorities with general information about the election and instructions to look for the information necessary for using the Internet voting system (on a polling card, also handed out to them at the beginning of the study).

As soon as the participants indicated that they were finished reading the instructions, they were asked to use the voting system installed on the lab computer. The system consists of the mock-ups of the interfaces for the corresponding system (that is, either the original or the improved interfaces).[5] The mock-ups simulate the German Parliament election (to be conducted in 2021) with the list of candidates from the 2017 election. The participants were instructed to cast a vote for a party outlined on their role card. For the participants in *Original-No-Manipulation, Improved-No-Manipulation* groups, no manipulation took place, so that voters were able successfully to complete the process of casting, verifying and confirming their votes. The time they took to complete casting the vote was noted by the examiner. The participants in the remaining groups were subjected to manipulation depending on their group – that is, the verification code was either removed or replaced, depending on experimental condition.

If a participant noticed the manipulation, they were asked how they would behave if this occurred in an actual election. If the participant answered that they would call the support number, they were asked whether they would use the number on the website, or the number given on the polling sheet. Afterwards, they were debriefed and told about the real purpose of the study. All participants were asked to fill in questionnaires assessing their satisfaction with the system, as well as being asked questions about whether they had issues with casting their votes and what they found positive or negative regarding the voting website and the polling sheet , participants who did not notice manipulations, as well as the participants who were not subjected to manipulations, were debriefed about the real purpose of the study.

---

[3] Germany's Social Democratic Party.

[4] Participants were asked to cast a vote for a specific party to preserve ballot secrecy.

[5] Cast votes were neither stored nor processed.

4.5   Recruitment and Ethics

The participants were recruited using snowball sampling. They were told that the study would take around 25 min and were offered a reimbursement of 10 Euros, which is above the minimum hourly German wage (around 9 Euro). The authors' institutional ethical and data protection guidelines were followed.

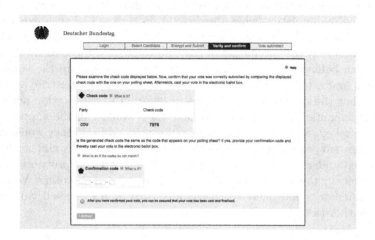

Fig. 4. The version of the verification web page, modeled after the original Swiss system and adjusted to resemble the German election scenario (translated from German).

5   Evaluation Results

144 participants took part. 16 were removed prior to the analysis due to deviations in the study procedure, such as the examiner handing out the materials for the wrong group by mistake. Of the remaining 128 participants, aged 20–81, with the mean age of 34.34 and standard deviation of 15.54. 66 were female and 62 male.

5.1   Manipulation Detection

In order to evaluate the hypotheses provided in Sect. 4.2, we consider the number of participants who detected a manipulation presented to them during the study (that is, either a replaced or an omitted verification code). We performed a comparison between the groups *Original-Replace* and *Improved-Replace*, as well as between the groups *Original-Remove* and *Improved-Remove*. An overview of the numbers of participants in each group who detected the corresponding manipulation is provided in Table 1. The results for both manipulations are analysed using a one-sided Fisher's exact test.

Replacing the Verification Code. While the majority of the participants in the *Original-Replace* group detected the manipulation, one fourth failed to do so. On the other hand, all participants in the *Improved-Replace* group detected the verification code replacement. $H_{replace}$ is therefore confirmed ($p = 0.0187$, odds ratio 95% CI: $[0, 0.662]$).

Reaction to Detected Misaligments. We asked all of the participants who detected the manipulation what they would do if they had such experience in real-world election. Some of the participants have noted that they are likely to login again and try one more time to cast the vote. An attacker can take advantage of such behaviour, for example, by trying to manipulate the vote during the voter's first attempt and leaving the vote intact if the voter tries again, thus ensuring that the manipulation remains unreported to the election authorities. Some participants further mentioned that they would call the support. However, when asked, which number they would use, several said they would call the number they saw on the website. As mentioned in Sect. 4, this number had also been altered under the assumption that an adversary would probably display a fake number on the voting interface to reassure concerned voters. Voters who call this number would likely reach the adversary him or herself, and not the election authorities.

Table 1. Number of participants detecting and not detecting the manipulation of replacing or removing the verification code

	Detected	Undetected		Detected	Undetected
Original-replace	16 (76.2%)	5 (23.8%)	Original-remove	2 (9.1%)	18 (90.9%)
Improved-replace	23 (100%)	0	Improved-remove	9 (43.48%)	12 (56.52 %)

Removing the Verification Code. The manipulation that involves removing the verification code was particularly hard for participants to detect. As such, only two of 20 participants managed to do so in the group using the original system. The results were better in the group using the improved system. Even so, more than half of these participants (12 out of 21) did not detect manipulation either. H_{remove} is therefore confirmed ($p = 0.02$, odds ratio 95% CI: $[0, 0.752]$). As there was no "Support" Button on this particular screen, as opposed to the *Replace*-Manipulation, we did not ask participants who they would call.

5.2   General Usability

As described in Sect. 4.2, we also consider general usability of the both systems in the absence of manipulations.

Effectiveness. We looked whether the participants that were not subjected the manipulation were able to cast their votes successfully. Of the 47 participants in groups *Original-No-Manipulation* and *Improved-No-Manipulation*, only one was not able to complete the vote casting process. The participant was interacting with the original system and thought that the displayed verification code was incorrect, resulting in a false positive result during verification.

Satisfaction. We compared the SUS scores of the *Original-No-Manipulation* and *Improved-No-Manipulation* groups (i.e those who experienced the system without being disrupted by a manipulation). We used only the scores from those who completed the vote casting process correctly. Both systems were awarded a high score (an average of 79.9 from 22 participants for the original system and an average of 80.9 from 20 participants for the improved), which is classified as "good" according to the scale proposed by Bangor *et al.* [4].

Efficiency. We measured the time it took participants from commencing the voting process to finalising their cast vote in absence of manipulation (i.e. groups *Original-No-Manipulation* and *Improved-No-Manipulation*). On average, the participants required 175.86 s using the original system and 180.35 s using the improved system.

5.3   Qualitative Feedback

In order to identify further potential improvements of the system, we considered the answers from the participants not subjected to manipulation to the following questions:

- Did you experience any issues with casting your vote? Which ones?
- What did you find positive about the polling sheet?
- What did you find positive about the voting website?
- What did you find negative about the polling sheet?
- What did you find negative about the voting website?

We summarised the responses to these questions for each one of the two systems below, providing the number of participants who mentioned each answer while omitting these numbers if an answer was only mentioned by either one or two participants.

Original System. The majority of the participants using the original system (18 out of 24) did not name any issues they had with casting their votes. The issues named by the rest of participants were related to the amount of codes, their complexity and difficulties in entering them without making errors, inability to distinguish between similar-looking characters in the codes (namely, i and l) and the font size being too small.

When asked about what they considered positive about the polling sheet, the participants mentioned the clarity of the instructions (11) and the comprehensibility of the polling sheet (7). Others commented on feeling secure due to assurance via different codes, the symbols for the codes being helpful, the sheet being compact, the presence of an emergency number and the choice of the headers. Five participants did not comment.

With respect to positive feedback on the voting website, the participants mostly commented on the system being fast (12) and easy to use (11). Further comments were related to the convenience of being able to cast their vote over the Internet (5), feeling secure in casting the vote, clarity of the instructions and the possibility of decreasing paper waste by using Internet voting. One participant did not give any positive feedback.

When asked about what the participants did not like about the polling sheet, the most common issues were the lack of information about the codes on the sheet, making the codes confusing without seeing the website (named by 7 of 24 participants) and the font being too small (named by 4 participants). Other issues were the complexity of the codes, too much information packed on the sheet, wanting more information about the technical aspects of the system, wanting to see a second polling sheet that outlines an example of how to cast a vote, not liking the use of the word "Support", finding the identification step illogical, general criticisms of the instructions and finding the term "verification code" confusing. Seven of 24 participants did not provide any negative feedback.

When asked for negative feedback about the voting website, five of 24 participants had doubts about the security of the system, such as a lack of control of whether the polling sheet is actually used by an authorised voter, the influence of third parties on the election outcome, or a general feeling of insecurity. Other issues were the design of the website looking untrustworthy, difficulties in navigating the help page, insufficient feedback when the vote was cast successfully, small font, lack of instructions regarding how many parties one is allowed to choose, lack of information about the parties on the ballot, finding the identification step illogical and feeling that one would miss the traditional aspects of voting, such as walking to the polling booth. Nine participants did not provide any negative feedback.

Improved System. Most of the participants using the improved system (20 out of 22) did not experience any issues during vote casting. The rest mentioned the overall inconvenience of the process, and the irritation with the system deleting entries after the Enter button was pressed.

When asked about positive feedback on the voting sheet, 11 of 22 participants commented on the enhanced comprehensibility and 5 mentioned the clear structure of the sheet. Three liked the check list on the right of the polling sheet, and the rest liked the use of color and the length of the polling sheet. Three did not give any positive feedback.

Similar to the original system, the most commonly named positive aspects of the voting website were the ability to cast a vote online (11 of 22 participants), the system being fast (5) and easy to use (10). Other positive mentions were the instructions for the system, overall clarity of the interface and the possibility of reducing paper waste.

Most of the participants did not mention any negative issues with the polling sheet (14 of 22). The remaining participants mentioned issues such as the complexity of writing down the codes, the large number of steps and the overall complexity of the procedure, design choices such as colors used in the table, the length of the instructions and the need to read them to avoid errors, and feeling that the instructions were redundant.

Among the negative issues with the voting website, the participants mentioned the complexity of the system, the inconvenience of having to check the codes, the number of steps required to traverse and the number of codes to enter, wanting a better user interface design (e.g. finding the party list too long), wanting a better understanding of the security that the system provides, general concerns with Internet voting and missing the social aspects of polling-station voting.

6 Discussion

Our study has shown that participants struggle to detect manipulations if an adversary manages to manipulate the voting interface, especially when the verification code was removed. Even after improvements, fewer than half of the participants detected this particular manipulation; only two detecting it using the original system. The detection rates are even worse than those reported by Gjøsteen and Lund [11], where a fifth of the participants detected a missing verification code that was supposed to be received via SMS. This is possibly because the manipulation we tested involved modifying interfaces, which fooled participants into believing that all was well. This demonstrates that even verifiable voting systems remain at high risk of undetected vote manipulations. It follows that usability (both of the systems in our study received high SUS scores, and many participants commented on their ease of use) is not the only factor that has to be considered in designing this kind of systems, confirming previous findings [17].

Future research into the design of these systems is needed in order to improve the manipulation detection rate and to address the issues related to participants' reaction to detected misalignments. Such research could focus on finding new ways to present the information about the proper voting procedure to the participants, such as an information flyer with examples of correct and incorrect voting procedures, or an interactive app.

Some users were unable to detect the manipulation to the verification code in the original system. This observation is different from the results of the study in [15], where all the participants were able to detect the manipulation using a code-based verification similar to the Swiss system. One possible explanation might be that the participants in the previous study were explicitly instructed to verify their vote, whereas in our study the focus was on casting a vote. A further explanation might be the intervening changes to the design of the Swiss polling sheet, so that the two studies tested different systems (actually in particular different polling sheets).

Although both the original and improved systems received high SUS scores, the complexity of the procedure and the codes was an issue, again confirming the findings from [15]. Voters might well be willing to accept complex systems and even trust them more if they are told that the complexity is necessary for security (see [16,26]). It is therefore worth investigating, whether including additional information about how the codes bolster security would be helpful to voters, and to find the best way of providing this information without overwhelming them. This might also help to address the issues we detected with participants reaction to detected misaligments.

Our study's sample consisted mostly of younger participants. This is not representative of the voting population, but if younger people, who are more comfortable with technology, fail to detect manipulations, the issue might be even more critical for older voters. We also note that Internet voting is usually implemented as an optional voting channel, available *in addition to* traditional paper-based voting, so that voters who are not confident in their ability to use technology can still cast their votes at polling stations. Nonetheless, investigating the human factors of Internet voting with an older sample remains an important direction for future work.

The study has the common limitations of studies that measure the usability of verification, in terms of differences between the lab and the real-life behaviour. As such, real-world verification might deliver different performances, perhaps because participants are more likely to read and follow the instructions when they know that they are being observed. On the other hand, they might be more incentivised to verify their vote in a real election, and therefore to pay more attention to the verification procedure and output codes, as the integrity of their votes is more important than in the lab setting. Still, conducting a study that involves introducing vote manipulations in a real-world election would pose critical ethical and legal issues, potentially undermining the participants' trust in the election authorities. A possible middle ground can be found, for example, by conducting remote studies where the participants are not directly observed during vote casting. Another way would be to conduct mock elections without telling the participants about the real purpose of the study before they cast their votes. However, one needs to choose a topic that participants will care about (otherwise they would not be incentivised to verify), yet, manipulation of votes on such a topic will most likely trigger an emotional response that will endure even after the debriefing. Given these considerations, the obstacles to in-the-wild testing seem almost insurmountable.

Finally, we focused on two kinds of attacks that, if successful, could jeopardize election integrity by allowing an adversary to replace cast votes with votes for a candidate of their choosing or merely reducing the number of votes that go to a candidate they do not approve of. Our study clearly does not attempt to improve verification in the face of all possible manipulation tactics, especially if one takes social engineering attacks into consideration. Investigating the scope and potential success of other attacks is an important and promising direction for future work.

7 Conclusion

Internet voting systems are a relatively new innovation in the history of democracy. To reassure voters, many systems build verifiability into the systems. However, achieving verifiability requires participation from the voters themselves, who now have to carry out extra steps in addition to casting their votes. The entire concept of verifiability stands or falls based on their ability to do this, and to spot any anomalies that manifest. The study reported here is the first to test whether voters can detect manipulations to the voting interface when voters verify using the code-based verification approach. To maximise the chances that people would spot manipulations, we first improved the paper-based instructions provided to walk people through the required steps. We then carried out a lab-based study with both the original and improved systems. While our refinements improved detection rates, participant voters did not universally detect the manipulations. There is clearly room for further refinements. One additional finding - which is likely to hold for any verifiable voting system - is that it is not enough to make people detect a manipulation if they then call the malicious support hotline or simply try again. This needs to be addressed as future work. What our investigation highlights is the need to consider the human in the loop when designing user interactions, especially where tasks are unfamiliar and different from the traditional way of doing things.

Acknowledgement. This work was partially conducted within the Center of Information Security and Trust at the IT University of Copenhagen and also supported by the German Federal Ministry of Education and Research within the Competence Center for Applied Security Technology (KASTEL).

References

1. Acemyan, C.Z., Kortum, P., Byrne, M.D., Wallach, D.S.: Usability of voter verifiable, end-to-end voting systems: baseline data for Helios, Prêt à Voter, and Scantegrity II. USENIX J. Election Technol. Syst. **2**(3), 26–56 (2014)
2. Acemyan, C.Z., Kortum, P., Byrne, M.D., Wallach, D.S.: From error to error: why voters could not cast a ballot and verify their vote with Helios, Prêt à Voter, and Scantegrity II. USENIX J. Election Technol. Syst. (JETS) **3**(2), 1–19 (2015)
3. Acemyan, C.Z., Kortum, P., Byrne, M.D., Wallach, D.S.: Summative usability assessments of STAR-Vote: a cryptographically secure e2e voting system that has been empirically proven to be easy to use. Hum. Factors **2018**, 1–24 (2018)
4. Bangor, A., Kortum, P., Miller, J.: Determining what individual SUS scores mean: adding an adjective rating scale. J. Usability Stud. **4**(3), 114–123 (2009)
5. Bär, M., Henrich, C., Müller-Quade, J., Röhrich, S., Stüber, C.: Real world experiences with bingo voting and a comparison of usability. In: IAVoSS Workshop On Trustworthy Elections (WOTE 2008), Leuven, Belgium (2008)

6. Bernhard, M., et al.: Can voters detect malicious manipulation of ballot marking devices? In: Proceedings of the 41st IEEE Symposium on Security and Privacy, Oakland (2020, To appear)

7. Budurushi, J., Renaud, K., Volkamer, M., Woide, M.: An investigation into the usability of electronic voting systems for complex elections. Ann. Telecommun. **71**(7–8), 309–322 (2016). https://doi.org/10.1007/s12243-016-0510-2

8. Budurushi, J., Woide, M., Volkamer, M.: Introducing precautionary behavior by temporal diversion of voter attention from casting to verifying their vote. In: Workshop on Usable Security, USEC 2014, San Diego, California, 23 February 2014. Internet Society, Reston (2014). ISBN 1-891562-37-1

9. Distler, V., Zollinger, M.-L., Lallemand, C., Roenne, P., Ryan, P., Koenig, V.: Security-visible, yet unseen? How displaying security mechanisms impacts user experience and perceived security. In: Proceedings of ACM CHI Conference on Human Factors in Computing Systems (CHI 2019), Glasgow, Scotland, pp. 605:1–605:13 (2019)

10. Giles, M.: US elections are still far too vulnerable to attack - at every level, 6 June 2019. https://www.technologyreview.com/s/613635/us-elections-are-still-far-too-vulnerable-to-attackat-every-level/. Accessed 23 June 2019

11. Gjøsteen, K., Lund, A.S.: An experiment on the security of the Norwegian electronic voting protocol. Ann. Telecommun. **71**(7–8), 299–307 (2016). https://doi.org/10.1007/s12243-016-0509-8

12. Halderman, J.A.: Practical attacks on real-world e-voting. In: Hao, F., Ryan, P.Y.A. (eds.) Real-World Electronic Voting. Design, Analysis and Deployment, pp. 143–170. Auerbach Publications, Boca Raton (2016)

13. Harada, M., Smith, D.M.: You have to pay to play: candidate and party responses to the high cost of elections in Japan. Electoral. Stud. **36**(2014), 51–64 (2014)

14. Karayumak, F., Olembo, M.M., Kauer, M., Volkamer, M.: Usability analysis of helios - an open source verifiable remote electronic voting system. In: Proceedings of the: Conference on Electronic Voting Technology/Workshop on Trustworthy Elections (EVT/WOTE 2011). USENIX Association, Berkeley (2011)

15. Kulyk, O., Henzel, J., Renaud, K., Volkamer, M.: Comparing "challenge-based" and "code-based" internet voting verification implementations. In: Lamas, D., Loizides, F., Nacke, L., Petrie, H., Winckler, M., Zaphiris, P. (eds.) INTERACT 2019. LNCS, vol. 11746, pp. 519–538. Springer, Cham (2019). https://doi.org/10.1007/978-3-030-29381-9_32

16. Kulyk, O., Neumann, S., Budurushi, J., Volkamer, M.: Nothing comes for free: how much usability can you sacrifice for security? IEEE Secur. Priv. **15**(3), 24–29 (2017)

17. Kulyk, O., Volkamer, M.: Usability is not enough: lessons learned from human factors in security - research for verifiability. E-Vote-ID 2018, pp. 66–81 (2018)

18. MacNamara, D., Gibson, P., Oakley, K.: A preliminary study on a DualVote and Prêt à Voter hybrid system. In: CeDEM 2012: Conference for E-Democracy and Open Government, 3–4 May 2012, p. 77. Edition-Donau-Univ. Krems, Danube-University Krems, Austria (2012)

19. MacNamara, D., Scully, T., Gibson, P.: DualVote addressing usability and verifiability issues in electronic voting systems (2011). http://citeseerx.ist.psu.edu/viewdoc/summary?doi=10.1.1.399.7284

20. Marky, K., Kulyk, O., Renaud, K., Volkamer, M.: What did i really vote for? In: 2018 Proceedings of the CHI Conference on Human Factors in Computing Systems, p. 176. ACM, Montreal (2018)

21. Olembo, M.M., Renaud, K., Bartsch, S., Volkamer, M.: Voter, what message will motivate you to verify your vote. In: Workshop on Usable Security. USEC, Okinawa (2014)
22. Oostveen, A.-M., Van den Besselaar, P.: Users' experiences with e-voting: a comparative case study. J. Electronic Gov. **2**(4), 357–377 (2009)
23. Schneider, S., Llewellyn, M., Culnane, C., Heather, J., Srinivasan, S., Xia, Z.: Focus group views on Prêt à Voter 1.0. In: International Workshop on Requirements Engineering for Electronic Voting Systems (REVOTE), pp. 56–65. IEEE, Trento (2011)
24. Schweitzer, E.J., Albrecht, S.: Das Internet im Wahlkampf: Eine Einführung. In: Schweitzer, E.J., Albrecht, S. (eds.) Das Internet im Wahlkampf, pp. 9–65. Springer, Heidelberg (2011). https://doi.org/10.1007/978-3-531-92853-1_1
25. Serdult, U., Germann, M., Mendez, F., Portenier, A., Wellig, C.: Fifteen years of internet voting in switzerland [history, governance and use]. In: 2nd International Conference on eDemocracy & eGovernment (ICEDEG), pp. 126–132. IEEE, Quito (2015)
26. Solvak, M., Krimmer, R.: The curse of knowledge. E-Vote-ID (2019)
27. Weber, J.-L., Hengartner, U.: Usability Study of the Open Audit Voting System Helios (2009). http://www.jannaweber.com/wpcontent/uploads/2009/09/858Helios.pdf. Accessed 22 Dec 2017
28. Winckler, M., et al.: Assessing the usability of open verifiable e-voting systems: a trial with the system Prêt à Voter. In: Proceedings of ICE-GOV, pp. 281–296 (2009)

Short Paper: Mechanized Proofs of Verifiability and Privacy in a Paper-Based E-Voting Scheme

Marie-Laure Zollinger$^{(\boxtimes)}$, Peter B. Rønne$^{(\boxtimes)}$, and Peter Y. A. Ryan$^{(\boxtimes)}$

SnT & University of Luxembourg, Esch-sur-Alzette, Luxembourg
{marie-laure.zollinger,peter.roenne,peter.ryan}@uni.lu

Abstract. Electryo is a paper-based voting protocol that implements the Selene mechanism for individual verifiability. This short paper aims to provide the first formal model of Electryo, with security proofs for vote-privacy and individual verifiability. In general, voting protocols are complex constructs, involving advanced cryptographic primitives and strong security guarantees, posing a serious challenge when wanting to analyse and prove security with formal verification tools. Here we choose to use the TAMARIN prover since it is one of the more advanced tools and is able to handle many of the primitives we encounter in the design and analysis of voting protocols.

1 Introduction

In this paper, we propose an initial model for the voting protocol Electryo [12]. Electryo is a paper-based e-voting protocol, where the voter experience remains close to a standard paper-ballot voting scheme, with the Selene mechanism [13] for individual verification.

The additional feature of Electryo is the link between paper ballots and electronic ballots, allowing the possibility to perform (comparison) Risk Limiting Audits [9] efficiently. From Selene it inherits a tracking number feature, allowing voters to verify that their vote has been correctly recorded and counted, but provides a much stronger dispute resolution, as a paper ballot exists which can be compared to the digital record in case of complaint. The voter casts a paper ballot printed at the polling station, which contains an encryption of her ID represented in a QR code. The ballots are scanned to create an encrypted digital version of the paper ballots on the bulletin board. From the data on the bulletin board an anonymous tally list of plaintext votes is created, each associated with a tracking number. After the election ends, each voter will be able to retrieve their tracker and hence check their vote. We will give details of the protocol in Sect. 3.

Among the available tools for formal verification, we chose the TAMARIN prover [1] to develop our model. TAMARIN has an expressive language based on multiset rewriting rules. This lets us represent a symbolic model of the adversary's knowledge and messages sent over the network. It also uses equational

© Springer Nature Switzerland AG 2020
M. Bernhard et al. (Eds.): FC 2020 Workshops, LNCS 12063, pp. 310–318, 2020.
https://doi.org/10.1007/978-3-030-54455-3_22

theories, that allow us to specify cryptographic operators, like encryption but also Pedersen commitments. We will detail the semantics of TAMARIN and our model in Sect. 4.

Our Contributions. In this paper, we provide a formal model of the Electryo protocol. We model the tracker commitments, encryption, signatures, and channels rules between entities. We provide proofs for ballot-secrecy and individual verification (see Sect. 5). This paper is still a work in progress and additional proofs for receipt-freeness are being developed.

Related Work. A TAMARIN model for a simplified version of Selene has already been developed [4]. The authors used the equational theory developed in [7] for the commitments in Selene, which we will use here as well. Vote-Privacy and Receipt-Freeness were proved for a protocol running over untappable channels.

Basin et al. in [3] have developed a protocol for random sample voting with the associated proofs in TAMARIN, and proved Receipt-Freeness and Verifiability. We use their definition of encryption with randomness.

Some other examples of voting protocol models in TAMARIN can be found in [7] where the equational theory for trapdoor commitments have been developed and applied in Okamoto's protocol [11] and the FOO protocol [8].

2   Outline of Selene

We now give a sketch of how voter-verification is achieved in the Selene voting protocol. Full details can be found in [13]. In Selene, the verification is much more direct and intuitive than is the case for conventional End-to-End Verifiability systems: rather than checking for the presence of her encrypted vote on the *BB*, the voter checks her vote in cleartext in the tally on the *BB* identified by a secret, deniable tracker.

During the setup phase the set of distinct trackers are posted on the *BB*, verifiably encrypted and mixed and then assigned to the voters according the resulting secret permutation. This ensures that each voter is assigned a unique, secret tracker. For each encrypted tracker, a trapdoor commitment is created for which the voter holds the secret trapdoor key. In essence this is the "β" term of an El Gamal encryption of the tracker, where the "α" term is kept secret for the moment.

Voting is as usual: an encryption of the vote is created, and sent to the server for posting to the *BB* against the voter (pseudo) ID. Once we are happy that we have the correct set of validly cast, encrypted votes, we can proceed to tabulation: the encrypted (vote, tracker) pairs are put through verifiable, parallel re-encryption mixes and decrypted, revealing the vote/tracker pairs in plaintext.

Later, the α terms are sent via an untappable channel to the voters to enable them to open the commitment using their secret, trapdoor key. If coerced, the voter can generate a fake α that will open her commitment to an alternative tracker pointing to the coercer's choice. With the trapdoor, creating such a fake

α is computationally straightforward. On the other hand, computing a fake α that will open the commitment to a given, valid tracker is intractable without the trapdoor. Thus, assuming that the voter's trapdoor is not compromised, the α term is implicitly authenticated by the fact that it opens to a valid tracker.

3   Electryo

In this paper we only give a very brief overview of Electryo [12] and refer the reader to the original paper for the details. The protocol is summarised in Fig. 1. It is assumed that each voter is equipped with an ID smart card holding their secret signing key and the corresponding verification key is publicly known. Further, Selene requires a separate public key and corresponding secret trapdoor key which the voter holds, e.g. in an app. In the polling station a registration clerk checks the ID card and this is read by a card reader connected to a ballot printer. From the smart card the printer receives an encryption of the ID and an encryption of a signature (e.g. of his PK or ID) from the voter. The printer now delivers a ballot with the re-encrypted ID and signature contained in a QR-Code bcode. Now the voter can fill out the paper ballot in a booth and proceed to a ballot box containing the scanner. The scanner sends the encrypted vote to the bulletin board together with both a re-encryption and a separate encryption of the ballot code. Further, a simple short receipt code is printed and an encryption of this code is sent with the other data to BB. At home the voter needs to enter the receipt code as an authentication token to be able to receive the Selene α term. The receipt code prevents a malicious printer to print another colluding voter's ID on the ballot. The encrypted vote will be associated with the voter via the corresponding encrypted ID, and the Selene mechanism described in the last section can be used.

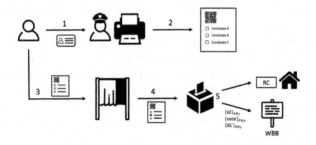

Fig. 1. The Electryo protocol.

4   Tamarin

4.1   Semantics

In TAMARIN, messages are represented as terms. A term is an element t or a function $f(t_1, ..., t_n)$ of arity n, where $t_1, \ldots, t_n$ are terms. We also define a set of operators, or functions, with their arities. An equation is a pair of terms s and t such as $s = t$. We define E as a set of equations. An equational theory is a smallest congruence closure containing all instances E.

Protocols are modeled through multiset rewriting rules. These rules use sets of Facts $F(t_1, ..., t_n)$ of arity n. We denote fresh values with $\sim$ and public values with \$. Facts are user-defined except: Fr, In and Out for inputs and outputs of a rule, and K is the attacker knowledge. An exclamation mark ! before a Fact will define it as persistent and can be consumed many times, while a linear Fact can be consumed only once.

4.2   The Electryo Model

In our model, we consider two voters V1 and V2, an Election Authority EA, the Tracker Retrieval Authority TRA and a scanner S. The ID cards, used to perform the ID encryption, are not distinguished from the printer. This is discussed below in the trust assumptions paragraph.

Channel Rules. We denote by $\bullet\!\!\rightarrow$ an *authentic* channel, that means the adversary cannot modify the messages or their sender, but he can access this data. This ensures that a message is correctly delivered but can be seen and copied by an adversary. More details about TAMARIN channel rules can be found on the manual web page [1].

We also define the *untappable* channel by $\boxed{\Longrightarrow}$, which means that a message is not readable nor modifiable over the network like a secure channel [10], but also the message won't be persistent and replayable later.

Trust Assumptions. In TAMARIN, the adversary is a standard Dolev-Yao style [6], that is controlling the network and can apply all operators. The adversary learns all messages sent by participants when they are output with the Out fact. He can send messages to the participants with the In fact, that is we assume that every input could be given by the adversary. The adversary can also generate fresh values and knows all public values. Finally, he can apply functions available in the set of operators. He will be provided with additional information depending on the trust assumptions below.

As a simplification in the current model, we merged the ID card and the printer into one entity. This means that the printer is reading this voter's ID card without changing the information. The adversary can still modify the information on the printed ballot which will correspond to the ID card and the printer colluding in the original model. We also assume that the voter is using her own ID card which is checked by polling station clerks in the Electryo protocol.

Equational Theories. To model Electryo, that is using the Selene mechanism, we need the trapdoor (td) commitments equations defined in [7]. This theory is defined as follows:

$$\text{open}(\text{commit}(m, r, td), r) = m$$
$$\text{commit}(m_2, \text{fake}(m_1, r, td, m_2), td) = \text{commit}(m_1, r, td)$$
$$\text{open}(\text{commit}(m_1, r, rd), \text{fake}(m_1, r, td, m_2)) = m_2$$
$$\text{fake}(m_1, \text{fake}(m, r, td, m_1), td, m_2) = \text{fake}(m, r, td, m_2)$$

From this equational theory, we can define the trapdoor commitments, which enables voters to fake their tracking number and α term.

We also define an asymmetric encryption scheme. We could not use the existing built-in *asymmetric-encryption* provided by Tamarin because the pre-defined version has no randomness, hence the adversary could learn the encrypted vote sent over the network by using the construction rule for encryption on the public value of candidate. This equation for a ciphertext cp is defined as follows:

$$\text{dcp}(\text{cp}(m, r, \text{pk}(sk)), sk) = m$$

Finally, we use the built-in package *multiset* to model the shuffling of messages as described in [4].

4.3   Tamarin Model of Electryo

An overview of the model is given in Fig. 2. Compared to the existing implementation of Bruni et al. [4], this model considers more cryptographic primitives and provides more data to the adversary as we will detail below. The EA generates tracking numbers and together with the TRA, computes the commitments. The TRA keeps the α-terms secret. The EA publishes the commitments with a persistant fact. Then, voters retrieve their ballot with a ballot code computed from their identity and signature, bcode = <cp($V, r, pkT),cp(sign($V, skV),s, pkT)>.

Voters input their ballot code and intended vote into the scanner, that computes an encryption of their ballot code *bcode*, an encryption of their vote, generates a receipt-code *RC* and encrypts it. Finally it calculates a re-encryption of the ciphertext buried in the ballot code.[1] In particular, it computes cp($V, r', pkT) and cp(sign($V, skV), s', pkT). The scanner sends all of this data to the EA, and gives the plaintext receipt-code to the voter.

When the EA receives the data for both voters, it decrypts and publishes the votes on the bulletin board with the tracking number and the encrypted RC.

When the votes are published, the TRA can send the α-term to the voter. We use an authentic channel to notify the voters.[2] Each voter can open the commitment and retrieve their tracker. A trace is written to provide a verifiability lemma, checking the validity of the receipt-code and of the vote (see Sect. 5).

---

[1] For readability, this does not appear in Fig. 2.

[2] Sufficient for Vote-privacy. To prove Receipt-Freeness, we will need a stronger assumption on channels.

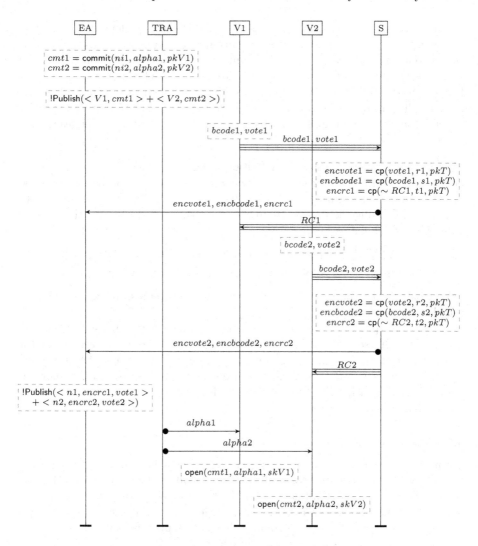

Fig. 2. An overview of the model.

5   Proofs

5.1   Privacy

To prove privacy properties, we need to prove indistinguishability between two executions of a system. In TAMARIN, this is done through observational equivalence [2]. For this, the tool uses a multiset rewriting system where terms can be written using a special operator $\mathsf{diff}(\cdot, \cdot)$. With this operator, we are able to instantiate two possible elements in one term. Then TAMARIN creates two systems, a left and a right, with identical rules where the difference is on the value of the term instantiated with diff.

To verify the observational equivalence, TAMARIN uses dependency graphs. A dependency graph represents the execution of a system. To each node corresponds one rule defined in the model, and there is a direct relation called edge from a rule r_1 to r_2 iff r_1 outputs a fact to r_2 input. The equivalence between two graphs depends on *mirroring*, that is: given a dependency graph, its mirrors contain all graphs on the other side (left or right) of the system defined with the diff operator, where nodes are instances of the same rules and edges are the same.

Vote-Privacy. First, we used the definition of Delaune et al. [5] for vote-privacy: an attacker cannot detect if voters V1 and V2 swap their votes. In our model, we use the diff operator during the setup phase when defining every entity knowledge: when defining the two voters in the setup rule, we swapped their intended vote. This is defined as follow:

$$St\_V\_1('V1', pkV1, {\sim}ltkV1, diff('candA', 'candB'), pkT)$$
$$St\_V\_1('V2', pkV2, {\sim}ltkV2, diff('candB', 'candA'), pkT)$$

where pkV· is the voter's public key, ~ltkV· is the voter's secret key and pkT is the election key.

In Electryo privacy is guaranteed (for covert adversaries) unless the ID card, printer and the scanner collude. Indeed, we found a trivial attack when the card/printer and the scanner collude. On the other hand, using the above definition, we have a proof in TAMARIN, when neither the card/printer nor the scanner collude with the adversary. Proofs for privacy when only one entity is misbehaving are in progress.

5.2   Electryo Verifiability

Verifiability is defined by individual verifiability, that is a voter can verify that her vote was really counted correctly, and universal verifiability, that is the outcome reflects the sum of all cast votes. In this model we only proved individual verifiability. To check verifiability properties, we can use *traces* and express properties as first order logic formulas. These formulas use the temporality of the protocol that let us use the order of events.

In this model, we defined individual verifiability as the ability of voters to correctly check their tracker and verifying that the recorded vote is correct. For Electryo, we also need to verify the correctness of the receipt-code. Given the action Vote, when the voter V casts his vote vote and receives his receipt-code rc, the action Learn when the voter V computes his tracker n, and the action BB, when votes, encrypted ballot-codes and trackers are published, we define individual verifiability as:

$$All\ V\ vote\ rc\ n\ \#i1\ \#i2.$$
$$Vote(V, vote, rc)\ @i1\ \&\ Learn(V, n)\ @i2$$
$$==> Ex\ othervote\ r\ pkT\ \#j.$$
$$BB(<n, cp(rc, r, pkT), vote> + othervote)\ @j$$

To verify this lemma, we used our model defined above, and we modeled a simple malicious behaviour either from the scanner or the card/printer allowing it to modify the ballot-code identity. The lemma remains proven for all traces.

6   Work in Progress

A more detailed implementation is still work in progress. In this paper, we provide proofs for verifiability aspects of Electryo with certain channel assumptions. We have shown that an attack from the scanner trying to modify the ballot code is detectable. We have also proven Vote-Privacy of the protocol. We are already using equational theories to model cryptographic primitives (commitments and encryption) but we aim at using these even further in a more detailed modelling of the cryptography. Finally, more proofs regarding privacy properties, in particular Receipt-Freeness, will be the scope of future work.

Acknowledgments. We would like to thank the Luxembourg National Research Fund (FNR) for funding, in particular MLZ was supported by the INTER-SeVoTe project and PBR by the FNR CORE project Q-CoDe and INTER-SURCVS. Also the experiments presented in this paper were carried out using the HPC facilities of the University of Luxembourg [14] – see https://hpc.uni.lu.

References

1. Basin, D.A., Cremers, C., Dreier, J., Meier, S., Sasse, R., Schmidt, B.: Tamarin prover manual (2019). https://tamarin-prover.github.io/manual/
2. Basin, D.A., Dreier, J., Sasse, R.: Automated symbolic proofs of observational equivalence. In: Proceedings of the 22nd ACM SIGSAC Conference on Computer and Communications Security (2015)
3. Basin, D.A., Radomirovic, S., Schmid, L.: Alethea: a provably secure random sample voting protocol. In: 31st IEEE Computer Security Foundations Symposium, CSF 2018 (2018)
4. Bruni, A., Drewsen, E., Schürmann, C.: Towards a mechanized proof of selene receipt-freeness and vote-privacy. In: Krimmer, R., Volkamer, M., Braun Binder, N., Kersting, N., Pereira, O., Schürmann, C. (eds.) E-Vote-ID 2017. LNCS, vol. 10615, pp. 110–126. Springer, Cham (2017). https://doi.org/10.1007/978-3-319-68687-5_7
5. Delaune, S., Kremer, S., Ryan, M.: Verifying privacy-type properties of electronic voting protocols. J. Comput. Secur. **17**, 435–487 (2009)
6. Dolev, D., Yao, A.C.: On the security of public key protocols. IEEE Trans. Inf. Theory **29**, 198–208 (1983)
7. Dreier, J., Duménil, C., Kremer, S., Sasse, R.: Beyond subterm-convergent equational theories in automated verification of stateful protocols. In: Maffei, M., Ryan, M. (eds.) POST 2017. LNCS, vol. 10204, pp. 117–140. Springer, Heidelberg (2017). https://doi.org/10.1007/978-3-662-54455-6_6
8. Fujioka, A., Okamoto, T., Ohta, K.: A practical secret voting scheme for large scale elections. In: Advances in Cryptology - AUSCRYPT 1992, Workshop on the Theory and Application of Cryptographic Techniques (1992)

9. Lindeman, M., Stark, P.B.: A gentle introduction to risk-limiting audits. IEEE Secur. Priv. **10**, 42–49 (2012)

10. Maurer, U.M., Schmid, P.E.: A calculus for secure channel establishment in open networks. In: Gollmann, D. (ed.) ESORICS 1994. LNCS, vol. 875, pp. 173–192. Springer, Heidelberg (1994). https://doi.org/10.1007/3-540-58618-0_63

11. Okamoto, T.: An electronic voting scheme. In: Advanced IT Tools, IFIP World Conference on IT Tools (1996)

12. Rønne, P.B., Ryan, P.Y., Zollinger, M.L.: Electryo, in-person voting with transparent voter verifiability and eligibility verifiability. In: Financial Cryptography and Data Security - FC 2018, Workshop on Voting (2018)

13. Ryan, P.Y.A., Rønne, P.B., Iovino, V.: Selene: voting with transparent verifiability and coercion-mitigation. In: Financial Cryptography and Data Security - FC 2016 (2016)

14. Varrette, S., Bouvry, P., Cartiaux, H., Georgatos, F.: Management of an academic HPC cluster: the UL experience. In: Proceedings of the 2014 International Conference on High Performance Computing & Simulation, HPCS 2014 (2014)

Sets of Half-Average Nulls Generate Risk-Limiting Audits: SHANGRLA

Philip B. Stark[✉]

University of California, Berkeley, CA, USA
stark@stat.berkeley.edu

Abstract. Risk-limiting audits (RLAs) for many social choice functions can be reduced to testing sets of null hypotheses of the form "the average of this list is not greater than 1/2" for a collection of finite lists of nonnegative numbers. Such social choice functions include majority, super-majority, plurality, multi-winner plurality, Instant Runoff Voting (IRV), Borda count, approval voting, and STAR-Voting, among others. The audit stops without a full hand count iff all the null hypotheses are rejected. The nulls can be tested in many ways. Ballot polling is particularly simple; two new ballot-polling risk-measuring functions for sampling without replacement are given. Ballot-level comparison audits transform each null into an equivalent assertion that the mean of re-scaled tabulation errors is not greater than 1/2. In turn, that null can then be tested using the same statistical methods used for ballot polling—applied to different finite lists of nonnegative numbers. The SHANGRLA approach thus reduces auditing different social choice functions and different audit methods to the same simple statistical problem. Moreover, SHANGRLA comparison audits are more efficient than previous comparison audits for two reasons: (i) for most social choice functions, the conditions tested are both necessary and sufficient for the reported outcome to be correct, while previous methods tested conditions that were sufficient but not necessary, and (ii) the tests avoid a conservative approximation. The SHANGRLA abstraction simplifies stratified audits, including audits that combine ballot polling with ballot-level comparisons, producing sharper audits than the "SUITE" approach. SHANGRLA works with the "phantoms to evil zombies" strategy to treat missing ballot cards and missing or redacted cast vote records. That also facilitates sampling from "ballot-style manifests," which can dramatically improve efficiency when the audited contests do not appear on every ballot card. Open-source software implementing SHANGRLA ballot-level comparison audits is available. SHANGRLA was tested in a process pilot audit of an instant-runoff contest in San Francisco, CA, in November, 2019.

Keywords: Sequential tests · Martingales · Kolmogorov's inequality

1 Introduction

A *risk-limiting audit* (RLA) of a reported election contest outcome is any procedure that guarantees a minimum probability of correcting the reported outcome

© Springer Nature Switzerland AG 2020
M. Bernhard et al. (Eds.): FC 2020 Workshops, LNCS 12063, pp. 319–336, 2020.
https://doi.org/10.1007/978-3-030-54455-3_23

if the reported winner(s) did not really win, but never alters a correct reported outcome. The largest probability that the procedure fail to correct the reported outcome if the reported outcome is wrong is the *risk limit*.

RLAs were introduced by [18] and named by [21]. RLA methods have been developed for a variety of social choice functions, to accommodate election equipment with different capabilities, and to comport with the logistics of ballot handling, organization, and storage in different jurisdictions.

RLAs are considered the gold standard for post-election tabulation audits, recommended by the National Academies of Science, Engineering, and Medicine [14], the Presidential Commission on Election Administration [17], the American Statistical Association [1], the League of Women Voters, Verified Voting Foundation, the Brennan Center for Justice, and other organizations concerned with election integrity.

Experience with RLAs. RLAs have been piloted dozens of times in 11 U.S. states and in Denmark. They are required by statute in Colorado, Nevada, Rhode Island, and Virginia, and authorized by statute in California and Washington.

Resources for RLAs. There is free and open-source software to help with the random selection of ballot cards for RLAs and to perform the risk calculations to determine when and if the audit can stop.[1]

Prerequisites for RLAs. A risk-limiting audit of a trustworthy paper record of voter intent can catch and correct wrong election outcomes. (Here, "trustworthy" means that a full hand count of the votes in the record would show the true winners.) But RLAs themselves check only the tabulation, not the trustworthiness of the paper records. If the paper trail is not trustworthy, it is not clear what a risk-limiting audit procedure accomplishes: while it can offer assurances that *tabulation error* did not alter the reported outcome, it cannot determine whether the reported outcome is right or wrong, nor can it promise any probability of correcting wrong outcomes. It therefore cannot limit the risk of certifying an outcome that is incorrect—the "risk" that a risk-limiting audit is supposed to limit.

Because all electronic systems are vulnerable to bugs, misconfiguration, and hacking, the paper trail can be trustworthy only if elections are conducted using *voter-verified paper ballots kept demonstrably secure* throughout the canvass and the audit. In particular, *compliance audits* [4, 12, 23, 25] are needed to assure that the paper trail remains inviolate from the time of casting through the completion of the audit.

---

[1] See, e.g., https://www.stat.berkeley.edu/users/stark/Vote/auditTools.htm, https://www.stat.berkeley.edu/users/stark/Vote/ballotPollTools.htm, https://github.com/pbstark/auditTools, https://github.com/pbstark/CORLA18/blob/master/code/suite_toolkit.ipynb, and https://github.com/votingworks/arlo (all last visited 10 November 2019); an implementation of SHANGRLA ballot-level comparison audits is available at https://github.com/pbstark/SHANGRLA.

However, that is not enough: the means of marking the paper matters. Recent experiments have shown that voters rarely check BMD printout and rarely notice errors in BMD printout, even when instructed to check—verbally, through written instructions, and through signage [6]. Most BMD output is evidently not voter-verified. Moreover, while voters who notice errors in BMD printout may request a fresh chance to mark a ballot, there is no way to tell whether the error was the voter's fault or the BMD's fault [2,5,10]. As a result, malfunctioning BMDs may go undetected by election officials. Applying RLA procedures to BMD printout cannot limit the risk that incorrect reported outcomes will go uncorrected, unless one simply defines "correct outcome" to be whatever an accurate tally of the paper would show, whether or not that reflects what voters indicated to the equipment.

What's New Here. SHANGRLA uses a new abstract framing of RLAs that involves constructing a set of *assertions* for each contest. If the assertions are true, the contest outcomes are correct. The assertions are predicates on the set of ballot cards, that is, they are either true or false, depending on what votes the whole set of trusted paper ballot cards shows.

Each assertion is characterized by an *assorter*, a function that assigns a nonnegative number to each ballot card,[2] again depending on the votes reflected on the ballot. The assertions that characterize the audit are of the form "the average value of the assorter for all the cast ballots is greater than $1/2$." In turn, each assertion is checked by testing the *complementary null hypothesis* that the average is less than or equal to $1/2$. To reject the entire set of complementary null hypotheses is to confirm the outcomes of all the contests under audit. Hence, the name of this method: Sets of Half-Average Nulls Generate RLAs (SHANGRLA).

By reducing auditing to repeated instances of a single, simple statistical problem—testing whether the mean of a list of nonnegative numbers is less than $1/2$—SHANGRLA puts ballot-polling audits, comparison audits, batch-level comparison audits, and stratified and "hybrid" audits on the same footing, and puts auditing a broad range of social choice functions on the same footing. Moreover, it makes it easy to incorporate statistical advances into RLAs: only one function needs to be updated.

Open-source software implementing SHANGRLA audits is available.[3] The software also implements the "phantoms to evil zombies" approach of [3] for dealing with missing cast-vote records and missing ballot cards. That also makes it possible to sample from "ballot-style manifests" [4,11], which facilitates efficient audits of contests that do not appear on every ballot card cast in the election. Despite the fact that they were developed more than 7 years ago, neither "phantoms-to-zombies" nor sampling from ballot-style manifests has been implemented before. The SHANGRLA software was tested in practice in a process pilot audit in San Francisco, CA, in November 2019.

---

[2] A ballot consists of one or more ballot cards. Below, "ballot," "card," and "ballot card" are used interchangeably, even though in most U.S. jurisdictions, a ballot consists of more than one ballot card.

[3] https://www.github.com/pbstark/SHANGRLA, last visited 22 November 2019.

2   Assorted Simplifications

An *assorter* A assigns a nonnegative value to each ballot card, depending on the marks the voter made on that ballot card.[4]

For instance, suppose that Alice and Bob are running against each other in a two-candidate first-past-the-post contest. The following function is an assorter: assign the value "1" to a ballot card if it has a mark for Alice but not for Bob; assign the value "0" if the card has a mark for Bob but not for Alice; assign the value $1/2$, otherwise (e.g., if the card has an overvote or an undervote in this contest or does not contain the contest). Then Alice beat Bob iff the average value of the assorter for the full set of cast ballot cards is greater than $1/2$: then Alice got more than 50% of the valid votes.

To express this more mathematically, let b_i denote the ith ballot card, and suppose there are N ballot cards in all. Let $1_{\text{Alice}}(b_i) = 1$ if ballot i has a mark for Alice, and 0 if not; define $1_{\text{Bob}}(b_i)$ analogously. The assorter could be written

$$A_{\text{Alice,Bob}}(b_i) \equiv \frac{1_{\text{Alice}}(b_i) - 1_{\text{Bob}}(b_i) + 1}{2}.$$

If b_i shows a mark for Alice but not for Bob, $A_{\text{Alice,Bob}}(b_i) = 1$. If it shows a mark for Bob but not for Alice, $A_{\text{Alice,Bob}}(b_i) = 0$. If it shows marks for both Alice and Bob (an overvote), for neither Alice nor Bob (an undervote), or if the ballot card does not contain the Alice v. Bob contest at all, $A_{\text{Alice,Bob}}(b_i) = 1/2$. The average value of A over all ballot cards is

$$\bar{A}^b_{\text{Alice,Bob}} \equiv \frac{1}{N} \sum_{i=1}^{N} A_{\text{Alice,Bob}}(b_i).$$

If Alice is the reported winner, the contest can be audited at risk limit α by testing the *complementary null hypothesis* that $\bar{A}^b_{\text{Alice,Bob}} \leq 1/2$ at significance level α. To reject the complementary null hypothesis is to conclude that Alice really won. If the complementary null hypothesis is true, Bob won or the contest was a tie: the assertion is false.

An assorter offers more flexibility than just counting votes. For instance, instead of either giving Alice one vote, half a vote, or no vote, an assorter could interpret a ballot card as giving Alice an arbitrary nonnegative value as a vote, depending on the marks on the ballot. This flexibility lets assorters solve the problem of auditing more complicated social choice functions, as we shall see.

2.1   Plurality Elections

In a plurality contest with $K \geq 1$ winners and $C > K$ candidates in all, a collection of candidates $\{w_k\}_{k=1}^{K}$ are the true winners and the remaining $C - K$ candidates $\{\ell_j\}_{j=1}^{C-K}$ are the true losers iff the assertions

---

[4] The value might also depend on what the voting system reported for that ballot card and others. See Sect. 3.2.

$$\bar{A}^b_{w_k,\ell_j} > 1/2, \quad \text{for all } 1 \le k \le K, \ 1 \le j \le C - K$$

all hold, where A_{w_k,ℓ_j} is defined as above, with w_k taking the role of Alice and ℓ_j taking the role of Bob. (This is essentially the approach taken in [12,18,20,22], reformulated and in different notation.) The contest can be audited to risk limit α by testing the $K(C - K)$ hypotheses $\bar{A}^b_{w_k,\ell_j} \le 1/2$ individually at significance level α. The audit stops only if all $K(C - K)$ complementary hypotheses are rejected; otherwise it requires a full hand count.

2.2   Approval Voting

Even though the voting rules are different, the same assorter functions can be used to audit approval voting and plurality voting. Candidates $\{w_k\}_{k=1}^K$ are the winners and the remaining $C - K$ candidates $\{\ell_j\}_{j=1}^{C-K}$ are the losers of a K-winner approval voting contest iff all the assertions

$$\bar{A}^b_{w_k,\ell_j} > 1/2, \quad \text{for all } 1 \le k \le K, \ 1 \le j \le C - K$$

hold.

2.3   Super-Majority

Suppose that a candidate must get at least a fraction $f \in (0,1)$ of the valid votes to win.[5] [18] shows how to audit this social choice function, but it can also be expressed in terms of the assertion that the average of an assorter applied to the cast ballot cards is greater than $1/2$.

Alice really won a super-majority contest with required winning fraction f iff

(valid votes for Alice) $> f \times$ ((valid votes for Alice) + (valid votes for everyone else)) .

Define an assorter as follows:

$$A(b_i) \equiv \begin{cases} \frac{1}{2f}, & b_i \text{ has a mark for Alice and no one else} \\ 0, & b_i \text{ has a mark for exactly one candidate and not Alice} \\ 1/2, & \text{otherwise.} \end{cases} \quad (1)$$

This assigns a nonnegative number to every ballot. Suppose that a fraction $p > f$ of the valid votes are for Alice, and that a fraction q of the ballots have valid votes. Then

$$\bar{A}^b \equiv pq/(2f) + (1-q)/2 \ge q/2 + (1-q)/2 = 1/2.$$

---

[5] Values $f \le 1/2$ are not technically "super-majorities," but the generality is useful. For instance, the rules of some primaries in the U.S. eliminate candidates who receive less than 15% of the vote. An RLA using $f = 0.15$ might be used to check whether the correct candidates were eliminated.

Again, using assorters reduces auditing to the question of whether the average of a list of nonnegative numbers is greater than $1/2$. The correctness of the outcome is implied by a single assertion, unlike plurality elections, which require (number of winners)×(number of losers) assertions.[6]

2.4 D'Hondt and Other Proportional Representation Schemes

[24] show how to reduce the problem of auditing D'Hondt and other proportional representation social choice functions to the problem of auditing a collection of two-candidate plurality contests. We have seen above that each such two-candidate contest can be expressed as the assertion that the average of an assorter applied to the ballots is greater than $1/2$, so auditing proportional representation contests can be reduced to auditing a collection of assertions that the averages of a set of assorters over the cast ballots is greater than $1/2$.

2.5 Borda Count, STAR-Voting, and Other Weighted Additive Voting Schemes

Borda count is one of several voting systems that assign points to candidates for each ballot, depending on what the ballot shows; the winner is the candidate who receives the most points in total across all cast ballots. This involves only a slight generalization of plurality contests to account for the fact that a ballot can give a candidate more than one "point," while for plurality a candidate either gets a vote or not. As before, the reported result is correct if the reported winner actually received more points than each reported loser, which we can test by constructing an assorter for each (winner, loser) pair.

Let $s_{\text{Alice}}(b_i)$ denote a nonnegative "score" for Alice on ballot i, and let $s_{\text{Bob}}(b_i)$ be the score for Bob. These need not be integers. Let s^+ be an upper bound on the score any candidate can get on a ballot. Alice beat Bob iff

$$\sum_{i=1}^{N} s_{\text{Alice}}(b_i) > \sum_{i=1}^{N} s_{\text{Bob}}(b_i),$$

i.e., iff

$$\bar{s}^b_{\text{Alice}} > \bar{s}^b_{\text{Bob}}.$$

Make the affine transformation

$$A(b_i) \equiv \frac{s_{\text{Alice}}(b_i) - s_{\text{Bob}}(b_i) + s^+}{2s^+}.$$

Then $A(b_i) \geq 0$ and $\bar{s}^b_{\text{Alice}} > \bar{s}^b_{\text{Bob}}$ iff $\bar{A}^b > 1/2$.

---

[6] To check whether K candidates all got at least a fraction $f \in (0, 1)$ of the valid votes (with $Kf < 1$) requires testing at most K assertions.

2.6   Ranked-Choice and Instant-Runoff Voting (RCV/IRV)

[7] show how to reduce the correctness of a reported IRV winner to the correctness of the reported winners of a set of two-candidate plurality contests. The "candidates" in those contests are not necessarily the candidates in the original contest; they are just two mutually exclusive (but not exhaustive) conditions that a ballot might satisfy.

Two types of assertions can be combined to give sufficient conditions for the reported winner of an IRV contest to have really won:

1. Candidate i has more first-place ranks than candidate j has total mentions.
2. After a set of candidates have been eliminated from consideration, candidate i is the top ranked candidate on more ballot cards than candidate j is.

Both of these can be written as $\bar{A}^b > 1/2$ by labeling the corresponding vote patterns "Alice" or "Bob" or "neither."

For instance, consider the first type of assertion. If b_i has candidate i ranked 1, the ballot is considered a vote for Alice. If b_i ranks candidate j at all, the ballot is considered a vote for Bob. Otherwise, the ballot is not a vote for either of them. If Alice beat Bob, candidate j cannot have beaten candidate i in the IRV contest.

In contrast to plurality, supermajority, approval, Borda, and d'Hondt, the assertions derived by [7] are sufficient for the reported winner to have won, but not necessary. Hence, it might be possible to sharpen such audits.

3   Auditing Assertions

We audit the assertion $\bar{A}^b > 1/2$ by testing the *complementary null hypothesis* $\bar{A}^b \leq 1/2$ statistically. We audit until either all complementary null hypotheses about a contest are rejected at significance level α or until all ballots have been tabulated by hand. This yields a RLA of the contest in question at risk limit α.

3.1   Ballot-Polling Audits

Ballot-polling audits select individual ballot cards at random, either with or without replacement. The BRAVO method of [13] uses Wald's Sequential Probability Ratio Test (SPRT) for sampling with replacement.

For each (reported winner, reported loser) pair, BRAVO tests the conditional probability that a ballot contains a vote for the reported winner given that it contains a vote for the reported winner or the reported loser. Using assorters allows us to eliminate the conditioning and opens the door to a broader collection of statistical tests, including tests based on sampling *without* replacement, which can improve the efficiency of the audit. Two such methods are presented below. In contrast to the SPRT (with or without replacement), these methods only require knowing the reported winners, not the reported vote shares.

First, we shall derive the Kaplan-Kolmogorov method for sampling without replacement, based on ideas in Harold Kaplan's (now defunct) website.[7] The method is based on the observation that a suitably constructed sequence is a nonnegative martingale, to which Kolmogorov's inequality for optionally stopped closed martingales can be applied.

We sample without replacement from a finite population of N nonnegative items, $\{x_1, \ldots, x_N\}$, with $x_j \geq 0$, $\forall j$. The population mean is $\mu \equiv \frac{1}{N} \sum_{j=1}^{N} x_j \geq 0$ and the population total is $N\mu \geq 0$. The value of the jth item drawn is X_j. On the hypothesis that $\mu = t$, $\mathbb{E}X_1 = t$, so $\mathbb{E}(X_1/t) = 1$. Conditional on $X_1, \ldots, X_n$, the total of the remaining $N - n$ items is $N\mu - \sum_{j=1}^{n} X_j$, so the mean of the remaining items is

$$\frac{Nt - \sum_{j=1}^{n} X_j}{N - n} = \frac{t - \frac{1}{N} \sum_{j=1}^{n} X_j}{1 - n/N}.$$

Thus, the expected value of X_{n+1} given $X_1, \ldots, X_n$ is $\frac{t - \frac{1}{N} \sum_{j=1}^{n} X_j}{1 - n/N}$. Define

$$Y_1(t) \equiv \begin{cases} X_1/t, & Nt > 0, \\ 1, & Nt = 0, \end{cases}$$

and for $1 \leq n \leq N - 1$,

$$Y_{n+1}(t) \equiv \begin{cases} X_{n+1} \cdot \frac{1 - \frac{n}{N}}{t - \frac{1}{N} \sum_{j=1}^{n} X_j}, & \sum_{j=1}^{n} X_j < Nt, \\ 1, & \sum_{j=1}^{n} X_j \geq Nt. \end{cases}$$

Then $\mathbb{E}(Y_{n+1}(t)|Y_1, \ldots Y_n) = 1$. Let $Z_n(t) \equiv \prod_{j=1}^{n} Y_j(t)$. Note that $Y_k(t)$ can be recovered from $\{Z_j(t), j \leq k\}$, since $Y_k(t) = Z_k(t)/Z_{k-1}(t)$. Now $\mathbb{E}|Z_k| \leq \max_j x_j < \infty$ and

$$\mathbb{E}\left(Z_{n+1}(t)|Z_1(t), \ldots Z_n(t)\right) = \mathbb{E}\left(Y_{n+1}(t)Z_n(t)|Z_1(t), \ldots Z_n(t)\right) = Z_n(t).$$

Thus

$$(Z_1(t), Z_2(t), \ldots, Z_N(t))$$

is a nonnegative closed martingale. By Kolmogorov's inequality, an application of Markov's inequality to martingales [8, p 242], for any $p > 0$ and any $J \in \{1, \ldots, N\}$,

$$\Pr\left(\max_{1 \leq j \leq J} Z_j(t) > 1/p\right) \leq p\, \mathbb{E}|Z_J|.$$

Since (Z_j) is a nonnegative martingale, $\mathbb{E}|Z_J| = \mathbb{E}Z_J = \mathbb{E}Z_1 = 1$. Thus a P-value for the hypothesis $\mu = t$ based on data $X_1, \ldots X_J$ is $(\max_{1 \leq j \leq J} Z_j(t))^{-1} \wedge 1$.

However, if $X_j = 0$ for some j, then $Z_k = 0$ for all $k \geq j$. To avoid that problem, we can shift everything to the right: pick $\gamma > 0$, find a lower confidence bound for $\delta = \mu + \gamma > 0$ from data $\{X_j + \gamma\}$, then subtract γ from the lower confidence bound to get a lower confidence bound for μ. There are tradeoffs involved in picking γ: if many X_j turn out to be small, especially for small j, it helps to have γ large, and vice versa.

Unpacking the math yields the P-value

$$p_{KK} \equiv 1 \wedge \left(\max_{1 \le j \le J} \prod_{k=1}^{j} (X_k + \gamma) \frac{1 - (k-1)/N}{t - \frac{1}{N}\sum_{\ell=1}^{k-1}(X_\ell + \gamma)} \right)^{-1}$$

for the hypothesis that $\mu \le t - \gamma$. This is implemented in the SHANGRLA software.

A related test that uses sampling without replacement, also introduced without proof on Kaplan's website, can be derived as follows. Let $S_j \equiv \sum_{k=1}^{j} X_k$, $\tilde{S}_j \equiv S_j/N$, and $\tilde{j} \equiv 1 - (j-1)/N$. Define

$$Y_n \equiv \int_0^1 \prod_{j=1}^{n} \left(\gamma \left[X_j \frac{\tilde{j}}{t - \tilde{S}_{j-1}} - 1 \right] + 1 \right) d\gamma.$$

This is a polynomial in γ of degree at most n, with constant term 1. Each X_j appears linearly. Under the null hypothesis that the population total is Nt, $\mathbb{E}X_1 = t$, and

$$\mathbb{E}(X_j \mid X_1, \ldots, X_{j-1}) = \frac{Nt - S_{j-1}}{N - j + 1} = \frac{t - \tilde{S}_{j-1}}{\tilde{j}}.$$

Now

$$Y_1 = \int_0^1 (\gamma[X_1/t - 1] + 1)\, d\gamma = \left[(\gamma^2/2)[X_1/t - 1] + \gamma \right]_{\gamma=0}^{1} = [X_1/t - 1]/2 + 1 = \frac{X_1}{2t} + 1/2.$$

Thus, under the null,

$$\mathbb{E}Y_1 = \frac{\mathbb{E}X_1}{2t} + 1/2 = 1.$$

Also,

$$\mathbb{E}(Y_n \mid X_1, \ldots, X_{n-1}) = \mathbb{E}\left[\int_0^1 \prod_{j=1}^{n} \left(\gamma \left[X_j \frac{\tilde{j}}{t - \tilde{S}_{j-1}} - 1 \right] + 1 \right) d\gamma \,\middle|\, X_1, \ldots, X_{n-1} \right]$$

$$= \int_0^1 \left(\gamma \left[\mathbb{E}(X_n \mid X_1, \ldots, X_{n-1}) \frac{\tilde{n}}{t - \tilde{S}_{n-1}} - 1 \right] + 1 \right) \prod_{j=1}^{n-1} \left(\gamma \left[X_j \frac{\tilde{j}}{t - \tilde{S}_{j-1}} - 1 \right] + 1 \right) d\gamma$$

$$= \int_0^1 \left(\gamma \left[\frac{t - \tilde{S}_{n-1}}{\tilde{n}} \frac{\tilde{n}}{t - \tilde{S}_{n-1}} - 1 \right] + 1 \right) \prod_{j=1}^{n-1} \left(\gamma \left[X_j \frac{\tilde{j}}{t - \tilde{S}_{j-1}} - 1 \right] + 1 \right) d\gamma$$

$$= \int_0^1 \prod_{j=1}^{n-1} \left(\gamma \left[X_j \frac{\tilde{j}}{t - \tilde{S}_{j-1}} - 1 \right] + 1 \right) d\gamma = Y_{n-1}.$$

Hence, under the null hypothesis, $(Y_j)_{j=1}^{N}$ is a nonnegative closed martingale with expected value 1, and Kolmogorov's inequality implies that for any $J \in \{1, \ldots, N\}$,

$$\Pr\left(\max_{1\leq j\leq J} Y_j(t) > 1/p\right) \leq p.$$

This method for finding a P-value for the hypothesis $\bar{A}^b \leq 1/2$ is also implemented in the SHANGRLA software, using a novel approach to integrating the polynomial recursively due to Steven N. Evans (U.C. Berkeley). This was the risk-measuring function used in the San Francisco IRV process pilot audit in November, 2019.

3.2 Ballot-Comparison Audits

Ballot-comparison audits require the voting system to export a *cast vote record* (CVR) for each physical ballot—the system's interpretation of that ballot—in such a way that the corresponding physical ballot can be retrieved, and vice versa.[8] Suppose that we apply the assorters for a contest to the CVRs (rather than the actual physical ballots), and every assorter has an average greater than $1/2$, i.e., the assertions are true for the CVRs. Then the assertions are true for the physical ballots provided the CVRs did not inflate the average value of the assorter by more than the *assorter margin*, twice the mean of the assorter applied to the reported CVRs, minus 1, as we shall see.

By how much could error in an individual CVR inflate the value of the assorter compared to the value the assorter has for the actual ballot? Since the assorter does not assign a negative value to any ballot, the *overstatement error* ω_i for CVR i is at most the value the assorter assigned to CVR i.

The existence of an upper bound for the overstatement error is key to auditing: otherwise, a single extreme value could make a contest result wrong, and it would take a prohibitively large sample to rule out that possibility.

If we can reject the hypothesis that the mean overstatement error for an assorter is large enough to account for the assorter margin, we may conclude that the assertion that the assorter mean exceeds $1/2$ is true, and the audit of that assertion can stop.

Let b_i denote the ith ballot, and let c_i denote the cast-vote record for the ith ballot. Let A denote an assorter, which maps votes on a ballot card or on a CVR into $[0, u]$, where u is an upper bound on the value A assigns to any ballot card or CVR. For instance, for plurality voting, $u = 1$; for super-majority, $u = 1/(2f)$, where f is the fraction of valid votes required to win.

The *overstatement error* for the ith ballot is

$$\omega_i \equiv A(c_i) - A(b_i) \leq A(c_i) \leq u. \tag{2}$$

It is the amount by which the assorter applied to the cast vote record overstates the value of the assorter applied to corresponding physical ballot.

Let

$$\bar{A}^c \equiv \frac{1}{N}\sum_{i=1}^{N} A(c_j) \text{ and } \bar{\omega} \equiv \frac{1}{N}\sum_{i=1}^{N} \omega_j.$$

---

[8] However, see section Sect. 3.4 below.

Now $\bar{A}^b = \bar{A}^c - \bar{\omega}$, so $\bar{A}^b > 1/2$ iff $\bar{\omega} < \bar{A}^c - 1/2$. We know that $\bar{A}^c > 1/2$ (or the assertion would not be true for the CVRs), so $\bar{\omega} < \bar{A}^c - 1/2$ iff

$$\frac{\bar{\omega}}{2\bar{A}^c - 1} < 1/2.$$

Define $v \equiv 2\bar{A}^c - 1$, the *reported assorter margin*. In a two-candidate plurality contest, v is the fraction of ballot cards with valid votes for the reported winner, minus the fraction with valid votes for the reported loser. This is the *diluted margin* of [12,22]. (Margins are traditionally calculated as the difference in votes divided by the number of valid votes. *Diluted* refers to the fact that the denominator is the number of ballot cards, which is greater than or equal to the number of valid votes.)

With this notation, the condition for the assertion to be true is:

$$\frac{\bar{\omega}}{v} < 1/2.$$

Let $\tau_i \equiv 1 - \omega_i/u \geq 0$, and $\bar{\tau} \equiv (1/N)\sum_{i=1}^{N} \tau_i = 1 - \bar{\omega}/u$. Then $\bar{\omega} = u(1 - \bar{\tau})$ and

$$\frac{\bar{\omega}}{v} = \frac{u}{v}(1 - \bar{\tau}).$$

Now $\omega/v < 1/2$ iff $\frac{u}{v}(1 - \bar{\tau}) < 1/2$, i.e.,

$$-\frac{u}{v}\bar{\tau} < 1/2 - \frac{u}{v}$$

$$\bar{\tau} > 1 - \frac{v}{2u}$$

$$\frac{\bar{\tau}}{2 - \frac{v}{u}} > 1/2.$$

Finally, define

$$B(b_i, c) \equiv \tau_i/(2 - v/u) = \frac{1 - \omega_i/u}{2 - v/u} > 0, \quad i = 1, \ldots, N.$$

Then B assigns nonnegative numbers to ballots, and the outcome is correct iff

$$\bar{B} \equiv \frac{1}{N}\sum_{i=1}^{N} B_i > 1/2.$$

It is an assorter! Any technique that can be used with ballot polling, including those in Sect. 3.1, can also be used to test the assertion $\bar{B} > 1/2$.

This assertion-based approach to comparison audits is sharper than methods that rely on the maximum across-contest relative overstatement of margins (MACRO) [22] in at least two ways: avoiding combining overstatements across candidates or contests gives a sharper upper bound on the total error in each (winner, loser) sub-contest, and the test statistic avoids combining overstatements across contests, which otherwise can lead to unnecessary escalation of the audit if an overstatement is observed in a contest with a wide margin.

3.3   Stratified Audits

Stratified sampling can be useful within a jurisdiction if the jurisdiction has a heterogenous mix of election equipment with different capability, e.g., ballot-polling for precinct-based optical scan, where it can be difficult to associate ballot cards with cast-vote records, and ballot-level comparisons for central-count optical scan. Stratification can also be useful auditing contests that cross jurisdictional boundaries by allowing those jurisdictions to sample independently from each other.

Stratified sampling for RLAs has been addressed in a number of papers, including [9, 16, 18–20]. The central idea of the approach taken in SUITE [16] can be used with SHANGRLA to accommodate stratified sampling and to combine ballot-polling and ballot-level comparison audits: Look at all allocations of error across strata that would result in an incorrect outcome. Reject the hypothesis that the outcome is incorrect if the maximum P-value across all such allocations is less than the risk limit.

SHANGRLA will generally yield a sharper (i.e., more efficient) test than SUITE, because it deals more efficiently with ballot cards that do not contain the contest in question, because it avoids combining overstatements across candidate pairs and across contests, and because it accommodates sampling without replacement more efficiently.

With SHANGRLA, whatever the sampling scheme used to select ballots or groups of ballots, the underlying statistical question is the same: is the average value of each assorter applied to all the ballot cards greater than $1/2$?

Suppose the cast ballot cards are partitioned into $S \geq 2$ *strata*, where stratum s contains N_s ballot cards, so $N = \sum_{s=1}^{S} N_s$. Let $\bar{A}_s^b$ denote the mean of the assorter applied to just the ballot cards in stratum s. Then

$$\bar{A}^b = \frac{1}{N} \sum_{s=1}^{S} N_s \bar{A}_s^b = \sum_{s=1}^{S} \bar{A}_s^b \frac{N_s}{N}.$$

We can reject the hypothesis $\bar{A}^b \leq 1/2$ if we can reject the hypothesis

$$\bigcap_{s \in S} \left\{ \bar{A}_s^b \frac{N_s}{N} \leq \beta_s \right\}$$

for all $(\beta_s)_{s=1}^{S}$ such that $\sum_{s=1}^{S} \beta_s \leq 1/2$. Let $P_s(\beta_s)$ be a P-value for the hypothesis $\bar{A}_s^b \leq \frac{N}{N_s} \beta_s$. That P-value could result from ballot polling, ballot-level comparison, batch-level comparison, or any other valid method. For instance, it could be produced by the methods described in Sect. 3.1 or Sect. 3.2.

Suppose that the samples from different strata are independent, so that $\{P_s(\beta_s)\}_{s=1}^{S}$ are independent random variables. Then Fisher's combining function (or any other method for nonparametric combination of tests) can be used to construct an overall P-value for the intersection null hypothesis $\bigcap_{s \in S} \left\{ \frac{N_s}{N} \bar{A}_s^b \leq \beta_s \right\}$. In particular, if the intersection hypothesis is true, then the probability distribution of

$$-2 \sum_{s=1}^{S} \ln P_s(\beta_s)$$

is dominated by the chi-square distribution with $2S$ degrees of freedom, as discussed in [16]. That makes it possible to assign a conservative P-value to the hypothesis $\bigcap_{s \in S} \left\{ \frac{N_s}{N} \bar{A}_s^b \leq \beta_s \right\}$ for every $(\beta_s)_{s=1}^{S}$ such that $\sum_{s=1}^{S} \beta_s \leq 1/2$. If all such S-tuples can be rejected, we may conclude that $\bar{A}_b > 1/2$.

3.4 Zombie Bounds II: Return of the Missing Ballot

[3] discuss how to conduct RLAs when not every ballot is accounted for or when a ballot cannot be retrieved. They cover both ballot-polling audits and ballot-level comparison audits. This section presents a brief but more systematic treatment for ballot-level comparison audits, reflecting what the SHANGRLA software implements. This method also makes it possible to use ballot-card style information to target the sampling to ballot cards that the voting system claims contain the contest, while protecting against the possibility that the voting system does not report that information accurately.

To conduct a RLA, it is crucial to have an upper bound on the total number of ballot cards cast in the contest. Absent such a bound, arbitrarily many ballots could be missing from the tabulation, and the true winner(s) could be any candidate(s). Let N denote an upper bound on the number of ballot cards that contain the contest. Suppose that $n \leq N$ CVRs contain the contest and that each of those CVRs is associated with a unique, identifiable physical ballot card that can be retrieved if that CVR is selected for audit. The phantoms-to-evil zombies approach is as follows.

If $N > n$, create $N-n$ "phantom ballots" and $N-n$ "phantom CVRs." Calculate the assorter mean for all the CVRs—including the phantoms—treating the phantom CVRs as if they contain no valid vote in the contest (i.e., the assorter assigns the value $1/2$ to phantom CVRs). Find the corresponding assorter margin (twice the assorter mean, minus 1).

To conduct the audit, sample integers between 1 and N.

– If the resulting integer is between 1 and n, retrieve and inspect the ballot card associated with the corresponding CVR.
  - If the associated ballot contains the contest, calculate the overstatement error as in Eq. 2.
  - If the associated ballot does not contain the contest, calculate the overstatement error using the value the assorter assigned to the CVR, but as if the value the assorter assigns to the physical ballot is zero (that is, the overstatement error is equal to the value the assorter assigned to the CVR).

– If the resulting integer is between $n + 1$ and N, we have drawn a phantom CVR and a phantom ballot. Calculate the overstatement error as if the value the assorter assigned to the phantom ballot was 0 (turning the phantom into an "evil zombie"), and as if the value the assorter assigned to the CVR was 1/2.

Proposition: if the risk is calculated based on this substitution of "evil zombies" for "phantoms," the result is still a RLA with risk limit α.

Proof: Every unaccounted for ballot card that might have or should have contained the contest is treated in the least favorable way. Every unaccounted for CVR is treated in exactly the way it was tabulated by the assorter, namely, it is assigned the value 1/2.

Some jurisdictions, notably Colorado, redact CVRs if revealing them might compromise vote anonymity. If such CVRs are omitted from the tally and the number of phantom CVRs and ballots are increased correspondingly, this approach still leads to a valid RLA. But if they are included in the tally, then if they are selected for audit they should be treated as if they had the value u (the largest value the assorter can assign) in calculating the overstatement error.

4   Discussion

4.1   From Many, One

Even though SHANGRLA may involve testing many assertions in the audit of one or more contests, there is no need to adjust for *multiplicity*. If any assertion is false, the chance that its complementary hypothesis will be rejected is at most α. If more than one assertion is false, the chance that all the complementary hypotheses will be rejected is at most α, because the probability of the intersection of a collection of events cannot exceed the probability of any event in the collection. Thus, if any of the reported winners did not really win, the chance that every complementary null hypothesis will be rejected is at most α: the chance that the audit will stop without a full hand count is not greater than the risk limit.

4.2   Sharpness and Efficiency

Extant comparison audit methods rely on MACRO, the maximum across-contest relative overstatement of margins [19]. MACRO is embedded in Colorado's CORLA audit tool, in the Arlo audit tool, and https://www.stat.berkeley.edu/~stark/Vote/auditTools.htm. MACRO involves combining discrepancies across pairs of candidates and across contests in a way that is conservative, but not sharp. That is, the condition that is tested is *necessary* for one or more reported outcomes to be incorrect, but not *sufficient*. In contrast, by keeping the pairwise margins separate, SHANGRLA is sharp for plurality, super-majority, approval,

Borda, STAR-Voting, D'Hondt, etc.—but in general not for RCV/IRV. The conditions it tests are both necessary and sufficient for one or more outcomes to be incorrect. This generally allows smaller sample sizes to confirm the results when the reported contest outcomes are correct.

4.3   The Power of Positivity

Working with assertions reduces election auditing to testing hypotheses of the form $\bar{A}^b < 1/2$: the only statistical issue is to test whether the mean of a finite list of nonnegative numbers is less than $1/2$. As new techniques for testing that hypothesis are developed, they can be applied immediately to election audits.

4.4   To Halve or Halve Not?

Assertions might look more elegant expressed as $\bar{A}^b > 1$ rather than $\bar{A}^b > 1/2$, which would just involve re-defining A by multiplying it by 2. However, keeping the connection between assorter means and getting more than 50% of the vote in a two-candidate majority contest seems to be a helpful mnemonic. It also might feel more natural to write an assertion as or $\bar{A}^b > 0$, but that would cut the connection to getting more than a 50% vote share and make the lower bound less natural than the nonnegativity constraint $A(b_i) \geq 0$ for all i.

Similarly, defining the "assorter margin" to be $v \equiv 2(\bar{A}^c - 1/2)$ rather than $\bar{A}^c - 1/2$ keeps the parallel to a two-candidate plurality contest, where the "margin" would generally be defined to be the winner's vote share minus the loser's vote share.

5   Conclusions

Risk-limiting audits of a broad variety of social choice functions can be reduced to testing whether the mean of any list among a set of finite lists of nonnegative numbers is less than or equal to $1/2$. That is, Sets of Half-Average Nulls Generate Risk-Limiting Audits (SHANGRLA). Those hypotheses can be tested directly, e.g., by ballot polling, or indirectly, by ballot-level comparisons or other methods. They can also be tested using Bernoulli sampling [15], stratified sampling, and "hybrid" methods following the same general approach as SUITE [16] (see 3.3), but SHANGRLA is generally more efficient. The sampling unit can be an individual ballot, or a cluster of ballots (e.g., all ballots cast in a single precinct or tabulated by a particular machine). Samples can be drawn with or without replacement.

Ballot-level comparison audits can also be framed as testing whether any of the means of a set of finite lists of nonnegative numbers is less than or equal to $1/2$, allowing exactly the same statistical tests to be used for ballot-polling audits and for ballot-level comparison audits, unifying the treatment of audits.

This paper proves the validity of two hypothesis tests for that statistical problem based on sampling without replacement, both of which were stated without proof in a now-defunct website of Harold Kaplan but apparently never published. Both proofs are based on Kolmogorov's inequality for optionally stopped martingales.

Even though auditing one or more contests generally involves testing many half-average nulls, no multiplicity adjustment is needed, because the audit only stops if all the nulls are rejected.

For many social choice functions (including plurality, multi-winner plurality, majority, super-majority, approval, D'Hondt, Borda count, and STAR-Voting), SHANGRLA comparison audits are sharper than previous comparison audit methods based on MACRO because the conditions it tests are both necessary and sufficient for the reported outcomes to be wrong, while previous methods tested conditions that were necessary but not sufficient. (MACRO bounds the maximum of a set of sums by the sum of the term-by-term maxima, both in the condition and in the test statistic; SHANGRLA keeps the maxima separate, both in the condition and in the test statistic.)

SHANGRLA also "plays nice" with the phantoms-to-zombies approach [3] for dealing with missing ballot cards and missing cast-vote records, which has two benefits: (i) it makes it easy to treat missing ballots rigorously, and (ii) it can substantially improve the efficiency of auditing contests that do not appear on every ballot card, by allowing the sample to be drawn just from cards that the voting system claims contain the contest, without having to trust that the voting system correctly identified which cards contain the contest.

Open-source software implementing SHANGRLA comparison audits and the phantoms-to-zombies approach is available; the software was tested in a process pilot audit of an IRV contest in San Francisco, CA, in November 2019.

Acknowledgments. I am grateful to Andrew Conway, Steven N. Evans, Kellie Ottoboni, Ronald L. Rivest, Vanessa Teague, Poorvi Vora, and Damjan Vukcevic for helpful conversations and comments on earlier drafts, and to Filip Zagorski for presenting the paper at the 5th Workshop on Advances in Secure Electronic Voting. The SHANGRLA software was a collaborative effort that included Michelle Blom, Andrew Conway, Dan King, Laurent Sandrolini, Peter Stuckey, and Vanessa Teague.

References

1. American Statistical Association: American Statistical Association statement on risk-limiting post-election audits. www.amstat.org/outreach/pdfs/Risk-Limiting_Endorsement.pdf (2010)
2. Appel, A., deMillo, R., Stark, P.B.: Ballot-marking devices cannot assure the will of the voters. Election Law J. (2020, in press)
3. Bañuelos, J., Stark, P.: Limiting risk by turning manifest phantoms into evil zombies. Technical report (2012). arXiv.org. http://arxiv.org/abs/1207.3413. Accessed 17 July 2012

4. Benaloh, J., Jones, D., Lazarus, E., Lindeman, M., Stark, P.: SOBA: secrecy-preserving observable ballot-level audits. In: Proceedings of the 2011 Electronic Voting Technology Workshop/Workshop on Trustworthy Elections (EVT/WOTE 2011), USENIX (2011). http://statistics.berkeley.edu/~stark/Preprints/soba11.pdf

5. Bernhard, M., et al.: Public evidence from secret ballots. In: Krimmer, R., Volkamer, M., Braun Binder, N., Kersting, N., Pereira, O., Schürmann, C. (eds.) E-Vote-ID 2017. LNCS, vol. 10615, pp. 84–109. Springer, Cham (2017). https://doi.org/10.1007/978-3-319-68687-5_6

6. Bernhard, M., et al.: Can voters detect malicious manipulation of ballot marking devices? In: 41st IEEE Symposium on Security and Privacy. IEEE (2020, in press)

7. Blom, M., Stuckey, P.J., Teague, V.: Risk-limiting audits for IRV elections. arXiv preprint arXiv:1903.08804 (2019). https://arxiv.org/abs/1903.08804

8. Feller, W.: An Introduction to Probability Theory and Its Applications, vol. II. Wiley, New York (1971)

9. Higgins, M., Rivest, R., Stark, P.: Sharper p-values for stratified post-election audits. Stat. Politics Policy 2(1) (2011). http://www.bepress.com/spp/vol2/iss1/7

10. Kaczmarek, T., et al.: Dispute resolution in accessible voting systems: the design and use of audiotegrity. In: Heather, J., Schneider, S., Teague, V. (eds.) Vote-ID 2013. LNCS, vol. 7985, pp. 127–141. Springer, Heidelberg (2013). https://doi.org/10.1007/978-3-642-39185-9_8

11. Lindeman, M., McBurnett, N., Ottoboni, K., Stark, P.: Next steps for the Colorado risk-limiting audit (CORLA) program. https://arxiv.org/abs/1803.00698 (2018)

12. Lindeman, M., Stark, P.: A gentle introduction to risk-limiting audits. IEEE Secur. Priv. 10, 42–49 (2012)

13. Lindeman, M., Stark, P., Yates, V.: BRAVO: Ballot-polling risk-limiting audits to verify outcomes. In: Proceedings of the 2011 Electronic Voting Technology Workshop/Workshop on Trustworthy Elections (EVT/WOTE 2011), USENIX (2012)

14. National Academies of Sciences, Engineering, and Medicine: Securing the Vote: Protecting American Democracy. The National Academies Press, Washington, September 2018. https://doi.org/10.17226/25120

15. Ottoboni, K., Bernhard, M., Halderman, J.A., Rivest, R.L., Stark, P.B.: Bernoulli ballot polling: a manifest improvement for risk-limiting audits. In: Bracciali, A., Clark, J., Pintore, F., Rønne, P., Sala, M. (eds.) Financial Cryptography and Data Security, FC 2019. LNCS, vol. 11599. Springer, Cham (2020). https://doi.org/10.1007/978-3-030-43725-1_16

16. Ottoboni, K., Stark, P.B., Lindeman, M., McBurnett, N.: Risk-limiting audits by stratified union-intersection tests of elections (SUITE). In: Krimmer, R., Volkamer, M., Cortier, V., Goré, R., Hapsara, M., Serdült, U., Duenas-Cid, D. (eds.) E-Vote-ID 2018. LNCS, vol. 11143, pp. 174–188. Springer, Cham (2018). https://doi.org/10.1007/978-3-030-00419-4_12

17. Presidential Commission on Election Administration: The American Voting Experience: Report and Recommendations of the Presidential Commission on Election Administration (2014). https://www.eac.gov/assets/1/6/Amer-Voting-Exper-final-draft-01-09-14-508.pdf

18. Stark, P.: Conservative statistical post-election audits. Ann. Appl. Stat. 2, 550–581 (2008). http://arxiv.org/abs/0807.4005

19. Stark, P.: A sharper discrepancy measure for post-election audits. Ann. Appl. Stat. 2, 982–985 (2008). http://arxiv.org/abs/0811.1697

20. Stark, P.: CAST: canvass audits by sampling and testing. IEEE Trans. Inform. Forensics Secur. Spec. Issue Electron. Voting **4**, 708–717 (2009)
21. Stark, P.: Risk-limiting post-election audits: P-values from common probability inequalities. IEEE Trans. Inf. Forensics Secur. **4**, 1005–1014 (2009)
22. Stark, P.: Super-simple simultaneous single-ballot risk-limiting audits. In: Proceedings of the 2010 Electronic Voting Technology Workshop/Workshop on Trustworthy Elections (EVT/WOTE 2010), USENIX (2010). http://www.usenix.org/events/evtwote10/tech/full_papers/Stark.pdf
23. Stark, P.: An introduction to risk-limiting audits and evidence-based elections, written testimony prepared for the Little Hoover Commission (2018). https://www.stat.berkeley.edu/~stark/Preprints/lhc18.pdf
24. Stark, P.B., Teague, V.: Verifiable European elections: risk-limiting audits for D'Hondt and its relatives. JETS: USENIX J. Election Technol. Syst. **3**(1) (2014). https://www.usenix.org/jets/issues/0301/stark
25. Stark, P.B., Wagner, D.A.: Evidence-based elections. IEEE Secur. Priv. **10**, 33–41 (2012)

A Note on Risk-Limiting Bayesian Polling Audits for Two-Candidate Elections

Sarah Morin[1], Grant McClearn[1], Neal McBurnett[1], Poorvi L. Vora[1(✉)], and Filip Zagórski[2]

[1] Department of Computer Science, The George Washington University, Washington, DC, USA
poorvi@gwu.edu
[2] Department of Computer Science, Wroclaw University of Science and Technology, Wroclaw, Poland

Abstract. This short paper provides a general form for a polling audit that is both Bayesian and risk-limiting: the *Bayesian Risk-Limiting (Polling) Audit*, which enables the use of a Bayesian approach to explore more efficient Risk-Limiting Audits. A numerical example illustrates the implications to practice.

Keywords: Election audits · Election security · Risk-limiting audits · Bayesian audits

1 Introduction

The framework of *risk-limiting audits (RLAs)*, as described by Lindeman and Stark [1], formalizes a rigorous approach to election verification. The purpose of an audit is to require a full hand count if the outcome is wrong; the *risk* is the rate at which it fails to do so, and depends on the (unknown) underlying true election tally. An *RLA* is an audit that guarantees that the worst-case risk—the largest value of the risk over all possible true election tallies—is smaller than a pre-specified bound.

The Bayesian audit, as described by Rivest and Shen [5], begins with an assumed prior probability distribution over the election tally. It guarantees a pre-specified upper bound on the *upset probability*, which is the weighted average of risk values, each risk value corresponding to an election tally inconsistent with the announced outcome and weighted by the corresponding prior probability. As an average of risks, the upset probability could be considerably smaller than the worst-case risk; limiting it does not, in general, limit the worst-case risk. The Bayesian framework is promising as a means of designing efficient audits

This material is based upon work supported in part by NSF Award CNS 1421373. Author was partially supported by Polish National Science Centre contract number DEC-2013/09/D/ST6/03927 and by Wroclaw University of Science and Technology [0401/0052/18].

© Springer Nature Switzerland AG 2020
M. Bernhard et al. (Eds.): FC 2020 Workshops, LNCS 12063, pp. 337–344, 2020.
https://doi.org/10.1007/978-3-030-54455-3_24

(requiring a small average sample size, we make this more precise later), and an important question is whether we can bound the worst-case (maximum) risk of a Bayesian audit given the upper bound on its upset probability.

The BRAVO audit [1] can be reduced to a comparison test as described in the classical work of Wald [7]. The CLIP audit of Rivest [4] is another RLA which may also be reduced to such a comparison, though the values are computed using simulations[1]. Before this work, it was not known if Bayesian audits could be reduced to comparison tests; they are generally computed using Pólya urn simulations.

In this short paper, while restricting ourselves to polling audits of two-candidate plurality elections with no invalid ballots, we state the following results without proof:

1. We define a class of Bayesian audits that are most efficient $RLAs$. Most efficient $RLAs$ are those that use the smallest expected number of ballots given either hypothesis: a correct election outcome or an incorrect one, if the election is drawn from the assumed prior. The expectation is computed over the randomness of the tally and the sampling process. We describe how the $BRAVO$ audit may be viewed as a special case of a generalized Bayesian RLA, based on a more general version of the Bayesian audit defined by Rivest and Shen.
2. The Bayesian audit can be reduced to a simple comparison test between the number of votes for the winner in the audit sample and two pre-computed values for this sample size (we denote this size n):
   - a minimum number of votes for the winner, $k_{min}(n)$, above which the election outcome is declared correct, and
   - a maximum number of votes for the winner, $k_{max}(n)$, below which the audit proceeds to a hand count.

We present an illustrative example of $k_{min}(n)$ values computed for various audits. Proofs of results 1 and 2 above and more illustrative examples may be found in [6].

1.1   Organization

This paper is organized as follows. Section 2 describes the model and establishes most of the notation. Section 3 describes $RLAs$ [1] and Bayesian audits [5]. Our contributions are to be found in Sect. 4, which states our theoretical results, and Sect. 5, which presents the illustrative example. Section 6 concludes.

2   The Model

We consider a plurality election with two candidates, N voters and no invalid ballots. Once the votes are cast, either the true outcome of the election is a tie, or

---

[1] Philip Stark has mentioned a CLIP-like audit which does not use simulations as work in progress.

there is a well-defined true winner. In the worst case, however, unless all votes are manually counted, the true winner is generally unknown. In the Bayesian approach, the true winner is modeled as a random variable, which we denote W. We further denote by w an instance of W, by w_a and ℓ_a the announced winner and loser respectively and by x the (true, unknown) number of votes obtained by w_a. Thus $w_a = w$ if and only if $x > \frac{N}{2}$.

A polling audit will estimate whether w_a is the true winner. Consider a sample of n votes drawn uniformly at random: $v_1, v_2, ..., v_n, n < N, v_i \in \{w_a, \ell_a\}$. The sample forms the *signal* or the *observation*; the corresponding random variable is denoted $\mathbf{S}_n \in \{w_a, \ell_a\}^n$, the specific value $\mathbf{s}_n = [v_1, v_2, ..., v_n]$. Let k_n denote the number of votes for w_a in the sample; then $n - k_n$ votes are for ℓ_a.

The audit computes a binary-valued estimate of the true winner from $\mathbf{s}_n$:

$$\hat{w}_n : \{w_a, \ell_a\}^n \to \{w_a, \ell_a\}$$

We will refer to the function $\hat{w}_n$ as the *estimator* and $\hat{w}_n(\mathbf{s}_n)$ as the *estimate*. The audit uses an error measure to compute the quality of the estimate.

- If $\hat{w}_n(\mathbf{s}_n) = w_a$ and the error measure is acceptable we are done (the audit stops) and declare that the election outcome was correctly announced.
- If $\hat{w}_n(\mathbf{s}_n) = \ell_a$ and the error measure is acceptable we stop drawing votes and proceed to perform a complete hand count.
- If the error measure is not acceptable we draw more votes to improve the estimate.

Thus, when we use the term *the audit stops*, we mean that the audit verified the election outcome. When we say the audit proceeds to a *hand count*, we mean that the tentative estimate is $\hat{w}_n(\mathbf{s}_n) = \ell_a$, we stop drawing samples and proceed to a full hand count.

In computing the audit we can make two types of errors:

1. *Miss:* A *miss* occurs when the announced outcome is incorrect, $w \neq w_a$, but the estimator misses this, $\hat{w}_n(\mathbf{s}_n) = w_a$, the error measure is small enough and the audit stops. We denote by P_M the probability of a miss—given that the announced outcome is incorrect, the probability that the audit will miss this:

$$P_M = Pr[audit\ stops\ ||\ w \neq w_a]$$

   P_M is the *risk* in risk limiting audits. If the audit is viewed as a statistical test, with the null hypothesis being $w = \ell_a$, when it stops, P_M is the Type I error.

2. *Unnecessary Hand Count:* Similarly, if $w = w_a$, but $\hat{w}_n(\mathbf{s}_n) = \ell_a$, acceptance of the estimate would lead to an unnecessary hand count. We denote the probability of an *unnecessary hand count* by P_U:

$$P_U = Pr[hand\ count\ ||\ w = w_a]$$

If the audit is viewed as a statistical test, with the null hypothesis being $w = \ell_a$, when the audit stops, P_U is the Type II error.

3   Defining the Audit

In this section, we describe two types of audits. We do not attempt to introduce any new ideas, but try to faithfully represent the existing literature.

3.1   Risk-Limiting Audits (RLAs) [1]

A *risk-limiting audit (RLA)* with *risk limit* α—as described by, for example, Lindeman and Stark [1]—is one for which the risk is smaller than α for all possible (unknown) true tallies in the election (or—equivalently for the two-candidate election—all possible values of x). For convenience when we compare audits, we refer to this audit as an α-*RLA*.

An example of an α-*RLA* for a two-candidate election with no invalid ballots and where ballots are drawn with replacement is the following, which is an instance of Wald's Sequential Probability Ratio Test (*SPRT*):

$$
\hat{w}_n = \begin{cases}
w_a & \frac{p^{kn}(1-p)^{n-kn}}{(\frac{1}{2})^n} > \frac{1-\beta}{\alpha} \\[2ex]
\ell_a & \frac{p^{kn}(1-p)^{n-kn}}{(\frac{1}{2})^n} < \frac{\beta}{1-\alpha} \qquad (1) \\[2ex]
undetermined\ (draw\ more\ samples) & else
\end{cases}
$$

We denote the above as the (α, β, p)-*SPRT RLA*. Note that a similar expression may be obtained for sampling without replacement, see, for example, [3].

Proposition:
When the only possible values of the true vote count, x, are pN when w_a wins, and $\frac{N}{2}$ otherwise, the (α, β, p) SPRT RLA has $P_M < \alpha$ and $P_U < \beta$, and is a most efficient test achieving these bounds.

Proof: This follows from Wald's argument [7].

Note that, in this case, there is no explicitly-assumed prior over the election tally; hence the term "most efficient test" here means one that requires the smallest expected number of ballots given either hypothesis: a correct election outcome or an incorrect one, if the tallies are pN when w_a wins and $\frac{N}{2}$ otherwise. The expectation is computed over the sampling process. While the test we denote the (α, β, p)-*SPRT RLA* is believed to be an *RLA*, we are not aware of this having been proven in the literature.

Lindeman and Stark recommend the use of the (α, β, p)-*SPRT RLA* with $p = s - t$ where s is the fractional vote count announced for the winner and t is a tolerance used to improve the performance of the audit when the vote tallies are not accurate, but the announced outcome is correct.

The *BRAVO* audit as described in [2] is the $(\alpha, 0, p)$-*SPRT RLA* which we denote the (α, p)-*BRAVO* audit. Note that $\beta = 0$, and p can be modified to be slightly smaller than the announced fractional vote count as described in [1].

Other *RLAs* include the CLIP audit [4] which may be expressed as a simple comparison test between the number of votes for the winner and a pre-computed value that depends on sample size.

3.2 Bayesian Audits [5]

Bayesian audits, defined by Rivest and Shen [5], assume knowledge of a *prior* probability distribution on x; we denote this distribution by f_X. Given the sample $\mathbf{s}_n$, W inherits a *posterior* distribution, $Pr[W \mid \mathbf{S}_n = \mathbf{s}_n]$, also known as the *a posteriori* probability of W. The Bayesian audit estimates the winning candidate that maximizes this probability (that is, the candidate for whom this value is largest), with the constraint that the probability of estimation error is smaller than γ, a pre-determined quantity, $0 < \gamma < \frac{1}{2}$. The election outcome is correct if the estimated winning candidate is w_a and the error smaller than γ. In this case, the estimation error is also termed the *upset probability*.

The *(computational) Bayesian Audit* assumes the audit draws votes without replacement and uses knowledge of f_X to simulate the distribution on the unexamined votes, conditional on $\mathbf{s}_n$, using Pólya urns. The estimated candidate is the one with the largest number of wins in the simulations, provided the fraction of wins is greater than $1 - \gamma$.

We study the general Bayesian audit and do not restrict ourselves to Pólya urn simulations or drawing samples without replacement. We will refer to the general Bayesian audit as the (γ, f_X)-Bayesian audit and specify whether ballots are drawn with or without replacement. Additionally, we assume that $Pr[w = w_a] = Pr[w = \ell_a]$ and denote the probability of error by γ.

4 Our Main Results

In this section we state our main results without proofs. For proofs, see [6].

4.1 Is BRAVO a Bayesian Audit?

Corollary 1. *The (γ, γ, p)-SPRT RLA with/without replacement is the (γ, f_X)-Bayesian audit with/without replacement for*

$$f_X = \frac{1}{2}\delta_{x,\frac{N}{2}} + \frac{1}{2}\delta_{x,pN}$$

Note that the (α, p)-*BRAVO* audit may not be represented as a special case of the above because the Bayesian audit as defined by Rivest and Shen requires $\alpha = \beta$. However, a more general definition of the Bayesian audit, where the probability of erring when the outcome is correct is zero and not equal to the probability of erring when the outcome is wrong, would correspond to the *BRAVO* audit for f_X as above.

4.2   The Bayesian Audit Is a Comparison Test

We observe (without proof here) that the decision rule for the Bayesian audit is a simple comparison test. In fact, we observe that the *SPRT RLA* and Bayesian audits may be defined in the form:

$$\hat{w}_n(\mathbf{s}_n) = \begin{cases} w_a & k_n \geq k_{min}(n) \\ \ell_a & k_n \leq k_{max}(n) \\ \text{undetermined} & else \\ \text{(draw more samples)} & \end{cases} \tag{2}$$

where $k_{min}(n)$ and $k_{max}(n)$ are determined by the specific audit. This follows from the fact that the likelihood ratio is monotone increasing with k_n for a fixed n.

4.3   Bayesian RLAs

Given a prior f_X of the vote count for election E, define the *risk-maximizing distribution corresponding to* f_X (denoted f_X^*) as follows.

$$f_X^* = \begin{cases} f_X(x) & x > \frac{N}{2} \\ \frac{1}{2} & x = \frac{N}{2} \\ 0 & else \end{cases} \tag{3}$$

Note that f_X^* is a valid distribution for the vote count of an election.

Theorem 1. *The* (α, f_X^*)-*Bayesian Audit is an* α-*RLA with* $P_U < \alpha$ *for election* E *with prior* f_X *and is a most efficient audit achieving* $P_M < \alpha$ *and* $P_U < \alpha$ *for the prior* f_X^*.

The above may be used to show that the (α, α, p)-*SPRT RLA* is an *RLA*. Additionally, a similar approach may be used to show that the (α, β, p)-*SPRT RLA* is an *RLA*. We are not aware of a proof of this in the literature on election audits. Note that, as mentioned in Sect. 1, most efficient *RLAs* are those that use the smallest expected number of ballots given either hypothesis: a correct election outcome or an incorrect one, if the election is drawn from the assumed prior. The expectation is computed over the randomness of the tally and the sampling process.

5   An Illustrative Example

We computed values of $k_{min}(n)$ for an election with $N = 100$ ballots cast, two candidates, no invalid ballots, $\alpha = 0.001$ and audit sample sizes (i.e. values of n) from 9–75.

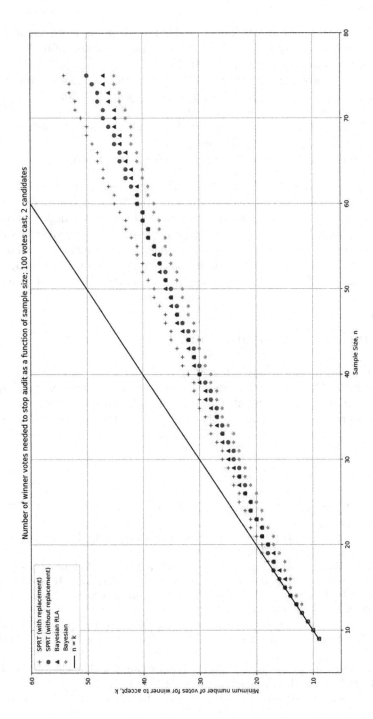

Fig. 1. Minimum number of winner votes as a function of sample size

We compared the following audits:

1. *SPRT RLA* with replacement, $p = 0.75$. That is, if the declared winner has won the election, we assume it is with a fractional vote count of 0.75.
2. *SPRT RLA* without replacement, $p = 0.75$.
3. Bayesian *RLA* corresponding to the uniform distribution. That is, the prior is uniform over all winning tallies, and the only possibility for $w \neq w_a$ is a fractional vote of 0.5 (a tie), with probability 0.5. The fractional vote of 0.75 in the *SPRT RLA* was chosen because the center of mass of the Bayesian prior when $w = w_a$ is a fractional vote of 0.75.
4. The Bayesian audit corresponding to the uniform distribution.

Figure 1 plots the values of $k_{min}(n)$ for samples sizes from 9 through 75. Note that each of (2) and (3) is the most efficient audit for its prior (when viewed as a Bayesian audit), so not much can be made of the number of samples needed. Note further that (1) is an audit with replacement and hence expected to require more samples than (2), which has the same assumed prior. Finally, note that (4) requires the fewest samples as expected because its upset probability is α, and it is not risk-limited. That is, its error bound is an average error bound, and not a worst-case one.

6   Conclusions and Future Work

We describe a risk-limiting Bayesian polling audit for two-candidate elections and describe how a Bayesian polling audit for two-candidate elections is a simple comparison test between the number of votes for the announced winner in a sample and a pre-computed value for that sample size. Open questions include the application of this model to more complex elections.

References

1. Lindeman, M., Stark, P.B.: A gentle introduction to risk-limiting audits. IEEE Secur. Priv. **10**(5), 42–49 (2012)
2. Lindeman, M., Stark, P.B., Yates, V.S.: BRAVO: ballot-polling risk-limiting audits to verify outcomes. In: EVT/WOTE (2012)
3. Ottoboni, K., Stark, P.B., Lindeman, M., McBurnett, N.: Risk-limiting audits by stratified union-intersection tests of elections (SUITE). In: Krimmer, R., et al. (eds.) E-Vote-ID 2018. LNCS, vol. 11143, pp. 174–188. Springer, Cham (2018). https://doi.org/10.1007/978-3-030-00419-4_12
4. Rivest, R.L.: ClipAudit–a simple post-election risk-limiting audit. arXiv:1701.08312
5. Rivest, R.L., Shen, E.: A Bayesian method for auditing elections. In: EVT/WOTE (2012)
6. Vora, P.L.: Risk-limiting Bayesian polling audits for two candidate elections. CoRR abs/1902.00999 (2019). http://arxiv.org/abs/1902.00999
7. Wald, A.: Sequential tests of statistical hypotheses. Ann. Math. Stat. **16**(2), 117–186 (1945)

Vote Selling Resistant Voting

Colin Boyd[1], Thomas Haines[1], and Peter B. Rønne[2(✉)]

[1] Norwegian University of Science and Technology, Trondheim, Norway
{colin.boyd,thomas.haines}@ntnu.no
[2] SnT, Université du Luxembourg, Luxembourg, Luxembourg
peter.roenne@uni.lu

Abstract. Creating a secure (purely) remote voting scheme which prevents active vote selling is an open problem. Observing that vote selling has a primarily economic motivation, we propose a novel approach to the problem which prevents a vote seller from profiting by allowing a different party to choose the seller's vote. As a proof of concept, we propose a concrete protocol which involves carefully restricting the ways the voter can prove how they voted and then penalising them for revealing it. With the assumption that the vote seller and vote buyer are mutually distrustful, we show that our protocol admits no situation where the buyer and seller can achieve a mutually agreeable selling price. We include a sample instantiation of our protocol demonstrating that it can be practically implemented including the outlay of a smart contract in Solidity.

Keywords: Vote buying resistance · Disincentives · Blockchain

1 Introduction

Coercion is a major security threat against electronic voting schemes, particularly for *remote* schemes where the voter is not isolated in a polling booth but can vote using any internet connection. A related, but in reality quite different, threat is *vote selling*. As with coercion, there is a malicious party whose goal is to influence or dictate the vote submitted by a valid voter. However, in contrast with a coercion scenario, the voter is willing to cooperate and indeed wants to vote in a way chosen by the malicious party, as long as the voter is paid (enough) for doing so. In this paper we address the vote selling threat.

A possible mechanism to mitigate the vote selling threat is to ensure that the voting scheme is *receipt free*, i.e. to ensure that voters are unable to prove to others how they voted, as suggested in the seminal paper by Benaloh and Tuinstra [4]. Denying the voter a receipt to prove how the vote was cast removes an instrument that the voter could use to negotiate or claim a payment from the buyer. However, we observe that this is not sufficient in many situations. In a remote setting the vote seller can perform the voting protocol in the presence of the buyer or can even hand over the voting credential required to vote and allow

© Springer Nature Switzerland AG 2020
M. Bernhard et al. (Eds.): FC 2020 Workshops, LNCS 12063, pp. 345–359, 2020.
https://doi.org/10.1007/978-3-030-54455-3_25

the buyer to vote on the seller's behalf. Indeed the scenario in which the voter hands over the voting credential for cash may at first seem impossible to avoid in the remote setting without some assumptions about what the voter is willing to sacrifice, or without a trusted setup phase such as is present in the JCJ scheme [11]. Further, even assuming a trusted setup-phase, a scheme like JCJ lacks good usability and intuitive individual verifiability [10] and the construction makes it harder to achieve eligibility verifiability without trust assumptions [15].

In this paper we propose a novel remote voting scheme which discourages voter selling **without** providing some form of receipt-freeness but instead by monetarily penalising the voter for revealing their vote. We believe this is interesting due to the general unavailability of useable end-to-end verifiable coercion-resistant e-voting schemes and the inherent assumption in the remote receipt-freeness definitions that the voter does not deviate from the honest vote casting protocol. We also hope to convince the reader that the problem is technically challenging from a cryptographic perspective.

We achieve vote selling resistance by having each voter deposit some amount of money which is automatically returned to them after a certain period of time has elapsed. However, anyone can claim half the money and donate the other half to a predetermined charity if they know a certain secret. This secret happens to be leaked whenever the voter proves how they voted. Strictly speaking the voter could always prove how they voted with general zero-knowledge since the question of which vote the ballot encodes is in NP, but we carefully choose the encryption scheme so that this is infeasible in practice. We note in passing that donating the money to charity is but one of a number of options. Alternatively, the money could be given to the government as a tax or transferred to a dead address effectively burning it.

The idea of using economic incentives to prevent security threats is certainly not new. Indeed, the Workshop on the Economics of Information Security[1] has been pointing out the connection between security and economics for over 15 years. Furthermore, there are a number of cryptographic protocols whose security relies on economic incentives for adversaries, see e.g. [6,8]. However, to our knowledge an economic approach to prevent vote buying has not been proposed before and seems natural given that the seller goal is to make a monetary profit.

Contribution

The overall contributions of this paper are to:

- introduce the idea of using economic incentives to mitigate the threat of vote buying;
- propose a concrete voting protocol incorporating an economic disincentive to vote selling and buying;
- demonstrate the feasibility of our approach by outlining an implementation in Solidity.

---

[1] https://econinfosec.org/.

2 Aims

The core aim is easy to state; have a secure remote scheme which prevents vote selling. However we relax this, instead desiring a secure scheme which disincentives the voters for selling their votes. Ideally, this would be possible even if the vote buyers and sellers trusted each other completely and the vote buyers were election authorities. However, it seems enormously difficult to construct such a scheme. We settle, in this paper, for a restricted setting in which the vote buyers and vote sellers are mutual distrusting and disincentivising vote selling during the election suffices.

In this section we will first define our assumptions about the parties and then talk informally about the security proprieties, we would like to achieve.

2.1 Authorities

We assume the election is run by a set of N_a authorities. As a basic requirement for any secure voting scheme, we require that *verifiability* holds even if all authorities are corrupt. This means that anyone can verify that only authorised voters took part, on the assumption that there is a valid registration process. However, as is usual in voting schemes, we assume that at least one voting authority is honest in order to maintain voter privacy and also will not collude with other authorities to steal the voters' deposits.

2.2 Voters and Vote Buyers

We assume that voters do not trust the vote buyers and are only willing to change their vote if they receive the payment with a time delay less than P_d. We, further, assume they want to be paid at least C_s.

We assume the vote buyers are interested in buying votes but are unwilling to buy them above, and including, the price point C_b. We assume they are unwilling to trust the voter and require evidence of what the vote was before releasing the payment.

We do not explicitly model the negotiation of the price P which the buyer will pay to the seller, which can happen with any protocol that the parties choose. However, we do assume that there is some P which both parties are willing to accept. This can be summarised in the following equation and, in particular note that the existence of an agreed price implies $C_b \geq C_s$.

$$P \in [C_s, C_b] \tag{1}$$

Note that the mutual distrust of the voters and vote buyers means it suffices to disincentivise vote selling during the election period. We further assume that there does not exist any escrow process which would allow the voters and vote buyers to overcome their mutual distrust. We claim the assumption of no escrow is reasonable because voting selling is illegal and hence any escrow must be privately conducted with a third party whom the voter already trusts and is willing to be engage in illegal activity. The assumption of no escrow also excludes the possibility of the voters and vote buyers creating a counter smart contract to overcome their distrust.

3   Preliminaries

In this section we will detail the building blocks and cryptographic primitives we need to build our scheme.

3.1   Smart Contract Enabled Blockchain

We use a blockchain, such as Ethereum [1], as our public bulletin board which allows us to integrate the deposit mechanism with the election. We rely on the universal verifiability of the blockchain to ensure that the steps of the election can be observed and checked by any party. The inbuilt payment mechanism available in typical blockchains, such at Ether in Ethereum, will be used to provide the economic incentives. Using similar techniques to those used in hash-locked contracts [9], voters will be required to provide a stake, or deposit, at the time of voting. The deposit will be recovered in full by honest voters a short time after the election is complete. As we will explain later in Sect. 5, voters trying to sell their votes will end up losing some or all of their deposit.

The required functionality can be achieved using a standard smart contract in Ethereum, which includes mechanisms for automatic payments and timing. The election authorities will construct the voting contract and post it to the blockchain. This will allow any party to verify its functionality.

3.2   Encryption Algorithm

Since voters will post their votes onto the blockchain, they must be encrypted first. This is not only in order to provide usual privacy of votes, but also so that the vote buyer cannot simply read the chosen vote. The encryption scheme chosen must also support certain proofs (see below for details of the proofs needed) and so a natural choice is ElGamal encryption [7] since it has the algebraic structure to support these proofs (and for that reason is often chosen for voting schemes). However, standard ElGamal encryption is not sufficient for our purposes since it allows an easy zero knowledge proof that the ciphertext takes on a certain value which could be used by the vote seller to convince the buyer that the desired choice has been made. We want instead to force the seller to release a specific value in order to convince the buyer.

Fortunately, there is a suitable solution already existing which is to use the OAEP 3-round (or simply OAEP3) transformation of Phan and Pointcheval [14]. Using similar principles to the well known OAEP transformation for trapdoor permutations (such as RSA), OAEP3 also works with ElGamal encryption. OAEP3 transformed ElGamal satisfies RCCA security [5] as proven by Phan and Pointcheval [14].

The OAEP3 transformation uses three hash function H_1, H_2, H_3. Its inputs are randomness r and the message m to be encrypted. Then the following values are computed:

$$s = m \oplus H_1(r) \quad t = r \oplus H_2(s) \quad u = s \oplus H_3(t) \quad c = (t, u).$$

To encrypt message m, we first compute the OAEP3 transform to derive c and then encrypt c using standard ElGamal.

The trick here is to observe that when the hash functions H_1, H_2, H_3 are ideal hash functions (thus using the Random Oracle Model) the OAEP3 output c, which is used as the input to the normal ElGamal encryption, is indistinguishable from a random string. This means that a normal ZK proof that the ciphertext contains a particular choice of vote cannot be used unless the randomness r is revealed so that $c = (t, u)$ can be reconstructed. We will use this observation to force a vote seller to give up the randomness r in order to convince the vote buyer.

Note that the ElGamal encryption uses its own randomness distinct from the r used in the OAEP3 transform. When we say we release the deposit to anyone who knows the randomness we mean the r value uses in OAEP3 transform not the randomness used in the ElGamal encryption.

3.3 Zero Knowledge Proofs

We need to use some standard proofs to provide verifiable evidence of correct working of the voting scheme. Although these proofs are usually applied to standard ElGamal, they can also be used with the OAEP3 transformed variant as pointed out by Pereira and Rivest [13].

NIZKP of correct encryption. We use a knowledge of discrete log zero knowledge proof to allow the voter to show they know the ballot inside their encrypted vote, these proofs should be inherently tied to the voter using signatures which will be submitted with the encrypted ballot.
Verifiable proof of shuffle. We use a zero knowledge proof of correct shuffle for ElGamal. This can be instantiated with known techniques [2,16].
NIZKP of correct decryption. We use a zero knowledge proof of correct decryption of ElGamal.

4 A Vote-Buying Resistant Scheme

We will now describe the phases of the scheme. We envision a smart contract on the bulletin board which enforces the public facing elements of the scheme. For simplicity we assume a pre-existing voter PKI though this can be removed with the expected loss of eligibility verification.

The contract is posted by the election authority to the blockchain (which may either be public or private). The contract describes the stages of voting analogous to the phases described below. In addition the contract describes what can/should occur in these stages. Essentially the contract functions as the bulletin board, while imposing certain constraints on who can do what when. Since verifiability occurs based on the data posted on the contract, the contract itself does not need to be correct for universal variability to hold. On the other hand, the eligibility verification is enforced by the contract and this component should be checked for correctness.

We have included a sketch of the contract in Appendix A.

Setup. In the setup phase the authorities jointly generate the public key pk to be used to encrypt votes [12]. The joint generation includes a shared set of decryption keys so that all authorities (possibly up to a threshold) need to cooperate to decrypt votes. The authorities also construct the contract and submit it to the blockchain. The voter credentials $\{pk_i\}_{i \in [1,n]}$ from the existing PKI are assumed to be known or can be included explicitly in the contract. The authorities also specify the deposit amount D.[2]

Submission. In the submission phase each voter may submit a ballot $\mathbf{Enc}_{pk}(m)$ by encrypting with OAEP3 and ElGamal and producing a zero knowledge proof of knowledge of the encrypted value (after OAEP3 transformation). In addition the voter creates a deposit of value D. All of these values are signed by the voter. The contract checks that the submission is well-formed by checking the proof and that the signature comes from an eligible voter who has not previously voted. If so, it accepts the ballot and marks the voter as having voted.

Claim. The claim phase runs from submission until the beginning of the proving phase. During this phase any party can submit an encrypted claim with respect to any vote. The contract will then perform a plaintext equivalence test and, if the test succeeds, the deposit is paid out half to the claimed party and half to the predetermined charity. This payout can only happen once according to the blockchain validity rules.

Note that since the messages in the ElGamal ciphertext are OAEP3 transformed, they are close to uniformly random in the message space and hence just guessing the message is infeasible. If denial of service attacks are a threat this claim process can be modified to require a small payment to submit. This payment should be small enough so that the money claimed if successful is higher than the fee.

Tallying. The authorities take turns to re-encrypt and shuffle the ciphertext using the verifiable shuffle to prove correctness. The authorities then jointly decrypt the ballots and publish the result. At this point they do not make public the proofs of correct decryption or reveal the randomness used in the OAEP3 transform.[3]

---

[2] It is possible to adjust the deposit amount during the election. The authorities may wish to do this if a significant number of successful claims are being made.

[3] It is significantly simpler if the tallying and proving phases are made into one phase. If they are separate, we either need to assume the authorities won't steal the deposits or develop someway for them to undo the OAEP3 transform using some distributed technique like MPC.

Proving. During the proving phase, which occurs at least P_d after the election closes, the authorities post the proofs of correct decryption and reveal the randomness used in the OAEP3 transform.

Verification. In the verification phase any party can check the publicly available evidence.

5 Security

In many ways the core of the scheme is a very similar to a standard e-voting scheme template based on mixnets. The small, but important, differences are designed to allow the disincentive mechanism to function. The basic voting security properties follow the standard pattern.

5.1 Verifiability

The argument for the universal verifiability of the election scheme is entirely standard. All ballots are signed by their respective voters and the bulletin board will accept only one ballot per eligible voter which ensures that the list of collected ballots is correct up to denial of service. The ballots are then verifiably mixed and verifiably decrypted which ensures they are counted as collected.

We do not specify any specific method for cast as intended verification. However, the standard methods like Benaloh challenges [3] can clearly be applied.

5.2 Privacy

The general privacy of the scheme follows for the ballot independence of the submitted ballots, the mixing of the ballots and the IND-CPA security of the encryption scheme.

5.3 Vote Buying Resistance

The scheme has vote buying resistance for the following reasons. First recall that the voter and vote buyer are mutually distrustful. In particular, both are economically incentivised, so the voter wants to maximise the price P paid while the buyer will try to minimise it. The strategy to show that our protocol provides vote buying resistance is to show that Eq. 1 cannot be satisfied, so that the buyer and seller are unable to agree on any suitable value for P.

We consider two mutually exclusive cases. Either (1) the voter produces the vote and later tries to convince the buyer of the choice of vote or (2) the buyer produces the vote with the help of the seller. For the first strategy, due to the usage of the OAEP3 transformation, the voter must reveal the OAEP3 transformed message, or equivalently the randomness r, to show how they voted. But this is precisely the information needed to claim the voter's deposit.

We need to consider two possible scenarios, which differ depending on what happens with the deposit. Note that the seller will not wait until the voting protocol finishes to reclaim the deposit because the seller knows that the buyer will try to claim it before then. However, the voter can also try to reclaim half the deposit in the **Claim** phase, so there will be a race condition between buyer and seller to try to get the deposit.

Scenario 1. The buyer pays P to the seller and the seller successfully executes a **Claim**.
   Outcome: Seller loses half deposit and gains P. Buyer pays P
Scenario 2. The buyer pays P to the seller and the buyer successfully executes a **Claim**.
   Outcome: Seller loses whole deposit and gains P. Buyer pays P but recovers half the deposit

Table 1 shows the payoff for each party in each of these scenarios.

Table 1. Payoff matrix

	Seller payoff	Buyer payoff
Scenario 1	$P - D/2 - C_s$	$C_b - P$
Scenario 2	$P - D - C_s$	$C_b - P + D/2$

Note that the vote seller and buyer will only proceed with the deal if the expected return is greater than 0, in other words their behaviour is determined only by their economic incentives. The question becomes: does there exist a price P such that both parties will have gained something?

Let $\Pr(\text{Buyer wins race}) = p$ so that $\Pr(\text{Seller wins race}) = 1 - p$. The analysis, and crucially the deposit amount, is independent of the expected success rates of the parties provided they are consistent, however, note that if both parties believe they will win the race condition all the time then no deposit amount suffices. The seller loses half the deposit in scenario 1 and all the deposit in scenario 2. Thus the seller is happy only if:

$$P - D/2 - p \cdot D/2 > C_s. \tag{2}$$

Consider then the buyer who gains half the deposit in scenario 2 and nothing in scenario 1. The buyer is happy only if:

$$P - p \cdot D/2 < C_b. \tag{3}$$

The event that the buyer and seller proceed will only occur if both inequalities (2) and (3) are satisfied. Therefore the vote selling attack occurs only if:

$$C_s + P - p \cdot D/2 < P - D/2 - p \cdot D/2 + C_b.$$

or $D < 2(C_b - C_s)$. To prevent the attack we therefore choose $D > 2(C_b - C_s)$.

Finally we consider case (2) where the buyer forms the ciphertext and the seller cooperates by signing the vote ciphertext and proofs, or the seller can even give the signing credential to the vote buyer. In this case only the buyer is able to make a successful claim. Either the buyer or seller must stake the deposit, assuming that the signing credential also allows payments on the blockchain. If the seller pays the deposit then Scenario 2 above applies since only the Buyer can make the claim. If the buyer makes the deposit then the roles are reversed and buyer will lose since the buyer will only be satisfied when $P \leq C_s$.

6   Conclusion

We have introduced a novel approach to vote buying resistance which utilises economic incentives to remove the economic motivation to buy voters rather than making it impossible to do so. We have, then, provided a reasonable instantiation of this scheme for distrusting vote buyers and sellers.

We believe that there are opportunities to optimise and refine our proposals in a number of different ways.

- A more formal analysis with formal definitions for security and a more comprehensive economic model may yield interesting insights.
- It may be possible to develop better protocols which remain secure against stronger adversaries. For example it would be good to allow the vote buyer and seller to collude rather than assuming they are mutually distrusting.
- We have assumed that values of C_s and C_b exist and are known to the implementor. This may not be reasonable in all situations. Increasing the value of the deposit allows a looser estimate of these values, but there is a limit to how large a deposit can reasonably be.
- Is it possible to construct an encryption system which allows efficient proofs of correct decryption without allowing efficient proofs of encryption to a particular message? Such a construction could be usefully applied in our protocol.
- It would be interesting to construct a variant of the scheme where each voter holds a long-term credential to authenticate their ballot, and it is this credential which is leaked to the vote buyer by a proof of the cast vote. In this case the deposit can be kept lower since the vote buyer can release the deposit in future elections, too.

Acknowledgements. PBR would like to thank Reto Koenig for discussions. The authors acknowledge support from the Luxembourg National Research Fund (FNR) and the Research Council of Norway for the joint project SURCVS.

A   Contract

For simplicity at present, we have described some functionality with comments and proofs of correct mixing are excluded from the contract. We stress that it is straightforward to extend this sketch to the full contract but we omit the fine details.

```solidity
1  pragma solidity >=0.3.0;
2
3  contract controlled { ///A contract which remembers the
       initial creator and allows functions to be restricted to
       the initial creator
4    address public electionCouncil;
5
6    function controlled() public {
7      electionCouncil = msg.sender;
8    }
9
10   modifier onlyElectionCouncil {
11     require(electionCouncil == msg.sender);
12     _;
13   }
14 }
15
16 ///This contract implements the voting scheme described
       previously
17 ///in the paper
18 contract Election is controlled {
19
20     uint256 public groupOrder
           =2188824287183927522224640574525727
21     508854836440041603434369820418657580849561 ;
22
23
24   function addEc (bytes32 point1x, bytes32 point1y, bytes32
       point2x, bytes32 point2y) private returns (bytes32,
       bytes32) {
25     bytes32 ret_1;
26     bytes32 ret_2;
27
28     assembly {
29       let size := mload(0x40)
30       mstore(size, point1x)
31       mstore(add(size, 32), point1y)
32       mstore(add(size, 64), point2x)
33       mstore(add(size, 96), point2y)
34
35       let res := call(1000, 6, 0, size, 128, size, 64)
36       ret_1 := mload(size)
37       ret_2 := mload(add(size, 32))
38     }
39
40     return (ret_1, ret_2);
41   }
```

```
42
43    function multiEc (bytes32 point1x, bytes32 point1y, bytes32
          scaler) private returns (bytes32, bytes32)  {
44      bytes32 ret_1;
45      bytes32 ret_2;
46
47      assembly {
48        let size := mload(0x40)
49        mstore(size, point1x)
50        mstore(add(size, 32), point1y)
51        mstore(add(size, 64), scaler)
52
53        let res := call(50000, 7, 0, size, 96, size, 64)
54        ret_1 := mload(size)
55        ret_2 := mload(add(size, 32))
56      }
57
58      return (ret_1, ret_2);
59    }
60
61    function negateScalaEc(bytes32 scala) private view returns
          (bytes32){
62      return bytes32(groupOrder-(uint256(scala)\%groupOrder));
63    }
64
65    function negatPointEc(bytes32 point1x, bytes32 point1y)
          private returns (bytes32,bytes32) {
66      uint256 con = groupOrder-1;
67      return multiEc(point1x, point1y, bytes32(con));
68    }
69
70    struct groupElement{
71      bytes32 x;
72      bytes32 y;
73    }
74
75    struct ElGamalCiphertext{
76    //ElGamal Ciphertext
77      bytes32 c1_x;    //g^r
78      bytes32 c1_y;
79      bytes32 c2_x;    //y^r v
80      bytes32 c2_y;
81    }
82
83    groupElement public pk;          //y = g^x
84
85    string public question;      //The question of the election
86    uint public totalVoted;
87
```

```
88     uint public maxNumVoters;
89     uint public numVoters;
90
91     uint public numTellers;
92
93     uint public deposit;
94     address public charity;
95
96     mapping(address => bool) public eligible;
97     mapping(address => bytes32[]) public vote;
98     mapping(uint => bytes32) public pkSharesStorage;
99
100    enum State { SETUP, VOTE, TALLYING, PROVING, FINISHED }
101    State public state;
102
103    modifier inState(State s) {
104      require(state == s);
105      _;
106    }
107
108    /// Create a new election
109    function Election(string elctionQuestion, bytes32[]
           pkShares, uint numberVoters, uint eldeposit, address
           elcharity) public  {
110      state = State.SETUP;
111      question = elctionQuestion;
112      deposit = eldeposit;
113      charity = elcharity;
114      require(pkShares.length %2 ==0 && pkShares.length >= 2);
115      var (temp1, temp2) = (pkShares[0], pkShares[1]);
116      pkSharesStorage[0] = pkShares[0];
117      pkSharesStorage[1] = pkShares[1];
118      for(uint i = 2; i < pkShares.length; i=i+2){
119        pkSharesStorage[i] = pkShares[i];
120        pkSharesStorage[i+1] = pkShares[i+1];
121        (temp1, temp2) = addEc(temp1, temp2, pkShares[i],
             pkShares[i+1]);
122      }
123      numTellers = pkShares.length/2;
124      pk = groupElement({x: temp1, y:temp2});
125
126      maxNumVoters = numberVoters;
127    }
128
129    function designateVoters(address[] voterRoll) public
                         onlyElectionCouncil inState(State.SETUP)
             {
130      require(maxNumVoters >= voterRoll.length + numVoters);
131      numVoters = numVoters + voterRoll.length;
132      for(uint i=0; i<voterRoll.length; i++) {
```

```
133        eligible[voterRoll[i]] = true;
134      }
135    }
136
137    function open() inState(State.SETUP) public
             onlyElectionCouncil  {
138      state = State.VOTE;
139    }
140
141    //cipher is expected to contain 4 elements and proofs is
           expected to contain n*2 (where n is the number of
           elements)
142    function Vote(bytes32[] cipher, bytes32[] proofs) public
           inState(State.VOTE)  {
143      require( //We should really change everthing else to
             require or we will take money from ineligable
             voters
144          msg.value >= deposit,
145          "In sufficent money deposited."
146        );
147
148      //Check the data is formatted as expected
149      require(cipher.length == 4);
150      require(proofs.length == 2);
151      //Prepare ciphertext
152      if(eligible[msg.sender]){ //Caller (voter) must be
             eligible and this must be there first time
153        if(Proof(cipher, proofs)){ //Check proof, and if it
               passes add the vote
154          vote[msg.sender] = cipher;
155          eligible[msg.sender] = false;
156          totalVoted++;
157        }
158      }
159    }
160
161    function Proof (ElGamalCiphertext cipher, bytes32 challenge
           , bytes32 response) private returns (bool) {
162      //We need to check the hash
163      var temp = [bytes32(hex"00"), bytes32(hex"00"),bytes32(
             hex"00")bytes32(hex"00")];
164      (temp[0], temp[1]) = multiEc(cipher.c1_x, cipher.c1_y,
             negateScalaEc(challenge));
165      (temp[2], temp[3]) = multiEc(hex"
             0000000000000000000000000000000
166      0000000000000000000000000000000001", hex"
             0000000000000000000000000000000000000000
167      0000000000000000000000002", response);
168      (temp[0], temp[1]) = addEc(temp[0], temp[1], temp[2],
             temp[3]);
169
```

```
170      bytes32 expectChallenge = keccak256(hex"
              00000000000000000000000000000
171      00000000000000000000000000000000000001", hex"
              00000000000000000000000000000000000000
172      00000000000000000000000002", cipher.c1_x, cipher.c1_y,
173      cipher.c2_x, cipher.c2_y, temp[0], temp[1], temp[2], temp
              [3]);
174      return(challenge == expectChallenge);
175   }
176
177   function close() inState(State.VOTE) public
          onlyElectionCouncil  {
178      state = State.TALLYING;
179   }
180
181   bool claimUnderway = false;
182   address targetsAddress;
183   address claimerAddress;
184
185
186   //Claim
187   function claim(address target, ElGamalCiphertext cipher)
          public returns (bool) {
188         claimUnderway = true;
189         targetsAddress = target;
190         claimerAddress = msg.sender;
191   }
192
193   function processClaim(bool correct) public
          onlyElectionCouncil returns (bool) {
194         claimUnderway = false;
195         if(correct){ //For simplicity and cost we assume the
                 PET occurs off chain
196            claimerAddress.transfer(deposit/2);
197            charity.transfer(deposit/2);
198         }
199   }
200
201   //Tally
202   function tally(bytes32[] result) inState(State.DECRYPT)
          public onlyElectionCouncil returns (bool)  {
203      state = State.PROVING; //Since the results are never used
              onchain inputting is sufficent
204   }
205
206   function prove(uint[] proofs) inState(State.PROVING)
          public onlyElectionCouncil returns (bool)  {
207      state = State.FINISHED; //Since the proofs are never used
              on chain inputting them is sufficent
208   }
209 }
```

References

1. Antonopoulos, A.M., Wood, G.: Mastering Ethereum: Building Smart Contracts and Dapps. O'Reilly Media, Newton (2018)
2. Bayer, S., Groth, J.: Efficient zero-knowledge argument for correctness of a shuffle. In: Pointcheval, D., Johansson, T. (eds.) EUROCRYPT 2012. LNCS, vol. 7237, pp. 263–280. Springer, Heidelberg (2012). https://doi.org/10.1007/978-3-642-29011-4_17
3. Benaloh, J.: Ballot casting assurance via voter-initiated poll station auditing. In: EVT. USENIX Association (2007)
4. Benaloh, J., Tuinstra, D.: Receipt-free secret-ballot elections. In: Proceedings of the Twenty-Sixth Annual ACM Symposium on Theory of Computing, pp. 544–553. ACM (1994)
5. Canetti, R., Krawczyk, H., Nielsen, J.B.: Relaxing chosen-ciphertext security. In: Boneh, D. (ed.) CRYPTO 2003. LNCS, vol. 2729, pp. 565–582. Springer, Heidelberg (2003). https://doi.org/10.1007/978-3-540-45146-4_33
6. van Dijk, M., Juels, A., Oprea, A., Rivest, R.L., Stefanov, E., Triandopoulos, N.: Hourglass schemes: how to prove that cloud files are encrypted. In: Yu, T., et al. (eds.) ACM Conference on Computer and Communications Security, CCS 2012, pp. 265–280. ACM (2012). https://doi.org/10.1145/2382196.2382227
7. Gamal, T.E.: A public key cryptosystem and a signature scheme based on discrete logarithms. IEEE Trans. Inf. Theory $31(4)$, 469–472 (1985)
8. Halpern, J.Y., Teague, V.: Rational secret sharing and multiparty computation: extended abstract. In: Babai, L. (ed.) Proceedings of the 36th Annual ACM Symposium on Theory of Computing, Chicago, IL, USA, 13–16 June 2004, pp. 623–632. ACM (2004). https://doi.org/10.1145/1007352.1007447
9. Herlihy, M.: Atomic cross-chain swaps. In: Newport, C., Keidar, I. (eds.) ACM Symposium on Principles of Distributed Computing, PODC, pp. 245–254. ACM (2018). https://dl.acm.org/citation.cfm?id=3212736
10. Iovino, V., Rial, A., Rønne, P.B., Ryan, P.Y.A.: Using selene to verify your vote in JCJ. In: Brenner, M., et al. (eds.) FC 2017. LNCS, vol. 10323, pp. 385–403. Springer, Cham (2017). https://doi.org/10.1007/978-3-319-70278-0_24
11. Juels, A., Catalano, D., Jakobsson, M.: Coercion-resistant electronic elections. In: Proceedings of the 2005 ACM Workshop on Privacy in the Electronic Society, pp. 61–70. ACM (2005)
12. Pedersen, T.P.: A threshold cryptosystem without a trusted party. In: Davies, D.W. (ed.) EUROCRYPT 1991. LNCS, vol. 547, pp. 522–526. Springer, Heidelberg (1991). https://doi.org/10.1007/3-540-46416-6_47
13. Pereira, O., Rivest, R.L.: Marked mix-nets. In: Brenner, M., et al. (eds.) FC 2017. LNCS, vol. 10323, pp. 353–369. Springer, Cham (2017). https://doi.org/10.1007/978-3-319-70278-0_22
14. Phan, D.H., Pointcheval, D.: OAEP 3-round:a generic and secure asymmetric encryption padding. In: Lee, P.J. (ed.) ASIACRYPT 2004. LNCS, vol. 3329, pp. 63–77. Springer, Heidelberg (2004). https://doi.org/10.1007/978-3-540-30539-2_5
15. Roenne, P.B.: JCJ with improved verifiability guarantees. In: The International Conference on Electronic Voting E-Vote-ID 2016 (2016)
16. Terelius, B., Wikström, D.: Proofs of restricted shuffles. In: Bernstein, D.J., Lange, T. (eds.) AFRICACRYPT 2010. LNCS, vol. 6055, pp. 100–113. Springer, Heidelberg (2010). https://doi.org/10.1007/978-3-642-12678-9_7

Short Paper: An Update on Marked Mix-Nets: An Attack, a Fix and PQ Possibilities

Thomas Haines[1], Olivier Pereira[2], and Peter B. Rønne[3(✉)]

[1] Norwegian University of Science and Technology, Trondheim, Norway
thomas.haines@ntnu.no
[2] Université catholique de Louvain, Louvain, Belgium
olivier.pereira@uclouvain.be
[3] Université du Luxembourg, Luxembourg, Luxembourg
peter.roenne@uni.lu

Abstract. Marked mix-nets were introduced by Pereira and Rivest as a mechanism to allow very efficient mixing that ensures privacy but at the cost of not guaranteeing integrity. This is useful in a number of e-voting schemes such as STAR-Vote and Selene. However, the proposed marked mix-net construction comes with no proof of security and, as we show in this paper, does not provide privacy even in the presence of a single corrupt authority. Fortunately, the attack that we present is easy to prevent and we show several possible ways to address it. Finally while the original marked mix-net paper worked with ElGamal, we identify conditions that the adopted encryption scheme should satisfy in order to be appropriate for a marked mix-net. This opens the possibility of building marked mix-nets based on intractability assumptions which are believed to hold in the presence of a quantum computer.

1 Introduction

Marked mixnets [9] are a technique proposed by Pereira and Rivest to enable faster mixing by only restricting attacks on privacy but not integrity attacks. At first it may seem strange to even consider a mix-net which only provides privacy but not integrity. However, in a variety of applications, we can (and sometimes must) independently check the output of a mix-net for correctness, and it then suffices to have privacy. This is notable the case in e-voting which schemes like STAR-vote [3] and Selene [11]. Another possible use case is to produce election results fast for public elections where tally time is often critical, and postpone the verifiability proofs until after the election result. In this case, the marked mixnet process constitute an accountable commitment to the result from each mixer server's side, and already offers some verifiable privacy guarantees (compared to a solution in which each mixer would simply shuffle ciphertexts).

The main idea of the marked mix-net is to have a sequence of mixing nodes that shuffle and reencrypt ciphertexts (as usual in any reencryption mixnet),

© Springer Nature Switzerland AG 2020
M. Bernhard et al. (Eds.): FC 2020 Workshops, LNCS 12063, pp. 360–368, 2020.
https://doi.org/10.1007/978-3-030-54455-3_26

with the twist that each mix node also a secret mark on its output ciphertexts. This mark prevents a later mix node from bypassing one or more earlier mixers by using their input ciphertexts. On top of this, voters are required to include a random value in each of their ciphertext, and to make each ciphertext somehow non-malleable, so that ciphertext copies (which could be a threat to privacy) can be identified at decryption time. This identification is expected to be a sufficient deterrent for cheating mixers (this is often called the *covert adversary* model [1]).

At present there is no rigorous security definition, and even less proof of correctness for the marked mix-net technique and, in this paper, we indeed present an attack. The essence of the attack is to exploit the homomorphic properties of ElGamal used in prime order groups to circumvent the marking mechanism, hence making it possible for the last mixer to bypass the earlier mixers and completely break privacy. We elaborate on the attack in Sect. 3.

We present two options that make it possible to prevent our attack: one is generic, and requires each mixer to add an extra dummy ciphertext as part of their mixing process. This should restore security as long as no adversary can guess which ciphertext is dummy with overwhelming probability. Our second option is to perform ElGamal encryption in a group of unknown order: it is not generic anymore, but keeps the marked mix-net protocol unchanged. We elaborate on this in Sect. 4.

Finally, whereas the original marked mix-net construction is based on a cryptosystem relying on classical hardness problems, we suggest that it would be possible to apply that construction to any publicly rerandomizable RCCA cryptosystem [5] meeting some minor additional constrains. This includes possible cryptosystems built on lattice based assumptions which are believed to hold even in the presence of large scale quantum computers. In the classical setting marked mixnets are only a small factor faster overall, though they are faster in the online phase by a factor of at least 100 compared to fully verifiable mixnets.[1] In the post-quantum setting, this efficiency gain is likely to be much higher.[2] Since we generalise a scheme with no rigorous security definition or proof of correctness, we claim only that our generalisation does not break the completeness of marked mix-nets nor does it invalidate any of the security arguments presented in the original paper.

2   Marked Mix-Net Construction

The original paper describes the scheme for the specific case of ElGamal encryption of OAEP3 transformed messages [10]. In this work we generalise this to (publicly) randomizable RCCA secure encryption schemes [5]; we make two

---

[1] This speed-up occurs because every verifiable mix requires at least one online exponentiation per ciphertext, while the marked mix-net only requires one online ciphertext multiplication per ciphertext.

[2] To our knowledge there is no published post-quantum verifiable mixnet with clear benchmarks and hence providing a concrete efficiency comparison is left as an interesting open problem.

additional requirements on the scheme but these appears to be hold for most currently known instantiations.

2.1 Primitives

Definition 1. *Rerandomisable Public Key Encryption scheme (Rand-PKE). A re-randomisable PKE is a tuple of five algorithms (Setup, KGen, Enc, Dec, Rand).*

- *Setup(1^λ) on input the security parameter λ outputs the public parameters prm.*
- *KGen(prm) on input the public parameters prm, outputs a key pair (pk, sk).*
- *Enc(pk, M) on input a public key pk and message M outputs a ciphertext C.*
- *Dec(sk, C) on input a public key pk, corresponding secret key sk, and ciphertext C, outputs a message M or error symbol $\bot$.*
- *Rand(pk, C) on input a public key pk and ciphertext C, outputs another ciphertext C'.*

Definition 2. *Rand-PKE correctness, We say a PKE scheme $\mathcal{PKE}$ is correct if*

$$\forall \lambda, prm \leftarrow Setup(1^\lambda), (pk, sk) \leftarrow KGen(prm), \forall M,$$
$$Dec(sk, Enc(pk, M)) = M.$$

We will now define the security properties for Rand-PKE. The first definition, Definition 3, is the standard definition of indistinguishability for Rand-PKE from Canetti et al.'s original paper [5]. The adversary chooses two messages based on the public key and with access to the decryption oracle $Dec^\diamond$. A ciphertext C is then created for the message M_b. The adversary must guess if b is equal to 0 or 1, it does this with the state st it gave when it created the messages, the ciphertext C and with access to the decryption oracle which will decrypt any ciphertext which does not decrypt to either M_0 or M_1.

The second definition, Definition 4, from Groth [8] captures the ability of an adversary who constructed the ciphertext to tell the difference between a re-encryption of the ciphertext or a new fresh encryption of the same message; the definition we use is weak in the sense that it does not capture an adversary that knows the private key material. Marked mixnets provide privacy under the first definition but cannot provide receipt-freeness without the second.

Definition 3 (Replayable CCA Security, [5]). *Consider the experiment in Fig. 1. We say a PKE scheme $\mathcal{PKE}$ is indistinguishable secure under replayable chosen-ciphertext attacks (RCCA-secure) if for all PPT adversaries $\mathcal{A}$:*

$$\boldsymbol{Adv}^{RCCA}_{\mathcal{A},\mathcal{PKE}}(\lambda) := \left| Pr[\boldsymbol{Exp}^{RCCA}_{\mathcal{A},\mathcal{PKE}}(\lambda) = 1] - \frac{1}{2} \right| \in \boldsymbol{negl}(\lambda).$$

$\mathbf{Exp}_{\mathcal{A},\mathcal{PKE}}^{RCCA}(\lambda)$	$Dec^{\diamond}(sk, \cdot)$
$prm \leftarrow Setup(1^{\lambda}), b \leftarrow_r \{0,1\};$	Upon input C;
$(pk, sk) \leftarrow KGen(prm);$	$M' \leftarrow Dec(sk, C);$
$(M_0, M_1, st) \leftarrow A^{Dec(sk, \cdot)}(pk);$	if $M' \in \{M_0, M_1\}$ then output $\diamond$,
$C \leftarrow Enc(pk, M_b);$	else output M'.
$b' \leftarrow A^{Dec^{\diamond}(sk, \cdot)}(st, C);$	
$return(b' = b^*).$	

Fig. 1. The RCCA security experiment

$Exp_{\mathcal{A},\mathcal{PKE}}^{Rand-wRCCA}(\lambda)$	$Dec^{\perp}(sk, \cdot)$
$prm \leftarrow Setup(1^{\lambda}), b \leftarrow_r \{0,1\};$	Upon input C;
$(pk, sk) \leftarrow KGen(prm);$	$M' \leftarrow Dec(sk, C);$
$C \leftarrow A^{Dec(sk, \cdot)}(pk);$	if $M' = M$ then output $\perp$,
$M \leftarrow Dec(sk, C);$	else output M'.
if $M = \perp$ return b;	
if $b = 0$ then $C^* \leftarrow Enc(pk, M),$	
else $C^* \leftarrow Rand(pk, C);$	
$b' \leftarrow A^{Dec^{\perp}(sk, \cdot)}(pk, C^*);$	
$return(b' = b^*).$	

Fig. 2. Weak Re-randomizable RCCA encryption

Definition 4 (Weak Rerandomisabilty [8]). *Consider the experiment in Fig. 2. Let $\mathcal{PKE}$ be a re-randomisable PKE scheme. $\mathcal{PKE}$ is rerandomizable under weak replayable chosen-ciphertext attacks (Rand-wRCCA secure) if for all PPT adversaries $\mathcal{A}$:*

$$\left| Pr[\mathbf{Exp}_{\mathcal{A},\mathcal{PKE}}^{Rand-wRCCA}(\lambda) = 1] - \frac{1}{2} \right| \in \mathbf{negl}(\lambda).$$

In addition to the standard properties of RCCA schemes, we additionally require that with knowledge of the secret key material it is possible to check if two ciphertexts are re-encryptions of the same original ciphertext (we note that this rules out anything stronger than Weak-RCCA Re-randomisabilty and hence receipt freeness in regards to the authorities is not possible to achieve if the input ciphertexts are directly linked to the voters.).

Marked mixnets, further, require that some subsection of the RCCA ciphertext space forms a homomorphic IND-CPA scheme. We note that this is almost always true since RCCA schemes are constructed from IND-CPA by adding a transform, a hash, or a signature.

Finally we assume that all the methods can be efficiently distributed among the authorities in a threshold way, which is also true of most RCCA schemes. Some examples of RCCA secure encryption schemes with Weak-RCCA are OAEP3 transformed ElGamal [10], the scheme of Faonio and Fiore [7], and the post quantum construction of [2].

We leave a formal definition of these requirements as future work.

2.2   Construction

We present the construction in a slightly simplified form; for most RCCA schemes it is possible to compute ahead of time most of **Rand** before seeing the particular ciphertext being re-randomised, this should be done in the setup phase. We refer the reader to the original paper [9] for the description in the concrete case of OAEP3 transformed ElGamal.

Setup. The authorities jointly run $Setup(1^\lambda)$ to produce the public parameters prm. They then run $KGen(prm)$ to produce the keys pk and sk. pk is published to the bulletin board.

Submission. Each sender encrypts their input M_i by running $Enc(pk, M_i)$ and receiving C_i. They then post their ciphertext to the bulletin board.

Mixing. In the mixing phase, each mixer chooses a single mark a_i—from the message space of RCCA scheme, and posts $Enc(pk, a_i)$ to the bulletin board. They then permute the list of inputs (or the output of the previous mix server), rerandomize them using $Rand$, and adds—in the case of OAEP3 transformed ElGamal multiplies—the plaintext mark to the homomorphic space.

Decryption. Once mixing is over, the authorities decrypts all the marks, which are then homomorphically removed from the ciphertexts. The authorities then check that the ciphertexts are valid and are independent.

Intuitively, it is expected that this mixing processes guarantees that all the decrypted ciphertexts have being rerandomized and shuffled by all the mixers, since the mark of every mixer appears on each ciphertext at decryption time. No correctness guarantee is offered, though: the first mixer, for instance, is perfectly free to mix whatever list of ciphertexts he likes, independently of its expected inputs.

3   Attack

For simplicity we present both the attack and the fix for the concrete RCCA scheme of OAEP3 transformed ElGamal which was suggested in the original marked mix-nets paper. We do not enter into the details of OAEP3-ElGamal encryption: for our purpose, it is sufficient to know that it is identical to the traditional ElGamal encryption algorithm, except that messages are preprocessed using the OAEP3 injective mapping before being encrypted with regular ElGamal: a ciphertext then looks like a pair $(g^r, OAEP3(m) \cdot h^r)$.

The proposed attack works by allowing any mixer, or indeed any party, to calculate the ciphertext of the mark of a previous mix using the homomorphic property of ElGamal. They are then free to use this ciphertext containing the previous mixer's mark to emulate the mixer and hence bypass these mixers without detection.

The initial input to the mix is a vector of N ciphertexts $c_1, \ldots, c_N$, containing the message $m_1, \ldots, m_N$ encrypted using randomness $r_1, \ldots, r_N$. If we multiply the ciphertexts together, we obtain $c_0^* = \prod_{i=1}^{N} c_i$, an encryption of the message $\prod_{i=1}^{N} OAEP3(m_i)$ using the randomness $\sum_{i=1}^{N} r_i$.

Consider the state after the first (presumed honest) mix, using a permutation π and whose mark was a_1, has occurred. We now have a vector of N ciphertexts $c'_1, \ldots, c'_N$, containing the message $a_1 \cdot OAEP3(m_{\pi_1}), \ldots, a_1 \cdot OAEP3(m_{\pi_N})$ using randomness $r'_1, \ldots, r'_N$. If we multiply the ciphertexts together, we obtain $c_1^* = \prod_{i=1}^{N} c'_i$, an encryption of the message $\prod_{i=1}^{N} a_1 \cdot OAEP3(m_i)$ using randomness $\sum_{i=1}^{N} r'_i$.

If we now take compute $c_{a_1^N} = c_1^*/c_0^*$ we have an encryption of the message a_1^N with randomness $\sum_{i=1}^{N} r_i - \sum_{i=1}^{N} r'_i$. Now, if the encryption is performed in a typical group of public prime order q, it is clear that $\gcd(N, q) = 1$, and it is therefore easy to compute $N^{-1} \bmod q$ (using the extended Euclidean algorithm) and to obtain an encryption of a_1 as $c_{a_1} = (c_{a_1^N})^{N^{-1}}$.

Now, c_{a_1} is precisely the rerandomization factor that an attacker would need to apply if he wants to bypass M_1. This attack continues to work for all following mixers. As a result, the last mixer M_k can de-anonymize all the ballots as follows: (1) Obtain encryptions $c_{a_1}, \ldots, c_{a_{k-1}}$ of all the marks produced by the previous mixers, as described above; (2) multiply all these ciphertexts, as well as fresh encryptions of its own mark, in order to obtain a rerandomization factor $c_a = Enc(pk, \prod_{i=1}^{k} a_i)$; (3) take all the ciphertexts that were the inputs of M_1, rerandomize them, multiply them by c_a, shuffle them, and output the resulting ciphertexts.

The resulting ciphertexts are perfectly valid and contain all the expected marks, but M_k knows the exact mapping between the ciphertexts submitted by the voters and those that will be decrypted by the trustees, since he is now the only person having actually shuffled those ciphertexts. Decryption would then break the secrecy of the votes for everyone.

4 Fixes

The attack described in the previous section relies upon the fact that product of all ciphertexts has a known relationship which allows computing an encryption of the mark. The intuition behind the fixes is to spoil this clean relationship. However, significant care must be taken not to introduce new problems while doing this.

4.1   Addition of Dummy Ciphertexts

A first possible approach is to require each mixer to add extra "decoy" cipher-texts to its output, placed in a random position, which would be an encryption of a specified plaintext (think "decoy mixer k") OAEP3-transformed, so that the ElGamal plaintext is unknown (the OAEP3 transformation is probabilistic). And adversary attempting to perform the attack described above would recover $Enc(a_1^N \cdot OAEP3(\text{"decoy mixer k"}))$, from which—due to the probabilistic nature of OAEP3—it could not recover the mark.

Once mixing is over all the ciphertexts are decrypted. It is expected that the dummy ciphertexts initially fail to open. They are then isolated and checked to ensure that after removing the marks added by latter mix servers they decrypt to the expected message. If this check fails then an investigation is launched.

This fix prevents the attack described above, because the product of the output ciphertexts now contains the extra decoy ciphertext, whose content is unknown thanks to the probabilistic nature of OAEP3. As a result, the attacker becomes unable to obtain an encryption of the marks (raised to a known power): doing so would require guessing the position at which the dummy ciphertext is added. However, the probability of guessing this position wrongly is non-negligible, actually close to one for a large number of ciphertexts to be mixed. Specifically, if n is the number of senders and d is the number of decoys the adversaries chance is $1 - \binom{n+d}{d}$.

4.2   DDH in Groups of Unknown Order

Another possibility to fix this issue is to prevent deriving an encryption of a_i from an encryption of a_i^N. This operation is easy to perform in the prime order groups that are typically used for ElGamal encryption.

The picture changes if we compute in groups of hidden order in which DDH is believed to be secure. A classical example [4,6] of such groups would be the group of quadratic residues modulo an RSA modulus $n = pq$ such that $(p-1)/2$ and $(q-1)/2$ are prime. Here, the order of the DDH group is $(p-1)(q-1)/4$, which is unknown to anyone ignoring the factors of n, and extracting N-th roots becomes a hard problem.

This solution makes it possible to use the marked-mixnet protocol without any change, but requires the generation of an RSA modulus of unknown factorisation, which may be an inconvenience, even though it can be performed using standard MPC protocols.

5   Remarks on Security

In this short paper, we refer to the original Marked Mix-net paper for further security discussions: they remain valid for our modified version of the protocol, both when generalising to RCCA Encryption systems, and when we include the fixes to the attacks.

To achieve a quantum-safe system we need to use a quantum safe RCCA encryption system which meets our additional constraints. The only quantum safe RCCA encryption scheme [2] in the literature does not appear to work. It is an interesting area of future work to modify or create a PQ RCCA encryption scheme to meet our constraints. Since the mix-net construction is simple compared to full verifiable mix-nets, especially not employing non-interactive zero-knowledge proofs, the marked mix-nets provide a good opportunity for an efficient way of quantum-safe privacy-preserving mixing, and the first fix suggested above should work with any PQ safe encryption system.

A full detailed security analysis of marked mix-nets is out of the scope of this short paper and remains an important piece of future work.

6   Conclusion and Future Work

We have shown that marked mix-nets as original presented are not secure but that there are straightforward fixes for the construction to prevent this attack. We also show that it is straightforward to generalise the construction to work with most rerandomisable CCA cryptosystems. In particular, this will also enable quantum-safe versions of marked mix-nets. It is an area of ongoing work to rigorously define and prove the security of the marked mix-nets construction.

Acknowledgements. This work was supported by the Luxembourg National Research Fund (FNR) and the Research Council of Norway for the joint project SUR-CVS, and by Belgium Fonds de la Recherche Scientifique for the joint FNR/F.R.S.-FNRS project SeVoTe.

References

1. Aumann, Y., Lindell, Y.: Security against covert adversaries: efficient protocols for realistic adversaries. In: Vadhan, S.P. (ed.) TCC 2007. LNCS, vol. 4392, pp. 137–156. Springer, Heidelberg (2007). https://doi.org/10.1007/978-3-540-70936-7_8

2. El Bansarkhani, R., Dagdelen, Ö., Buchmann, J.: Augmented learning with errors: the untapped potential of the error term. In: Böhme, R., Okamoto, T. (eds.) FC 2015. LNCS, vol. 8975, pp. 333–352. Springer, Heidelberg (2015). https://doi.org/10.1007/978-3-662-47854-7_20

3. Benaloh, J., et al.: Star-vote: a secure, transparent, auditable, and reliable voting system. In: EVT/WOTE. USENIX Association (2013)

4. Boneh, D.: The Decision Diffie-Hellman problem. In: Buhler, J.P. (ed.) ANTS 1998. LNCS, vol. 1423, pp. 48–63. Springer, Heidelberg (1998). https://doi.org/10.1007/BFb0054851

5. Canetti, R., Krawczyk, H., Nielsen, J.B.: Relaxing chosen-ciphertext security. In: Boneh, D. (ed.) CRYPTO 2003. LNCS, vol. 2729, pp. 565–582. Springer, Heidelberg (2003). https://doi.org/10.1007/978-3-540-45146-4_33

6. Damgård, I., Jurik, M.: A length-flexible threshold cryptosystem with applications. In: Safavi-Naini, R., Seberry, J. (eds.) ACISP 2003. LNCS, vol. 2727, pp. 350–364. Springer, Heidelberg (2003). https://doi.org/10.1007/3-540-45067-X_30

7. Faonio, A., Fiore, D.: Optimistic mixing, revisited. Cryptology ePrint Archive, Report 2018/864 (2018). https://eprint.iacr.org/2018/864

8. Groth, J.: Rerandomizable and replayable adaptive chosen ciphertext attack secure cryptosystems. In: Naor, M. (ed.) TCC 2004. LNCS, vol. 2951, pp. 152–170. Springer, Heidelberg (2004). https://doi.org/10.1007/978-3-540-24638-1_9

9. Pereira, O., Rivest, R.L.: Marked mix-nets. In: Brenner, M., et al. (eds.) FC 2017. LNCS, vol. 10323, pp. 353–369. Springer, Cham (2017). https://doi.org/10.1007/978-3-319-70278-0_22

10. Phan, D.H., Pointcheval, D.: OAEP 3-round: a generic and secure asymmetric encryption padding. In: Lee, P.J. (ed.) ASIACRYPT 2004. LNCS, vol. 3329, pp. 63–77. Springer, Heidelberg (2004). https://doi.org/10.1007/978-3-540-30539-2_5

11. Ryan, P.Y.A., Rønne, P.B., Iovino, V.: Selene: voting with transparent verifiability and coercion-mitigation. In: Clark, J., Meiklejohn, S., Ryan, P.Y.A., Wallach, D., Brenner, M., Rohloff, K. (eds.) FC 2016. LNCS, vol. 9604, pp. 176–192. Springer, Heidelberg (2016). https://doi.org/10.1007/978-3-662-53357-4_12

Performance of Shuffling: Taking It to the Limits

Rolf Haenni$^{(\boxtimes)}$ and Philipp Locher

Bern University of Applied Sciences, 2501 Biel, Switzerland
{rolf.haenni,philipp.locher}@bfh.ch

Abstract. In this paper, we propose further performance improvements for Wikström's shuffle proof. Compared to an implementation based on general-purpose exponentiation algorithms, we show that the overall shuffle operation can be accelerated by approximately one order of magnitude. The improvements result partly from applying special-purpose algorithms for fixed-based and product exponentiations in the right way and partly from other optimization techniques. Given that shuffling is often one of the most time-consuming tasks in cryptographic voting protocols, the achieved speed-up is significant for practical implementations of electronic voting systems.

1 Introduction

Current proposals for cryptographic voting protocols are often based on verifiable re-encryption mix-nets. At the core of this approach is a cryptographic shuffle process under encryption, which is usually used to unlink the decryption of ciphertext votes from their submission by the voters. It is therefore a method to establish vote secrecy under the assumption that the mix-net includes sufficiently many independent mix-nodes performing single shuffle steps in sequential order. In such a setting, only a coalition of all mix-nodes can break vote secrecy, i.e., a single non-colluding mix-node is sufficient for achieving the desired security.

Generating and verifying the cryptographic shuffles of a mix-net for a large number of encrypted votes is often the most time-consuming operation in a voting protocol. Performance improvements at the core of this method are therefore relevant for the overall performance of the voting protocol. As an example, consider the verification of the shuffle proofs for an input size of $N = 100\,000$ ElGamal ciphertexts and a mix-net with four mix-nodes. Verifying a single Wikström shuffle proof requires approximately $9N$ exponentiations, i.e., $36N = 3\,600\,000$ exponentiations are needed for verifying all four proofs. Assuming that computing modular exponentiations on 3072-bits integers lasts approximately 9 ms on regular hardware (according to measurements conducted in [11] using the fastest available libraries), we obtain approximately 9 h of computations as a rough overall estimate. This result shows that performance optimizations of one or more orders of magnitude are more than welcome for improving the shuffle proof performance in practical implementations.

M. Bernhard et al. (Eds.): FC 2020 Workshops, LNCS 12063, pp. 369–385, 2020.
https://doi.org/10.1007/978-3-030-54455-3_27

1.1 Related Work

There are several competing proposals for non-interactive shuffle proofs[1] in the literature. Provably secure methods by Furukawa and Sako [8], by Wikström and Terelius [18,19], and by Bayer and Groth [1] are among the most efficient ones in the *random oracle model* (ROM). Methods discovered more recently based on bilinear pairings are provably secure in the *common reference string model* (CRS) [5,10] or the *generic bilinear group model* (GBGM) [6,7]. While the performance of pairing-based methods has improved in recent years, they are still slightly less efficient than comparable ROM methods (see Table 1). Furthermore, their dependence to pairing-friendly elliptic curves may pose a restriction in voting protocols, which require the encoding of votes in groups or fields of integers. Nevertheless, reports on remarkable performance results have demonstrated their maturity and potential for practical applications [6].

Table 1. Performance comparison of shuffle proofs for ElGamal ciphertexts. N denotes the size of the shuffle and $m = N/n$ an algorithm parameter from Bayer and Groth's method for trading-off performance against proof size.

Task	Operation	[8]	[18,19]	[1]	[5]	[6]
Shuffling	Exponentiations	$2N$	$2N$	$2N$	$2N$	$2N$
Proof generation	Exponentiations	$8N$	$8N$	$2N \log m$	$16N$	$8N$
Proof verification	Exponentiations	$10N$	$9N$	$4N$	$2N$	$7N$
	Pairings	–	–	–	$18N$	$3N$
Security model		ROM	ROM	ROM	CRS	GBGM

For achieving performance results similar to [6], it is important to implement optimization techniques in a systematic manner. Special-purpose algorithms for fixed-base and product exponentiations are two of the most obvious and most rewarding techniques. Corresponding algorithms such as the *comb method* by Lim and Lee [14,15] have been available for quite some time, but they are still not available very frequently in common libraries for large number arithmetic. A systematic analysis and comparison of fixed-base and product exponentiation algorithms have been conducted in [11]. For a given use case, the presented results are useful for selecting the best algorithm and optimal algorithm parameters.

The particular use case of Wikström's shuffle proof is also briefly discussed in [11]. For the 2048-bits setting and an input size of $N = 100\,000$ ciphertexts,

---

[1] Some authors distinguish between *zero-knowledge proofs* with statistical soundness and *zero-knowledge arguments* with computational soundness. According to this definition, many existing methods for proving the correctness of a shuffle are actually shuffle arguments. This is also the case for Wikström's method, which depends on computationally binding Pedersen commitments and therefore offers computational soundness only under the discrete logarithm assumption. By calling it a shuffle proof throughout this paper, we adopt the terminology of Wikström's original publications.

a speed-up by a factor of 12.5 is reported for the proof generation. The proof verification also benefits from the optimizations, but the reported speed-up by a factor of 3.85 is much more moderate.

1.2 Contribution and Paper Overview

This paper takes the discussion of Wikström's shuffle proof from [11] as a starting point for a more detailed and systematic analysis of possible performance optimizations. In addition to the aforementioned exponentiation algorithms, we also use batch verification techniques and methods for performing membership tests in groups of quadratic residues with minimal overhead. The main goal is to further speed up the performance of the proof verification algorithm, which seems to offer the greatest potential for further improvements.

In Sect. 2, we summarize existing optimization techniques. With respect to exponentiation algorithms, we mainly refer to the recently published survey paper [11] and adopt its notation and results. We also give a summary of existing batch verification techniques and demonstrate their potential in combination with efficient group membership tests.[2] In Sect. 3, we apply these techniques in a systematic way to Wikström's shvffle proof. Our analysis, which demonstrates that regular exponentiations can be avoided almost entirely, is based on counting the number of necessary multiplications in a prime-order group, for which the decisional Diffie-Hellman (DDH) assumption is believed to hold. The results of our analysis are therefore applicable to all groups commonly used in combination with the ElGamal encryption scheme. We conclude the paper in Sect. 4 with a summary of the achieved results and outlook to future research.

2 Performance Optimization Techniques

Computing exponentiations $z = \mathsf{Exp}(b, e) = b^e$ in a given mathematical group is often the most time-consuming operation in applications of public-key cryptography. For 2048-bits or 3072-bits numbers, computing a single modular exponentiation natively on off-the-shelf hardware is a matter of a few milliseconds. Other execution environments such as JavaScript engines are up to 30 times less efficient [11]. While this is still sufficiently efficient for simple tasks such as signing or encrypting a message, it may lead to a bottleneck in more complex tasks such as shuffling a large list of encrypted votes. Computations on elliptic curves are about one order of magnitude more efficient, but they are less frequently used in voting protocols.

2.1 Product and Fixed-Base Exponentiation

The recommended general-purpose algorithm for computing $z = b^e$ for a base $b \in \mathcal{G}$ and exponent $e \in \mathbb{Z}_q$ in a multiplicative group $(\mathcal{G}, \cdot, ^{-1}, 1)$ of prime order

---

[2] The idea of applying batch verification to shuffle proofs is due to Groth [9].

q is the *sliding window method* [16, Alg.14.85]. By referring to it as HAC 14.85, we adopt the notation from [11]. It has a single parameter $1 \leq k \leq \ell$ (the *window size*), which can be maximized for a given bit length $\ell = \|e\|$ of the exponent. Table 2 shows the running time of HAC 14.85 as a function of ℓ and k and optimal values k for some typical values ℓ. Running times are measured in expected number $M_k(\ell)$ of group multiplications (thus assuming that squarings and general multiplications are equally expensive).

Table 2. Expected number of multiplications and optimal algorithm parameters for plain, product, and fixed-based exponentiation algorithms. The expressions for $M_k(\ell)$, $\widetilde{M}_m(\ell, N)$, and $\widetilde{M}_{k,m}(\ell, N)$ have been slightly simplified for improved readability.

Algorithm		Number of Multiplications	112	128	224	256	2048	3072
Plain	HAC 14.85	$M_k(\ell) = 2^{k-1} + \ell + \dfrac{\ell}{k+2}$	$k = 3$		$k = 4$		$k = 6$	$k = 7$
Product	HLG 2	$\widetilde{M}_m(\ell, N) = \dfrac{2^m + \ell}{m} + \dfrac{\ell}{N}$	$m = 5$		$m = 6$		$m = 9$	
Fixed-base	HLG 3.2 HAC 14.117	$\widetilde{M}_{k,m}(\ell, N) = \dfrac{\ell}{N}\left(\dfrac{2^m}{km} + 1\right) + \dfrac{\ell}{m} + k$	maximize over $1 \leq k \leq \ell$ and $1 \leq m \leq \frac{\ell}{k}$					

The particular task of computing the product $z = \mathsf{ProductExp}(\boldsymbol{b}, \boldsymbol{e}) = \prod_{i=1}^{N} b_i^{e_i}$ of exponentiations $z_i = b_i^{e_i}$ for $\boldsymbol{b} = (b_1, \ldots, b_N) \in \mathcal{G}^N$ and $\boldsymbol{e} = (e_1, \ldots, e_N) \in \mathbb{Z}_q^N$ can be computed much more efficiently than computing the N exponentiations individually using a general-purpose algorithm such as HAC 14.85. The most efficient *product exponentiation* (also called *simultaneous multi-exponentiation*) algorithm for small problem sizes N is the *interleaving method* from [17], but the precomputation table of size $O(2^N)$ prevents the algorithm from scaling.

For large problem instances, Algorithm 2 from [11] offers much better performance. In the remainder of this paper, we will refer to it as HLG 2. It has a single algorithm parameter $1 \leq m \leq N$, which denotes the size of the sub-tasks into which the problem is decomposed. If $M_m(\ell, N)$ denotes the total number of multiplications needed to solve a problem instance of size N and maximal exponent length $\ell = \max_{i=1}^{N} \|e_i\|$, then $\widetilde{M}_m(\ell, N) = M_m(\ell, N)/N$ denotes the *relative running time* of HLG 2. As shown in Table 2, $\widetilde{M}_m(\ell, N)$ depends on both ℓ and N, but the impact of N vanishes for large values N. Optimizing m is therefore largely independent of N. The parameters m shown in Table 2 are optimal for $N \geq 210$ (and nearly optimal for smaller values).

A second type of special-purpose exponentiation algorithms results from the problem of computing multiple exponentiations $z_i = b^{e_i}$ for a fixed base $b \in \mathcal{G}$. We denote this problem by $\boldsymbol{z} = \mathsf{FixedBaseExp}(b, \boldsymbol{e})$, where $\boldsymbol{z} = (z_1, \ldots, z_N) \in \mathcal{G}^N$ denotes the resulting exponentiations and $\boldsymbol{e} = (e_1, \ldots, e_N) \in \mathbb{Z}_q^N$ the given exponents. For solving this problem most efficiently, two *fixed-base exponentiation* algorithms exist with equivalent running times, the *comb method* by Lim and Lee [15] and Algorithm 3.2 from [11]. We refer to them as HAC 14.177 and

HLG 3.2, respectively. Both of them are parametrized by two values, for example $1 \leq k \leq \ell$ (window size) and $1 \leq m \leq \ell/k$ (sub-task size) in the case of HLG 3.2. The relative running time $\widetilde{M}_{k,m}(\ell, N)$ of HLG 3.2 is shown in Table 2. If N tends towards infinity, we get optimal parameters $k = 1$ and $m = \ell$, but otherwise the choice of k and m depends on both ℓ and N. For example, $k = 32$ and $m = 12$ are optimal for $\ell = 3072$ and $N = 1000$, i.e., $\widetilde{M}_{32,12}(3072, 1000) = 320$ group multiplications is the best possible performance in this particular case. Further exemplary performance results are depicted in Table 3, which also shows the benefits of special-purpose algorithms for product and fixed-base exponentiation. While HLG 2 performs between 5 to 9 times better than HAC 14.85 for product exponentiation, HLG 3.2/HAC 14.117 perform up to 25 times better than HAC 14.85 for fixed-base exponentiation.

Table 3. Comparison between exponentiation algorithms. For each exponent length $\ell \in \{112, 128, 224, 256, 2048, 3072\}$, the number of necessary group multiplications is shown in the left column, whereas the benefit of the optimization algorithm relative to HAC 14.85 is shown in the right column. All values are either taken or derived from [11].

	$\ell = 112$		$\ell = 128$		$\ell = 224$		$\ell = 256$		$\ell = 2048$		$\ell = 3072$		
HAC 14.85	138	1.00	157	1.00	269	1.00	306	1.00	2336	1.00	3477	1.00	
HLG 2	26	0.19	30	0.19	46	0.17	51	0.17	282	0.12	396	0.11	
HLG 3.2	22	0.16	27	0.17	43	0.16	49	0.16	313	0.13	449	0.13	$N = 100$
HAC 14.117													
	14	0.10	17	0.11	29	0.11	35	0.11	225	0.10	320	0.09	$N = 1\,000$
	11	0.08	12	0.08	22	0.08	25	0.08	176	0.08	255	0.07	$N = 10\,000$
	7	0.05	8	0.05	16	0.06	19	0.06	143	0.06	210	0.06	$N = 100\,000$
	5	0.04	6	0.04	12	0.04	15	0.05	120	0.05	176	0.05	$N = 1\,000\,000$

2.2 Batch Verification

A particular task which sometimes appears in cryptographic protocols is testing for a batch of input triples $(z_1, b_1, e_1), \ldots, (z_N, b_N, e_N)$ whether $z_i = b_i^{e_i}$ holds for all N instances. We denote this problem by $\mathsf{BatchVerif}(\boldsymbol{z}, \boldsymbol{b}, \boldsymbol{e})$, where $\boldsymbol{z} \in \mathcal{G}^N$, $\boldsymbol{b} \in \mathcal{G}^N$, and $\boldsymbol{e} \in \mathbb{Z}_q^N$ denote respective vectors of input values. The trivial solution of computing all N exponentiations $b_i^{e_i}$ individually and comparing them with the given values z_i is not the most efficient one. The *small exponent test* (SET) from [2] solves $\mathsf{BatchVerif}(\boldsymbol{z}, \boldsymbol{b}, \boldsymbol{e})$ using a single equality test

$$\mathsf{ProductExp}(\boldsymbol{z}, \boldsymbol{s}) \overset{?}{=} \mathsf{ProductExp}(\boldsymbol{b}, \boldsymbol{s'}) \tag{1}$$

between two product exponentiations of size N, where $\boldsymbol{s} = (s_1, \ldots, s_N) \in_R \mathbb{Z}_{2^s}^N$ is picked uniformly at random and $\boldsymbol{s'} = (s'_1, \ldots, s'_N)$ is derived from $\boldsymbol{s}$ and $\boldsymbol{e}$ by computing $s'_i = s_i e_i \bmod q$ over all N inputs.[3] The bit length s of the random

---

[3] Note that the algorithm given in [2] for solving $\mathsf{ProductExp}(\boldsymbol{z}, \boldsymbol{s})$ is not the most efficient one. Replacing it by HLG 2 improves the reported running times significantly.

exponents determines the failure probability 2^{-s} of the test. A failed test is one that returns true for a problem instance containing at least one $z_i \neq b_i^{e_i}$. Note that one product exponentiation deals with (short) exponents of length s and one with (long) exponents of length $\ell = \|q\|$. Therefore, the relative running time for solving $\mathsf{BatchVerif}(z, b, e)$ in this ways corresponds to

$$\widetilde{M}_{m_1, m_2}(s, \ell, N) = \widetilde{M}_{m_1}(s, N) + \widetilde{M}_{m_2}(\ell, N)$$

group multiplications per input (plus one modular multiplication in $\mathbb{Z}_q$ for computing $s_i' = s_i e_i \bmod q$). Optimal algorithm parameters m_1 and m_2 can be selected from Table 1 independently of N, for example $m_1 = 5$ and $m_2 = 9$ for solving a problem with parameters $s = 128$ and $\ell = 3072$. In this particular case, we obtain a total of $30 + 396 = 426$ multiplications in $\mathcal{G}$ (see Table 3) to perform the full batch verification. Compared to a naive implementation, this is approximately 8.5 times more efficient.

The small exponent test as described in [2] is defined for the special-case of a single fixed base b, in which the right-hand side of (1) can be replaced by a single exponentiation $\mathsf{Exp}(b, s')$ for $s' = \sum_{i=1}^{N} s_i' \bmod q$. Another special case arises in problems with a fixed exponent e, where the right-hand side of (1) becomes equivalent to $\mathsf{Exp}(\mathsf{ProductExp}(b, s), e)$. As shown in [13], these techniques can also be used in combination, for example if input values

$$z = (z_1, \ldots, z_n), \quad b = (b_1, \ldots, b_N), \quad \hat{b} = (\hat{b}, \ldots, \hat{b}), \quad \tilde{b} = (\tilde{b}_1, \ldots, \tilde{b}_N),$$
$$e = (e_1, \ldots, e_N), \quad \hat{e} = (\hat{e}_1, \ldots, \hat{e}_N), \quad \tilde{e} = (\tilde{e}, \ldots, \tilde{e}),$$

are given ($\hat{b}$ and $\tilde{e}$ are fixed) and the problem consists in testing $z_i = b_i^{e_i} \hat{b}^{\hat{e}_i} \tilde{b}_i^{\tilde{e}}$ for all $1 \leq i \leq N$. We denote this particular combination of batch verification problems, which we will encounter in Sect. 3 in exactly this form, by $\mathsf{BatchVerif}(z, b, e, \hat{b}, \hat{e}, \tilde{b}, \tilde{e})$. Solving it using the small exponent test means to perform the following equality test:

$$\mathsf{ProductExp}(z, s) \stackrel{?}{=} \mathsf{ProductExp}(b, s') \cdot \mathsf{Exp}(\hat{b}, s') \cdot \mathsf{Exp}(\mathsf{ProductExp}(\tilde{b}, s), \tilde{e}).$$

Based on the algorithms described in Sect. 2.1, the relative running time of this combined test consists of

$$\widetilde{M}_{k, m_1, m_2}(s, \ell, N) = 2\widetilde{M}_{m_1}(s, N) + \widetilde{M}_{m_2}(\ell, N) + \frac{2M_k(\ell) + 2}{N}$$

multiplications per input, which converges towards $2\widetilde{M}_{m_1}(s, N) + \widetilde{M}_{m_2}(\ell, N)$ when N increases. In the example from above with $s = 128$ and $\ell = 3072$, we get a total of $2 \cdot 30 + 396 = 456$ multiplications, which is approximately 23 times more efficient than computing $3N$ exponentiations without optimization.

Applications of the small exponent test are based on two critical preconditions [3]. First, $\mathcal{G}$ must be a prime-order group, which implies for example that the small exponent test is not applicable to the group $\mathbb{Z}_p^*$ of integers modulo p, which is of order $p-1$. Second, every z_i from z must be an element of $\mathcal{G}$. For arbitrary prime-order groups $\mathcal{G}$, group membership $z_i \in \mathcal{G}$ can be tested by $z_i^q = 1$

using one exponentiation with an exponent of maximal length $\ell = \|q\|$. But by executing this test N times for all values $z_1, \ldots, z_N$, the potential performance benefit of the small exponent test is no longer available.

2.3 Efficient Group Membership Tests for Quadratic Residues

Group membership in elliptic curves can be tested efficiently by checking if a given point satisfies the curve equation. For the subgroup $\mathbb{G}_q \subset \mathbb{Z}_p^*$ of integers modulo a safe prime $p = 2q + 1$, which is the most commonly used cryptographic setting for the ElGamal encryption scheme in voting protocols, group membership $z_i \in \mathbb{G}_q$ can be tested more efficiently using the Jacobi symbol $\left(\frac{z_i}{p}\right) \in \{-1, 0, 1\}$. For $\ell = 2048$, common $O(\ell^2)$ time algorithms for computing the Jacobi symbol run approximately twenty times faster than modular exponentiation [16]. This largely solves the above-mentioned group membership problem of the short exponent test in this particular setting.

To avoid different sorts of attacks, group membership tests are also required in many other cryptographic primitives. Performing such tests in a systematic way over *all* input values is therefore a best practice in the design and implementation of cryptographic applications. For very large inputs, even efficient Jacobi symbol algorithms may then become a target for performance optimizations.

Since elements of $\mathbb{G}_q$ are quadratic residues modulo p, we can reduce the cost of the group membership test to a single modular multiplication in $\mathbb{Z}_p^*$. The improvement is based on the observation that every quadratic residue $x \in \mathbb{G}_q$ has two square roots in $\mathbb{Z}_p^*$, whereas quadratic non-residues $x \notin \mathbb{G}_q$ have no square roots in $\mathbb{Z}_p^*$. Group membership $x \in \mathbb{G}_q$ can therefore be demonstrated by presenting one of the two square roots $\sqrt{x} = \pm x^{\frac{q+1}{2}} \bmod p$ as a *membership witness* and by checking that $\sqrt{x}^2 \equiv x \ (\bmod \ p)$ holds. Thus, provided that such a membership witness is available "for free", group membership can be tested using a single modular multiplication.[4]

To implement this idea in practice, elements $x \in \mathbb{G}_q$ can be represented as pairs $\hat{x} = (\sqrt{x}, x)$, for which group membership can be tested as described above using a single multiplication.[5] For such pairs, multiplication $\hat{z} = \hat{x}\hat{y}$, exponentiation $\hat{z} = \hat{x}^e$, and computing the inverse $\hat{z} = \hat{x}^{-1}$ can be implemented based on corresponding computations on the square roots:

$$\sqrt{xy} \equiv \sqrt{x}\sqrt{y} \ (\bmod p), \quad \sqrt{x^e} \equiv \sqrt{x}^e (\bmod p), \quad \sqrt{x^{-1}} \equiv \sqrt{x}^{-1}(\bmod p).$$

---

[4] While group membership testing based on square roots has been used in protocols for outsourcing modular exponentiations to malicious servers [4], we are not aware of any proposal or implementation of this technique as a general method for representing elements of $\mathbb{G}_q \subset \mathbb{Z}_p^*$. However, given the simplicity of the approach, we can not exclude it from being folklore.

[5] To disallow the encoding of an additional bit of information into the square root representation of a quadratic residue, we suggest normalizing the representation by taking always either the smaller or the larger of the two values.

Thus, only a single additional multiplication $z = \sqrt{z}^2 \bmod p$ is needed in each case to obtain the group element itself. In such an implementation, it is even possible to compute groups elements only when needed, for example before decoding a decrypted ElGamal message or for equality tests. In this way, additional multiplications and can be avoided almost entirely during the execution of a cryptographic protocol, during which all computations are conducted on the square roots. Restricting the representation to the square root is also useful for avoiding additional memory and communication costs. In other words, group membership in $\mathbb{G}_q \subset \mathbb{Z}_p^*$ can be guaranteed at almost no additional cost. This maximizes the benefit of the small exponent test in batch verification.

3   Optimizing the Performance of Shuffling

A *cryptographic shuffle* transforms a list of input ciphertexts $e = (e_1, \ldots, e_N)$ into a permuted list $\tilde{e} = (\tilde{e}_1, \ldots, \tilde{e}_N)$ of re-encrypted output ciphertexts, in which every $\tilde{e}_j = \mathsf{ReEnc}_{pk}(e_i, \tilde{r}_i)$, $j = \psi(i)$, is a re-encryption of exactly one e_i under the given public key pk. The whole shuffle operation can be denoted by

$$\tilde{e} = \mathsf{Shuffle}_{pk}(e, \tilde{r}, \psi),$$

where $\tilde{r} = (\tilde{r}_1, \ldots, \tilde{r}_N)$ denotes the vector of re-encryption randomizations and $\psi \in \Psi_N$ the randomly selected permutation (which determines the order of the elements in $\tilde{e}$). For proving the correctness of $\tilde{e}$ relative to e, a non-interactive zero-knowledge proof of knowledge of $\tilde{r}$ and ψ must be generated along with $\tilde{e}$. Such a *shuffle proof*

$$\pi = NIZKP\,[(\tilde{r}, \psi) : \tilde{e} = \mathsf{Shuffle}_{pk}(e, \tilde{r}, \psi)]$$

can be constructed in various ways (see Table 1). In this paper, we only focus on the shuffle proof by Wikström and Terelius [18, 19], which is one of the most prominent and efficient approaches in the literature. Based on the pseudo-code algorithms from [12], we first provide a detailed list of all the exponentiations required for generating and verifying the shuffle. We will then discuss possible improvements in the light of the optimization techniques presented in Sect. 2. The goal is to reduce the overall running times to the greatest possible extent.

3.1   Performance Analysis

The shuffle proof by Wikström and Terelius is very flexible in various aspects. It supports different types of encryption schemes, different mathematical groups, and different operations to be performed on each ciphertext. The *Verificatum Mix-Net* implementation, for example, supports a combination of re-encryption and decryption with a shared private key [20]. In this particular setting, the mix-net outputs a list of decrypted plaintext messages, which correspond to the plaintext messages included in the input ciphertexts.

In our analysis, we restrict ourselves to the classical case of performing a re-encryption shuffle of ElGamal ciphertexts. Each ciphertext included in e is therefore a pair $e_i = (a_i, b_i) \in \mathcal{G}^2$ of two group elements $a_i = m_i \cdot pk^{r_i}$ and $b_i = g^{r_i}$ and re-encrypting e_i with a fresh randomization $\tilde{r}_i \in \mathbb{Z}_q$ means to multiply it with an encryption of the identity element $1 \in \mathcal{G}$:

$$\mathsf{ReEnc}_{pk}(e_i, \tilde{r}_i) = e_i \cdot \mathsf{Enc}_{pk}(1, \tilde{r}_i) = (a_i, b_i) \cdot (pk^{\tilde{r}_i}, g^{\tilde{r}_i}) = (a_i \cdot pk^{\tilde{r}_i}, b_i \cdot g^{\tilde{r}_i}).$$

On the other hand, we do not restrict the analysis to a particular mathematical group, i.e., the presented results are applicable to any DDH secure group. As in Sect. 2, the performance is measured in number of group multiplications, i.e., without making a distinction between general multiplication and squaring.

Slightly modified versions of the pseudo-code algorithms GenShuffle, Gen-Proof, and CheckProof from [12] are included in Appendix A. For better readability, two sub-algorithms have been merged into GenProof and some variables have been renamed for better consistency with the rest of the paper. To avoid negative exponents $-c$ in CheckProof, we have swapped all appearances of c and $-c$ in both algorithms. The benefit of this modification is computations with smaller exponents. If λ denotes the security parameter and $\ell = \|q\|$ an appropriate group size in bits, for example $\lambda = 128$ and $\ell = 3072$, we get much smaller exponents of length $\|c\| = \lambda$ instead of $\|-c\| = \ell$. This improves the running time of CheckProof independently of any optimization techniques.

Based on the algorithms as given in the appendix, Table 4 provides a complete list of all exponentiations required for generating a cryptographic shuffle of size N and the corresponding shuffle proof. The lengths of the involved exponents are indicated in each case. As a general rule, randomizations such as r_i or ω_i are of length $\ell = \|q\|$, whereas challenges such as $\tilde{u}_i$ are of length λ, where λ is the security parameter of the shuffle proof. The rightmost column of Table 4 shows the number of necessary group membership tests to conduct on the input values. It is assumed that independent generators $g, h, h_1, \ldots, h_N \in \mathcal{G}$ are publicly known.

In Table 5, a similar overview of exponentiations and group membership tests is given for algorithm CheckProof, again by distinguishing between exponents of length ℓ and λ. By comparing Table 5 with Table 4, it seems that generating and verifying a shuffle is almost equally expensive. In each case, there are exactly N plain exponentiations and $3N$ product exponentiations with large ℓ-bits exponents, and roughly N plain exponentiations with small λ-bits exponents. The main difference lies in the number of product exponentiations with small exponents and fixed-base exponentiations with large exponents, but the total sum of all exponentiations is almost identical ($10N + 5$ for generating the shuffle vs. $9N + 11$ for verifying the shuffle). A major difference lies in the number of group membership tests ($2N + 1$ vs. $7N + 6$).

3.2 Performance Improvements

The analysis of the previous subsection give us a precise map of how to apply the special-purpose exponentiation algorithms from Sect. 2.1 for improving the

Table 4. Overview of exponentiations and group membership tests in the shuffle and shuffle proof generation algorithms. The column PLE lists the number of plain exponentiations, the column PRE the number of product exponentiations, the column FBE the number of fixed-based exponentiations, and the column GMT the number of group membership tests for an input size of N ciphertexts, a group $\mathcal{G}$ of size $\ell = \|q\|$ bits, and a security parameter λ.

Algorithm	Line	Computation	PLE		PRE	FBE		GMT
			ℓ	λ	ℓ	ℓ	b	
GenShuffle	1a	$(a_i, b_i) \in \mathcal{G}^2$	–	–	–	–	–	$2N$
	1b	$pk \in \mathcal{G}$	–	–	–	–	–	1
	5	$\tilde{a}_i \leftarrow a_i \cdot pk^{\tilde{r}_i}$	–	–	–	N	pk	–
	6	$\tilde{b}_i \leftarrow b_i \cdot g^{\tilde{r}_i}$	–	–	–	N	g	–
GenProof	4	$c_{j_i} \leftarrow h_i \cdot g^{r_{j_i}}$	–	–	–	N	g	–
	11	$\hat{c}_i \leftarrow g^{\hat{r}_i} \cdot \hat{c}_{i-1}^{\tilde{u}_i}$	–	N	–	N	g	–
	15	$\hat{t}_i \leftarrow g^{\hat{\omega}_i} \cdot \hat{c}_{i-1}^{\tilde{\omega}_i}$	N	–	–	N	g	–
	17	$t_1 \leftarrow g^{\omega_1}$	–	–	–	1	g	–
	18	$t_2 \leftarrow g^{\omega_2}$	–	–	–	1	g	–
	19	$t_3 \leftarrow g^{\omega_3} \cdot \prod_{i=1}^{N} h_i^{\tilde{\omega}_i}$	–	–	N	1	g	–
	20	$t_{4,1} \leftarrow pk^{-\omega_4} \cdot \prod_{i=1}^{N} \tilde{a}_i^{\tilde{\omega}_i}$	–	–	N	1	pk	–
	21	$t_{4,2} \leftarrow g^{-\omega_4} \cdot \prod_{i=1}^{N} \tilde{b}_i^{\tilde{\omega}_i}$	–	–	N	1	g	–
Total			$10N + 5$					$2N + 1$

performance of generating and verifying a cryptographic shuffle. Based on this map, we can compute the total number of multiplications required for an input size of N ElGamal ciphertext. By dividing this number by N, we obtain *relative running times* for generating and verifying the shuffle, which measures the average number of multiplications *per* input ciphertext. The columns in the middle of Tables 6 and 7 show corresponding numbers for $\lambda = 128$ and $\ell = 3072$ and $\lambda = 128$ and $\ell = 256$, which are typical settings today for modular groups respectively elliptic curves. Compared to the numbers for an unoptimized implementation shown in the left hand columns, generating the shuffle becomes up to 5.5 times and verifying the shuffle up to 3.5 times more efficient. Generally, the speed-up for $\ell = 256$ is slightly smaller than for $\ell = 3072$, and it grows moderately for an increasing N.

Given the potential of product and fixed-base exponentiation algorithms (between 10 and 20 times more efficient for $\ell = 3072$, see Table 3), the maximum performance improvement has not yet been achieved. The most problematic exponentiations in Tables 4 and 5 are the $2N$ plain exponentiations, and among them especially those with exponents of length ℓ. Apparently, computing them without optimizations creates a significant bottleneck that prevents even better performances. Here is a proposal for removing the bottleneck in all cases:

Table 5. Overview of exponentiations and group membership tests in the shuffle verification algorithm. The column PLE lists the number of plain exponentiations, the column PRE the number of product exponentiations, the column FBE the number of fixed-based exponentiations, and the column GMT the number of group membership tests for an input size N, a group $\mathcal{G}$ of size $\ell = \|q\|$ bits, and a security parameter λ.

Algorithm	Line	Computation	PLE		PRE		FBE		GMT
			ℓ	λ	ℓ	λ	ℓ	b	
CheckProof	1a	$t \in \mathcal{G} \times \mathcal{G} \times \mathcal{G} \times \mathcal{G}^2 \times \mathcal{G}^N$	–	–	–	–	–	–	$N+5$
	1b	$c \in \mathcal{G}^N,\ \hat{c} \in \mathcal{G}^N$	–	–	–	–	–	–	$2N$
	1c	$(a_i, b_i) \in \mathcal{G}^2,\ (\tilde{a}_i, \tilde{b}_i) \in \mathcal{G}^2$	–	–	–	–	–	–	$4N$
	1d	$pk \in \mathcal{G}$	–	–	–	–	–	–	1
	7	$\hat{c} \leftarrow \hat{c}_N \cdot h^{-u}$	–	–	–	–	1	h	–
	8	$\tilde{c} \leftarrow \prod_{i=1}^N c_i^{u_i}$	–	–	–	N	–	–	–
	9	$\tilde{a} \leftarrow \prod_{i=1}^N a_i^{u_i}$	–	–	–	N	–	–	–
	10	$\tilde{b} \leftarrow \prod_{i=1}^N b_i^{u_i}$	–	–	–	N	–	–	–
	13	$\hat{t}'_i \leftarrow \hat{c}_i^c \cdot g^{\hat{s}_i} \cdot \hat{c}_{i-1}^{\tilde{s}_i}$	N	N	–	–	N	g	–
	14	$t'_1 \leftarrow \bar{c}^c \cdot g^{s_1}$	–	1	–	–	1	g	–
	15	$t'_2 \leftarrow \hat{c}^c \cdot g^{s_2}$	–	1	–	–	1	g	–
	16	$t'_3 \leftarrow \tilde{c}^c \cdot g^{s_3} \cdot \prod_{i=1}^N h_i^{\tilde{s}_i}$	–	1	N	–	1	g	–
	17	$t'_{4,1} \leftarrow \tilde{a}^c \cdot pk^{-s_4} \cdot \prod_{i=1}^N \tilde{a}_i^{\tilde{s}_i}$	–	1	N	–	1	pk	–
	18	$t'_{4,2} \leftarrow \tilde{b}^c \cdot g^{-s_4} \cdot \prod_{i=1}^N \tilde{b}_i^{\tilde{s}_i}$	–	1	N	–	1	g	–
Total			$9N+11$						$7N+6$

- The second exponentiation in the assignment $\hat{t}_i \leftarrow g^{\hat{\omega}_i} \cdot \hat{c}_{i-1}^{\tilde{\omega}_i}$ in Line 15 of GenProof is based on the commitment chain $\hat{c}_0, \hat{c}_1, \ldots, \hat{c}_N$, which is defined recursively by $\hat{c}_0 \leftarrow h$ in Line 8 and $\hat{c}_i \leftarrow g^{\hat{r}_i} \cdot \hat{c}_{i-1}^{\tilde{u}_i}$ in Line 11. By raising the recursion to the exponent, we can reformulated this definition into $\hat{c}_i \leftarrow g^{R_i} \cdot h^{U_i}$, where exponents $R_i = \hat{r}_i + \tilde{u}_i R_{i-1} \bmod q$ and $U_i = \tilde{u}_i U_{i-1} \bmod q$ are computed recursively from $R_0 = 0$ and $U_0 = 1$ in time linear to N. By changing Line 11 accordingly, we obtain two fixed-base exponentiations—one for base g and one for base h—with exponents of length $\ell = \|q\|$.
- Based on the same exponents R_i and U_i, we can also change Line 15 of GenProof into $\hat{t}_i \leftarrow g^{R'_i} \cdot h^{U'_i}$ with exponents $R'_i = \hat{\omega}_i + \tilde{\omega}_i R_{i-1} \bmod q$ and $U'_i = \tilde{\omega}_i U_{i-1} \bmod q$, which again consists of two fixed-base exponentiations with exponents of length ℓ. Therefore, all plain exponentiations from algorithm GenProof can be replaced by fixed-base exponentiations. Together with GenShuffle, we obtain a total of $3N$ product exponentiations and $7N+5$ fixed-base exponentiations ($N+1$ for pk, $4N+4$ for g, $2N$ for h) for generating the shuffle and its proof. All exponents are of length $\ell = \|q\|$.
- The two plain exponentiations of algorithm CheckProof are both contained in the assignment $\hat{t}'_i \leftarrow \hat{c}_i^c \cdot g^{\hat{s}_i} \cdot \hat{c}_{i-1}^{\tilde{s}_i}$ of Line 13. The purpose of computing the values $\hat{t}'_i$ is to compare them in Line 19 with the values $\hat{t}_i$ included in

Table 6. Comparison of relative running times for generating and verifying a cryptographic shuffle in a typical setting for modular groups with $\lambda = 128$ and $\ell = 3072$.

Not optimized				Partly optimized				Fully optimized				N
Generate		Verify		Generate		Verify		Generate		Verify $s = \lambda$		
31622	1.00	18221	1.00	6742	0.21	5406	0.30	3908	0.12	1861	0.10	100
31465	1.00	18027	1.00	6264	0.20	5233	0.29	3230	0.10	1740	0.10	1 000
31450	1.00	18007	1.00	5971	0.19	5162	0.29	2817	0.09	1730	0.10	10 000
31448	1.00	18007	1.00	5782	0.18	5117	0.28	2546	0.08	1729	0.10	100 000
31448	1.00	18005	1.00	5640	0.18	5083	0.28	2346	0.07	1729	0.10	1 000 000

Table 7. Comparison of relative running times for generating and verifying a cryptographic shuffle in a typical setting for elliptic curves with $\lambda = 128$ and $\ell = 256$.

Not optimized				Partly optimized				Fully optimized				N
Generate		Verify		Generate		Verify		Generate		Verify $s = \lambda$		
2926	1.00	2184	1.00	822	0.28	768	0.35	445	0.15	374	0.17	100
2913	1.00	2161	1.00	763	0.26	742	0.34	362	0.12	356	0.16	1 000
2911	1.00	2158	1.00	725	0.25	731	0.34	308	0.11	354	0.16	10 000
2911	1.00	2158	1.00	699	0.24	725	0.33	270	0.09	354	0.16	100 000
2911	1.00	2158	1.00	683	0.23	721	0.33	248	0.09	354	0.16	1 000 000

the proof. They must all be equal for the proof to succeed. Instead of conducting explicit equality tests as suggested in algorithm CheckProof, it is also possible to apply the batch verification method from Sect. 2.2. Note that the given use case in Line 19 corresponds precisely to the particular combination of batch verification problems discussed at the end of Sect. 2.2, which tests three exponentiations simultaneously (one with a fixed base g, one with a fixed exponent c, and one general case). For $\hat{t} = (\hat{t}_1, \ldots, \hat{t}_N)$, $\hat{c} = (\hat{c}_1, \ldots, \hat{c}_N)$, and $\hat{c}_0 = (\hat{c}_0, \ldots, \hat{c}_{N-1})$, we can therefore execute the combined small exponent test from Sect. 2.2 to perform $\mathsf{BatchVerif}(\hat{t}, \hat{c}_0, \tilde{s}, g, \hat{s}, \hat{c}, c)$, which requires three product exponentiations of size N (one with exponents of length ℓ and two with exponents of length s), and two single plain exponentiations. This implies that CheckProof can be implemented using nine product exponentiations of size N (four with exponents of lengths ℓ, three with exponents of length λ, and two with exponents of length s) and 13 single exponentiations (which become negligible for large problem instances). When implementing batch verification into the non-interactive verification algorithm in this way, care has to be taken that the process of picking s uniformly at random can not be influenced by the prover.

Rewriting GenProof and CheckProof using these optimization leads to the performance results shown in the right hand columns of Tables 6 and 7. Note that the change in CheckProof increases the probability for an invalid proof to pass the verification by 2^{-s} (see Sect. 2.2). To preserve the soundness of the proof, it is therefore important to select s in accordance with the security parameter

λ. For $s = \lambda = 112$ and $\ell = 3072$, a speed-up by a factor of 10 and more can be observed for both generating and verifying the shuffle. For $s = \lambda = 128$ and $\ell = 256$, the speed-up is slightly more moderate, but still significant.

With the above optimizations, it seems that the potential for improvements based on special-purpose exponentiations algorithms has been exhausted. In groups $\mathbb{G}_q \subseteq \mathbb{Z}_p^*$ of integers modulo a safe prime $p = 2q + 1$, an area for further improvements are the group membership tests, which need to be conducted on all group elements included in the algorithm inputs (we mentioned earlier that membership tests in elliptic curves are almost for free). Recall from Tables 4 and 5 and from Sect. 2.3 that an ElGamal shuffle of size N requires $2N + 1$ such membership tests for generating and $7N + 6$ tests for verifying the shuffle.

If membership testing $z \in \mathbb{G}_q$ is implemented naïvely by computing $z^q \bmod p$ using plain modular exponentiation, then the added cost of this test completely outweighs the performance improvements achieved so far. Therefore, we assume that any practical implementation at leasts includes an algorithm for computing the Jacobi symbol, which is up to 20 times faster than plain modular exponentiation for 3072-bits integers. Given that HAC 14.85 requires 3477 modular multiplications, we can estimate the cost of computing the Jacobi symbol as equivalent to approximately 175 multiplications. Therefore, $2 \cdot 175 + 1 = 351$ and $7 \cdot 175 + 6 = 1231$ multiplications need to be added to the cost of generating and verifying the shuffle, respectively. Compared to the numbers from Table 6, this demonstrates that the cost for computing Jacobi symbols is not negligible, especially for verifying a proof. For large N, we obtain a total of $1729 + 1231 = 2960$ multiplications per input ciphertext, which is approximately 1.7 less efficient than without performing the membership test. This loss can be avoided by implementing the membership test based on the membership witness method from Sect. 2.3, which reduces the relative cost to a single multiplication.

4 Conclusion

Based on recent work on special-purpose algorithms for computing exponentiations, we have shown in this paper that generating and verifying a cryptographic shuffle can be accelerated by approximately one order of magnitude. A combination of optimization techniques is necessary to obtain the best possible performance. Given the importance of shuffling in voting protocols and the high computational costs of the available methods, this improvement is significant for practical implementations. We have shown how to achieve this benefit for Wikström's shuffle proof, but we expect similar benefits for other methods.

Many of the algorithms and methods discussed in this paper are not yet available in libraries for large integer arithmetic. We were therefore not able to evaluate the performance of the proposed method on real machines. But recent work on similar topics has shown that theoretical performance estimations based on counting multiplications can often be confirmed rather easily in practical experiments. Implementing all algorithms and conducting such experiments is an area for further research.

Further performance improvements can be achieved by executing the exponentiation tasks in parallel on multiple cores or multiple machines. There are many ways of implementing parallelization into a shuffling procedure, but finding a clever way of distributing the total cost optimally to all available resources is a complex problem. This is another area for further research.

A   Pseudo-Code Algorithms

---

1 **Algorithm:** GenShuffle(e, pk)

Input: ElGamal ciphertexts $e = (e_1, \ldots, e_N)$, $e_i = (a_i, b_i) \in \mathcal{G}^2$
Encryption key $pk \in \mathcal{G}$

2 $\psi \leftarrow$ GenPermutation(N)

3 **for** $i = 1, \ldots, N$ **do**

4 $\quad$ $\tilde{r}_i \in_R \mathbb{Z}_q$

5 $\quad$ $\tilde{a}_i \leftarrow a_i \cdot pk^{\tilde{r}_i}$

6 $\quad$ $\tilde{b}_i \leftarrow b_i \cdot g^{\tilde{r}_i}$

7 $\quad$ $\tilde{e}_i \leftarrow (\tilde{a}_i, \tilde{b}_i)$

8 $\tilde{e} \leftarrow (\tilde{e}_{j_1}, \ldots, \tilde{e}_{j_N})$

9 $\tilde{r} \leftarrow (\tilde{r}_1, \ldots, \tilde{r}_N)$

10 **return** $(\tilde{e}, \tilde{r}, \psi)$ $\qquad\qquad\qquad$ // $\tilde{e} \in (\mathcal{G}^2)^N$, $\tilde{r} \in \mathbb{Z}_q^N$, $\psi \in \Psi_N$

Algorithm A.1: Performs a re-encryption shuffle to a given list of ElGamal ciphertexts.

1 **Algorithm:** GenProof($e, \tilde{e}, \tilde{r}, \psi, pk$)

Input: ElGamal ciphertexts $e = (e_1, \ldots, e_N)$, $e_i = (a_i, b_i) \in \mathcal{G}^2$
Shuffled ElGamal ciphertexts $\tilde{e} = (\tilde{e}_1, \ldots, \tilde{e}_N)$, $\tilde{e}_i = (\tilde{a}_i, \tilde{b}_i) \in \mathcal{G}^2$
Re-encryption randomizations $\tilde{r} = (\tilde{r}_1, \ldots, \tilde{r}_N)$, $\tilde{r}_i \in \mathbb{Z}_q$
Permutation $\psi = (j_1, \ldots, j_N) \in \Psi_N$
Encryption key $pk \in \mathcal{G}$

2 **for** $i = 1, \ldots, N$ **do**

3     $r_{j_i} \in_R \mathbb{Z}_q$

4     $c_{j_i} \leftarrow h_i \cdot g^{r_{j_i}}$

5 $c = (c_1, \ldots, c_N)$

6 **for** $i = 1, \ldots, N$ **do**

7     $u_i \leftarrow \mathsf{Hash}((e, \tilde{e}, c), i)$

8 $\hat{c}_0 \leftarrow h$

9 **for** $i = 1, \ldots, N$ **do**

10     $\hat{r}_i \in_R \mathbb{Z}_q$, $\tilde{u}_i \leftarrow u_{j_i}$

11     $\hat{c}_i \leftarrow g^{\hat{r}_i} \cdot \hat{c}_{i-1}^{\tilde{u}_i}$

12 $\hat{c} = (\hat{c}_1, \ldots, \hat{c}_N)$

13 **for** $i = 1, \ldots, N$ **do**

14     $\hat{\omega}_i \in_R \mathbb{Z}_q$, $\tilde{\omega}_i \in_R \mathbb{Z}_q$

15     $\hat{t}_i \leftarrow g^{\hat{\omega}_i} \cdot \hat{c}_{i-1}^{\tilde{\omega}_i}$

16 $\omega_1 \in_R \mathbb{Z}_q$, $\omega_2 \in_R \mathbb{Z}_q$, $\omega_3 \in_R \mathbb{Z}_q$, $\omega_4 \in_R \mathbb{Z}_q$

17 $t_1 \leftarrow g^{\omega_1}$

18 $t_2 \leftarrow g^{\omega_2}$

19 $t_3 \leftarrow g^{\omega_3} \cdot \prod_{i=1}^{N} h_i^{\tilde{\omega}_i}$

20 $t_{4,1} \leftarrow pk^{-\omega_4} \cdot \prod_{i=1}^{N} \tilde{a}_i^{\tilde{\omega}_i}$

21 $t_{4,2} \leftarrow g^{-\omega_4} \cdot \prod_{i=1}^{N} \tilde{b}_i^{\tilde{\omega}_i}$

22 $t \leftarrow (t_1, t_2, t_3, (t_{4,1}, t_{4,2}), (\hat{t}_1, \ldots, \hat{t}_N))$

23 $c \leftarrow \mathsf{Hash}(e, \tilde{e}, c, \hat{c}, pk, t)$

24 $v_N \leftarrow 1$

25 **for** $i = N, \ldots, 1$ **do**

26     $v_{i-1} \leftarrow \tilde{u}_i v_i \bmod q$

27 $r \leftarrow \sum_{i=1}^{N} r_i \bmod q$, $s_1 \leftarrow \omega_1 - c \cdot r \bmod q$

28 $\hat{r} \leftarrow \sum_{i=1}^{N} \hat{r}_i v_i \bmod q$, $s_2 \leftarrow \omega_2 - c \cdot \hat{r} \bmod q$

29 $\bar{r} \leftarrow \sum_{i=1}^{N} r_i u_i \bmod q$, $s_3 \leftarrow \omega_3 - c \cdot \bar{r} \bmod q$

30 $\tilde{r} \leftarrow \sum_{i=1}^{N} \tilde{r}_i u_i \bmod q$, $s_4 \leftarrow \omega_4 - c \cdot \tilde{r} \bmod q$

31 **for** $i = 1, \ldots, N$ **do**

32     $\hat{s}_i \leftarrow \hat{\omega}_i - c \cdot \hat{r}_i \bmod q$, $\tilde{s}_i \leftarrow \tilde{\omega}_i - c \cdot \tilde{u}_i \bmod q$

33 $s \leftarrow (s_1, s_2, s_3, s_4, (\hat{s}_1, \ldots, \hat{s}_N), (\tilde{s}_1, \ldots, \tilde{s}_N))$

34 $\pi \leftarrow (t, s, c, \hat{c})$

35 **return** $\pi \in (\mathcal{G} \times \mathcal{G} \times \mathcal{G} \times \mathcal{G}^2 \times \mathcal{G}^N) \times (\mathbb{Z}_q \times \mathbb{Z}_q \times \mathbb{Z}_q \times \mathbb{Z}_q \times \mathbb{Z}_q^N \times \mathbb{Z}_q^N) \times \mathcal{G}^N \times \mathcal{G}^N$

Algorithm A.2: Generates an ElGamal shuffle proof.

---

1 **Algorithm:** CheckProof$(\pi, e, \tilde{e}, pk)$

Input: Shuffle proof $\pi = (t, s, c, \hat{c})$
  - $t = (t_1, t_2, t_3, (t_{4,1}, t_{4,2}), (\hat{t}_1, \ldots, \hat{t}_N)) \in \mathcal{G} \times \mathcal{G} \times \mathcal{G} \times \mathcal{G}^2 \times \mathcal{G}^N$
  - $s = (s_1, s_2, s_3, s_4, (\hat{s}_1, \ldots, \hat{s}_N), (\tilde{s}_1, \ldots, \tilde{s}_N)) \in \mathbb{Z}_q \times \mathbb{Z}_q \times \mathbb{Z}_q \times \mathbb{Z}_q \times \mathbb{Z}_q^N \times \mathbb{Z}_q^N$
  - $c = (c_1, \ldots, c_N) \in \mathcal{G}^N$, $\hat{c} = (\hat{c}_1, \ldots, \hat{c}_N) \in \mathcal{G}^N$
  ElGamal ciphertextes $e = (e_1, \ldots, e_N)$, $e_i = (a_i, b_i) \in \mathcal{G}^2$
  Shuffled ElGamal ciphertexts $\tilde{e} = (\tilde{e}_1, \ldots, \tilde{e}_N)$, $\tilde{e}_i = (\tilde{a}_i, \tilde{b}_i) \in \mathcal{G}^2$
  Encryption key $pk \in \mathcal{G}$

2 **for** $i = 1, \ldots, N$ **do**

3 $\quad\lfloor\ u_i \leftarrow \mathsf{Hash}((e, \tilde{e}, c), i)$

4 $\hat{c}_0 \leftarrow h$

5 $\bar{c} \leftarrow \prod_{i=1}^N c_i / \prod_{i=1}^N h_i$

6 $u \leftarrow \prod_{i=1}^N u_i \bmod q$

7 $\hat{c} \leftarrow \hat{c}_N \cdot h^{-u}$

8 $\tilde{c} \leftarrow \prod_{i=1}^N c_i^{u_i}$

9 $\tilde{a} \leftarrow \prod_{i=1}^N a_i^{u_i}$

10 $\tilde{b} \leftarrow \prod_{i=1}^N b_i^{u_i}$

11 $c \leftarrow \mathsf{Hash}(e, \tilde{e}, c, \hat{c}, pk, t)$

12 **for** $i = 1, \ldots, N$ **do**

13 $\quad\lfloor\ \hat{t}_i' \leftarrow \hat{c}_i^c \cdot g^{\hat{s}_i} \cdot \hat{c}_{i-1}^{\tilde{s}_i}$

14 $t_1' \leftarrow \bar{c}^c \cdot g^{s_1}$

15 $t_2' \leftarrow \hat{c}^c \cdot g^{s_2}$

16 $t_3' \leftarrow \tilde{c}^c \cdot g^{s_3} \cdot \prod_{i=1}^N h_i^{\tilde{s}_i}$

17 $t_{4,1}' \leftarrow \tilde{a}^c \cdot pk^{-s_4} \cdot \prod_{i=1}^N \tilde{a}_i^{\tilde{s}_i}$

18 $t_{4,2}' \leftarrow \tilde{b}^c \cdot g^{-s_4} \cdot \prod_{i=1}^N \tilde{b}_i^{\tilde{s}_i}$

19 **return**

$$(t_1 = t_1') \wedge (t_2 = t_2') \wedge (t_3 = t_3') \wedge (t_{4,1} = t_{4,1}') \wedge (t_{4,2} = t_{4,2}') \wedge \left[\bigwedge_{i=1}^N (\hat{t}_i = \hat{t}_i')\right]$$

Algorithm A.3: Checks the correctness of an ElGamal shuffle proof.

References

1. Bayer, S., Groth, J.: Efficient zero-knowledge argument for correctness of a shuffle. In: Pointcheval, D., Johansson, T. (eds.) EUROCRYPT 2012. LNCS, vol. 7237, pp. 263–280. Springer, Heidelberg (2012). https://doi.org/10.1007/978-3-642-29011-4_17

2. Bellare, M., Garay, J.A., Rabin, T.: Fast batch verification for modular exponentiation and digital signatures. In: Nyberg, K. (ed.) EUROCRYPT 1998. LNCS, vol. 1403, pp. 236–250. Springer, Heidelberg (1998). https://doi.org/10.1007/BFb0054130

3. Boyd, C., Pavlovski, C.: Attacking and repairing batch verification schemes. In: Okamoto, T. (ed.) ASIACRYPT 2000. LNCS, vol. 1976, pp. 58–71. Springer, Heidelberg (2000). https://doi.org/10.1007/3-540-44448-3_5

4. Di Crescenzo, G., Khodjaeva, M., Kahrobaei, D., Shpilrain, V.: Practical and secure outsourcing of discrete log group exponentiation to a single malicious server. In: 9th ACM Cloud Computing Security Workshop, CCSW 2017, Dallas, USA, pp. 17–28 (2017)

5. Fauzi, P., Lipmaa, H.: Efficient culpably sound NIZK shuffle argument without random oracles. In: Sako, K. (ed.) CT-RSA 2016. LNCS, vol. 9610, pp. 200–216. Springer, Cham (2016). https://doi.org/10.1007/978-3-319-29485-8_12

6. Fauzi, P., Lipmaa, H., Siim, J., Zając, M.: An efficient pairing-based shuffle argument. In: Takagi, T., Peyrin, T. (eds.) ASIACRYPT 2017. LNCS, vol. 10625, pp. 97–127. Springer, Cham (2017). https://doi.org/10.1007/978-3-319-70697-9_4

7. Fauzi, P., Lipmaa, H., Zając, M.: A shuffle argument secure in the generic model. In: Cheon, J.H., Takagi, T. (eds.) ASIACRYPT 2016. LNCS, vol. 10032, pp. 841–872. Springer, Heidelberg (2016). https://doi.org/10.1007/978-3-662-53890-6_28

8. Furukawa, J., Sako, K.: An efficient scheme for proving a shuffle. In: Kilian, J. (ed.) CRYPTO 2001. LNCS, vol. 2139, pp. 368–387. Springer, Heidelberg (2001). https://doi.org/10.1007/3-540-44647-8_22

9. Groth, J.: A verifiable secret shuffle of homomorphic encryptions. J. Cryptol. 23(4), 546–579 (2010). https://doi.org/10.1007/s00145-010-906

10. Groth, J., Lu, S.: A non-interactive shuffle with pairing based verifiability. In: Kurosawa, K. (ed.) ASIACRYPT 2007. LNCS, vol. 4833, pp. 51–67. Springer, Heidelberg (2007). https://doi.org/10.1007/978-3-540-76900-2_4

11. Haenni, R., Locher, P., Gailly, N.: Improving the performance of cryptographic voting protocols. In: 4th Workshop on Advances in Secure Electronic Voting, Voting 2019, Basseterre, St. Kitts and Nevis (2019)

12. Haenni, R., Locher, P., Koenig, R., Dubuis, E.: Pseudo-code algorithms for verifiable re-encryption mix-nets. In: Brenner, M., et al. (eds.) FC 2017. LNCS, vol. 10323, pp. 370–384. Springer, Cham (2017). https://doi.org/10.1007/978-3-319-70278-0_23

13. Hoshino, F., Abe, M., Kobayashi, T.: Lenient/strict batch verification in several groups. In: Davida, G.I., Frankel, Y. (eds.) ISC 2001. LNCS, vol. 2200, pp. 81–94. Springer, Heidelberg (2001). https://doi.org/10.1007/3-540-45439-X_6

14. Lee, P.J., Lim, C.H.: Method for exponentiation in a public-key cryptosystem. United States Patent No. 5999627, December 1999

15. Lim, C.H., Lee, P.J.: More flexible exponentiation with precomputation. In: Desmedt, Y.G. (ed.) CRYPTO 1994. LNCS, vol. 839, pp. 95–107. Springer, Heidelberg (1994). https://doi.org/10.1007/3-540-48658-5_11

16. Menezes, A.J., van Oorschot, P.C., Vanstone, S.A.: Handbook of Applied Cryptography. CRC Press, Boca Raton (1996)

17. Möller, B.: Algorithms for multi-exponentiation. In: Vaudenay, S., Youssef, A.M. (eds.) SAC 2001. LNCS, vol. 2259, pp. 165–180. Springer, Heidelberg (2001). https://doi.org/10.1007/3-540-45537-X_13

18. Terelius, B., Wikström, D.: Proofs of restricted shuffles. In: Bernstein, D.J., Lange, T. (eds.) AFRICACRYPT 2010. LNCS, vol. 6055, pp. 100–113. Springer, Heidelberg (2010). https://doi.org/10.1007/978-3-642-12678-9_7

19. Wikström, D.: A commitment-consistent proof of a shuffle. In: Boyd, C., González Nieto, J. (eds.) ACISP 2009. LNCS, vol. 5594, pp. 407–421. Springer, Heidelberg (2009). https://doi.org/10.1007/978-3-642-02620-1_28

20. Wikström, D.: User Manual for the Verificatum Mix-Net - VMN Version 3.0.3. Verificatum AB, Stockholm, Sweden (2018)

WTSC 2020: Fourth Workshop on Trusted Smart Contracts

Characterizing Types of Smart Contracts in the Ethereum Landscape

Monika di Angelo$^{(\boxtimes)}$ and Gernot Salzer

TU Wien, Vienna, Austria
{monika.di.angelo,gernot.salzer}@tuwien.ac.at

Abstract. After cryptocurrencies, smart contracts are the second major innovation of the blockchain era. Leveraging the immutability and accountability of blockchains, these event-driven programs form the basis of the new digital economy with tokens, wallets, exchanges, and markets, but facilitating also new models of peer-to-peer organizations. To judge the long-term prospects of particular projects and this new technology in general, it is important to understand how smart contracts are used. While public announcements, by their nature, make promises of what smart contracts might achieve, openly available data of blockchains provides a more balanced view on what is actually going on.

We focus on Ethereum as the major platform for smart contracts and aim at a comprehensive picture of the smart contract landscape regarding common or heavily used types of contracts. To this end, we unravel the publicly available data of the main chain up to block 9 000 000, in order to obtain an understanding of almost 20 million deployed smart contracts and 1.5 billion interactions. As smart contracts act behind the scenes, their activities are only fully accessible by also considering the execution traces triggered by transactions. They serve as the basis for this analysis, in which we group contracts according to common characteristics, observe temporal aspects and characterize them quantitatively and qualitatively. We use static methods by analyzing the bytecode of contracts as well as dynamic methods by aggregating and classifying the communication between contracts.

Keywords: Bytecode analysis · Empirical study · EVM · Execution trace · Smart contract · Transaction data

1 Introduction

Smart contracts (SCs) are small, event-triggered programs that run in a trustless environment on a decentralized P2P network. They may be self-sufficient in offering a service or may be part of a decentralized application (dApp). In the latter scenario, they implement trust-related parts of the application logic like the exchange of assets, while the off-chain frontend interacts with users and other applications. Frequently, SCs extend the concept of cryptocurrencies by implementing tokens as a special purpose currency.

© Springer Nature Switzerland AG 2020
M. Bernhard et al. (Eds.): FC 2020 Workshops, LNCS 12063, pp. 389–404, 2020.
https://doi.org/10.1007/978-3-030-54455-3_28

Information on the purpose of SCs is often scarce. Colorful web pages advertise business ideas without revealing technical details, whereas technical blogs are anecdotal and selective. A comprehensive, but not readily accessible source is the blockchain data itself, growing continuously. Ethereum as the most prominent platform for SCs has recorded so far half a billion transactions, among them millions of contract creations. Although Ethereum is a well-researched platform, many questions about the usage of SCs remain unanswered.

Our work contributes to a deeper understanding of the *types of contracts* on the Ethereum blockchain, of their *quantities*, and of their *activities*. Starting from the publicly available transaction data of Ethereum's main chain we draw a comprehensive picture that accounts for the major phenomena. Along the way, we also investigate two claims frequently put forward: 'In Ethereum, the majority of deployed contracts remain unused' (claim 1), and 'Tokens are the killer application of Ethereum' (claim2).

Blockchain activities are usually described in terms of transactions clustered into blocks. This view is too coarse as contract activities become only visible when taking into account internal messages like calls, creates, and self-destructs. We base our static and dynamic analysis on the bytecode of contracts and their execution traces, define classes of contracts with common behavior or purpose, and observe their temporal evolution.

Roadmap. The next section summarizes related work. Section 3 clarifies terms, while Sect. 4 defines the types of contracts we intend to investigate. Section 5 describes our methods in detail. We start our analysis with general statistics in Sect. 6 before we examine various contract groups in Sect. 7. Section 8 puts the pieces together to arrive at the general picture. Finally, Sect. 9 summarizes our findings and concludes.

2   Previous Smart Contract Analyses

Contract Types. The authors of [13] find groups of similar contracts employing the unsupervised clustering techniques *affinity propagation* and *k-medoids*. Using the program *ssdeep*, they compute fuzzy hashes of the bytecodes of a set of verified contracts and determine their similarity by taking the mean of the Levenshtein, Jaccard, and Sorenson distance. After clustering, the authors identify the purpose of a cluster by the associated names (and a high transaction volume). With k-medoids, they are able to identify token presale, DAO withdrawal, some gambling, and empty contracts. The analysis is based on the bytecode deployed until February 2017.

The authors of [1] provide a comprehensive survey of Ponzi schemes on the Ethereum blockchain. They start from bytecode with known source code and extend their analysis to bytecode that is similar regarding normalized Levenshtein distance, collecting 191 Ponzi schemes in total. The analysis is based on the bytecode deployed until July 2017. The authors of [4] also detect Ponzi schemes, with data until October 2017.

The authors of [5] investigate the lifespan and activity patterns of SCs on Ethereum. They identify several groups of contracts, provide quantitative and qualitative characteristics for each identified type, and visualize them over time. The analysis is based on bytecode and messages until December 2018.

Topology. In the empirical analysis [2], the authors investigate platforms for SCs, cluster SC applications on Bitcoin and Ethereum into six categories, and evaluate design patterns for SCs of Solidity code until January 2017.

The authors of [9] measure "the control flow immutability of all smart contracts deployed on Ethereum." They apply "abstract interpretation techniques to all bytecode deployed on the public Ethereum blockchain, and synthesize the information in a complete call graph of static dependencies between all smart contracts." They claim that debris from past attacks biases statistics of Ethereum data. Their analysis is based on bytecode of 225000 SCs until May 2017.

In a graph analysis [3], the authors study Ether transfer, contract creation, and contract calls. They compute metrics like degree distribution, clustering, degree correlation, node importance, assortativity, and strongly/weakly connected components. They conclude that financial applications dominate Ethereum. The analysis is based on the messages until June 2017.

In their empirical study on Ethereum SCs [12], the authors find that SCs are "three times more likely to be created by other contracts than they are by users, and that over 60% of contracts have never been interacted with" and "less than 10% of user-created contracts are unique, and less than 1% of contract-created contracts are so." The analysis is based on the messages until January 2018.

3   Terms

We assume familiarity with blockchain technology. For Ethereum basics, we refer to [8,14].

Accounts, Transactions, and Messages. Ethereum distinguishes between externally owned accounts, often called *users*, and contract accounts or simply *contracts*. Accounts are uniquely identified by addresses of 20 bytes. Users can issue *transactions* (signed data packages) that transfer Ether to users and contracts, or that call or create contracts. These transactions are recorded on the blockchain. Contracts need to be triggered to become active, either by a transaction from a user or by a call (a *message*) from another contract. Messages are not recorded on the blockchain, since they are deterministic consequences of the initial transaction. They only exist in the execution environment of the EVM and are reflected in the execution trace and potential state changes.

For the sake of uniformity, we use the term message as a collective term for any (external) transaction or (internal) message, including SELFDESTRUCT operations that also may transfer Ether.

The Lifecycle of a Contract. For a contract to exist, it needs to be created by an account via *deployment code* (see below). As part of this deployment, the so-called *deployed code* is written to the Ethereum state at the contract's address. The contract exists upon the successful completion of the CREATE operation.

A contract may call other contracts, may create further contracts or may destruct itself by executing a SELFDESTRUCT operation. This results in a state change because the code at the contract's address is cleared. It is worth noting that this change happens only at the end of the whole transaction; until then the contract may still be called.

Deployment Code. A CREATE message passes bytecode to the EVM, the so-called deployment code. Its primary purpose is to initialize the storage and to provide the code of the new contract (the deployed code). However, deployment code may also call other contracts and may even contain CREATE instructions itself, leading to a cascade of contract creations. All calls and creates in the deployment code will seem to originate from the address of the new contract, even though the account contains no code yet. Moreover, the deployment code need not provide reasonable code for the new contract in the end. In particular, it may destruct itself or just stop the execution.

Gas. Users are charged for consumed resources. This is achieved by assigning a certain number of *gas units* to every instruction and each occupied storage cell, which are supposed to reflect the costs to the network of miners. Each transaction specifies the maximum amount of gas to be used as well as the amount of Ether the user is willing to pay per gas unit. The amount of gas limits the runtime of contracts, whereas the gas price influences the likelihood of a transaction to be processed by miners.

4   Definitions

We define the types of contracts that we will investigate in subsequent sections.

Dormant: a contract that has never been called since deployment. More precisely, we check the condition that the code (deployment or deployed) neither self-destructs in the transaction creating it nor receives a call later on.

Active: a contract that has received at least one successful call after the transaction creating it.

Self-destructed: a contract that successfully executed the operation SELFDESTRUCT at some point in time.

Short-Lived: a contract with an extremely short lifespan. More precisely, a short-lived contract self-destructs in the same transaction that has created it.

Prolific: a contract that creates at least 1 000 contracts.

Token: a contract that maintains a mapping from accounts to balances of token ownership. Moreover, it offers functions for transferring tokens between accounts. We approximate this informal notion by defining a token to be a contract that implements the mandatory functions of the token standards ERC-20 or ERC-721, or that is a positive instance of our ground truth [6].

Wallet: a contract that provides functionality for collecting and withdrawing Ether and tokens via its address. We consider a contract a wallet if it corresponds to one of the blueprints that we identified in earlier work as wallet code [7].

GasToken: a contract with the sole purpose of self-destructing when called from a specific address, this way causing a gas refund to the caller because of the freed resources. GasToken contracts can be identified by their behavior (numerous deployments and self-destructions) and subsequent code analysis.

Attack: a contract involved in an attack. Attack contracts stick out by unusual behavior (like executing certain instructions in a loop until running out of gas, or issuing an excessive number of specific messages); subsequent code analysis reveals the intention.

ENS Deed: a contract created by another contract, the so-called ENS Registrar, that registers a name for an Ethereum address.

5   Methods for Identifying Contracts

Contract groups characterized by their function (like wallets) are detected mainly statically by various forms of code analysis; transactional data may yield further clues but is not essential. Groups characterized by operational behavior, on the other hand, require a statistical analysis of dynamic data, mostly contract interactions. This section describes the data forming the basis of our analysis as well as the methods we use. As a summary, Table 1 relates the contract groups defined above to the methods for identifying them.

5.1   The Data

Our primary data are the messages and log entries provided by the Ethereum client `parity`, which we order chronologically by the triple of block number, transaction id within the block, and message/entry id within the transaction.

A message consists of type, status, context, sender, receiver, input, output, and value. Relevant message types are contract creations, four types of calls, and self-destructions. The status of a message can be 'success' or some error. 'Context' is the address affected by value transfers and self-destructs, whereas 'sender' is the user or contract issuing the message. The two addresses are identical except when the contract sending a message has been invoked by DELEGATECALL or CALLCODE. In this case, the sender address identifies the contract, whereas the context is identical to the context of the caller. For calls, 'receiver' is the address of the user or contract called, 'input' consists of a function identifier and argument values, and 'output' is the return value. For create, 'receiver' is the address of the newly created contract, 'input' is the deployment code, and 'output' is the deployed code of the new contract. 'Value' is the amount of Ether that the message transfers from 'context' to 'receiver'.

Log entries arise whenever the EVM executes a LOG instruction. They contain the context, in which the instruction was executed, and several fields with event-specific information. The most frequent log entries are those resulting from a 'Transfer' event. In this case, the context is the address of a token contract, whereas the fields contain the event identifier as well as the sender, the receiver, and the amount of transferred tokens.

A second source of data is the website etherscan.io, which provides the source code for 76.5 k deployments (0.4% of all deployments), as well as supplementary information for certain addresses. The website speeds up the process of understanding the purpose of contracts, which otherwise has to rely on disassembled/decompiled bytecode.

5.2   Static Analysis

Code Skeletons. To detect functional similarities between contracts we compare their *skeletons*, a technique also used in [5,11]. They are obtained from the bytecodes of contracts by replacing meta-data, constructor arguments, and the arguments of push operations uniformly by zeros and by stripping trailing zeros. The rationale is to remove variability that has little to no impact on the functional behavior. Skeletons allow us to transfer knowledge gained for one contract to others with the same skeleton.

As an example, the 19.7 M contract deployments correspond to just 112 k distinct skeletons. This is still a large number, but more manageable then 247 k distinct bytecodes. By exploiting creation histories and the similarity via skeletons, we are able to relate 7.7 M of these deployments to some source code on Etherscan, an increase from 0.4 to 39.2%.

Function Signatures. The vast majority of deployed contracts adheres to the convention that the first four bytes of call data identify the function to be executed. Therefore, most deployed code contains instructions comparing this function signature to the signatures of the implemented functions. We developed a pattern-based tool that reliably [1] extracts these signatures from the bytecode. Thus we obtain for each deployed contract the list of signatures that will trigger the execution of specific parts of the contract. The signatures are computed as the first four bytes of the Keccak-256 hash of the function name concatenated with the parameter types. Given the signature, it is not possible in general to recover name and types. However, we have compiled a dictionary of 328 k function headers with corresponding signatures that allows us to find a function header for 59% of the 254 k distinct signatures on the main chain. [2] Since signa-

---

[1] For the 76.5 k source codes from Etherscan, we observe 50 mismatches between the signatures extracted by our tool and the interface there. In all these cases our tool works actually correctly, whereas the given interface on Etherscan is inaccurate.

[2] An infinity of possible function headers is mapped to a finite number of signatures, so there is no guarantee that we recover the original header. The probability of collisions is low, however. E.g., of the 328 k signatures in our dictionary, only 19 appear with a second function header.

tures occur with varying frequencies and codes are deployed in different numbers, this ratio increases to 91% (or 89%) when picking a code (or a deployed contract) at random.

Event Signatures. On source code level, so-called events are used to signal state changes to the outside world. On machine level, events are implemented as LOG instructions with the unabridged Keccak-256 hash of the event header as identifier. We currently lack a tool that can extract the event signatures as reliably as the function signatures. We can check, however, whether a given signature occurs in the code section of the bytecode, as the 32-byte sequence is virtually unique. Even though this heuristic may fail if the signature is stored in the data section, it performs well: For the event *Transfer* and the 76.5 k source codes from Etherscan, we obtain just 0.2 k mismatches.

Code Patterns. Some groups of bytecodes can be specified by regular expressions that generalize observed code patterns. A prime example are the code prefixes that characterize contracts and libraries generated by the Solidity compiler, but also gasTokens, proxies, and some attacks can be identified by such expressions.

Symbolic Execution. To a limited extent, we execute bytecode symbolically to detect code that will always fail or always yield the same result, a behavior typical e.g. of early attacks targeting underpriced or poorly implemented instructions.

5.3   Dynamic Analysis

Time Stamps. Each successful create message gives rise to a new contract. We record the time stamps of the start and the end of deployment, of the first incoming call, and of any self-destructs. There are several intricacies, since self-destructs from and calls to a contract address before and after deployment have different effects. Moreover, since March 2019 different bytecodes may be deployed successively at the same address, so contracts have to be indexed by their creation timestamp rather than their address.

Message Statistics. By counting the messages a contract/code/skeleton sends or receives according to various criteria like type or function signature, we identify excessive or otherwise unusual behavior.

Temporal Patterns of Messages. Certain types of contacts can be specified by characteristic sequences of messages. This approach even works in cases where the bytecode shows greater variance. E.g., a group of several million short-lived contracts exploiting token contracts can be detected by three calls with particular signatures to the target contract followed by a self-destruct.

Log Entry Analysis. In contrast to the static extraction of event signatures from the bytecode, log entries witness events that have actually happened. For transfer events, the log information reveals token holders. Log analysis complements static extraction as it uncovers events missed by extraction as soon as they are used, whereas the extraction detects events even if they have not been used yet.

5.4   Combined Approaches

Grouping contracts by their purpose is a complex task and usually requires a combination of methods.

Interface Method. Some application types, like tokens, use standardized interfaces. Given unknown bytecode, one can detect the presence of such an interface and then draw conclusions regarding the purpose of the code. In [10], the authors show that testing for the presence of five of six mandatory signatures is an effective method for identifying ERC20 tokens. As many token contracts are not fully compliant, we can lower the threshold for signatures even further. To maintain the level of reliability, we can additionally check, statically and dynamically, for standardized events.

Blueprint Fuzzing. Many groups of contracts are heterogeneous. As an example, wallets have a common purpose, but there are hardly any similarities regarding their interfaces. In such a situation, we start from samples with available source code or from frequently deployed bytecode that we identify as group members by manual inspection (blueprints). We then identify idiosyncratic signatures of these blueprints and collect all bytecodes implementing the same signatures. By checking their other signatures and sometimes even the code, we ensure that we do not catch any bytecode outside of the group. If bytecode has been deployed by other contracts, we can detect variants of such factories by the same method; the contracts deployed by these variants are usually also members of the group under considerations. Altogether, this method turned out to be quite effective, though more laborious than the interface method. As an example, starting from 24 Solidity wallets and five wallets available only as bytecode we identified more than four million wallets [7] deployed on the main chain.

Table 1. Methods for identifying groups of contracts

	Function signatures	Event signatures	Eode patterns	Symbolic execution	Time stamps	Message stats	Message patterns	Log entries	Interface	Blueprint fuzzing	Ground truth
Dormant					✓						
Active					✓						
Self-destructed					✓						
Short-lived					✓		✓				
Prolific						✓					
Token	✓	✓				✓		✓	✓		✓
Wallet	✓					✓			✓	✓	✓
ENS deed	✓		✓								
GasToken			✓								✓
Attack			✓	✓		✓					

Ground Truth. For the validation of methods and tools as well as conclusions about contract types, we compiled a ground truth, i.e. a collection of samples known to belong to a particular group [6,7]. This required the manual classification of bytecodes (or more efficiently, skeletons) that are particularly active or otherwise prominent. A further approach is to rely on adequate naming of source code on Etherscan. Moreover, samples identified as positive instances of one group can serve as negative instances for another one.

6   Messages and Contracts

Messages. The 9 M blocks contain 590 M transactions, which gave rise to 1448 M messages. That is, about 40% of the messages are from users, who in turn send about two thirds of the messages to contracts. Regarding contract-related messages, of the 1176 M messages to, from, or between contracts, 81.9% were successful, while 18.1% failed.

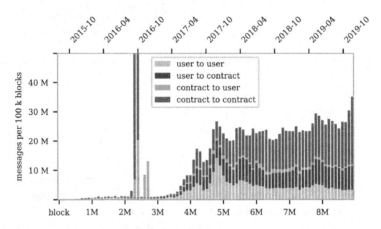

Fig. 1. Stackplot of user-messages (transactions) in blue and contract-sent messages in grey. The two clipped peaks around block 2.4 M depict 137 M and 89 M messages. (Color figure online)

Figure 1 shows the distribution of the messages over time in bins of 100 k blocks (corresponding to about two weeks). Messages initiated by users are depicted in blue, while messages emanating from contracts are depicted in grey. The activities on the blockchain steadily increased in the course of the year 2017 and remained on the elevated level since the year 2018, but with more and more activities happening behind the scenes as the share of internal messages slightly keeps increasing. The peak after block 2 M shows the DoS attack in 2016 with the bloating of the address space in the first two elevated light grey bins and the countermeasure in the next two elevated light grey bins, both touching user addresses. At the same time, the unusually high contract interaction indicated by the two huge dark grey bins was also part of this attack.

Contracts. Figure 2 depicts the 19.7 M successful deployments over time, differentiated into user-created contracts in blue and contract-created ones in grey. Interestingly, 111 k different users created about 3 M (15.2%) contracts, whereas just 21 k distinct contracts deployed 16.7 M (84.8%) contracts.

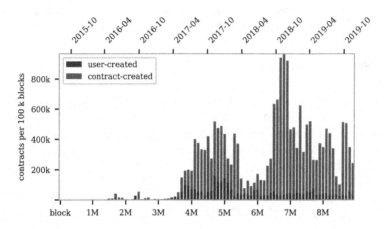

Fig. 2. Stackplot of user-created contracts in blue and contract-created ones in grey. (Color figure online)

7   Groups of Contracts

In this section, we explore groups of contracts with specific properties that we defined in Sect. 4. The methods for identifying the groups are indicated and described in Sect. 5. Interesting properties are a high number of deployments with similar functionality, a high number of specific operations like CREATE, SELFDESTRUCT, or calls, as well as special bytecode or call patterns.

Dormant and Active Contracts. It has been observed (e.g. [5,12]) that many deployed contracts have never been called. As of November 2019, 62.4% (12.3 M) of the successfully created contracts never received a call. On closer inspection, however, the picture is more differentiated (see Sect. 8).

Self-destructed Contracts. We count 7.3 M self-destructed contracts, which include 4.2 M short-lived contracts, 2.8 M GasTokens, and 0.2 M ENS deeds. The remaining 9 k self-destructed contracts contain a few (778) wallets. We arrive at about 8 k contracts that self-destructed for other reasons. Self-destructed contracts show minimal average activity.

Short-Lived Contracts. We count almost 4.2 M short-lived contracts that were created by less than 1 k distinct addresses, mostly contracts. So far, the short-lived contracts predominantly harvested tokens, while some are used to gain advantages in gambling. The main reason for designing such a short-lived contract is to circumvent the intended usage of the contracts with which they interact.

Short-lived contracts appear in two types. Type 1 never deploys a contract and just executes the deployment code. With a total of 4.2 M, almost all short-lived contracts are type 1. Technically, they show no activity (as deployed contract). Type 2 actually deploys a contract that receives calls within the creating transaction, which includes the instruction SELFDESTRUCT that eventually destructs the contract at the end of the transaction. Type 2 is rare (52 k) and was mainly used during the DoS attack in 2016 with high activity.

Prolific Contracts. Interestingly, the set of contracts that deploy other contracts is small, while the number of their deployments is huge. Only 21 k contracts created a total of 16.7 M other contracts, which corresponds to 84.8% of all Ethereum deployments. Still, the vast majority of these deployments (16.3 M) originate from the very small group of 460 prolific contracts, each of which created at least 1 k other contracts. Thus, the prolific contracts leave about 0.4 M deployments to non-prolific contracts and 3.0 M to users. Apart from over 16.3 M contract creations, the prolific contracts made 65 M calls, so in total, they sent about 4.5% of all messages.

Tokens. We identified 226 k token contracts that comprise the 175.6 k fully compliant tokens overlapping with the 108.7 k contracts (23.5 k distinct bytecodes) from the ground truth. Tokens are a highly active group since they were involved in 455.5 M calls, which amounts to 31.5% of all messages.

Wallets. On-chain wallets are numerous, amounting to 4.3 M contracts (21.7% of all contracts). Two-thirds of the on-chain wallets (67.7%) are not in use yet. It might well be that wallets are kept in stock and come into use later. We define wallets to be *not in use* when they have never been called, neither received any token (which can happen passively), nor hold any Ether (which might be included in the deployment or transferred beforehand). Some never called wallets do hold Ether (385), or tokens (20 k), or both (40). Wallets show a low average activity with 30.8 M messages in total, which amounts to 2.1% of all messages.

ENS Deeds. The old ENS registrar created 430 k deeds, of which about half (200 k) are already destructed. They exhibit almost no activity.

GasTokens. We identified 5.3 M deployments. About half of them (2.8 M) were already used and thus destructed, while the other half (2.5 M) are still dormant and wait to be used. GasTokens have 16 k distinct bytecodes that can be reduced to 16 skeletons. Naturally, gasTokens are to be called only once.

Attacks. Remnants of attacks also populate the landscape. Some argue that this debris puts a bias on statistics [9]. On the other hand, attacks are a regular usage scenario in systems with values at stake. We identified 49 k attacking contracts that were involved in almost 30 M calls, which amount to 2% of all messages.

8   Overall Landscape

Dormant, Active, and Short-Lived Contracts. For a deployed contract to become active, it has to receive a call. Therefore, contracts fall into three disjoint groups regarding activity: short-lived contracts that are only active during deployment, dormant contracts that get deployed but have not yet been called, and active contracts that have been called at least once.

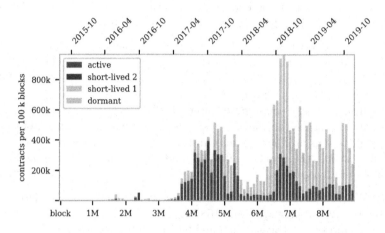

Fig. 3. Deployments of active, short-lived and dormant contracts.

Figure 3 depicts the 7.4 M active contracts in bright colors and the 12.3 M dormant ones in light colors. Regarding the short-lived contracts, the common type 1 is shown in light pink, while the rare type 2 is shown in bright pink.

Weaken claim 1: a) A few wallets are used also passively when receiving tokens. b) The numerous gasTokens are in use *until* they are called. c) The numerous short-lived contracts type 1 are improper contracts as they were never intended to be contracts and actually were active without being called directly. If we disregard the 4.2 M short-lived contracts, the share of never-called contracts drops to 41.1% (8.1 M).

Groups with Plentiful Contracts. Some groups of contracts are deployed in large quantities with a clear usage scenario. At the same time, they are not overly active. Figure 4 shows the deployments of the larger groups wallets, gasTokens, short-lived contracts, and ENS deeds. We also included the highly active, but smaller group of 0.2 M tokens in light green to facilitate the comparison of group sizes. The most common contract type with 5.3 M deployments is the gasToken in blue (dark blue for the already used ones, and light blue yet unused). The second largest group of 4.3 M wallets is depicted in dark green. The almost equally common group of 4.2 M short-lived contracts is depicted in light and bright pink. Finally, there are the 0.4 M ENS deeds in yellow and brown.

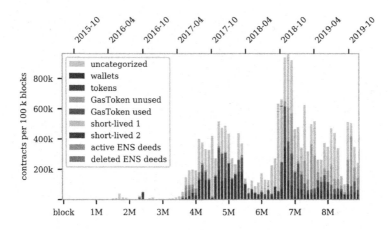

Fig. 4. Deployments of large groups.

Groups with High Activity. Of the total of 1 448 M messages, 21% are transactions, i.e. they come from users. The remaining 79% can be attributed to contracts that generate the further messages as an effect of being called. Attributing the messages (calls) to the identified groups delivers a somewhat incomplete picture. First, we can clearly map only about half of the message to the groups. Secondly, some of the groups contain contracts that belong to a (decentralized) application that employs other contracts as well. This is especially true for the tokens that are part of a dApp. Third, we have not yet characterized exchanges, markets, and DAOs, that may make up a substantial part of the messages. Lastly, some quite active dApps may not fall into the mentioned groups.

As depicted in Fig. 5, the 225.7 k tokens account for 31.5% of all messages (calls from users included). This is followed by the 460 prolific contracts (4.5%). Due to overlaps, we did not include wallets (2.4%), short-lived (1%) and attacking contracts (2%) in the plot.

Regarding exchanges, Etherscan lists 180 addresses (164 user and 16 contract accounts) as well as 111 token accounts. The token activities are already included in our token count. According to Etherscan, the 180 exchange addresses had 76.5 M transactions (!), which corresponds to 12.9% of the overall 590 M transactions. Of these, 6.6 M transactions (1.1%) stem from the 16 contracts.

Corroborate claim 2: a) Token interactions are overwhelmingly high. b) Tokens are the base of an ecosystem that includes also wallets for managing tokens and exchanges for trading them. The contracts and messages of the token ecosystem account for such a large part of the activity that tokens justifiably are referred to as the killer application of SCs.

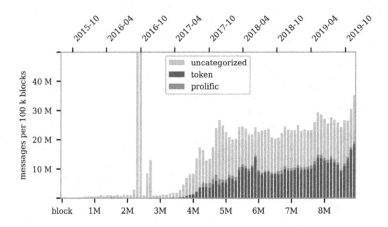

Fig. 5. Group-related message distribution as stackplot.

9   Conclusion

We defined groups of smart contracts with interesting properties. Furthermore, we summarized methods for identifying these groups based on the bytecode and call data that we extracted from the execution trace. With this, we characterized many of the smart contracts deployed in Ethereum until November 2019. Based on the identified groups and their interactions, we elaborated an overall picture of the landscape of smart contracts and tested two claims.

Compared to [12], this work draws a much more detailed and recent picture. This work extends the analysis of [5], as it uses similar groups, but adds further groups and methods. For tokens, it builds on [6,10], for wallets on [7]. In summary, the added value lies in the detail concerning both, temporal aspects and number of groups, as well as in the variety of the employed methods.

Observations. We conclude with some observations resulting from our analysis.

Code variety. As has been widely observed, code reuse on Ethereum is high. Therefore, it is surprising that some authors still evaluate their methods on samples of several hundred thousand *contracts*. Picking one bytecode for each of the 112 k skeletons results in a *complete coverage*, with less effort. By weighting quantitative observations with the multiplicity of skeletons, it is straight-forward to arrive also at conclusions about contracts.

Creations. Deployment is dominated by just a few groups of contracts: gasTokens, wallets, short-lived contracts, and ENS deeds. GasTokens make gas tradable; they are actually in use, even though it is debatable whether they constitute a reasonable use scenario. Wallets are a frequent and natural use case. Short-lived contracts, only active during the creating transaction, are borderline: the contracts they are targeting were probably not intended to be used this way. The ENS deeds were replaced by a more efficient solution without mass deployment. Claim 1 that the majority of contracts remains unused may seem true on a superficial level but becomes less so upon closer inspection.

Calls. Concerning contract activity, there is one dominating group. Tokens form a lively ecosystem resulting in numerous wallets on-chain (and also off-chain) and highly active crypto exchanges (albeit with most of it being non-contract activity). Our work thus confirms that tokens are the killer application before anything else (claim 2). The other groups contribute comparatively little to the call traffic. However, there are still large grey areas in the picture of messages.

Self-destructions. Our work gives a near-complete account of self-destructing contracts. The majority are contracts that fulfill their purpose during deployment and self-destruct to save resources. After further discounting gasTokens and ENS deeds, only 8 k contracts (of 7.3 M) remain that self-destructed for other reasons.

Future Work. Exchanges should be examined in more detail with respect to activity and regulations. Moreover, markets and DAOs seem worth exploring more closely regarding governance and usage scenarios. Furthermore, a focus on dApps would be interesting. Finally, our methodology would be well complemented by a behavioral analysis of contract activity.

References

1. Bartoletti, M., Carta, S., Cimoli, T., Saia, R.: Dissecting Ponzi schemes on Ethereum: identification, analysis, and impact. arXiv:1703.03779 (2017)
2. Bartoletti, M., Pompianu, L.: An empirical analysis of smart contracts: platforms, applications, and design patterns. In: Brenner, M., et al. (eds.) FC 2017. LNCS, vol. 10323, pp. 494–509. Springer, Cham (2017). https://doi.org/10.1007/978-3-319-70278-0_31
3. Chen, T., et al.: Understanding Ethereum via graph analysis. In: IEEE INFOCOM 2018-IEEE Conference on Computer Communications, pp. 1484–1492. IEEE (2018). https://doi.org/10.1109/INFOCOM.2018.8486401
4. Chen, W., Zheng, Z., Cui, J., Ngai, E., Zheng, P., Zhou, Y.: Detecting Ponzi schemes on Ethereum: towards healthier blockchain technology. In: Proceedings of the 2018 World Wide Web Conference. WWW 2018, International World Wide Web Conferences Steering Committee, Republic and Canton of Geneva, Switzerland, pp. 1409–1418 (2018). https://doi.org/10.1145/3178876.3186046
5. Di Angelo, M., Salzer, G.: Mayflies, breeders, and busy bees in Ethereum: smart contracts over time. In: Third ACM Workshop on Blockchains, Cryptocurrencies and Contracts (BCC 2019). ACM Press (2019). https://doi.org/10.1145/3327959.3329537
6. Di Angelo, M., Salzer, G.: Tokens, types, and standards: identification and utilization in Ethereum. In: International Conference on Decentralized Applications and Infrastructures (DAPPS). IEEE (2020). https://doi.org/10.1109/DAPPS49028.2020.00-11
7. Di Angelo, M., Salzer, G.: Wallet contracts on Ethereum. arXiv preprint arXiv:2001.06909 (2020)
8. Ethereum Wiki: A Next-Generation Smart Contract and Decentralized Application Platform. https://github.com/ethereum/wiki/wiki/White-Paper. Accessed 02 Feb 2019

9. Fröwis, M., Böhme, R.: In code we trust? In: Garcia-Alfaro, J., Navarro-Arribas, G., Hartenstein, H., Herrera-Joancomartí, J. (eds.) ESORICS/DPM/CBT -2017. LNCS, vol. 10436, pp. 357–372. Springer, Cham (2017). https://doi.org/10.1007/978-3-319-67816-0_20

10. Fröwis, M., Fuchs, A., Böhme, R.: Detecting token systems on Ethereum. In: Goldberg, I., Moore, T. (eds.) FC 2019. LNCS, vol. 11598, pp. 93–112. Springer, Cham (2019). https://doi.org/10.1007/978-3-030-32101-7_7

11. He, N., Wu, L., Wang, H., Guo, Y., Jiang, X.: Characterizing code clones in the Ethereum smart contract ecosystem. arXiv preprint (2019) arXiv:1905.00272

12. Kiffer, L., Levin, D., Mislove, A.: Analyzing Ethereum's contract topology. In: Proceedings of the Internet Measurement Conference 2018 (IMC 2018), pp. 494–499. ACM, New York (2018). https://doi.org/10.1145/3278532.3278575

13. Norvill, R., Awan, I.U., Pontiveros, B.B.F., Cullen, A.J. et al.: Automated labeling of unknown contracts in Ethereum. In: 26th International Conference on Computer Communication and Networks (ICCCN). IEEE (2017). https://doi.org/10.1109/ICCCN.2017.8038513

14. Wood, G.: Ethereum: a secure decentralised generalised transaction ledger. Technical report, Ethereum Project Yellow Paper (2018). https://ethereum.github.io/yellowpaper/paper.pdf

Smart Contract Development from the Perspective of Developers: Topics and Issues Discussed on Social Media

Afiya Ayman, Shanto Roy, Amin Alipour, and Aron Laszka[✉]

University of Houston, Houston, USA
alaszka@uh.edu

Abstract. Blockchain-based platforms are emerging as a transformative technology that can provide reliability, integrity, and auditability without trusted entities. One of the key features of these platforms is the trustworthy decentralized execution of general-purpose computation in the form of smart contracts, which are envisioned to have a wide range of applications. As a result, a rapidly growing and active community of smart-contract developers has emerged in recent years. A number of research efforts have investigated the technological challenges that these developers face, introducing a variety of tools, languages, and frameworks for smart-contract development, focusing on security. However, relatively little is known about the community itself, about the developers, and about the issues that they face and discuss. To address this gap, we study smart-contract developers and their discussions on two social media sites, Stack Exchange and Medium. We provide insight into the trends and key topics of these discussions, into the developers' interest in various security issues and security tools, and into the developers' technological background.

1 Introduction

The popularity and adoption of blockchain based platforms are growing rapidly both in academia and industry. This growth is driven by the unique features of blockchains: providing integrity and auditability for transactions in open, decentralized systems. While earlier blockchains, such as Bitcoin [42], used these features to establish cryptocurrencies, more recent blockchains, such as Ethereum, also function as distributed computational platforms [56,61]. These platforms enable developers to deploy general-purpose computational code in the form of smart contracts, which can then be executed by a decentralized but trustworthy system. Smart contracts are envisioned to have a range of innovative applications, such as asset tracking in the Internet of Things [10], privacy-preserving transactive energy systems [31,59], and various financial applications [51].

Since the security of these applications hinges on the correctness of the underlying contracts, it is crucial that developers are able to create correct contracts.

© Springer Nature Switzerland AG 2020
M. Bernhard et al. (Eds.): FC 2020 Workshops, LNCS 12063, pp. 405–422, 2020.
https://doi.org/10.1007/978-3-030-54455-3_29

Sadly, the development of smart contracts has proven to be a challenging and error-prone process, in large part due to the unusual semantics of smart contract platforms and languages [4,36]. Studies have found that a large number of contracts that are deployed on the main Ethereum network suffer from various security issues [36,44]. Such issues may manifest as security vulnerabilities, some of which have led to security incidents with financial losses in the range of hundreds of millions of dollars worth of cryptocurrencies [20,43]. As a response, the research community has stepped forward and introduced a number of tools (e.g., [2,36,44,55]), frameworks (e.g., [37–39]), and even new languages (e.g., [45]) to help developers.

While the technical capabilities of these tools and frameworks have been evaluated by multiple surveys (e.g., [9,13,23,29,35]), relatively little is known about whether developers use them in practice or even whether developers are aware of them. In fact, to the best of our knowledge, no prior work has studied the smart contract developers' awareness of security issues and tools or about which issues they are most concerned. In light of this, there is a clear gap in research regarding the developers' perspective of smart contract development. Further, very little is known about the developers' technological background and interests, and about their online communities. Such information is crucial for enabling researchers to better understand the potential entry barriers for smart contract technology and for guiding researchers to address the developers' needs.

To address this gap, we study the smart contract developers' online communities, the topics that they discuss, and their interest in various security issues and tools. To this end, we collect data from three social media sites: *Stack Overflow*, the most popular Q&A site for software developers [3,6,54]; *Ethereum Stack Exchange*, a site focusing on Ethereum from the leading network of Q&A sites [17], and *Medium*, a popular blog hosting site [11]. In particular, we collect and analyze discussions about smart contracts (e.g., posted questions, answers, blog entries, comments) as well as information about the users who participate in these discussions. We seek to answer the following research questions:

Q1 Trends: What are the main trends in smart contract related discussions? How do they compare to discussions related to other technologies?

Q2 Security: Which common security issues and tools do developers discuss? Do discussions about security issues and tools coincide?

Q3 Developers: What are the smart contract developers' technological background and interests besides smart contracts?

We answer the above questions in our analysis (Sect. 3); here, we highlight a few interesting results. We find that the intensity of smart contract related discussions reached its peak in early 2018 and has been slowly declining since then (while discussions about other technologies have remained stable). This coincides with the decline of ETH price, which peaked in January 2018. In the terminology of the so-called 'hype cycle' [19], this suggests that smart contracts may have passed the 'peak of inflated expectations' and are now in the 'trough of disillusionment' phase. This is in interesting contrast with a 2019 July Gartner report [33], which placed smart contracts at the peak of expectations. On Stack Overflow and Ethereum Stack Exchange, we find that most questions about smart contracts receive at least one answer, while the majority of questions about other technologies remain unanswered; however, questions about smart contracts are less likely to lead to lengthy discussions. We also find that very few discussions are related to security, with re-entrancy being the most discussed vulnerability (in part due to the so-called "DAO attack", as evidenced by our findings). There are even fewer mentions of security tools, even in security related discussions. However, we find a significantly higher number of security related posts on Medium. On all sites, smart contract related discussions are dominated by a few key technologies and languages (e.g., Solidity, web3.js, Truffle). Besides smart contracts, the topics that are most discussed by smart contract developers on Stack Overflow are related to web (e.g., jQuery, HTML, CSS). On Medium, we find that smart contract developers are also interested in non-technical topics related to entrepreneurship (e.g., startups, finance, investing).

Outline. The remainder of this paper is organized as follows: In Sect. 2, we describe our data collection and analysis methodology. In Sect. 3, we present the results of our study. In Sect. 4, we give a brief overview of related work. Finally, in Sect. 5, we discuss our findings and provide concluding remarks.

2   Study Design

2.1   Data Collection

Research Ethics. Our study is based on publicly available data, and we report statistical results that contain no personally identifiable information.

Stack Exchange is a network of question-and-answer (Q&A) websites. We collect data from two Stack Exchange sites: *Stack Overflow*[1], the most popular generic site for developers [3,6,54], and *Ethereum Stack Exchange*[2], the site that focuses on Ethereum. On these two websites, posts have the same structure: each post includes a question, a title, a set of associated tags, a set of answers, and a set of comments. Only registered users can post new questions or answer existing ones, which enables us to study the developers. To facilitate searching and categorizing posts, Stack Exchange requires users to associate one or more tags with each question. These tags are unstructured and chosen by the users, so they include a wide range of terms (e.g., *Python, linked-list*).

From Ethereum Stack Exchange, we collect all posts and users using Stack Exchange Data Explorer (SEDE) [1]. We also collect all posts and users from Stack Overflow using the quarterly archives hosted on the Internet Archive [24], which we complement with the latest data from SEDE. Since Stack Overflow is a generic site for developers, we need to find posts that are related to smart

---

[1] https://stackoverflow.com/.
[2] https://ethereum.stackexchange.com/.

contracts. To this end, we use a snowballing methodology. First, we find all posts whose tags contain *smartcontract*. Then, we extract other tags from the collected posts, identify the most frequently used tags that are strictly related to smart contracts, and extend our search with these tags. We continue repeating this process until we cannot collect any more related posts. In the end, we search for posts whose tags contain the following strings (except for *ether*, which needs to be an exact match to avoid finding, e.g., *ethernet*): *smartcontract*, *solidity*, *ether*, *ethereum*, *truffle*, *web3*, *etherscan*. Finally, we manually check a random sample of the collected posts to confirm that they are indeed related to smart contracts. In total, we collect 30,761 smart contract related questions, 38,152 answers, and 73,608 comments as well as the 56,456 users who posted these. Our dataset includes everything up to November 22, 2019.

Medium[3] is a popular blog platform [11], where registered users can publish posts on a variety of subjects, and other users may read, respond (i.e., comment), clap, or vote. A Medium post typically contains a title, a text body, tags, reader responses, number of claps and votes, author's name and profile URL, reading time based on word count, and publication date. Since Medium is a generic blog site, we again use a snowballing methodology to collect smart contract related posts, similar to Stack Overflow. We first search for posts that contain the tag *smart contract*, and then iteratively extend our search with new tags, finally stopping at the following list of tags: *solidity*, *smart contract*, *smart contracts*, *vyper*, *metamask*, *truffle*, *erc20*, *web3*. Again, we manually check a random sample to confirm that the collected post are indeed related to smart contracts. In total, we collect 4,045 unique posts from 2,165 authors, which have been posted on Medium between January 2014 and November 24, 2019.

2.2 Methodology

Statistical Analysis. First, we analyze various statistics of smart contract related posts and the posting users from Stack Exchange and Medium. Statistics for posts include the rate of new posts over time, the distributions of tags, number of answers, etc., while statistics for users include the distribution of tags in all of their posts. For the Stack Exchange dataset, we also compare smart contract related posts to posts about other subjects on Stack Overflow.

Textual Data Analysis. Next, we preprocess the data to prepare the posts for text analysis. First, for each Stack Exchange post, we combine the title, question, answers, comments, and tags together; for each Medium post, we combine the title, text, and tags together. Second, we remove HTML tags and code snippets from all posts. After this step, we search for occurrences of certain keywords in the posts, such as mentions of common security issues and tools.

---

[3] https://medium.com/.

3   Results

3.1   Discussion Trends (Q1)

We begin our analysis by comparing trends in posts about smart contracts with trends in posts about other technologies (e.g., Java and Python). Specifically, we study how interest in smart contracts (measured as the number of new posts) has evolved over time and how active smart contract related discussions are (measured using distributions of answers and comments), showing significant differences compared to other technologies.

Figure 1 compares the number of questions related to smart contracts (vertical bars) posted on Stack Exchange with the total number of questions (black line) posted on Stack Overflow each month. For the sake of comparison, the figure also shows numbers of questions about other, more mature technologies, namely Java (dotted blue), Python (dashed red), and JavaScript (dash-dotted green). The first smart contract related questions were posted in May 2015, but users did not start posting in significant numbers until Ethereum Stack Exchange launched in January 2016. From 2017 to early 2018, there is a clear upward trend; however, the rate of new questions has been steadily declining since then,

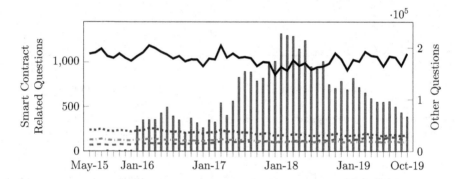

Fig. 1. Number of smart contract related questions (vertical bars) posted on Stack Exchange, number of all questions (black line) and Java (dotted blue), Python (dashed red), and JavaScript (dash-dotted green) related questions posted on Stack Overflow each month. Please note the different scales. (Color figure online)

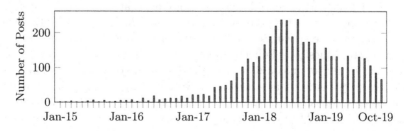

Fig. 2. Number of smart contract related posts on Medium each month.

which suggests that interest in smart contracts on Stack Exchange peaked in early 2018. Meanwhile, the overall rate of new questions on Stack Overflow has remained steady since 2015. Similarly, the rates of new questions about Java, Python, and JavaScript have remained relatively steady, with only slightly increasing (Python) and decreasing (Java) trends. These results suggest that the significant fluctuations observed in smart contract related questions are not due to the varying popularity of Stack Overflow. Finally, Fig. 2 shows the number of new Medium posts related to smart contracts in each month. Again, we observe a clear upward trend from 2017 to early 2018, peaking in the first half of 2018, and a steady decrease since then.

The close similarity between Figs. 1 and 2 suggests that our observations are robust in the sense that they are not artifacts of our data sources, our measurement, or our analysis; rather, the trends that we observe may be signs of declining developer interest in smart contracts. Further, this finding is corroborated by a third data source, the price of Ethereum (ETH). Indeed, we can see a very similar trend in the price of ETH[4] over the past years: ETH reached its highest value on January 12, 2018 [16] and has been mostly declining since then.

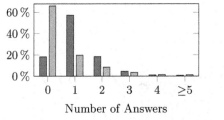 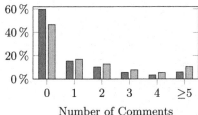

Fig. 3. Number of answers and comments received by smart contract related questions (blue ▮) and by other questions (red ▯) on Stack Exchange. (Color figure online)

To gain insight into the level of interactions in the smart contract developer community, we analyze the distributions of answers and comments in smart contract related posts. Figure 3 shows the number of answers and comments received by smart contract related questions (blue ▮) on Ethereum Stack Exchange and Stack Overflow and by other questions (red ▯) on Stack Overflow. We observe that 82% of smart contract related questions have at least one answer. This ratio is very high compared to other questions, of which less than 34% have at least one answer. We speculate that this difference could be explained by smart contract related questions being simpler and easier to answer, asking mostly about basic issues; or it could be explained by the community of smart contract developers being more active. However, we also observe that few smart contract related questions receive more than one answer, and very few receive five or more, especially in comparison with other questions. This suggests that

---

[4] www.coinbase.com/price/ethereum.

the more likely explanation is that smart contract related questions are indeed simpler since developers rarely post improved or conflicting answers. We also observe that smart contract related questions tend to receive fewer comments than other questions, and receiving five or more comments is very rare (5.9% of smart-contract questions vs. 10.6% of other questions). While the difference compared to other questions is not as pronounced as in the case of answers, this difference indicates that smart contract related questions rarely spark lengthy debates or discussions. This might again suggest that questions pertain to simpler issues.

Table 1. Most frequent tags in smart contract related posts

Stack Exchange						Medium				
Tag	Num.	Average				Tag	Num.	Average		
		Score	View	Ans.	Com.			Resp.	Clap	Voter
Solidity	9323	0.48	752	1.2	1.14	Ethereum	2643	2.37	388	37.10
Go-Ethereum	4946	0.55	1047	1.09	1.19	Blockchain	2585	2.06	423	35.91
web3js	3948	0.48	880	1.16	1.37	Smart Contracts	1274	1.68	311	32.03
Contract-development	2973	0.70	845	1.29	1.04	Solidity	907	1.62	290	29.26
Blockchain	2539	0.88	1232	1.53	1.37	Crypto-currency	659	2.48	577	41.32
Ethereum	2530	1.55	3023	3.73	3.94	Security	476	0.81	194	16.50
Truffle	2430	0.40	750	1.28	1.46	ERC20	467	3.63	836	54.46
Transactions	1743	0.94	1382	1.31	1.1	Web3	401	1.75	429	41.03
Remix	1642	0.29	593	1.15	1.34	Bitcoin	369	5.04	730	74.07
Contract-design	1522	1.12	873	1.34	0.92	MetaMask	296	0.76	216	16.97

Finally, we study what topics are at the center of smart contract related discussions. Posts from both Stack Exchange and Medium have tags to identify the topic of discussion. Although these tags do not necessarily capture the exact topic of discussion, they can indicate what technologies, issues, etc. are discussed. Table 1 lists ten tags that are most frequently used in smart contract related posts on each site. For Stack Exchange, the table lists the average score[5] and the average number of views, answers, and comments received by questions with each tag. For Medium, it lists the average number of responses, claps, and number of voters for each tag. The list is dominated by a few smart contract technologies, such as *Solidity* (high-level language for smart contracts), *Go-Ethereum* (official implementation of Ethereum), *web3js* (JavaScript library for Ethereum), and *Truffle* (development environment for smart contracts). We found very few mentions of other smart-contract languages, such as Vyper or

---

[5] Score is the difference between the number of upvotes and downvotes for a post.

Plutus [25,57]. This may suggest the existence of a monoculture: most developers might be familiar with only a small set of technologies. Alternatively, it may indicate that some technologies are discussed mostly on alternative forums.

3.2   Security Issues and Tools (Q2)

Next, we focus on discussions related to security. Our goal is to gauge the smart contract developers' level of concern and awareness about various security issues and tools. To this end, we search for posts related to common security issues and tools, using the numbers of related posts as indicators for concern about security and for awareness about tools.

Table 2. Posts mentioning common security issues

Security issues	Stack Exchange		Medium	
	Number	Percentage	Number	Percentage
Re-entrancy	126	0.41%	164	4.05%
Denial of service	95	0.31%	111	2.74%
Race condition	35	0.11%	34	0.84%
Integer overflow	16	0.05%	95	2.35%
Transaction-ordering dependence	4	0.01%	66	1.63%
Timestamp dependence	4	0.01%	49	1.21%
Integer underflow	2	0.007%	12	0.30%

Security Issues. To gauge how concerned smart contract developers are about security, we first search for mentions of *security* and *vulnerability* in smart contract related posts. We search in the preprocessed texts of the posts, which include tags, titles, comments, etc. by considering all common variations of these terms (e.g., *vulnerabilities* and *vulnerable*). On Stack Exchange, we find 1,211 and 236 posts that mention *security* and *vulnerability*, respectively, which constitute only 3.9% and 0.77% of all smart contract related posts. On Medium, we find 1,429 and 470 posts that mention *security* and *vulnerability*, respectively, which constitute 32% and 11% of all smart contract related posts. Based on these findings, we speculate that security awareness on Stack Exchange is rather low, while it is comparatively high on Medium. Unfortunately, many developers use Stack Exchange as their primary source of information [6].

Next, we consider specific types of vulnerabilities. Based on prior surveys of smart contract vulnerabilities [4,9,32,36,63], we establish the following list of common issues to search for: *re-entrancy, timestamp dependence, transaction-ordering dependence, integer overflow, integer underflow, race condition,* and *denial of service*. Again, we search for mentions of these issues in the preprocessed posts by considering all common variations (e.g., *DoS, dependence* and *dependency*). Table 2 shows the number of smart contract related Stack Exchange and

Medium posts that mention these issues. We find that Stack Exchange not only suffers from generally low security concern, but discussions are also restricted to only a few issues, such as *re-entrancy*; meanwhile, Medium posts discuss a broader range of issues. To explain Stack Exchange users' fascination with the *re-entrancy* vulnerability, consider Fig. 4, which shows the number of new posts mentioning *re-entrancy* for each month. There is a significant peak in 2016 June, which is when one of the most famous Ethereum security incidents happened, the so-called "DAO attack," which exploited a *re-entrancy* vulnerability [20]. A significant number of security discussions on Stack Exchange seem to be driven by this incident. Also note that Fig. 4 shows relatively high interest in security back in 2016. However, while the number of smart contract related posts on Stack Exchange rapidly rose in 2017, interest in security rather declined.

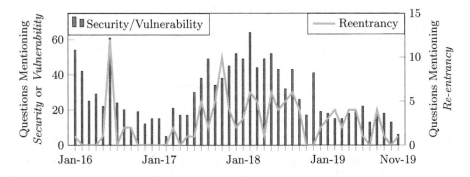

Fig. 4. Number of smart contract posts per month on Stack Exchange mentioning *security* or *vulnerability* and *re-entrancy*. Please note the different scales.

Security Tools, Frameworks, and Design Patterns. We complement our results on security issues by studying the smart contract developers' awareness of security tools (e.g., which tools they ask about or suggest in answers). We compile a comprehensive list of security tools based on relevant evaluation and survey papers (e.g., [9,13,23,29,35,47]) and other sources (e.g., [12]), and search for mentions of the following (in alphabetical order): ContractFuzzer [26], ContractLarva [15], echidna[6], EtherTrust [21], EthIR, Ethlint (formerly known as Solium)[7], FSolidM [37], MAIAN [44], Manticore [40], Mythril (as well as the service MythX and the client Mythos) [41], Octopus[8], Osiris [53], Oyente [36], Rattle [50], ReGuard [34], SASC [62], sCompile [8], Securify [55], Slither [18], Smar-

---

[6] github.com/crytic/echidna.
[7] www.ethlint.com.
[8] github.com/quoscient/octopus.

Table 3. Number of posts mentioning various security tools and patterns

Tools and pattern	Stack Exchange	Medium	Tools and pattern	Stack Exchange	Medium
Mythril	12	98	solcheck	2	5
Oyente	10	64	Maian	2	3
Smartcheck	4	57	Octopus	0	3
Security	6	46	teEther	6	2
Solhint	8	39	Vandal	2	2
Ethlint/Solium	6	36	EthIR	2	2
scompile	0	33	SASC	1	2
Checks-effects-interactions	22	17	VeriSolid	0	2
Manticore	3	16	Zeus	1	1
Slither	0	10	Rattle	1	1
Solgraph	2	7	ContractFuzzer	1	1
Solint	2	6	SonarSolidity	3	0
Surya (Sūrya)	0	6	echidna	1	0

tAnvil [14], SmartCheck [52], solcheck[9], solgraph[10], solint[11], Solhint[12], SonarSo-lidity[13], Sūrya (also spelled as Surya)[14], teEther [30], Vandal [7], VeriSolid [39], VerX [48], VULTRON [58], Zeus [28]. Note that our goal is not to evaluate or compare the technical quality of these tools and frameworks (for that we refer the reader to surveys, e.g., [47]); we are only interested in whether they are discussed by developers. We also search for mentions of the *checks-effects-interactions* design pattern—considering again variations in spelling—which is meant to prevent the re-entrancy vulnerability [49].

Table 3 shows the number of smart contract related posts on Stack Exchange and Medium that mention the above tools. We again find low awareness on Stack Exchange: Mythril and Oyente are mentioned by only 12 and 10 posts, and other tools are mentioned by even fewer. However, we do find 22 posts that mention the *checks-effects-interactions* pattern, which is most likely due to interest in the *re-entrancy* vulnerability (see Table 2). Similarly, we again find higher awareness on Medium: there are 7 tools that are mentioned at least 33 times, with Mythril being mentioned the most.

---

[9] github.com/federicobond/solcheck.
[10] github.com/raineorshine/solgraph.
[11] github.com/SilentCicero/solint.
[12] protofire.github.io/solhint.
[13] github.com/sagap/sonar-solidity.
[14] github.com/ConsenSys/surya.

Table 4. Co-occurrence of security issues and tools in posts

Security tools	Security/vulnerability		Re-entrancy		Timestamp dependency		Transaction ordering dependency	
	Stack Overflow	Medium	Stack Overflow	Medium	Stack Overflow	Medium	Stack Overflow	Medium
Mythril	6	95	2	36	2	19	2	17
Oyente	6	63	2	37	1	26	1	3
Smartcheck	3	57	0	45	1	34	1	2
Securify	4	45	1	26	1	20	1	3
Solhint	2	38	1	34	1	26	1	1
Ethlint/Solium	4	28	1	10	1	6	1	3
Manticore	3	16	1	5	1	1	1	0
Slither	0	10	0	7	0	3	0	2
solgraph	2	7	1	4	1	1	1	0
Surya	0	6	0	2	0	1	0	0
solint	2	5	1	1	1	0	1	0
Solcheck	2	4	1	2	1	1	1	0
Maian	0	3	0	2	0	1	0	1
SASC	0	2	0	1	0	1	0	1
VeriSolid	0	2	0	1	0	0	0	0
Vandal	2	2	0	1	0	0	0	0
teEther	2	1	0	0	0	0	0	0
EthIR	2	1	0	1	0	0	0	0

Co-Occurrence of Security Issues and Tools. Finally, we investigate if users recommend these tools against certain vulnerabilities and if they are aware of which vulnerabilities these tools address. To this end, we study which security issues and tools are mentioned together. Table 4 shows the number of posts on Stack Exchange and Medium that mention various pairs of security issues and tools (focusing on pairs mentioned by the most posts, omitting less frequent pairs). Again, we find low awareness on Stack Exchange: Mythril and Oyente are each mentioned only in 6 posts that also mention *security* or *vulnerability*, which means that these tools are suggested for security issues less than 0.5% of the time; other tools are mentioned even fewer times. These tools are not mentioned even in conjunction with vulnerabilities that they address (see, e.g., *re-entrancy*). On the other hand, we find much higher awareness on Medium, as security issues and tools are often mentioned together.

3.3 Developers' Background and Interests (Q3)

For many developers, it is easier to adopt new tools, languages, and platforms that resemble ones with which they are already familiar. Hence, adoption of new technologies can hinge on the developers' technological background. To discover with which technologies smart contract developers are familiar, we study what tags they use in posts that are *not* related to smart contracts.

For each smart contract developer, we retrieve all of the developer's posts (i.e., questions and answers, or blog posts) that are *not* related to smart contracts, collecting a total of 1,250,325 posts from Stack Overflow and 44,684 posts

Table 5. Other tags used by smart contract developers on SO & Medium

Stack Overflow		Medium					
		Blockchain		Technical (Other)		Non-technical	
Tag	Freq.	Tag	Freq.	Tag	Freq.	Tag	Freq.
jQuery	8787	Blockchain	17877	Technology	2167	Startup	1897
HTML	6503	Cryptocurrency	8957	Artificial Intelligence	1331	Investing	958
CSS	5657	Bitcoin	5013	Fintech	1232	Finance	820
Node.js	5040	Crypto	2511	IoT	697	Business	786
.NET	4247	ICO	2256	Programming	646	Entrepreneurship	582
Android	3739	Security	630	JavaScript	635	Exchange	527
Objective-C	3727	Cryptocurrency Investment	620	Machine Learning	479	Marketing	493
MySQL	3330	Token Sale	616	Software Development	376	Innovation	488
Ruby	3281	Decentralization	525	Privacy	342	News	467
JSON	3231	Tokenization	220	Data	329	Travel	428

from Medium. Table 5 lists the 10 most frequently used tags in the smart contract developers' Stack Overflow posts. The most frequent tags are all related to web development (*jQuery, HTML, CSS, Node.js*). Other popular tags correspond to major platforms (*.NET, Android*). Table 5 lists the most frequent tags from the smart contract developers' Medium posts in three categories: blockchain related, other technical, and non-technical (i.e., everything else). Note that since Medium is a generic blog site, there are many non-technical posts (e.g., tagged with *Business* or *Travel*). Unsurprisingly, the most popular tags are related to blockchains and cryptocurrencies. Other technical terms are led by the area of *Artificial Intelligence* and *Machine Learning*, and by tags related to software development (e.g., *Programming* and *JavaScript*). The most frequent non-technical terms are related to entrepreneurship (*Startup, Finance, Business, Investing*, etc.).

On both sites, we observe that a significant number of posts are related to JavaScript (highlighted in blue in Table 5): on Medium, *JavaScript* is the only programming language in the top 10 tags; on Stack Exchange, related technologies (*jQuery* and *Node.js*) are at the top. These results suggest that many smart contract developers have a background in JavaScript and related technologies, which may be explained by the similarity between JavaScript and Solidity, the most widely used high-level language for smart contract development.

4   Related Work

Smart Contract Development Practices. Bartoletti et al. [5] were the first to quantitatively investigate the usage of design patterns and the major categories of smart contracts, providing a categorized and tabulated repository of data related to smart contracts. To this end, they examined smart contract platforms, applications, and design patterns, aggregated articles about smart contracts from coindesk.com, and identified nine common design patterns used in some combination by most of the smart contracts that they found. Atzei et al. [4] presented a study of security vulnerabilities in Ethereum smart contracts, based on analysis of academic literature, Internet blogs, discussion forums about Ethereum, and practical experience in programming smart contracts. Based on their study, they provided a taxonomy for the root causes of vulnerabilities and techniques to mitigate them. Wohrer et al. [60] examined design patterns for smart contracts in Ethereum, focusing on two questions: which design patterns are common in the ecosystem and how they map to Solidity coding practices. They employed a multivocal literature review, which considered various sources from academic papers to blogs and forums about Ethereum. Their analysis yielded 18 distinct design patterns. Jiang et al. [27] performed a preliminary study of blockchain technology as interpreted by developers and found that blockchain related questions represent a growing minority of posts on Stack Overflow. The most common problems with blockchain are related to configuration, deployment, and discussion, followed by ten less common categories. However, they did not consider the development of smart contracts.

Smart Contract Security Issues and Tools. Parizi et al. [46] conducted an empirical analysis of smart contract programming languages based on usability and security from the novice developers' point of view. They considered three programming languages: Solidity, Pact, and Liquidity. The study concluded that although Solidity is the most useful language to a novice developer, it is also the most vulnerable to malicious attacks as novice developers often introduce security vulnerabilities, which can leave the contracts exposed to threats. More recently, in another study, Parizi et al. [47] carried out an assessment of various static smart contract security testing tools for Ethereum and its programming language, Solidity. Their results showed that the SmartCheck tool is statistically more effective than the other automated security testing tools. However, their study considers only the effectiveness, usability, etc. of the tools, but not whether developers are aware of them in practice. Groce et al. [22] summarized the results of security assessments (both manual and automated) performed on smart contracts by a security company. The authors argued that their results pertain to more important contracts (in contrast to prior surveys) since developers were willing to pay for the assessments. Based on the results, they categorized security issues and provided statistics on their frequency, impact, and exploitability. Li et al. [32] studied a wide range of security issues in blockchain technology. They conducted a systematic examination of security risks to blockchain by studying popular blockchain platforms (e.g., Ethereum, Bitcoin, Monero).

5 Discussion and Conclusion

Based on the volume of smart contract related discussions on Stack Exchange (i.e., Stack Overflow and Ethereum Stack Exchange) and Medium, we found that interest in smart contracts—at least from the developers' perspective—seems to have peaked in the first few months of 2018, and has been slowly declining since then. This trend also coincides with a decline in the price of ETH. It will be interesting to see whether this negative trend will continue into the future, or if the decline was just a temporary disillusionment after the initial hype.

We also found that even though most smart contract related questions on Stack Exchange receive at least one answer, extended discussions that would include many answers or comments are rare. The topics of smart contract related discussion on Stack Exchange seem to be dominated by a narrow stack (e.g., Solidity, Go Ethereum, Truffle, web3.js), and we observe the prevalence of similar topics on Medium. For example, on both sites, alternative languages (e.g., Vyper) are rarely discussed.

We also observed limited discussion of security-related topics on Stack Exchange, which is very concerning since many smart contracts suffer from security vulnerabilities in practice and since many developers rely on Stack Overflow and similar sites. On Stack Exchange, less than 5% of posts mention security or vulnerabilities; while on Medium, the ratio is around 41%. On Stack Exchange, re-entrancy is the most discussed vulnerability, which seems to be in large part due to the infamous "DAO attack." Similarly, Stack Exchange posts rarely mention security tools. Further, security tools are even less frequently mentioned in response to question about vulnerabilities (e.g., in conjunction with question about re-entrancy, even though some of the tools can detect re-entrancy vulnerabilities). Fortunately, Medium has a lot more posts that discuss security tools. We find Oyente and Mythril to be the most popular among those tools.

Finally, studying what other topics smart contract developers discuss, we found a significant number of posts about JavaScript and related technologies (and web technologies more generally). This suggests that many smart contract developers have background and interest in JavaScript. We will explore the relationship between the JavaScript and smart-contract developer communities deeper in future work. Similarly, we will also study the relation between smart-contract and safety-critical technologies from the perspective of developers in future work.

Acknowledgment. We thank the anonymous reviewers of our manuscript for their insightful comments.

References

1. Stack Exchange Data Explore. https://data.stackexchange.com/. Accessed 22 Nov 2019
2. di Angelo, M., Salzer, G.: A survey of tools for analyzing Ethereum smart contracts (2019). https://pdfs.semanticscholar.org/5fcd/6089a4973d3ddd7ca831b7129046c87f33c6.pdf
3. Ashutosh, K.S.: Top 10 Sites to Ask All Your Programming Questions (2017). https://www.hongkiat.com/blog/programming-questions-websites/. Accessed 23 Sept 2019
4. Atzei, N., Bartoletti, M., Cimoli, T.: A survey of attacks on ethereum smart contracts (SoK). In: Maffei, M., Ryan, M. (eds.) POST 2017. LNCS, vol. 10204, pp. 164–186. Springer, Heidelberg (2017). https://doi.org/10.1007/978-3-662-54455-6_8

5. Bartoletti, M., Pompianu, L.: An empirical analysis of smart contracts: platforms, applications, and design patterns. In: Brenner, M., et al. (eds.) FC 2017. LNCS, vol. 10323, pp. 494–509. Springer, Cham (2017). https://doi.org/10.1007/978-3-319-70278-0_31

6. Barua, A., Thomas, S.W., Hassan, A.E.: What are developers talking about? An analysis of topics and trends in stack overflow. Empirical Softw. Eng. 19(3), 619–654 (2014)

7. Brent, L., et al.: Vandal: a scalable security analysis framework for smart contracts. arXiv preprint arXiv:1809.03981 (2018)

8. Chang, J., Gao, B., Xiao, H., Sun, J., Yang, Z.: sCompile: Critical path identification and analysis for smart contracts. arXiv preprint arXiv:1808.00624 (2018)

9. Chen, H., Pendleton, M., Njilla, L., Xu, S.: A survey on Ethereum systems security: vulnerabilities, attacks and defenses. arXiv preprint arXiv:1908.04507 (2019)

10. Christidis, K., Devetsikiotis, M.: Blockchains and smart contracts for the Internet of Things. IEEE Access 4, 2292–2303 (2016)

11. Colwell, A.: How Medium became a leading blogging platform - Salesflare blog. https://blog.salesflare.com/how-medium-became-a-leading-blogging-platform-9b4b08d9d3ac. Accessed 26 Nov 2019

12. ConsenSys: Security tools. Ethereum Smart Contract Best Practices (2019). https://consensys.github.io/smart-contract-best-practices/security_tools/

13. Di Angelo, M., Salzer, G.: A survey of tools for analyzing Ethereum smart contracts. In: Proceedings of the 2019 IEEE International Conference on Decentralized Applications and Infrastructures (DAPPCON) (2019)

14. Ducasse, S., Rocha, H., Bragagnolo, S., Denker, M., Francomme, C.: SmartAnvil: Open-source tool suite for smart contract analysis (2019)

15. Ellul, J., Pace, G.: Runtime verification of Ethereum smart contracts. In: Conjunction with 14th European Dependable Computing Conference (EDCC), Workshop on Blockchain Dependability (WBD) (2018)

16. EthereumPrice.org: Ethereum price, charts & history. https://ethereumprice.org/. Accessed 12 Apr 2019

17. FeedreaderObserve: Ethereum Stack Exchange news. https://feedreader.com/observe/ethereum.stackexchange.com. Accessed 12 Oct 2019

18. Feist, J., Grieco, G., Groce, A.: Slither: a static analysis framework for smart contracts. In: Proceedings of the 2nd IEEE/ACM International Workshop on Emerging Trends in Software Engineering for Blockchain (WETSEB), pp. 8–15. IEEE (2019)

19. Fenn, J., Raskino, M.: Mastering the Hype Cycle: How to Choose the Right Innovation at the Right Time. Harvard Business Press (2008)

20. Finley, K.: A $50 million hack just showed that the DAO was all too human. Wired, June 2016. https://www.wired.com/2016/06/50-million-hack-just-showed-dao-human/

21. Grishchenko, I., Maffei, M., Schneidewind, C.: EtherTrust: sound static analysis of Ethereum bytecode. Technische Universität Wien, Technical report (2018)

22. Groce, A., Feist, J., Grieco, G., Colburn, M.: What are the actual flaws in important smart contracts (and how can we find them)? arXiv preprint arXiv:1911.07567 (2019)

23. Harz, D., Knottenbelt, W.: Towards safer smart contracts: a survey of languages and verification methods. arXiv preprint arXiv:1809.09805 (2018)

24. Internet Archive: Stack Exchange Directory Listing. https://archive.org/download/stackexchange. Accessed 23 Sept 2019

25. IOHK: Plutus: a functional contract platform. https://testnet.iohkdev.io/en/plutus/. Accessed 11 Mar 2020
26. Jiang, B., Liu, Y., Chan, W.: ContractFuzzer: fuzzing smart contracts for vulnerability detection. In: Proceedings of the 33rd ACM/IEEE International Conference on Automated Software Engineering (ASE), pp. 259–269. ACM (2018)
27. Jiang, H., Liu, D., Ren, Z., Zhang, T.: Blockchain in the eyes of developers (2018)
28. Kalra, S., Goel, S., Dhawan, M., Sharma, S.: ZEUS: analyzing safety of smart contracts. In: Proceedings of the 2018 Network and Distributed Systems Security Symposium (NDSS) (2018)
29. Kirillov, D., Iakushkin, O., Korkhov, V., Petrunin, V.: Evaluation of tools for analyzing smart contracts in distributed ledger technologies. In: Misra, S., et al. (eds.) ICCSA 2019. LNCS, vol. 11620, pp. 522–536. Springer, Cham (2019). https://doi.org/10.1007/978-3-030-24296-1_41
30. Krupp, J., Rossow, C.: teEther: gnawing at ethereum to automatically exploit smart contracts. In: Proceedings of the 27th USENIX Security Symposium, pp. 1317–1333 (2018)
31. Laszka, A., Eisele, S., Dubey, A., Karsai, G., Kvaternik, K.: TRANSAX: a blockchain-based decentralized forward-trading energy exchange for transactive microgrids. In: Proceedings of the 24th IEEE International Conference on Parallel and Distributed Systems (ICPADS), December 2018
32. Li, X., Jiang, P., Chen, T., Luo, X., Wen, Q.: A survey on the security of blockchain systems. Future Gener. Comput. Syst. **107**, 841–853 (2017)
33. Litan, A., Leow, A.: Hype cycle for blockchain technologies, 2019. Technical report G00383155, Gartner Research, July 2019. https://www.gartner.com/en/documents/3947355/hype-cycle-for-blockchain-technologies-2019
34. Liu, C., Liu, H., Cao, Z., Chen, Z., Chen, B., Roscoe, B.: ReGuard: finding reentrancy bugs in smart contracts. In: Proceedings of the 40th International Conference on Software Engineering: Companion Proceedings (ICSE), pp. 65–68. ACM (2018)
35. Liu, J., Liu, Z.: A survey on security verification of blockchain smart contracts. IEEE Access **7**, 77894–77904 (2019)
36. Luu, L., Chu, D.H., Olickel, H., Saxena, P., Hobor, A.: Making smart contracts smarter. In: Proceedings of the 23rd ACM SIGSAC Conference on Computer and Communications Security (CCS), pp. 254–269, October 2016
37. Mavridou, A., Laszka, A.: Designing secure ethereum smart contracts: a finite state machine based approach. In: Meiklejohn, S., Sako, K. (eds.) FC 2018. LNCS, vol. 10957, pp. 523–540. Springer, Heidelberg (2018). https://doi.org/10.1007/978-3-662-58387-6_28
38. Mavridou, A., Laszka, A.: Tool demonstration: FSolidM for designing secure ethereum smart contracts. In: Bauer, L., Küsters, R. (eds.) POST 2018. LNCS, vol. 10804, pp. 270–277. Springer, Cham (2018). https://doi.org/10.1007/978-3-319-89722-6_11
39. Mavridou, A., Laszka, A., Stachtiari, E., Dubey, A.: VeriSolid: correct-by-design smart contracts for Ethereum. In: Goldberg, I., Moore, T. (eds.) FC 2019. LNCS, vol. 11598, pp. 446–465. Springer, Cham (2019). https://doi.org/10.1007/978-3-030-32101-7_27
40. Mossberg, M., et al.: Manticore: a user-friendly symbolic execution framework for binaries and smart contracts. arXiv preprint arXiv:1907.03890 (2019)
41. Mueller, B.: Smashing Ethereum smart contracts for fun and real profit. In: 9th Annual HITB Security Conference (HITBSecConf) (2018)

42. Nakamoto, S.: Bitcoin: A Peer-to-Peer Electronic Cash System (2008)
43. Newman, L.H.: Security news this week: $280m worth of Ethereum is trapped thanks to a dumb bug. WIRED, November 2017. https://www.wired.com/story/280m-worth-of-ethereum-is-trapped-for-a-pretty-dumb-reason/
44. Nikolić, I., Kolluri, A., Sergey, I., Saxena, P., Hobor, A.: Finding the greedy, prodigal, and suicidal contracts at scale. In: Proceedings of the 34th Annual Computer Security Applications Conference (ACSAC), pp. 653–663 (2018)
45. O'Connor, R.: Simplicity: a new language for blockchains. In: Proceedings of the 2017 Workshop on Programming Languages and Analysis for Security, pp. 107–120. PLAS (2017)
46. Parizi, R.M., Amritraj, Dehghantanha, A.: Smart contract programming languages on blockchains: an empirical evaluation of usability and security. In: Chen, S., Wang, H., Zhang, L.J. (eds.) Proceedings of the 1st International Conference on Blockchain (ICBC), vol. 10974, pp. 75–91. Springer, Cham (2018). https://doi.org/10.1007/978-3-319-94478-4_6
47. Parizi, R.M., Dehghantanha, A., Choo, K.K.R., Singh, A.: Empirical vulnerability analysis of automated smart contracts security testing on blockchains. In: Proceedings of the 28th Annual International Conference on Computer Science and Software Engineering (CASCON) (2018)
48. Permenev, A., Dimitrov, D., Tsankov, P., Drachsler-Cohen, D., Vechev, M.: VerX: safety verification of smart contracts. In: Proceedings 41st IEEE Symposium on Security and Privacy (S&P) (2020)
49. Solidity Documentation: Security considerations - use the Checks-Effects-Interactions pattern. http://solidity.readthedocs.io/en/develop/security-considerations.html#use-the-checks-effects-interactions-pattern (2018). Accessed 23 Sept 2019
50. Stortz, R.: Rattle - an Ethereum EVM binary analysis framework. REcon Montreal (2018)
51. Tapscott, A., Tapscott, D.: How blockchain is changing finance. Harvard Bus. Rev. 1(9), 2–5 (2017)
52. Tikhomirov, S., Voskresenskaya, E., Ivanitskiy, I., Takhaviev, R., Marchenko, E., Alexandrov, Y.: SmartCheck: static analysis of Ethereum smart contracts. In: Proceedings of the 1st IEEE/ACM International Workshop on Emerging Trends in Software Engineering for Blockchain (WETSEB), pp. 9–16. IEEE (2018)
53. Torres, C.F., Schütte, J., et al.: Osiris: hunting for integer bugs in Ethereum smart contracts. In: Proceedings of the 34th Annual Computer Security Applications Conference (ACSAC), pp. 664–676. ACM (2018)
54. Tryfanava, D.: 25 Best Active Forums for Programmers (2018). https://vironit.com/best-active-forums-for-programmers/. Accessed on 23 Sept 2019
55. Tsankov, P., Dan, A., Cohen, D.D., Gervais, A., Buenzli, F., Vechev, M.: Securify: Practical security analysis of smart contracts. In: 25th ACM Conference on Computer and Communications Security (CCS) (2018)
56. Underwood, S.: Blockchain beyond bitcoin. Commun. ACM 59(11), 15–17 (2016)
57. Vyper Team: Vyper documentation. https://vyper.readthedocs.io/en/latest/. Accessed 11 Mar 2020
58. Wang, H., Li, Y., Lin, S.W., Ma, L., Liu, Y.: VULTRON: catching vulnerable smart contracts once and for all. In: Proceedings of the 41st International Conference on Software Engineering: New Ideas and Emerging Results (ICSE-NIER), pp. 1–4 (2019)

59. Wang, N., et al.: When energy trading meets blockchain in electrical power system: the state of the art. Appl. Sci. **9**(8), 1561 (2019). https://doi.org/10.3390/app9081561
60. Wöhrer, M., Zdun, U.: Design patterns for smart contracts in the Ethereum ecosystem. In: Proceedings of the 2018 IEEE Conference on Blockchain, pp. 1513–1520 (2018)
61. Wood, G.: Ethereum: a secure decentralised generalised transaction ledger. Technical report EIP-150, Ethereum Project - Yellow Paper, April 2014
62. Zhou, E., et al.: Security assurance for smart contract. In: Proceedings of the 9th IFIP International Conference on New Technologies, Mobility and Security (NTMS), pp. 1–5. IEEE (2018)
63. Zhu, L., et al.: Research on the security of blockchain data: a survey. arXiv preprint arXiv:1812.02009 (2018)

Bypassing Non-Outsourceable Proof-of-Work Schemes Using Collateralized Smart Contracts

Alexander Chepurnoy[1,2]([⊠]) and Amitabh Saxena[1]

[1] Ergo Platform, Sestroretsk, Russia
kushti@protonmail.ch, amitabh123@gmail.com
[2] IOHK Research, Sestroretsk, Russia
alex.chepurnoy@iohk.io

Abstract. Centralized pools and renting of mining power are considered as sources of possible censorship threats and even 51% attacks for decentralized cryptocurrencies. Non-outsourceable Proof-of-Work (PoW) schemes have been proposed to tackle these issues. However, tenets in the folklore say that such schemes could potentially be bypassed by using escrow mechanisms. In this work, we propose a concrete example of such a mechanism which is using collateralized smart contracts. Our approach allows miners to bypass non-outsourceable PoW schemes if the underlying blockchain platform supports smart contracts in a sufficiently advanced language. In particular, the language should allow access to the PoW solution. At a high level, our approach requires the miner to lock some collateral covering the reward amount and protected by a smart contract acting as an escrow. The smart contract allows the pool to collect the collateral as soon as the miner collects any block rewards. We propose two variants of the approach depending on when the collateral is bound to the block solution. Using this, we show how to bypass previously proposed non-outsourceable Proof-of-Work schemes (with the notable exception for strong non-outsourceable schemes) and show how to build mining pools for such schemes.

1 Introduction

Security of Bitcoin and many other cryptocurrencies relies on so called Proof-of-Work (PoW) schemes (also known as scratch-off puzzles), which are mechanisms to reach fast consensus and guarantee immutability of the ledger. Security of such consensus mechanisms is based on the assumption that no single entity controls a large part of the mining power. For example, if a single entity controls 33% then it can earn unproportionally more rewards using *selfish mining* [1], and with more than 50% an adversary can do double spending or filter out certain transactions. Mining pools are the primary cause of such concentration of mining power. However, individually, it is more beneficial for miners to join pools despite the fact that they are detrimental to the system. Another threat, especially for new

M. Bernhard et al. (Eds.): FC 2020 Workshops, LNCS 12063, pp. 423–435, 2020.
https://doi.org/10.1007/978-3-030-54455-3_30

cryptocurrencies are potential Goldfinger attacks using hosted mining services to rent mining power in order to mine (or attack) a cryptocurrency [2].

Non-outsourceable scratch-off puzzles have been proposed to address these issues [3,4]. A notable example of a real world implementation of this idea is Ergo [5], whose PoW, Autolykos [6], is based on [4]. The primary technique in such approaches is to discourage pooled mining by tying the rewards to some trapdoor information needed for solution generation. In this work, we describe how to bypass the non-outsourceability of many such schemes, including Ergo's. More importantly, while our solution bypasses non-outsourceability, which gives the ability to form pools, it retains the *censorship resistance* property of non-outsourceable puzzles. That is, a pool cannot conduct 51% attacks even if it handles more than 51% of the mining power (see Sect. 2.2 for details).

The rest of the paper is organized as follows. Section 2 contains an overview of the current state of affairs in proof-of-work schemes and pooled mining along a high level overview of non-outsourceable puzzles. Section 3 describes one approach for creating mining pools in many types of non-outsourceable puzzles, specifically those of [4]. Section 4 describes another approach that covers a wider range of puzzles [3,4]. We conclude the paper in Sect. 5 along with pointers for future research.

2   Background

2.1   Proofs of Work

We first describe the vanilla proof-of-work (PoW) mechanism used in Bitcoin. In order to generate a block in Bitcoin, a miner collects a number of unconfirmed transactions and organizes them into a Merkle tree. The digest of this tree, denoted t here, is stored in a section of the block called the *block header*, which also includes h, the hash of the previous block's header, and n, a random string called the nonce. We use the term m to denote the puzzle made of the concatenation of the Merkle tree digest and the hash of the previous block. That is, $m = t\|h$ and then the header is of the form $m\|n$. The solution is also determined by another parameter $\lambda > 1$, called the *difficulty*. Let H be a collision resistant hash function with output of 256 bits. The header $m\|n$ is considered a valid solution if $H(m\|n) \leq 2^{256}/\lambda$. A miner repeatedly tries different values of n (and possibly m) until a solution is found. Since H is like a random oracle, the probability of finding a solution in one attempt is $1/\lambda$. All PoW systems use the above idea of finding a value from a uniform distribution that falls within some narrower range based on the difficulty parameter.

2.2   Pooled Mining

Bitcoin allows mining pools, which roughly work as follows. The pool distributes work based on a some m that it decides. Each miner tries to find a solution for the given m and any solution found is sent to the network. A miner actually tries to find a *share*, which is like a solution but with reduced difficulty (also decided by the pool). Some of the shares may also be real solutions, which result in valid blocks. A miner gets paid by the number of shares submitted. This is possible because the Bitcoin PoW puzzle is a *scratch-off puzzle* [3], a type of PoW puzzle that can be processed in parallel by multiple non-communicating entities with an appropriate reduction in search time.

The pool generates the potential block candidates as if it was solo mining, and then distributes that candidate to its miners for solving, which can be considered workers for the pool. The shares have no actual value and are just an accounting tool used by the pool to keep track of the work done by each worker. The key observation with pools is that miners do work for some other entity who then distributes the rewards back to the workers. Since the pool selects the transactions that are to be included, this gives the pool greater control over the entire blockchain network. We define this using three levels of (de)centralization that a pool may operate at.

1. *Level 1 (Centralized):* The pool operator defines both m and the reward address. Thus, a pool operator has full control over which transactions are included (censorship) and also carries the risk of losing the rewards.
2. *Level 2 (Censorship Resistant):* The pool operator does not define m but collects the rewards. This is resistant to censorship but still carries the risk of losing the rewards.
3. *Level 3 (Decentralized):* There is no centralized pool operator but rather another decentralized oracle that emulates the pool operator and rewards are automatically given to the participants based on the shares they submitted (see P2Pool [7] for Bitcoin and SmartPool [8] for Ethereum). In P2Pool, this oracle is implemented using another blockchain, while in SmartPool, it is implemented using a smart contract.

The following table summarizes the concepts.

Pool level	Censorship	Reward theft risk	Example
L1 (Centralized)	Yes	Yes	BTC.com
L2 (Censorship Resistant)	No	Yes	ErgoPool (this work)
L3 (Decentralized)	No	No	SmartPool [8], P2Pool [7]

The primary issue with pools is that they increase the potential of transaction censorship and 51 percent attacks. One way to address this issue is to disallow pools entirely. This is what non-outsourceable puzzles aim to achieve, and Ergo is the first practical implementation of such puzzles [5]. Thus, such puzzles are designed to provide the same level of security as an L3 pool.

We, however, note that disallowing pools entirely comes with its own set of problems. For instance, at Ergo launch, the difficulty went up so quickly that miners with single GPUs could not find any blocks in a reasonable time. Since

Ergo does not allow pools, such miners had no incentive to continue mining. In fact, this research was motivated from the need to create a mining pool for Ergo. However, we also want our solution to retain the security offered by lack of pools, that is, resistance to censorship and 51% attacks.

Our solution is based on the observation that another way to address censorship and 51 percent attacks is to have pools operate at levels L2 or L3, where these issues are not present. Thus, not only can we have decentralization in mining but also have all the benefits of pools (such as regular income for miners and thereby, stronger network). Our solution is designed for L2 but can also be trivially extended to operate at L1. Additionally, it may be possible to extend it to L3 using approaches similar to SmartPool or P2Pool, which we leave as a topic for further research.

2.3   Non-Outsourceable Puzzles

We start with overviewing (non-)outsourceability definitions in existing literature expressed in different works, such as Non-outsourceable Scratch-Off Puzzles [3], 2-Phase Proof-of-Work (2P-PoW) [9], PieceWork [4], Autolykos [6]. The details of these approaches are described in Sects. 3 and 4. However, at a high level, all these approaches can be broadly classified into two categories.

In the first one [4,6,9], which we call **Type 1**, a PoW scheme is considered non-outsourceable if it is not possible to iterate over the solution space without knowing some trapdoor information (such as a secret key) corresponding to some public information (such as a public key) contained in the block header, with block rewards locked by that trapdoor information. The reasoning here is that in order to send the reward to a pool's address, each miner must know the secret corresponding to that address. However, a pool does not trust miners and so will not give the secret away to them.

In the other category [3], called **Type 2**, a PoW scheme is considered non-outsourceable if for any solved block, a miner can generate another block efficiently with non-negligible probability. The motivation behind this definition is that a miner can get paid for shares by trying to generate a block that pays the reward to the pool. In case of successful block generation, however, the miner could generate and broadcast another block that sends the reward elsewhere. We further classify Type 2 into *weak* if the identity of the miner stealing the rewards can be ascertained and *strong* if the identity remains secret.

At a technical level, both Type 1 and 2 approaches rely on a miner's ability to steal the pool's rewards. The difference lies in the way this occurs. In Type 1 schemes, the miner is able to steal the reward *after* the block gets finalized. In Type 2, the reward can only be stolen *before* a block is finalized.

We note that all Type 2 schemes have an inherent problem that allows malicious actors to flood the network with a large number of valid but distinct solutions, thereby causing network partitions and instability. This causes the network to converge very slowly or result in several forks. Hence, we don't consider Type 2 schemes to be robust in reaching consensus, thereby making them impractical in the real world. We call this the *forking attack*. Strong Type 2 schemes are even more prone to this attack because there is no fear of detection.

In this work, we bypass the non-outsourceability of all Type 1 and weak Type 2 schemes assuming that their platforms support some minimal smart contract capability. The following table summarizes this.

Puzzle type	Thief's identity	When rewards stolen	Forking attack	Bypassed
1	Revealed	After block acceptance	No	Yes
2 (weak)	Revealed	Before block acceptance	Yes	Yes
2 (strong)	Secret	Before block acceptance	Yes	No

2.4 Execution Context in Smart Contracts

To give understanding of how a smart contract can bypass non-outsourceability, we first explain what kind of data the contract can access.

In PoW currencies, a block contains a compact section called the *header*, which is enough to verify the PoW solution and check integrity of other sections (such as block transactions).

Execution context is what is available to a contract during execution. Considering UTXO-based cryptocurrencies, such as Bitcoin and Ergo, we can think about following components of the execution context. At the bare minimum, the first level, the smart contract should have access to the contents of the UTXO it is locking (i.e., its monetary value and any other data stored in it). At the second level, the smart contract may additionally have access to the spending transaction, that is, all its inputs and outputs. At the third level, the smart contract may have access to block header data in addition to the data at the second level. For example, in Ergo, the last ten block headers and also some parts of the next block header (which are known in advance before the next block is mined) are also available in the execution context. Finally, at the fourth level, the execution context may contain the entire block with all sibling transactions. Note that since the execution context must fit into random-access memory of commodity hardware, accessing the full blockchain is not a realistic scenario. The following table summarizes possible execution context components.

Context level	UTXO	Transaction	Header	Block	Example
C1	Yes	No	No	No	Bitcoin [10]
C2	Yes	Yes	No	No	–
C3	Yes	Yes	Yes	No	Ergo [5]
C4	Yes	Yes	Yes	Yes	–

3 Pooled Mining in Type 1 Puzzles

In a nutshell, Type 1 puzzles use a combination of two approaches. The first approach is to replace the hash function with a digital signature (i.e., use public-key cryptography instead of symmetric key cryptography for obtaining the final solution). The second approach is to tie the public key to the rewards.

3.1 Using Public-Key Cryptography

The method requires a randomized signature scheme that is strongly unforgeable under adaptive chosen message attacks (s-UFCMA) and outputs signatures uniformly spread over some range irrespective of how the signer behaves. Schnorr signature is one such scheme [11].

A candidate block header is constructed using transactions as in Bitcoin along with a public key p. A valid block header is a candidate block header along with a signature d that verifies with this public key and satisfies the difficulty constraints as before (i.e., is less than a certain value). The difficulty parameter is automatically adjusted as in Bitcoin.

One real-world implementation of this concept is Autolykos [6], the PoW algorithm of Ergo [5]. Autolykos uses a variation of Schnorr signatures [11], where the goal of a miner is to output d such that $d < 2^{256}/\lambda$ and λ is the difficulty parameter. The value d is to be computed as follows. First compute $r = H(m\|n\|p\|w)$ where m is the transactions digest, n is a nonce, p is a public key (an elliptic curve group element) and w is an ephemeral public key that should never be reused in two different blocks. Let x be the corresponding private key of w. Compute $d = xr - s$, where s is the private key corresponding to p.

3.2 Tying Public-Key to Rewards

The second technique in making a Type 1 pool-resistant scheme is to tie the rewards to the public key p contained in the block solution. That is, the platform enforces that any mining rewards are protected by the statement *prove knowledge of secret key corresponding to the public key p (from the block solution)*

We consider Ergo as an example here. Rather than enforcing this logic within the protocol, Ergo uses smart contracts to enforce it. In particular, this rule is enforced in a so called **Emission box**[1], a UTXO which contains all the ergs (Ergo's primary token) that will ever be emitted in rewards. The box is protected by a script that enforces certain conditions on how the rewards must be collected. In particular, it requires that a reward transaction has exactly two outputs, such that the first is another emission box containing the remaining ergs and the second is a box with the miners reward protected with the following script: *prove knowledge of the discrete logarithm (to some fixed base g) of group element p AND height is greater than or equal to the box-creation height plus 720.* This is possible because Ergo's (level C3) context includes the block solution. Note that

---

[1] A box is just a fancy name for a UTXO. We will use these two terms interchangeably.

the requirement of 720 blocks (which is roughly a day) is to prevent spending of rewards until they have almost no chance of being invalidated due to forks.

The above approach ensures that the private key used for finding the block solution is also needed for spending the rewards. Consequently, anyone who finds a block also has the ability to spend those rewards. If we try to create any standard type of pool, we find that anyone having the ability to find a solution also has the ability to spend (i.e., steal) the reward. In fact, any standard pool must share the same private key among all participants, thereby making it impossible to determine the actual spender. This restriction also applies to decentralized schemes such as P2Pool and SmartPool because they both require that rewards be sent to addresses not under the miner's control.

3.3   Creating a Mining Pool

We now describe a pooling strategy for bypassing any Type 1 scheme, provided that the underlying smart contract language supports context level C3 or higher (see Sect. 2.4). Hence one way to mitigate our method would be to restrict the smart contract language to level C2 or lower. Our concrete implementation uses Ergo as the underlying platform, which supports C3 context.

We will follow the *pay-per-share* approach, where the reward is distributed among the miners based on the number of shares they submitted since the last payout. Our pool is designed to operate at centralization level L2, where the pool only collects the rewards but does not select transactions (see Sect. 2.2). Hence, it provides resistance against censorship and does not encourage 51% attacks that are possible at L1. Note that the pool could also operate at L1 by creating miner-specific blocks using pair-wise shared public keys. However, this increases computational load on the pool and overall network usage.

Basic Variant: We first describe a basic version that is insecure. We then patch the vulnerability to obtain the full version.

The key observation in our approach is that in a valid share, the reward need not necessarily be sent directly to the pool's address. What is actually necessary is that an amount equivalent to the reward is sent to the pool's address. This simple observation allows us to create a pool with the following rules:

1. Each miner can send the reward to his own public key p, whose secret key only he knows (*reward transaction*).
2. The block must also have another transaction sending the same amount as the reward to the pool address (*pool transaction*).

A valid share is a solution to a block with the above structure. A miner can efficiently prove that a share is valid without having to send the entire block to the pool. It can simply send the pool transaction along with the Merkle proof that validates that the transaction [12]. A pool operator collects such shares (along with the proofs) and any funds thus received when a block is solved are distributed among the miners using the pay-per-share algorithm. To ensure that miners generate valid blocks, the pool randomly asks miners to provide full blocks corresponding to some of their shares and penalize those who cannot.

One drawback of this is that each miner must have sufficient collateral to cover the reward amount at any time, even though the reward becomes spendable only after a 'cooling-off period' (720 blocks in Ergo). Thus, there is a minimum period during which the collateral is spent but the reward is locked and cannot be used as further collateral. Therefore, for uninterrupted mining, each miner must keep the reserved amount of at least 2 rewards (possibly more depending on the expected time to find a block).

To overcome this drawback, a pool may provide incentives such as allowing the miner to keep a fraction of the reward (example for the current reward of 67.5 ergs in Ergo, the pool may require only 65 ergs to be sent to it).

The broadcast attack: Let Alice be a miner with public key `alice`. If such a system is used in, say, Bitcoin, then the system becomes insecure. Once the pool-paying transaction is publicized, anyone (not necessarily Alice) may broadcast it (possibly by using it as their own pool transaction).

Enhanced variant: The enhanced protocol mitigates the above attack. This is possible because ErgoScript allows us to use the block solution in the context, using which we can secure the pool transaction as follows. Instead of paying to the pool from an arbitrary box (or boxes), Alice will instead store this collateral in a special box protected by the following script:

```
minerPubKey == alice
```

A box with this script does not require a signature because the above statement only fixes the miner's public key to `alice` and does not enforce any other spending condition. Thus, anyone can create a transaction spending this box. However the transaction is valid only if the block that includes it is mined by Alice. This ensures that the box can only be spent if and when Alice mines a block. Alice creates her pool transaction using this box as input and submits her shares and proofs to the pool as before. She need not even use a private channel for this purpose and can broadcast this publicly. This enables the possibility of L3 decentralization level that requires public shares [7,8] (see Sect. 2.2).

The above variant prevents the broadcast attack because knowing the pool transaction does not help the attacker in any way (since anyone can create that transaction without Alice's help). An attacker might try to spend Alice's collateral in a transaction paying to some address other than the pool address. However, Alice will discard such transactions when creating a candidate block and only include her pool paying transaction that spends the collateral. In the worst case, if Alice does not check for others spending her collateral, the mined block will still include her own pool-paying transaction double-spending the same collateral, thereby making the entire block invalid.

Full variant: Observe that the above collateral box is not spendable until Alice actually mines a block. Depending on her hardware and the global hash rate, this may take a very long time, and her funds will be stuck till then. We would like Alice to be able to withdraw her collateral at any time she decides to stop participating in the pool. This can be done as follows. Alice first sets another public key `aliceWithdraw` that she will use to withdraw the collateral (it is possible to keep `aliceWithdraw = alice`). The modified script is:

`(minerPubKey == alice) || aliceWithdraw`

The first condition, `minerPubKey == alice`, ensures that when used to fund the pool output, the miner must be Alice as in the enhanced variant. The second condition, `bob`, ensures that the coins are not stuck till Alice finds a block, because it allows Alice may withdraw the collateral at any time. Alice should fund the pool transaction by satisfying only the first condition and never the second condition, otherwise the broadcast attack becomes possible. The second condition is be used only for withdrawing collateral.

Note that the above allows everyone to create a transaction spending Alice's collateral box as long as Alice mines the transaction. Alice may have more than one collateral box protected by identical scripts. Thus, an attacker may try to spend Alice's box that is not used in the pool funding transaction. Of course, Alice should not include such transactions in her block. This requires Alice to implement additional checks. An easier solution is for Alice to use another public key, `aliceLock`, as below to ensure that only she can create a valid transaction.

`((minerPubKey == alice) && aliceLock) || aliceWithdraw`

The above broadcast attack mitigation strategy requires C3 context level (i.e., access to `minerPubKey`) and will not work in lower levels. One may envisage a hiding strategy at C2 context level, where the pool transaction is not revealed in a share (only a commitment is revealed). The actual transaction is revealed only if a block is found or when a miner later proves to the pool that the shares were correct. However, this is also insecure. First note that there are two types of broadcast attacks. The first is the *leak-from-share* attack. The second is the *leak-from-orphaned-block* attack, where the transaction is extracted from a mined block that ends up getting orphaned. The hiding strategy mitigates the first attack but not the second.

Weak Broadcast Security: We can obtain a weaker form of broadcast security for C2 context level by assuming a trusted pool as follows. A pool-paying transaction is created as before by spending some arbitrary input and paying to the pool address. The miner sends the shares along with the proofs to the pool over a private channel. The pool is trusted not to misuse the transaction. This addresses the leak-from-share attack. To address the leak-from-orphaned-block attack, the following strategy is used. Assume that the box funding the pool transaction contains a unique identifier of Alice (such as her public key) and a script that enforces any spending transaction to pay the pool. Lets us call this *Alice's funding box*. The pool then enforces the following rules internally.

1. Any transaction it receives from Alice's funding box that was not mined by Alice is considered *irregular*.

2. Any irregular transaction using Alice's funding box is not considered for pool reward disbursement and the funds are refunded back to Alice.

It is possible for everyone to verify that a given pool transaction is irregular if everyone knows Alice's public key. Thus, a pool cannot deny the existence of an irregular transaction. Refunds can also be made verifiable in many ways, such as by requiring the pool to create another funding box for Alice, which can be publicly verified. We can additionally require that the new funding box be created in a transaction that consumes the irregular transaction's output.

4 Pooled Mining with Type 2 Puzzles

In Type 2 puzzles, a miner can produce (with non-negligible probability) an alternative block for the same PoW solution [3]. For concreteness, we will use public key cryptography to illustrate this, as we did for Type 1 puzzles. However, our approach will work for any other implementation of such puzzles.

Recall that a Type 1 puzzle comprises of two steps: (1) embedding a public key p in the block header, whose private key is needed in generating the solution, and (2) tying the block rewards to p. A Type 2 puzzle can be considered a variation of a Type 1 puzzle, where Step 1 remains the same but Step 2 is modified so that the block rewards are not tied to p but instead to another public key a that is certified by p. In other words, the complete solution is defined using a tuple $(p, a, \text{cert}_p(a))$, where $\text{cert}_p(a)$ is a signature on a that verifies with p.

The rationale behind non-outsourceability is that a cheating miner knowing the private key of p can steal the reward as follows. When claiming shares, the miner behaves correctly. That is, it constructs the block so that rewards go to the pool public key a. However, if a real solution is found, the rewards are sent to the miner public a' by creating a certificate $\text{cert}_p(a')$. Thus, as in Type 1 puzzles, the pool risks losing rewards if it shares secrets with miners.

Watermarking: In the basic Type 2 scheme, a pool can make it possible to identify stolen rewards by publicly fixing a watermark identifying its blocks in advance [3]. A watermark in this context is something that is preserved even if the pool key a is replaced by the miner key a'. A few examples are the certifying key p or, say, half the bits of the nonce. If such a watermark is used then it becomes possible to identify the cases when the block rewards are stolen.

Strong Type 2 puzzles: In the above design, it is possible to determine when the rewards are stolen. For instance, using the public key p as a watermark, a pool may declare in advance that for a given p, it only considers the pair (p, a) as valid and any other pair (p, a') indicates a theft. The stronger variant of Type 2 puzzles replaces signatures with zero knowledge proofs so that the two cases (block rewards stolen or not) become indistinguishable. Any Type 2 puzzle that is not strong is called *weak*.

We describe a smart contract that bypasses both Type 1 and (weak) Type 2 schemes. For sake of brevity, however, we only describe the Type 2 solution here. Recall that for such schemes, it is possible to detect when a particular watermark is being used in the block. In our approach, this watermark is attached to the miner instead of the pool. Thus, the pool with share pair-wise watermarks with every miner. Similar to the previous approach, we will also require the miner to lock some collateral that can be used by the pool to cover any rewards taken by the miner. We also require the smart contract language to make available in the execution context the block solutions for not only the current block header but also the last L block header prior to the current one.

Then a weak Type 2 scheme can be bypassed as follows. In order to participate in the pool, Alice creates an unspent box that locks collateral with the guard script: *payable to pool public key if at least one of the last L headers contains the watermarked solution*. The same solution will also work for Type 1 schemes there because the block header cannot be efficiently altered without also altering the embedded public key. In ErgoScript, for example, this can be implemented as: `poolPubKey && lastHeaders.exists(h => h.minerPubKey == alice)`.

The method `exists` of `lastHeaders` takes as input another method, say f, that takes as input an header and outputs a `Boolean`. The method f is applied to every element of `lastHeaders` and the output of `exists` is the OR of the outputs of f. In this case, f outputs true if the miner public key in the header is Alice's public key.

A miner is permitted to send the reward to any chosen address, since as soon as a valid block is generated, the collateral becomes spendable by the pool. One way the miner can try to save the collateral is to generate L blocks after the one with the watermark, but this case is unlikely for a pool user if L is big enough. In Ergo, for example, $L = 10$, and the chance to generate 11 consecutive blocks is very small [10].

Note that the above script locks the collateral until Alice find a block, which may never happen. Hence, as in the Type 1 case, we need to allow Alice to withdraw collateral if she desires. However, the solution used in Type 1 (i.e., simply appending '`|| aliceWithdraw`') will not work here because the pool does not immediately get the collateral when Alice gets the reward, but rather after at most L blocks. If we allow Alice to withdraw the collateral at any time, the she can withdraw it in the same block as the reward. One solution would be to allow Alice to withdraw the collateral only after some fixed height H, while her participation in the pool using this collateral ends at height $H - L$, after which she must use new collateral. For simplicity, we skip this deadline condition for withdrawing the collateral by the miner in case a block is not found for a long time. However, a real world implementation must consider this.

5   Conclusion and Further Work

Non-outsourceable puzzles have been proposed as a possible workaround for attacks that arise due to pool formation in PoW blockchains. Such solutions fall into two broad categories: Type 1, where the reward is directly bound to some trapdoor information used for generating the block solution (and thus, that information is needed while spending), and Type 2, where the reward is indirectly bound to the trapdoor information via a certificate. Type 2 schemes can be further classified into weak, where the identity of the miner is revealed, and strong, where the identity remains hidden.

In this paper we proposed two approaches to bypass non-outsourceability of Type 1 and weak Type 2 schemes to create mining pools, thereby 'breaking' them. Our pools operates at level L2 (censorship resistance), where the pool does not control transactions to be included in blocks but only collects the rewards (see Sect. 2.2). Such pools do not pose stability threats that L1 level pools do. Although our pools are most efficient when operating at L2, they can operate at L1 simply by having the pool create miner-specific blocks using their public keys. Note that both L1 and L2 carry the risk of funds loss due to operator compromise. A topic of further investigation is to have the pools operate at L3, where there is no risk of losing funds.

Only strong Type 2 schemes (where a miner does not provide a block solution in the clear, but rather provides an encrypted solution along with zero-knowledge proof of its correctness) remain unbroken. However, it should also be noted that strong schemes are not very practical as they require a generic zero-knowledge proof system which imposes heavy burden on both the prover and verifier. Thus, such schemes currently have no implementations in the real world. Additionally, we note that Type 2 schemes in their entirety have an inherent weakness that make them impractical for real world use: the high possibility of forking attacks.

Both our approaches rely on smart contracts acting as decentralized escrows and require the underlying programming language to allow predicates at context level C3 or higher (i.e., access to the block solution; see Sect. 2.4). Thus, one way to invalidate our methods would be to restrict the language context to level C2 or lower. Note that even level C2 contracts allow sophisticated applications such as non-interactive mixing, rock-paper-scissors, and even an ICO [13].

Another open issue in mining pools is that of block withholding [14], where the miner tries to attack the pool by submitting valid shares but discarding actual solutions. The need for collateral in our schemes may possibly affect the attacker's strategy. This will be considered in a follow-up work.

Acknowledgements. We would like to thank Mohammad Hasan Samadani and the ergopool.io team for building a pool based on this paper and highlighting real-world issues in regards with high-level scheme descriptions.

References

1. Eyal, I., Sirer, E.G.: Majority is not enough: bitcoin mining is vulnerable. CoRR, abs/1311.0243 (2013)
2. Paul, D.M.: We need a financial James Bond to prevent a 'goldfinger' attack on bitcoin (2017). https://www.americamagazine.org/politics-society/2017/10/31/we-need-financial-james-bond-prevent-goldfinger-attack-bitcoin
3. Miller, A., Kosba, A., Katz, J., Shi, E.: Nonoutsourceable scratch-off puzzles to discourage bitcoin mining coalitions. In: Proceedings of the 22nd ACM SIGSAC Conference on Computer and Communications Security, pp. 680–691. ACM (2015)

 4. Daian, P., Eyal, I., Juels, A., Sirer, E.G.: (Short Paper) PieceWork: generalized outsourcing control for proofs of work. In: Brenner, M., Rohloff, K., Bonneau, J., Miller, A., Ryan, P.Y.A., Teague, V., Bracciali, A., Sala, M., Pintore, F., Jakobsson, M. (eds.) FC 2017. LNCS, vol. 10323, pp. 182–190. Springer, Cham (2017). https://doi.org/10.1007/978-3-319-70278-0_11
 5. Ergo Developers. Ergo: a resilient platform for contractual money (2019). https://ergoplatform.org/docs/whitepaper.pdf
 6. Autolykos: the ergo platform pow puzzle (2019). https://docs.ergoplatform.com/ErgoPow.pdf
 7. Chesterman, X.: The P2POOL mining pool. PhD thesis, Ghent University (2018)
 8. Luu, L., Velner, Y., Teutsch, J., Saxena, P.: Smartpool: practical decentralized pooled mining. In: 26th {USENIX} Security Symposium ({USENIX} Security 17), pp. 1409–1426 (2017)
 9. How to disincentivize large bitcoin mining pools (2014). http://hackingdistributed.com/2014/06/18/how-to-disincentivize-large-bitcoin-mining-pools/
10. Nakamoto, S.: Bitcoin: a peer-to-peer electronic cash system (2008). https://bitcoin.org/bitcoin.pdf
11. Schnorr, C.P.: Efficient signature generation by smart cards. J. Cryptol. 4(3), 161–174 (1991). https://doi.org/10.1007/BF00196725
12. Hearn, M., Corallo, M.: Bitcoin improvement proposal 0037. Web document (October 2012)
13. Advanced Ergoscript Tutorial (2019). https://docs.ergoplatform.com/sigmastate_protocols.pdf
14. Courtois, N.T., Bahack, L.: On subversive miner strategies and block withholding attack in bitcoin digital currency. arXiv preprint (2014). arXiv:1402.1718

Scalable Open-Vote Network
on Ethereum

Mohamed Seifelnasr[✉], Hisham S. Galal, and Amr M. Youssef

Concordia Institute for Information Systems Engineering, Concordia University,
Montréal, QC, Canada
M_SEIFEL@encs.concordia.ca

Abstract. McCorry *et al.* (Financial Cryptography 2017) presented the
first implementation of a decentralized self-tallying voting protocol on
Ethereum. However, their implementation did not scale beyond 40 voters since all the computations were performed on the smart contract. In
this paper, we tackle this problem by delegating the bulk computations
to an off-chain untrusted administrator in a verifiable manner. Specifically, the administrator tallies the votes off-chain and publishes a Merkle
tree that encodes the tallying computation trace. Then, the administrator submits the Merkle tree root and the tally result to the smart
contract. Subsequently, the smart contract transits to an intermediate
phase where at least a single honest voter can contend the administrator's claimed result if it was not computed correctly. Then, in the worst
case, the smart contract verifies the dispute at the cost of an elliptic
curve point addition and scalar multiplication, and two Merkle proofs of
membership which are logarithmic in the number of voters. This allows
our protocol to achieve higher scalability without sacrificing the public
verifiability or voters' privacy. To assess our protocol, we implemented
an open-source prototype on Ethereum and carried out multiple experiments for different numbers of voters. The results of our implementation
confirm the scalability and efficiency of our proposed solution which does
not exceed the current block gas limit for any practical number of voters.

Keywords: Open Vote Network · Merkle tree · Smart contract

1 Introduction

A blockchain is a decentralized append-only immutable ledger over a peer-to-
peer network. It utilizes a consensus algorithm that ensures different users have
access to a consistent ledger state. Furthermore, mining nodes have an economic
incentive to behave honestly and compete in solving a cryptographic puzzle,
referred to as Proof of Work (PoW), to receive block rewards.

As of November 2019, Ethereum capitalization exceeds 16 billion USD, which
makes it the second most valuable blockchain after Bitcoin [2]. Ethereum is
considered as a platform for running smart contracts in a world computer referred
to as Ethereum Virtual Machine (EVM). Once a smart contract is deployed on

© Springer Nature Switzerland AG 2020
M. Bernhard et al. (Eds.): FC 2020 Workshops, LNCS 12063, pp. 436–450, 2020.
https://doi.org/10.1007/978-3-030-54455-3_31

the EVM, it becomes immutable, i.e., its code cannot be changed or patched afterward. Furthermore, it stays dormant until triggered either by a transaction submitted from an Externally Owned Account (EOA) (i.e., a user account) or by a call from another contract. The underlying consensus protocol ensures that the smart contract state gets modified only as its code dictates.

In all transactions, the sender has to pay upfront in Ether for the execution of the contract's code. The computational complexity of a transaction is measured in gas, which can be bought for a *gas price* specified by the sender. Therefore, the transaction fee is the gas cost multiplied by the gas price. Furthermore, the sender also has to specify a *gas limit* which does not allow the transaction to burn more gas than the specified limit. During execution, if a transaction runs out of gas, then all the state changes are reverted while the transaction fee is paid to the miner. On the other hand, if the transaction is successful, then the sender gets the remaining gas.

Additionally, there exists a block gas limit, which limits the computational complexity of transactions in one block. Currently, the block gas limit is about 10,000,000 gas [1]. Obviously, it is important to minimize the gas cost of transactions in order to spend as little as possible on transaction fees. Furthermore, small gas costs are also crucial from a scalability point of view, since the less gas burnt for each transaction, the more transaction can fit into a single block.

McCorry *et al.* [12] presented the first implementation of the Open Vote Network protocol on the Ethereum blockchain. To hide their votes, voters send encrypted votes to the smart contract. These encrypted votes are accompanied by one-out-of-two Zero Knowledge Proof (ZKP) of either a 0 or 1 to prove the validity of the vote. Although their implementation tackles the voter privacy on Ethereum, it barely scaled up to 40 voters before exceeding the block gas limit. We identified two main reasons for this scalability problem from computation and storage perspectives. First, the smart contract computes the tally which involves running elliptic curve operations. Furthermore, this computation scales linearly with the number of voters. Secondly, at the deployment phase, the administrator sends the list of the eligible voters to be stored on the smart contract which also scales linearly with the number of voters.

Contribution. In this paper, we propose a protocol that efficiently reduces the computation and storage cost of the Open Vote Network without sacrificing its inherent security properties. More precisely, we make the following modifications:

1. We utilize a Merkle tree to accumulate the list of eligible voters. Thus, the smart contract stores only the tree root rather than the full list. Certainly, each voter will have to provide a proof-of-membership along with their votes.
2. We delegate the tally computation to an untrusted administrator in a verifiable manner even in the presence of a malicious majority. In fact, we require only a single participant, which could be a regulator or one of the voters, to be honest in order to maintain the protocol's security.

The rest of this paper is organized as follows. Section 2 presents a very brief review of some related work on voting protocols implemented on the Ethereum blockchain. Section 3 presents the cryptographic primitives utilized in our protocol. Section 4 provides the design of the election contract and its execution phases. Also, it provides an analysis of the gas used in every transaction by the voter/election administrator. Lastly, Sect. 5 presents our conclusions.

2   Related Work

A cryptographic voting system is one that provides proof to each voter that her vote was included in the final tally. Public verifiability requires that the tallying process can be validated by anyone who wants to do so, even those who did not vote. Cryptographic voting systems should not leak any information about how the voter voted, beyond what can be inferred from the tally alone, including the cases where voters may deliberately craft their ballot to leak how they voted. Based on his mix network protocol [5], Chaum proposed the first cryptographic voting system in 1981. Interestingly, blind signature schemes [4], which formed the basis for the first cryptographic payment systems, have also been applied extensively in the design of e-voting protocols. Traditionally, e-voting protocols rely on a trusted authority for collecting the encrypted votes from the voters to maintain the voters' privacy. Later, that trusted authority computes the final tally from the casted votes. The problem in this approach is giving a single centralized authority the full control of collecting and computing the tally. Instead, multiple authorities can be utilized for collecting the votes and in the tally computation phase, e.g., see Helios [3]. Yet, the collusion of the tally authorities is still a threat against voters' privacy. Removing the tally authorities completely was first accomplished by Kiayias and Yung [11] who introduced a boardroom self-tallying protocol. In a self-tallying voting protocol, once the vote casting phase is over, any voter or a third-party can perform the tally computation. Self-tallying protocols are regarded as the max-privacy voting protocols since breaching the voter privacy requires full collusion of all the other voters.

McCorry et al. [12] implemented the Open Vote Network protocol to build the first Boardroom voting on Ethereum. The protocol does not require a trusted party to compute the tally, however, it is a self-tallying protocol. Furthermore, each voter is in control of her vote's privacy such that it can only be breached by full collusion involving all other voters. To ensure the correct execution of votes tallying, the authors developed a smart contract that computes the votes tallying. Certainly, the consensus mechanism of Ethereum secures the tallying computation, however, running elliptic curve operations in smart contracts are cost-prohibitive. Therefore, the smart contract can tally a relatively small number of votes, up to 40, before consuming the block gas limit. Furthermore, a second drawback with this implementation is that at the deployment phase, the smart contract stores the list of all eligible voters. Technically speaking, storing large data on smart contracts is prohibitively expensive as the op-code SSTORE costs 20000 gas to store non-zero 32 bytes. For instance, storing a list of 500 voters' addresses will exceed the current block gas limit (≈ 10 million gas).

3   Preliminaries

In this section, we briefly review the cryptographic primitives utilized in our protocol.

3.1   Merkle Tree

Merkle trees [13] are cryptographic accumulators with efficient proofs of set membership. Generally speaking, to accumulate a set of elements, one builds a binary tree where the leaf nodes correspond to the hash values of the elements. The *parent* nodes are assigned the hash of their children using a collision-resistant hash function. The set membership proof, known as *Merkle proof*, has a logarithmic size in terms of the number of leaves. For example, given a Merkle tree MT with a root r, to prove that an element $x \in MT$, the prover sends to the verifier a Merkle proof π which consists of the sibling nodes on the path from x to r as illustrated in Fig. 1. The verifier initially computes $r' \leftarrow H(x)$. Then, she iterates sequentially over each hash in π and reconstructs the parent r'. Finally, the verifier accepts the proof π if $r' = r$.

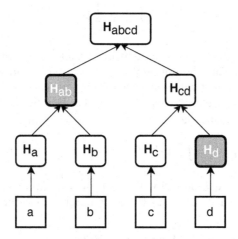

Fig. 1. An example illustrating the Merkle proof for element $c \in MT$ which consists of the nodes H_d and H_{ab}

3.2   Schnorr Zero-Knowledge Proof of Discrete Log Knowledge

A Zero-Knowledge Proof of Knowledge is an interactive protocol that runs between a prover and a verifier. It enables the prover to convince the verifier of her knowledge of a secret without revealing that secret to the verifier. Schnorr protocol [14] is a Σ protocol that consists of three interactions between the prover and verifier. These interactions are: commit, challenge and response. Let $v = g^s \bmod P$ where $s \in \mathbb{Z}_p$. In Schnorr ZKP, the prover knows a secret s (the discrete log of v) and she wants to convince the verifier of her knowledge without telling him the secret. ZKP protocol must achieve three properties: completeness, soundness, and zero-knowledge.

The Schnorr ZKP proceeds as follows: it starts by a commit phase where the prover sends the verifier her commitment $x = g^r \bmod p$ where $r \in \mathbb{Z}_p$. Then, the verifer sends back her challenge e where $e \in \mathbb{Z}_p$. Then, the prover responds with $y = (r - se) \bmod p$. In the end, the verifier checks $x = g^y \cdot v^e$.

3.3   Open Vote Network

The Open Vote Network is a two-round self-tallying protocol that does not require a trusted party. In the first round, the administrator generates a cyclic group $\mathbb{G}$ of prime order q and a generator g. Then, each voter picks a random value $x_i \in \mathbb{Z}_q$ as a secret key and publishes her voting keys as g^{x_i} along with a Schnorr proof of knowledge of discrete log. In the second round, each voter computes her blinding key as

$$Y_i = \prod_{j=1}^{i-1} g^{x_j} / \prod_{j=i+1}^{n} g^{x_j}$$

By implicitly setting $Y_i = g^{y_i}$, then it is clear that $\prod_i Y_i^{x_i} = g^{\sum_i x_i y_i} = g^0 = 1$. Subsequently, using the blinding key Y_i, each voter broadcasts her encrypted vote as $c_i = g^{v_i} Y_i^{x_i}$ along with a zero-knowledge proof of validity to prove that c_i is formed correctly and the vote $v \in \{0, 1\}$. Finally, one can compute the tally by simply exploiting the homomorphic property in the encrypted votes as follows:

$$\prod_i c_i = \prod_i g^{x_i y_i} g^{v_i} = g^{\sum_i x_i y_i + v_i} = g^{\sum_i v_i}$$

The tally result $\sum_i v_i$ can be easily obtained by performing an exhaustive search on the discrete log which is bounded by the number of voters.

3.4   Proof of Validity on Encrypted Vote

As mentioned above, in our implementation, each voter needs to provide a zero knowledge proof that the encrypted vote is either one or zero, and it is generated correctly. Similar to [12], we utilize the zero-knowledge proof of validity presented in [7]. More precisely, the terms of our protocol are analogous to the form of ElGamal encryption in the exponent. By treating the g^{y_i} terms as public keys and using the previously published voting keys g_{x_i}, we form

$$(g^{x_i}, (g^{y_i})^{x_i} \cdot g^{v_i})$$

If voter i is playing by the rules, this will be an ElGamal encryption of g or 1 with public key g^{y_i} and randomisation x_i. In other words, given an ElGamal

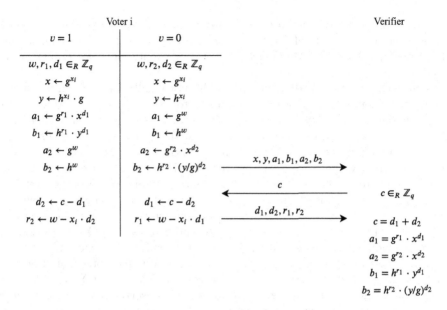

Fig. 2. Proof of valid encrypted vote [6].

encryption $(x, y) = (g^{x_i}, h^{x_i} m)$, the protocol shown in Fig. 2 proves that m is either $m_0 = 1$ or $m_1 = g$, without revealing which, by proving the following OR statement

$$\log_g x = \log_h (y/m_0) \vee \log_g x = \log_h (y/m_1)$$

Applying the Fiat–Shamir's heuristics [9], by letting $c = H(i, x, y, a_1, b_1, a_2, b_2)$ where H is a publicly secure hash function, makes the protocol non-interactive.

4 Protocol Design and Implementation

In this section, we present the design of our proposed protocol and explain the various details regarding its implementation.

4.1 Protocol Overview

To bring scalability and efficiency to the deployment of Open Vote Network on Ethereum, we have to solve the computational and storage problems that we identified in [12]. First, we delegate the votes tallying process to an off-chain [8] untrusted administrator in a verifiable and efficient way. The proof verification of the delegated tally computation is logarithmic in the number of voters and involves a single elliptic curve point addition. Secondly, to significantly reduce the storage requirements of the smart contract deployment, we accumulate the list of eligible voters in a Merkle tree and store its root, which corresponds to a 256-bit hash value.

Our voting protocol is divided into six chronologically ordered phases. Starting with the deployment phase, the administrator Alice constructs a Merkle tree of all eligible voters $MT_{\mathcal{E}}$ and generates a set of public parameters. Then, she deploys the smart contract and initializes it with the $root_{\mathcal{E}} = root(MT_{\mathcal{E}})$ and a set of public parameters. Afterward, in the registration phase, all voters have to register their voting keys within its time window. For instance, suppose that Bob, who is one of the eligible voters, wants to cast his vote. Bob generates a voting key g^x along with Schnorr proof of discrete log knowledge π_x. Then, he submits g^x, π_x, in addition to a Merkle proof of membership π_{Bob}. Next, in the vote casting phase, the voters cast their encrypted votes $c = g^v Y^x$ to the smart contract along with a zero-knowledge proof that c is formed correctly.

In the votes tallying phase, Alice obtains the encrypted votes stored on the smart contract, tallies them, and brute-forces the discrete log $\sum_i v_i$, which is bounded by the number of registered voters. We observe that the tally computation can be represented as a program that loops over the encrypted votes and accumulates their multiplications at each iteration. As a result, Alice can efficiently encode her the program execution trace by building a Merkle tree $MT_{\mathcal{C}}$ over the intermediate accumulated multiplication result of each iteration. Subsequently, she publishes $MT_{\mathcal{C}}$, for example, on the Interplanetary file system (IPFS) for public verifiability. Finally, she submits the $root_{\mathcal{C}} = root(MT_{\mathcal{C}})$ in addition to $\sum_i v_i$ to the smart contract.

Once $MT_{\mathcal{C}}$ is published, any voter or regulatory body can verify the tally computation trace done by Alice to determine whether the result has been computed correctly. One needs to count for scenarios where Alice could maliciously alter the inputs in one of the trace steps to affect the final tally result. Consequently, Bob, as an honest voter, can verify her computation trace and dispute her on the first invalid step i he finds. In other words, Bob does not have to verify the whole computation trace, instead, he simply disputes the first erroneous step. When the smart contract transits to the dispute phase, Bob submits Merkle proofs for the inputs at step i encoded by Alice in $MT_{\mathcal{C}}$. After verifying the Merkle proofs, the smart contract will recompute the step i using the encrypted votes in its storage to detect whether Alice acted maliciously. If so, the smart contract will penalize her and reward Bob. On the other hand, if Bob tries to dispute a correct operation, the smart contract will simply reject Bob's transaction. Therefore, it is irrational for Bob to pay gas in that case. Eventually, in the reclaim phase, honest parties can request the release of their collateral deposits. In what follows, we explain the different phases of our protocol in more detail.

4.2 Phase 1: Smart Contract Deployment

In the beginning, Alice sets the interval for the phases: voters registration, vote casting, tally computation, dispute, and fund reclaim. She also establishes a list of all eligible voters. Then, she constructs a Merkle tree $MT_{\mathcal{E}}$ of the voters in this list. Then, Alice publishes it so that each voter can construct her own Merkle proof of membership. Upon deploying the contract, Alice sends the interval of each phase and the $root_{\mathcal{E}} = Root(MT_{\mathcal{E}})$ to the contract rather than storing the full list in the smart contract permanent storage.

Initialize: upon receiving $(root_{\mathcal{E}}, T_1, T_2, T_3, T_4, T_5)$ from administrator A:
Assert $value = F$
Store $root_{\mathcal{E}}, T_1, T_2, T_3, T_4, T_5$
Init $voters := \{\}$, $votes := \{\}$, $keys := \{\}$ $index := 1$

Fig. 3. Pseudocode for deployment of the smart contract.

As illustrated in Fig. 3, the voting administrator deploys the voting contract on Ethereum with the following set of parameters:

1. $root_{\mathcal{E}}$: Root of the Merkle tree of the eligible voters.
2. T_1, T_2, T_3, T_4, T_5: The block heights which define the end of the phases: registration, vote casting, tally computation, dispute, and reclaim, respectively.
3. F: A collateral deposit that is paid by Alice and the voters. This deposit is used to penalize malicious behavior if any.

4.3 Phase 2: Voters Registration

This phase starts immediately after the contract deployment where interested voters can participate by registering their voting keys. For instance, Bob as one of the eligible voters generates a voting key g^x along with Schnorr proof of DL π_x. Then, he submits a transaction containing g^x, π_x, a Merkle proof of membership π_{Bob} as parameters, and pays a collateral deposit F as shown in Fig. 4. The smart contract ensures that registration transactions are accepted only within the allowed interval and verifies both the Schnorr proof of DL knowledge and the Merkle proof of membership. For verifying membership of voters in the $MT_{\mathcal{E}}$, we use the *VerifyMerkleProof* algorithm implemented in [10]. Furthermore, recall that in the Open Vote Network, voters have fixed positions which allow them to properly compute Y_i. In our protocol, we impose that each voter takes the order at which his voting keys were stored in the smart contract (i.e., an index in the array of voting keys).

RegisterVoter: upon receiving (g^x, π_x, π_B) from voter B:
```
          Assert value = F
          Assert T < T₁
          Assert verifyMerkleProof( πB, B, rootℰ)
          Assert verifyDL( gˣ, πₓ)
          Set keys[index] := gˣ
          Set voters[index] := B
          Set index := index + 1
```

Fig. 4. Pseudocode for register voter function

4.4 Phase 3: Vote Casting

After all the voting keys have been submitted, voters generate their encrypted votes. More precisely, suppose Bob's voting key is stored at index i, then he computes:

$$Y_i = \prod_{j=1}^{i-1} g^{x_j} / \prod_{j=i+1}^{n} g^{x_j}$$

Bob encrypts his vote v as $c = g^v Y_i^{x_i}$, and submits a transaction containing c, Y_i, and a zero-knowledge proof π_v that c is formed correctly and v is either 0 or 1. The smart contract will store the encrypted vote c if the transaction is sent within the right time window, the value Y_i is computed correctly, and the proof π_v is verified successfully as shown in Fig. 5.

CastVote: upon receiving (c, Y, π_v) from voter B
```
          Assert T₁ < T < T₂
          Set index := IndexOf(B, voters)
          Assert verifyY(Y, index)
          Assert verifyEncryptedVote(c, Y, πᵥ)
          Set votes[index] := c
```

Fig. 5. Pseudocode for cast vote function

4.5 Phase 4: Tally Computation

This is the phase in our implementation which aims to bring scalability to the Open Vote Network protocol. Basically, we show how to significantly reduce the transaction fees by delegating the tally computation to an untrusted administrator, Alice, in a publically verifiable manner. Suppose that the vector $\mathbf{c} = (c_1, ..., c_n)$ contains the n encrypted votes sent to the smart contract. We observe that the tally computation $\prod_i c_i = \prod_i g^{v_i} Y_i^{x_i}$ can be computed by a program that iterates over the vector **c** and accumulates intermediate multiplication result as shown in Fig. 6.

```
def TallyVotes(c: array[]):
    t = 1
    for i=1 to n:
        t = Mul(c[i], t)
    return t
```

Fig. 6. Program tally function

The program execution trace is represented as a $4 \times n$ array where the first column denotes the step number, and the remaining columns denote the two input operands and the accumulated multiplication result as shown in Table 1.

Table 1. Computation tally execution trace

Step i	c_i	t_{i-1}	t_i
1	c_1	$t_0 = 1$	$t_1 = c_1$
2	c_2	t_1	$t_2 = c_2 \cdot t_1$
.	.	.	...
n	c_n	t_{n-1}	$t_n = c_n \cdot t_{n-1}$

```
SetTally:        upon receiving (res, root_C) from administrator A:
                 Assert sender = A
                 Assert T_2 < T < T_3
                 Store res, root_C
                 Set tallySubmitted := true
```

Fig. 7. Pseudocode for set tally function

Afterwards, Alice constructs a Merkle tree MT_C to encode the result t_i at each row. Specifically, the data for each leaf node is formatted as $(i||t_i)$ where $||$ denotes concatenation. Furthermore, she brute-forces $log_g(t_n) = \sum_i v_i$ which corresponds to the sum of the encrypted votes. Finally, she creates a transaction to the smart contract with the parameters $root_C = root(MT_C)$ and the tally result $res = \sum_i v_i$ as shown in Fig. 7. The smart contract stores these parameters provided that the transaction within the interval of this phase.

4.6   Phase 5: Tally Dispute

After publishing the Merkle tree MT_C on IPFS, any voter or regulatory body can verify the correctness of the intermediate accumulated multiplication result of each trace step. Alice could attempt to maliciously affect the tally result by using a different encrypted vote c_i' which is different from the c_i stored on the smart contract. For example, suppose Alice incorrectly set $t_i = c_i' \cdot t_{i-1}$. Note that, she could make multiple errors, however, it is sufficient to dispute the first one. Bob disputes her by sending i, t_i, t_{i-1} along with Merkle proofs π_i, π_{i-1} to the smart contract as shown in Fig. 8.

Dispute: upon receiving $(i,\ t_i,\ t_{i-1},\ \pi_i,\ \pi_{i-1})$ from voter B:
  Assert $T_3 < T < T_4$
  Assert $disputed \neq true$
  Assert VerifyMerkleProof$(\pi_i,\ (i\|t_i),\ root_C)$
  Set $c_i := votes[i]$
  Set $n := votes.length$
  IF $(i > 1$ and $i \leq n)$
         Assert VerifyMerkleProof$(\pi_i,\ (i-1\|t_{i-1}),\ root_C)$
         IF $t_i \neq c_i \cdot t_{i-1}$
              Set $disputed := true$
  IF $(i = 1$ and $t_i \neq c_i)$
         Set $disputed := true$
  IF $(i = n$ and $g^{res} \neq t_i)$
         Set $disputed := true$
  IF $disputed := true$
         B.transfer(F)

Fig. 8. Pseudocode for the dispute function

There are three different cases for how the smart contract handles the dispute based on the parameter i:

1. When the disputed step is the first one (i.e., $i = 1$), then the smart contract will only verify whether $t_1 \neq c_1$ since we assume $t_0 = 1$.
2. For other steps where $i \in [2, n]$, the smart contract will verify the Merkle proofs π_{i-1} and checks if $t_i \neq c_i \cdot t_{i-1}$.
3. Finally, the last step is related to the case where Alice has encoded the correct computation trace. However, she submitted an incorrect discrete log res in the previous phase. Thus, the smart contract will test whether $g^{res} \neq t_n$.

If any of these cases is verified successfully, the smart contract will reward Bob and set the flag *disputed* to prevent Alice from reclaiming her collateral deposit in the reclaim phase.

4.7   Phase 6: Reclaim

After the dispute phase, each honest participant can submit a transaction to reclaim her collateral deposit. The smart contract checks whether the sender has not been refunded before. Then, it checks whether the sender has behaved honestly in following the specified protocol steps. More precisely, if the sender is one of the voters, then the smart contract checks if that voter has already submitted the encrypted vote. On the other hand, if the sender is the administrator, then it checks whether the flag disputed is not set. On success, the smart contract sends the deposit back to the sender as shown in Fig. 9.

Reclaim:	upon receiving() from a sender: Assert $T_4 < T < T_5$ Assert $refund[sender] = false$ Assert ($sender \in voters$ and $votes[sender] \neq null$) or ($sender = A$ and $tallySubmitted$ and $disputed = false$) Set $refund[sender] := true$ $sender.transfer(F)$

Fig. 9. Pseudocode for reclaiming collateral deposit

4.8   Gas Cost Analysis

In order to assess our protocol, we developed a prototype and tested it with a local private Ethereum blockchain. The prototype is available as open-source on the Github repository[1]. On the day of carrying out our experiments, during November 2019, the ether exchange rate to USD is 1 ether $\approx$ 140\$ and the gas price is approximately 10 $Gwei = 10 \times 10^{-9}$ ether. The genesis initialization file of the local blockchain contains {"*byzantiumBlock*": 0} attribute in order to support our elliptic curve point addition and scalar multiplication over *alt_bn128* curve [15]. The test scenario is implemented with 40 local Ethereum accounts to compare our results with the implementation of McCorry *et al.* [12]. In Table 2, we show the gas used per voter/administrator for every function in the smart contract and the corresponding gas cost in USD.

It should be noted that, in our implementation, the total gas paid by the administrator is constant. In particular, the administrator pays the gas for the deployment of two smart contracts: CryptoCon and VoteCon, in addition to a

---

[1] https://github.com/HSG88/eVoting.

Table 2. The gas cost for functions in the voting contract

Function	Gas units	Gas cost (USD)
CryptoCon	1,002,399	1.40
VoteCon	2,439,158	3.41
RegisterVoter	206,478	0.29
CastVote	492,425	0.69
SetTallyResult	64,723	0.09
Dispute	60,464	0.08
Reclaim	50,148	0.07

transaction `setTallyResult`. Neither any of these transactions involve operations that depend on the number of voters. On the other hand, for the voters, the transaction cost of `RegisterVote` scales logarithmically with the number of voters since it verifies the Merkle proof of membership. Similarly, the transaction `Dispute` scales logarithmically as it verifies two Merkle proofs in addition to carrying two elliptic curve operations (one point addition and one scalar multiplication) at maximum. All the other transactions have a constant cost.

Although the Open Vote Network protocol is suitable for a small number of voters, we carried out some experiments to determine the highest number of voters that can be supported in our prototype without exceeding the block gas limit. Recall that all transactions have constant gas cost except `RegisterVoter` and `Dispute` which scales logarithmically with the number of voters due to verification of Merkle proofs. Furthermore, the primitive unit of storage on Ethereum is `uint256`, hence theoretically the largest number of voters supported by the smart contract is 2^{256}. Therefore, in the `RegisterVoter` transaction, the voter sends a Merkle proof of membership which consists of 256 hash values (i.e., 256×32 bytes). Interestingly, we found the total gas cost in this theoretical case to be $667,254 \approx 6.6\%$ of the current block gas limit. Furthermore, we followed the same approach to find the gas cost for the `Dispute` transaction. In that case, the smart contract verifies two Merkle proofs and carries out elliptic curve single scalar multiplication and point addition at a total estimated gas cost $1,426,593 \approx 14.3\%$ of the current block gas limit. Since these two numbers serve as upper bounds for the gas cost in any practical scenario, the results of this experiment clearly confirm that the operations within the smart contract in our prototype does not limit the number of supported voters in practice.

In McCorry *et al.* implementation, all computations are performed on the smart contract. Thus, while there is no dispute phase, the number of voters it can support is significantly limited. For the administrator, the gas used comes from VoteCon, CryptoCon, Eligible, Begin Signup, Begin Election and Tally transactions [12] which is equal to about 12 million gas units. For the voter, the gas cost comes from Register, Commit and Vote transactions which sum to 3 million gas units. Table 3 compares the total gas cost in our implementation versus theirs for the same number of the 40 voters.

Table 3. Gas cost comparison between the two implementations

Sender	Our Implementation	McCorry *et al.* [12]
Voter	809,515	3,323,642
Admin	3,506,280	12,436,190

5 Conclusion

In this paper, we presented a protocol that efficiently reduces the computation and storage cost of the Open Vote Network without sacrificing its inherent security properties. More precisely, we utilize a Merkle tree to accumulate the list of eligible voters. Additionally, we delegate the tally computation to an untrusted administrator in a verifiable manner even in the presence of a malicious majority. In fact, we require only a single participant, which could be a regulatory body or one of the voters, to be honest in order to maintain the protocol's security. Also, we developed a prototype to assess our protocol and carried out multiple experiments. The results of our experiments confirm that our prototype is efficient and can support a very large number of voters without exceeding the current block gas limit. Furthermore, the limitation of Open-vote networks are inherited in our protocol. Thus, we stress that our protocol is feasible for a university scale voting, and it is not applicable for a nation wide voting.

References

1. Ethereum gaslimit history (2018). https://etherscan.io/chart/gaslimit. Accessed 24 Nov 2019
2. Top 100 Cryptocurrencies by Market Capitalization. https://coinmarketcap.com. Accessed 22 Nov 2019
3. Adida, B.: Helios: web-based open-audit voting. In: USENIX Security Symposium, vol. 17, pp. 335–348 (2008)
4. Chaum, D.: Blind signatures for untraceable payments. In: Chaum, D., Rivest, R.L., Sherman, A.T. (eds.) Advances in Cryptology, pp. 199–203. Springer, Boston, MA (1983). https://doi.org/10.1007/978-1-4757-0602-4_18
5. Chaum, D.: Untraceable electronic mail, return addresses and digital pseudonyms. In: Gritzalis, D.A. (ed.) Secure Electronic Voting. ADIS, vol. 7, pp. 211–219. Springer, Boston (2003). https://doi.org/10.1007/978-1-4615-0239-5_14
6. Cramer, R., Damgård, I., Schoenmakers, B.: Proofs of partial knowledge and simplified design of witness hiding protocols. In: Desmedt, Y.G. (ed.) CRYPTO 1994. LNCS, vol. 839, pp. 174–187. Springer, Heidelberg (1994). https://doi.org/10.1007/3-540-48658-5_19
7. Cramer, R., Gennaro, R., Schoenmakers, B.: A secure and optimally efficient multi-authority election scheme. Eur. Trans. Telecommun. 8(5), 481–490 (1997)
8. Eberhardt, J., Tai, S.: On or off the blockchain? Insights on off-chaining computation and data. In: De Paoli, F., Schulte, S., Broch Johnsen, E. (eds.) ESOCC 2017. LNCS, vol. 10465, pp. 3–15. Springer, Cham (2017). https://doi.org/10.1007/978-3-319-67262-5_1

9. Fiat, A., Shamir, A.: How to prove yourself: practical solutions to identification and signature problems. In: Odlyzko, A.M. (ed.) CRYPTO 1986. LNCS, vol. 263, pp. 186–194. Springer, Heidelberg (1987). https://doi.org/10.1007/3-540-47721-7_12

10. Galal, H.S., ElSheikh, M., Youssef, A.M.: An efficient micropayment channel on ethereum. In: Pérez-Solà, C., Navarro-Arribas, G., Biryukov, A., Garcia-Alfaro, J. (eds.) DPM/CBT -2019. LNCS, vol. 11737, pp. 211–218. Springer, Cham (2019). https://doi.org/10.1007/978-3-030-31500-9_13

11. Kiayias, A., Yung, M.: Self-tallying elections and perfect ballot secrecy. In: Naccache, D., Paillier, P. (eds.) PKC 2002. LNCS, vol. 2274, pp. 141–158. Springer, Heidelberg (2002). https://doi.org/10.1007/3-540-45664-3_10

12. McCorry, P., Shahandashti, S.F., Hao, F.: A smart contract for boardroom voting with maximum voter privacy. In: Kiayias, A. (ed.) FC 2017. LNCS, vol. 10322, pp. 357–375. Springer, Cham (2017). https://doi.org/10.1007/978-3-319-70972-7_20

13. Merkle, R.C.: Protocols for public key cryptosystems. In: 1980 IEEE Symposium on Security and Privacy, pp. 122–122. IEEE (1980)

14. Schnorr, C.P.: Efficient signature generation by smart cards. J. Cryptol. 4(3), 161–174 (1991). https://doi.org/10.1007/BF00196725

15. Ethereum Project Team: Ethereum improvement proposals (2017). https://github.com/ethereum/EIPs

How to Dynamically Incentivize Sufficient Level of IoT Security

Jianan Su[✉], Michael Bartholic, Andrew Stange, Ryosuke Ushida, and Shin'ichiro Matsuo

Georgetown University, Washington, D.C., USA
{js4488,mwb70,ars316,ru64,sm3377}@georgetown.edu

Abstract. This paper propose an incentive mechanism to secure large numbers of devices through the use of insurance based on smart contracts. It consists of the automated security evaluation of enterprise IoT devices and the creation of a dynamic insurance premium. To automate the security evaluation of enterprise IoT devices, we collect and store IoT device status data with privacy preservation on blockchain. Then, we track and assess the risk associated with IoT devices with the use of a smart contract. By monitoring this risk over time, we present a means to incentivize the resolution of vulnerabilities by measuring the latent risk in an environment as well as the vigilance of the devices' managers in resolving these vulnerabilities. In this way, we produce a dynamic cyber insurance premium that more accurately captures the risk profile associated with an environment than existing cyber insurance. Through the use blockchain and smart contracts, this framework also provides public verification for both insured and insurer and provides a level of risk management for the insurer. We also present regulatory considerations in order for this scheme to meet supervisory requirements.

Keywords: Smart contract · Blockchain · Cyber insurance · Information security · Cyber security · Privacy preservation · Regulation awareness

1 Introduction

1.1 Background

Smart contracts are a mechanism originally proposed by Nick Szabo to process business logic autonomously. The automation of business processes provides compounded benefits to large-scale systems with multiple stakeholders as it eliminates many negotiations between these stakeholders. The implementation of this concept necessitates a shared place to record and update a common data set. Blockchain technology is a significant breakthrough to realize such a distributed ledger that was originally developed as part of Bitcoin [13]. Blockchain forms the foundation of smart contracts between any number of stakeholders and allows the development of smart contract platforms such as Ethereum.

© Springer Nature Switzerland AG 2020
M. Bernhard et al. (Eds.): FC 2020 Workshops, LNCS 12063, pp. 451–465, 2020.
https://doi.org/10.1007/978-3-030-54455-3_32

In a similar manner to crytoassets as an application of blockchain technology, the use of smart contracts has garnered the attention of the financial industry. A large number of experimental proof-of-concept systems have been built upon smart contract platforms. Insurance is one promising application area for smart contracts because it consists of different types of stakeholders such as insurance companies, insurers, insured persons/corporations, and auditor. This business requires negotiation in deciding the insurance fee at the time of contract, and deciding the amount of actual payment at the time of accident. Automating such processes for huge numbers of stakeholders is required.

As an example target for such an insurance product, there is the cyber security of huge numbers of devices that are becoming increasingly essential to business and our lives in general. Since first becoming practical to produce, market, and distribute inexpensive internet-connected appliances, the realm of "Internet of Things" has grown immensely. In almost all instances, there is a stark lack of attention paid to the security of these devices. Usually, security incidents occur by attacks on the weakest link of the system. Nowadays, most devices have functionality such as an update mechanism to apply security patch, however, the application of the security patch cannot be automated because it may inject another bugs and vulnerabilities. In practice, if it takes more time to apply the security patch than expected there may be additional security risks. In the worst case scenario, the entity completely neglects to update some of the devices they manages. Properly securing Internet of Things (IoT) devices involves identifying the presence of compromised devices on a network as well as tracking and resolving the risk they present. In the era of IoT, the task of managing all devices in a system that need to be updated is becoming increasingly difficult from security viewpoint, and sometimes it becomes an impossible mission, while stakeholders expect the system to operate securely. To resolve these issues, we need an automated system to help humans manage the huge number of devices and provide them sufficient incentives to make their own devices securely updated.

1.2   Related Works

Since we cannot assure 100% security for any system, designing insurance for cyber security is an essential building block to ensure secure and safe use of the system. There are a number of existing research works on such cyber insurance. Sasha and et al. [18] answered fundamental questions of cyber insurance such as how insurance carriers write insurance policies and calculate premiums. In [19], Danial and et al. have proved that cyber insurance will promote security best practice. While questions remain regarding how cyber insurance as a means of transferring cyber risk could provide incentives of proper adoption of security controls over time, several authors [2,21] have indicated that insured parties take several security controls required by insurance carrier in return for reduced premium. However, the premium discount is applied at the beginning when an insurance contract is signed and insurers can not track and evaluate security postures of insured party. Continuous incentives of the adoption of security controls are necessary.

There are several proof-of-concept level trials in this direction. Existing work on cyber insurance involving smart contracts and high resolution data, in general, maintains a distinct scope from our focus on dynamic pricing. For example, the Smart Contract Insurance project from ASU Blockchain Research [12] focuses primarily on automating the negotiation of settlements based on predefined triggers and the Smart Cyber Excess Insurance from Corvus [10] which uses data to aid the underwriting process but not to create a fully dynamic insurance premium.

There are existing discussions about the regulatory implications of applying smart contract to financial services and products in general such as Finck [7]. However, as far as we investigate, there is no academic discussion on the in-depth regulation issues of cyber insurance based on smart contracts.

1.3 Contributions

In this paper, we offer an approach for how one can increase the security level of IoT devices with sufficient incentives by using smart cyber insurance. The inclusion of dynamic pricing mechanism creates incentives for the proactive patching and resolution of security vulnerabilities. When compared to penetration testing and other in-depth surveys that are performed annually, our proposal dramatically reduces the cost of obtaining high-resolution vulnerability information about a insured client's environment. Other methods of obtaining this information only represent the state of a insured client's environment at a given time and cannot quantify the vigilance or responsiveness of an insured company when new vulnerabilities are discovered. In addition, we identify key considerations on how our scheme can meet regulatory requirements.

2 Smart Insurance for Cyber Security

2.1 Overview of Cyber Insurance

Thousands of data breaches and security incidents occur each year and cost hundreds of millions of dollars. To mitigate these losses, organizations turn to cyber insurance to transfer their risk to an insurer. Insured organizations benefit from this risk protection while insurers profit from premiums. Insurers can also encourage increased security investments from insured organizations by sharing information regarding cyber-attacks and offering premium discounts for applicants that adopt security controls dictated by the insurer [20]. As a result, cyber insurance drives improvements in cyber security. In general, cyber insurance is for covering risks in the real operation of a system. ISO/IEC TR27103 [1] describes a framework of such operation. Cyber insurance is thought to cover risks in this framework. Such risks are caused by many factors such as costs, liability, and loss by business interruption. Most existing cyber insurance products try to cover such risks, but they do not cover everything, e.g. penalty against data breach regulated by GDPR. Risk factors are categorized into two types: technical and human. This paper concentrates on the technical factor.

2.2 Challenges of Cyber Insurance

2.2.1 Soundness
The soundness of cyber insurance is indicated by five aspects:

- Insurance contract is based on the agreement of stakeholders.
- Agreed contract cannot be altered.
- Insurance premium and claim should be in accordance with signed contract.
- Insured party cannot obtain more insurance coverage than the defined coverage in the original contract.
- Insurance carrier cannot pay lower coverage to insured party than the defined coverage in the original contract.

2.2.2 Privacy
The insured party must be able to provide information about their security status in a manner that does not compromise their system's integrity or significantly confide in another party. It is undesirable for a vulnerable party to broadcast such information. Therefore, the sharing of the high resolution information that enables the dynamic nature of the cyber insurance scheme must be protected from unknown external parties. However, it is crucial for the insured party to share a minimum level of detail that is required by the insurer to implement such a dynamic system. There exists an optimal level of detail that is a balance between providing high resolution dynamic information to the insurer while simultaneously limiting the scope of this information in order to protect the insured party.

2.2.3 Difficulties of Existing Cyber Insurance Business
Despite increasing demand, the cyber insurance market still accounts for less than one percent of total U.S. insurance premiums. According to EIOPA [11], even existing cyber insurance shows a low conversion rate. This implies that the cyber insurance products do not meet policyholders needs and/or policyholders do not have sufficient level of understanding of the products. In a conventional cyber insurance scheme, the insurance premium is based on simple surveys, industry evaluations, and the coverage level. This analysis is static and only reevaluated on renewal of the insurance contract.

EU-U.S. Insurance Dialogue Project [17] stated several obstacles that insurers have been facing. One of the biggest problems is the lack of historical claims data and resulting weak risk modeling, which makes adequate pricing difficult. This is mainly due to lack of reporting and relatively new, complex, and changing nature of cyber risk. Though some insurers make efforts to gather data from external providers, difficulties are observed in collecting sufficient amounts of data of advanced systems and measuring the relevance to the current or future cyber landscape. In consequence, the majority of existing insurance products rely on insufficient qualitative model and do not provide incentives for policyholders to proactively secure their network environment. In this regard, a scheme which has quantitative modelling and proper incentive mechanism could play a important role in improving cyber insurance business.

2.2.4   Regulation

Insurance regulators are paying increasing attention to the risks associated with underwriting cyber insurance as the market expands[1]. In the U.S. all registered insurance companies who write cyber insurance are required to report associated data such as direct premiums written and earned to the National Association of Insurance Commissioners (NAIC) [14]. State regulators use this data to review how insurers set prices and policy terms for new cyber insurance business in order to confirm that the insurer properly understands and controls the risk.

Regulators have taken several steps to identify key challenges and improve supervisory practices. According to EIOPA [11], there is a need for both insurers and policyholders to deepen their understanding of cyber risk to support better underwriting and purchasing decisions. Some insurers underwrite cyber risk without the use of any modeling while policyholders choose insurance by price rather than the assessment of indemnity. Aggregation of risk is another concern as the increase in connectivity of IoT devices could cause unexpected insurance loss in distressed situations where catastrophic cyber incidents break out on a global scale. In addition, IAIS [15] pointed out that insurers are prime targets for cyber criminals who seek information that later can be used for financial gain through extortion, identity theft, or other criminal activities.

In this regard, the smart cyber insurance scheme can play a positive role in aspects such as sophisticating underwriting practices of cyber insurance and mitigating the concentrated risk of sensitive information. However, given the relatively complex nature of the scheme and the limited expertise of examiners with blockchain technology, smart cyber insurance products are likely to be thoroughly reviewed in many jurisdictions to confirm their positive or negative impacts on an insurer's business, financial stability, and policyholder protection.

2.3   Dynamic Pricing and Incentive Mechanism

To address the challenges discussed in Sect. 2.2, we introduce a dynamic pricing mechanism to cyber insurance based on smart contracts. Using smart contracts provides transparency between the insurer and the insured, allowing for increased efficiency in the insurance marketplace by removing the asymmetrical knowledge of an insured organization's vulnerabilities. Allowing insurance companies more insight into the insured party's network ecosystem permits more accurate and potentially lower insurance premiums for the insured party.

The smart insurance scheme also records the responsiveness of an insured party to vulnerabilities that have been discovered in their environment. The time taken to address vulnerabilities is then factored into the calculation of

---

[1] U.S. direct premiums written for cyber risk coverage were approximately 2.03 billion dollars in 2018, a 10% increase over 2017's 1.84 billion.

an insured party's insurance premium. In conjunction with the increased detail provided to the insurance company, this time-scaled insurance scheme can be adapted to provide dynamic insurance pricing to an insured organization. Since the smart insurance scheme is informed by the state of an insured system's security, updated insurance contracts can be created on any interval the insured party and insurance provider agree on, even daily or hourly. Compared to offering premium discounts to incentivize security postures of organizations, this dynamic insurance scheme provides a more clear financial incentive for an insured party to proactively secure their network environment, resulting in lower premiums for the insured party and lower risk for the insurance provider. Depending on the vulnerabilities encountered, this scheme may help avoid the widespread use of botnets and increase the overall security of the Internet.

3   System Design for Smart Cyber Insurance

3.1   Stakeholders

The system consists of numerous stakeholders with distinct roles:

- Security organizations and security vendors: provide security information to end users as a service.
- Organizations (or individuals) with IoT devices: value their own privacy and desire to minimize the cost of any breach.
- Insurance companies: underwrite a cyber insurance policy and provide insurance as a service.
- Manufacturers and developers: produce hardware and software products.

3.2   System Model

The smart cyber insurance system consists of vulnerability information management, IoT device status management, and cyber insurance management. The security information management platform allows NIST and other security organizations to publish security and vulnerability information and allows entities in the network to access this information. The IoT device status management platform allows individuals or the IoT device manager to record encrypted device data and allows the insurance company to access that encrypted data. Insurance management allows the insurance company to manage cyber insurance policies of the insured party, and allows the insured party to view their insurance policies.

The primary components of a smart cyber insurance system are a blockchain to store the installed software database, a vulnerability database populated with information published by NIST, smart contracts for interacting with the blockchain, an application local to the IoT devices for software identification, the risk score calculation, and the insurance premium and coverage calculation. The primary components and stakeholders of the system are illustrated in Fig. 1.

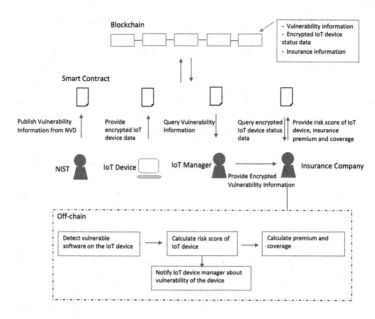

Fig. 1. System model of smart cyber insurance

3.3 Detailed Process

The system functions such that when a security organization publishes vulnerability information from a national vulnerability database (NVD) to the blockchain. Each entry of vulnerability information includes CVE ID, affected product information, impact metrics, and timestamp. Examples of vulnerability information are illustrated in Table 1. Each IoT device will possess a list of its installed-software records. Each record includes device ID, vendor name, product name, version value, current risk score of device, and timestamp. Examples of installed-software records are illustrated in Table 2. To protect the privacy of the IoT device, records of device data will be encrypted before they are stored on blockchain. The IoT manager will store encrypted IoT device status data and provide proper tokens of vulnerability information to the insurance company. The insurance company will use those tokens and encrypted IoT device status data from the blockchain to measure a device's risk level and calculate its risk score. At the end, the insurance company will use risk scores of all insured IoT devices as an input of insurance model to calculate premiums as well as coverage. We describe details of two triggers of the system in the following paragraphs.

In one scenario, the security organization publishes a vulnerable software such as first entry in Table 1 to the blockchain. The IoT device manager notices this event and generates a token of vendor name, product name, version value, and impact score of the entry and sends it to the insurance company. The insurance company searches this token over encrypted IoT device status data from blockchain and stores it to a local database for future use. If a match is detected,

Table 1. Examples of vulnerability information

CVE ID	Vendor name	Product name	Version value	Impact score	Publish time
CVE-2019-1	debian	debian_linux	8.0	5.9	08/01/2019
CVE-2019-2	libexpat	expat	1.95.1	3.6	08/02/2019
CVE-2019-2	google	android	4.4.4	3.6	08/02/2019

Table 2. Examples of installed-software record of IoT device

Device ID	Vendor name	Product name	Version value	Current risk score	Install time
1	debian	debian_linux	8.0	0	08/01/2019
1	google	android	4.4.4	5.9	08/02/2019
2	libexpat	expat	1.95.1	2.8	08/01/2019

the insurance company will recalculate the risk score of the vulnerable device and write it to the blockchain. Note that for every new vulnerable software the insurance company needs a new token. Each token is unique and it is issued for a specific vulnerability. With the updated risk score, the insurance company uses the insurance model to calculate a new premium and writes this information to the blockchain as part of the insurance policy for insured party.

In another scenario, new software is installed on an insured party's IoT device and the encryption of the software information is stored on the blockchain. To measure the latest risk level of the IoT device, the insurance company scans all tokens from local vulnerability database and checks if a match exists. If the newly installed software is vulnerable, the insurance company will update the risk score of the device and recalculate the premium and write it to the blockchain.

3.4 Privacy Protection

3.4.1 Requirement

To insure the security of IoT devices, we also need to protect the information stored on the blockchain. There are two types of data in this system that require privacy protection: the IoT device software information and the cyber insurance policy information. The software information is used in vulnerability detection to find vulnerable software on the IoT devices. Only the insured party who manages IoT devices has access to the devices' data. As for information of each insurance policy, they should be available to both the insurer and the insured party. Device software data and cyber insurance policy data are stored on blockchain for public verification, providing each stakeholder with proper access to those data is critical. There are several secure public key encryption introduced in [3,6,8] that in some cases resist selective opening attacks and also faulty randomness. However, we also need to insure that stakeholders with proper access are able to search over the encrypted IoT devices information for matching vulnerabilities. In order to do so we use public key encryption with keyword search (PEKS) [5,9,16].

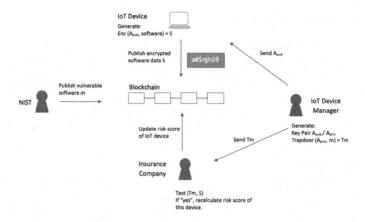

Fig. 2. PEKS in smart cyber insurance system

3.4.2   Realization Using PEKS

PEKS is a public key encryption scheme that enables parties to search over encrypted data without revealing any additional information about the plaintexts. PEKS was first introduced by Boneh *et al.* [4] and consists of four algorithms: KeyGen, Enc, Trapdoor, Test.

- KeyGen: generates public key pk and private key sk.
- Enc: takes public key pk and keyword m and outputs encrypted keyword c.
- Trapdoor: takes sk and keyword m' and generates a trapdoor td for m'.
- Test: takes trapdoor td and encrypted keyword c corresponding to keyword m outputs 'yes' if td is the trapdoor for keyword m, otherwise it outputs 'no'.

In this paper, the use of PEKS enables insurance companies to detect vulnerable software on IoT devices without revealing software data on the IoT devices. The insurance company is provided a trapdoor for each vulnerability, searches the encrypted IoT device data, and only learns whether or not an IoT device has the specific vulnerability or not. The use of PEKS in the smart cyber insurance system is illustrated in Fig. 2 and details are as follows:

1. KeyGen: a company's IoT device manager generates a A_{pub}/A_{priv} key pair for all managed IoT devices, where A_{pub} is company's public key and A_{priv} is the company's private key.
2. Enc(A_{pub}, software): Each data entry from an IoT device is encrypted using PEKS scheme with A_{pub}. It is then stored on blockchain via smart contract.
3. Trapdoor(A_{pub}, m): When the security organization publishes security information m on the blockchain, IoT devices manager will listen to this event and fetch m via the smart contract. The IoT device manager uses A_{priv} to generate a trapdoor T_m and sends T_m to insurance company.
4. Test(S, T_m): Given S = Enc(A_{pub}, software) from the blockchain and T_m, the insurance company can test if IoT device software matches with the vulnerability data. If 'yes', they will recalculate risk score of the device.

3.5   Risk Rating Scheme

3.5.1   Basic Summation

A naive Smart Insurance risk rating scheme would simply calculate the current risk based on the vulnerabilities present on the devices in a network at a given time. Although this is a functional approach to determining the security of a network at a given time, this simple count does not truly reflect the insured party's risk over time nor the insured party's responsiveness to these risks.

3.5.2   Time Scaling

Since risk can be thought of as "having a vulnerability over time," if you can incentivize the timely resolution of vulnerabilities, you can decrease the risk to both the insured company and the insurer. In order to develop these incentives, the risk rating scheme increases the impact of a vulnerability the longer it is left unresolved. By reducing the amount of time each vulnerability is present, the insured party can reduce their overall risk score. This scheme also allows a vigilant party to prevent a single vulnerability from significantly impacting their overall risk score and therefore their insurance premium.

Parameters:

- I = Interval of relevance: the interval in which we care about counting risk scores of vulnerabilities. For example, some number of months.
- C = Score reduction time constant: Exponential functions have the feature of scaling to a limit. Using a time constant to divide the exponent, we can set how quickly this diminishing occurs.
- Δt = time period of vulnerability: this is the interval of time between when a vulnerability is detected on a client's system and when it is resolved.
- Sampling interval: The interval in which the smart insurance system receives new information. This is the highest precision time period in which we can measure vulnerability resolutions.

Calculation:

1. Δt = (time of vulnerability resolution) − (time of vulnerability detection)
2. C = choice of time constant to shape the scaling (Fig. 3)
3. Individual vulnerability risk = (raw impact score as published) × $(1 - e^{\Delta t/C})$
4. Risk score = sum of all individual vulnerability risks in the interval of interest

4   Implementation and Evaluation

4.1   Implementation Using Ethereum

The smart cyber insurance system implementation consists of two smart contracts and several java classes. We implemented smart contracts in Solidity and deployed them on a private Ethereum blockchain. The security management

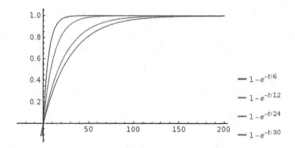

Fig. 3. Examples for various values for C

smart contract (SIManagement.sol) provides functions for storing vulnerability data to blockchain and retrieving that data from blockchain. The IoT device management smart contract (IoTManagement.sol) provides functions for storing the encrypted software data on and retrieving it from the blockchain.

We implemented the primary components of the system following the design described in Sect. 3. First, the functions of PEKS, then functions to set up connection with remote Ethereum node, load credentials, and shut down the connection for each stakeholder. In addition, we implemented a Java wrapper for the smart contracts and specific functions for each stakeholder such for the insurance company to scan the encrypted software data and against the trapdoors of vulnerable software and calculate the risk score of IoT devices.

4.2   Evaluation

4.2.1   Soundness

After the insured party first signs insurance contract with insurer and the contract is stored on blockchain, no part of the contract can be changed by any party. Using the vulnerability data, IoT device status data, and the insurance policy rules from blockchain, both parties can perform risk score verification or insurance policy verification. Because of the public verifiability of the system, the insurer and the insured party have to follow the agreed contract without exception. In other words, insurer cannot pay lower coverage and insured party cannot obtain more coverage for any reasons which are not covered in the claim.

4.2.2   Privacy

The encryption of an IoT device's information using PEKS prevents the access of this sensitive information by other parties on the network. Since a blockchain provides authentication through a public key signature scheme, an adversary cannot fake any vulnerable IoT device to falsely raise the rate of the insurance of the insured party. Crucially, the insurance company is only given access to the information that is necessary to calculate the risk scores but has no access to additional sensitive information regarding the IoT devices.

4.2.3   Risk Rating Scheme as an Incentive Mechanism

As discussed previously, standard (cyber) insurance has a mostly predefined level of risk based on a small number of data points and observations such as surveys. With a static (or at least infrequently renewed) risk evaluation, insurance products are stuck having to charge premiums that reflect that standard risk in the entire market with only low levels of adjustment for the individual risk of the client. Since the insurance premium primarily reflects this analysis, insured parties have little incentive to improve their cyber security environment as they will benefit from the insurance regardless and will have the same premium cost without regard for security improvements[2]. In a Risk Rating Scheme such as the one described in this paper, we have the benefit of far more data points and being able to dynamically track both software vulnerability states as well as the vigilance with which clients attempt to resolve these vulnerabilities. By dynamically tracking and updating a client's insurance premium using these features, clients can see a direct economic benefit from routinely evaluating and resolving security problems in a timely manner. In this way, we create an incentive mechanism that provides an economic benefit to clients who actively resolve problems and improve the security state of their environment.

Based on the smart cyber scheme, expected profit/loss of insured company, insurers, and society could be quantified with a certain formula. The insured company will benefit from the decrease in the insurance premium when the risk score improves, though it may require additional operating costs in order to maintain a good security environment. In addition, it is likely that the expected loss caused by cyber incidents goes down as the probability of cyber attack decreases in a better security state. In a simple situation where contract is concluded at t=0 and the insurance premium (=f(Risk Score)) is adjusted only once at t=1 based on the change in risk score between t=0 and t=1, the calculation for the expected profit/loss for insured company is:

– Expected profit/loss = (Insurance premium at the time of contract) $\times \Delta f$(Risk Score) $- \Delta$(Operational costs) $+ \Delta$(Probability of cyber attack) $\times$ (Expected loss rate) $\times$ (Total exposure)

As for insurers, they will benefit from the decrease in the expected insurance loss incurred by cyber incidents, while their revenue goes down when the risk score decreases.

– Expected profit/loss = (Total coverage) $\times \Delta$(Expected insurance loss) $-$ (Insurance premium at the time of contract) $\times \Delta f$(Risk Score)

The impact on social welfare is difficult to estimate. However, decreases in the risk score will entail a decrease in the number of vulnerable IoT devices,

---

[2] It is not to say that insurance companies cannot adjust premiums based on security improvements that are observed in a client's environment, but that there is usually no practical way to access this information in a reliable way that provides a faithful representation of the client's efforts or accomplishments.

implying that the likelihood of catastrophic cyber attack and resulting social costs will go down. Thus, the insured company could be incentivized to improve the risk score when the positive effects, the decrease in premium and expected loss incurred by cyber attack, exceed the increase in operational costs. Likewise, insurers would have incentive to provide this type of products to mitigate cyber risk underwritten. Further study is needed to specify proper parameters and formula for the calculation of the premium so as to create sufficient level of incentives to each stakeholder.

4.3 Consideration on Regulation Issues

As discussed earlier, insurance products utilizing the smart cyber insurance scheme need to comply with regulatory requirement in order to get approval from insurance regulators. Given the traits of the scheme, issues we discuss in this section should be especially considered before commercialization.

4.3.1 Validity and Accountability for the Calculation

Regulators might ask insurers to report details such as calculation model, risk score, premium, and back data so as to assess the validity of dynamic pricing policy. In contrast to traditional insurance products where the premium is fixed, the premium of smart cyber insurance products is periodically adjusted based on dynamic pricing model. Insurers and regulators would have to agree in advance on the degree and interval for the adjustment as regulators might deem that too volatile and frequent change in premium could harm interest of the policyholder[3]. Moreover, regulators might ask detailed explanation if the degree of discount by the risk score is much larger than the impact of other coefficients.

In addition, insurers are accountable for verifying that the scheme adequately captures the underwriting risk including accumulation risks and that the risks are covered its capital. It should be noted that the risk and associated costs of cyber incidents such as data breaches could vary depending on multiple factors such as the IT development and regulation, indicating that insurers are required to address the change in situation (e.g. unexpected insurance loss incurred) by modifying the risk rating model or parameters.

On the other hand, it is desirable to achieve mitigated concentration risk of holding sensitive data with insurance companies having only encrypted data. Therefore, stakeholders of smart cyber insurance system should work together to strike a balance between privacy protection and insurer's accountability. For example, it is possible that other stakeholders such as IoT device managers provide regulators with necessary information for the supervisory purposes on behalf of insurance companies without sharing such data.

---

[3] A smart cyber insurance scheme could be more difficult to understand than a traditional one. From policyholder protection perspective, regulators might ask insurers to refrain from using complex pricing model especially when the products are sold to individuals.

4.3.2   Future Work: Designing Optimal Supervisory Framework

While various regulators are trying to develop policy framework for the cyber insurance market [4], there are still limited guidelines or standards that fits for new types of cyber insurance like the smart cyber insurance scheme. For example, risk factors with regard to cyber insurance are not stipulated in law and regulation in many jurisdictions. It might make regulators face challenges in evaluating the appropriateness of the selected data, resulting in conservative judgement. Even though it is technically feasible to solve these issues, existing legal and supervisory framework may not allow such arrangement. Another example is the security evaluation of smart contracts used in smart cyber scheme, which is quite challenging for insurance regulators with limited knowledge and expertise about the technology. In order to design and develop better regulatory environments, all stakeholders involved in the ecosystem should have a dialogue to develop common language and mutual understandings.

5   Conclusion

As the use of Internet of Things devices proliferates in all aspects of business operations and personal electronics, the security risk they pose remains a prominent concern. The usage of a smart cyber insurance scheme allows for the development of strong financial incentives to maintain safer IoT ecosystems. The scheme should be applied to actual product design with considerations for regulatory goals and requirements. The inclusion of time-scaled premium calculations, the increased transparency between organizations and their insurers, and the potential of dynamic insurance schemes acts to further the development of a more stable and secure Internet of Things ecosystem.

References

1. Information technology - security techniques - cybersecurity and ISO and IEC standards. Report ISO/IEC TR 27103:2018, ISO/IEC JTC1 (2018)
2. Baer, W.: Rewarding it security in the marketplace. Contemp. Secur. Policy **24**(1), 190–208 (2003)
3. Bellare, M., Yilek, S.: Encryption schemes secure under selective opening attack. Cryptology ePrint Archive, Report 2009/101. https://eprint.iacr.org/2009/101 (2009)
4. Boneh, D., Di Crescenzo, G., Ostrovsky, R., Persiano, G.: Public key encryption with keyword search. In: Cachin, C., Camenisch, J.L. (eds.) EUROCRYPT 2004. LNCS, vol. 3027, pp. 506–522. Springer, Heidelberg (2004). https://doi.org/10. 1007/978-3-540-24676-3_30

---

[4] As an example, The EU-U.S. Insurance Dialogue Project began as an initiative by multiple organization including EIOPA, FIO and NAIC to enhance mutual understanding and cooperation between the European Union (EU) and the United States for the benefit of insurance consumers and business.

5. Boneh, D., Kushilevitz, E., Ostrovsky, R., Skeith, W.E.: Public key encryption that allows PIR queries. In: Menezes, A. (ed.) CRYPTO 2007. LNCS, vol. 4622, pp. 50–67. Springer, Heidelberg (2007). https://doi.org/10.1007/978-3-540-74143-5_4
6. Cao, N., O'Neill, A., Zaheri, M.: Toward RSA-OAEP without random oracles. In: Kiayias, A., Kohlweiss, M., Wallden, P., Zikas, V. (eds.) PKC 2020. LNCS, vol. 12110, pp. 279–308. Springer, Cham (2020). https://doi.org/10.1007/978-3-030-45374-9_10
7. Finck, M.: Blockchain Regulation and Governance in Europe. Cambridge University Press, Cambridge (2018)
8. Hoang, V.T., Katz, J., O'Neill, A., Zaheri, M.: Selective-Opening Security in the Presence of Randomness Failures. In: Cheon, J.H., Takagi, T. (eds.) ASIACRYPT 2016. LNCS, vol. 10032, pp. 278–306. Springer, Heidelberg (2016). https://doi.org/10.1007/978-3-662-53890-6_10
9. Hofheinz, D., Weinreb, E.: Searchable encryption with decryption in the standard model. *IACR Cryptology ePrint Archive*, 2008:423. (2008)
10. Corvus Insurance. Insurtech corvus launches smart cyber excess insurance with $10mlimit. Insurance Journal (2019)
11. European Insurance and Occupational Pensions Authority. Understanding cyber insurance – a structured dialogue with insurance companies (2018). https://eiopa.europa.eu/Publications/Reports
12. Jevtic, P., Lanchier, N.: Smart contract insurance. https://blockchain.asu.edu/smart-contract-insurance/
13. Nakamoto, S.: Bitcoin: a peer-to-peer electronic cash system. Cryptography Mailing list (2009). https://metzdowd.com
14. National Association of Insurance Commissioners. Report on the cybersecurity insurance and identity theft coverage supplement (2019). https://content.naic.org
15. International Association of Insurance Supervisors. Application paper on supervision of insurer cybersecurity (2018). https://www.iaisweb.org/page/supervisory-material/application-papers
16. Ostrovsky, R., Skeith, W.E.: Private searching on streaming data. In: Shoup, V. (ed.) CRYPTO 2005. LNCS, vol. 3621, pp. 223–240. Springer, Heidelberg (2005). https://doi.org/10.1007/11535218_14
17. EU-U.S. Insurance Dialogue Project. The cyber insurance market (2018). https://eiopa.europa.eu/Publications
18. Romanosky, S., Ablon, L., Kuehn, A., Jones, T.: Content analysis of cyber insurance policies: How do carriers write policies and price cyber risk? SSRN Electron. J. (2017)
19. Woods, D., Agrafiotis, I., Nurse, J.R.C., Creese, S.: Mapping the coverage of security controls in cyber insurance proposal forms. J. Internet Serv. Appl. 8(1), 1–13 (2017). https://doi.org/10.1186/s13174-017-0059-y
20. Woods, D., Simpson, A.: Policy measures and cyber insurance: a framework. J. Cyber Policy 2(2), 209–226 (2017)
21. Yurcik, W., Doss, D.: Cyber insurance: a market solution to the internet security market failure. In Proceedings of The 1st Workshop on the Economics of Information Security (2002)

Confidential and Auditable Payments

Tatsuo Mitani[1,2(✉)] and Akira Otsuka[1]

[1] Institute of Information Security, Yokohama, Japan
{dgs187101,otsuka}@iisec.ac.jp
[2] Mitsubishi Chemical Systems, Inc., Tokyo, Japan

Abstract. In this paper, we construct the Confidential and Auditable Payments (CAP) scheme. We keep the transaction confidential by writing ciphertexts of transactions in a ledger. We realize the soundness of the CAP scheme by the soundness of the zero-knowledge proof. A court or an authority controls a unique secret key of the ciphertexts written in the ledger. They can enforce confidential transactions open with the secret key according to the legal procedure. There are many works for protecting the transaction's privacy strictly. However, these works do not have a forcibly auditable function, to the best of our knowledge. The proposed scheme is both confidential and auditable. It eliminates concerns about money laundering caused by excessively confidential transactions and contributes to the sound use of blockchain.

Keywords: Blockchain · Homomorphic encryption · Zero-knowledge proof

1 Introduction

Bitcoin [13] has spread around the world in the past decade. This underlying technology is called the blockchain. Bitcoin makes transaction information public. For this reason, Bitcoin is transparent. A bank typically keeps the customer's transaction information confidential. People hope that a blockchain also keeps transaction information concealed. Many works realize anonymity and confidentiality in the blockchain. However, these works have rarely a forcibly auditable function. It is a problem that excessive confidentiality of transaction information may cause money laundering.

In this paper, we construct the Confidential and Auditable Payments (CAP) scheme that allows a court or an authority to audit transactions while keeping the transaction information confidential. Every participant writes their account balance as a ciphertext of homomorphic encryption in a ledger with a unique public key. They realize transactions by calculating ciphertexts. The court controls its secret key and can forcefully decrypt the ciphertexts and confirm the information.

Supported by Mitsubishi Chemical Corporation.

1.1 Related Work

In Bitcoin, transaction information is open. For this reason, there are some works for concealing transaction information. Zerocoin [10] and Zerocash [15] are extensions based on Bitcoin. They realized strong anonymity and confidentiality by designing anonymous coins that skillfully combined commitments. Zerocash uses the zero-knowledge succinct non-interactive argument of knowledge (zk-SNARK) [6] to show to others that there is no fraud such as double-spending. Recently, Zether [4], a cryptocurrency that can conceal transaction information, has been proposed as an extension based on Ethereum. Zether has also used the zero-knowledge proof Bulletproofs [5] proposed by their group. However, neither Zerocoin, Zerocash, nor Zether is forcibly auditable because of their strong anonymity and confidentiality.

Mitani and Otsuka expressed the state transition of a permissioned blockchain using homomorphic encryption [11,12]. In their scheme, a zero-knowledge proof of plaintext knowledge shows that the equation of the encrypted model is established to outsiders of the blockchain, and can prove the validity of the state transition. So their scheme is auditable concerning the permissioned blockchain.

1.2 Our Approach

Many works protect transaction privacy strictly and do not have a forcibly auditable function. The proposed scheme is not only confidential but also auditable. It eliminates concerns about money laundering caused by confidentiality and contributes to the sound use of blockchain.

Let us state our approach. We describe auditability at first. A pair of a public key pk_0 and a secret key sk_0 of homomorphic encryption is issued. The court controls this secret key sk_0. They can decrypts ciphertexts according to the judicial procedure when requested. In this sense, the scheme is auditable.

Next, we state confidentiality. As shown in Fig. 1, we consider that a column vector of each participant's account balance $\vec{x}$ is updated to the next time state $\vec{x}'$ by the transition matrix A. That is, $\vec{x}' = \vec{x}A$. The transition matrix A corresponds to the remittance by each participant. Each participant uses the public key pk_0 in common. Each participant writes their balance in the ledger as ciphertext $\vec{\mathbf{x}}$. As for the transition matrix, each participant writes each element in the ledger as ciphertext $\mathbf{A}$. Then, each participant writes their balance of the next time, reflecting the remittance in the ledger as a ciphertext $\vec{\mathbf{x}}'$. All the ciphertexts in the ledger are the ciphertexts of homomorphic encryption. $\vec{\mathbf{x}}' - \vec{\mathbf{x}}\mathbf{A}$ is the ciphertext of zero if and only if $\vec{x}' = \vec{x}A$.

Let us confirm the remittance procedure when a sender i transfers to a recipient j. The element a_{ij} of the transition matrix A corresponds to this remittance. We use zero-knowledge proof of plaintext knowledge of ciphertext to show that the remittance is legitimate. The sender also writes the proof regarding a_{ij} in the ledger. This proof shows that the sender has not sent more than their account balance. Knowledge corresponds to the randomness in creating the ciphertext

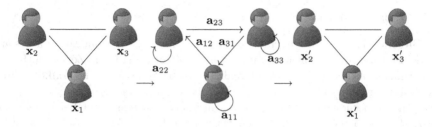

Fig. 1. Illustration of a state transition for three participants. $\vec{x} = (x_1, x_2, x_3), \vec{x}' = (x_1', x_2', x_3')$ and $A = (a_{ij})$ are plaintexts. The corresponding ciphertexts are $\vec{\mathbf{x}}, \vec{\mathbf{x}}'$ and $\mathbf{A}$. Because of the homomorphic encryption, $\vec{\mathbf{x}}' - \vec{\mathbf{x}}\mathbf{A}$ is the ciphertext of zero if and only if $\vec{x}' = \vec{x}A$.

of homomorphic encryption. At the time of remittance, the sender encrypts the randomness with the recipient's public key pk_j. Then the sender sends it to the recipient. The recipient decrypts with their secret key sk_j and obtains the randomness of the remittance. From the knowledge of the randomness collected, the recipient proves that their updated account balance x_j' is correct by the operation $\vec{x}' = \vec{x}A$.

We organize the rest of this paper as follows. Section 2 describes two ingredients: the ring learning with errors (RLWE) and the zero-knowledge proof (ZKP). Section 3 describes the definitions for a secure CAP scheme. Section 4 describes the construction of the CAP scheme, including data structures, algorithms, and security proofs. Section 5 states the conclusion and future work.

2   Building Blocks

Notation. We summarize the parameters and notation in this paper in Table 1. We identify a vector $(a_0, \ldots, a_{n_d-1})$ with a polynomial $a_0 + a_1 X + \cdots + a_{n_d-1} X^{n_d-1}$.

RLWE. Fully homomorphic encryption is capable of both addition and multiplication in ciphertexts. Gentry realized it in 2009 [7]. The RLWE scheme [9] is one of the most promising forms. We introduce the definitions used in this paper.

Definition 1 (Syntax of the RLWE scheme (Definition 6 in [2])). *We describe the RLWE scheme represented by a tuple of PPT algorithms*

$$\mathsf{RLWE} := (\mathsf{RLWE.Gen}, \mathsf{RLWE.Enc}, \mathsf{RLWE.Dec})$$

with the following syntax. We denote a message space as $\mathbf{M}$ *and a ciphertext space as* $\mathbf{C}$.

- *$\mathsf{RLWE.Gen}(1^\lambda)$ returns a key pair $(\mathsf{pk}, \mathsf{sk})$ from an input 1^λ.*
- *$\mathsf{RLWE.Enc}(\mathsf{pk}, m, r)$ returns a ciphertext $\mathbf{c} \in \mathbf{C}$ from an input of the public key pk, a message $m \in \mathbf{M}$ and a randomness r.*

Table 1. List of Parameters and Notation

Parameters	Explanation
$\mathbb{N}, \mathbb{Z}, \mathbb{Q}$ and $\mathbb{R}$	The sets of natural numbers, integers, rational numbers and real numbers
$\mathbb{Z}_q = \mathbb{Z}/q\mathbb{Z}$	The finite field $\{0, 1, \ldots, q-1\}$
n_d	The degree of the polynomial
$\mathbf{R} = \mathbb{Z}[X]/\langle X^{n_d} + 1\rangle$	The ring of integers
$\mathbf{R}_q = \mathbb{Z}_q[X]/\langle X^{n_d} + 1\rangle$	The ring of integers modulo q
$\lvert a \rvert = \sqrt{a_0^2 + a_1^2 + \cdots + a_{n_d-1}^2}$	l_2-norm of $a \in \mathbf{R}_q$. a_i is the coefficient of X^i
$\mathrm{negl}(n)$	A negligible function f such that $\forall n > n_c, f(n) < 1/n^c$ under $\forall c \in \mathbb{N}, \exists n_c$
$a \xleftarrow{\$} A$	Randomly sampled from the distribution A or from a uniform distribution over the set A
$\tilde{\mathcal{O}}(\cdot)$	Bachmann-Landau notation
$\omega(f(n))$	The ω notation is a function growing asymptotically faster than $f(n)$
$\mathcal{O}$	An oracle
$D_{v,\sigma} = \rho_{v,\sigma}^{n_d}(x)/\rho_{0,\sigma}^{n_d}(\mathbb{Z}^{n_d})$ and $D_\sigma = \rho_{0,\sigma}^{n_d}(x)/\rho_{0,\sigma}^{n_d}(\mathbb{Z}^{n_d})$	D_σ and $D_{v,\sigma}$ are discrete gaussian distributions on $\mathbf{R}$ with mean 0, v and standard deviation σ $$\rho_{v,\sigma}^{n_d}(x) = (\tfrac{1}{\sqrt{2\pi}\sigma})^{n_d} e^{\frac{-\lvert x-v\rvert^2}{2\sigma^2}} \text{ over } \mathbb{R}^{n_d}$$ $$\rho_{0,\sigma}^{n_d}(\mathbb{Z}^{n_d}) = \Sigma_{z \in \mathbb{Z}^{n_d}} \rho_{0,\sigma}^{n_d}(z)$$
Adv	The advantage of an adversary in a game
Exp	The experiment in a game
$\Pr[E]$	The probability that an event E occurs

- RLWE.Dec(sk, $\mathbf{c}$) *returns a message* $m \in \mathbf{M}$ *or* $\perp$ *from an input of the secret key* sk *and a ciphertext* $\mathbf{c} \in \mathbf{C}$.

Definition 2 (Pseudorandomness of ciphertexts (Definition 7 in [2])).
We say a RLWE scheme RLWE := (RLWE.Gen, RLWE.Enc, RLWE.Dec) *satisfies pseudorandomness of ciphertexts or simply* RLWE *is secure, if for every PPT adversary* $\mathcal{A}$ *the advantage*

$$\mathrm{Adv}^{\mathsf{pr}}_{\mathsf{RLWE},\mathcal{A}}(\lambda) := \lvert \Pr[\mathrm{Exp}^{\mathsf{pr}}_{\mathsf{RLWE},\mathcal{A}}(\lambda) = 1] - 1/2 \rvert$$

is negligible in λ, *where* $\mathrm{Exp}^{\mathsf{pr}}_{\mathsf{RLWE},\mathcal{A}}(\lambda)$ *is as defined in Fig. 2.*

$$\begin{array}{l|l}
\mathrm{Exp}_{\mathsf{RLWE},\mathcal{A}}^{\mathsf{pr}}(\lambda): & \mathcal{O}_{\mathsf{RLWE.Enc}}(m): \\
\hline
(\mathsf{pk},\mathsf{sk}) \leftarrow \mathsf{RLWE.Gen}(1^{\lambda}) & \text{if } \beta = 0 \\
\beta \leftarrow \{0,1\} & \quad \mathbf{c} \leftarrow \mathsf{RLWE.Enc}(\mathsf{pk}, m) \\
\beta' \leftarrow \mathcal{A}^{\mathcal{O}_{\mathsf{RLWE.Enc}}(\cdot)}(1^{\lambda}, \mathsf{pk}) & \text{else} \\
\text{if } \beta = \beta' \text{ return } 1 & \quad \mathbf{c} \xleftarrow{\$} \mathbf{R}_q^2 \\
\text{else return } 0 & \text{return } \mathbf{c}
\end{array}$$

Fig. 2. Security challenge experiment for pseudorandomness of ciphertexts.

Table 2. Brakerski-Vaikuntanathan (BV) scheme

Parameters	Explanation
$\mathbf{M} = \mathbf{R}_p$	The plaintext space
(a,b) and s	(a,b) is a public key. s is a secret key. Then, $a, s \xleftarrow{\$} \mathbf{R}_q,\ e_s \xleftarrow{\$} D_\sigma,\ b = as + e_s$
$\mathbf{c} = (c_1, c_2) = (bv + pe + m, av + pf)$	The ciphertext of a plaintext $m \in \mathbf{M}$ Then, a set of randomness $v, e, f \xleftarrow{\$} D_\sigma$
$m = (c_1 - s \cdot c_2 \mod q) \mod p$	Decryption of $\mathbf{c} = (c_1, c_2)$

Remark 1. We consider RLWE scheme that is secure in the sense of Definition 2. We write a ciphertext $\mathbf{c}$ in the boldface like this. We concretely consider Brakerski-Vaikuntanathan (BV) scheme [3] in Table 2.

ZKP. Goldwasser *et al.* originally formulated this method [8]. ZKP is an interactive protocol that a prover that has a secret can inform a verifier of the fact that the proposition on the secret is correct. A prover can prevent the secret from being leaked. A verifier can reject a malicious prover with no secret.

Benhamouda *et al.* originally proposed the zero-knowledge proof of knowledge of randomness in RLWE encryption [1]. Then, Mitani and Otsuka adopt its scheme for the zero-knowledge proof of plaintext $m = 0$ knowledge in RLWE encryption [11,12]. We state this detail in Appendix A. In this paper, we denote the zero-knowledge proof and its verification as below syntax.

- Prove$(\mathbf{x}; r)$ inputs the ciphertext $\mathbf{x}$ and its randomness r and outputs the proof π for the knowledge of RLWE.Dec$(\mathsf{sk}, \mathbf{x}) = 0$. We denotes Prove$(\mathbf{x}; r_1, \ldots, r_n)$ if there are some randomnesses $r_1, \ldots, r_n$.
- Verify(π) inputs the proof π and outputs 1 if it is valid, otherwise 0.

3   Secure CAP Scheme

In this section, we define the security of a CAP scheme. Regarding security, we follow Zerocash [15]. Zerocash defines and satisfies the three properties; ledger indistinguishability, transaction non-malleability, and balance. In this sense, the DAP scheme of Zerocash is secure. We adjust the three properties for a CAP scheme. We modify ledger indistinguishability. Balance corresponds to the proof regarding the transition matrix, according to Lemma 1. We combine transaction non-malleability and balance into non-malleability. In this sense, a CAP scheme Π is secure. Let us confirm the below definitions.

Definition 3 (Ledger indistinguishability). *A CAP scheme*

$$\Pi := (\mathsf{Setup}, \mathsf{CreateAccount}, \mathsf{Transition}, \mathsf{Send}, \mathsf{Receive})$$

satisfies ledger indistinguishability, if for any $\lambda \in \mathbb{N}$ and any PPT adversary $\mathcal{A}$, the advantage

$$\mathsf{Adv}_{\Pi,\mathcal{A}}^{\mathsf{L-IND}}(\lambda) := \mid \Pr[\mathsf{Exp}_{\Pi,\mathcal{A}}^{\mathsf{L-IND}}(\lambda) = 1] - 1/2 \mid$$

is negligible in λ, where $\mathsf{Exp}_{\Pi,\mathcal{A}}^{\mathsf{L-IND}}(\lambda)$ is defined in Fig. 3.

In Fig. 3, a pair of the queries (Q, Q') must be the same type; CreateAccount or Transition. If the query type is Transition, then $Q = (\mathsf{Transition}, A)$ and $Q' = (\mathsf{Transition}, A')$. A and A' must be same size. Each element is generally different. That is, $A \neq A'$. $\vec{Q}$ and $\vec{Q}'$ are the lists of all the queries that $\mathcal{A}$ sent to the oracles. Append is the function to append the latest query to the lists.

$\mathsf{Exp}_{\Pi,\mathcal{A}}^{\mathsf{L-IND}}(\lambda)$:

$\mathsf{pp}, \mathsf{cp} \leftarrow \mathsf{Setup}(1^\lambda)$
$L_0 \leftarrow \mathcal{O}_0^\Pi(\mathsf{pp}); L_1 \leftarrow \mathcal{O}_1^\Pi(\mathsf{pp})$
$b \xleftarrow{\$} \{0, 1\}$
while:
$\quad (Q, Q') \leftarrow \mathcal{A}(\mathsf{pp}, \vec{Q}, \vec{Q}', L_b, L_{1-b})$
$\quad L_b \leftarrow \mathcal{A}^{\mathcal{O}_b^\Pi(\cdot)}(\mathsf{pp}, Q, L_b); L_{1-b} \leftarrow \mathcal{A}^{\mathcal{O}_{1-b}^\Pi(\cdot)}(\mathsf{pp}, Q', L_{1-b})$
$\quad \vec{Q} \leftarrow \mathsf{Append}(\vec{Q}, Q); \vec{Q}' \leftarrow \mathsf{Append}(\vec{Q}', Q')$
$\quad c \leftarrow \mathcal{A}(\mathsf{pp}, \vec{Q}, \vec{Q}', L_b, L_{1-b})$
$\quad$ if $c = 1$ break
$\quad$ else continue
$b' \leftarrow \mathcal{A}(\mathsf{pp}, \vec{Q}, \vec{Q}', L_b, L_{1-b})$
if $b = b'$ return 1
else return 0

Fig. 3. Security challenge experiment for ledger indistinguishability

Definition 4 (Non-malleability). *A CAP scheme*

$$\Pi := (\mathsf{Setup}, \mathsf{CreateAccount}, \mathsf{Transition}, \mathsf{Send}, \mathsf{Receive})$$

satisfies non-malleability, if for any $\lambda \in \mathbb{N}$ and any PPT adversary $\mathcal{A}$, the advantage

$$\mathrm{Adv}^{\mathsf{NM}}_{\Pi,\mathcal{A}}(\lambda) := \Pr[\mathrm{Exp}^{\mathsf{NM}}_{\Pi,\mathcal{A}}(\lambda) = 1]$$

is negligible in λ, where $\mathrm{Exp}^{\mathsf{NM}}_{\Pi,\mathcal{A}}(\lambda)$ is defined in Fig. 4. Besides, $\mathcal{O}^{\Pi}$ and Append are the same as Definition 3.

We lead the below definition of a secure CAP scheme.

$\mathrm{Exp}^{\mathsf{NM}}_{\Pi,\mathcal{A}}(\lambda)$:

pp, cp $\leftarrow$ Setup(1^{λ})
$L \leftarrow \mathcal{O}^{\Pi}(\mathsf{pp})$
while:
    $Q \leftarrow \mathcal{A}(\mathsf{pp}, \vec{Q}, L)$
    $L \leftarrow \mathcal{A}^{\mathcal{O}^{\Pi}(\cdot)}(\mathsf{pp}, Q, L)$
    $\vec{Q} \leftarrow \mathsf{Append}(\vec{Q}, Q)$
    $c \leftarrow \mathcal{A}(\mathsf{pp}, \vec{Q}, L)$
    if $c = 1$ break
    else continue
$A^* \leftarrow \mathcal{A}(\mathsf{pp}, \vec{Q}, L)$
$L' \leftarrow \mathcal{A}^{\mathcal{O}^{\Pi}(\cdot)}(\mathsf{pp}, (\mathsf{Transition}, A^*), L)$
if (Verify(π^a) or Verify($\vec{\pi}^b$) or Verify(Π^c) or Verify($\vec{\pi}'$))
    and ($\sum_i (\mathbf{x}'_i - \mathbf{x}_i) \notin \mathbf{C}_0$) in L'
    return 1
else return 0

Fig. 4. Security challenge experiment for non-malleability

Definition 5 (Security). *A CAP scheme*

$$\Pi := (\mathsf{Setup}, \mathsf{CreateAccount}, \mathsf{Transition}, \mathsf{Send}, \mathsf{Receive})$$

is secure if it satisfies ledger indistinguishability of Definition 3 and non-malleability of Definition 4.

4   Construction

In this section, we describe data structures, algorithms, and security analysis.

4.1   Data Structures

In this subsection, we describe data structures of the CAP scheme. Following the ideas of Mitani and Otsuka [11], we consider that the state of the assets held by each participant will transition to the next state.

- $\vec{x} = (x_1, x_2, \ldots, x_n) \in \mathbb{Q}^n$. $\vec{x}$ is the amount of assets in the blockchain at time t. n is the number of the participants in a blockchain.
- $\vec{x}' = (x_1', x_2', \ldots, x_n') \in \mathbb{Q}^n$. $\vec{x}'$ is the amount of assets in the blockchain at time $t+1$.
- $A = (a_{ij})$ is a transition matrix such that $\vec{x}' = \vec{x}A$. Its size is $n \times n$. We suppose that the total volume moving from x_i to x_j' is v. That is, $x_i' = x_i - v$ and $x_j' = x_j + v$. We define the distribution rate $a_{ij} := v/x_i$. In particular, we consider a_{ii} as the "staying" rate ($x_i \to x_i'$). In the transition, the amount x_i is distributed to $x_1', \ldots, x_i', \ldots, x_n'$ at the ratio of $a_{i1}, \ldots, a_{ii}, \ldots, a_{in}$. The sum of all the ratios must be equal 1 because of the preservation. That is, $\sum_{j=1}^n a_{ij} = 1$. Let us confirm the following lemma.

Lemma 1 (Lemma 1 in [11]). *If $\vec{x}' = \vec{x}A$ and $\sum_{j=1}^n a_{ij} = 1$, then the equation $\sum_{i=1}^n x_i' = \sum_{i=1}^n x_i$ holds.*

- Ledger L is a distributed ledger each participants in the blockchain holds and updates. L contains the ciphertexts $\vec{\mathsf{x}}, \vec{\mathsf{x}}', \mathbf{A}$ and related proofs.

Remark 2. It is impractical to force all participants to join the transition matrix A every time. We assume a transition matrix A' that pertains only to participants trading at a particular time t. That is, A' is the submatrix of the transition matrix A for all participants. Since there is essentially no difference, we will discuss A and A' indiscriminately.

4.2 Algorithms

We describe the CAP scheme

$$\Pi := (\mathsf{Setup}, \mathsf{CreateAccount}, \mathsf{Transition}, \mathsf{Send}, \mathsf{Receive})$$

as follows. We can verify the completeness of the CAP scheme Π by confirming the construction.

Definition 6 (The CAP scheme). *Tha CAP scheme*

$$\Pi := (\mathsf{Setup}, \mathsf{CreateAccount}, \mathsf{Transition}, \mathsf{Send}, \mathsf{Receive})$$

is as follows.

Setup

- *Inputs: security parameter λ*
- *Outputs: public parameters* pp *and court parameters* cp

1. *Compute* $(\mathsf{pk}_0, \mathsf{sk}_0) := \mathsf{RLWE.Gen}(1^\lambda)$.
2. *Set* $\mathsf{pp} := \mathsf{pk}_0$.
3. *Set* $\mathsf{cp} := \mathsf{sk}_0$.
4. *Output* pp *and* cp.

CreateAccount

- *Inputs: public parameters* pp *and security parameter* λ
- *Outputs: account ciphertext* $\mathbf{x}$, *proof* π^a *in* L *and key pair* $(\mathsf{pk}, \mathsf{sk})$

1. *Choose randomly* $r_{\mathbf{x}}$.
2. *Compute* $\mathbf{x} := \mathsf{RLWE.Enc}(\mathsf{pk}_0, 0, r_{\mathbf{x}})$.
3. *Compute* $\pi^a := \mathsf{Prove}(\mathbf{x}; r_{\mathbf{x}})$.
4. *Compute* $(\mathsf{pk}, \mathsf{sk}) := \mathsf{RLWE.Gen}(1^\lambda)$.
5. *Output* $\mathbf{x}$, π *and* $(\mathsf{pk}, \mathsf{sk})$.

Transition

- *Inputs:*
    - *public parameters* pp
    - *old accounts state* $\vec{\mathbf{x}} = (\mathbf{x}_1, \ldots, \mathbf{x}_n)$ *in* L
    - *accounts randomness* $r_{\mathbf{x}_1}, \ldots, r_{\mathbf{x}_n}$
- *Outputs in* L:
    - *new accounts state* $\vec{\mathbf{x}}' = (\mathbf{x}_1', \ldots, \mathbf{x}_n')$
    - *new transition matrix* $\mathbf{A} = (\mathbf{a}_{ij})$
    - *balance proofs* $\vec{\pi}^b = (\pi_1^b, \ldots, \pi_n^b)$
    - *accounts copy proofs* $\Pi^c = (\pi_{ij}^c)$
    - *transition proofs* $\vec{\pi}' = (\pi_1', \ldots, \pi_n')$

1. *For* $i \in \{1, \ldots, n\}$ *(i sends v to j.)*
    (a) *For* $j \in \{1, \ldots, n\}$
        i. $\mathsf{Send}(\mathsf{pp}, \mathbf{x}_i, r_{\mathbf{x}_i}, x_i, v, \mathsf{pk}_j)$.
        ii. *Write* $\pi_{ij}^c, \mathbf{x}_{ij}^c, \mathbf{a}_{ij}$ *in* L.
    (b) *Compute* $\pi_i^b := \mathsf{Prove}(\sum_j \mathbf{a}_{ij} - \mathbf{1}; r_{\mathbf{a}_{i1}}, \ldots, r_{\mathbf{a}_{in}})$.
    (c) *Write* π_i^b *in* L.
2. $\mathsf{Verify}(\Pi^c)$
3. $\mathsf{Verify}(\vec{\pi}^b)$
4. *For* $j \in \{1, \ldots, n\}$ *(j receives v from i.)*
    (a) *For* $i \in \{1, \ldots, n\}$
        i. $\mathsf{Receive}(\mathsf{pp}, \mathsf{sk}_j, \mathbf{x}_i^c, \mathbf{a}_{ij}, \mathbf{v}, \mathbf{r}_{\mathbf{v}}, \pi_{ij}^c)$.
    (b) *Compute* $x_j' := \sum_i v_{ij}$.
    (c) *Choose* $r_{\mathbf{x}_j'}$ *randomly.*
    (d) *Compute* $\mathbf{x}_j' := \mathsf{RLWE.Enc}(\mathsf{pk}_0, x_j', r_{\mathbf{x}_j'})$.
    (e) *Compute* $\pi_j' := \mathsf{Prove}(\mathbf{x}_j' - \sum_i \mathbf{a}_{ij} \cdot \mathbf{x}_i; r_{\mathbf{x}_j'}, r_{\mathbf{v}_{1j}}, \ldots, r_{\mathbf{v}_{nj}})$.
    (f) *Write* $\mathbf{x}_j', \pi_j'$ *in* L.
5. $\mathsf{Verify}(\vec{\pi}')$

Send

- *Inputs:*
    - *public parameters* pp
    - *account ciphertext* $\mathbf{x}$ *in Ledger* L
    - *randomness* $r_{\mathbf{x}}$

- *plaintext x*
- *sending volume v*
- *public key* pk_j
  - *Outputs:*
    - *copy proof* π^c
    - *copy account* $\mathbf{x}^c$
    - *distribution ratio* $\mathbf{a}_{ij}$
    - *volume* $\mathbf{v}$
    - *randomness* $\mathbf{r_v}$

1. *Choose randomly* $r_{\mathbf{x}^c}$, *where* $r_{\mathbf{x}^c} \neq r_{\mathbf{x}}$.
2. *Compute* $\mathbf{x}^c := \mathsf{RLWE.Enc}(\mathsf{pk}_0, x, r_{\mathbf{x}^c})$.
3. *Compute* $\pi^c := \mathsf{Prove}(\mathbf{x}^c - \mathbf{x}; r_{\mathbf{x}^c} - r_{\mathbf{x}})$.
4. *Compute* $a := v/x$.
5. *Choose randomly* $r_{\mathbf{a}_{ij}}$.
6. *Compute* $\mathbf{a}_{ij} := \mathsf{RLWE.Enc}(\mathsf{pk}_0, a, r_{\mathbf{a}_{ij}})$.
7. *Compute* $r_{\mathbf{v}}$ *from* $r_{\mathbf{x}^c}$ *and* $r_{\mathbf{a}_{ij}}$.
8. *Compute* $\mathbf{v} := \mathsf{RLWE.Enc}(\mathsf{pk}_j, v, r_{\mathbf{v}})$.
9. *Compute* $\mathbf{r_v} := \mathsf{RLWE.Enc}(\mathsf{pk}_j, r_{\mathbf{v}}, r_{\mathbf{r_v}})$.
10. *Output* $\pi^c, \mathbf{x}^c, \mathbf{a}_{ij}, \mathbf{v}, \mathbf{r_v}$.

Receive

- *Inputs:*
  - *public parameters* pp
  - *secret key* sk_j
  - *ciphertexts* $\mathbf{x}^c, \mathbf{a}_{ij}, \mathbf{v}, \mathbf{r_v}$
  - *proof* π^c *in* L
- *Outputs:*
  - *volume v*
  - *randomness* $r_{\mathbf{v}}$

1. *Compute* $v := \mathsf{RLWE.Dec}(\mathsf{sk}_j, \mathbf{v})$.
2. *Compute* $r_{\mathbf{v}} := \mathsf{RLWE.Dec}(\mathsf{sk}_j, \mathbf{r_v})$.
3. *If* $\mathbf{a}_{ij} \cdot \mathbf{x}^c = \mathsf{RLWE.Enc}(\mathsf{pk}_0, v, r_{\mathbf{v}})$ *and* $|r_{\mathbf{v}}|$ *is small: Output* $v, r_{\mathbf{v}}$.
4. *Else: Output* $\perp$.

4.3   Security Analysis

We describe the below lemmas for the security of the CAP scheme Π in Definition 6.

Lemma 2 (Ledger indistinguishability). *The CAP scheme Π in Definition 6 satisfies ledger indistinguishability in Definition 3.*

Proof. We consider the games in Fig. 5. We denote events as follows.

- $E_0 : \mathrm{G}^0_{\mathsf{CPA},\mathcal{A}}(\lambda) = 1$

$$G^0_{\mathsf{CPA},\mathcal{A}}(\lambda):$$
$(\mathsf{pk},\mathsf{sk}) \leftarrow \mathsf{RLWE.Gen}(1^\lambda)$
$\beta \leftarrow \{0,1\}$
$\beta' \leftarrow \mathcal{A}^{\mathcal{O}^{\mathsf{CPA}}_0(\cdot,\cdot)}(1^\lambda,\mathsf{pk})$
if $\beta = \beta'$ return 1
else return 0

$$G^1_{\mathsf{CPA},\mathcal{A}}(\lambda):$$
$(\mathsf{pk},\mathsf{sk}) \leftarrow \mathsf{RLWE.Gen}(1^\lambda)$
$\beta \leftarrow \{0,1\}$
$\beta' \leftarrow \mathcal{A}^{\mathcal{O}^{\mathsf{CPA}}_1(\cdot,\cdot)}(1^\lambda,\mathsf{pk})$
if $\beta = \beta'$ return 1
else return 0

$$\mathcal{O}^{\mathsf{CPA}}_0(m_0, m_1):$$
if $\beta = 0$
   Choose r randomly.
   $\mathbf{m} \leftarrow \mathsf{RLWE.Enc}(\mathsf{pk}, m_0, r)$
else
   Choose r randomly.
   $\mathbf{m} \leftarrow \mathsf{RLWE.Enc}(\mathsf{pk}, m_1, r)$
return $\mathbf{m}$

$$\mathcal{O}^{\mathsf{CPA}}_1(m_0, m_1):$$
$\mathbf{m} \xleftarrow{\$} \mathbf{R}^2_q$
return $\mathbf{m}$

Fig. 5. Security challenge experiment for plaintexts

- $E_1 : G^1_{\mathsf{CPA},\mathcal{A}}(\lambda) = 1$
- $B_0 : \beta = 0$
- $B_1 : \beta = 1$

Since B_0 and B_1 are disjoint events, we have

$$\Pr[E_i] = \Pr[E_i \cap B_0] + \Pr[E_i \cap B_1] = \Pr[E_i|B_0] \cdot \Pr[B_0] + \Pr[E_i|B_1] \cdot \Pr[B_1].$$

where $i = \{0, 1\}$. We construct an adversary $\mathcal{B}$ from an adversary $\mathcal{A}$ who can distinguish $G^0_{\mathsf{CPA},\mathcal{A}}(\lambda)$ and $G^1_{\mathsf{CPA},\mathcal{A}}(\lambda)$. That is,

$$| \Pr[G^0_{\mathsf{CPA},\mathcal{A}}(\lambda) = 1] - \Pr[G^1_{\mathsf{CPA},\mathcal{A}}(\lambda) = 1] |$$
$$= | \Pr[E_0] - \Pr[E_1] |$$
$$= | (\Pr[E_0|B_0] \cdot \Pr[B_0] + \Pr[E_0|B_1] \cdot \Pr[B_1])$$
$$\quad - (\Pr[E_1|B_0] \cdot \Pr[B_0] + \Pr[E_1|B_1] \cdot \Pr[B_1]) |$$
$$= | \Pr[B_0] \cdot (\Pr[E_0|B_0] - \Pr[E_1|B_0]) + \Pr[B_1] \cdot (\Pr[E_0|B_1] - \Pr[E_1|B_1]) |$$
$$\leq \Pr[B_0] \cdot | \Pr[E_0|B_0] - \Pr[E_1|B_0] | + \Pr[B_1] \cdot | \Pr[E_0|B_1] - \Pr[E_1|B_1] |$$
$$= (\Pr[B_0] + \Pr[B_1]) \cdot \mathsf{Adv}^{\mathsf{pr}}_{\mathsf{RLWE},\mathcal{B}}(\lambda)$$
$$= \mathsf{Adv}^{\mathsf{pr}}_{\mathsf{RLWE},\mathcal{B}}(\lambda)$$

where we applied $\Pr[B_0] + \Pr[B_1] = 1$ in the last equation. Since the game $G^1_{\mathsf{CPA},\mathcal{A}}(\lambda)$ is independent of β, we have thus $\Pr[G^1_{\mathsf{CPA},\mathcal{A}}(\lambda) = 1] = 1/2$. Moreover, $\mathsf{Exp}^{\mathsf{L-IND}}_{\Pi,\mathcal{A}}(\lambda)$ consists of the game $G^0_{\mathsf{CPA},\mathcal{A}}(\lambda)$. Because of Definition 2, we obtain

$$\mathsf{Adv}^{\mathsf{L-IND}}_{\Pi,\mathcal{A}}(\lambda) \leq | \Pr[G^0_{\mathsf{CPA},\mathcal{A}}(\lambda) = 1] - 1/2 | \leq \mathsf{Adv}^{\mathsf{pr}}_{\mathsf{RLWE},\mathcal{B}}(\lambda) < \mathsf{negl}(\lambda).$$

Lemma 3 (Non-malleability). *The CAP scheme Π in Definition 6 satisfies non-malleability in Definition 4.*

Proof. Let us consider the below violations of verification in the cases $\mathcal{A}$ wins without the knowledge of randomness.

- $\mathcal{A}$ wins but violates Verify(π^a) in CreateAccount.
- $\mathcal{A}$ wins but violates Verify($\vec{\pi}^b$) in Transition.
- $\mathcal{A}$ wins but violates Verify(Π^c) in Transition.
- $\mathcal{A}$ wins but violates Verify($\vec{\pi}'$) in Transition.

Any violations result from the violation of zero-knowledge proof, that is, the knowledge error of zero-knowledge proof. From Lemma 6, the knowledge error of zero-knowledge proof is negligible.

Finally, we can lead the below theorem from Lemma 2 and Lemma 3.

Theorem 1 (The secure CAP scheme). *The CAP scheme Π in Definition 6 is secure in the sense of Definition 5.*

5   Conclusion

In this paper, we have constructed the confidential and auditable payments (CAP) scheme that allows a court or an authority to audit transactions while keeping the transaction information confidential. We have proposed that every participant writes the ciphertexts of transaction information in a ledger. Besides, we have confirmed the ledger indistinguishability, which is the concealment of the transaction information. Moreover, we have confirmed the soundness of the CAP scheme by the soundness of the zero-knowledge proof. The CAP scheme is secure in this sense. A court or an authority can forcibly clarify transaction information with a unique secret key. In this sense, we realized auditability in the CAP scheme.

Future Work. In the CAP scheme, the secret key of a court can decrypt all transaction information. Therefore, we expect the court to disclose minimum requisite information. Building a decryptable scheme for each account is an open problem.

A   Non-interactive Zero-Knowledge Proof

Following Benhamouda *et al.* [1], and Mitani and Otsuka [11,12], we describe the non-interactive zero-knowledge proof of plaintext $m = 0$ knowledge. First, we describe the formal definition of the Σ'-protocol, the protocol and its theorem proving this relationship.

Definition 7 (Definition 2.5. in [1]). *Let (P, V) be a two-party protocol, where V is a PPT, and let $L, L' \subseteq \{0,1\}^*$ be languages with witness relations R, R' such that $R \subseteq R'$. Then (P, V) is called a Σ'-protocol for L, L' with completeness error α, a challenge set $\mathbb{C}$, a public input x and a private input w, if and only if it satisfies the following conditions:*

- *Three-move form: The prover P, on input (x,w), computes a commitment t and sends it to V. The verifier V, on input x, then draws a challenge $c \leftarrow \mathbb{C}$ and sends it to P. The prover sends a response s to the verifier. Depending on the protocol transcript (t,c,s), the verifier finally accepts or rejects the proof. The protocol transcript (t,c,s) is called accepting, if the verifier accepts the protocol run.*
- *Completeness: Whenever $(x,w) \in R$, the verifier V accepts with probability at least $1-\alpha$.*
- *Special soundness: There exists a PPT algorithm E (the knowledge extractor) which takes two accepting transcripts $(t,c',s'),(t,c'',s'')$ satisfying $c' \neq c''$ as inputs, and outputs w' such that $(x,w') \in R'$.*
- *Special honest verifier zero knowledge (HVZK): There exists a PPT algorithm S (the simulator) taking $x \in L$ and $c \in \mathbb{C}$ as inputs, that outputs (t,s) so that the triple (t,c,s) is indistinguishable from an accepting protocol transcript generated by a real protocol run.*
- *High-entropy commitments: For all $(y,w) \in R$ and for all t, the probability that an honestly generated commitment by P takes on the value t is negligible.*

Let us introduce Pedersen commitments [14] for the zero-knowledge proof. we make use of the commitments as an auxiliary commitment scheme. We denote it as (aCSetup, aCCommit, aCOpen).

Pedersen Commitments. Given a family of prime order groups $\{\mathbb{G}(\lambda)\}_{\lambda \in \mathbb{N}}$ such that the discrete logarithm problem is hard in $\mathbb{G}(\lambda)$ with security parameter λ, let $\tilde{q} = \tilde{q}(\lambda)$ be the order of $\mathbb{G} = \mathbb{G}(\lambda)$. To avoid confusion, we denote all elements with order $\tilde{q}$ with a tilde in the following. We will write the group $\mathbb{G}(\lambda)$ additively.

- aCSetup: This algorithm chooses $\tilde{g}, \tilde{h} \overset{\$}{\leftarrow} \mathbb{G}$ and outputs $cpars = (\tilde{g}, \tilde{h})$.
- aCommit: To commit to a message $m \in \mathbb{Z}_{\tilde{q}}$, it first chooses $r \overset{\$}{\leftarrow} \mathbb{Z}_{\tilde{q}}$. It then outputs a pair $(\widetilde{cmt}, o) = (m\tilde{g} + r\tilde{h}, r)$.
- aCOpen: Given a commitment $\widetilde{cmt}$, an opening o, a public key $cpars$ and a message m, it outputs accept if and only if $(\widetilde{cmt}, o) \overset{?}{=} (m\tilde{g} + r\tilde{h}, r)$.

Lemma 4 (Theorem 2.1. in [1]). *Under the discrete logarithm assumption for $\mathbb{G}$, the Pedersen commitment scheme is perfectly hiding and is computationally binding.*

We show a non-interactive zero-knowledge proof of ciphertext of zero in Fig. 6. h is a cryptographic hash function. This protocol satisfies Lemma 5. The parallel protocol satisfies Lemma 6.

Lemma 5 (Lemma 5 in [12]). *The protocol in Fig. 6 is an HVZK Σ'-protocol for the following relations:*

$$R_0 = \{((c_1,c_2),(v,e,f)) : (c_1,c_2) = (bv+pe, av+pf) \wedge |v|,|e|,|f| \leq \tilde{\mathcal{O}}(\sqrt{n_d}\alpha)\}$$
$$R_0' = \{((c_1,c_2),(v,e,f)) : (2c_1, 2c_2) = (2bv+2pe, 2av+2pf)$$
$$\wedge |2v|,|2e|,|2f| \leq \tilde{\mathcal{O}}(n_d^2\alpha)\}$$

Common input: the public key (a, b), the ciphertext (c_1, c_2)

Relation: $R_0 = \{((c_1, c_2), (v, e, f)) : (c_1, c_2) = (bv + pe, av + pf)$
$$\land |v|, |e|, |f| \leq \tilde{\mathcal{O}}(\sqrt{n_d}\alpha)\}$$

Prover	Verifier

$r_v, r_e, r_f \xleftarrow{\$} D_{\tilde{\mathcal{O}}(\sqrt{n_d}\alpha)}$

$t_1 = br_v + r_e$

$t_2 = ar_v + r_f$

$(c_{\text{aux}}^{(1)}, d_{\text{aux}}^{(1)}) = \mathsf{aCommit}(t_1)$

$(c_{\text{aux}}^{(2)}, d_{\text{aux}}^{(2)}) = \mathsf{aCommit}(t_2)$

$$\xrightarrow{\quad c_{\text{aux}}^{(1)}, c_{\text{aux}}^{(2)} \quad}$$

$c = h(t_1, t_2, c_{\text{aux}}^{(1)}, d_{\text{aux}}^{(1)}, c_{\text{aux}}^{(2)}, d_{\text{aux}}^{(2)})$

$s_v = r_v + X^c v$

$s_e = r_e + X^c pe$

$s_f = r_f + X^c pf$

accept with probability
$$\frac{D_{\tilde{\mathcal{O}}(\sqrt{3n_d}\alpha)}((s_v, s_e, s_f))}{M D_{(X^c v, X^c e, X^c f), \tilde{\mathcal{O}}(\sqrt{3n_d}\alpha)}((s_v, s_e, s_f))}$$

$$\xrightarrow{\quad t_1, t_2, d_{\text{aux}}^{(1)}, d_{\text{aux}}^{(2)}, (s_v, s_e, s_f) \quad}$$

$c = h(t_1, t_2, c_{\text{aux}}^{(1)}, d_{\text{aux}}^{(1)}, c_{\text{aux}}^{(2)}, d_{\text{aux}}^{(2)})$

$X^c c_1 + t_1 \overset{?}{=} bs_v + s_e$

$X^c c_2 + t_2 \overset{?}{=} as_v + s_f$

$\mathsf{aCOpen}(t_1, c_{\text{aux}}^{(1)}, d_{\text{aux}}^{(1)}) \overset{?}{=} \mathsf{accept}$

$\mathsf{aCOpen}(t_2, c_{\text{aux}}^{(2)}, d_{\text{aux}}^{(2)}) \overset{?}{=} \mathsf{accept}$

$|s_v|, |s_e|, |s_f| \leq \tilde{\mathcal{O}}(n_d\alpha)$

Fig. 6. Non-interactive zero-knowledge proof of a ciphertext of zero regarding RLWE encryption (Figure 3 in [12])

where $2v, 2e$ and $2f$ are reduced modulo q. The protocol has a knowledge error of $1/(2n_d)$, a completeness error of $1 - 1/M$, and high-entropy commitments.

Lemma 6 (Theorem 6 in [12]). *Let us apply the protocol in Fig. 6 for λ times in parallel (the parallel protocol). Let the parallel protocol be accepting if and only if at least $\lambda/2M$ out of λ proofs were valid under the condition that an honest verifier rejects no proofs. Then, the parallel protocol has both a completeness error and knowledge error of $\mathrm{negl}(\lambda)$ under the condition $n_d \geq 2M$.*

References

1. Benhamouda, F., Camenisch, J., Krenn, S., Lyubashevsky, V., Neven, G.: Better zero-knowledge proofs for lattice encryption and their application to group signatures. In: Sarkar, P., Iwata, T. (eds.) ASIACRYPT 2014. LNCS, vol. 8873, pp. 551–572. Springer, Heidelberg (2014). https://doi.org/10.1007/978-3-662-45611-8_29

2. Boyle, E., Kohl, L., Scholl, P.: Homomorphic secret sharing from lattices without FHE. In: Ishai, Y., Rijmen, V. (eds.) EUROCRYPT 2019. LNCS, vol. 11477, pp. 3–33. Springer, Cham (2019). https://doi.org/10.1007/978-3-030-17656-3_1

3. Brakerski, Z., Vaikuntanathan, V.: Fully homomorphic encryption from ring-LWE and security for key dependent messages. In: Rogaway, P. (ed.) CRYPTO 2011. LNCS, vol. 6841, pp. 505–524. Springer, Heidelberg (2011). https://doi.org/10.1007/978-3-642-22792-9_29

4. Bünz, B., Agrawal, S., Zamani, M., Boneh, D.: Zether: towards privacy in a smart contract world. IACR Cryptology ePrint Archive 2019/191 (2019)

5. Bünz, B., Bootle, J., Boneh, D., Poelstra, A., Wuille, P., Maxwell, G.: Bulletproofs: short proofs for confidential transactions and more. In: 2018 IEEE Symposium on Security and Privacy (SP), pp. 315–334. IEEE (2018)

6. Gennaro, R., Gentry, C., Parno, B., Raykova, M.: Quadratic span programs and succinct NIZKs without PCPs. In: Johansson, T., Nguyen, P.Q. (eds.) EUROCRYPT 2013. LNCS, vol. 7881, pp. 626–645. Springer, Heidelberg (2013). https://doi.org/10.1007/978-3-642-38348-9_37

7. Gentry, C.: Fully homomorphic encryption using ideal lattices. In: Proceedings of the Forty-First Annual ACM Symposium on Theory of Computing. STOC 1909, pp. 169–178. Association for Computing Machinery, New York (2009). https://doi.org/10.1145/1536414.1536440

8. Goldwasser, S., Micali, S., Rackoff, C.: The knowledge complexity of interactive proof systems. SIAM J. Comput. **18**(1), 186–208 (1989)

9. Lyubashevsky, V., Peikert, C., Regev, O.: On ideal lattices and learning with errors over rings. J. ACM (JACM) **60**(6), 43 (2013)

10. Miers, I., Garman, C., Green, M., Rubin, A.D.: Zerocoin: anonymous distributed e-cash from bitcoin. In: 2013 IEEE Symposium on Security and Privacy, pp. 397–411. IEEE (2013)

11. Mitani, T., Otsuka, A.: Traceability in permissioned blockchain. In: 2019 IEEE International Conference on Blockchain (Blockchain), pp. 286–293, July 2019. https://doi.org/10.1109/Blockchain.2019.00045

12. Mitani, T., Otsuka, A.: Traceability in permissioned blockchain. IEEE. Access **8**, 21573–21588 (2020). https://doi.org/10.1109/ACCESS.2020.2969454

13. Nakamoto, S., et al.: Bitcoin: A Peer-to-peer Electronic Cash System (2008)

14. Pedersen, T.P.: Non-interactive and information-theoretic secure verifiable secret sharing. In: Feigenbaum, J. (ed.) CRYPTO 1991. LNCS, vol. 576, pp. 129–140. Springer, Heidelberg (1992). https://doi.org/10.1007/3-540-46766-1_9

15. Sasson, E.B., et al.: Zerocash: decentralized anonymous payments from bitcoin. In: 2014 IEEE Symposium on Security and Privacy, pp. 459–474. IEEE (2014)

MAPPCN: Multi-hop Anonymous and Privacy-Preserving Payment Channel Network

Somanath Tripathy$^{(\boxtimes)}$ and Susil Kumar Mohanty

Department of Computer Science and Engineering, Indian Institute of Technology
Patna, Bihta, Patna 801106, India
{som,susil_1921cs05}@iitp.ac.in

Abstract. Payment channel network (PCN) has become an indispensable mechanism to resolve scalability issues in blockchain-based cryptocurrencies. On the other hand, PCNs do not provide adequate security and privacy guarantee. Most of the existing payment schemes leak information about payer or payee to the nodes in the payment path. To address this issue, we propose a simple but effective, multi-hop, anonymous, and privacy-preserving PCN *(MAPPCN)*. MAPPCN construction is based on Elliptic curve cryptography (ECC) and is proved to be secure while achieving payment path privacy, sender, and receiver anonymity. MAPPCN can be performed in $(3 \cdot n + 5)$ Elliptic curve scalar multiplication (ECSM) operations for an off-chain payment operation.

Keywords: Blockchain · Security · Payment channel network · Hash time lock contract

1 Introduction

Blockchain-based cryptocurrencies including Bitcoin [18], Ethereum [21] are increasing their popularity. The number of transactions in Bitcoin and Ethereum are 256,253 K (lowest) TPD, 351,791 K (highest) TPD[1], and 571,769 K (lowest) TPD, 751,354 K (highest) TPD[2] in 30th Oct, 2019 respectively. This rapid growth of transactions would lead to scalability and privacy issues. A payment channel is a suitable alternative and widely deployed solution at the present system, in which a sequence of the transaction(s) can be performed between two users without updating each on the blockchain.

Two users can establish a payment channel by depositing a fixed amount and creating a 2-party ledger ($2PL$). Later on, they can use this $2PL$ to transfer within themselves, without involving blockchain for every payment. After completion of the transactions, they set the last state into the blockchain to

---

[1] Bitcoin transactions chart per day. https://www.blockchain.com/en/charts/n-transactions.

[2] Ethereum transactions chart per day. https://etherscan.io/chart/tx.

© Springer Nature Switzerland AG 2020
M. Bernhard et al. (Eds.): FC 2020 Workshops, LNCS 12063, pp. 481–495, 2020.
https://doi.org/10.1007/978-3-030-54455-3_34

get the corresponding coins. This idea can be extended for two users to execute a transaction through intermediate hops by establishing a Payment Channel Network (PCN). Several PCNs are proposed, but most of them fail to provide adequate security and privacy guarantee. Therefore, there is a call for developing an anonymous multi-hop and privacy-preserving PCN.

Lightning network [5] and Raiden network [4] are the most popular PCN widely deployed on Bitcoin and Ethereum, respectively. There are many practical deployments of PCNs, including [1–4,16,17], and some survey work on layer-2 or off-chain scalability solutions are proposed in [9,11]. Privacy and security of PCNs are crucial and need to be addressed carefully. Recently many privacy-preserving mechanisms for PCNs including [8,10,14,15,22], are presented with their advantages and limitations.

This work proposes a simple but effective, anonymous multi-hop and privacy-preserving PCN ($MAPPCN$). Like AMHL [15], $MAPPCN$ uses Elliptic curve group-based operation. Unlike, $AMHL$ the sender in our proposed scheme does not require to communicate directly with intermediate nodes other than its immediate neighbor. It is showed that the proposed mechanism achieves consumer privacy and resistant to different attacks.

The remaining part of this paper is organized as follows. Section 2 describes the related work. The background concept including payment channel network, Hash Time Lock Contract ($HTLC$) are presented in Sect. 3. The adversary model and security requirements are discussed in Sect. 4 and the proposed $MAPPCN$ technique is described in Sect. 5. Security analysis is presented in Sect. 6. Section 7 discusses conclusions and future scope of the paper.

2   Related Work

Recently, many payment channel networks [1–3] are based on Lightning network [5] in Bitcoin, while [4,16,17] are based on Ethereum. Recently, the authors in [8] and [14] observed that the techniques presented in [1–3] are not privacy-preserving and prone to security attacks. Further, different privacy-preserving PCNs have been proposed recently.

Blind Off-chain Lightweight Transactions ($BOLT$) [8] consists of a set of techniques for constructing privacy-preserving payment channels for a decentralized currency. These techniques ensure that multiple payments on a single channel are unlinkable to each other, and the channels are funded with anonymized capital. It imposes a communication overhead of around 5 MB upon each node, which hinders its deployability. TumbleBit [10] is an unidirectional unlinkable anonymous off-chain payment hub protocol that uses untrusted intermediary called *Tumbler*. It is fully compatible with Bitcoin and provides atomicity. Security of TumbleBit follows from the standard assumption of RSA and ECDSA.

Zhang *et al.* [23] proposed an anonymous off-blockchain micropayment mechanism, in which the payee receives payment from an *"honest-but-curious"* intermediary T by solving (RSA assumption based) puzzles. It achieves strong unlinkability and unforgeability. A secure, privacy-preserving and interoperable payment channel hub (PCH) has been proposed in [20] called A^2L. A^2L has been built on the three-party protocol for conditional transactions, where the intermediary pays the receiver, only if the latter solves the assigned cryptographic challenge with the help of the sender.

Malavolta et al. [14] presented an alternative security and privacy approach for payment channel networks called *Multi-HTLC* (MHTLC), but requires more communication overhead. In [15], they reported the *wormhole attack* in *HTLC* based payment channel network, and proposed a privacy-preserving mechanism called anonymous multi-hop locks (AMHL). Also, they demonstrated the practicality of their approach and its impact on the security, privacy, interoperability, and scalability of today's cryptocurrencies. Recently, authors in [22] proposed a Chameleon Hash Time-Lock Contract (*CHTLC*), for addressing the payment path privacy issues in PCNs. *CHTLC* outperforms than *MHTLC* [14] as, five times faster for payment data initialization, and reduced communication overhead from 17, 000 KB to just 7.7 KB.

TEEChain [13] is another off-chain payment protocol that utilizes trusted execution environments (*TEEs*) to perform secure, efficient, and scalable payments on the top of a blockchain, with asynchronous blockchain access. *AMCU* [7] is the first protocol for achieving atomic multi-channel updates and *state privacy*. Moreover, the reduced collateral mitigates the consequences of griefing attacks in PCNs. Meanwhile, the (multi-payment) atomicity achieved by AMCU opens the door to new applications such as credit re-balancing and crowdfunding that are not possible otherwise. *Sprites* [17] is an alternative PCN technique that supports partial withdrawals and deposits in the payment channel without interruption. It reduces the delay to the expiry timeout period, and funds (collateral cost) locked at intermediate payment channels, and it improves throughput and decentralization. *PISA* [16] is a generic state channel which can be used to build applications like payments, auctions, boardroom voting, gaming, using a new third party agent called *custodian*. The custodian is designed to help alleviate a new assumption in state channels, which require every participating party to remain online (synchronized with the blockchain).

3   Background

The section delivers the background information related to payment channel network (PCN). For the sake of readability, the frequently used notations are presented in Table 1.

3.1   Payment Channel Network (PCN)

As shown in Fig. 1, a payment channel locks up the collateral cost between two parties in a *multisig* address on the blockchain to facilitate the participants to send or withdraw in the future, through off-chain transactions. A payment channel has three states; these are ❶ open channel, ❷ update channel (off-chain transactions) and ❸ close channel as marked with shaded region in Fig. 1. Two on-chain transactions (to open and to close the channel) are required to access the blockchain. Between these two transactions, users can make a vast number of transactions by exchanging signatures on updated states of the collateral cost. The deposited funds can be settled by any party according to the last updated state while closing the channel.

Table 1. Notations

Notation	Description	Notation	Description
F_p	Finite field	v	Actual amount payer wants to pay payee
E_p	Elliptic curve Group	γ_i	Balanced amount or Collateral fund with user u_i
P	Base point on E_p	v_i	Updated payment amount after deducting transaction fee of user u_i
r	Secret or random number	$c_{<u_i, u_j>}$	Payment channel (between users u_i and u_j) identifier
$f(u_i)$	Transaction fee of user u_i	t_i	Expiration time of the transaction corresponding to user u_i
u_i	User or Intermediate user	S & R	Sender or Payer (u_0) & Receiver or Payee (u_{n+1})

A PCN is a path of payment channels, used to perform off-chain transactions between two users (the payer or sender S and payee or receiver R), without existing of direct payment channel between them. In Fig. 1, Sender S wants to pay $v = \$30$ to Receiver R through the payment path $S \rightarrow u_1 \rightarrow u_2 \rightarrow u_3 \rightarrow R$ (we assume the transaction fees for all the intermediate users are set to $f = \$0.1$). The payer S sends a payment request $\text{Pay}(S, u_1, v_1, s, t_1)$, where, $v_1 = v + \left(\sum_{i=1}^{n} f(u_i)\right)$ (i.e., $\$30.3 = \$30 + \sum_{i=1}^{3} 0.1$) to the next neighbor u_1. For a successful payment, each intermediate user u_i in the path must have a collateral cost (γ_i) not less than the payment amount to be forwarded next, *i.e.*, $\gamma_i \geq v_{i+1}$ ($\gamma_1 = \$80$ and $v_2 = \$30.2$), where $v_i = v_1 - \sum_{j=1}^{i-1} f(u_j)$, otherwise *aborts* the payment request. In Fig. 1, the intermediate user u_1 deducts transaction fee $f = \$0.1$ and forwards $v_2 = \$30.2$ to user u_2 and so on. Thus, R receives correctly v coins from that sender S initiates the payment with the amount v_1.

3.2 Routing in PCNs

The foremost essential task to construct a payment path with enough capacity between the payer and payee is an interesting problem. We are assuming the network topology is known to every user, and a gossip protocol between users can be carried out to broadcast the existence of any payment channel [19]. Furthermore, the fees charged by every user can be made public by similar means. Under these conditions, the sender can locally calculate the path to the receiver.

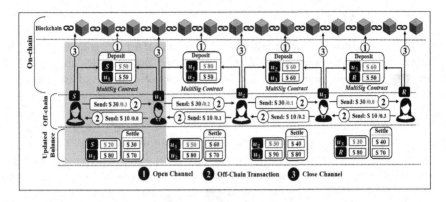

Fig. 1. PCN: Payment Channel Network

3.3   Atomicity in Multi-hop Payments

One of the fundamental properties in a multi-hop payment is *atomicity*, which means either all channel's capacity (each user's collateral cost of the corresponding channel $c_{<u_i,u_{i+1}>}$) in the path will update or none. A user would lose some coins if it transfers an amount to its next neighbor but never receives the corresponding coins from the preceding user in the same path. To avoid such issues, Lightning Network introduced a solution called Hash Time-Lock Contract *HTLC* [5] to achieve this property.

Here the Contract is executed between two users. In Fig. 2, S pays $v to R through the payment channel network. For simplicity, we assume that each user u_i charges a transaction fee of $f(u_i)$ coins. At the beginning, the receiver R sends a hashed random secret s, $s = H(r)$ to sender S. In the second step, sender S creates a payment contract $HTLC(S, u_1, v_1, s, t_1)$ where $v_1 = v + \sum_{i=1}^{n} f(u_i)$ with the right neighbor u_1 asking to forward the payment to user u_2, otherwise the payment is refunded back to sender S if time t elapsed. After receiving the payment, the user u_1, first deducts its transaction fee from the payment amount and creates a similar payment between himself and the next neighbor user u_2. When the *HTLC* condition meets (i.e., the secret r is reached to the sender) in reverse direction, the sender releases the locked v coins. The HTLC condition is based on a one-way hash function H, a hash value $s = H(r)$, the amount of coins v, and timeout t.

4   Adversary Model and Security Requirements

We assume that attacker $\mathcal{A}$ is computational efficient to corrupt a subset of existing users in PCN. $\mathcal{A}$ can extract the internals states of those corrupted users and all the information flow through them. The corrupted users can cooperate to compromise the security of PCN. $\mathcal{A}$ can send arbitrary message impersonating any corrupted user. But, the communication among the honest (not-corrupted) users occur through secure channels and thus confidential to $\mathcal{A}$.

4.1 Security Model

We consider the ideal functionality $\mathcal{F}$ defined in *MHTLC* [14] to prove the security and privacy of *MAPPCN*. $\mathcal{F}$ is a trusted functionality interact with users (u_i) and maintains two lists $\mathcal{L}$ and $\mathcal{C}$. Input $\mathcal{F}$ consists of the following three operations:

1. **_OpenChannel_**: The *open channel* operation accepts $(open, c_{<u_i,u_j>}, \gamma_i, u_j, t, f(u_j))$ from user u_i, where γ_i is the collateral cost of user u_i of the channel $c_{<u_i,u_j>}$, t and $f(u_j)$ are the expiration time and transaction fee respectively. $\mathcal{F}$ verifies whether $c_{<u_i,u_j>}$ is unique and valid identifier, and then, sends $(c_{<u_i,u_j>}, \gamma_i, t, f(u_j))$ to u_j. If u_j authorizes the operation, $\mathcal{F}$ chooses a random number h and appends tuple $(c_{<u_i,u_j>}, \gamma_i, t, f(u_j))$ and $(c_{<u_i,u_j>}, v, t, h)$ respectively to $\mathcal{B}$ and $\mathcal{L}$. Finally $\mathcal{F}$ returns h to u_i and u_j.

2. **_CloseChannel_**: Consequent upon receiving the inputs $(close, c_{<u_i,u_j>}, h)$ from either user u_i or u_j, $\mathcal{F}$ verifies $\mathcal{B}$ for an entry $(c_{<u_i,u_j>}, \gamma_i, t, f(u_j))$ and $\mathcal{L}$ for an entry $(c_{<u_i,u_j>}, \gamma_i', t', h)$, where $h \neq \bot$. If $c_{<u_i,u_j>} \in \mathcal{C}$ or $t \geq |\mathcal{B}|$ or $t' > |\mathcal{B}|$, $\mathcal{F}$ aborts, otherwise $\mathcal{F}$ appends $(c_{<u_i,u_j>}, u_i, v', t')$ to $\mathcal{B}$ and $c_{<u_i,u_j>}$ to $\mathcal{C}$. Then $\mathcal{F}$ informs both u_i, u_j with message $(c_{<u_i,u_j>}, \bot, h)$.

3. **_Payment_**: In this operation, after receiving $(pay, v, (c_{<S,u_1>}, \cdots, c_{<u_n,R>}), (t_0, \cdots, t_n))$ from S, $\mathcal{F}$ performs the following protocol:

   (a) $\mathcal{F}$ randomly picks h_i for each $i \in \{0, \cdots, n\}$ and searches for an entry $(c_{<u_{i-1},u_i>}, v_i, t_i', f(u_j))$ in $\mathcal{B}$. If found, $\mathcal{F}$ sends $\langle h_i, h_{i+1}, c_{<u_{i-1},u_i>}, c_{<u_i,u_{i+1}>}, v - \sum_{j=i}^{n} f(u_j), t_{i-1}, f(u_j) \rangle$ to user u_i and $\langle h_n, c_{u_n,R}, v, t_n \rangle$ to R through a separate secure channel. Then $\mathcal{F}$ checks if all the entries of the form $(c_{<u_{i-1},u_i>}, v_i')$ exists in $\mathcal{L}$ and the corresponding $(\delta_i = v_i' - (v - \sum_{j=i}^{n} f(u_j)) \geq 0$ and $(t_{i-1} \geq t_i)$. Then, $\mathcal{F}$ adds $(d_i = (c_{<u_{i-1},u_i>}, \delta_i, t_i, \bot)$ to $\mathcal{L}$, where $(c_{<u_{i-1},u_i>}, v_i') \in \mathcal{L}$ is the entry with the lowest u_i'. If any of the conditions fails $\mathcal{F}$ removes all d_i entries added in this phase to $\mathcal{L}$ and aborts.

   (b) $\mathcal{F}$ queries each user u_i $\forall i \in \{(n+1), \cdots, 1\}$ with (h_i, h_{i+1}) through secure channel. Each user can replies with either $\bot$ or $\top$. Let j be the index of user that returns $\bot$, s.t. $\forall i > j$, u_i returned $\top$. If no user returned $\bot$, then set $j = 0$.

   (c) $\forall i \in \{(j+1), \cdots, n\}$, $\mathcal{F}$ updates $d_i \in \mathcal{L}$ to $(\_, \_, \_, h_i)$ and informs the user with the message $(success, h_i, h_{i+1})$, $\forall i \in \{0, \cdots j\}$ $\mathcal{F}$ removes d_i from $\mathcal{L}$ and notifies the user with the message $(\bot, h_i, h_{i+1})$.

4.2 Security and Privacy Requirements

The security and privacy requirements in payment channel networks are summarised as follows:

1. **Balance Privacy**: No honest user loses coins even if some involving participants are corrupted.
2. **Privacy (Off-Path)**: For a pay operation, involving only honest users, no
   user outside the payment path learn about the payment related information.
3. **Privacy (On-Path)**: For a payment operation, the honest but curious users
   (not colluding) inside the payment path, learn no information about the user
   who is sending or receiving party.
4. **Hash-lock Decorrelation**: In the payment path $\boxed{S \rightarrow u_1 \rightarrow u_2 \rightarrow u_3 \rightarrow R}$
   shown in Fig. 2, as the hash-lock is same through out the route, the users can
   know that this is the same payment they got from S and get more information
   on that.
5. **Stealing Transfer Fee Attack**: Let us consider a payment path used by S
   $\boxed{\rightarrow u_1 \rightarrow u_2 \rightarrow u_3 \rightarrow R}$, to pay v coins to R. Thus, the sender S needs
   to send total v_1 coins, where $\boxed{v_1 = v + \sum_{i=1}^{n} f(u_i)}$. Suppose user u_1 and user
   u_3 are colluded on this payment path, to eliminate intermediate user u_2
   from participating in the successful completion of payment, thereby stealing
   the payment forwarding charges $f(u_2)$, which was contracted for honest nodes
   of the payment path. An illustrative example of *stealing transfer fee attack* is
   depicted in Fig. 2 with red coloured arrow (step 7 and 8) during lock releasing
   phase.

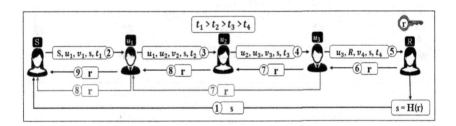

Fig. 2. HTLC & stealing transfer fee attack

5   The Proposed MAPPCN

This section presents our proposed simple, but effective Multi-hop Anonymous
and Privacy-Preserving Payment Channel Network named ($MAPPCN$). MAP-
PCN uses Elliptic curve cryptography (ECC) [12]. Let E_p be an additive elliptic
curve group over a finite field F_p. The scalar multiplication on the group E_p is
defined as $c \cdot P = P + P + \cdots + P (c - times)$, where $c \in z_p$ and P is a base point
on E_p. The Elliptic curve discrete logarithmic problem ($ECDLP$) is defined as
given P and $c \cdot P$, it is computationally infeasible to find c. The security of
$MAPPCN$ relies on $ECDLP$ problem.

5.1   Assumptions

We focus on the design of a privacy-preserving PCN mechanism, but the efficiency of the routing protocols in PCNs is beyond the scope of this work. We assume that each pair of users communicate through a secure and authenticated channel for sharing the payment channel. Unlike *MHTCL* [14] and *CHTLC* [22], we are not considering the existence of a secure channel between the sender and each intermediate user for *setup* phase. Each intermediate node has only knowledge about its previous neighbor and next neighbor of the corresponding payment path. But sender has complete information about each and every node information; like user identifier (public key), lock-time (t_i), transaction fee ($f(u_j)$), channel identifier ($c_{<u_i,u_{i+1}>}$), channel capacity or collateral cost (γ_i) of user u_i of the corresponding channel ($c_{<u_i,u_{i+1}>}$).

5.2   MAPPCN Construction Overview

As shown in Fig. 3, consider a payment channel network in which the payment to be occurred between user **S** (sender or payer) and **R** (receiver or payee) through three intermediate users u_1, u_2 and u_3. Thus the payment path of five users exists as $S \to u_1 \to u_2 \to u_3 \to R$.

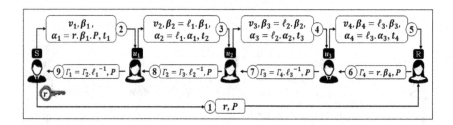

Fig. 3. MAPPCN: anonymous multi-hop privacy-preserving PCN

At first, sender **S** generates a random number r and base point P in Elliptic curve group E_p. Sender **S** sends $<r, P>$ to receiver **R** through a secure channel. Next **S** sends $S, u_1, v_1, \beta_1, \alpha_1, t_1$ to its next neighbor u_1. Each user u_i generates a random number ℓ_i and computes $\beta_{i+1} = \ell_i \cdot \beta_i$ and $\alpha_{i+1} = \ell_i \cdot \alpha_i$, sends $<\beta_{i+1}, \alpha_{i+1}>$ to its next neighbor u_{i+1}. Consequent upon receiving the tuple $<\beta_{n+1}, \alpha_{n+1}>$ from its neighbor u_n, the receiver **R** verifies if $r \cdot \beta_{n+1} \cdot P \overset{?}{=} \alpha_{n+1}$ then computes $\Gamma_{n+1} = r \cdot \beta_{n+1}$ and returns to its previous neighbor. The neighbor u_n upon receiving Γ_{n+1} from **R**, verifies if $\Gamma_{n+1} \cdot P \overset{?}{=} \alpha_{n+1}$ and releases the locked coins accordingly, and sends $\Gamma_n = \ell_n^{-1} \cdot \Gamma_{n+1}$ to its previous neighbor. Each intermediate neighbor u_i performs the similar operations and releases the locked amount and returns $\Gamma_i = \ell_i^{-1} \cdot \Gamma_{i+1}$ to its previous neighbor. Thus each user in the path receives the committed coins.

Algorithm 1: MAPPCN Payment Protocol

Sender's Payment Routine:

1: **Generate** a random number r and a *Elliptic curve* base point P
2: **Send** $\boxed{< r, P >}$ to receiver 🅁 via a secured channel
3: $v_1 = v + \sum_{i=1}^{n} f(u_i)$
4: **if** $(v_1 \leq \gamma_0)$ **then**
5:     $\gamma_0 = \gamma_0 - v_1$
6:     $t_0 = t_{now} + \Delta \cdot n$
7:     **Generate** a random value β_1
8:     **Compute** $\alpha_1 = r \cdot \beta_1 \cdot P$
9:     $ETLC(\boxed{S}, \boxed{u_1}, v_1, \beta_1, \alpha_1, t_1)$
10: **else**
11:     **Abort**
12: **end if**

Receiver's Payment Routine:

1: **if** $((r \cdot \beta_{n+1} \cdot P == \alpha_{n+1})$ and $(t_{n+1} > t_{now} + \Delta))$ **then**
2:     **Compute** $\Gamma_{n+1} = r \cdot \beta_{n+1}$
3:     **Send** $\boxed{< \Gamma_{n+1}, P >}$ to user $\boxed{u_n}$

4: **else**
5:     **Abort**
6: **end if**

Intermediate's Payment Routine:

1: **if** $((v_{i+1} \leq \gamma_i)$ and $(t_{i+1} == t_i - \Delta))$ **then**
2:     $\gamma_i = \gamma_i - v_{i+1}$
3:     **Generate** a random value ℓ_i
4:     **Compute** $\beta_{i+1} = \ell_i \cdot \beta_i$ and $\alpha_{i+1} = \ell_i \cdot \alpha_i$
5:     $ETLC(\boxed{u_i}, \boxed{u_{i+1}}, v_{i+1}, \beta_{i+1}, \alpha_{i+1}, t_{i+1})$
6: **else**
7:     **Abort**
8: **end if**
9: **if** $(\Gamma_{i+1} \cdot P == \alpha_{i+1})$ **then**
10:     $\Gamma_i = \Gamma_{i+1} \cdot \ell_i^{-1}$
11:     **Send** $\boxed{< \Gamma_i, P >}$ to user $\boxed{u_{i-1}}$
12: **else**
13:     **Abort**
14: **end if**

/*Δ: For some positive value, $\boxed{u_0} = \boxed{S}$, $\boxed{u_{n+1}} = \boxed{R}$*/

MAPPCN Construction: The primary three operations of *MAPPCN* are discussed here as follows:

1. *OpenChannel*($\boxed{u_i}$, $\boxed{u_j}$, γ, t, $f(u_j)$): This operation is to open a payment channel between users $\boxed{u_i}$ and $\boxed{u_j}$. For this $\boxed{u_i}$, $\boxed{u_j}$ create a joint-wallet depositing collateral cost. Both the users agreed upon the initial capacity of the channel (γ), channel expiration timeout (t), the fee charged to use the channel ($f(u_j)$) and a channel identifier ($c_{<u_i,u_j>}$). Subsequently the transaction is added to the blockchain, and the operation returns *true*. If any of the previous steps is not carried out, the operation returns *false*.

2. *CloseChannel*($c_{<u_i,u_j>}, v$): This operation is used by two users ($\boxed{u_i}$, $\boxed{u_j}$) sharing an open payment channel ($c_{<u_i,u_j>}$) to close it at the state defined by v and accordingly update their balances in the blockchain. It returns *true* if it is successfully included in to the blockchain, otherwise *false*.

3. *Pay*(($c_{<S,u_1>}, \cdots, c_{<u_n,R>}), v$) $\rightarrow \{false, true\}$: This operation takes a list of payment channels ($c_{<S,u_1>}, c_{<u_1,u_2>}, \cdots, c_{<u_n,R>}$) to the corresponding payment path from payer $\boxed{S}$ to payee $\boxed{R}$ and the payment amount v. In each payment channel $c_{<u_i,u_i+1>}$ in the path, it has at least a current balance $\gamma_i \geq v_i$, where $v_i = v - \sum_{j=1}^{i-1} f(u_j)$, for each intermediate user $\boxed{u_i}$, the pay

operation deducts it's transaction fee from the amount v_i' and returns $true$. Otherwise, none of the balances of payment channel be updated and the pay operation returns $false$.

Algorithm 1 depicts $MAPPCN$ payment protocol. The detailed protocol steps for all the parties (sender, receiver, and intermediate users) are discussed as under.

Sender's Payment Routine: We assume that there exists a payment channel network or payment path denoted as $\boxed{\mathcal{P} = \{S, u_1, u_2, \cdots, u_n, R\}}$. Payer ⬛S generates a random number r and a base point P in an Elliptic curve group E_p and sends it to payee ⬛R in a secured channel. Further, ⬛S generates a random value β_1 and computes $\boxed{\alpha_1 = r \cdot \beta_1 \cdot P}$ (Steps 7–8). Then, it creates an Elliptic curve based time-lock commitment or contract i.e., $\boxed{\text{ETLC}(⬛S, \boxed{u_1}, v_1, \beta_1, \alpha_1, t_1)}$ to the next neighbor $\boxed{u_1}$ (Step 9) and promising that if $\boxed{u_1}$ can provide a pair of value $\boxed{< \Gamma_1, P >}$ within t_1 time such that $\boxed{\Gamma_1 \cdot P \overset{?}{=} \alpha_1}$, user ⬛S pays v_1 coins to $\boxed{u_1}$.

Intermediate's Payment Routine: At the time of locking or commitment phase, each intermediate user $\boxed{u_i}$ receives the payment request from its previous neighbor $\boxed{u_{i-1}}$, then it checks (i) if the commitment request of user $\boxed{u_{i-1}}$ is fulfilled, and it has enough amount of coins (γ_i) i.e., $\boxed{\gamma_i \geq v_{i+1}}$ (v_{i+1}: after deducting transaction fee from v_i, $\boxed{v_i = v_1 - \sum_{j=1}^{i-1} f(u_j)}$). (ii) Correctness of the lock-time commitment t_{i+1} i.e., $\boxed{t_{i+1} \overset{?}{=} t_i - \Delta}$, otherwise it aborts. Then, the intermediate user $\boxed{u_i}$ generates a random value ℓ_i ($1 \leq i \leq n$) and computes $\boxed{\beta_{i+1} = \ell_i \cdot \beta_i}$ and $\boxed{\alpha_{i+1} = \ell_i \cdot \alpha_i}$. Then, it creates a time-lock commitment i.e., $\boxed{\text{ETLC}(\boxed{u_i}, \boxed{u_{i+1}}, v_{i+1}, \beta_{i+1}, \alpha_{i+1}, t_{i+1})}$ to the next neighbor $\boxed{u_{i+1}}$ (Step 5). During lock release, user $\boxed{u_i}$ waits for a pair of value $\boxed{< \Gamma_{i+1}, P >}$ from user $\boxed{u_{i+1}}$, to fulfill the condition $\boxed{\Gamma_{i+1} \cdot P \overset{?}{=} \alpha_i}$ and claims the coins from user $\boxed{u_i}$ (Step 9). With the help of Γ_{i+1}, user $\boxed{u_i}$ computes $\boxed{\Gamma_i = \Gamma_{i+1} \cdot \ell^{-1}}$ for releasing left-lock, and sends $\boxed{< \Gamma_i, P >}$ to user $\boxed{u_{i-1}}$ and claims the coins.

Receiver's Payment Routine: Once the payee ⬛R, receives the ETLC commitment from its previous neighbor $\boxed{u_n}$, it checks the validity of the commitment $\boxed{r \cdot \beta_{n+1} \cdot P \overset{?}{=} \alpha_{n+1}}$ and $\boxed{t_{n+1} \overset{?}{>} t_{now} + \Delta}$ i.e., it can meet the condition within time t_{n+1} (Step 1). Then it computes $\boxed{\Gamma_{n+1} = r \cdot \beta_{n+1}}$ and sends $\boxed{< \Gamma_{n+1}, P >}$ to $\boxed{u_n}$ to claim the coins (Steps 2–3). It aborts otherwise.

Since each intermediate user $\boxed{u_i}$ ($1 \leq i \leq n$), redeems the amount by generating the collision with the arguments $\boxed{< \Gamma_i, P >}$ it received from the next neighbors, and waits for the next neighbor to redeem the amount. Thus, all the users are paid with the promised amount after completion of protocol.

5.3 Discussion

MAPPCN achieves the following properties:

1. **Atomicity:** Every user in the path (u_1, u_2, u_3) would be able to release its left lock by computing $\Gamma_i = \ell_i^{-1} \cdot \Gamma_{i+1}$, thus by releasing the right lock Γ_{i-1} only.

2. **Consistency:** No user (u_1 or u_2 or u_3) can release the lock i.e., compute Γ_i without its corresponding right lock Γ_{i-1}.

3. **Relationship anonymity:** Intermediate user has no information about the set of users in PCN path except its right neighbor. Moreover, unlike *MHTLC* [14] and *CHTLC* [22], in *MAPPCN* sender/ receiver does not send any information to all intermediate users except its direct neighbor.

4. **Balance Privacy:** Let u_i be an intermediate user in a payment $pay((c_{<S,u_1>}, c_{<u_1,u_2>}, \cdots, c_{<u_n,R>}), v)$. In lock releasing phase, if the user u_{i+1} multiply some value (or send the same value which was received) rather than ℓ_{i+1}^{-1} (step 10, Intermediate Node Payment Routine of Algorithm 1) maliciously, then the user u_i gets the incoming message $< \Gamma'_{i+1} \neq \Gamma_{i+1}, P >$, thus fails during verification so does not release the lock.

5. **Privacy (Off-Path):** In the off-chain or layer-2 payment channel network, all the communications that happened between the users is in the secured channel. Therefore any intermediate user u_i involved in the payment does not learn about the payment value except the neighbor information.

6. **Privacy (On-Path):** In the state-of-the-art off-chain payment channel network like MHTLC [14] and CHTLC [22], the sender sends some path specific secret information to each user of the payment. So, each user knows the sender. But, in the proposed MAPPCN payment network, each intermediate user u_i has only information about its previous and next neighbor information. Therefore any (corrupted or honest) user cannot determine the correct sender-receiver pair, thus MAPPCN and achieves sender and receiver anonymity.

The proposed *MAPPCN* payment protocol gives the same level of security as that of *MHTLC* [14] and *CHTLC* [22] without requiring zero-knowledge proofs (*ZKP*) or chameleon hash (which require exponential operations). The security of *MAPPCN* follows the security model used by *MHTLC* [14] and *CHTLC* [22] according to the universal composable (*UC*) security paradigm [6] and relies on ECDLP. On the top, MAPPCN achieves following interesting properties.

1. **No Setup Phase:** The proposed payment protocol, we does not opt setup phase. In MHTLC, the sender computes zero-knowledge proofs (π takes 309 ms per NIZK proof) for communication (1.65 MB data per NIZK proof) between the intermediate users to ensure the correctness of the received message. At the same time, in CHTLC, the sender computes chameleon hash (256 bytes, $\approx$ 55 ms per user) for each user and sends it in a private channel. MAPPCN protocol is efficient; as, the sender does not compute any intensive operations. Therefore the computational overhead of the sender is very less as compared to the aforementioned *atomic swap* protocols.

2. **Sender and Receiver Anonymity:** In both the MHTLC and CHTLC, the sender sends some path specific secret information to each intermediate user. So each intermediate user knows the sender, thus loses sender anonymity. But in the proposed *atomic swap* protocol, the sender does not send any information to each intermediate user except its next neighbor, therefore, achieves strong *sender* and *receiver* anonymity.

3. **Stealing Transfer Fee Attack Resistance:** Let $\mathcal{P} = \{\boxed{S}, \cdots, \boxed{u_{i-1}}, \boxed{u_i}, \boxed{u_{i+1}}, \cdots, \boxed{R}\}$ be a payment path. Suppose user $\boxed{u_{i-1}}$ and $\boxed{u_{i+1}}$ colluded to steal the transaction fees of honest user $\boxed{u_i}$. But, neither of them can derive the secret used ℓ_i or release the lock that they took part in the corresponding payment without the intervention of the user $\boxed{u_i}$.

Table 2. Computation overhead comparison

Schemes	Setup phase	Commitment phase	Releasing phase	Total operations
MAPPCN	$\cdots$	$(n+1)$ ECSM	$(2 \cdot n + 4)$ ECSM	$(3 \cdot n + 5)$ ECSM
MHTLC [14]	$(n+1)$ H, n NIZK	$(k \cdot n + 1)$ H	$\cdots$	$((k+1) \cdot n + 2)$ H, n NIZK
CHTLC [22]	$(n+2)$ CH	$(n+1)$ CH	$(3 \cdot n + 3)$ CH	$(5 \cdot n + 6)$ CH

CH: Chameleon Hash   1 CH = $2\times$ Exponentiation operations   H: Hash (SHA256)
n: number of intermediate users/ hops   NIZK: Non-Interactive Zero-Knowledge
ECSM: Elliptic Curve Scalar Multiplication k: Constant

6   Security and Performance Analysis

6.1   Security Analysis

Theorem 1. MAPPCN *UC-realizes the ideal functionality* $\mathcal{F}$, *if* ECDLP *is computationally difficult.*

Proof. Consider a simulator $\mathcal{S}$ which simulates the (real world) execution *MAPPCN*, while interacting with the ideal functionality $\mathcal{F}$. $\mathcal{S}$ also handles the users corrupted by the adversary $\mathcal{A}$. The following PCN operations are to be simulated.

$\underline{OpenChannel}(c_{<u_i,u_j>}, \gamma, t, f(u_j))$: Let the request be initiated by $\boxed{u_i}$, there would be two cases arise:

- *Corrupted* $\boxed{u_i}$: $\mathcal{A}$ impersonates $\boxed{u_i}$ and sends a request $\boxed{(c_{<u_i,u_j>}, \gamma, t, f(u_j))}$ to $\mathcal{S}$. Consequently, $\mathcal{S}$ initiates an agreement protocol with $\mathcal{A}$ and sends $\boxed{(open, c_{<u_i,u_j>}, \gamma, t, f(u_j))}$ to $\mathcal{F}$. $\mathcal{F}$ returns $(c_{<u_i,u_j>}, h)$.

- *Corrupted* $\boxed{u_j}$: $\mathcal{F}$ sends message $\boxed{(c_{<u_i,u_j>}, v, t, f(u_j))}$ to $\mathcal{S}$. Upon receiving this message, $\mathcal{S}$ initiates an agreement protocol with $\mathcal{A}$, on behalf of $\boxed{u_i}$, for opening a channel. If it is successful $\mathcal{S}$ sends a successful message to $\mathcal{F}$, which returns $(c_{<u_i,u_j>}, h)$. Then $\mathcal{S}$ initializes the list $\mathcal{L}_{c_{<u_i,u_j>}}$ and appends $(h, v, \perp, \perp)$, otherwise it outputs $\perp$.

CloseChannel$(c_{<u_i,u_j>}, v)$: Like open channel, two cases would arise:

- *Corrupted* $\blacksquare_i$: $\mathcal{A}$ (impersonates $\blacksquare_i$) sends close channel request. Consequently $\mathcal{S}$ retrieves $\mathcal{L}_{c_{<u_i,u_j>}}$ for some value $(h, v, \_, \_)$ if could not found aborts. Otherwise, $\mathcal{S}$ sends close $(c_{<u_i,u_j>}, v, h)$ to $\mathcal{F}$.
- *Corrupted* $\sqcap_{|}$: $\mathcal{F}$ sends $(c_{<u_i,u_j>}, h, \perp)$ to $\mathcal{S}$. $\mathcal{S}$ informs $\mathcal{A}$ as closing of channel $c_{<u_i,u_j>}$.

Pay$(c_{S,u_1}, c_{u_1,u_2}, \cdots, c_{u_n,R}, v)$: Each user acts according to its role in the protocol as defined below:

- *Sender*: To initiate the payment, $\mathcal{A}$ provides $\boxed{m_1 = (c_{<S,u_1>}, v_1, t_1, \beta_1, \alpha_1)}$ to $\blacksquare_1$ notifying the path information i.e., the next hop address to be forwarded. If $\boxed{t_0 \geq t_1}$, then simulator $\mathcal{S}$ sends pay $\boxed{(v_i, c_{<u_{i-1},u_i>}, t_i)}$ to $\mathcal{F}$, otherwise aborts. For each $\blacksquare_i$, the simulator $\mathcal{S}$ confirms the payment only when it receives Γ_i from $\blacksquare_i$ such that $\boxed{\Gamma_{i+1} \cdot \ell_i^{-1} \cdot P = \alpha_i}$, and thus, for receiver $\blacksquare$ if $\boxed{\ell_n \cdot \beta_n \cdot r \cdot P = \alpha_n}$. For each confirmed payment, the entry in $\mathcal{L}_{c_{<u_i,u_j>}}$ containing $(h_i^*, v^*, \_, \_)$ with lowest v^* is updated by $(h_i, v^* - v_i, \Gamma_i)$.
- *Receiver*: $\mathcal{F}$ sends $\boxed{(h, c_{<u_n,R>}, v, t_n)}$ to simulator $\mathcal{S}$. Consequently simulator $\mathcal{S}$ chooses ℓ, r randomly and sends a triple as $\boxed{(\alpha, \beta, \beta \cdot r \cdot P)}$. If $\mathcal{A}$ returns $\boxed{<\Gamma, P>}$ s.t. $\boxed{\Gamma \cdot P = \alpha}$, then $\mathcal{S}$ returns $\top$ to $\mathcal{F}$, otherwise it sends $\perp$.
- *Intermediate user*: $\mathcal{F}$ informs $\mathcal{S}$ about the corrupted users in the payment with a message of the form $\boxed{m = (h_i, h_{i+1}, c_{<u_{i-1},u_i>}, c_{<u_i,u_{i+1}>}, v, t_{i-1}, t_i)}$. Simulator $\mathcal{S}$ chooses randomly ℓ_i and sends $\boxed{\langle c_{<u_{i-1},u_i>}, c_{<u_i,u_{i+1}>}, \ell_i, \alpha_i =}$ $\boxed{r \cdot \ell_i \cdot P, \ell_{i+1}, \alpha_{i+1} = r \cdot \ell_{i+1} \cdot P, v, t_{i-1}, t_i \rangle}$ to $\mathcal{A}$. If $\mathcal{A}$ outputs r^* such that $\boxed{r^* \cdot \ell_i \cdot P = \alpha_i}$ then aborts.

Now it is trivial to observe the *indistinguishability* in both *OpenChannel* and *CloseChannel*. Moreover, the payment chain never stops at the honest node, so the simulation does not abort. Therefore, $\mathcal{A}$ could succeed to interrupt the payment or abort the simulation outputting the correct Γ_i such that $\boxed{\Gamma_{i+1} \cdot \ell_i^{-1} \cdot P = \alpha_i}$. In such case $\mathcal{A}$ could break *ECDLP* as communication in channel is private.

Thus MAPPCN is secure as long as ECDLP assumption holds.

6.2 Performance Analysis

Here, we discuss the performance of *MAPPCN* payment protocol in terms of computation overhead. Table 2 presents the comparison of different phases (Setup phase, Commitment or Locking phase and Lock releasing phase) of the multi-hop payment schemes.

MHTLC [14] requires $(n+1)$ hash (SHA256) operations and n zero-knowledge proof (NIZK) operations, while CHTLC [22] requires $(n + 2)$ chameleon hash (CH) operations (where n is the number of intermediate users, 1 CH = 2 $\times$ Exponentiation operations). On the other hand, MAPPCN protocol does not need setup phase. Also, zero-knowledge proofs and chameleon hash operations are the most expensive operations as compared to Elliptic curve point multiplication. In commitment or locking phase MHTLC requires constant operations (as reported by the authors, sender requires 309 ms to compute a NIZK proof π_i of size 1.65 MB and to verify π_i intermediate user takes 130 ms time), CHTLC requires $(n+1)$ chameleon hash operations and MAPPCN requires $(n+1)$ Elliptic curve scalar multiplication (ECSM) operations. At the time of lock releasing phase MHTLC, CHTLC, and MAPPCN requires $(3 \cdot n + 3)$ chameleon hash operations, and $(2 \cdot n + 4)$ Elliptic curve scalar multiplication operations respectively.

Thus, the overall computation overheads are $((k+1) \cdot n + 2)$ hash (SHA256) operations and n zero-knowledge proof (NIZK) operations are required to execute an instance of MHTLC, while $(5 \cdot n + 6)$ chameleon hash operations required for CHTLC. On the other hand, MAPPCN requires only $(3 \cdot n + 5)$ Elliptic curve scalar multiplication operations. Therefore, MAPPCN would achieve better performance.

7   Conclusion

In this paper, we proposed a novel anonymous privacy-preserving payment protocol called *MAPPCN* to address the payment path privacy and sender anonymity issues in PCNs. Security of *MAPPCN* relies on ECDLP and analysed using universal composable paradigm. *MAPPCN* requires lesser computation i.e., $(3 \cdot n + 5)$ Elliptic curve scalar multiplication operations for preserving sender and receiver anonymity. The implementation of *MAPPCN* is under progress.

Acknowledgement. We acknowledge the Ministry of Human Resource Development, Government of India for providing fellowship under Ph. D. programme to complete this work.

References

1. A scala implementation of the lightning network. https://github.com/ACINQ/eclair
2. c-lightning - a lightning network implementation in c. https://github.com/ElementsProject/lightning
3. Lightning network daemon. https://github.com/lightningnetwork/lnd
4. Raiden Network. https://raiden.network/
5. The Bitcoin Lightning Network: Scalable Off-Chain Instant Payments. https://lightning.network/lightning-network-paper.pdf
6. Canetti, R.: Universally composable security: a new paradigm for cryptographic protocols. In: Proceedings of the 42nd IEEE Symposium on Foundations of Computer Science. FOCS 2001, p. 136. IEEE Computer Society, Washington (2001)
7. Egger, C., Moreno-Sanchez, P., Maffei, M.: Atomic multi-channel updates with constant collateral in bitcoin-compatible payment-channel networks. In: Proceedings of the 2019 ACM SIGSAC Conference on Computer and Communications Security, CCS 2019, London, UK, 11–15 November 2019, pp. 801–815 (2019). https://doi.org/10.1145/3319535.3345666

8. Green, M., Miers, I.: BOLT: anonymous payment channels for decentralized currencies. In: Proceedings of the 2017 ACM SIGSAC Conference on Computer and Communications Security, pp. 473–489. ACM (2017)
9. Gudgeon, L., Moreno-Sanchez, P., Roos, S., McCorry, P., Gervais, A.: SoK: off the chain transactions. IACR Cryptology ePrint Archive, p. 360 (2019)
10. Heilman, E., Alshenibr, L., Baldimtsi, F., Scafuro, A., Goldberg, S.: Tumblebit: an untrusted bitcoin-compatible anonymous payment hub. In: 24th Annual Network and Distributed System Security Symposium, NDSS 2017, San Diego, California, USA, 26 February–1 March 2017 (2017)
11. Jourenko, M., Kurazumi, K., Larangeira, M., Tanaka, K.: SoK: a taxonomy for layer-2 scalability related protocols for cryptocurrencies. IACR Cryptology ePrint Archive 2019/352 (2019)
12. Koblitz, N.: Elliptic curve cryptosystems. Math. Comput. **48**(177), 203–209 (1987)
13. Lind, J., Naor, O., Eyal, I., Kelbert, F., Sirer, E.G., Pietzuch, P.: Teechain: a secure payment network with asynchronous blockchain access. In: 27th ACM Symposium on Operating Systems Principles, SOSP, pp. 63–79. ACM, New York (2019). https://doi.org/10.1145/3341301.3359627
14. Malavolta, G., Moreno-Sanchez, P., Kate, A., Maffei, M., Ravi, S.: Concurrency and privacy with payment-channel networks. In: Proceedings of the 2017 ACM SIGSAC Conference on Computer and Communications Security, CCS 2017, Dallas, TX, USA, 30 October–03 November 2017, pp. 455–471 (2017). https://doi.org/10.1145/3133956.3134096
15. Malavolta, G., Moreno-Sanchez, P., Schneidewind, C., Kate, A., Maffei, M.: Anonymous multi-hop locks for blockchain scalability and interoperability. In: 26th Annual Network and Distributed System Security Symposium, NDSS 2019, San Diego, California, USA, 24–27 February 2019 (2019)
16. McCorry, P., Bakshi, S., Bentov, I., Meiklejohn, S., Miller, A.: Pisa: arbitration outsourcing for state channels. In: Proceedings of the 1st ACM Conference on Advances in Financial Technologies, AFT 2019, Zurich, Switzerland, 21–23 October 2019, pp. 16–30 (2019). https://doi.org/10.1145/3318041.3355461
17. Miller, A., Bentov, I., Bakshi, S., Kumaresan, R., McCorry, P.: Sprites and state channels: Payment networks that go faster than lightning. In: Financial Cryptography and Data Security - 23rd International Conference, FC. pp. 508–526 (2019). https://doi.org/10.1007/978-3-030-32101-7_30
18. Nakamoto, S.: Bitcoin: a peer-to-peer electronic cash system. http://bitcoin.org/bitcoin.pdf
19. Prihodko, P., Sakhno, K., Ostrovskiy, A., Zhigulin, S., Osuntokun, O.: Flare: an approach to routing in lightning network (2016)
20. Tairi, E., Moreno-Sanchez, P., Maffei, M.: A^2L: anonymous atomic locks for scalability and interoperability in payment channel hubs. IACR Cryptology ePrint Archive, p. 589 (2019)
21. Wood, G., et al.: Ethereum: a secure decentralised generalised transaction ledger. https://ethereum.github.io/yellowpaper/paper.pdf
22. Yu, B., Kermanshahi, S.K., Sakzad, A., Nepal, S.: Chameleon hash time-lock contract for privacy preserving payment channel networks. In: Steinfeld, R., Yuen, T.H. (eds.) ProvSec 2019. LNCS, vol. 11821, pp. 303–318. Springer, Cham (2019). https://doi.org/10.1007/978-3-030-31919-9_18
23. Zhang, D., Le, J., Mu, N., Liao, X.: An anonymous off-blockchain micropayments scheme for cryptocurrencies in the real world. IEEE Trans. Syst. Man Cybern.: Syst. 1–11 (2018). https://doi.org/10.1109/TSMC.2018.2884289

Marlowe: Implementing and Analysing Financial Contracts on Blockchain

Pablo Lamela Seijas[1]([✉]), Alexander Nemish[3], David Smith[1],
and Simon Thompson[1,2]

[1] IOHK, Hong Kong, China
{pablo.lamela,simon.thompson}@iohk.io,
david.smith@tweag.io
[2] School of Computing, University of Kent, Canterbury, UK
s.j.thompson@kent.ac.uk
[3] IOHK, Kyiv, Ukraine
alexander.nemish@iohk.io

Abstract. Marlowe is a DSL for financial contracts. We describe the implementation of Marlowe on the Cardano blockchain, and the Marlowe Playground web-based development and simulation environment.

Contracts in Marlowe can be exhaustively analysed prior to running them, thus providing strong guarantees to participants in the contract. The Marlowe system itself has been formally verified using the Isabelle theorem prover, establishing such properties as the conservation of money.

Keywords: Cardano · DSL · Functional · Haskell · SMT · Static analysis

1 Introduction

Marlowe [11] is a domain-specific language (DSL) for implementing financial contracts on blockchain: our initial target is Cardano, but it could be implemented on many distributed ledgers (DLT platforms), including Ethereum. Marlowe is embedded in Haskell, allowing users selectively to use aspects of Haskell – typically definitions of constants and simple functions – to express contracts more readably and succinctly. Section 2 gives an overview of the language, and the changes made to it since it was originally introduced in [9].

Marlowe is specified by a reference semantics for the language written in Haskell, and we can use that in a number of ways. We can interpret Marlowe contracts in Haskell itself, but we can also use that implementation, compiled into Plutus [6], to interpret Marlowe directly on the Cardano blockchain, see Sect. 3. We can also execute the semantics – translated into PureScript – directly in a browser, to give an interactive simulation environment, see Sect. 6.

Because Marlowe is a DSL, we are able to build special purpose tools and techniques to support it. Crucially in a financial environment, we are able to *exhaustively analyse contracts* without executing them, so that we can, for

M. Bernhard et al. (Eds.): FC 2020 Workshops, LNCS 12063, pp. 496–511, 2020.
https://doi.org/10.1007/978-3-030-54455-3_35

instance, check whether any particular contract is able to make all the payments it should: in the case it is not, we get an explicit example of how it can fail. This analysis (Sect. 4) is built into the Marlowe Playground. Finally (Sect. 5) we are able to use formal verification to prove properties of the implementation of Marlowe, including a guarantee that "money in = money out" for all contracts.

Building on [9], the specific contributions of this paper are threefold. We describe revised versions of Marlowe and its Playground, we describe the implementation of Marlowe on the Cardano blockchain, and we present both automated static analysis and machine-supported verification for Marlowe.

2   Marlowe Revised: Version 3.0

Since first publication, we have revised the language design: this section gives a brief overview of the current (3.0) version of the language and its semantics.

The Marlowe Model. Contracts are built by putting together a small number of constructs that in combination can describe many different financial contracts.

The parties to the contract, also called the participants, can engage in various actions: they can be asked to deposit money, or to make a choice between various alternatives. In some cases, any party will be able to trigger the contract just to notify it that some condition has become true (e.g., a timeout has occurred).

The Marlowe model allows for a contract to control money in a number of disjoint accounts: this allows for more explicit control of how the money flows in the contract. Each account is owned by a particular party to the contract, and that party receives a refund of any remaining funds in the account when the contract is closed.

Marlowe contracts describe a series of steps, typically by describing the first step, together with another (sub-) contract that describes what to do next. For example, the contract Pay a p v cont says "make a payment of v Lovelace to the party p from the account a, and then follow the contract cont". We call cont the continuation of the contract.

In executing a contract, we need to keep track of the current contract: after making a step in the example above, the current contract would be cont. We also have to keep track of some other information, such as how much is held in each account: this information together is the state, which generally changes at each step. A step can also see an action taking place, such as money being deposited, or an effect being produced, e.g. a payment. It is through their wallets that users are able to interact with Marlowe contracts running on the blockchain, making deposits and receiving payments.

Marlowe Step by Step. Marlowe has five ways of building contracts, we call these *contract constructs*. *Contract constructs*, in turn, can also contain *values*, *observations* and *actions*.

Values, observations and actions are used to supply external information and inputs to a running contract to control how it will evolve.

Values include some quantities that change with time, like the current slot number, the current balance of an account, and any choices that have already been made. Values can be combined using addition, subtraction and negation.

Observations are Boolean expressions that compare values, and can be combined using the standard Boolean operators. It is also possible to observe whether any choice has been made (for a particular identified choice). Observations will have a value at every step of execution.

Actions happen at particular points during execution and can be (i) depositing money, (ii) making a choice between various alternatives, or (iii) notifying the contract that a certain observation has become true.

Contract constructs are the main building block of contracts, and there are five of them: four of these – Pay, Let, If and When – build a complex contract from simpler contracts, and the fifth, Close, is a simple contract. At each step of execution we will obtain a new state and continuation contract and, in some it is possible that effects, like payments and warnings, can be generated too.

Pay: A payment contract Pay a p v cont will make a payment of value v from the account a to a payee p, which will be one of the contract participants or another account in the contract. Warnings will be generated if the value v is not positive, or if there is not enough in the account to make the payment in full. In the first case, nothing will be transferred; in the later case, a partial payment (of all the money available) is made. The contract will continue as cont.

Close: A contract Close provides for the contract to be closed (or terminated). The only action that is performed is to refund the contents of each account to their respective owners. This is performed one account per step, but all accounts will be refunded in a single transaction. All contracts eventually reduce to Close.

If: The conditional If obs cont1 cont2 will continue as cont1 or cont2, depending on the Boolean value of the observation obs on execution.

When: This is the most complex constructor for contracts, with the form When cases timeout cont. It is a contract that is triggered on actions, which may or may not happen at any particular slot: the permitted actions and their consequences are described by cases.

The list cases contains a collection of cases of the form Case ac co, where ac is an action and co a continuation (another contract). When the action ac is performed, the state is updated accordingly and the contract will continue as described by co.

In order to make sure that the contract makes progress eventually, the contract When cases timeout cont will continue as cont as soon as any valid transaction is issued after the timeout (a slot number) is reached.

Let: A let contract Let id val cont causes the expression val to be evaluated, and stored with the name id. The contract then continues as cont.

3   Implementation of Marlowe on Cardano

Marlowe is specified by an executable semantics written in Haskell, but to make it usable in practice with financial contracts, it needs to be implemented on a blockchain. In this section, we explain how Marlowe is executed on the Cardano blockchain using an interpreter[1] written in the Plutus programming language.

3.1   Cardano and Plutus

Cardano is a third-generation blockchain that solves the energy usage issue by moving to an energy efficient *Proof of Stake* protocol [2].

Cardano aims to support smart contracts during its Shelley release in 2020. Cardano smart contract platform is called *Plutus*, and it uses Haskell programming language to generate a form of $SystemF_\omega$, called *Plutus Core*, by extending GHC using its plugin support [8, Section 13.3].

To implement Marlowe contracts, we use the PlutusTx compiler, which compiles Haskell code into serialized *Plutus Core* code, to create a Cardano *validator script* that ensures the correct execution of the contract. This form of implementation relies on the extensions to the UTxO model described in [6].

3.2   Extended UTxO

Cardano is a UTxO-based (unspent transaction output) blockchain, similar to Bitcoin [5]. It extends the Bitcoin model by allowing transaction outputs to hold a *Datum*. As the name suggests, this is a serialised data value used to store and communicate a contract state. This allows us to create complex multi-transactional contracts. In a nutshell, the EUTxO model looks like this:

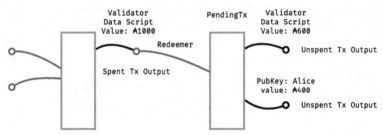

Validator(Data Script, Redeemer, PendingTx) = True

where black circles represent *unspent transaction outputs*, and red lines show *transaction inputs* that reference existing *transaction outputs*. Each transaction output contains a *Value*, and is protected either by a *public key*, or by a *Validator*.

---

[1] The implementation is available at https://github.com/input-output-hk/plutus/blob/0ca9af4f6614d591de7ebbe4dd759ce122d74efd/marlowe/src/Language/Marlowe/Semantics.hs.

In order to spend an existing transaction output protected by a *Validator*, one must create a transaction (a *Context*) that has an *input* that references the transaction output, and contains a *Redeemer*, such that `Validator(Datum, Redeemer, Context)` evaluates to *True*. A valid signature is required to spend a *public key* transaction output.

3.3 Design Space

There are several ways to implement Marlowe contracts on top of Plutus. We could write a Marlowe to Plutus compiler that would convert each Marlowe contract into a specific Plutus script. Instead, we chose to implement a Marlowe interpreter as a single Plutus script. This approach has a number of advantages:

- It is simple: having a single Plutus script that implements all Marlowe contracts makes it easier to implement, review, and test what we have done.
- Implementation is close to the semantics of Marlowe, as sketched above and in more detail in [9], which makes it easier to validate.
- The same implementation can be used for both on- and off-chain (wallet) execution of Marlowe code.
- It facilitates client-side contract evaluation, where we reuse the same code to do contract execution emulation in an IDE, and compile it to WASM/-JavaScript on the client side, e.g. in the Marlowe Playground.
- Having a single interpreter for all (or a particular group of) Marlowe contracts allows us to monitor the blockchain for these contracts, if required.
- Finally, Cardano nodes could potentially use an optimised interpreter (e.g: native) just for Marlowe contracts, which would save processing time.

Marlowe contract execution on the blockchain consists of a chain of transactions where, at each stage, the remaining contract and its state are passed through the *Datum*, and actions/inputs (i.e. *choices* and *money deposits*) are passed via the *Redeemer*. Each step in contract execution is a transaction that spends a Marlowe contract transaction output by providing a valid input as *Redeemer*, and produces a transaction output with a the remaining Marlowe contract and the updated state.

We store the remaining contract in the *Datum*, which makes it visible to everyone. This simplifies contract reflection and retrospection.

3.4 Contract Lifecycle on the Extended UTxO Model

As described above, the Marlowe interpreter is realised as a *Validation script*. We can divide the execution of a Marlowe Contract into two phases: creation and execution.

Creation. Contract creation is realised as a transaction with at least one script output, with the particular Marlowe contract in the *Datum*, and protected by the Marlowe validator script. Note that we do not place any restriction on the transaction inputs, which could use any other transaction outputs, including other scripts. This gives this model optimal flexibility and composability.

```
data MarloweData = MarloweData {
    marloweState    :: State,
    marloweContract :: Contract }
```

The contract has a state

```
data State = State { accounts    :: Map AccountId Ada
                   , choices     :: Map ChoiceId ChosenNum
                   , boundValues :: Map ValueId Integer
                   , minSlot     :: Slot }
```

where `accounts` maps account ids to their balances, `choices` stores user made choice values, `boundValues` stores evaluated `Value`'s introduced by `Let` expressions, and `minSlot` holds a minimal slot number that a contract has seen, to avoid 'time travel to the past'.

Execution. Marlowe contract execution consists of a chain of transactions, where the remaining contract and state are passed through the *Datum*, and input actions (i.e. `choices`) are passed as *redeemer scripts*.

Each execution step is a transaction that spends a Marlowe contract transaction output by providing an expected input in a redeemer script, and produces a transaction output with a Marlowe contract as continuation.

The Marlowe interpreter first validates the current contract state: i.e. we check that the contract locks at least as much as specified by the contract balances (the `accounts` field in `State`), and that balances are strictly positive.[2]

We then apply `computeTransaction` to the contract inputs, the contract continuation, and new state to compute the expected transaction outcomes:

```
computeTransaction ::
    TransactionInput -> State -> Contract -> TransactionOutput
```

where a `TransactionInput` consists of the current slot interval, together with other ontract inputs, and the outputs combine any payments and warnings with the resulting output state and contract.

Given a list of `Input`'s from *Redeemer*, the interpreter reduces a contract until it becomes quiescent: either it evaluates to `Close`, or it expects a user input in a `When` construct. All `Pay`, `If`, `Let`, `Close` constructs are evaluated immediately.

The evaluation function returns a new contract state, contract continuation, a list of warnings (such as partial payments), and a list of expected payments (i.e. one for each of the `Pay` constructs evaluated).

The on-chain *Validator* code cannot generate transaction outputs, but can only validate whatever a user provides in a transaction. Consider this simple zero coupon bond example.

---

[2] Using the Isabelle proof assistant, we have formally verified that given a state with positive balances, it is impossible for any possible contract and inputs to result in non-positive balances. This is described in more detail in Sect. 5.2.

```
When [ Case (Deposit aliceAccount alicePubKey (Constant 850_000_000))
     (Pay aliceAccount (Party bobPubKey) (Constant 850_000_000)
        (When
           [ Case
              (Deposit aliceAccount bobPubKey (Constant 1000_000_000))
              Close
           ] (Slot 200) Close
        ))] (Slot 100) Close
```

Here we expect Alice to deposit 850 Ada (850,000,000 Lovelace) into her account
`aliceAccount` before slot 100. Otherwise, we `Close` the contract.

If Alice deposits the money before slot 100, money immediately goes to Bob,
by requiring a transaction output of 850 Ada to Bob's public key address. Alice
must produce the following *Redeemer* to satisfy the Marlowe validator:

```
[IDeposit aliceAccount alicePubKey 850000000]
```

Bob is then expected to deposit 1000 Ada into Alice's account before slot 200.
If he does, the contract is closed, and all remaining balances must be paid out
to their respective owners; in this case, 1000 Ada must be paid to Alice. If Bob
does not pay, then Alice has lost her money, because this is an unsecured loan.

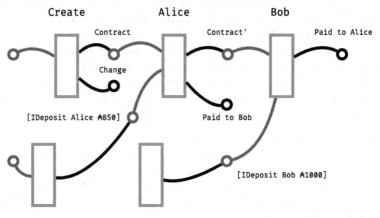

Note, that it is possible to provide multiple inputs at a time, allowing as many
steps of a contract execution as necessary to be merged. This gives atomicity to
some operations, and saves on transaction fees.

Ensuring Execution Validity. Except for the transaction that closes a Marlowe
contract, the Marlowe validator script checks that a spending transaction contains a valid continuation output, i.e: the hash of the output validator is the
same (same hash), and the new state and contract are the expected ones: the
ones resulting from applying the `computeTransaction` to the given inputs.

Closing a Contract. When a contract evaluates to `Close`, all remaining balances
the accounts of the contract are payed out to the respective owners of each
account, and the contract is removed from the set of unspent transaction outputs.

Future Work. Cardano extends its ledger rules to support *forging* of custom currencies and tokens. Simple token creation gives interesting possibilities of representing Marlowe contract parties by tokens. This tokenization of contract participants abstracts away concrete public keys into contract *roles*. In turn, those roles could be traded independently of a contract. We are working on adding *multicurrency* or *roles* support to Marlowe.

4   Static Analysis of Contracts

Marlowe semantics use types to prevent many non-sensical contracts from being written. But there are potential problems which are harder to detect until runtime, for example, whether there will be enough money to issue all the payments declared in the contract. At that point, it may already be too late to fix them, particularly in the case of blockchain.

Fortunately, in the case of Marlowe, a computer can decidedly determine whether a particular contract satisfies certain property before executing it, and it can provide a counter-example when it does not.

Our implementation relies on the Haskell library SBV, which in turn relies on existing SMT solvers to check satisfiability of properties.

4.1   SBV Library

SBV [7] (SMT Based Verification) library provides a high-level API that allows developers to automatically prove properties about Haskell programs, among other functionalities. The SBV library translates these properties to SMTLib queries, passes them to one or several SMT solvers, and translates the results back to the format in which the queries were written.

SBV monad. SBV provides a monad called `SBV`, a function can use parameters wrapped in this monad to represent symbolic values. Functions that take symbolic values can be used as properties and passed to the solver, which will replace the symbolic values with concrete values that satisfy or falsify the property.

4.2   Using SBV to Analyse Marlowe Contracts

Marlowe semantics represents errors that can be found at runtime as `Warnings`.

The property that we have implemented using SBV library can be enunciated as: "the given contract will not need to issue warnings at runtime no matter the inputs it receives".

This property is essentially a symbolic version of the semantics that returns a list of the warnings produced by a symbolic trace (a symbolic list of transactions input to the contract):

```
warningsTraceWB :: Bounds -> SSlotNumber -> SList NTransaction
                -> Contract -> SList NTransactionWarning
```

where types that begin with S, like SSlotNumber, are abbreviations for the symbolic versions of types: in this case SBV SlotNumber. The types that begin with N are *nested* types, which we explain in the *Custom datatypes* section below.

Custom Datatypes. SBV does not currently seem to support in general the use of custom datatypes. Fortunately, SBV supports tuples and the Either type. We can represent all types that Marlowe requires as combinations of Either and tuples, with the exception of the Contract type, but we do not need a symbolic version of the Contract type because we know its value at the time of analysis. For example, the TransactionResult type:

```
data TransactionResult
  = TransactionProcessed [TransactionWarning]
                         [TransactionEffect]
                         State
  | TransactionError TransactionError
```

becomes the nested type synonym NTransactionResult:

```
type NTransactionResult =
  Either ([NTransactionWarning], [NTransactionEffect], NState)
         NTransactionError
```

Because working with nested types is much more error prone than working with the original data-types, we used Template Haskell [15] to implement functions that transform the custom datatypes into nested types and generate the appropriate conversion functions.

Bounds for the State and the Inputs. The recursion in the execution of the semantics is bounded by the Contract, and because the Contract is not a symbolic parameter, the translation will terminate.

However, in both the input and the State record there are several lists (representing finite maps) that are not explicitly bounded in the implementation. Some parts of the semantics are bounded by the length of these lists (or maps), such as the implementation of Close. In order for the symbolic implementation to be finite, we need to find a bound for the length of these lists or maps.

Fortunately, we can infer a bound for all this lists quite straightforwardly. The least obvious one is the length of the list of transactions; we discuss the proof for this bound in Sect. 5.4.

Returning Non-Symbolic Contract Values. Values that rely on symbolic values have to be themselves symbolic, and the continuation Contract after each step depends on the Inputs and State, which are both symbolic. But having the contract as a symbolic parameter would be inconvenient since it is recursive, we know it in advance, and we use it to bound the execution of the symbolic semantics.

We work around this problem by modifying the signature of the function to receive a *continuation function* instead, and instead of just returning a value, we return the result of applying the *continuation function* to the result we were planning to return.

For example, the original type signature for the `apply` function was:

```
apply :: Environment -> State -> Input -> Contract -> ApplyResult
```

and the symbolic version of the `apply` function has the following signature:

```
apply :: SymVal a => Bounds
         -> SEnvironment -> SState -> SInput -> Contract
         -> (SApplyResult -> DetApplyResult -> SBV a) -> SBV a
```

where `DetApplyResult` contains the parts of `ApplyResult` that are not symbolic (like the `Contract`).

5   Formal Verification of the Marlowe Semantics

We can also use proof assistants to demonstrate that the Marlowe semantics presents certain desirable properties, such as that money is preserved and anything unspent is returned to users by the end of the execution of any contract. Formal statements and proofs of these properties are given in [11].

Currently, we have translated the Haskell Marlowe semantics to Isabelle while keeping both versions as close as possible, but we decided to make them different in two main aspects:

- We use *integers for identifiers* because they are easier to handle than strings.
- We use a *custom implementation of maps and sets* that use lists because Isabelle already provides many theorems that are proved for lists.

5.1   Termination Proof

Isabelle automatically proves termination for most function. This is not the case for `reductionLoop`. This function repeatedly calls `reduceContractStep` until it returns `NotReduced`, so proving overall termination requires a proof that `reduceContractStep` will eventually do that. In order to prove this, we defined a measure for the size of a pair of `Contract` and `State`:

```
fun evalBound :: "State ⇒ Contract ⇒ nat" where
"evalBound sta cont = length (accounts sta) + 2 * (size cont)"
```

where `size` is a measure already generated automatically by Isabelle.

We need the number of accounts in the `State` because the size of the contract `Close` will not decrease when calling `reduceContractStep`, but the number of accounts will, unless they are all empty.

And we needed to multiply the size of the `Contract` by two because the primitive `Deposit` may increase the number of accounts by one, so we need to multiply the effect of the reduction of the size of the contract in order to compensate that.

5.2   Valid State and Positive Account Preservation

There are some values for `State` that are allowed by its type but make no sense, especially in the case of Isabelle semantics where we use lists instead of maps:

1. The lists represent maps, so they should have no repeated keys.
2. We want two maps that are equal to be represented the same, so we force keys to be in ascending order.
3. We only want to record those accounts that contain a positive amount.

We call a value for `State` *valid* if the first two properties are true. And we say it has *positive accounts* if the third property is true.

We have proved that functions in the semantics preserve all three properties.

Quiescent Result. A contract is *quiescent* if and only if the root construct `When`, or if the contract is `Close` and all accounts are empty. We have proved that, if an input `State` is valid and accounts are positive, then the output will be quiescent.

5.3   Money Preservation and Contract Timeout

One of the dangers of using smart contracts is that a badly written one can potentially lock its funds forever. By the end of the contract, all the money paid to the contract must be distributed back, in some way, to a subset of the participants of the contract. To ensure this is the case we proved two properties:

Money Preservation. Money is not created or destroyed by the semantics. More specifically, the money that comes in plus the money in the contract before the transaction must be equal to the money that comes out plus the contract after the transaction, except in the case of an error.

Timeout Closes a Contract. For every Marlowe `Contract` there is a slot number after which an empty transaction can be issued that will close the contract and refund all the money in its accounts.

A conservative upper bound for the expiration slot number can be calculated efficiently by using the function `maxTime` (or `maxTimeContract` in the Isabelle semantics), essentially by taking the maximum of all the timeouts in the contract.

We proved that this conservative upper bound is general enough for every contract, by showing that, if the contract is not closed and empty, then an empty transaction sent after `maxTime` will close the contract and empty the accounts.

5.4   Bound on the Maximum Number of Transactions

Another property of Marlowe is that any given `Contract` has an implicit finite bound on the maximum number of `Transactions` that it accepts. This is a convenient property for two reasons.

First, it reduces the danger of Denial of Service (DoS) attacks, because the number of valid inputs is limited, an attacker participant cannot arbitrarily block the contract by issuing an unbounded amount of useless `Transactions`. Secondly, the number of transactions bounds the length of traces that symbolic execution (see Sect. 4) needs to explore. We state the property as follows:

```
lemma playTrace_only_accepts_maxTransactionsInitialState :
"playTrace sl c l = TransactionOutput txOut
  ⟹ length l ≤ maxTransactionsInitialState c"
```

where `maxTransactionsInitialState` is essentially the maximum number of nested `When` constructs in the contract plus one.

This property implies that any trace that is longer than this is guaranteed to produce at least one error. Because transactions that produce an error do not alter the state of the contract, such a list of transactions (a trace) will be equivalent to a list of transactions that does not have the erroneous transaction. Thus, we do not lose generality by only exploring shorter traces.

5.5   Future Work

At the time of writing, we are actively trying new optimisations and approaches for implementing static analysis that are more efficient in practise than the approach described in this paper. As a consequence, in some cases, the static analysis implementation can deviate considerably from the Haskell semantics. Our intention is to keep using property-based testing and formal verification to ensure that both implementations are consistent.

6   The Marlowe Playground

For Marlowe to be usable in practice, users need to be able to design and develop Marlowe contracts, and also to understand how contracts will behave once deployed to the blockchain, but without actually deploying them.

The Marlowe Playground, a web-based tool that supports the interactive construction, revision, and simulation of smart contracts written in Marlowe, provides these facilities, as well as access to a static analysis of contracts (as described in the previous section), an online tutorial for Marlowe and a set of example contracts. The playground is available at https://prod.meadow. marlowe.iohkdev.io/.[3]

At the top level, the playground offers three panes: the main *Simulation* pane, as well as panes for developing Marlowe contracts, embedded in *Haskell* or using the *Blockly* visual language.

---

[3] Development of the playground is rapid, and the latest, unstable, version is also available at https://alpha.marlowe.iohkdev.io/.

Development. On the simulation pane, "pure" Marlowe contacts can be developed directly, not embedded in another language. Two reasons for doing this are:

- There is a shallower learning curve for users who are new to Haskell or programming languages in general. The Marlowe constructs are quite simple, and there is no need, at least initially, to learn about Haskell syntax or even variables, functions etc.
- As we step through the execution of a contract in a simulation, the contract is reduced; it is very useful to be able to view, or even edit, the reduced contract during this execution.

As contracts become larger it makes sense to use another editor in the *Haskell* pane. Here contracts can be written using facilities from *Haskell* to abbreviate and make more readable the description of the contracts. These contracts can then be transferred as a pure Marlowe data structure into the simulation pane.

Contracts can also be written using Google's *Blockly* visual programming language, as was earlier described in Meadow [9]. Blockly gives an easy way to introduce the concepts of Marlowe to users who have no programming knowledge, and in particular the editor gives users a set of options for each construct as the contract is built. Once a contract has been constructed in Blockly it is possible to transfer that contract to the simulation pane. It is also possible to transfer a Marlowe contract to Blockly for further editing.

The Marlowe editor in the unstable version of the playground has a feature called *holes* to aid writing contracts. If we enter the contract `?mycontract` we will be presented with a dropdown list of values that could be used.

In our case `?mycontract` must be a `Contract` of some sort, and so we are offered a choice of `Contract` constructors from a dropdown list. If we choose `Pay` then the Marlowe editor will automatically fill in a skeleton `Pay` contract with new holes where we need to provide values.

```
Pay ?accountId_1_1 ?payee_1_2 ?value_1_3 ?contract_1_4
```

New options will be presented, one for each hole, and each will have a dropdown list of all the possible values.

A complete contract can be written in this guided way with the user needing only to fill in strings and numbers by hand. This approach to writing holes in your code and "asking" the compiler what you could put in there is easy to implement in a DSL because there are very limited options, however is also becoming popular with more complex languages such as Haskell and Idris.

Users can at any point save the current contract directly to a Github Gist, as well as being able to re-load contracts from Github Gists. There are also some demo contracts that can be loaded in their Haskell and Marlowe versions.

Simulation. Contracts written in the Marlowe editor are parsed in real-time and if there are no errors (and no holes) then the contract is analysed to discover which actions a user could take to progress the contract. These actions are displayed in the "Input Composer" above the editor. Consider the following example contract:

```
When [Case (Deposit (AccountId 0 "investor")
            "guarantor" (Constant 1000_000000)) Close] 10 Close
```

In this case, the only action a user can take to progress the contract is to accept a deposit of 1000 ADA from the guarantor to the investor's account. Because of this, the playground can display this action in the input composer.

The user can then choose to add this action to a transaction being prepared. Once the action is added other inputs become possible; these are displayed in the input composer, and again they can be added to the transaction being composed. In this way, multiple actions can be added to a transaction before it is applied.

A user can then apply this transaction and in the example above this would result in the state pane showing a single payment and in addition the contract in the Marlowe editor will have been reduced to `Close`.

At any point in the simulation, the user can undo any steps made: in this particular case, they can undo the application of the transaction, and iteratively undo more steps. At any point, they can also reset the contract to its initial state. This enables users to apply transactions, see their effects, step back, and try different transactions to see the effects of the changes on the result. They can also change the reduced contract to investigate variants of the original.

The final feature that we would like to present is the static analysis of contracts. As described in the previous section, it is possible to carry out a symbolic execution of a contract and then use a SMT solver to look for cases that could cause unwanted situations. The playground uses this to search for situations where contract execution would cause warnings. For example, suppose you write a contract that causes a payment of 450 Lovelace from Alice to Bob but the contract allows a situation where Alice has only deposited 350 Lovelace. The static analysis will find this partial payment case and report it to the playground user with an example of how it could occur.

7 Related Work

Our work is inspired by the work of Peyton Jones et al. [14] to describe financial contracts using a DSL embedded in Haskell. In the remainder of this section we look at a number of recent systems that bear direct comparison with Marlowe; an earlier paper [10] gives a detailed review of smart contracts on blockchain.

The Findel project [4] examines financial contracts on the Ethereum platform, and is also based on [14]. The authors note that payments need to be bounded; this is made concrete in our account by our notion of commitments. They take no account of commitments or timeouts as our approach does, and so are unable to guarantee some properties – such as a finite lifetime – built into Marlowe by design. Nxt [12], is special-purpose in providing a "fat" high-level API, containing built-in transaction types and transactions that support some 250 primitives; these can be "scripted" in a client using a binding to the API, which is available, e.g., in JavaScript. In providing such specificity this bears comparison with our implementation of contracts from the ACTUS standard [1].

BitML [3] is a DSL for specifying Marlowe-like contracts that regulate transfers on the Bitcoin blockchain, and is implemented via a compiler that translates contracts into Bitcoin transactions plus strategies. Participants execute a contract by appending these transactions on the Bitcoin blockchain, according to their strategies, which involve the exchange of bitstrings that guarantee to a very high probability the correctness of contract execution. Marlowe is directly implemented by an interpreter which could also be implemented on a covenant-based [13] extension of the Bitcoin blockchain.

8   Conclusions and Future Work

Rather than aiming to be general-purpose, Marlowe is a DSL designed to support financial contracts on blockchain. We leverage its specificity in our work on static analysis and verification, where we are able to deliver much greater impact and focus than we could for a general-purpose language. We are able to shape the development and simulation environment to give stronger user support too. Moreover, Marlowe presents a model for how other DSLs can be built in this space, supporting different domains such as provenance in the supply chain.

Defining the language by means of an executable reference semantics means that we can, as well as directly executing this semantics, generate an on-chain interpreter for it and simulate it in browser using the Haskell-like languages Plutus and PureScript. This is particularly straightforward when working with a subset of Haskell that is represented in the same way on these languages.

Our medium term aim is launching on Cardano blockchain itself, by which time we expect to have added multiple currencies to Marlowe, as well as making (roles in) Marlowe contracts tradeable, through tokenising contract roles.

References

1. ACTUS. https://www.actusfrf.org. Accessed 9 Dec 2019
2. Badertscher, C., et al.: Ouroboros genesis: composable proof-of-stake blockchains with dynamic availability. In: CCS 2018 (2018)

3. Bartoletti, M., Zunino, R.: BitML: a calculus for bitcoin smart contracts. In: CCS 2018. ACM (2018)
4. Biryukov, A., Khovratovich, D., Tikhomirov, S.: Findel: secure derivative contracts for Ethereum. In: Brenner, M., et al. (eds.) FC 2017. LNCS, vol. 10323, pp. 453–467. Springer, Cham (2017). https://doi.org/10.1007/978-3-319-70278-0_28
5. Bonneau, J., et al.: SoK: research perspectives and challenges for bitcoin and cryptocurrencies. In: IEEE Symposium on Security and Privacy (SP). IEEE (2015)
6. Chakravarty, M., et al.: Functional blockchain contracts (2019). https://iohk.io/en/research/library/papers/functional-blockchain-contracts/
7. Erkök, L.: SBV: SMT based verification in Haskell (2010). http://leventerkok.github.io/sbv/. Accessed 3 Dec 2019
8. GHC: User's Guide (2019). https://downloads.haskell.org/~ghc/8.6.3/docs/html/users_guide/index.html. Accessed 20 Feb 2019
9. Lamela Seijas, P., Thompson, S.: Marlowe: financial contracts on blockchain. In: Margaria, T., Steffen, B. (eds.) ISoLA 2018. LNCS, vol. 11247, pp. 356–375. Springer, Cham (2018). https://doi.org/10.1007/978-3-030-03427-6_27
10. Lamela Seijas, P., Thompson, S., McAdams, D.: Scripting smart contracts for distributed ledger technology. Cryptology ePrint Archive, Report 2016/1156 (2016). https://eprint.iacr.org/2016/1156
11. Marlowe github (2018). https://github.com/input-output-hk/marlowe. Accessed 27 Jan 2020
12. Nxt (2013). https://nxtplatform.org/. Accessed 26 Mar 2018
13. O'Connor, R., Piekarska, M.: Enhancing bitcoin transactions with covenants. In: Brenner, M., et al. (eds.) FC 2017. LNCS, vol. 10323, pp. 191–198. Springer, Cham (2017). https://doi.org/10.1007/978-3-319-70278-0_12
14. Peyton Jones, S., et al.: Composing contracts: an adventure in financial engineering (functional pearl). In: Proceedings of the Fifth ACM SIGPLAN ICFP. ACM (2000)
15. Sheard, T., Peyton Jones, S.: Template meta-programming for Haskell. In: Proceedings of the 2002 Haskell Workshop, Pittsburgh. ACM SIGPLAN (2002)

Load Balancing for Sharded Blockchains

Naoya Okanami[1,2](✉), Ryuya Nakamura[2,3](✉), and Takashi Nishide[1](✉)

[1] University of Tsukuba, Ibaraki, Japan
nishide@risk.tsukuba.ac.jp
[2] LayerX Inc., Tokyo, Japan
{naoya.okanami,ryuya.nakamura}@layerx.co.jp
[3] The University of Tokyo, Tokyo, Japan

Abstract. Sharding is an approach to designing a highly scalable blockchain. A sharded blockchain achieves parallelism by dividing consensus nodes (validators) into groups called shards and making them process different transactions in each shard. In this paper, we economically analyze users' behavior on sharded blockchains and identify a phenomenon that users' accounts and smart contracts eventually get concentrated in a few shards, making shard loads unfair. This phenomenon leads to bad user experiences, such as delays in transaction inclusions and increased transaction fees. To solve the above problem, we propose a load balancing framework in sharded blockchains in which accounts and contracts are frequently reassigned to shards to reduce the difference of loads between shards. We formulate the contract reassignment as an optimization problem and present the algorithm to solve it. Further, we apply the framework to an existing sharding design (Ethereum 2.0) and modify the protocol to do load balancing. Finally, we simulate the protocol and observe smaller transaction delays and fees.

Keywords: Sharding · Blockchain · Load balancing · Game theory · Heuristics · Simulated annealing

1 Introduction

Traditional distributed ledgers do not increase transaction processing capacity, no matter how many participants exist in the network. In order to improve the scalability of the distributed ledger, methods such as off-chain protocols and Directed Acyclic Graph (DAG) based blockchains and sharded blockchains have been proposed. One of them, sharding, implements parallelization by dividing validators that verify transactions into different groups and processing different transactions in each shard. Sharding was first proposed at Elastico [13], followed by sharded blockchains such as OmniLedger [12], Chainspace [2], and Rapid-Chain [17]. It will be used in Ethereum [5] in the future.

There are two blockchain transaction models, the Un-spent Transaction-Output (UTXO) model and the account/balance model. The blockchain with the account/balance model is more compatible with implementing smart contract

© Springer Nature Switzerland AG 2020
M. Bernhard et al. (Eds.): FC 2020 Workshops, LNCS 12063, pp. 512–524, 2020.
https://doi.org/10.1007/978-3-030-54455-3_36

functions, and Ethereum most used among blockchains that currently implement smart contracts adopts the account/balance model.

Sharded blockchains with the account/balance model allow users to choose the shard to which their account belongs freely. Users spend less fee and have less latency when their accounts belong to the same shard as the contracts that frequently trade with them. Therefore, in reality, it is easier to collect accounts for shards to which popular contracts belong. As a result, the load on the shard is increasingly imbalanced. On the other hand, in a shard, the higher the load is, the more the fee increases. Users don't want to use shards with high fees, so no extreme imbalances occur. In other words, when users act to improve their user experience (UX), there is no extreme imbalance that all accounts are concentrated in one shard, and some load balancing is performed. A user can actually have multiple accounts, but so does this.

We thought that, due to these two characteristics, the account behaves selfishly, and the account assignment state converges approximately to a state where all users have no incentive to go to another shard (ϵ-Nash equilibrium). The sharding protocol already has a mechanism that performs load balancing when the user acts selfishly. In theoretical computer science and distributed systems, the fact that load balancing is performed by users acting selfishly as described above is called *selfish load balancing* [1,3,15].

If the load on each shard is imbalanced, sharding protocols have the following issues.

- Due to the load imbalance, the hardware specs required for the validator will be higher than when the load is balanced. This prevents new validators from entering.
- The gas price differs across shards and worsen the UX of cross-shard communications.
- Validators favor an environment, e.g., on Amazon Web Services (AWS), which can efficiently scale in/out.
- The incentive analysis around parameterization of rewards or gas costs might become complicated.

Monoxide is one of the sharded blockchains in the account/balance model [16]. When a popular decentralized application (Dapps) exists in a sharded blockchain with smart contract functionality, the load is concentrated in the shard to which the application belongs, which is stated in the Monoxide paper as a "single address hotspot" issue. The Monoxide paper mentions a solution by the upper layers, where application operators create one address for each shard and distribute the load.

However, as explained earlier, there is not only an imbalance because there is a heavily loaded account. If the user is selfish, the imbalance will be more widespread, and the load will be concentrated in a few shards. Also, considering previous research, selfish load balancing is performed and converges to the ϵ-Nash equilibrium.

Since selfish load balancing is one of the congestion games in terms of game theory, it cannot equalize shard loads. If the shard load is not equal, the overall UX is worse than when the load is equal. To solve the above problem, we propose in-protocol load balancing to reduce shard load imbalance by frequently reassigning accounts within the protocol.

With frequent account reassignments, even if a user self-changes a shard, it is immediately reassigned to another shard by the protocol. Since there is a fee for the act of moving the shard itself, the incentive for the user to change the shard themselves becomes very small, and the user does not want to change the shard themselves.

In order to do in-protocol load balancing, we formulate load balancing as an optimization problem. Moreover, as a result of the formulation, it is shown that this problem is NP-hard. Since it is NP-hard, there is no polynomial-time algorithm for finding an exact solution for the load balancing problem. Thus, it is necessary to use an approximation algorithm or heuristics, but it is very computationally expensive to obtain a good solution. Doing the calculation itself on-chain is not worth the cost. Therefore, in-protocol load balancing is done in a competition format where the problem is disclosed and delegated to the outside, and the best solution is adopted. This provides a better solution than on-chain.

We define the objective function of the optimization problem to minimize the load of the shard with the highest load. The reason is that the minimum computer specifications required to become a validator are proportional to the maximum load that can occur in a shard. In addition, it is because the UX of many accounts deteriorates because the commission becomes high, and the delay occurs in the shard where the transaction is concentrated.

Finally, we apply this load balancing framework to Ethereum 2.0 [16] and construct an algorithm that solves the load balancing problem using simulated annealing, which is one of metaheuristics. In addition, comparing selfish load balancing with the proposed algorithm, we show that the total transaction fee and total transaction delay can be smaller.

In summary, our contributions are:

- We show that the load concentrates on a small number of shards when the user acts selfishly in sharded blockchains with the account/balance model.
- We show that shard imbalance increases user transaction fees and latency.
- In order to solve this problem, we propose in-protocol load balancing, which performs load balancing by reassigning accounts in sharded blockchains. In-protocol load balancing formulates load balancing as an optimization problem, and a blockchain can obtain a good solution by competing players with the solution in a competition.
- We apply this framework to Ethereum 2.0, an existing sharding design, and demonstrate that transaction fees and latencies can be reduced over selfish load balancing.

2   Preliminaries

2.1   Task Assignment Problem (TAP)

There is a mathematical optimization problem called *task assignment problem*. For example, there are the following problems.

M resources and N tasks are given. It takes c_i to execute task i. Further, when task i and task j are assigned to different resources, the resources to which task i and task j are assigned cost d_{ij} and d_{ji}, respectively. Each task can be assigned to one resource. What is the shortest time to complete all the tasks?

TAP is a well-known NP-hard problem in the field of mathematical optimization, and various algorithms for solving it have been proposed [4,9,14].

2.2   Cross Shard Transaction

A transaction sent from one shard to another is called a *cross-shard transaction*. A cross-shard transaction has to go through another shard or parent chain and has a higher fee and latency than a single-shard transaction. For example, the problem of how to handle hotel room reservations and train seat reservations atomically is called *train-and-hotel problem*. In sharding, it is a problem of handling contracts in one shard and contracts in another shard atomically.

2.3   Ethereum 2.0

The Ethereum community is now actively working on the Ethereum 2.0 project [11], which upgrades the Ethereum protocol to introduce proof-of-stake, sharding, etc. Ethereum 2.0 consists of one **beacon chain** and multiple **shard chains**. A shard chain is a sharded blockchain, and a beacon chain is a blockchain that manages the shard chain. Beacon chain mediates cross-shard communications. For simplicity, we assume smart contracts exist on the shard chains but not on the beacon chain.

Yank Operation. Ethereum 2.0 solves the train-and-hotel problem by introducing an operation called *yank* [7]. A yank is to delete a contract on one shard, issue a transaction receipt, and instantiate the contract on another shard. Then perform some operation on the shard to which it is yanked. For example, yank a contract to reserve a room for a hotel to a shard that has a contract to reserve a train and make an atomic reservation.

3   In-Protocol Load Balancing

The process flow of in-protocol load balancing is as follows.

1. Competition coordinators collect necessary transaction load information of accounts.
2. Coordinators formulate load balancing as an optimization problem.
3. Competition participants calculate a good account assignment.
4. Coordinators move accounts based on the new assignment.

3.1 Problem Definition

The formulation of the optimization problem varies depending on what metrics the community and users value.

We formulate minimizing the highest load among loads of shards as an optimization problem. Let S be a mapping from account to shard id. Let l_{ij} be the load of a shard that accounts i and j belong to when they belong to the same shard. Further, let l'_{ij} be a load for the shard to which the account i belongs when the accounts i and j belong to different shards. The total load $L_k(S)$ in shard k per unit time is

$$L_k(S) := \sum_{i,j,S(i)=k\wedge S(j)=k} l_{ij} + \sum_{i,j,S(i)=k\wedge S(j)\neq k} l'_{ij} \tag{1}$$

There is a correlation between shard fees and shard load. Let the overall load of the shard be L, the fee for processing the load l be $C(L,l)$. In reality, the function C cannot be determined exactly because the fees are proposed by users, and the auction determines which transaction is incorporated into the block by validators.

There are several optimization problems that can be used to improve UX while equalizing the load on all users—for example, minimizing the load on the heaviest shard. Shards with heavy loads have higher transaction fees, and reducing them can significantly reduce overall fees. We formulate this as follows.

$$\text{minimize} \qquad \max_k L_k(S) \tag{2}$$

We name this optimization problem *maximum load minimization problem* (MLMP). TAP is a polynomial-time reducible to MLMP with simple formula transformations. If MLMP could be solved in polynomial time, TAP can be solved in polynomial time using that algorithm. Therefore, MLMP is NP-hard.

Good results can also be obtained by minimizing the overall fee. In order to reduce the overall cost, it is necessary to reduce the load on the shard, which is the bottleneck and has the highest load. Thus, the load on all the shards is equalized, and the overall fee is reduced. In addition, the fee is reduced when the number of cross-shard transactions is reduced. Therefore, that optimization is performed so that the number of cross-shard transactions is reduced. This also reduces latency. We formulate this as follows.

$$\text{minimize} \qquad \sum_k C(L_k(S), L_k(S)) \tag{3}$$

This problem is as difficult as MLMP.

3.2 Competition

Since the above optimization problems are difficult, heuristics and approximate algorithms must be used to find a good solution. However, running such heavy processing algorithms on-chain is not worth the cost, so in our design, anyone can submit a solution, and we build a game that rewards the player who submitted the best solution.

For each epoch, the account assignment at the next epoch is determined using the information of the previous epoch. If too old information is used for the past epoch information, load balancing suitable for the transaction in the next epoch is not performed, so it is necessary to use appropriate information of the previous.

If we use transaction load information for all accounts, the amount of information is $O(n^2)$, where n is the number of accounts. In actual operation, the transaction information of the account selected by some algorithm is used for each epoch because of the limited capacity of the beacon chain. For example, there is a method of randomly selecting half of the active accounts, or selecting 10% of contracts in descending order of load.

To host a competition, we have nodes that act as competition coordinators. The coordinators formulate and publicize the account assignment as an optimization problem using past epoch transaction load information. The competition players understand the optimization problem, work on optimization, and submit a solution when the time limit is approaching. After the epoch, the coordinators evaluate the solution and rewards the player who submits the best solution. Rewards are paid for pool or newly issued coins. Since a malicious player may submit a poorly evaluated solution and put unnecessary load on the coordinators, the player must pay a fee when submitting the solution. Also, if there are multiple players who have both submitted the best solution, the winner is the one with the fastest submission time.

Coordinators are elected for each epoch. In Ethereum 2.0, a coordinator is the validator who was elected the first block proposer in an epoch.

Collecting Transaction Data. Every shard has transaction load information for accounts belonging to that shard. To perform in-protocol load balancing, this information must be passed to the competition coordinators. The method differs depending on the sharding protocol.

In Ethereum 2.0, the state of each shard is committed as a Merkle root called *crosslink* [6,8] that is stored in the beacon chain. The validity and data availability are checked by the shard's validator set.

Since the beacon chain cannot handle transaction load information for all accounts, all shards build data as follows:

1. Every epoch, a shard i randomly samples k contracts $A_i = \{a_{i,1}, a_{i,2}, ..., a_{i,k}\}$.

2. Accounts not selected by random sampling are merged as a single virtual account as $a_{i,\text{rest}}$. Let R be the unselected set and C_{i_x,j_y} be the cross-shard transaction load from shard i account x to shard j account y.

$$C_{i_{\text{rest}},j_y} = \sum_{x \in R} C_{i_x,i_y} \tag{4}$$

The shard chain sends the information constructed in this way to the beacon chain by crosslink.

Player Algorithms. The player selects themselves the algorithm that they will use. Examples of the algorithm include hill climbing, simulated annealing, and genetic algorithm. Alternatively, players can use a mathematical optimization solver or a combination of the solver and their algorithm. The longer the sharding protocol that introduced in-protocol load balancing operates, the more efficiently the player's algorithm will evolve, and the better the load balancing will be.

Commit-Reveal Scheme. If the solution is submitted, another player may copy the solution and submit an improved solution starting from that solution. If the commit-reveal scheme is adopted, this problem can be solved by releasing the solution and verifying the best solution after the competition is over. That is, the player submits the commitment of (**solution** ∥ **signature**). However, there must be at least one honest player in order for the user to benefit from in-protocol load balancing.

3.3 Security Analysis

The above protocol only changes the state transition rules, so it does not affect the safety, liveness, and validity properties of the blockchain. Also, the consensus protocol and validator validation rules have not changed radically. On the other hand, there is room for validators to selfishly choose a solution to make a profit by external opportunity such as front-running. The analysis of such potential attacking vectors is left as future work.

4 Experiments

In this section, we show that applying in-protocol load balancing to Ethereum 2.0, modeling users, and simulating them actually reduces shard imbalance and reduces fees and latency. The optimization problem used in the experiment is formulation (3), which minimizes the overall fee.

4.1 Simulation Settings

This subsection describes the user strategy, the algorithm used by the player, and the sharded blockchain model to be simulated.

User Strategy. We use Berenbrink's method [3] to model how a user behaves. Let m be the number of accounts, n be the number of shards and $m \gg n$. In one unit time, a user moves an account with the following strategy.

Let i be a shard to which the user belongs, and j be a destination shard, and j is selected at random. Let C_i and C_j are the loads of i and j per unit time, respectively. if $C_j < C_i$, it moves with probability $1 - \frac{C_j}{C_i}$. If not, do not move.

When performing in-protocol load balancing, the shard allocation is changed by the protocol, so the cost of moving the shard cannot be ignored. If C_t is the cost of moving the shard, and the time until the next allocation, that is, epoch time is T, if $C_j + C_t/T < C_i$, then the probability $1 - \frac{C_j + C_t/T}{C_i}$ to move. If not, do not move. As T becomes shorter, C_t/T becomes so large that the user has no incentive to change the shard.

Simulated Annealing Approach. We use the simulated annealing approach for this simulation. Simulated annealing is a generalization of hill climbing and is a metaheuristic used for difficult problems such as NP-hard problems [10]. It is difficult to find the global optimal solution by using hill climbing, but simulated annealing can obtain a value close to the global optimal solution. The algorithm is such that a solution in the neighborhood of the provisional solution is selected at random, and the transition is always made when the score is improved.

The pseudo code is as follows (see Algorithm 1). Let T be the time to execute this algorithm. NEIGHBOR is a function that randomly selects a nearby solution, SCORE is a function that evaluates the solution, and GETTIME is a function that returns how much time has passed since this algorithm was executed. The evaluation value of the score function moves to the better one. Therefore, SCORE(assignment) is $-$(whole total fee). The PROBABILITY is a function that returns the probability of transition based on the current time t, the current_assignment score, and the next_assignment score. The RANDOM function returns a uniform random number between 0 and 1.

Also, no competition will be held, i.e., one person submits one solution.

Sharded Blockchain Model. Ethereum 2.0 will generate one block every 12 s, with 64 shards planned to be introduced first. Ethereum currently trades $300,000$ accounts a day. Simulating all of them requires a lot of computational resources, so this time we set $T = 0.1$ s and simulate with 8 shards and $1,000$ accounts. Also, the load information of all active accounts is used.

We model how accounts trade with other accounts in a directed graph. The vertex in the graph represents an account, and the directed edge extending from account i to account j represents the average load on account i in all transactions between account i and account j in one unit time (block). This load includes not only the transaction from account i to account j, but also the load at the time of transaction from account j to account i. In reality, transactions are concentrated on very popular accounts such as Maker DAO, so we set a parameter called account popularity, so that the more popular the account is, the more easily transactions to that account are sent. The popularity of the account

Algorithm 1. Simulated annealing approach

1: $t \leftarrow 0$
2: **while** $t < T$ **do**
3:      next_assignment $\leftarrow$ NEIGHBOR(current_assignment)
4:      $s_c \leftarrow$ SCORE(current_assignment)
5:      $s_n \leftarrow$ SCORE(next_assignment)
6:      **if** $s_n > s_c$ **then**
7:          current_assignment $\leftarrow$ next_assignment
8:      **else**
9:          $p \leftarrow$ PROBABILITY(t, s_c, s_n)
10:         **if** $p >$ RANDOM() **then**
11:             current_assignment $\leftarrow$ next_assignment
12:         **end if**
13:     **end if**
14:     $t \leftarrow$ GETTIME()
15: **end while**

---

is simply a quadratic function. In other words, the popularity of account i is popularity$_i = i^2$. Popularity was used to weight the load when trading. However, it is impossible in reality that one account is trading with all other accounts. Therefore, considering the total number of accounts 1000, an account accounts for 5% of all accounts.

We believe this setting is sufficient to show the effect of our in-protocol load balancing (Table 1).

Table 1. Simulation parameters

Parameter	Value
Number of shards	8
Number of accounts	1000
Load balancing interval	0.1 s
Number of accounts traded by one account	5%
Number of epochs	1000

4.2   Results and Comparisons

As a result of the simulation, the sum of account fees and the number of cross-shard transactions have reduced. Although this setting was small, the effect of in-protocol load balancing was confirmed.

Figures 1 and 2 show selfish load balancing and in-protocol load balancing when all accounts selfishly move between shards at each epoch. Both have converged to specific values, but in-protocol load balancing has reached better values. This is a natural result because selfish load balancing converges to ϵ-Nash

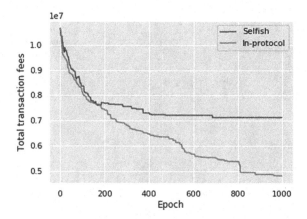

Fig. 1. Decrease of total transaction fees when all accounts selfishly move between shards at each epoch (blue: selfish load balancing, orange: in-protocol load balancing) (Color figure online)

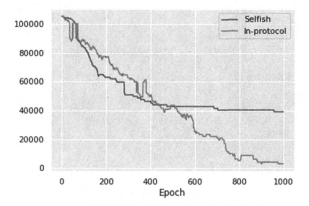

Fig. 2. Decrease of number of cross-shard transactions when all accounts selfishly move between shards at each epoch (blue: selfish load balancing, orange: in-protocol load balancing) (Color figure online)

equilibrium, while in-protocol load balancing can obtain a Pareto optimal solution.

Figures 3 and 4 show selfish load balancing and in-protocol load balancing when all accounts selfishly move between shards at each epoch. Even if the user acts selfishly, in-protocol load balancing achieves better results than selfish load balancing, similarly to the above results. It is thought that the result will depend on the implementation, but it is a result that the effect of in-protocol load balancing has been raised by the user acting selfishly.

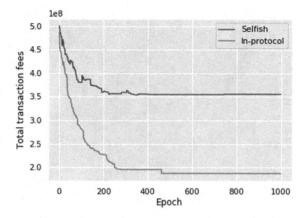

Fig. 3. Decrease of total transaction fees when half accounts selfishly move between shards at each epoch (blue: selfish load balancing, orange: in-protocol load balancing) (Color figure online)

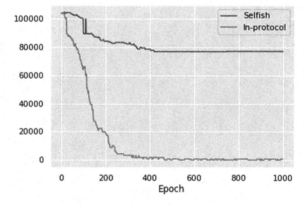

Fig. 4. Decrease of number of cross-shard transactions when half accounts selfishly move between shards at each epoch (blue: selfish load balancing, orange: in-protocol load balancing) (Color figure online)

5   Discussions

Other Algorithms

In this paper, simulated annealing is used, but it may be possible to find a more efficient solution by using another heuristic algorithm or by using mixed-integer optimization with a mathematical optimization solver. Moreover, the simulation used here does not speed up, such as updating the difference or implementing it with C++ or Rust. The algorithm actually used for in-protocol sharding will be refined as players compete. What is important is not the efficiency of the algorithm used, but the use of our proposed in-protocol load balancing can improve total fees and latency over selfish load balancing.

Simulation Settings

The settings we tried this time have room for experimentation in modeling the number of shards and accounts, and various settings are possible using statistical distributions, game theory, and more measured data from Ethereum 1.0. Improvements include varying the statistical distribution of load over time and using transaction-level simulation. A more strict simulation may show that in-protocol load balancing is more effective. It may also indicate cases where in-protocol load balancing is not effective, as well as cases where it is effective. The reality is that we need to deal with even larger data, so the results obtained by in-protocol load balancing may not be worth the cost.

Application to Other Sharded Blockchains

In addition, although one level of sharding was considered, there is room to consider how effective hierarchical sharding such as CBC Casper [18] can be compared with plain sharding.

6   Conclusion

We confirmed the phenomenon by modeling and simulating users with the expectation that a few shard accounts would be concentrated by acting selfishly in sharded blockchains with the account/balance model. We also showed that the shard load imbalance worsens UX, due to higher transaction fees and increased latency. To solve this problem, we proposed a load balancing framework for sharded blockchains. This framework achieves in-protocol load balancing by taking advantage of the incentive to change shards by changing account assignments frequently. We also proposed a method for efficiently obtaining good account assignments in the competition format. Although small, simulations show that transaction fees and latency are lower than the selfish load balancing that occurs when users act on their own with this in-protocol load balancing.

References

1. Adolphs, C.P., Berenbrink, P.: Distributed selfish load balancing with weights and speeds. In: Proceedings of the Annual ACM Symposium on Principles of Distributed Computing, pp. 135–144 (2012). https://doi.org/10.1145/2332432. 2332460
2. Al-Bassam, M., Sonnino, A., Bano, S., Hrycyszyn, D., Danezis, G.: Chainspace: a sharded smart contracts platform. Internet Society (2018). https://doi.org/10. 14722/ndss.2018.23241
3. Berenbrink, P., Friedetzky, T., Ann Goldberg, L., Goldberg, P.W., Hu, Z., Martin, R.: Distributed selfish load balancing. SIAM J. Comput. **37**(4), 1163–1181 (2007). https://doi.org/10.1137/060660345
4. Billionnet, A., Costa, M.C., Sutter, A.: An efficient algorithm for a task allocation problem an efficient algorithm for a task allocation problem. J. Assoc. Comput. Mach. **39**(3), 50–518 (1992)

5. Buterin, V.: A next generation smart contract & decentralized application platform whitepaper. Ethereum Foundation (2013)
6. Buterin, V.: Cross-links between main chain and shards - Sharding - Ethereum research. https://ethresear.ch/t/cross-links-between-main-chain-and-shards/1860
7. Buterin, V.: Cross-shard contract yanking - Sharding - Ethereum Research. https://ethresear.ch/t/cross-shard-contract-yanking/1450
8. Buterin, V.: Serenity Design Rationale. https://notes.ethereum.org/9l707paQQEeI-GPzVK02lA#Beacon-committees
9. Chaudhary, V., Aggarwal, J.K.: A generalized scheme for mapping parallel algorithms. IEEE Trans. Parallel Distrib. Syst. **4**(3), 328–346 (1993). https://doi.org/10.1109/71.210815
10. Dowsland, K.A., Thompson, J.M.: Simulated annealing. In: Rozenberg, G., Back, T., Kok, J.N. (eds.) Handbook of Natural Computing. Springer, Berlin (2012)
11. Eth2.0: ethereum/eth2.0-specs: Ethereum 2.0 Specifications. https://github.com/ethereum/eth2.0-specs
12. Kokoris-Kogias, E., Jovanovic, P., Gasser, L., Gailly, N., Syta, E., Ford, B.: OmniLedger: a secure, scale-out, decentralized ledger via Sharding. In: Proceedings - IEEE Symposium on Security and Privacy, pp. 583–598. IEEE (2018). https://doi.org/10.1109/SP.2018.000-5
13. Luu, L., Chu, D.H., Olickel, H., Saxena, P., Hobor, A.: Making smart contracts smarter. In: Proceedings of the 2016 ACM SIGSAC Conference on Computer and Communications Security – CCS 2016, pp. 254–269. ACM Press, New York (2016). https://doi.org/10.1145/2976749.2978309
14. Salman, A., Ahmad, I., Al-Madani, S.: Particle swarm optimization for task assignment problem. Microprocess. Microsyst. **26**(8), 363–371 (2002). https://doi.org/10.1016/S0141-9331(02)00053-4
15. Suri, S., Tóth, C.D., Zhou, Y.: Selfish load balancing and atomic congestion games. Annu. ACM Symp. Parallel Algorithms Architectures **16**, 188–195 (2004). https://doi.org/10.1145/1007912.1007941
16. Wang, G., Shi, Z.J., Nixon, M., Han, S.: SOK: Sharding on blockchain. AFT 2019 – Proceedings of the 1st ACM Conference on Advances in Financial Technologies, pp. 41–61 (2019). https://doi.org/10.1145/3318041.3355457
17. Zamani, M., Movahedi, M., Raykova, M.: RapidChain: scaling blockchain via full Sharding. In: Proceedings of the ACM Conference on Computer and Communications Security, pp. 931–948. Association for Computing Machinery (2018). https://doi.org/10.1145/3243734.3243853
18. Zamfir, V., Rush, N., Asgaonkar, A., Piliouras, G.: cbc-casper/cbc-casper-paper: an introduction to CBC Casper Consensus Protocols. https://github.com/cbc-casper/cbc-casper-paper

The Extended UTXO Model

Manuel M. T. Chakravarty[1]([✉]), James Chapman[2], Kenneth MacKenzie[3],
Orestis Melkonian[3,5], Michael Peyton Jones[4], and Philip Wadler[5]

[1] IOHK, Utrecht, The Netherlands
manuel.chakravarty@iohk.io
[2] IOHK, Glasgow, Scotland
james.chapman@iohk.io
[3] IOHK, Edinburgh, Scotland
{kenneth.mackenzie,orestis.melkonian}@iohk.io
[4] IOHK, London, England
michael.peyton-jones@iohk.io
[5] University of Edinburgh, Edinburgh, Scotland
orestis.melkonian@ed.ac.uk, wadler@inf.ed.ac.uk

Abstract. Bitcoin and Ethereum, hosting the two currently most valuable and popular cryptocurrencies, use two rather different ledger models, known as the *UTXO model* and the *account model*, respectively. At the same time, these two public blockchains differ strongly in the expressiveness of the smart contracts that they support. This is no coincidence. Ethereum chose the account model explicitly to facilitate more expressive smart contracts. On the other hand, Bitcoin chose UTXO also for good reasons, including that its semantic model stays simple in a complex concurrent and distributed computing environment. This raises the question of whether it is possible to have expressive smart contracts, while keeping the semantic simplicity of the UTXO model.

In this paper, we answer this question affirmatively. We present *Extended UTXO (EUTXO)*, an extension to Bitcoin's UTXO model that supports a substantially more expressive form of *validation scripts*, including scripts that implement general state machines and enforce invariants across entire transaction chains.

To demonstrate the power of this model, we also introduce a form of state machines suitable for execution on a ledger, based on Mealy machines and called Constraint Emitting Machines (CEM). We formalise CEMs, show how to compile them to EUTXO, and show a *weak bisimulation* between the two systems. All of our work is formalised using the Agda proof assistant.

Keywords: Blockchain · UTXO · Functional programming · State machines

1 Introduction

Bitcoin, the most widely known and most valuable cryptocurrency, uses a graph-based ledger model built on the concept of *UTXOs (unspent transaction out-*

© Springer Nature Switzerland AG 2020
M. Bernhard et al. (Eds.): FC 2020 Workshops, LNCS 12063, pp. 525–539, 2020.
https://doi.org/10.1007/978-3-030-54455-3_37

puts) [2,17]. Individual *transactions* consist of a list of *inputs* and a list of *outputs*, where outputs represent a specific *value* (of a cryptocurrency) that is available to be spent by inputs of subsequent transactions. Each output can be spent by (i.e., connect to) exactly one input. Moreover, we don't admit cycles in these connections, and hence we can regard a collection of transactions spending from each other as a directed acyclic graph, where a transaction with m inputs and n outputs is represented by a node in the graph with m edges in and n edges out. The sum of the values consumed by a transaction's inputs must equal the sum of the values provided by its outputs, thus value is conserved.

Whether an output can be consumed by an input is determined by a function ν attached to the output, which we call the output's *validator*. A transaction input proves its eligibility to spent an output by providing a *redeemer* object ρ, such that $\nu(\rho) = \mathsf{true}$; redeemers are often called *witnesses* in Bitcoin. In the simplest case, the redeemer is a cryptographic hash of the spending transaction signed by an authorised spender's private key, which is checked by the validator, which embeds the corresponding public key. More sophisticated protocols are possible by using more complex validator functions and redeemers—see [3] for a high-level model of what is possible with the functionality provided by Bitcoin.

The benefit of this graph-based approach to a cryptocurrency ledger is that it plays well with the concurrent and distributed nature of blockchains. In particular, it forgoes any notion of shared mutable state, which is known to lead to highly complex semantics in the face of concurrent and distributed computations involving that shared mutable state.

Nevertheless, the UTXO model, generally, and Bitcoin, specifically, has been criticised for the limited expressiveness of programmability achieved by the validator concept. In particular, Ethereum's *account-based ledger* and the associated notion of *contract accounts* has been motivated by the desire to overcome those limitations. Unfortunately, it does so by introducing a notion of shared mutable state, which significantly complicates the semantics of contract code. In particular, contract authors need to understand the subtleties of this semantics or risk introducing security issues (such as the vulnerability to recursive contract invocations that led to the infamous DAO attack [5]).

Contributions. The contribution of the present paper is to propose an extension to the basic UTXO ledger model, which (a) provably increases expressiveness, while simultaneously (b) preserving the dataflow properties of the UTXO graph; in particular, it forgoes introducing any notion of shared mutable state. More specifically, we make the following contributions:

- We propose the *EUTXO model*, informally in Sect. 2 and formally in Sect. 3.
- We demonstrate that the EUTXO model supports the implementation of a specific form of state machines (*Constraint Emitting Machines*, or CEMs), which the basic UTXO model does not support, in Sect. 4.
- We provide formalisations of both the EUTXO model and Constraint Emitting Machines. We prove a weak bisimulation between the two using the Agda proof[1] assistant, building on previous work by Melkonian et al. [11].

---

[1] https://github.com/omelkonian/formal-utxo/tree/a1574e6.

Section 5 summarises related work.

The EUTXO model will be used in the ledger of Cardano, a major blockchain system currently being developed by IOHK. It also provides the foundation of Cardano's smart contract platform *Plutus*[2], which includes a small functional programming language *Plutus Core* which is used to implement Scripts. Although a technical description of Cardano itself is beyond the scope of this paper, one can try out the Plutus Platform in an online playground.[3]

Other future work includes a formal comparison of EUTXO with Ethereum's account-based model.

2   Extending UTXO

Various forms of state machines have been proposed to characterise smart contract functionality that goes beyond what is possible with the basic UTXO model—see, for example, [8,16] using Ethereum's account-based model. However, we might wonder whether we can extend the basic UTXO model in such a way as to support more expressive state machines without switching to an account-based model.

Given that we can regard the individual transactions in a continuous chain of transactions as individual steps in the evolution of a state machine, we require two pieces of additional functionality from the UTXO model: (a) we need to be able to maintain the machine state, and (b) we need to be able to enforce that the same contract code is used along the entire sequence of transactions—we call this *contract continuity*.

To maintain the machine state, we extend UTXO outputs from being a pair of a validator ν and a cryptocurrency value *value* to being a triple $(\nu, value, \delta)$ of validator, value, and a *datum* δ, where δ contains arbitrary contract-specific data. Furthermore, to enable validators to enforce contract continuity, we pass the entirety of the transaction that attempts to spend the output locked by a validator to the validator invocation. Thus a validator can inspect the transaction that attempts to spend its output and, in particular, it can ensure that the contract output of that transaction uses validator code belonging to the same contract—often, this will be the same validator. Overall, to check that an input with redeemer ρ that is part of the transaction tx is entitled to spend an output $(\nu, value, \delta)$, we check that $\nu(value, \delta, \rho, tx) = \mathsf{true}$.

As we are allowing arbitrary data in δ and we enable the validator ν to impose arbitrary validity constraints on the consuming transaction tx, the resulting Extended UTXO (EUTXO) model goes beyond enabling state machines. However, in this paper we restrict ourselves to the implementation of state machines and leave the investigation of further-reaching computational patterns to future work.

As a simple example of a state machine contract consider an n–of–m multi-signature contract. Specifically, we have a given amount $value_{\mathrm{msc}}$ of some cryptocurrency and we require the approval of at least n out of an a priori fixed set of

---

[2] https://github.com/input-output-hk/plutus.

[3] https://prod.playground.plutus.iohkdev.io/.

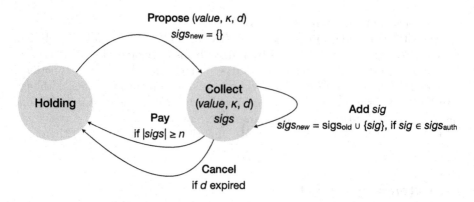

Fig. 1. Transition diagram for the multi-signature state machine; edges labelled with input from redeemer and transition constraints.

$m \geq n$ owners to spend $value_{\mathrm{msc}}$. With plain UTXO (e.g., on Bitcoin), a multi-signature scheme requires out-of-band (off-chain) communication to collect all n signatures to spend $value_{\mathrm{msc}}$. On Ethereum, and also in the EUTXO model, we can collect the signatures on-chain, without any out-of-band communication. To do so, we use a state machine operating according to the transition diagram in Fig. 1, where we assume that the threshold n and authorised signatures $sigs_{\mathrm{auth}}$ with $|sigs_{\mathrm{auth}}| = m$ are baked into the contract code.

In its implementation in the EUTXO model, we use a validator function ν_{msc} accompanied by the datum δ_{msc} to lock $value_{\mathrm{msc}}$. The datum δ_{msc} stores the machine state, which is of the form Holding when only holding the locked value or Collecting$((value, \kappa, d), sigs)$ when collecting signatures $sigs$ for a payment of $value$ to κ by the deadline d. The initial output for the contract is $(\nu_{\mathrm{msc}}, value_{\mathrm{msc}}, \mathsf{Holding})$.

The validator ν_{msc} implements the state transition diagram from Fig. 1 by using the redeemer of the spending input to determine the transition that needs to be taken. That redeemer (state machine input) can take four forms: (1) Propose$(value, \kappa, d)$ to propose a payment of $value$ to κ by the deadline d, (2) Add(sig) to add a signature sig to a payment, (3) Cancel to cancel a proposal after its deadline expired, and (4) Pay to make a payment once all required signatures have been collected. It then validates that the spending transaction tx is a valid representation of the newly reached machine state. This implies that tx needs to keep $value_{\mathrm{msc}}$ locked by ν_{msc} and that the state in the datum δ'_{msc} needs to be the successor state of δ_{msc} according to the transition diagram.

The increased expressiveness of the EUTXO model goes far beyond simple contracts such as this on-chain multi-signature contract. For example, the complete functionality of the Marlowe domain-specific language for financial contracts [15] has been successfully implemented as a state machine on the EUTXO model.

3 Formal Model

3.1 Basic Types and Notation

Figure 2 defines some basic types and notation used in the rest of the paper; we have generally followed the notation established by Zahnentferner in [17].

$\mathbb{B}$	the type of booleans
$\mathbb{N}$	the type of natural numbers
$\mathbb{Z}$	the type of integers
$(\phi_1 : T_1, \ldots, \phi_n : T_n)$	a record type with fields $\phi_1, \ldots, \phi_n$ of types $T_1, \ldots, T_n$
$t.\phi$	the value of ϕ for t, where t has type T and ϕ is a field of T
$\mathsf{Set}[T]$	the type of (finite) sets over T
$\mathsf{List}[T]$	the type of lists over T, with $\_[\_]$ as indexing and $\|\_\|$ as length
$h :: t$	the list with head h and tail t
$x \mapsto f(x)$	an anonymous function
$c^{\#}$	a cryptographic collision-resistant hash of c
$\mathsf{Interval}[A]$	the type of intervals over a totally-ordered set A

Fig. 2. Basic types and notation

The Data Type. We will make particular use of a primitive type Data which can be used to pass information into scripts. This is intended to be any relatively standard structured data format, for example JSON or CBOR [6].

The specific choice of type does not matter for this paper, so we have left it abstract. The intention is that this should be well supported by all the programming languages we are interested in, including whatever language is used for scripts, and whatever languages are used for off-chain code that interacts with the chain.

We assume that for every (non-function) type T in the scripting language we have corresponding toData and fromData functions.

3.2 EUTXO: Enhanced Scripting

Our first change to the standard UTXO model is that as well as the validator we allow transaction outputs to carry a piece of data called the *datum* (or *datum object*), which is passed in as an additional argument during validation. This allows a contract to carry some state (the datum) without changing its "code" (the validator). We will use this to carry the state of our state machines (see Sect. 2).

The second change is that the validator receives some information about the transaction that is being validated. This information, which we call the *context*, is passed in as an additional argument of type Context. The information supplied in the context enables the validator to enforce much stronger conditions than is possible with a bare UTXO model—in particular, it can inspect the *outputs* of the current transaction, which is essential for ensuring contract continuity (see Sect. 2).

The third change is that we provide some access to time by adding a *validity interval* to transactions. This is an interval of ticks (see Subsect. 3.3) during which a transaction can be processed (a generalisation of a "time-to-live"). Thus, any scripts which run during validation can assume that the current tick is within that interval, but do not know the precise value of the current tick.

Finally, we represent all the arguments to the validator (redeemer, datum, Context) as values of type Data. Clients are therefore responsible for encoding whatever types they would like to use into Data (and decoding them inside the validator script).

3.3   A Formal Description of the EUTXO Model

In this section we give a formal description of the EUTXO model. The description is given in a straightforward set-theoretic form, which (1) admits an almost direct translation into languages like Haskell for implementation, and (2) is easily amenable to mechanical formalisation. We will make use of this in Sect. 4.

The definitions in this section are essentially the definitions of UTXO-based cryptocurrencies with scripts from Zahnentferner [17], except that we have made the changes described above.

Figure 3 lists the types and operations used in the the the basic EUTXO model. Some of these are defined here, the others must be provided by the ledger ("ledger primitives").

Addresses. We follow Bitcoin in referring to the targets of transaction outputs as "addresses". In this system, they refer only to *script* addresses (likely a hash of the script), but in a full system they would likely include public-key addresses, and so on.

Ticks. A tick is a monotonically increasing unit of progress in the ledger system. This corresponds to the "block number" or "block height" in most blockchain systems. We assume that there is some notion of a "current tick" for a given ledger.

Inputs and Outputs. Transactions have a Set of inputs but a List of outputs. There are two reasons that we do not also have a Set of outputs although they are conceptually symmetrical:

- We need a way to uniquely identify a transaction output, so that it can be referred to by a transaction input that spends it. The pair of a transaction id and an output index is sufficient for this, but other schemes are conceivable.

LEDGER PRIMITIVES

Quantity	an amount of currency
Tick	a tick
Address	an "address" in the blockchain
Data	a type of structured data
DataHash	the hash of a value of type Data
TxId	the identifier of a transaction
txId : Tx $\rightarrow$ TxId	a function computing the identifier of a transaction
Script	the (opaque) type of scripts
scriptAddr : Script $\rightarrow$ Address	the address of a script
dataHash : Data $\rightarrow$ DataHash	the hash of an object of typeData
$\llbracket\_\rrbracket$: Script $\rightarrow$ Data $\times$ Data $\times$ Data $\rightarrow$ $\mathbb{B}$	applying a script to its arguments

DEFINED TYPES

$$Output = (value : \text{Quantity},$$
$$addr : \text{Address},$$
$$datumHash : \text{DataHash})$$

$$OutputRef = (id : \text{TxId}, index : \mathbb{N})$$

$$Input = (outputRef : \text{OutputRef},$$
$$validator : \text{Script},$$
$$datum : \text{Data},$$
$$redeemer : \text{Data})$$

$$Tx = (inputs : \text{Set[Input]},$$
$$outputs : \text{List[Output]},$$
$$validityInterval : \text{Interval[Tick]})$$

$$Ledger = \text{List[Tx]}$$

Fig. 3. Primitives and types for the EUTXO model

– A Set requires a notion of equality. If we use the obvious structural equality on outputs, then if we had two outputs paying X to address A, they would be equal. We need to distinguish these—outputs must have an identity beyond just their address and value.

The Location of Validators and Datum Objects. Validator scripts and full datum objects are provided as parts of transaction *inputs*, even though they are conceptually part of the output being spent. The output instead specifies them by providing the corresponding address or hash.[4]

This strategy reduces memory requirements, since the UTXO set must be kept in memory for rapid access while validating transactions. Hence it is desirable to keep outputs small—in our system they are constant size. Providing the much larger validator script only at the point where it is needed is thus a helpful saving. The same considerations apply to datum objects.

---

[4] That these match up is enforced by Rules 7 and 8 in Fig. 6.

An important question is how the person who spends an output *knows* which validator and datum to provide in order to match the hashes on the output. This can always be accomplished via some off-chain mechanism, but we may want to include some on-chain way of accomplishing this.[5] However, this is not directly relevant to this paper, so we have omitted it.

Fees, Forge, and Additional Metadata. Transactions will typically have additional metadata, such as transaction fees or a "forge" field that allows value to be created or destroyed. These are irrelevant to this paper, so have been omitted.[6]

Ledger Structure. We model a ledger as a simple list of transactions: a real blockchain ledger will be more complex than this, but the only property that we really require is that transactions in the ledger have some kind of address which allows them to be uniquely identified and retrieved.

3.4   The Context Type

Recall from the introduction to Sect. 3.2 that when a transaction input is being validated, the validator script is supplied with an object of type Context (encoded as Data) which contains information about the current transaction. The Context type is defined in Fig. 4, along with some related types.

$$
\begin{aligned}
\text{OutputInfo} &= (value : \text{Quantity}, \\
&\quad validatorHash : \text{Address}, \\
&\quad datumHash : \text{DataHash}) \\[1em]
\text{InputInfo} &= (outputRef : \text{OutputRef}, \\
&\quad validatorHash : \text{Address}, \\
&\quad datum : \text{Data}, \\
&\quad redeemer : \text{Data}, \\
&\quad value : \text{Quantity}) \\[1em]
\text{Context} &= (inputInfo : \text{Set}[\text{InputInfo}], \\
&\quad outputInfo : \text{List}[\text{OutputInfo}], \\
&\quad validityInterval : \text{Interval}[\text{Tick}], \\
&\quad thisInput : \mathbb{N})
\end{aligned}
$$

Fig. 4. The Context type for the EUTXO model

---

[5] Cardano will provide a mechanism in this vein.
[6] Adding such fields might require amending Rule 4 to ensure value preservation.

The Contents of Context. The Context type is a summary of the information contained in the Tx type in Fig. 3, situated in the context of a validating transaction, and made suitable for consumption in a script. That results in the following changes:

1. The InputInfo type is augmented with information that comes from the output being spent, specifically the value attached to that output.
2. The Context type includes an index that indicates the input currently being validated. This allows scripts to identify their own address, for example.
3. Validators are included as their addresses, rather than as scripts. This allows easy equality comparisons without requiring script languages to be able to represent their own programs.

We assume that there is a function toContext : Tx × Input × Ledger → Context which summarises a transaction in the context of an input and a ledger state.

Determinism. The information provided by Context is entirely determined by the transaction itself. This means that script execution during validation is entirely deterministic, and can be simulated accurately by the user *before* submitting a transaction: thus both the outcome of script execution and the amount of resources consumed can be determined ahead of time. This is helpful for systems that charge for script execution, since users can reliably compute how much they will need to pay ahead of time.

A common way for systems to violate this property is by providing access to some piece of mutable information, such as the current time (in our system, the current tick has this role). Scripts can then branch on this information, leading to non-deterministic behaviour. We sidestep this issue with the validation interval mechanism (see the introduction to Sect. 3.2).

$\mathsf{lookupTx} : \mathsf{Ledger} \times \mathsf{TxId} \rightarrow \mathsf{Tx}$
$\mathsf{lookupTx}(l, id) \qquad = \text{the unique transaction in } l \text{ whose id is } id$

$\mathsf{unspentTxOutputs} : \mathsf{Tx} \rightarrow \mathsf{Set}[\mathsf{OutputRef}]$
$\mathsf{unspentTxOutputs}(t) = \{(\mathsf{txId}(t), 1), \ldots, (\mathsf{txId}(id), |t.outputs|)\}$

$\mathsf{unspentOutputs} : \mathsf{Ledger} \rightarrow \mathsf{Set}[\mathsf{OutputRef}]$
$\mathsf{unspentOutputs}([]) \quad = \{\}$
$\mathsf{unspentOutputs}(t :: l) = (\mathsf{unspentOutputs}(l) \setminus t.inputs) \cup \mathsf{unspentTxOutputs}(t)$

$\mathsf{getSpentOutput} : \mathsf{Input} \times \mathsf{Ledger} \rightarrow \mathsf{Output}$
$\mathsf{getSpentOutput}(i, l) \quad = \mathsf{lookupTx}(l, i.outputRef.id).outputs[i.outputRef.index]$

Fig. 5. Auxiliary functions for EUTXO validation

3.5   Validity of EUTXO Transactions

Figure 6 defines what it means for a transaction t to be valid for a valid ledger l during the tick currentTick, using some auxiliary functions from Fig. 5. Our definition combines Definitions 6 and 14 from Zahnentferner [17], differing from the latter in Rule 6.

A ledger l is *valid* if either l is empty or l is of the form $t :: l'$ with l' valid and t valid for l'.

---

1. **The current tick is within the validity interval**

$$\text{currentTick} \in t.validityInterval$$

2. **All outputs have non-negative values**

$$\text{For all } o \in t.outputs, \; o.value \geq 0$$

3. **All inputs refer to unspent outputs**

$$\{i.outputRef : i \in t.inputs\} \subseteq \text{unspentOutputs}(l).$$

4. **Value is preserved**

$$\text{Unless } l \text{ is empty,} \sum_{i \in t.inputs} \text{getSpentOutput}(i, l).value = \sum_{o \in t.outputs} o.value$$

5. **No output is double spent**

$$\text{If } i_1, i_2 \in t.inputs \text{ and } i_1.outputRef = i_2.outputRef \text{ then } i_1 = i_2.$$

6. **All inputs validate**

$$\text{For all } i \in t.inputs, \; ⧫i.validator⧫(i.datum, i.redeemer, \text{toData}(\text{toContext}(t, i, l))) = \text{true}.$$

7. **Validator scripts match output addresses**

$$\text{For all } i \in t.inputs, \; \text{scriptAddr}(i.validator) = \text{getSpentOutput}(i, l).addr$$

8. **Each datum matches its output hash**

$$\text{For all } i \in t.inputs, \; \text{dataHash}(i.datum) = \text{getSpentOutput}(i, l).datumHash$$

Fig. 6. Validity of a transaction t in the EUTXO model

Creating Value. Most blockchain systems have special rules for creating or destroying value. These are usually fairly idiosyncratic, and are not relevant to this paper, so we have provided a simple genesis condition in Rule 4 which allows the initial transaction in the ledger to create value.

Lookup Failures. The function getSpentOutput calls lookupTx, which looks up the unique transaction in the ledger with a particular id and can of course fail. However Rule 3 ensures that during validation all of the transaction inputs refer to existing unspent outputs, and in these circumstances lookupTx will always succeed for the transactions of interest.

4   Expressiveness of EUTXO

In this section, we introduce a class of state machines that can admit a straight-forward modelling of smart contracts running on an EUTXO ledger. The class we choose corresponds closely to Mealy machines [9] (deterministic state trans-ducers). The transition function in a Mealy machine produces a value as well as a new state. We use this value to model the emission of constraints which apply to the current transaction in the ledger. We do not claim that this class captures the full power of the ledger: instead we choose it for its simplicity, which is sufficient to capture a wide variety of use cases.

We demonstrate how one can represent a smart contracts using Mealy machines and formalise a *weak bisimulation* between the machine model and the ledger model. Furthermore, we have mechanised our results in Agda[7], based on an executable specification of the model described in Sect. 3.

4.1   Constraint Emitting Machines

We introduce Constraint Emitting Machines (CEM) which are based on Mealy machines. A CEM consists of its type of states S and inputs I, a predicate function final : $S \rightarrow$ Bool indicating which states are final and a valid set of transitions, given as a function step : $S \rightarrow I \rightarrow$ Maybe $(S \times$ TxConstraints$)$[8] from source state and input symbol to target state and constraints and denoted $s \xrightarrow{i} (s', tx^{\equiv})$.

The class of state machines we are concerned with here diverge from the typical textbook description of Mealy Machines in the following aspects:

- The set of states can be infinite.
- There is no notion of **initial state**, since we would not be able to enforce it on the blockchain level. Therefore, each contract should first establish some initial trust to bootstrap the process. One possible avenue for overcoming this limitation is to build a notion of *trace simulation* on top of the current relation between single states, thus guaranteeing that only valid sequences starting from initial states appear on the ledger. For instance, this could be used to establish inductive properties of a state machine and carry them over to the ledger; we plan to investigate such concerns in future work.
- While **final states** traditionally indicate that the machine *may* halt at a given point, allowing this possibility would cause potentially stale states to clutter the UTXO set in the ledger. Thus, a CEM final state indicates that

---

[7] https://github.com/omelkonian/formal-utxo/tree/a1574e6/Bisimulation.agda.

[8] The result may be Nothing, in case no valid transitions exist from a given state/input.

the machine *must* halt. It will have no continuing transitions from this point onward and the final state will not appear in the UTXO set. This corresponds to the notion of a *stopped* process [14] which cannot make any transitions.

- The set of output values is fixed to *constraints* which impose a certain structure on the transaction that will implement the transition. Our current formalisation considers a limited set of first-order constraints, but these can easily be extended without too many changes in the accompanying proofs.

4.2 Transitions-as-Transactions

We want to compile a smart contract C defined as a CEM into a smart contract that runs on the chain. The idea is to derive a validator script from the step function, using the datum to hold the state of the machine, and the redeemer to provide the transition signal. A valid transition in a CEM will correspond to a single valid transaction on the chain. The validator is used to determine whether a transition is valid and the state machine can advance to the next state. More specifically, this validator should ensure that we are transitioning to a valid target state, the corresponding transaction satisfies the emitted constraints and that there are no outputs in case the target state is final:

$$\mathsf{validator}_C(s, i, \mathit{txInfo}) = \begin{cases} \mathsf{true} & \mathit{if}\ s \xrightarrow{\ i\ } (s', \mathit{tx}^\equiv) \\ & \mathit{and}\ \mathsf{satisfies}(\mathit{txInfo}, \mathit{tx}^\equiv) \\ & \mathit{and}\ \mathsf{checkOutputs}(s', \mathit{txInfo}) \\ \mathsf{false} & \mathit{otherwise} \end{cases}$$

Note that unlike the step function which returns the new state, the validator only returns a boolean. On the chain the next state is provided with the transaction output that "continues" the state machine (if it continues), and the validator simply validates that the correct next state was provided.[9]

4.3 Behavioural Equivalence

We have explained how to compile state machines to smart contracts but how do we convince ourselves that these smart contracts will behave as intended? We would like to show (1) that any valid transition in a CEM corresponds to a valid transaction on the chain, and (2) that any valid transaction on the chain corresponds to a valid transition. We refer to these two properties as soundness and completeness below.

While state machines correspond to automata, the automata theoretic notion of equivalence—trace equivalence—is too coarse when we consider state machines as running processes. Instead we use bisimulation, which was developed in concurrency theory for exactly this purpose, to capture when processes behave the same [14]. We consider both the state machine and the ledger itself to be running processes.

---

[9] A user can run the step function locally to determine the correct next state off-chain.

If the state machine was the only user of the ledger then we could consider so-called strong bisimulation where we expect transitions in one process to correspond to transitions in the other and vice-versa. But, as we expect there to be other unrelated transactions occurring on the ledger we instead consider weak bisimulation where the ledger is allowed to make additional so-called *internal* transitions that are unrelated to the behaviour we are interested in observing.

The bisimulation proof relates steps of the CEM to new transaction submissions on the blockchain. Note that we have a *weak* bisimulation, since it may be the case that a ledger step does not correspond to a CEM step.

Definition 1 (Process relation). *A CEM state s corresponds to a ledger l whenever s appears in the current UTXO set, locked by the validator derived from this CEM:*

$$l \sim s$$

Definition 2 (Ledger step). *Concerning the blockchain transactions, we only consider valid ledgers.*[10] *Therefore, a valid step in the ledger consists of submitting a new transaction tx, valid w.r.t. to the current ledger l, resulting in an extended ledger l':*

$$l \xrightarrow{\ tx\ } l'$$

Proposition 1 (Soundness). *Given a valid CEM transition $s \xrightarrow{\ i\ } (s', tx^{\equiv})$ and a valid ledger l corresponding to source state s, we can construct a valid transaction submission to get a new, extended ledger l' that corresponds to target state s':*

$$\frac{s \xrightarrow{\ i\ } (s', tx^{\equiv}) \quad l \sim s}{\exists tx\ l' \ .\ l \xrightarrow{\ tx\ } l' \ \wedge l' \sim s'} \text{ SOUND}$$

Note. We also require that the omitted constraints are satisfiable in the current ledger and the target state is not a final one, since there would be no corresponding output in the ledger to witness $l' \sim s'$. We could instead augment the definition of correspondence to account for final states, but we have refrained from doing so for the sake of simplicity.

Proposition 2 (Completeness). *Given a valid ledger transition $l \xrightarrow{\ tx\ } l'$ and a CEM state s that corresponds to l, either tx is irrelevant to the current CEM and we show that the extended ledger l' still corresponds to source state s, or tx is relevant and we exhibit the corresponding CEM transition $s \xrightarrow{\ i\ } (s', tx^{\equiv})$*[11]*:*

$$\frac{l \xrightarrow{\ tx\ } l' \quad l \sim s}{l' \sim s \ \vee \ \exists i\ s'\ tx^{\equiv} \ .\ s \xrightarrow{\ i\ } (s', tx^{\equiv})} \text{ COMPLETE}$$

---

[10] In our formal development, we enforce validity statically at compile time.

[11] We cannot provide a correspondence proof in case the target state is final, as explained in the previous note.

Together, soundness and completeness finally give us weak bisimulation. Note, however, that our notion of bisimulation differs from the textbook one (e.g. in Sangiorgi [14]), due to the additional hypotheses that concern our special treatment of constraints and final states.

5   Related Work

Bitcoin Covenants [12] allow Bitcoin transactions to restrict how the transferred value can be used in the future, including propagating themselves to ongoing outputs. This provides contract continuity and allows the implementation of simple state machines. Our work is inspired by Covenants, although our addition of a datum is novel and simplifies the state passing.

The Bitcoin Modelling Language (BitML) [3] is an idealistic process calculus that specifically targets smart contracts running on Bitcoin. The semantics of BitML contracts essentially comprise a (labelled) *transition system*, aka a state machine. Nonetheless, due to the constrained nature of the plain UTXO model without any extensions, the construction is far from straightforward and requires quite a bit of off-chain communication to set everything up. Most importantly, the BitML compilation scheme only concerns a restricted form of state machines, while ours deals with a more generic form that admits any user-defined type of states and inputs. BitML builds upon an abstract model of Bitcoin transactions by the same authors [2]; one of our main contributions is an extended version of such an abstract model, which also accounts for the added functionality apparent in Cardano.

Ethereum and its smart contract language, Solidity [4], are powerful enough to implement state machines, due to their native support for global contract instances and state. However, this approach has some major downsides, notably that contract state is global, and must be kept indefinitely by all core nodes. In the EUTXO model, contract state is localised to where it is used, and it is the responsibility of clients to manage it.

Scilla [16] is a intermediate-level language for writing smart contracts as state machines. It compiles to Solidity and is amendable to formal verification. Since Scilla supports the asynchronous messaging capabilities of Ethereum, Scilla contracts correspond to a richer class of automata, called *Communicating State Transition Systems* [13]. In the future, we plan to formally compare this class of state machines with our own class of CEMs, which would also pave the way to a systematic comparison of Ethereum's account-based model against Cardano's UTXO-based one.

Finally, there has been an attempt to model Bitcoin contracts using *timed automata* [1], which enables semi-automatic verification using the UPPAAL model checker [7]. While this provides a pragmatic way to verify temporal properties of concrete smart contracts, there is no formal claim that this class of automata actually corresponds to the semantics of Bitcoin smart contracts. In contrast, our bisimulation proof achieves the bridging of this semantic gap.

References

1. Andrychowicz, M., Dziembowski, S., Malinowski, D., Mazurek, Ł.: Modeling bitcoin contracts by timed automata. In: Legay, A., Bozga, M. (eds.) FORMATS 2014. LNCS, vol. 8711, pp. 7–22. Springer, Cham (2014). https://doi.org/10.1007/978-3-319-10512-3_2

2. Atzei, N., Bartoletti, M., Lande, S., Zunino, R.: A formal model of Bitcoin transactions. In: Meiklejohn and Sako [10], pp. 541–560. https://doi.org/10.1007/978-3-662-58387-6_29

3. Bartoletti, M., Zunino, R.: BitML: a calculus for bitcoin smart contracts. In: Proceedings of the 2018 ACM SIGSAC Conference on Computer and Communications Security, pp. 83–100. ACM (2018)

4. Ethereum Foundation: Solidity documentation (2016–2019). https://solidity.readthedocs.io/

5. Falkon, S.: The story of the DAO – its history and consequences (2017). medium.com. https://medium.com/swlh/the-story-of-the-dao-its-history-and-consequences-71e6a8a551ee

6. IETF: RFC 7049 - Concise Binary Object Representation (CBOR), October 2013. https://tools.ietf.org/html/rfc7049 . Accessed 01 Jan 2020

7. Larsen, K.G., Pettersson, P., Yi, W.: UPPAAL in a nutshell. Int. J. Softw. Tools Technol. Transfer 1(1–2), 134–152 (1997). https://doi.org/10.1007/s100090050010

8. Mavridou, A., Laszka, A.: Designing secure Ethereum smart contracts: a finite state machine based approach. In: Meiklejohn and Sako [10], pp. 523–540. https://doi.org/10.1007/978-3-662-58387-6_28

9. Mealy, G.H.: A method for synthesizing sequential circuits. The Bell Syst. Tech. J. 34(5), 1045–1079 (1955)

10. Meiklejohn, S., Sako, K. (eds.): FC 2018. LNCS, vol. 10957. Springer, Heidelberg (2018). https://doi.org/10.1007/978-3-662-58387-6

11. Melkonian, O., Swierstra, W., Chakravarty, M.M.: Formal investigation of the Extended UTxO model (Extended Abstract) (2019). https://omelkonian.github.io/data/publications/formal-utxo.pdf

12. Möser, M., Eyal, I., Gün Sirer, E.: Bitcoin covenants. In: Clark, J., Meiklejohn, S., Ryan, P.Y.A., Wallach, D., Brenner, M., Rohloff, K. (eds.) FC 2016. LNCS, vol. 9604, pp. 126–141. Springer, Heidelberg (2016). https://doi.org/10.1007/978-3-662-53357-4_9

13. Nanevski, A., Ley-Wild, R., Sergey, I., Delbianco, G.A.: Communicating state transition systems for fine-grained concurrent resources. In: Shao, Z. (ed.) ESOP 2014. LNCS, vol. 8410, pp. 290–310. Springer, Heidelberg (2014). https://doi.org/10.1007/978-3-642-54833-8_16

14. Sangiorgi, D.: Introduction to Bisimulation and Coinduction. Cambridge University Press, Cambridge (2012)

15. Lamela Seijas, P., Thompson, S.: Marlowe: financial contracts on blockchain. In: Margaria, T., Steffen, B. (eds.) ISoLA 2018. LNCS, vol. 11247, pp. 356–375. Springer, Cham (2018). https://doi.org/10.1007/978-3-030-03427-6_27

16. Sergey, I., Nagaraj, V., Johannsen, J., Kumar, A., Trunov, A., Hao, K.C.G.: Safer smart contract programming with Scilla. In: Proceedings of the ACM on Programming Languages 3(OOPSLA) (2019). Article No: 185

17. Zahnentferner, J.: An abstract model of UTxO-based cryptocurrencies with scripts. IACR Cryptology ePrint Archive 2018, p. 469 (2018). https://eprint.iacr.org/2018/469

Privacy-Preserving Cross-Chain Atomic Swaps

Apoorvaa Deshpande$^{(\boxtimes)}$ and Maurice Herlihy

Brown University, Providence, USA
{acdeshpa,maurice}@cs.brown.edu

Abstract. Recently, there has been a lot of interest in studying the transfer of assets across different blockchains in the form of *cross-chain atomic swaps*. Unfortunately, the current candidates of atomic swaps (hash-lock time contracts) offer no privacy; the identities as well as the exact trade that happened between any two parties is publicly visible.

In this work, we explore the different notions of privacy that we can hope for in an atomic swap protocol. Concretely, we define an atomic swap as a two-party protocol and formalize the different notions of privacy in the form of *anonymity*, *confidentiality* and *indistinguishability* of swap transactions.

As a building block, we abstract out the primitive of *Atomic Release of Secrets* (ARS) which captures atomic exchange of a secret for a predecided transaction. We then show how ARS can be used to build privacy-preserving cross-chain swaps.

We also show that the recently introduced notion of *adapter signatures* [Poe18, War17] is a concrete instantiation of ARS under the framework of Schnorr signatures [Sch91] and thus, construct a private cross-chain swap using Schnorr signatures.

1 Introduction

A key attraction of distributed ledgers is that they can replace a trusted party or an escrow service, for parties wishing to transact. Assets can be held and transferred according to programmable logic that the network evaluates a.k.a through a *smart contract*. A natural scenario to consider is the transfer of assets across different blockchains. Such a transfer is often referred to as an *cross-chain atomic swap*. Unfortunately, such a protocol offers no privacy; the identities as well as the exact trade that happened between any two parties is publicly visible. In this work, we explore the different notions of privacy that we can hope for in an atomic swap protocol. We might want to hide the identities of the parties involved in the swap so that we have an *anonymous* swap, we may want to hide the amounts transferred as part of the swap so that we have *confidential transactions* in a swap. We may also want to hide the fact that an atomic swap ever happened. These different notions of privacy may not be comparable and maybe specific to individual chains that are part of the swap, and in fact the different notions may have some trade-offs as we soon elaborate.

© Springer Nature Switzerland AG 2020
M. Bernhard et al. (Eds.): FC 2020 Workshops, LNCS 12063, pp. 540–549, 2020.
https://doi.org/10.1007/978-3-030-54455-3_38

Suppose that Alice and Bob want to engage in an atomic cross-chain swap as follows: Alice is willing to trade her 5 ether for Bob's 2 BTC. Typically, they can proceed to do such an atomic swap through a hash-lock time contract (HTLC) [PD16]. An HTLC is a contract with a hash value y associated with it, and on input a value s such that $H(s) = y$, the contract is executed and the specified amount gets transferred as per the contract. HTLC also has a time-out T associated such that if a valid s is not produced until time T then the amount is refunded to the party that initiates the contract.

The atomic swap protocol comprises of the following steps: First, Alice chooses a secret s and publishes on the Bitcoin blockchain an HTLC with $y = H(s)$ paying Bob 2 BTC, and with time-out T_B. After confirming that this contract satisfies pre-decided conditions, Bob publishes on the Ethereum blockchain an HTLC with the same y paying Alice 5 ether with timelock $T_A = T_B - \Delta$. Bob chooses Δ such that it leaves enough time for Bob to claim 2 BTC after Alice has claimed her ether amount. If the contract looks correct, Alice claims 5 ether and in the process reveals s. Bob can then claim the 2 BTC using the same s.

Unfortunately, such a protocol offers no privacy; the identities as well as the exact trade that happened between any two parties is publicly visible. In this work, we explore the different notions of privacy that we can hope for in an atomic swap protocol. We might want to hide the identities of the parties involved in the swap so that we have an *anonymous* swap, we may want to hide the amounts transferred as part of the swap so that we have *confidential transactions* in a swap. We may also want to hide the fact that an atomic swap ever happened. These different notions of privacy may not be comparable and maybe specific to individual chains that are part of the swap, and in fact the different notions may have some trade-offs as we soon elaborate.

1.1 Our Contributions

In this work, we initiate the study of privacy in cross-chain swaps. Concretely, our contributions are as follows:

- Formalizing Privacy in Cross-Chain Atomic Swaps. We define an atomic swap as a two-party protocol and formalize the different notions of privacy in the form of *anonymity*, *confidentiality* and *indistinguishability* of swap transactions.
- Private Swaps from Atomic Release of Secrets. We abstract out the primitive of *Atomic Release of Secrets* (ARS) which captures atomic exchange of a secret for a pre-decided transaction. We then show how ARS can be used to build privacy-preserving cross-chain swaps.
- Instantiating Atomic Release of Secrets. We show that the recently introduced notion of *adapter signatures* [Poe18, War17] is a concrete instantiation of ARS under the framework of Schnorr signatures [Sch91]. This in turn enables a private cross-chain swap using Schnorr signatures.

1.2   Related Work

Poon and Dryja [PD16] gave the first atomic swap protocol in the form of an HTLC contracts, several works [Nol13, BCD+14] have extended that protocol. Herlihy [Her18] formalized the notion of cross-chain atomic swaps for the first time, and generalized the definition to a swap across multiple parties. Cross-chain swap for some specific cases has been studied, for example Bitcoin and Ethereum [Pre18].

There has been a lot of work around ensuring fairness in atomic swaps [DEF, HLY19]. These works focus on appropriate punishments to the misbehaving party, whereas the guarantees that we want in a two-party swap are that either both assets are transferred or none of them are.

There has been extensive work on how different chains can communicate with each other [Kwo15, HHK18, Tho15]. Though privacy has been extensively studied in context of individual blockchains [SCG+14, NM+16, GM17, Max15], there has been no formal study of privacy in the context of cross-chain swaps.

1.3   A Simple Privacy-Preserving Atomic Cross-Chain Swap

As a starting point, we describe a protocol for an atomic cross-chain swap with the following privacy guarantee: It is impossible to link transactions across two chains that are part of an atomic swap. Moreover, the transactions on both the chains are indistinguishable from regular transactions on that chain.

Note that in the HTLC-based contract described above, the same hash value y is associated with both the contracts and hence, the transactions on both the chains are easily identifiable as being part of one atomic swap. We use a similar framework as above for our protocol, but instead of using the same value y, we use two different values y_A, y_B such that $z = y_A - y_B$ is computable only by Alice, Bob, and for any other observer the values y_A, y_B are unlinkable.

We assume public-key infrastructure (PKI); When Alice and Bob decide (off-chain) to execute an atomic swap, they can find each other's public key $\mathsf{pk}_A, \mathsf{pk}_B$. Alice and Bob can use the PKI to then execute a key-exchange protocol such as Diffie-Hellman key-exchange [DH76], to agree on a shared key.

We also assume that Alice and Bob agree on a (possibly pseudorandom) value $z \in \mathbb{Z}_p^*$ which could be a time-stamp of their off-chain communication or some function of key-exchange value of their public-keys (For instance, z can be a function of g^{ab} which is the value of Diffie-Hellman key-exchange between Alice and Bob). Note that this z is computable or known to only Alice and Bob.

The protocol is as follows:

1. Alice chooses a secret s_A and publishes on the Bitcoin blockchain an HTLC with $Y_A = g^{s_A}$ paying Bob 2 BTC, and with time-out T_B. Note that the hash function we are using here is modular exponentiation $H(s_A) = g^{s_A}$.
2. After confirming that this contract satisfies predecided conditions, Bob publishes on the Ethereum blockchain an HTLC with $y_B = y_A \cdot g^z = g^{s_A+z}$ paying Alice 5 ether with timelock $T_A = T_B - \Delta$.

3. If the contract looks correct, Alice computes $s_B = s_A + z$. She then claims 5 ether from Bob's contract, and in the process reveals s_B.
4. Bob can then claim the 2 BTC from Alice's contract using $s_A = s_B - z$.

Since z is computable or known only to Alice and Bob, the values s_A, s_B are unlinkable to any other observer, thus the transactions on either of the chains are indistinguishable from regular transactions.

2   Formalizing Privacy in Atomic Swaps

We will now formally define a private atomic swap protocol over two independent ledgers each with certain privacy properties. The underlying ledger will be captured through an abstract primitive of a *Transaction* over a distributed ledger.

Let coin be the native currency of the underlying ledger L. Let $\mathsf{tx}(A, B, x, L)$ denote a transaction that transfers x coins from A to B. A transaction tx should satisfy the following properties:

- *Correctness*: A tx is a proof of transfer of assets on the ledger, namely unconditional transfer of x coins from A to B on L.
- *Transaction Non-malleability.* This property requires that no bounded adversary can alter any of the data or any of the transactions published so far.
- *Balance.* This property requires that no bounded adversary can own more money than what he minted or received via payments from others.

A transaction may additionally satisfy following properties:

- *Confidentiality*: A transaction tx hides the amount of assets being transferred that is, two transactions between A and B for two different amounts look indistinguishable, denoted by $\approx$. More formally, for any two amounts x_0, x_1,

$$\mathsf{tx}(A, B, x_0, L) \approx \mathsf{tx}(A, B, x_1, L)$$

- *Anonymity*: A transaction tx hides the identities of the parties involved in it. More formally, for any two pairs of identities $(A_0, B_0), (A_1, B_1)$,

$$\mathsf{tx}(A_0, B_0, x, L) \approx \mathsf{tx}(A_1, B_1, x, L)$$

2.1   Private Atomic Swap Protocol

We will now formalize a private atomic swap protocol PAS over two ledgers L_1, L_2 with native currencies $\mathsf{coin}_1, \mathsf{coin}_2$ respectively. Assume that the swap takes place between parties Alice(A) and Bob(B), where Alice is willing to trade z_1 coin_1 with z_2 coin_2 of Bob. Such a protocol will be denoted by $\mathsf{PAS}(A, B, z_1, z_2, L_1, L_2)$. In more detail,

$$\mathsf{PAS}(A, B, z_1, z_2, L_1, L_2) \equiv \langle \mathsf{tx}_1(A, B, z_1, L_1), \mathsf{tx}_2(B, A, z_2, L_2) \rangle$$

where PAS can be characterized as a pair of transactions over L_1 and L_2 such that A transfers z_1 coin$_1$ to Bob ($\mathsf{tx}_1(A, B, z_1, L_1)$) and B transfers z_2 coin$_2$ to Alice ($\mathsf{tx}_2(B, A, z_2, L_2)$).

Informally the different properties that we want from an atomic swap protocol are as follows:

- *Correctness.* If both Alice and Bob follow the steps of the protocol correctly, then swap takes place with Alice receiving z_1 coin$_1$ and Bob receiving z_2 coin$_2$.
- *Soundness.* If either of the parties deviate from the protocol, the honest party does not end up worse off. More concretely, either both $\mathsf{tx}_1(A, B, z_1, L_1)$, $\mathsf{tx}_2(B, A, z_2, L_2)$ take place or neither.
- *Privacy (Indistinguishability of Swap Transactions).* The transactions that are part of the PAS protocol that is, $\mathsf{tx}_1, \mathsf{tx}_2$ should be indistinguishable to regular transactions on both the ledgers of L_1, L_2.
  We can decouple the privacy of the entire PAS protocol, and require *indistinguishability of swap transactions* to hold for either of the ledgers individually.
- *Confidential Swap.* Protocol PAS hides the amounts exchanged in the swap transaction.
- *Anonymous Swap.* Protocol PAS hides the identities of the parties involved in the swap transaction.

Note that the indistinguishability property for any ledger will also depend on the confidentiality and anonymity properties of that ledger. For example, all the amounts in a Bitcoin transaction are in clear, and Bitcoin does not offer any confidentiality. Hence, if an atomic swap protocol involves the Bitcoin chain and it satisfies indistinguishability of transactions with respect to Bitcoin, then the swap protocol cannot satisfy confidentiality of transactions.

Lemma 1. *Let PAS be a private atomic swap protocol over two ledgers L_1, L_2. PAS satisfies both* indistinguishability of transactions *and* confidentiality *if and only if the transactions in that ledger satisfy confidentiality.*

Lemma 2. *Let PAS be a private atomic swap protocol over two ledgers L_1, L_2. PAS satisfies both* indistinguishability of transactions *and* anonymity *if and only if the transactions in that ledger satisfy anonymity.*

Let us now formalize these privacy notions.

Privacy (Indistinguishability of Swap Transactions). Let $\mathsf{PAS}(A, B, z_1, z_2, L_1, L_2) \equiv \langle \mathsf{tx}_1(A, B, z_1, L_1), \mathsf{tx}_2(B, A, z_2, L_2) \rangle$ be the atomic swap protocol between parties Alice(A) and Bob(B), where Alice is willing to trade z_1 coin$_1$ with z_2 coin$_2$ of Bob. For both ledgers L_1, L_2 we require that for any A', B', z_1', z_2',

$$\mathsf{tx}(A, B, z_1, L_1) \approx \mathsf{tx}(A', B', z_1', L_1) \text{ and } \mathsf{tx}(B, A, z_2, L_2) \approx \mathsf{tx}(B', A', z_2', L_2)$$

Recall that $\mathsf{tx}(A', B', z_1', L_1)$ and $\mathsf{tx}(B', A', z_2', L_2)$ are transactions on L_1 and L_2 respectively.

Confidential Swap. Let $\langle \mathsf{tx}_1(A, B, z_1, L_1), \mathsf{tx}_2(B, A, z_2, L_2) \rangle$ be part of the $\mathsf{PAS}(A, B, z_1, z_2, L_1, L_2)$ protocol, and let $\langle \mathsf{tx}_1(A, B, z_1', L_1), \mathsf{tx}_2(B, A, z_2', L_2) \rangle$ be part of the $\mathsf{PAS}(A, B, z_1', z_2', L_1, L_2)$ protocol. For any A, B and for any amounts z_1, z_2, z_1', z_2', the following holds:

$$\langle \mathsf{tx}_1(A, B, z_1, L_1), \mathsf{tx}_2(B, A, z_2, L_2) \rangle \approx \langle \mathsf{tx}_1(A, B, z_1', L_1), \mathsf{tx}_2(B, A, z_2', L_2) \rangle$$

Anonymous Swap. Let $\langle \mathsf{tx}_1(A, B, z_1, L_1), \mathsf{tx}_2(B, A, z_2, L_2) \rangle$ be part of the $\mathsf{PAS}(A, B, z_1, z_2, L_1, L_2)$ protocol, and let $\langle \mathsf{tx}_1(A', B', z_1, L_1), \mathsf{tx}_2(B', A', z_2, L_2) \rangle$ be part of the $\mathsf{PAS}(A', B', z_1, z_2, L_1, L_2)$ protocol. For any z_1, z_2 and for any participants $A, B A', B'$, the following holds:

$$\langle \mathsf{tx}_1(A, B, z_1, L_1), \mathsf{tx}_2(B, A, z_2, L_2) \rangle \approx \langle \mathsf{tx}_1(A', B', z_1, L_1), \mathsf{tx}_2(B', A', z_2, L_2) \rangle$$

3   Atomic Release of Secrets

We now define the new primitive of *Atomic Release of Secrets* (ARS) which is a two-party protocol that enables a *conditional exchange* between two entities without a trusted intermediary. The setting is as follows: Alice and Bob agree on a transaction tx that pays Alice some predecided amount z on a ledger L $(\mathsf{tx}(A, B, z, L))$. For example, suppose Bob agrees to pay Alice some Bitcoins for a rare audio recording that Alice has. The guarantee of an ARS protocol is that tx will be published on L if and only if Bob learns Alice's secret s. In the previous example, tx will be published on the Bitcoin blockchain if and only if Bob gets the audio file (or learns a link address that gives him access to the file). Such a primitive can be directly useful in realizing cross-chain atomic swaps as we elaborate later in the section.

3.1   Definition: Atomic Release of Secrets

Let Alice, Bob be two entities that agree on a transaction tx and let s be Alice's secret. Let com be a homomorphic commitment scheme. Let $\mathsf{ARS}(B, A, z, \mathsf{com}(s))$ denote an ARS protocol between Alice and Bob for $\mathsf{tx}(B, A, z, L)$ and secret s. Such a protocol is a valid ARS protocol if the following property holds:

Atomic Release: The transaction tx is published if and only if Bob learns Alice's secret s.

In other words, if Alice and Bob engage in an ARS protocol then it is not possible that tx is published and Bob does not learn s or vice versa. It also means that knowledge of secret s gives the power to publish the tx.

Privacy of ARS: The transaction tx is indistinguishable from a regular transaction on the ledger. In particular, there is no way to tell if any tx was part of an ARS protocol or not.

Theorem 1 (Informal). *Protocols* $\mathsf{ARS}(B, A, z, \mathsf{com}(s))$ *and* $\mathsf{PAS}(A, B, z_1, z_2, L_1, L_2)$ *are equivalent; One can implement either from the other.*

Proof Sketch.

Claim. $\mathsf{ARS}(A, B, z, \mathsf{com}(s))$ implies $\mathsf{PAS}(A, B, z_1, z_2, L_1, L_2)$

Let $\mathsf{PAS}(A, B, z_1, z_2, L_1, L_2) = \langle \mathsf{tx}_1(A, B, z_1), \mathsf{tx}_2(B, A, z_2) \rangle$ be the the private swap protocol that we want to execute. Bob chooses a secret s and initiates an ARS protocol as $\mathsf{ARS}(A, B, z_1, \mathsf{com}(s))$. Bob then sends $\mathsf{com}(s)$ to Alice through a private channel. Alice homomorphically computes $\mathsf{com}(s')$ for a secret invertible function $f(s) = s'$ of her choosing. She then initiates $\mathsf{ARS}(B, A, z_2, \mathsf{com}(s'))$. If Bob publishes tx_1 then by the property of the ARS, Alice learns s and correspondingly $s' = f(s)$ as well thereby publishing tx_2 atomically. Correctness, soundness and privacy of the PAS follow from the properties of the underlying ARS and the homomorphic commitments.

Claim. $\mathsf{PAS}(A, B, z_1, z_2, L_1, L_2)$ implies $\mathsf{ARS}(A, B, z, \mathsf{com}(s))$

Alice chooses secret s and sends $\mathsf{com}(s)$ to Bob. If Bob later learns secret s from Alice, he executes $\mathsf{PAS}(A, B, z_1, z_2, L_1, L_2)$.

3.2 Instantiation: Atomic Release of Secrets

We now describe an instantiation of ARS in the form of *Adapter Signatures*. These are based on the classic construction of Schnorr signatures.

Schnorr Signatures. We first recall Schnorr Signatures [Sch91]. Let $\mathbb{G}$ be a group of prime order q with generator g and let $H : \{0, 1\}^{\mathsf{poly}(k)} \to \{0, 1\}^k$ be any collision-resistant hash function.

Key Generation $(s, g^s) \leftarrow \mathsf{KeyGen}(1^k)$. The key generation algorithm takes in the security parameter, and outputs secret key sk chosen uniformly as $s \leftarrow \mathbb{Z}_q^*$ and public key pk as g^s.

Signing $(R, \sigma) \leftarrow \mathsf{Com}(\mathsf{sk}, \mathsf{msg})$. The signing algorithm takes as input secret key sk and the message msg and outputs signature $\mathsf{sig} = (R, \sigma)$ computed as follows:
  – Choose $r \leftarrow \mathbb{Z}_q^*$ and $R = g^r$.
  – Compute $\sigma = r + H(pk \mid R \mid \mathsf{msg}) \cdot s$

Verification $0/1 \leftarrow \mathsf{Verify}(\mathsf{pk}, \mathsf{sig}, \mathsf{msg})$. The verification algorithm takes as input the public key pk, message msg and the signature sig and checks if

$$g^\sigma = R \cdot \mathsf{pk}^{H(pk \mid R \mid \mathsf{msg})}$$

Schnorr signatures are the primary tool for checking validity of transactions on Bitcoin as well as on most other blockchains. If Alice wants to transfer money to Bob, she needs to sign that transaction with her secret key. Anyone can then verify the signature confirming that Alice is the rightful owner of the account from which she is transferring money. If the signature verifies, then the transaction will be published on the blockchain.

3.3   Adapter Signatures

At a high level, an adaptor signature is a partial signature with a secret associated with it. It is a commitment such that if a predecided signature is published then the underlying secret of the adaptor signature can be derived. An adaptor signature functions as a kind of "promise" that a signature you agree to publish will reveal a secret. Such a signature can in turn be used for multiple applications such as atomic swaps as we elaborate later.

In more detail, an adapter signature is a protocol between two parties Alice and Bob that works as follows:

- Alice chooses $r, t \leftarrow \mathbb{Z}_q^*$ and sends $R = g^r, T = g^t$ to Bob.
- Bob computes the challenge $c = H(B \mid R + T \mid \mathsf{msg})$ and sends $c \cdot b$ to Alice, where (B, b) is the public-private key pair for Bob ($\mathsf{pk}_B, \mathsf{sk}_B$) and msg is any message that Alice and Bob want to sign jointly.
- Alice can now compute the adapter signature $\sigma_{\mathsf{adapt}} = c \cdot b + r$ and send it to Bob.
- Note that σ_{adapt} is not a valid signature, but Bob can still verify the correctness of the adapter signature by checking:

$$g^{\sigma_{\mathsf{adapt}}} = R \cdot \mathsf{pk}_B^{H(pk_B \mid R+T \mid \mathsf{msg})}$$

Alice now publishes a valid signature $\sigma = r + t + c \cdot b$ as part of a transaction published on the blockchain, and this signature can be verified by anyone. Once Bob sees this, Bob can derive the secret t as $\sigma - \sigma_{\mathsf{adapt}}$.

Theorem 2 (Informal). *The adapter signature protocol described above implies an* ARS *protocol for Alice and Bob.*

Proof Sketch. Alice and Bob agree on a desired transaction transferring assets from Bob to Alice and on secret t. This transaction needs a valid signature from Bob to be accepted by the blockchain. The adapter signature protocol guarantees that the signature is published if and only if Bob learns the secret t. Also the signature generated is a valid Schnorr signature, indistinguishable from any other signature, which ensures privacy of the corresponding ARS protocol.

3.4   Atomic Cross-Chain Swap Using Adapter Signatures

We proved that adapter signatures directly give an ARS protocol for two parties Alice and Bob. We also proved that if there exists an ARS protocol and homomorphic commitments, then Alice and Bob can engage in a private cross-chain swap. Note that the signature itself acts as a homomorphic commitment in this case.

We now describe a concrete protocol for completeness. Recall that Alice is willing to trade z_1 coin_1 with z_2 coin_2 of Bob. The corresponding transactions are $\mathsf{tx}_1(A, B, z_1, L_1)$ and $\mathsf{tx}_2(B, A, z_2, L_2)$ respectively. The protocol will be as follows:

- Alice and Bob generate ephemeral (Schnorr) verification keys $\mathsf{pk}_A^1, \mathsf{pk}_A^2$ and $\mathsf{pk}_B^1, \mathsf{pk}_B^2$. Note that these are generated by choosing $s \leftarrow \mathbb{Z}_q^*$ and $\mathsf{pk} = g^s$. Thus, Alice knows a_1, a_2, whereas Bob knows b_1, b_2.
  The key for tx_1 is assigned as $\mathsf{pk}_A^1 + \mathsf{pk}_B^1$ and the key for tx_2 is assigned as $\mathsf{pk}_A^2 + \mathsf{pk}_B^2$. In other words, we set up two 2-out-of-2 multi-signature transactions.
- Alice chooses $t, r_1, r_2 \leftarrow \mathbb{Z}_q^*$. Let c_1, c_2 be the challenge for the two signatures corresponding to $\mathsf{tx}_1, \mathsf{tx}_2$ respectively. Alice sends $R_1 = g^{r_1}, R_2 = g^{r_2}, T = g^t$ and $c_1 \cdot a_1$ and $c_2 \cdot a_2$ to Bob.
- Bob adds his part of the keys to generate $c_1 \cdot (a_1 + b_1)$ and $c_2 \cdot (a_2 + b_2)$. Note that Bob can compute the challenges c_1, c_2 on his own.
- Alice creates two adapter signatures $\sigma_{\mathsf{adapt}}^1 = r_1 + c_1 \cdot (a_1 + b_1)$ and $\sigma_{\mathsf{adapt}}^2 = r_2 + c_2 \cdot (a_2 + b_2)$ and sends to Bob. Bob can verify both of these with respect to R_1, R_2 that Alice sent before.
- Finally, when Alice publishes tx_2 using $\sigma_2 = \sigma_{\mathsf{adapt}}^2 + t$, that atomically reveals t to Bob and thus enabling him to publish $\sigma_1 = \sigma_{\mathsf{adapt}}^1 + t$ and in turn, publishing tx_1.

4   Conclusion

In this work, we initiate the study of privacy in cross-chain atomic swaps. We formalize the different notions of privacy that we can expect from a cross-chain swap and we show the different trade-offs between these notions. In particular, we show how these notions of privacy depend heavily on the privacy of the underlying chains. We also give a concrete instantiation of a private swap protocol.

While we look at two-party swaps as a starting point, the next step is to study privacy of swaps across multiple chains. It may also be worthwhile to look at specific blockchains and study the exact privacy properties achievable for cross-chain swaps involving those chains.

References

[BCD+14] Back, A., et al.: Enabling blockchain innovations with pegged sidechains, p. 72 (2014). http://www.opensciencereview.com/papers/123/enablingblockchain-innovations-with-pegged-sidechains

[DEF]   Dziembowski, S., Eckey, L., Faust, S.: FairSwap: how to fairly exchange digital goods. In: Proceedings of the 2018 ACM SIGSAC Conference on Computer and Communications Security, CCS 2018, pp. 967–984 (2018)

[DH76]   Diffie, W., Hellman, M.: New directions in cryptography. IEEE Trans. Inf. Theory **22**(6), 644–654 (1976)

[GM17]   Green, M., Miers, I.: Bolt: anonymous payment channels for decentralized currencies. In: Proceedings of the 2017 ACM SIGSAC Conference on Computer and Communications Security, pp. 473–489. ACM (2017)

[Her18] Herlihy, M.: Atomic cross-chain swaps. In: Proceedings of the 2018 ACM Symposium on Principles of Distributed Computing, pp. 245–254. ACM (2018)

[HHK18] Hosp, J., Hoenisch, T., Kittiwongsunthorn, P.: COMIT - cryptographically-
         secure off-chain multi-asset instant transaction network. CoRR (2018)
[HLY19] Han, R., Lin, H., Yu, J.: On the optionality and fairness of atomic swaps.
         In: Proceedings of the 1st ACM Conference on Advances in Financial Tech-
         nologies, pp. 62–75. ACM (2019)
[Kwo15] Buchman, E., Kwon, J.: Cosmos: a network of distributed ledgers (2015).
         https://github.com/cosmos/cosmos/blob/master/WHITEPAPER.md
[Max15] Maxwell, G.: Confidential transactions (2015). https://people.xiph.org/
         ~greg/confidential_values.txt
[NM+16] Noether, S., Mackenzie, A., et al.: Ring confidential transactions. Ledger **1**,
         1–18 (2016)
[Nol13] Nolan, T.: Alt chains and atomic transfers (2013). https://bitcointalk.org/
         index.php?topic=193281.msg2224949#msg2224949
[PD16]   Poon, J., Dryja, T.: The bitcoin lightning network: scalable off-chain instant
         payments (2016)
[Poe18] Poelstra, A.: Mimblewimble and scriptless scripts, Real World Crypto
         (2018). https://www.youtube.com/watch?v=ovCBT1gyk9c&t=0s
[Pre18] Prestwich, J.: Non-atomic swaps, Bitcoin Expo (2018). https://www.
         youtube.com/watch?v=njGSFAOz7F8&feature=emb_logo
[SCG+14] Sasson, E.B., et al.: Zerocash: decentralized anonymous payments from
         bitcoin. In: 2014 IEEE Symposium on Security and Privacy, pp. 459–474.
         IEEE (2014)
[Sch91] Schnorr, C.P.: Efficient signature generation by smart cards. J. Cryptol.
         4(3), 161–174 (1991). https://doi.org/10.1007/BF00196725
[Tho15] Schwartz, E., Thomas, S.: A protocol for interledger payments (2015).
         https://interledger.org/interledger.pdf
[War17] Warwing: Flipping the scriptless script on Schnorr (2017). https://
         joinmarket.me/blog/blog/flipping-the-scriptless-script-on-schnorr/

A Blockchain Based Approach to Resource Sharing in Smart Neighbourhoods

Kumaramangalam Muni Venkateswarlu$^{(\boxtimes)}$, Sepideh Avizheh,
and Reihaneh Safavi-Naini

University of Calgary, Calgary, Canada
{munivenkateswarlu.ku,sepideh.avizheh1,rei}@ucalgary.ca

Abstract. Sharing resources is a growing trend in today's world. Sharing allows larger groups of individuals to benefit from available resources, hence optimizing the resource consumption. Sharing however demands a level of trust and control on the outcome: one needs to have confidence that a shared item will be used according to a prior agreement. In this paper we rely on geographic proximity of users to provide as an initial level of trust, and use this trust to develop a platform for sharing digital goods in a geographic neighbourhood. We require the platform to allow users to express their preferences and be confident about the sharing outcome. Our proposed platform uses a permissioned blockchain that is maintained by network providers whose subscribers are in the same geographic area, and use attribute-based access control to specify and control accesses to the shared items. Our proposed system uses smart contracts to enforce the conditions of access. We analyze security of the proposed design and discuss directions for future work.

Keywords: Access control · Permissioned blockchain · Resource sharing

1 Introduction

As sharing economy grows [9,16,23] more users are willing to share their resources and being compensated for a reward, or simply acknowledged for being a good citizen. Sharing requires some level of trust so that the owner of the resource has confidence about the outcome. Sharing services Uber [22] and Airbnb [1] are examples of sharing for reward, and rely on a trusted intermediary to ensure that the sharing conditions are enforced. There are also community sharing [11] that find ways of sharing things from clothing to hardware to digital goods, and advocate for a cultural shift toward widespread sharing. These systems offer different levels of support for users expressing their preferences, and rely on intermediaries to achieve the required guarantees.

We consider a neighborhood that consists of a set of residential units in close geographic proximity, and use this proximity as an initial basis for trust and

© Springer Nature Switzerland AG 2020
M. Bernhard et al. (Eds.): FC 2020 Workshops, LNCS 12063, pp. 550–567, 2020.
https://doi.org/10.1007/978-3-030-54455-3_39

convenience for sharing. In support of our approach we refer to [14] that states "Collocation facilitates trust formation, largely because of greater opportunity of face-to-face [7,12]". Authors also noted that, "Storper and Venables [19] argue that the type of interaction enabled by physical proximity requires that the actors invest time and effort in personal relationships and this form of exchange renders greater understanding and human closeness."

We assume each residential unit uses an Internet Service Provider (ISP) to connect to the Internet using what we call an *EdgeHub*, a smart Hub that can support smart services. The EdgeHub can also act as a first point of network connectivity for smart devices in the home. Our goal is to build on this initial trust that is engendered by being in the same neighbourhood, and provide a platform to allow home users to share their items with confidence that their personal preferences (policies) are respected.

The sharing problem above can be easily solved if there is a trusted authority (TA) that acts as the intermediary in all sharing interactions; that is:

- Alice with resource R can specify a policy p (conditions of access) for accessing R, digitally sign (R, p) and send it to the TA.
- The TA will verify if Alice is in possession of R, and if verified, will publish (R, p). Verification can be performed by Alice by providing sufficient evidence, or making a deposit that will be taken away if her claim is found to be false.
- Users in the neighborhood can see published items. Bob who is interested in the item will contact the TA with his credentials.
- TA verifies Bob's credentials and if it satisfies the policy, grants access to the resource (e.g. by notifying Alice of Bob's interest and establishing a link between them).

This is a fully centralized system with the following drawbacks:

(i) TA will be responsible for verifying credentials of users, quality of items, as well as evaluating policies and must be capable and trusted for doing all these. These multiple roles and responsibilities could at times become conflicting;

(ii) TA requires significant processing and management, and the ability to handle many requests simultaneously;

(iii) TA will become a single point of failure for the system and target for various denial of service attacks.

To avoid the above shortcomings, we consider a blockchain-based architecture that replaces the trusted authority with a decentralized system of computing nodes. The users in this architecture are represented by smart homes that they reside in.

Smart Homes. Smart homes are one of the fastest growing areas of Internet of Things (IoT) with many providers such as Apple Home [3], Samsung Smart-Things [18] and Amazon AWS (Amazon Web Services) [2]. Smart homes use a *Hub* as a first point of connecting smart devices in the home to the Internet. Existing smart homes are cloud-based: the main intelligence and processing is in cloud and the Hub primarily provides the networking interface for the devices. In [4] and [6], the cloud-based architecture of smart homes was analyzed and a wide range of attacks on security and resiliency of smart homes were identified. Authors suggested to expand the Hub with sufficient computing power to act as an edge computing node to perform basic computational tasks. Inspired by this proposal, we assume the smart home is equipped with a smart Hub that we call *EdgeHub*. For simplicity, we assume each EdgeHub is associated with a single network subscriber, and we use the two terms interchangeably. A set of smart homes in a neighbouring geographic area form a *smart neighborhood*.

A Distributed Ledger (DL) System for Smart Neighborhood. We consider a permissioned blockchain, and refer to it as neighborhood blockchain or *N-chain*. We consider an N-chain that is established and managed by a set of ISPs with subscribers in the neighbourhood. Each ISP acts as a *consensus node* (*C-nodes*) that is responsible for verifying the identity of a requester (subscriber to the ISP), verifying (the signature of the signer) and validating (conditions that must be satisfied) received request. If the request passes verification and validation requirements, it will be submitted to other C-nodes for approval and publishing it on the N-chain. Establishing such an N-chain by ISPs will be an attractive proposition for ISPs, and can be further used as a platform for new paid services. Using ISPs for secure identity verification is well justified as ISPs have long-term relationship with EdgeHubs, and can implement secure identity verification mechanisms based on these relationships.

1.1   Our Contribution

We design a system that smart home users can use to share and manage their resources in a smart neighborhood, according to their preferences. The design uses a blockchain based distributed ledger system to present the users preferences (access policies), and evaluating and enforcing them in a distributed setting. We consider a permissioned blockchain setting that is managed and maintained by a set of C-nodes that aim to provide computing and storage space for smart home communities. We assume that the following external entities are available to provide trusted services:

- **Enrolment Service (EnS)** will provide certificate for the public key of an EdgeHub in the neighbourhood. We assume EdgeHubs generate their own public and private key pair. In practice, this service will be provided by the ISPs, that is, each ISP will be a certificate authority for its own subscribers.
- **Attribute Authority Service (AAS)** will verify and generate certificates for the attributes of the users and resources. Users will obtain certificates for their own attributes (e.g. age > 18) and their resources (e.g. a high definition video clip) from relevant authorities. The resource attributes can also be certified by its owner only. These certificates will form the basis of confidence that a requester indeed has the claimed properties. AAS can interact with a set of trusted authorities, each responsible for certifying one or more type of attributes.

The N-chain will be used to store, (i) information about resources (name of the resource, type and attributes of the resource, attributes of the resource owner (e.g. public key)), (ii) access control policies (e.g., resource α can be accessed by users with attribute β) that governs the access rules and conditions to the resources, and (iii) authenticated supplementary information (e.g. state of the resource, such as "occupied") for evaluation of the policies.

The N-chain will perform the following tasks: (i) advertising shareable resources (in the form of events), (ii) handling access requests from the interested users for a shared resource, (iii) evaluating access requests using the stored access policies, (iv) enforcing the access decision (e.g., informing Alice and Bob, and triggering offchain resource sharing by sending Alice's IP address to Bob) as well as (v) handling misbehavior and penalties in case of a detected misbehaviour (e.g., when Bob tries to access Alice's resource more than once, his access is blocked).

We use smart contracts to achieve distributed and trustworthy access request evaluation according to the defined policies. We develop the following smart contracts to implement the required functionalities: (i) *Registration Contract* (RC) holds addresses of other smart contracts and the functions that are associated to resources (each resource is identified by a unique identifier). It also provides functions to register a new resource and update or delete an existing resource. (ii) *Attribute Repository Contract* (ARC) stores attributes of shared resources or a user. (iii) *Access Control Contract* (ACC) stores access control policies and their evaluation procedures for the resources. The ACCs also provide functions for adding, updating, and deleting access control policies. (iv) *Adjudicator Contract* (ADJ) handles the defined misbehaviours according to the specified policy (e.g. imposes penalties if misbehaviour is detected).

Users interested in a shared resource will send a query to RC for the required ACC information such as ACC's address, its associated functions and their input requirements, and the resource availability. The user then invokes the corresponding ACC function, which will be executed and verified by the C-nodes, ensuring the security (safety) of the access control. For evaluating the access policy, ACC retrieves the required attributes of the resource, the resource provider and requester using their respective ARCs (addresses), and makes the access decision (e.g., grant or deny). ACC also performs the task of detecting misbehaviour, and provides the misbehaviour report to ADJ which enforces the specified (penalty) policy. In this work, we use *Attribute-based access control (ABAC)* model to describe allowed accesses. More details on the above smart contracts are given in Sect. 4, and in Sect. 4.2, the security and privacy of the system are analyzed. In Sect. 5, we consider the example scenario of sharing a movie and present a proof of concept implementation of the system using private Ethereum blockchain.

1.2   Related Work

The idea of using smart contract for access control has been proposed in [13,15, 24]. All these systems rely on permissionless blockchain (e.g. Ethereum) where proof-of-work is used to achieve consensus. In contrast, our proposal is based on permissioned blockchain and C-nodes work together to reach consensus. This will significantly increase the rate of transactions that can system handle and it is much greener compared to proof-of-work blockchain which requires significant energy consumption. Furthermore, a permissioned blockchain allows a level of access control on blockchain data and helps with privacy of users in the system.

The closest work among these compared to ours is [24] that uses a smart contract-based access control framework for IoT. There are, however, major differences between the two works; apart from using a permissioned blockchain, we use ABAC model to represent access control policies. The access control model in [24] is based on the basic access control matrix which is defined for subject-object pairs. We use ABAC to provide a fine-grained access control and ability to express a wide range of access conditions. Another difference to note is ADJ contract in our system, which has the same role as the judge contract in [13], but it follows different adjudication rules.

Organization of Paper. Next section introduces the preliminary definitions and concepts. Section 3 introduces our system model, configuration, and architecture. Section 4 presents the system design and its security analysis, and discusses privacy issues. Section 5 provides a proof of concept implementation, and Sect. 6 concludes the paper.

2   Preliminaries

EdgeHub is a hub that connects the smart home to the Internet, and provides the network connection point for smart devices. It connects the home to cloud and its services, and also to the neighbourhood to share and/or use a resource. EdgeHub can provide a range of functionalities including edge computing services that improves efficiency and timeliness of communication and enables smart home to perform basic functions, removing the total reliance on cloud. In this paper, we assume EdgeHub is a registered node in a permissioned blockchain network, N-chain, representing the smart home resources that are offered for sharing.

Blockchain and Smart Contracts. A blockchain is a decentralized, distributed, and often times public, trusted ledger that records transactions across the system in a sequential form. Transactions are stored in units of block which include hash of the previous blocks. C-Nodes, who use a consensus protocol (e.g., PBFT, RAFT) are responsible to agree on the order of blocks and maintain a consistent view in all nodes, so that any involved record cannot be altered retroactively, without the alteration of all subsequent blocks. Blockchains are of two types, permissionless and permissioned blockchains.

Permissioned Blockchain. In permissioned blockchains, data is stored according to an access policy that is written by the blockchain administrators. The policy determines the read and write accesses of users and parts of a transaction that will be observable to parties. The task of executing and verifying transactions is performed by a designated set of nodes (C-nodes in our design). An EdgeHub is a subscriber to an ISP that is a C-node, who can authenticate the subscriber, and together with other C-nodes, provide the task of verifying transactions and executing them. The entry C-node for EdgeHub provides an initial verification of the EdgeHub signature on the transaction, and if successful, signs and broadcasts to other C-nodes. This will trigger the consensus protocol, at the end of which the transactions will appear on the ledger while enforcing the access control policy of the blockchain.

Smart Contract. A smart contract [5] is a public piece of code that resides on the blockchain and specifies a protocol that is run on the underlying consensus computer that guarantees trusted execution, and handles the required transfer of coins if the blockchain is associated with its own coins. Smart contracts provide an attractive solution to achieve distributed and trustworthy operations for smart home networks. A smart contract is normally deployed in bytecode and uses Application Binary Interface (ABI) to represent its functions. A smart contract includes data and functions that can be invoked by the EdgeHub's transactions, or by other smart contracts though passing messages. A transaction is a package of data that is signed by an account and is aimed at an another account, or to execute the ABIs of a contract. A message is similar to a transaction, but is sent by a contract to another contract to run the ABIs of the contract.

Attribute Based Access Control Policy (ABAC). Controlling access to resources by authorized users will be provided by access control systems. Access control systems must provide expressibility for the policy designer and security and efficiency for enforcement. There have been many access control proposals including capability-based [8] and Role-Based Access Control (RBAC) [17] to provide the required efficiency and security. An access control system with growing significance and adoption is ABAC [10]. ABAC assigns attributes to subjects, objects, and environment. Attributes are in the form of key-value pairs. Attributes are used in defining policies which are written as boolean expressions, and specify the attributes of the subjects who can access an object with a given attribute set under the stated environmental conditions. We use ABAC to be able to write expressive access control policies that capture complex access conditions. In addition, ABAC supports designing a fine-grained access control policies that well match the dynamicity and flexibility of the smart home environment.

3   System Architecture and Assumptions

We consider a neighborhood of smart homes, each equipped with an EdgeHub as illustrated in Fig. 2. Each EdgeHub is connected to the Internet through an ISP (to access cloud services) who is also a C-node in the N-chain. To register in the system, the EdgeHub generates a private and public key pair, and obtains certificate for its public key from EnS. Each public key represents an EdgeHub in the system. Each EdgeHub acts as a node in the blockchain network running an instance of the blockchain software and communicate with the blockchain using transactions through its ISP.

The smart home owner (represented by EdgeHub) will write two smart contracts: (i) *Attribute Repository Contract* (ARC) and (ii) *Access Control Contract* (ACC), that will be deployed on the blockchain through EdgeHub. ARC is used to store the attribute values of both the users and the resources, and ACC to present access policies on the resources. The attributes, including user attributes (e.g., *age* > 18) and resource attributes (e.g., *movieType* = *Cartoon*), that will be stored on the blockchain must first be certified by the AAS. AAS verifies the information (using external trusted parties if required) and supplies the certificates to the user. The user then stores his attributes and certificates on the blockchain in the form of ARC contracts. The interactions with the trusted services, EnS and AAS, are illustrated in Fig. 1.

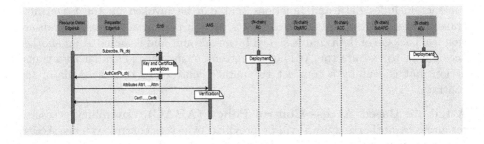

Fig. 1. Registration process

We refer (i) to the resources that can be shared by users as *Objects*, and (ii) to the users who seek the access to the resources as *Subjects*. Also, we refer to the smart contracts storing attributes of an object and a subject as ObjARC and SubARC respectively. We assume that the user uses only one ObjARC to store all the attributes of multiple resources that he wants to share. Also, we consider each certificate has a life-time and is verified by C-nodes when an access request is evaluated. If the certificates are expired, C-nodes do not proceed with the evaluation and deny further access requests to the resources.

A user who wishes to share their resources and has published ObjARC, use one ACC to publish all access control policies for different shareable resources.

The blockchain administrators (C-nodes) develop and publish two smart contracts: *Register Contract* (RC) and *Adjudicator Contract* (ADJ). RC contract maintains the list of shared resources in the system. The users use RC to register and manage their shared resources and also information to access the resources. The resource information stored on RC can be updated (or deleted) only by the respective resource owner. ADJ contract handles misbehaviour and enforces the misbehaviour policy, if it is detected. The ACC sends to ADJ the records of

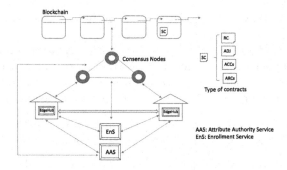

Fig. 2. Different entities in the proposed infrastructure

the misbehaving subject, that will be verified by ADJ and appropriate punitive steps (e.g., slash the deposit of the subject) will be taken. The smart contracts functions are discussed in details in Sect. 4. The process of invoking smart contracts functions by the resource owner to store attributes and associated access conditions is presented in Fig. 3.

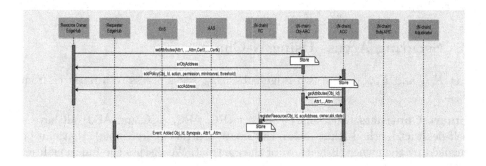

Fig. 3. Invoking smart contracts functions

3.1 Security Goals and Trust Assumptions

We consider four types of entities: (i) Smart home users, EdgeHub, (ii) C-Nodes, (iii) Trusted authorities and services, and (iv) outsiders.

Security Goal: The general security goal of the system is to provide access according to the stated access policy.

Privacy Goal: We note that in a sharing platform, the information about the resources will be voluntarily shared and so we assume that the published information on the blockchain will be accessible by all EdgeHubs (ISP subscribers). However, we do expect that transactions do not reveal un-necessary information. For start we impose the following restrictions:

- C-nodes do not learn the identity of EdgeHub owners that are not their subscribers;
- The two sides of a transaction only learn the necessary information to complete the transaction. In particular if the transaction fails, none of the parties learn any new information, and if the transaction is successful, they only learn the required link or access information for the requested resource.

Our analysis in Sect. 4 shows, our design provides security and privacy, in its basic form and without using extra cryptographic protection.

Trust Assumptions. We assume EdgeHubs are implemented as tamper-evident boxes that will ensure that the installed software will be run as specified. However, the smart home user will not be trusted in their sharing claims: they may offer resources, or attributes of resources, that they do not have. They are also interested in learning details of other users in the system through their interaction with the N-chain, or through transactions that may have been unsuccessful. The C-nodes and other authorities are honest but curious: they follow the prescribed protocol, but attempt to learn extra information about participants (EdgeHub), and transactions including real identities of subscribers. We assume the communication between EdgeHub and the C-node is secure (e.g. is over TLS).

4   Securing Access Using N-Chain

Let E_{obj} and E_{sub} denote two EdgeHubs: E_{sub} seeks access to a resource from E_{obj}.

Smart Contracts. The smart contract (RC, ARC, ACC and ADJ) all have a self-destruct method (that makes the smart contract inaccessible), that can be invoked by the owner (EdgeHub) of the contract. We discuss the functionalities of each smart contract below.

(1) ARC. We require that each requester only sees the information that is needed for evaluating the request and accepting or rejecting the access. To facilitate this, we store the attributes of the users and the resources in different contracts. While the resource contract is visible to all subscribers, the user attribute contract become available only to C-nodes for evaluation of the access. Table 1 presents attributes and their certificates of an exemplary resource with a movie identifier M_i.

Table 1. ObjARC look up table

Obj_Id	$Attr_1$	...	$Attr_n$	$Cert_1$	...	$Cert_k$
M_i	*title*: Tom and Jerry	...	*Description*: Cartoon	0xabc....	...	0xa89....

Although our design considers two types of ARC, that is ObjARC and SubARC, they both have the same set of functions and for simplicity we represent them as ARC contract. The abstract of this contract is shown in Fig. 4.

```
pragma solidity >=0.4.25 <0.6.0;
contract ARC{
mapping (string ⇒ string) attributes
function setAttributes(string memory Obj/Sub_Id, attributes[ ] memory attr, string memory
certificate) public onlyOwner
function updateAttributes(string memory Obj/Sub_Id, attributes[ ] memory attr, string
memory certificate) public onlyOwner
function getUserAttributes(string memory Obj/Sub_Id) public onlyOwnerCnode view
returns (attributes[ ] memory attr, address creator, string memory certificate)
function getResourceAttributes(string memory Obj_Id) public view returns (attributes[ ]
memory attr, address creator, string memory certificate)
function deleteAttributes(string memory Obj/Sub_Id) public onlyOwner
function selfDestruct() public onlyOwner;
}
```

Fig. 4. Abstract ARC smart contract.

- *setAttributes():* is used to set the attributes (in the form of key-value pair) and their certificates for a user or resource. For example, user attributes would be public key, address, age, etc, and resource attributes would be index, name, type, etc.
- *updateAttributes():* is used to update the attributes of a user or a resource. (For example, when a certificate is revoked the resource owner is responsible to get a new one and update the certificate stored in the contract.)
- *getUserAttributes() and getResourceAttributes():* is used to retrieve the attributes and certificates of a user or a resource when the associated policies are evaluated. For a user, the function's scope is defined using a derived modifier *onlyOwnerCnode* to limit the access only to the owner of the contract and C-nodes. Whereas, for a resource, the function's scope is public.
- *deleteAttributes():* is used to delete the attributes of a user or a resource. (For example, when the resource is no longer shareable and the user wants to delete the resource.)

(2) ACC. This smart contract stores access control policies that are expressed using the ABAC model for accessing multiple resources and the functions required to manage these policies. Important functions of ACC are presented in Fig. 5.

- *setADJ():* is used to set the address of the ADJ contract.
- *setARC():* is used to record the address of ObjARC contract which is used to retrieve the attributes of a resource.

```
pragma solidity >=0.4.25<0.6.0;
contract ACC{
function setADJ(address adj) public onlyOwner
function setARC(address objARC) public onlyOwner
function addPolicy(string memory Obj_Id, string memory action, string memory permission,
uint minInterval, uint threshold) public onlyOwner
function getPolicy(string memory Obj_Id, string memory action) public view returns (string
memory permission, uint minInterval, uint threshold)
function updatePolicy(string memory Obj_Id, string memory action, string memory
newPermission) public onlyOwner
function deletePolicy(string memory Obj_Id) public onlyOwner
function accessControl(string memory Obj_Id, string memory action, string memory Sub_Id,
address arSub) public
function getRequestHistory(string memory Obj_Id) public onlyModifier view returns
(address arSub, uint ToLR, uint NoFR, bool res, uint8 errcode)
function selfDestruct() public onlyOwner;
}
```

Fig. 5. Abstract ACC smart contract.

- *addPolicy():* is used by E_{obj} to specify the actions that are permissible for each resource.
- *getPolicy() and updatePolicy:* are used to read or update an existing policy identified using its identifier.
- *deletePolicy:* is used to delete an existing policy for a specific resource. Resource owner can also set the minimum time interval that a requester can send consecutive requests, and the number of requests that each requester can send. These information can be used for misbehavior detection.
- *accessControl():* will be invoked by E_{sub} to send access request for accessing interested resource providing its identifier and its ACC address. E_{sub} attributes are retrieved by C-nodes while evaluating its request. This function outputs either Grant or Deny. When the access is granted, the state of the resource is updated (for e.g., unavailable) by invoking *updateState()* method in RC.
- *getRequestHistory():* is used by E_{obj} or ADJ and is defined using a derived modifier known as *onlyModifier* that limits the access to this function to the resource owner and ADJ. This function is used to obtain the information about a resource for which access is requested, address of E_{obj}, Time of Last Request (*ToLR*), Number of Frequent Requests (*NoFR*), result of the request (*res*), and an error message (*errcode*).

(3) RC. This contract stores the information about shareable resources such as resource identifier, the corresponding ACC address and its ABI, address of the resource owner (public key) and the state of the resource (for e.g., available or unavailable). When a new resource is registered, this contract emits an event to inform all (or listening) EdgeHubs in the neighbourhood about the resource. The event advertises the resource information such as, resource identifier, resource name, owner, deposit information, and synopsis of resource characteristics, allowing the listening EdgeHub to learn about the resource. The EdgeHubs listening to the events on the blockchain will store the resource information locally. Table 2 presents an example entry of a resource in RC. Figure 6 presents the important ABIs of RC.

Table 2. RC look up table

Obj_Id	ACC address	Pk_r	ABI	state
M_i	0xf2453jddkkd..	0x456788433...	accessControl_1(M_i,..), Inputs:[]	unavailable

```
pragma solidity >=0.4.25<0.6.0;
contract RC{
function registerResource (string memory Obj_Id, address accAddress, address owner ,
string memory abi, string memory state) public
function updateResource (string memory Obj_Id, address accAddress, address owner ,
string memory abi, string memory state) public onlyResOwner
function deleteResource (string memory Obj_Id) public onlyResOwner
function getContractInfo (string memory Obj_Id) public view returns (address accAddress,
string memory abi, string memory state)
function updateState (string memory Obj_Id, string memory newState) public onlyModifier
function getState (string memory Obj_Id) public
function selfDestruct () public onlyOwner;
}
```

Fig. 6. Abstract *RC* smart contract.

- *registerResource():* is used to add a new resource to RC.
- *updateResource():* is used to update the stored information of a resource.
- *deleteResource():* is used to delete an existing resource information.
- *getContractInfo():* is used by E_{sub} to retrieve the information (ACC address, ABI, and state) of an existing resource.
- *getState():* is used to get the resource state.
- *updateState():* is used to update the resource state.

The functions which have the derived modifier, *onlyResOwner*, are accessible only by the resource owner, which is considered as the party who has registered the resource before.

(4) ADJ. This contract is triggered if a misbehaviour is detected, providing misbehaviour reports including the information about the resource, the misbehaving party, and misbehavior description and time. ADJ verifies the misbehavior information and applies the respective stated actions. Table 3 presents the information stored by ADJ. Important functions of the contract are presented in Fig. 7.

Table 3. Adjudicator look up table

Obj_Id	Pk_s	Misbehavior	Time	Penalty
M_i	0xf2453jddkkd..	Frequent access	7:43 12-10-2019	slash P coins

```
pragma solidity >=0.4.25<0.6.0;
contract ADJ{
function reportMisbehavior (address requester, address resOwner, string memory Obj_Id,
string memory action, string memory misbehavior, uint time) public returns (uint penalty)
function getLatestMisbehaviorInfo (string memory Obj_Id) public view returns (address
requester, address resOwner, string memory Obj_Id, string memory action, string memory
misbehavior, uint time)
function selfDestruct () public onlyOwner;
}
```

Fig. 7. Abstract ADJ smart contract.

- *reportMisbehaviour()*: is used to report information about a misbehaviour. For example, if E_{sub} sends more than the permitted number of requests in a given time interval, this is marked as a misbehavior, and ADJ will be notified.
- *getLatestMisbehaviourInfo()*: ADJ uses this method to retrieve the misbehavior information of a misbehaving entity, verify and apply the required action.

4.1 Requesting an Access

To request access for a specific resource, EdgeHub E_{sub}, searches its local database for the identifier of the resource. It then sends a request to RC and obtains the address of the ACC with the ABI, or an error message.

E_{sub} receives an error message: (i) if the requested resource is not found in the list of shared resources (for e.g., it maybe be deleted by the owner), or (ii) the resource is not available at the moment. In the other case, the E_{sub} invokes the *accessControl()* method supplying the required input such as resource identifier and address of its SubARC. The access policy presented in ACC is evaluated against E_{sub} attributes and issues an event which shows the result of the evaluation (Grant or Deny). The process of access requesting is presented in Fig. 8.

$E_{sub} \rightarrow RC : Obj\_Id$
$RC \rightarrow E_{sub} : accAddress, abi, state$
$E_{sub} \rightarrow ACC : accessControl(Obj\_Id, read, Sub\_Id, arSub)$
$Event\{ "AccessResult" : ...\}$

Connecting to Resource Owner: If access is granted, the E_{obj} encrypts its IP address (or any link to the resource) with the public key of E_{sub} and sends it to the N-chain. E_{sub} decrypts the message, connects to the E_{obj}, and retrieves the resource.

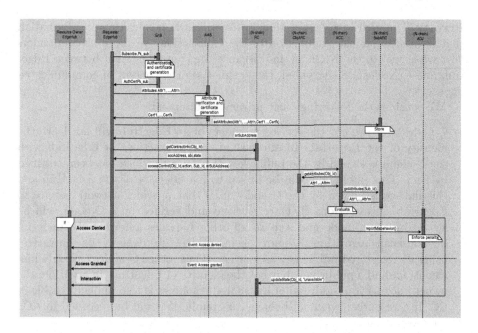

Fig. 8. Subject EdgeHub requesting for access

4.2   Security Analysis

Security. The goal is to ensure that access to resources are granted in accordance with the access policy of the resource in the corresponding ACC. We assume access to resources is restricted to the subscriber EdgeHubs. That is we require that, (i) outsiders will not be able to access any resource, (ii) requests that do not satisfy the policy should be denied, and (ii) requests that satisfy the policy are granted.

For (i), we note that permissioned blockchain access policy can be designed to ensure outsiders cannot access the system (their requests without appropriate credentials will be dropped by the C-nodes). We assume EnS is a secure and trusted service and only registered users have the required credentials. (ii) and (iii) follow from the fact that according to the above protocol flow, users and resource attributes are verified before the access policies are evaluated, and that the C-nodes are trusted and will correctly evaluate the access requests.

Recall that the real identity of each EdgeHub is known by the C-node that EdgeHub has subscribed to. So, if a cheating is detected, the corresponding EdgeHub can be tracked and the required policy be applied by the judge. To detect misbehavior, ACC keeps track of requests, and checks the request history for each new request. If a requesting EdgeHub E_{sub} misbehaves (for e.g., by sending frequent access requests for a resource in given interval of time), the resource proving EdgeHub E_{obj} sends the history of E_{sub} access interactions to ADJ. If the misbehavior is proved, ADJ will enforce penalties on E_{sub}.

Privacy. The goal is to ensure that transactions do not leak more information that is needed for the completion of the transaction. We note that outsiders do have access to the N-Chain and because the communication between Edge-Hub and C-Nodes are encrypted, they cannot see the content of communicated messages.

We consider the following basic privacy requirements:

- C-nodes that are not the service providers of an EdgeHub will not learn the identity of the EdgeHub. In our system, the interactions of EdgeHub with the N-chain is signed by the public key of EdgeHub which has been certified by EnS. This public key will be linked to real identity of the EdgeHub and this linkage is known by the C-node (ISP) that provides network service to EdgeHub. Transactions that are received and verified by a C-node, will be signed by the C-node and sent to all other C-nodes following the underlying consensus algorithm. Resource owner (EdgeHub) deploys the contract(s) using its registered public key as a owner. Thus, other C-nodes can only link a contract and a public key, but not the identity of EdgeHub. In addition, the owner information (address) of the shared resources is also publicly visible in RC. If a resource owner misbehaves, its public key will be recorded in ADJ for prosecution.
- EdgeHubs that participate in a transaction learn only the necessary information to process the transaction. C-nodes retrieves the attributes and certificates of a requesting EdgeHub to evaluate its access requests. Therefore, the details retrieved are only observable by C-nodes in the system. If the access request is successful, C-nodes notify both the EdgeHubs involved in the transaction and trigger further communication as outlined in Sect. 4.1. Otherwise, an error message is sent to the requesting EdgeHub.

5   Proof of Concept Implementation

In this section we consider the case of sharing a movie (ignoring copyright issues for simplicity) in a smart neighbourhood to show feasibility of the proposed system.

Truffle and Ganache. Truffle provides a development environment for building, testing, and deploying Ethereum smart contract and decentralized applications (dApp) [20]. Ganache is a personal blockchain that allows developers to create smart contracts, dApps, and test software [21]. The smart contracts: RC, ARC, ACC and ADJ are developed and tested on Truffle and Ganache.

Experiment. We simulate a neighbourhood of 5 smart homes each equipped with an EdgeHub. Public-keys generated by EdgeHubs (for registering in the system) are certified by the enrolment service, and are used for authenticating transaction to the blockchain. Let us consider that an EdgeHub E_{obj} would like to share a movie with the other EdgeHubs in the neighbourhood. For this, E_{obj} provides the movie attributes (for e.g., movie name, type of the movie (adult or kids), size of the movie, etc) as $\{key, value\}$ pairs to AAS which verifies and provides a certificate that certifies these attributes. E_{obj} then stores these attributes including their certificate on the blockchain using the ARC smart contract and obtains its address.

E_{obj} then deploys the ACC contract with access policies including an *accessControl*() function that handles the access request evaluation. The function retrieves the attributes of the requesting EdgeHub, E_{sub}, and the resource attributes from their respective ARCs. After publishing the ACC on the blockchain, E_{obj} assigns a unique identifier to its movie, and calls the function *registerResource*() to register the movie with RC, providing the resource identifier, the ACC address, E_{obj} address, ABI and the state of the resource.

After successful execution of *registerResource*(), the RC generates an event including the movie index, ACC address, ABI and synopsis of the movie to advertise with all the EdgeHubs in the neighbourhood. This information will help the requester to find the resource according to its will.

EdgeHub E_{sub} interested in the movie, sends a request to RC to get more information like the ABI that it requires to request for the access. Using this information, E_{sub} sends its access request calling *accessControl*() with the parameters *movieName* and its ARC address, subARC. The function evaluates the request and makes a decision based on the attributes. The ACC also provides a function that identifies the misbehaviour of E_{sub}. For instance, if an E_{sub} sends more than 1 access request in 100 ms, it is considered as misbehavior. This is similar to what is discussed in [24]. When the number of requests exceeds the limit, a report including the time of the last request and time of the current access request by the E_{sub} is provided to ADJ. On verifying this information, if the misbehaviour is validated, ADJ denies the access request and block further requests from the E_{sub}. If no misbehaviour is detected, the ACC grants the access and informs both E_{obj} and E_{sub}. Then the interaction between the EdgeHubs is off-chain and they share the movie using a secure communication link.

6   Concluding Remarks

We proposed a neighborhood sharing platform using a premissioned blockchain that allows users to leverage trust in their (geographic) neighbors to benefit from a resource sharing service that respects their personal preferences. Users employ attribute-based access control to specify the conditions and terms of access for their items, and the access control is enforced by the smart contracts on the blockchain. We gave details of the system, and discussed its security. Although our focus is on sharing and does not consider exchange of money, our work can be extended to include exchange of goods and services for money.

Acknowledgement. This research is in part supported by Natural Sciences and Engineering Research Council of Canada, Industrial Research Chair Program, supported by Telus Communications.

References

1. Airbnb: Book homes, hotels, and more on Airbnb (2019). https://www.airbnb.ca/
2. Amazon: AWS IoT Framework (2018). https://aws.amazon.com/iot
3. Apple: The smart home just got smarter (2018). http://www.apple.com/ios/home/
4. Avizheh, S., Doan, T.T., Liu, X., Safavi-Naini, R.: A secure event logging system for smart homes. In: Proceedings of the 2017 Workshop on Internet of Things Security and Privacy, pp. 37–42. ACM (2017)
5. Buterin, V., et al.: A next-generation smart contract and decentralized application platform. White paper **3**, no. 37 (2014)
6. Doan, T.T., Safavi-Naini, R., Li, S., Avizheh, S., Fong, P.W., et al.: Towards a resilient smart home. In: Proceedings of the 2018 Workshop on IoT Security and Privacy, pp. 15–21. ACM (2018)
7. Dupuy, J.C., Torre, A.: Cooperation and trust in spatially clustered firms. In: Trust and Economic Learning, pp. 141–61. Edward Elgar, Cheltenham (1998)
8. Gusmeroli, S., Piccione, S., Rotondi, D.: A capability-based security approach to manage access control in the Internet of Things. Math. Comput. Model. **58**(5–6), 1189–1205 (2013)
9. Higginbottom, J.: Governments finally embrace the sharing economy (2018). https://www.ozy.com/fast-forward/governments-finally-embrace-the-sharing-economy/89688/
10. Hu, V.C., et al.: Guide to attribute based access control (ABAC) definition and considerations (draft), vol. 800, no. 162. NIST special publication (2013)
11. Johnson, C.: The rise of the sharing communities (2012). https://www.shareable.net/the-rise-of-the-sharing-communities/
12. Lazaric, N., Lorenz, E.: Trust and Economic Learning. Edward Elgar Publishing, Cheltenham (1998)
13. Maesa, D.D.F., Mori, P., Ricci, L.: Blockchain based access control services. In: 2018 IEEE International Conference on Internet of Things (iThings) and IEEE Green Computing and Communications (GreenCom) and IEEE Cyber, Physical and Social Computing (CPSCom) and IEEE Smart Data (SmartData), pp. 1379–1386. IEEE (2018)
14. Nilsson, M.: Proximity and the trust formation process. Eur. Plan. Stud. **27**(5), 841–861 (2019)
15. Ouaddah, A., Abou Elkalam, A., Ait Ouahman, A.: FairAccess: a new blockchain-based access control framework for the Internet of Things. Secur. Commun. Netw. **9**(18), 5943–5964 (2016)
16. Rinne, A.: 4 big trends for the sharing economy in 2019 (2019). https://www.weforum.org/agenda/2019/01/sharing-economy/
17. Sandhu, R.S., Coyne, E.J., Feinstein, H.L., Youman, C.E.: Role-based access control models. Computer **29**(2), 38–47 (1996)
18. SmartThings: How it works-SmartThings (2018). https://www.smartthings.com/getting-started
19. Storper, M., Venables, A.J.: Buzz: face-to-face contact and the urban economy. J. Econ. Geogr. **4**(4), 351–370 (2004)
20. truffle: truffle suite (2019). https://www.trufflesuite.com/truffle
21. truffle: truffle suite (2019). https://www.trufflesuite.com/ganache
22. Uber: Drive with Uber, earn on your schedule (2019). https://www.uber.com/ca/en/

23. Williams, R.: Forrester: millennials boost growth of sharing economy (2018). https://www.mobilemarketer.com/news/forrester-millennials-boost-growth-of-sharing-economy/515851/
24. Zhang, Y., Kasahara, S., Shen, Y., Jiang, X., Wan, J.: Smart contract-based access control for the Internet of Things. IEEE Internet Things J. **6**(2), 1594–1605 (2018)

Enforcing Determinism of Java Smart Contracts

Fausto Spoto[✉]

Dipartimento di Informatica, Università di Verona, Verona, Italy
fausto.spoto@univr.it

Abstract. Java is a high-level, well-known and powerful object-oriented language, with a large support library and a comfortable toolbelt. Hence, it has been proposed for writing smart contracts in blockchain. However, its support library is non-deterministic, which is a blocking issue for its application to smart contracts. This paper discusses the kind of (non-)determinism of the methods of the Java library and how a deterministic fragment of that library can be specified. It shows that some relevant parts are deterministic only under specific conditions on runtime values. It concludes with the description of an instrumentation, for the Takamaka blockchain, that enforces such conditions, statically or dynamically, reporting experiments with its implementation.

1 Introduction

Smart contracts are programs that specify the effects of running blockchain transactions. They are written in specialized languages, that take into account the fact that they operate on data kept in blockchain. They must support some special concepts, such as a reference to the caller of a transaction, monetary transfers between contracts and payment of code execution through *gas*. Such concepts are not natively available in traditional programming languages. Instead, the Bitcoin bytecode [5,14] can be seen as a language for smart contracts, although non-Turing equivalent and mostly limited to coin transfers. The more powerful Solidity [6], compiled into Ethereum bytecode, allows one to code complex smart contracts in an imperative high-level language, and is one of the main reasons behind the success of Ethereum.

Recently, there have been efforts towards the use of traditional high-level languages for writing smart contracts. A notable example is Hyperledger Fabric [4,18], that allows one to write smart contracts in Java, among other languages. Quoting from [4], "blockchain domain-specific languages are difficult to design for the implementer and require additional learning by the programmer. Writing smart contracts in a general-purpose language (*e.g.*, Go, Java, C/C++) instead appears more attractive and accelerates the adoption of blockchain solutions". In particular, Java is a well-known programming language, with modern features such as generics, inner classes, lambda expressions and lazy streams. For instance, a Solidity contract for a Ponzi pyramid scheme consists of 39

© Springer Nature Switzerland AG 2020
M. Bernhard et al. (Eds.): FC 2020 Workshops, LNCS 12063, pp. 568–583, 2020.
https://doi.org/10.1007/978-3-030-54455-3_40

non-blank non-comment lines of code (page 155 of [11]), while its translation into Java is only 19 lines long. Java has a large and powerful toolbelt and an active community. Also other blockchains [1,2,17] let programmers code in a limited subset of Java. Solidity has native features for smart contracts, such as `payable` functions, but the same can be obtained in Java through instrumentation [17]. One of the most compelling reasons for writing smart contracts in a mainstream language such as Java is that it comes with a large support library, that provides general solutions to typical programming problems. Many programmers are familiar with that library and appreciate the possibility of using it also for developing smart contracts. This reduces development time and errors, since the library has been widely tested in the last decades and its semantics is well-known. There is, however, a big issue here. Namely, the support library of Java is non-deterministic, in general. For most blockchains, non-determinism leads to a fork of the network, since consensus cannot be reached. Hyperledger Fabric allows instead non-determinism, in the sense that code execution, if non-deterministic, gets rejected [18]. Hence, also in this case, programmers should avoid non-determinism, if they want their code to be run. Non-determinism can be allowed in smart contracts for the generation of random numbers [9], but that technique does not extend to other forms of non-determinism. Non-determinism is obvious for library classes and methods that perform, explicitly, parallel or random computations. But the real problem is that also some library parts, that are explicitly sequential, might lead to non-deterministic results. This is well-known to Java programmers and has been at the origin of subtle bugs also in traditional software. For smart contracts, however, this situation cannot be tolerated: the execution of the same code, from the same state, *must* lead to the same result in any two distinct blockchain nodes.

A possible solution could be to write a special Java library, whose methods are made deterministic. But this is far from simple, since the Java library is huge and determinism would require to modify very low-level aspects of the same virtual machine, such as its memory allocation strategy and its garbage collectors. The process should be repeated at each new version of Java. Moreover, programmers should be aware to use a non-standard library, with a different semantics. Finally, one should be sure to have fixed *all* possible sources of non-determinism in the (immense) Java library. Instead, this paper advocates the use of a standard, fixed Java library, restricted to a white-listed fragment and with the addition of a verification layer that enforces some run-time conditions. It must be ensured that this fragment is deterministic, which is typically small (but still large if compared to, say, Solidity, that has *no* native support library and only very rudimentary third-party libraries; in particular, Solidity's `library` keyword only allows one to define stateless libraries). One needn't prove to have caught every single potential case of non-determinism in the library, but only that the white-listed sandbox is safe.

Namely, the contributions of this paper are a discussion of the (non-)determinism of the Java library methods; a way for specifying deterministic fragments of that library; a technique to enforce some run-time conditions for determinism, statically or dynamically; an implementation of the technique, currently part of the verification layer for Java smart contracts of the Takamaka blockchain; experiments with that implementation. Our deterministic fragment has been selected manually, since there is currently no automatic way to prove that a method is deterministic. The Takamaka blockchain verifies, instruments and installs in blockchain the code of the smart contracts, in instrumented form [17]. Later, transactions execute the instrumented code, never the original one. All nodes perform verification and instrumentation and must agree on the result. An attacker cannot modify the instrumented program or its execution semantics after it has been installed in blockchain. The motivation of the original instrumentation goes beyond the issue on determinism; we refer to [17] for its description: this paper describes its use for enforcing determinism only.

This work is organized as follows. Section 2 discusses the (non-)determinism of some examples of Java library methods. Section 3 defines the notion of *deterministic white-listed fragment* of the Java library. Its definition can use run-time conditions on the way its methods are called. Section 4 provides a technique for enforcing such conditions, dynamically or statically, through bytecode instrumentation. Section 5 reports experiments with an implementation. This paper is *not* about Java smart contracts themselves. The interested reader is referred to the references provided above and, in particular, to [17] and to the tutorial about Takamaka smart contracts in Java (https://www.takamaka.dev/docs/Takamaka.html).

2   Determinism for Java Methods in Smart Contracts

This section discusses the different kinds of determinism of methods from the Java library and what must be required if they are used in a language for smart contracts. We recall that the Java library exists in different versions, from its first 1.0 edition of 1996 to its 14 edition of March 2020. Each version has different implementations, with OpenJDK probably being the most used, nowadays. Some classes and methods exist only in some versions of the library. For instance, class `java.lang.Integer` exists from the very first 1.0 edition, while class `java.util.Collection` was only introduced with version 1.2.

Let us discuss the meaning of *determinism*. The state σ of the Java interpreter is typically defined as a function from variables and object fields into values. Then the goal is to guarantee that the execution ϕ of a piece of code, from the same state σ but in two different blockchain nodes, yields the same result, *i.e.*, same next state σ' and same value r (if the code is an expression): $\phi(\sigma) = \langle \sigma', r \rangle$ in all nodes of the network. This definition, however, is too strict. Consider the constructor `String()` of `java.lang.String`, that instantiates and returns a new empty `String` object. It is an expression whose execution, from any given state σ but in two different blockchain nodes, will very likely yield two distinct pointers r in RAM: the heap allocation will likely pick two distinct free locations. But both references will refer to a brand new empty string. As long as the programming language does not allow one to distinguish the exact pointer, but only the object it refers to, then such two next states and results can be considered *equivalent*. This notion of state and reference equivalence is actually borrowed from [7,8]. With this interpretation in mind, `String()`, applied to two equivalent states but in two distinct blockchain nodes, yields equivalent states and equivalent results (two references to brand new empty strings), and is consequently deterministic.

Method	Deterministic?			
	always	platform	platform + conditions	never
`Number.intValue()`	✓			
`Object()`	✓			
`String()`	✓			
`HashSet<E>()`	✓			
`String(String original)`	✓			
`String.concat(String other)`	✓			
`String.length()`	✓			
`Integer.valueOf(int i)`		✓		
`Object.hashCode()`			✓	
`Object.toString()`			✓	
`Collection<E>.iterator()`			✓	
`Collection<E>.stream()`			✓	
`Collection<E>.add(E e)`			✓	
`StreamSupport.stream(Spliterator<T> s, boolean p)`			✓	
`System.currentTimeMillis()`				✓
`BaseStream<T,S>.parallel()`				✓
`Thread.start()`				✓

potentially white-listed

Fig. 1. Some methods of the Java library, with their behavior *wrt.* determinism. *Always* means that a method does not compromise code determinism. *Platform* means that a method does not compromise determinism, but only if a specific implementation of the library is fixed. *Platform + conditions* means that a method does not compromise determinism, but only if an implementation of the library is fixed *and* the program satisfies extra conditions, that typically refer to the actual arguments passed to that method or to other methods at run time. *Never* means that a method can have different behaviors in distinct executions, even on a specific library implementation, and no condition can be sensibly devised to make its behavior deterministic.

Figure 1 reports examples of Java library methods, classified on the basis of the kind of determinism that holds for them. We discuss them below. We recall that, in Java, a method call `o.m(pars)` specifies its *receiver* `o` and its *static target* `C.m(types)`, that is, a signature reporting the class `C` from where method `m` with formal arguments of type `types` must be looked for. Note that `C` and `types` do not include generic type parameters, if any, since they are erased during compilation into Java bytecode and our instrumentation works on bytecode. Since Java is an object-oriented language, the static target is just the specification of the method implementation that must be run (the *dynamic* target): a non-static method call runs the implementation of C.m(types) that is selected by looking up m(types) from the run-time class of o upwards, along the superclass chain[1]. Hence, any implementation of m(types) in C or in any of its subtypes can be run. For instance, a call o.intValue() with static target Number.intValue() can be called on any object o that extends java.lang.Number. At run time, it might execute any implementation of intValue() in any subtype of Number, such as in Integer or in java.lang.Double, depending on the run-time type of o. Hence, when Fig. 1 classifies Number.intValue() as always deterministic, this applies to every implementation of intValue() in the subtypes of Number of the Java library.

Many methods of the Java library are clearly deterministic. Their behavior is fixed by the official documentation by Oracle and does not change across distinct versions of the library. An example is the unwrapping method intValue() of Number (Fig. 1). It yields the primitive int value corresponding to an instance of the abstract class Number, such as objects of class Integer or Double. For instance, new Integer(3).intValue() == 3 holds in any version of the Java library, as well as new Double(3.14).intValue() == 3 since, in Java, truncation of double into int is machine-independent. Hence, a language for smart contracts, that must require determinism, can safely allow the use of that method, always. Other examples are the constructors of String, java.lang.Object and java.util.HashSet reported in Fig. 1, or methods String.concat(String other), that yields the concatenation of strings this and other, and String.length(), that yields the length of a string. If only these methods are used, then any Java library can be used by any node of a blockchain, even distint versions in distinct nodes.

The static method Integer.valueOf(int i) wraps a primitive int value into an object of class Integer. It might be surprising, but its result can be different in two blockchain nodes, if they use distinct implementations of the Java library. For instance, while Integer.valueOf(3) == Integer.valueOf(3) holds in every implementation of the library, since the official documentation *requires* this method to cache values between −128 and 127, inclusive, there is instead no guarantee that caching is used outside that range. Hence Integer.valueOf(2019) == Integer.valueOf(2019) might be true in some implementations of the Java library and false in others (such as in Oracle JDK 13.0.1). We call *platform deterministic* such methods, since they are deterministic only once a specific implementation (*platform*) of the Java library is fixed. If only methods of this and of the previous category are used, then all nodes of a blockchain must run on a given, fixed Java library, to guarantee determinism.

Consider method Object.hashCode() of class Object now. It yields an int hash of its receiver. Its implementation computes that hash from the

---

[1] Java also allows so-called *special* calls, such as super.m(), that start the look-up from a given *static* type; as well as calls embedded in closures, such as method references (corresponding to invokedynamic in Java bytecode). For simplicity, these calls are not discussed here, but our implementation deals with them.

RAM pointer value of the object reference. Since two blockchain nodes will likely use different RAM pointers, this method is non-deterministic. In other terms, this method exposes an execution detail (the exact RAM pointer) that was meant to be invisible for state equivalence. For instance, `int i = new Object().hashCode()` will likely assign different values to `i` in two distinct blockchain nodes (and even in repeated executions on the same node). The same problem occurs for `Object.toString()` that, inside `Object`, is implemented in terms of `Object.hashCode()` (its implementation concatenates the name of the run-time class of its receiver with its hash and returns it). Hence, `String s = new Object().toString()`, in two distinct blockchain nodes, will likely assign different strings to variable `s`. However, banning calls to `Object.hashCode()` or `Object.toString()` from smart contracts would be unacceptable to programmers, that heavily use such calls in their programs, without incurring in nondeterminism. The reason is that programmers normally take care of calling such methods only on objects that redefine the default (non-deterministic) implementation of `hashCode()` and `toString()` from class `Object`. If that is the case, the calls will actually execute the deterministic redefinitions. Hence, it seems sensible to allow calls to such methods in smart contracts, but only if their receiver redefines them in a deterministic way, as in: `String o = ...; int h = o.hashCode()`, where o holds a `String`, that redefines `hashCode()`. Hence, such methods are *platform-deterministic under certain conditions*: they are deterministic if a given Java library is fixed *and* some run-time conditions hold. Section 4 shows how such conditions can be enforced.

Consider methods `iterator()` and `stream()` of the generic `Collection<E>`. They provide two ways for processing the elements, of type E, of a collection. The former implements the traditional *iterator pattern* and yields an object that enumerates the elements. The latter yields a *stream*, *i.e.*, a lazy algorithm on the elements, that can be subsequently programmed and executed. Streams implement the map/filter/reduce pattern, making heavy use of lamba expressions. Interestingly, neither method guarantees a fixed enumeration order. There are collections for which they guarantee an order, such as instances of `java.util.List<E>`: on lists, enumeration proceeds from head to tail; or instances of `java.util.LinkedHashSet<E>`, on which they proceed in insertion order. For collections such as `java.util.HashSet<E>`, instead, the order varies with the library version *and* at each execution. The reason is that `HashSet` uses a hashmap [10] to store elements with the same `hashCode()` in the same bucket. Since `hashCode()`, as shown above, is non-deterministic, then the distribution of elements in the buckets varies from run to run and their enumeration as well, being the lexicographic scan of the buckets' elements. One could forbid `HashSet` and only allow its more expensive sibling `LinkedHashSet`, whose iteration order is fixed. But then method `add()` would still be non-deterministic, since its gas consumption is affected by the shape of the buckets, as discussed later. Moreover, programmers use `HashSet` extensively (it is possibly the fifth most used library class: https://javapapers. com/core-java/top-10-java-classes) and would be annoyed if it were banned. It is much better to observe that, if the `hashCode()` of all its elements has been redefined in a deterministic way and if a specific library version is fixed, then the behavior of `HashSet` becomes deterministic, since the shape of the buckets is the same in every run. This means that one can allow, in smart contracts, calls to `iterator()` and `stream()` on any collection, but only under such conditions. Section 4 shows how such conditions can be enforced.

Consider method `add(E e)` of `Collection<E>`. It adds an element `e` to the collection. For a given library version, it is deterministic on lists: it adds `e` to the end of the list. However, on `HashSet` and `LinkedHashSet` it scans the bucket selected for `e.hashCode()` and checks if an equal element was already in that bucket, by calling `equals()` against each of its elements. Hence `add(E e)` on a hashset consumes an amount of gas that depends on the shape of its buckets. Again, the solution is to require that all elements of the set and `e` redefine `hashCode()` in a deterministic way, which must be enforced at run time (Sect. 4).

Consider the static method `stream(Spliterator<T> s, boolean p)` of class `java.util.stream.StreamSupport`. It yields a stream for processing the elements specified by the given `Spliterator`. If the `Spliterator` is deterministic, the resulting stream is deterministic as well, on a given library version, but only if it is sequential. Passing true for `p` would yield a parallel stream instead, that is inherently non-deterministic. Hence, this method can be used only if a specific library is used and if it is enforced that false is passed for `p` at run time (Sect. 4).

If only methods of this and of the previous two categories are used, then all nodes of a blockchain must be run on a given, fixed Java library, *and* the run-time conditions that entail determinism must be somehow enforced.

Static method `System.currentTimeMillis()`, in `java.lang.System`, yields the number of milliseconds elapsed since the beginning of 1970. Not surprisingly, it will yield different values for different runs. Such an inherently non-deterministic method cannot be used in a smart contract. Consider method `parallel()` of `java.util.stream.BaseStream` now. It yields a parallel version of a stream. For instance, if `list` is a list with at least two distinct positive `Integer`s:

```
int pos = list.stream().parallel().mapToInt(Integer::intValue)
  .filter(i -> i > 0).findAny().getAsInt();
```

processes `list` with a parallel algorithm that unwraps each `Integer` element of the list into its corresponding `int` primitive value, filters only the positive values and selects any of them. The result of `findAny()` is an optional value, hence the `getAsInt()` call at the end. Since the algorithm is parallel, each execution of this code might select a different positive element, depending on thread scheduling. Hence, `parallel()` introduces non-determinism and cannot be allowed in smart contracts. Note that even the gas consumption of the code is not deterministic, since it depends on how many elements are checked before a thread encounters a positive value and terminates the look-up.

In general, methods that introduce parallelism are never deterministic. Another example is `Thread.start()` in `java.lang.Thread`, that spawns a parallel execution thread. If methods of this category are used, then the code cannot be used in blockchain, since there is not way to make it deterministic.

3   White-Listed Fragments of the Java Library

Section 2 has shown that some Java library methods can be used in smart contracts, at least if a specific version of the library is fixed and some run-time conditions are enforced. Such methods can hence be *white-listed* for smart contracts (Fig. 1).

Definition 1. *A white-listed fragment WL is a set of method signatures (constructors are considered methods named as their defining class), with associated run-time conditions (if any).*

The consensus rules must specify a white-listed fragment WL: each node verifies that smart contracts *obey WL*, or otherwise aborts their execution in blockchain.

Definition 2. *A program P obeys a white-listed fragment WL if and only if*

1. *every method call in P has a static target that is either in contract code, or in WL or overrides a signature in WL (syntactical check); and*
2. *in every execution of P, WL's run-time conditions hold (semantical check).*

A program P that obeys a white-listed fragment WL cannot call signatures outside WL, but can call signatures in WL that, indirectly, call methods outside WL. In other terms, Definition 2 constrains only the library API allowed in P.

Definition 3. *Given a Java library version V, a white-listed fragment WL is deterministic for V if and only if any Java program that obeys WL is deterministic, when executed over V.*

A very simple example of white-listed fragment is $WL_1 = \emptyset$. It is deterministic for every Java library version. Namely, a program P that obeys WL_1 cannot call any library method nor constructor (condition 1 of Definition 2). P cannot contain classes, since Java classes have always at least a constructor that calls the constructor of `Object`, possibly indirectly. Hence, P consists of interfaces only, with default and static methods that do not call any library code, and is hence deterministic. A deterministic white-listed fragment is $WL_2 = \{\texttt{Object()}\}$. This time, one can write programs P that obey WL_2, with classes that extend `Object` and whose constructors call `Object()`. But no other library methods nor contructors can be called, which is an irrealistic constraint. The white-listed fragment $WL_3 = \{\texttt{Object()}, \texttt{System.currentTimeMillis()}\}$ is not deterministic, since it is possible to write a program, that obeys WL_3, consisting of a single class with a method that uses `System.currentTimeMillis()` to return a random value. A deterministic white-listed fragment that allows, at least, simple string manipulations is $WL_4 = \{\texttt{Object()}, \texttt{String.concat(String other)}, \texttt{String.length()}\}$. It allows one to write Java programs whose classes extend `Object` and whose code performs computations such as `"hello".concat(s).length()`, where s is a string.

Up to now, we have not used run-time conditions in white-listed fragments. In order to specify such conditions, it is possible to use Java annotations on method signatures. An annotation can be applied to a formal parameter, meaning that the condition must hold for the corresponding actual parameter; or to a non-static method itself, meaning that the condition must hold for the receiver of the method. Let us introduce for instance the following annotations:

@MustRedefineHashCode: the annotated value is null or belongs to a class that redefines Object.hashCode();

@MustRedefineHashCodeOrToString: the annotated value is null or belongs to a class that redefines Object.hashCode() or Object.toString() (or both);

@MustBeFalse: the annotated value is false.

Then one can define

$$
WL_5 = \left\{ \begin{array}{c} \texttt{Object(),HashSet<E>(),} \\ \texttt{@MustRedefineHashCodeOrToString Object.toString(),} \\ \texttt{Collection<E>.add(@MustRedefineHashCode E e)} \end{array} \right\}
$$

that constrains Object.toString() to be called on values that redefine at least one of hashCode() and toString(), and Collection<E>.add(E e) to be called with an actual parameter, for e, that redefines hashCode(). WL_5 is deterministic for any given Java library version, thanks to such constraints. For instance, the following code is deterministic on any Java library:

```
Set<Object> set = new HashSet<>();
set.add("hello"); set.add(BigInteger.ONE); set.add(new HashSet<String>());
String s = set.toString();
```

It creates a hashset and populates it with a String, a java.math.BigInteger and an empty HashSet. These redefine hashCode(), hence the constraint on add() holds. At the end, it calls toString() on the set, that is a HashSet that redefines toString(), hence the constraint on toString() holds. By using, for instance, the OpenJDK 14 library, variable s will always hold the string "[[], 1, hello]". Other versions of the library might compute different strings but, once a library version is fixed, always the same string is computed. The reason of this determinism is that the shape of the buckets of the hashset is fixed since the hashCode() of its elements is redefined in a deterministic way in String, BigInteger and HashSet. Moreover, toString on HashSet has been redefined in a way that iterates on the elements of the hashset and concatenates their toString(), which is redefined and deterministic in String, BigInteger and HashSet.

The justification above for the determinism of the code follows from a manual investigation of the library's source code. It is not automated. What can be automated is, instead, the verification that a program P obeys a given WL. Namely, condition 1 of Definition 2 can be verified by following the static target of each call in P, upwards, and checking if the method is in the smart conrtacts or in WL. Condition 2 of Definition 2 is more complex and Sect. 4 shows how it can be enforced.

A white-listed fragment WL must be specified in a way that is easily machine-readable. WL is a set of method signatures, hence it can be provided as a set of Java abstract classes and interfaces. For each library class C that defines some methods to white-list, one writes an abstract class whitelisted.C; for each interface I, one write an interface whitelisted.I. That is, one defines, in package whitelisted, *mirrors* declaring the white-listed signatures and their annotations, if any. The advantage of using such mirrors is that they can be written by copying and pasting signatures from the source code of the mirrored library classes. Moreover, they can be compiled, which helps spotting typos. Finally, a blockchain node can query such classes by reflection, which is both simple and efficient, compared for instance to querying textual or XML specifications.

For instance, Fig. 2 specifies a white-listed fragment of Object, Collection, Set, List, HashSet and ArrayList[2]. It is deterministic for a given fixed version of the Java library: thanks to its annotations, this fragment guarantees that elements in collections (hence also in sets and lists) redefine hashCode(), which makes iterators on collections, streams derived from collections and toString() on collections deterministic. The latter can be called on collections since they redefine it, hence satisfying the constraint for Object.

Interestingly, method contains(Object o) in Collection (Fig. 2) requires o to redefine hashCode() or otherwise, for hashsets, the bucket where o is looked for might be different for different runs, with subsequent non-determinism. That constraint is not needed for contains(Object o) in List (Fig. 2), that scans the list from its head, looking for an equals() element, deterministically, regardless of o having redefined hashCode() or not. This is consistent with Liskov's substitution principle [12] that, for formal arguments, works by generalization: hence white-listing constraints on formal arguments can be weakened, not strengthened, in subclasses. The same for remove(Object o), passing from Collection to List.

There is no largest deterministic fragment for a given set of classes and interfaces: another deterministic fragment is identical to Fig. 2 but for allowing any elements in lists, possibly not redefining hashCode() (hence more permissive); forbidding Object.toString() and Object.hashCode() altogether, since it would now be non-deterministic on lists (hence more restrictive); and forbidding the constructor HashSet(Collection<? extends E> c) (Fig. 2), that allows a hashset to be built from a list and hence contain elements whose hashCode() has not been redefined, with consequent non-determinism (hence more restrictive). Choosing a specific deterministic fragment is often a question of personal taste. One should choose that allowing more methods of frequent use. In this example, forbidding Object.toString() and Object.hashCode() would hardly be acceptable.

4   Enforcing Run-Time Conditions for Determinism

Section 3 shows that a deterministic fragment of the Java library can require run-time conditions on the values of the receiver or parameters of its methods. A blockchain node must enforce that such conditions hold at run time for the smart contracts that it executes. Hence each condition is a proof-obligation that must

---

[2] These signatures are copy and paste from the library source code. For the use of generics, wildcards and Object in these signatures, we refer to [13].

```
public abstract class whitelisted.java.lang.Object {
  public Object() {}
  public abstract boolean equals(java.lang.Object other);
  public abstract @MustRedefineHashCodeOrToString java.lang.String toString();
  public abstract @MustRedefineHashCode int hashCode();
}

public interface whitelisted.java.util.Collection<E> {
  int size();
  boolean isEmpty();
  java.lang.Object[] toArray();
  <T> T[] toArray(T[] a);
  <T> T[] toArray(java.util.function.IntFunction<T[]> generator);
  boolean add(@MustRedefineHashCode E e);
  boolean contains(@MustRedefineHashCode java.lang.Object o);
  boolean remove(@MustRedefineHashCode java.lang.Object o);
  boolean containsAll(java.util.Collection<?> c);
  boolean addAll(java.util.Collection<? extends E> c);
  boolean removeAll(java.util.Collection<?> c);
  boolean removeIf(java.util.function.Predicate<? super E> filter);
  boolean retainAll(java.util.Collection<?> c);
  void clear();
  java.util.stream.Stream<E> stream();
  java.lang.Iterator<E> iterator();
}

public interface whitelisted.java.util.Set<E> {
  boolean containsAll(java.util.Collection<?> c);
  boolean addAll(java.util.Collection<? extends E> c);
  boolean retainAll(java.util.Collection<?> c);
  boolean removeAll(java.util.Collection<?> c);
}

public interface whitelisted.java.util.List<E> {
  E get(int index);
  E remove(int index);
  boolean remove(java.lang.Object o);
  boolean contains(java.lang.Object o);
  void sort(java.util.Comparator<? super E> c);
  E set(int index, @MustRedefineHashCode E element);
  void add(int index, @MustRedefineHashCode E element);
  int indexOf(java.lang.Object o);
  int lastIndexOf(java.lang.Object o);
  java.util.ListIterator<E> listIterator();
  java.util.ListIterator<E> listIterator(int index);
  java.util.List<E> subList(int fromIndex, int toIndex);
  java.util.Spliterator<E> spliterator();
}

public abstract class whitelisted.java.util.HashSet<E> {
  public HashSet() {}
  public HashSet(java.util.Collection<? extends E> c) {}
  public HashSet(int initialCapacity, float loadFactor) {}
  public HashSet(int initialCapacity) {}
}

public abstract class whitelisted.java.util.ArrayList<E> {
  public ArrayList() {}
  public ArrayList(int size) {}
  public ArrayList(java.util.Collection<? extends E> c) {}
  public abstract void trimToSize();
  public abstract void ensureCapacity(int minCapacity);
}
```

Fig. 2. White-listed methods of Object, Collection, Set, List, HashSet and ArrayList.

be discharged: if this is not possible, the smart contract cannot be executed or, at least, its execution must be aborted. This section shows how this is possible.

Very likely, a blockchain node receives the compiled contract in Java byte-code. The idea is to let it instrument such bytecode, only the first time it is installed in blockchain, with checks that, at each subsequent run, verify the run-time conditions. For simplicity, this section presents the instrumentation at source-code level, but it actually works at bytecode level.

Assume that a blockchain node verifies that smart contracts obey to the deterministic fragment in Fig. 2. Assume that a user installs in blockchain a smart contract whose code contains `collection.remove(element)`, whose static target is `Collection<E>.remove(Object o)`. The node spots this syntactically[3]. The node consults its white-listed fragment and recognizes the call as white-listed, but having a run-time constraint `@MustRedefineHashCode` on `o` (Fig. 2). Hence, during installation of the smart contract, the node instruments its code by adding a brand new verification method:

```
private static boolean remove_0(Collection<E> receiver, Object par_0) {
  Support.mustRedefineHashCode(par_0);
  return receiver.remove(par_0);
}
```

and replaces `collection.remove(element)` with `remove_0(collection, element)`. Each time that code will later be executed, `Support.mustRedefineHash Code(par_0)` will check (through Java reflection) that the actual argument to `remove(Object o)` redefines `hashCode()` and aborts the current transaction otherwise. The node includes a `Support` class for that, whose code is not reported for space limitations.

For another example, assume the smart contract to call `x.toString()`, with static target `Object.toString()`. The blockchain node spots this syntactically, consults its white-listed fragment and recognizes the call as white-listed, but having a run-time constraint `@MustRedefineHashCodeOrToString` on `x` (Fig. 2). Hence, it replaces `x.toString()` with `toString_0(x)` and adds the method:

```
private static toString_0(Object receiver) {
  Support.mustRedefineHashCodeOrToString(receiver);
  return receiver.toString();
}
```

At each run of the contract, `Support.mustRedefineHashCodeOrToString(receiver)` will be executed, to check the condition, by reflection.

Assume the smart contract to contain a static call `StreamSupport.stream(s, p)`, whose static target is `StreamSupport.stream(Spliterator<T> s, boolean p)`, and that the white-listed fragment of the blockchain node allows that signature, but has a run-time condition on `p` to avoid creation of parallel streams: `StreamSupport.stream(Spliterator<T> s, @MustBeFalse boolean p)`. The node replaces `StreamSupport.stream(s, p)` with `stream_0(s, p)` and adds the method:

---

[3] The Java bytecode of the smart contract will contain an instruction `invokeinterface` `java.util.Collection.remove(Object):boolean`, or a similar one for a subtype of `Collection`.

```
private static Stream<T> stream_0(Spliterator<T> par_0, boolean par_1) {
    Support.mustBeFalse(par_1); // aborts transaction if par_1 is false
    return StreamSupport.stream(par_0, par_1);
}
```

4.1 Static vs. Dynamic

The instrumentation technique described above adds dynamic checks on run-time values, triggered during each subsequent transaction. Hence, checks are performed repeatedly, every time an annotated white-listed method is executed. This can incur in a performance penalty. It would be better to check, once and for all, if a run-time condition holds, definitely, when smart contracts are installed in blockchain. This can be done with static analysis [15], a technique that infers properties of programs, before they are actually run. Since the verification of non-trivial run-time program properties is in general undecidable [16], static analysis provides a definite answer only in some cases. Hence, a blockchain node can use static analysis to discharge the proof-obligations due to run-time conditions on white-listed methods. If it succeeds with a definite answer, stating that a given condition definitely holds, the node needn't generate any verification method for that condition. Otherwise, it adds the verification method. More aggressive static analyses discharge more proof-obligations statically, which is desirable since the smart contract's code will check less conditions at run-time. However, aggressive analyses are typically more expensive (although they are executed only once, when the smart contract is installed in blockchain). In practice, a good trade-off should be found between the power of the analysis and its cost.

Our implementation uses static types to infer if @MustRedefineHashCode or @MustRedefineHashCodeOrToString holds for a variable v, statically. If the static type τ of v is a class that redefines Object.hashCode() or Object.toString(), the same must hold for v's dynamic type τ', that can only be an instance of τ (since Java and Java bytecode are strongly-typed): the run-time condition holds, always. Otherwise, a verification method is added for that condition. For @MustBeFalse, our implementation looks, intra-procedurally, for the producers of the annotated value. If these are always the literal false, then the condition holds. If, instead, at least one producer is the literal true or a complex expression, the static analysis gives up and the verification method is added.

5   Experiments

We have implemented the technique of Sect. 4 at bytecode level, by using the BCEL library for bytecode manipulation [3]. Experiments have been performed on an Intel 4-Core i3-4150 at 3.50 GHz with 16 GB of RAM, running Linux Ubuntu 18.04. Figure 3 reports the Java archives (jars) for experiments. They contain contracts for auction (auctions.jar), for storage of objects in blockchain (basicdependencies.jar), for the use of such objects as a library (basic.jar), uses of Takamaka's collection classes (collections.jar), contracts for crowdfunding

archive of smart contracts	#m	#c	#d	without	with	instr. time
auctions.jar	20	0	0	11997	11997	4
basicdependencies.jar	38	3	0	7265	7505	26
basic.jar	38	8	0	8109	8464	31
collections.jar	0	0	0	8909	8909	4
crowdfunding.jar	0	0	0	10043	10043	4
io-takamaka-code.jar	348	18	5	88101	89177	223
javacollections.jar	38	17	0	3040	3635	18
lambdas.jar	45	3	0	4570	4745	27
ponzi.jar	69	7	0	12964	13556	43
purchase.jar	0	0	0	5362	5362	4
tictactoe.jar	40	0	0	6745	6745	27
voting.jar	8	1	0	7210	7305	20

Fig. 3. The jars used for the experiments. Each contains one or more contracts. For each jar, #m is the number of calls to signatures of the Java library; #c is the number of white-listing conditions that must be checked for those calls; #d is the subset of #c that has been discharged statically, at instrumentation time; *without* is the size (in bytes) of the instrumented jar without the addition of run-time checks for the remaining #c−#d conditions; *with* is the size (in bytes) of the instrumented jar with that addition; *instr. time* is the time for computing such instrumented jars (in milliseconds).

(crowdfunding.jar), the run-time support of Takamaka (io-takamaka-code.jar), contracts using Java collections (javacollections.jar), contracts testing lambda expressions (lambdas.jar), Ponzi contracts (ponzi.jar), a remote purchase contract (purchase.jar), a tic-tac-toe game (tictactoe.jar) and contracts for electronic voting (voting.jar).

Column #m of Fig. 3 counts the calls to constructors or methods of the Java library. Our implementation uses an extension of the fragment in Fig. 2 and verifies that all those calls are white-listed. However, a few of them require to enforce run-time conditions for determinism (Sect. 4): column #c counts such conditions; of these, our implementation statically discharged #d, at instrumentation time, through static analysis; that is, these needn't be checked at run time, since these checks are eliminated by the static analysis of Sect. 4.1. The remaining #c−#d require to add run-time checks in the instrumented jar. Consequently, when #c − #d > 0, extra code is instrumented into the jars, as it can be seen by comparing columns *without* and *with* in Fig. 3. These show that the extra checks induce a small inflation of the jars. Finally, Fig. 3 reports time for instrumentation, in milliseconds. We computed it for columns *with* and *without*, but the results (reported in the figure) were identical. This means that the time for checking if method calls are white-listed and for adding run-time checks for white-listing conditions is very small. In order to investigate if the extra run-time checks for the #c − #d conditions slow down the code, we have run 113 JUnit tests, that trigger blockchain transactions that execute the instrumented code of the jars in Fig. 3. The total time for running the tests (115 s) was the same both with and without the addition of the run-time checks, which shows that these do not actually slow down the execution. Note that the code without run-time checks is still instrumented for running on a blockchain. Hence, we cannot compare with fully uninstrumented code since it cannot be run [17].

6   Conclusion

The technique in this paper allows a simple specification of a deterministic fragment of the Java library and enforces its run-time constraints. Experiments show that it works in practice and does not incur in size or time degradation of the compiled code. Current work consists in enlarging the white-listed fragment. We will perform this task on demand, while writing smart contracts in Takamaka, in order to concentrate only on library portions that are relevant for that.

References

1. Hello World...from the Aion Virtual Machine! https://aion.theoan.com/blog/hello-world-from-the-aion-virtual-machine/
2. How to Use Java to Write a NEO Smart Contract. https://docs.neo.org/docs/en-us/sc/devenv/getting-started-java.html
3. BCEL. https://commons.apache.org/proper/commons-bcel. Accessed December 2017
4. Androulaki, E., et al.: Hyperledger fabric: a distributed operating system for permissioned blockchains. In: Proceedings of the Thirteenth EuroSys Conference, EuroSys 2018, Porto, Portugal, pp. 30:1–30:15. ACM (2018)
5. Antonopoulos, A.M.: Mastering Bitcoin: Programming the Open Blockchain, 2nd edn. Oreilly & Associates Inc., Boston (2017)
6. Antonopoulos, A.M., Wood, G.: Mastering Ethereum: Building Smart Contracts and Dapps, 1st edn. Oreilly & Associates Inc., Boston (2018)
7. Banerjee, A., Naumann, D.A.: Stack-based access control and secure information flow. J. Funct. Program. **15**(2), 131–177 (2005)
8. Barthe, G., Pichardie, D., Rezk, T.: A certified lightweight non-interference Java bytecode verifier. Math. Struct. Comput. Sci. **23**(5), 1032–1081 (2013)
9. Chatterjee, K., Goharshady, A.K., Pourdamghani, A.: Probabilistic smart contracts: secure randomness on the blockchain. In: Proceedings of the IEEE International Conference on Blockchain and Cryptocurrency (ICBC 2019), Seoul, South Korea, pp. 403–412. IEEE (2019)
10. Cormen, T.H., Leiserson, C.E., Rivest, R.L., Stein, C.: Introduction to Algorithms, 3rd edn. MIT Press, Cambridge (2009)
11. Iyer, K., Dannen, C.: Building Games with Ethereum Smart Contracts. Apress, New York (2018)
12. Liskov, B., Wing, J.M.: A behavioral notion of subtyping. ACM Trans. Program. Lang. Syst. **16**(6), 1811–1841 (1994)
13. Naftalin, M., Wadler, P.: Java Generics and Collections. O'Reilly, Cambridge (2006)
14. Nakamoto, S.: Bitcoin: a peer-to-peer electronic cash system. https://bitcoin.org/bitcoin.pdf. Accessed October 2008

15. Nielson, F., Nielson, H.R., Hankin, C.: Principles of Program Analysis. Springer, Heidelberg (1999). https://doi.org/10.1007/978-3-662-03811-6
16. Rice, H.G.: Classes of recursively enumerable sets and their decision problems. Trans. Am. Math. Soc. **74**(2), 358–366 (1953)
17. Spoto, F.: A Java framework for smart contracts. In: Bracciali, A., Clark, J., Pintore, F., Rønne, P.B., Sala, M. (eds.) FC 2019. LNCS, vol. 11599, pp. 122–137. Springer, Cham (2020). https://doi.org/10.1007/978-3-030-43725-1_10
18. Vukolić, M.: Rethinking permissioned blockchains. In: Proceedings of the ACM Workshop on Blockchain, Cryptocurrencies and Contracts (BCC 2017), Abu Dhabi, United Arab Emirates, pp. 3–7. ACM, April 2017

Albert, An Intermediate Smart-Contract Language for the Tezos Blockchain

Bruno Bernardo, Raphaël Cauderlier, Basile Pesin, and Julien Tesson[✉]

Nomadic Labs, Paris, France
{bruno.bernardo,raphael.cauderlier,
basile.pesin,julien.tesson}@nomadic-labs.com

Abstract. Tezos is a smart-contract blockchain. Tezos smart contracts are written in a low-level stack-based language called Michelson. In this article we present Albert, an intermediate language for Tezos smart contracts which abstracts Michelson stacks as linearly typed records. We also describe its compiler to Michelson, written in Coq, that targets Mi-Cho-Coq, a formal specification of Michelson implemented in Coq.

Keywords: Certified programming · Certified compilation ·
Programming languages · Linear types · Blockchains · Smart contracts

1 Introduction

Tezos is an account-based public blockchain and smart-contract platform. It was launched in June 2018 and an open-source implementation is available [3]. The Tezos blockchain distinguishes itself through its on-chain amendment procedure by which a super-majority of stakeholders can modify a large part of the codebase, through its liquid Proof-of-Stake consensus algorithm [2], and through its focus on formal methods which is especially visible in the design and implementation of Michelson, its smart-contract language.

Indeed, the Michelson interpreter is implemented using a GADT that statically ensures the subject reduction property. Moreover, Michelson is formally specified in the Coq proof assistant. This Coq specification is called Mi-Cho-Coq [17] and its main application today is the certification of Michelson smart contracts by deductive verification [7].

However, the stack paradigm used by Michelson is too low-level for complex applications. For this reason, several high-level languages have been developed [5,6,10,13,15,16]. Unfortunately, their compilers to Michelson are not formally verified which limits the application of formal methods for these languages.

In this article, we propose an intermediate language named Albert to avoid the duplication of effort put into compilers to Michelson and to ease the certification of these compilers. The main feature of Albert is that the Michelson stack is abstracted through named variables. The duplication and destruction of resources are however explicit operations in both Albert and Michelson, this is reflected in Albert by the use of a linear type system.

M. Bernhard et al. (Eds.): FC 2020 Workshops, LNCS 12063, pp. 584–598, 2020.
https://doi.org/10.1007/978-3-030-54455-3_41

We have formally specified the Albert language in the Ott tool [20] from which the Albert lexer, parser, and LaTeX documentation are generated. Ott can also generate typing and semantic rules for Coq and other proof assistants. We have written the Albert compiler in Coq as a function from the generated Coq output for the Albert grammar to the Michelson syntax defined in Mi-Cho-Coq.

This article is organised as follows: Sect. 2 gives an overview of the Michelson smart-contract language. Section 3 presents the Albert intermediate language, the figures of this section have been produced by the LaTeX output of Ott. The Albert compiler is then presented in Sect. 4. Section 5 discusses some related work and finally Sect. 6 concludes the article by listing directions for future work.

The Albert specification and compiler are available at https://gitlab.com/nomadic-labs/albert/tree/WTSC20.

2 Overview of Michelson

Smart contracts are Tezos accounts of a particular kind. They have private access to a memory space on the chain called the *storage* of the smart contract, each transaction to a smart contract account contains some data, the *parameter* of the transaction, and a *script* is run at each transaction to decide if the transaction is valid, update the smart contract storage, and possibly emit new operations on the Tezos blockchain.

Michelson is the language in which the smart contract scripts are written. The most important parts of the implementation of Michelson, the typechecker and the interpreter, belong to the economic ruleset of Tezos which evolves through the Tezos on-chain amendment voting process.

2.1 Design Rationale

Smart contracts operate in a very constrained context: they need to be expressive, evaluated efficiently, and their resource consumption should be accurately measured in order to stop the execution of programs that would be too greedy, as their execution time impacts the block construction and propagation. Smart contracts are non-updatable programs that can handle valuable assets, there is thus a need for strong guarantees on the correctness of these programs.

The need for efficiency and more importantly for accurate account of resource consumption leans toward a low-level interpreted language, while the need for contract correctness leans toward a high-level, easily auditable, easily formalisable language, with strong static guarantees.

To satisfy these constraints, Michelson was made a Turing-complete, low-level, stack based interpreted language (*à la* Forth), facilitating the measurement of computation costs, but with some high-level features *à la* ML: polymorphic products, options, sums, lists, sets and maps data-structures with collection iterators, cryptographic primitives and anonymous functions. Contracts are pure functions that take a stack as input and return a stack as output. This side-effect free design is an asset for the conception of verification tools.

The language is statically typed to ensure the well-formedness of the stack at any point of the program. This means that if a program is well typed, and if it is being given a well-typed stack that matches its input expectation, then at any point of the program execution, the given instruction can be evaluated on the current stack.

Moreover, to ease the formalisation of Michelson, ambiguous or hidden behaviours have been avoided. In particular, unbounded integers are used to avoid arithmetic overflows and division returns an option (which is None if and only if the divisor is 0) so that the Michelson programmer has to specify the behaviour of the program in case of division by 0; she can however still *explicitly* reject the transaction using the **FAILWITH** Michelson instruction.

2.2   Quick Tour of the Language

The full language syntax, type system, and semantics are documented in [1], we give here a quick and partial overview of the language.

Contracts' Shape. A Michelson smart contract script is written in three parts: the parameter type, the storage type, and the code of the contract. A contract's code consists of one block that can only be called with one parameter, but multiple entry points can be encoded by branching on a nesting of sum types and multiple parameters can be paired into one.

When the contract is deployed (or *originated* in Tezos lingo) on the chain, it is bundled with a data storage which can then only be changed by a contract's successful execution. The parameter and the storage associated to the contract are paired and passed to the contract's code at each execution. The execution of the code must return a list of operations and the updated storage.

Seen from the outside, the type of the contract is the type of its parameter, as it is the only way to interact with it.

Michelson Instructions. As usual in stack-based languages, Michelson instructions take their parameters on the stack. All Michelson instructions are typed as a function going from the expected state of the stack, before the instruction evaluation, to the resulting stack. For example, the **AMOUNT** instruction used to obtain the amount in μtez (*i.e.* a millionth of a *tez*, the smallest token unit in Tezos) of the current transaction has type 'S $\rightarrow$ mutez:'S meaning that for any stack type 'S, it produces a stack of type mutez:'S. Michelson uses an ordered type system which means that the number of times values are used and the order in which they are introduced and consumed matter and are visible at the type level. Some operations such as **SWAP** :: 'a:'b:'S $\rightarrow$ 'b:'a:'S, **DUP** :: 'a:'S $\rightarrow$ 'a:'a:'S, and **DROP** :: 'a:'S $\rightarrow$ 'S have to be used to respectively change the order of the values on the Michelson stack, to duplicate a value, and to pop a value from the stack without actually using it. Some instructions, like comparison or arithmetic operations, exhibit non-ambiguous ad-hoc polymorphism: depending on the input arguments' type, a specific implementation of the instruction is selected, and the return type is fixed. For example **SIZE** has the following types:

$$\texttt{bytes:'S} \rightarrow \texttt{nat:'S}$$
$$\texttt{string:'S} \rightarrow \texttt{nat:'S}$$

$$\texttt{set 'elt:'S} \rightarrow \texttt{nat:'S}$$
$$\texttt{map 'key 'val:'S} \rightarrow \texttt{nat:'S}$$
$$\texttt{list 'elt:'S} \rightarrow \texttt{nat:'S}$$

While computing the size of a string or an array of bytes is similarly implemented, under the hood, the computation of map size has nothing to do with the computation of string size.

Finally, the contract's code is required to take a stack with a pair *parameter-storage* and returns a stack with a pair *operation list-storage*:

$$(\texttt{parameter\_ty*storage\_ty}):[] \rightarrow (\texttt{operation list*storage\_ty}):[].$$

The operations listed at the end of the execution can change the delegate of the contract, originate new contracts, or transfer tokens to other addresses. They will be executed right after the execution of the contract. The transfers can have parameters and trigger the execution of other smart contracts: this is the only way to perform *inter-contract* calls.

3 The Albert Intermediate Language

Michelson, as a stack-based language, is a difficult and unusual target for compiler writers. In addition to the usual effort to translate high-level constructions to lower-level types and control-flow, they have to deal with stack manipulation to make values available at the right stack position when calling an Michelson opcode, and to cope with the consumption of values by the opcode execution.

These additional difficulties also hinder the effort of teams developing static analysers and verification frameworks.

As a first simplification step, we have decided to build an intermediate language that abstracts away the ordering of values in the stack and provides a named binding to values. This intermediate language still keeps track of the resources as variables are typed by a linear type system, which enforces each value to be consumed exactly once. When a value is needed more than once, it must be explicitly duplicated with a dup operation. Generation of dups is left to a future higher-level intermediate language.

In the process of defining the language, we thought that it would also be helpful to define some abstractions over the datatypes so we provide support for *records* which compile to nestings of Michelson's binary product type pair and *variants* which compile to nestings of Michelson's binary sum type or.

We also offer to define separate non-recursive function definitions used to define programming libraries. These functions are inlined at compile time.

3.1 Base Language

The Albert language is defined as a collection of small language fragments that can be studied independently. Each fragment is defined in a separate Ott file.

The first fragment to consider is called the *base* fragment. As its name suggests, this fragment is the basis on top of which the other fragments are defined.

The base fragment contains the two main features of Albert: the stack is abstracted by named variables and Michelson binary pairs are generalized as records. We use the metavariable l to denote record labels and the metavariable x to denote variables but these two notions are unified in Albert.

Records and Linear Typing. As we have seen it Sect. 2.2, Michelson uses an ordered type system that tracks both the order of the values on the stack and the number of uses of the values. Most high-level languages however bind values to named variables and implicitly handle the ordering and number of uses of variables. The required stack manipulation instructions are introduced at compile time. Albert is an intermediate language between these two extremes. In Albert, the order of values is abstracted but not the number of uses which is still explicitly handled.

This choice is reflected in Albert's type system by the use of linear typing. Each expression of the Albert language is typed by a pair of record types whose labels are the variables touched by the instruction or expression; the first record type describes the consumed values and the second record type describes the produced values.

Thanks to the unification of variable names and record labels, records in Albert generalize both the Michelson stack types and the Michelson pair type. In the base fragment of Albert, all types are possibly-empty record types.

The grammar of types of the base fragment given in Fig. 1.

$$
\begin{array}{llll}
label,\ l\ ::= & \text{Label / variable} & ty\ ::= & \text{Type} \\
\mid & id & \mid\ rty & \text{Record type}
\end{array}
$$

$$
\begin{array}{ll}
rty\ ::= & \text{Record type} \\
\mid\ \{l_1\ :\ ty_1;\ ..\ ;\ l_n\ :\ ty_n\} &
\end{array}
$$

Fig. 1. Syntax of the record types

In the record type $\{l_1\ :\ ty_1;\ ..\ ;\ l_n\ :\ ty_n\}$, we assume the labels to be distinct and lexicographically ordered.

This constraint is formalized by the well-formedness judgement $\Gamma \vdash ty$ defined in Fig. 2. The typing context Γ is always empty here but other cases for typing contexts will be added in other language fragments.

The grammar for the base fragment is defined in Fig. 3. Albert's grammar is more stratified than Michelson's grammar because we adopt from imperative languages the usual distinction between expressions and instructions. An instruction is either the **noop** instruction that does nothing, a sequence of instructions separated by semicolons, or an assignment *lhs=rhs* where the left-hand side *lhs* is either a variable or a record of variables and the right-hand side is an expression.

$$\boxed{\Gamma \vdash ty} \quad \text{Type well-formedness}$$

$$\frac{\begin{array}{c} l_1 < .. < l_n \\ \Gamma \vdash ty_1 \quad .. \quad \Gamma \vdash ty_n \\ \Gamma \vdash \end{array}}{\Gamma \vdash \{l_1 \; : \; ty_1; \; ..; \; l_n \; : \; ty_n\}}$$

Fig. 2. Type well-formedness judgment

Contrary to usual imperative expressions, arbitrary nesting of expressions is not allowed and intermediate values should be named. This restriction, inspired by the static single assignment form commonly used in intermediate compilation languages, is designed to ease the production of Michelson code and to allow for more optimisations at the level of the Albert language in the future. In practice, this restriction means that an expression is either a variable x, a value val, the application of a user-defined function to a variable $f\,x$, a record projection $x.l$, or a record update $\{var\, \text{with}\, l_1{=}var_1; \; ...; \; l_n{=}var_n\}$.

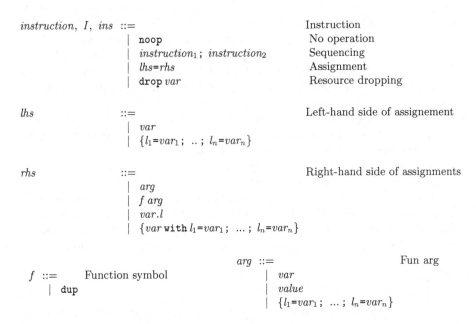

Fig. 3. Syntax of the base fragment

The type system of the base fragment is presented in Fig. 4. In the case of instruction sequencing $instruction;\ instruction'$, we do not want to restrict $instruction'$ to consume exactly the values produced by $instruction$. To avoid this limitation, we have added the framing rule FRAME. This rule can be used to extend both record types *rty* and *rty'* used for typing an instruction *instruction* by the same record type *rty''*. This extension is performed by the join operator ⊙, a partial function computing the disjoint union of two record types.

Operational Semantics. The semantics of the Albert base language is defined in big-step style in Fig. 5. The definition of this semantic relation is unsurprising because the base fragment is very simple and the type system does not let much freedom at this point.

3.2   Language Extensions

The full Albert language is obtained by adding to the base fragment that we have just defined a series of language extensions. The main purpose of these extensions is to reflect all the features available in Michelson. The only new main feature compared to Michelson is the generalisation of the binary sum type or into n-ary non-recursive variants with named constructors.

Albert's variant types generalize the or, option, and bool types of Michelson. Variants are the dual of records, with the caveat that it is not possible to construct an empty variant as Michelson does not have an empty type it could correspond to. Variants offer two main operations to the user: constructing a variant value using a constructor, and pattern-matching on a variant value.

Constructors are determined by a label, and applied as a function on a single value. When constructing a variant value, the user must indicate the full type of the variant value because the same constructor name is allowed to appear in different variant types. We use the syntax $[C_1 : ty_1 \mid .. \mid C_n : ty_n]$ for the variant type whose constructors are the $C_1, \ldots, C_n$ where each C_k expects an argument of type ty_k. The types or a b, option a, and bool in Albert are aliases for the variant types [Left : a | Right : b], [Some : a | None : {}] and [False : {} | True : {}] respectively.

Pattern matching can be used on variants either as a right-hand side or as an instruction. In both cases, the Albert syntax for pattern matching is similar to the OCaml syntax of pattern matching; for right-hand sides, the syntax is match x with | pattern_1 →rhs_1 | ... | pattern_n →rhs_n end.

3.3   Example: A Voting Contract

We present in Fig. 6 a simple voting contract written in Albert. The user of the contract can vote for a predefined set of options by sending tokens and its choice (represented by a string) to the contract.

The storage of the contract (line 1) is a record with two fields: a **threshold** that represents a minimum amount that must be transferred to the contract for the vote to be considered, and an associative map, **votes**, with strings as keys (the options of the vote) and integers as values (the number of votes for each associated key).

$$\boxed{\Gamma \vdash instruction \; : \; ty \Rightarrow ty'}$$
Instruction typing

$$\frac{\begin{array}{c} \Gamma \vdash rty_1 \\ \Gamma \vdash rty_2 \\ rty \odot rty''=rty_1 \\ rty' \odot rty''=rty_2 \\ \Gamma \vdash instruction \; : \; rty \Rightarrow rty' \end{array}}{\Gamma \vdash instruction \; : \; rty_1 \Rightarrow rty_2} \; \text{FRAME}$$

$$\overline{\Gamma \vdash \mathtt{noop} \; : \; \{\,\} \Rightarrow \{\,\}}$$

$$\frac{\begin{array}{c} \Gamma \vdash instruction \; : \; ty_1 \Rightarrow ty_2 \\ \Gamma \vdash instruction' \; : \; ty_2 \Rightarrow ty_3 \end{array}}{\Gamma \vdash instruction; \; instruction' \; : \; ty_1 \Rightarrow ty_3}$$

$$\frac{\begin{array}{c} \Gamma \vdash rhs \; : \; a \Rightarrow b \\ \Gamma \vdash lhs \; : \; b \Rightarrow c \end{array}}{\Gamma \vdash lhs{=}rhs \; : \; a \Rightarrow c}$$

$$\overline{\Gamma \vdash \mathtt{drop} \; var \; : \; \{var : ty\} \Rightarrow \{\,\}}$$

$$\boxed{\Gamma \vdash lhs \; : \; ty \Rightarrow ty'}$$
Left-hand sides typing

$$\overline{\Gamma \vdash var \; : \; ty \Rightarrow \{var : ty\}}$$

$$\overline{\Gamma \vdash \{l_1{=}x_1; \; ..; \; l_n{=}x_n\} \; : \; \{l_1 : ty_1; \; ..; \; l_n : ty_n\} \Rightarrow \{x_1 : ty_1; \; ..; \; x_n : ty_n\}}$$

$$\boxed{\Gamma \vdash rhs \; : \; ty \Rightarrow ty'}$$
Right-hand side typing

$$\frac{\Gamma \vdash_a arg \; : \; ty \Rightarrow ty'}{\Gamma \vdash arg \; : \; ty \Rightarrow ty'}$$

$$\frac{\begin{array}{c} \Gamma \vdash_a arg \; : \; ty \Rightarrow ty' \\ \Gamma \vdash f \; : \; ty' \Rightarrow ty'' \end{array}}{\Gamma \vdash f \; arg \; : \; ty \Rightarrow ty''}$$

$$\frac{\begin{array}{c} \{l : ty\} \odot rty{=}rty' \\ \Gamma \vdash rty' \end{array}}{\Gamma \vdash var.l \; : \; rty' \Rightarrow ty}$$

$$\frac{\begin{array}{c} \Gamma \vdash rty' \\ \{l_1 : ty_1; \; ..; \; l_n : ty_n\} \odot rty{=}rty' \end{array}}{\Gamma \vdash \{var \, \mathtt{with} \, l_1{=}var_1; \; ..; \; l_n{=}var_n\} \; : \; \{var : rty'; \; var_1 : ty_1; \; ..; \; var_n : ty_n\} \Rightarrow rty'}$$

$$\boxed{\Gamma \vdash f \; : \; ty \Rightarrow ty'}$$
Function symbol typing

$$\overline{\Gamma \vdash \mathtt{dup} \; : \; ty \Rightarrow \{\mathtt{car} : ty; \; \mathtt{cdr} : ty\}}$$

$$\boxed{\Gamma \vdash_a arg \; : \; ty \Rightarrow ty'} \quad \text{Argument typing}$$

$$\overline{\Gamma \vdash_a var \; : \; \{var : ty\} \Rightarrow ty}$$

$$\frac{\Gamma \vdash value \; : \; ty}{\Gamma \vdash_a value \; : \; \{\,\} \Rightarrow ty}$$

$$\overline{\Gamma \vdash_a \{l_1{=}x_1; \; ..; \; l_n{=}x_n\} \; : \; \{x_1 : ty_1; \; ..; \; x_n : ty_n\} \Rightarrow \{l_1 : ty_1; \; ..; \; l_n : ty_n\}}$$

Fig. 4. Typing rules for the base fragment

$$\boxed{lhs/val \implies val'}\quad \text{Left-hand side evaluation}$$

$$\overline{var/val \implies \{var\text{=}val\}}$$

$$\overline{\{l_1\text{=}x_1;\ ..;\ l_n\text{=}x_n\}/\{l_1\text{=}val_1;\ ..;\ l_n\text{=}val_n\} \implies \{x_1\text{=}val_1;\ ..;\ x_n\text{=}val_n\}}$$

$$\boxed{arg/_a val \implies val'}\quad \text{Argument evaluation}$$

$$\overline{var/_a\{var\text{=}val\} \implies val}$$

$$\overline{val/_a\{\} \implies val}$$

$$\overline{\{l_1\text{=}x_1;\ ..;\ l_n\text{=}x_n\}/_a\{x_1\text{=}val_1;\ ..;\ x_n\text{=}val_n\} \implies \{l_1\text{=}val_1;\ ..;\ l_n\text{=}val_n\}}$$

$$\boxed{f/val \implies val'}\quad \text{Function symbol evaluation}$$

$$\overline{\mathtt{dup}/val \implies \{\mathtt{car}\text{=}val;\ \mathtt{cdr}\text{=}val\}}$$

$$\boxed{rhs/val \implies val'}\quad \text{Right-hand side evaluation}$$

$$\frac{arg/_a val \implies val'}{arg/val \implies val'}$$

$$\frac{arg/_a val \implies val'\quad f/val' \implies val''}{f\ arg/val \implies val''}$$

$$\frac{\{l\text{=}val\} \odot rval\text{=}rval'}{var.l/rval' \implies val}$$

$$\frac{\{l_1\text{=}val_1';\ ..;\ l_n\text{=}val_n'\} \odot rval\text{=}rval'\quad \{l_1\text{=}val_1;\ ..;\ l_n\text{=}val_n\} \odot rval\text{=}rval''}{\{var\ \mathtt{with}\ l_1\text{=}var_1;\ ..;\ l_n\text{=}var_n\}/\{var\text{=}rval';\ var_1\text{=}val_1;\ ..;\ var_n\text{=}val_n\} \implies rval''}$$

$$\boxed{instruction/val \implies val'}\quad \text{Instruction evaluation}$$

$$\frac{instruction/rval \implies rval'\quad rval \odot rval''\text{=}rval_1\quad rval' \odot rval''\text{=}rval_2}{instruction/rval_1 \implies rval_2}$$

$$\overline{\mathtt{noop}/\{\} \implies \{\}}$$

$$\frac{I_1/val \implies val'\quad I_2/val' \implies val''}{I_1;\ I_2/val \implies val''}$$

$$\frac{rhs/val \implies val'\quad lhs/val' \implies val''}{lhs\text{=}rhs/val \implies val''}$$

$$\overline{\mathtt{drop}\ var/\{var\text{=}val\} \implies \{\}}$$

Fig. 5. Big-step operational semantics of the base fragment

If the user sends less tokens that the threshold or if the parameter sent is not one of the options (the keys of the votes map), then the call to the contract will fail.

The contract contains two functions, vote and **guarded_vote**. Both functions respect Michelson's call conventions: they take as input the parameter and the storage combined and return a list of operations and an updated storage.

vote checks that the parameter is one of the voting options (l. 9 and 10). If not, the contract fails (due to assert_some in l.10). Otherwise, the number of votes associated to the parameter is increased by one (l. 11 and 12). vote returns an updated storage as well as an empty list of operations.

guarded_vote, the main function, checks that the amount of tokens sent (obtained with the amount primitive instruction l.21) is greater or equal to the threshold (l.22). If so, then vote is applied. Otherwise, it fails.

```
1    type storage_ty = { threshold : mutez; votes: map string nat }
2
3    def vote :
4      { param : string ; store : storage_ty } →
5      { operations : list operation ; store : storage_ty } =
6          {votes = state; threshold = threshold } = store ;
7          (state0, state1) = dup state;
8          (param0, param1) = dup param;
9          prevote_option = state0[param0];
10         { res = prevote } = assert_some { opt = prevote_option };
11         one = 1; postvote = prevote + one; postvote = Some postvote;
12         final_state = update state1 param1 postvote;
13         store = {threshold = threshold; votes = final_state};
14         operations = ([] : list operation)
15
16   def guarded_vote :
17     { param : string ; store : storage_ty } →
18     { operations : list operation ; store : storage_ty } =
19        (store0, store1) = dup store;
20        threshold = store0.threshold;
21        am = amount;
22        ok = am >= threshold0;
23        match ok with
24            False f →failwith "you_are_so_cheap!"
25          | True t →drop t;
26              voting_parameters = { param = param ; store = store1 };
27              vote voting_parameters
28        end
```

Fig. 6. A voting contract, in Albert

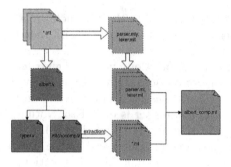

Fig. 7. Compiler architecture: dashed frames designate generated component, solid arrows represent relevant library dependencies.

4   Compilation to Michelson

4.1   Compiler Architecture

As we want to be able to prove the correctness of our compiler in a near future, we decided to implement it in Coq. This allows us to easily take advantage of Ott's definitions automatically translated to Coq, as well as to easily compile to Mi-Cho-Coq's AST. Moreover, using Coq's extraction facilities, our compiler transpiles to OCaml code, which is more efficient and easier to use as a library.

The global architecture of the compiler is depicted in Fig. 7. The compiler pipeline, defined using OCaml glue code, roughly follows a classic architecture, notwithstanding the peculiar tools used: the lexer-parser, automatically generated from the grammar described in Ott, produces an AST which is then checked and annotated by the typer, extracted from a Coq development. Then, the compilation function, also written in Coq and extracted to OCaml, translates the typed Albert AST into an untyped Mi-Cho-Coq AST. Finally, the extracted Mi-Cho-Coq pretty-printer is used to produce a string which is a Michelson program, and which the glue code dumps into a file ready to be injected in the Tezos blockchain.

Typechecker. The type checker phase can be divided in three steps.

First, type aliases declared by the user are replaced by their actual definition. This will simplify the verification of type equivalence in the next phases, as we will not have to worry about type variables. As declared types are simple aliases - types can't be recursively declared – this amounts to inlining the type aliases wherever they are found in the program.

The second step normalises type declarations by sorting in lexicographic order both the fields of records and the constructors of variants.

Finally, the third step checks that all defined functions are well typed. Currently, this type-checking proceeds in one pass from top to bottom and it does not perform any type inference. It checks the linearity of variable usage, the compatibility of operands' types with their operator and the exhaustiveness of pattern matching. Each instruction is annotated with an input and output environments. The environment being a record type, associating a type to each variable name. One can note here that this record type is actually a description of the Michelson stack at each point of the program where position have been replaced by names.

The type checker is defined as a Coq function, thus is a total function. Its implementation uses an error monad to deal with ill-typed programs. If a program does not type check, an error message is returned instead of the typed version of the AST.

The lack of type inference is not too much of a limitation since the higher-level languages that will target Albert have enough type information to produce the explicit type annotations that are mandatory, as for example on variant constructors.

4.2   Compilation Scheme

To compile an Albert program to a Michelson program, we need first to convert Albert's types to Michelson's types and Albert's data to Michelson's data, then to translate Albert instructions to an equivalent Michelson sequence of instructions.

Types and Data. Because Albert's primitive types reflect Michelson types, their translation is obvious. Only the translation of records and variants is not trivial. Records are translated into nested pairs of values, whereas variants are translated into a nesting of sum types. For the sake of simplicity, we use a comb shaped nesting, making access to records' fields and size of variant constructor linear in the size of the Albert type. A future task will be to provide a syntax to control the shape of the Michelson translation or to use a balanced tree shape.

Instructions. The compilation scheme of instructions is rather straightforward. Projections of records fields are translated into a sequence of projections over the relevant parts of a pair. Pattern matching over variants are translated into a nesting of IF_LEFT branchings. Each branch of an Albert pattern-matching is translated in Michelson and inserted in the associated position of the Michelson IF_LEFT branchings tree.

At every point of the program we memorise a mapping from variable names to their positions in the stack. Each operation is then translated to the equivalent operation in Michelson, prefixed by DIG n operations that move the operands on top of the stack, n being the index of the variables used as operands.

Function arguments are brought back on top of the stack if they are variables and are pushed on it if they are literals. The Michelson translation of the function is then inlined.

Assignment instructions translate into a translation of the right hand side computation, followed by a reordering of data, guided by the shape of the left hand side: simple variable assignments DUG the result deeper in the stack for later use, while record patterns translate to a pairing destruction and then some stack reorganisation.

Our mapping from variable names to stack positions is currently naive and enforces the invariant that the elements of the stack are ordered by the lexicographic order of the variable names. This requires too much stack reorganisation and will be later replaced by an optimising placement algorithm.

5   Related Work

Formal verification of smart contracts is a recent but active field. The K framework has been used to formalise [12] the semantics of both low-level and high-level smart-contract languages for the Ethereum and Cardano blockchains. These formalisations have been used to verify common smart contracts such as Casper, Uniswap, and various implementations of the ERC20 and ERC777 standards. A formalization of Michelson in the K framework [21] is also under development.

In the case of Cardano, the high-level language is called Plutus and the low-level one is called Plutus Core. The metatheory of System $F_{\omega\mu}$, an extension of System F very similar to Plutus Core, has been formalized [9] in the Agda proof assistant. Moreover, parts of the Plutus compiler [14] are also defined (but not certified) in Agda.

Note also a formalisation of the EVM in the F* dependently-typed language [11], that was validated against the official Ethereum test suite. This formalisation effort led to formal definitions of security properties for smart contracts (call integrity, atomicity, etc).

Ethereum smart contracts, written in the Solidity high-level language, can also be certified using a translation to F* [8].

The Zen Protocol [4] directly uses F* as its smart-contract language so that smart contracts of the Zen Protocol can be proved directly in F*. Moreover, runtime tracking of resources can be avoided since computation and storage costs are encoded in the dependent types.

The Scilla [18] language of the Zilliqa blockchain has been formalised in Coq as a shallow embedding. This intermediate language is higher-level (it is based on λ-calculus) but also less featureful (it is not Turing-complete as it does not feature unbounded loops nor general recursion) than Michelson and Albert. Its formalisation includes inter-contract interaction and contract lifespan properties. This has been used to show safety properties of a crowdfunding smart contract. Moreover, Scilla's framework for writing static analyses [19] can be used for automated verification of some specific properties.

In the particular case of the Tezos platform, several high-level languages are being developed [5,6,10,13,15,16] to ease the development of smart contracts. Formal specification is featured in the Archetype language [10], the specification is then translated to the Why3 platform for automated verification. In Juvix [15], dependent types can be used to specify and verify smart contracts and resources are tracked in a similar fashion to Albert's linear type system thanks to a variant of quantitative type theory in Juvix's core language.

6   Conclusion and Future Work

The Albert intermediate language has been formally specified in a very modular way using the Ott framework. This formal specification is the unique source from which Albert's parser (written in Menhir), Albert's typechecker and compiler (written in Coq) and the Sect. 3 of this article (written in LaTeX) are generated.

The current implementation of the compiler is rather naive and we plan to improve the performance of the produced code by sorting the values on the Michelson stack not by the name of the corresponding Albert variable but by their last use so that no work is performed after a variable assignment to dive it back to its position in the stack. This will however add some complexity in the compiler when several branches of a pattern-matching construction are joined because we will need to permute the stack in all but one of them to recover matching stack types in all branches.

The Coq versions of the language specification and the compiler open the possibility of certifying the compiler correctness and meta-properties of the Albert language such as subject reduction and progress. We have started proving these properties in Coq to improve the trust in the Albert tools.

Finally, we would like to add to Albert a specification language and support for deductive verification through the use of ghost code so that functional verification of Tezos smart contracts can be performed with the very high level of confidence offered by Coq and Mi-Cho-Coq but at a higher level than Michelson.

References

1. Michelson: the language of Smart Contracts in Tezos. https://tezos.gitlab.io/whitedoc/michelson.html
2. Proof-of-stake in Tezos. https://tezos.gitlab.io/whitedoc/proof_of_stake.html
3. Tezos code repository. https://gitlab.com/tezos/tezos
4. An introduction to the Zen protocol (2017). https://www.zenprotocol.com/files/zen_protocol_white_paper.pdf
5. Alfour, G.: LIGO: a friendly smart-contract language for Tezos. https://ligolang.org. Accessed 12 Dec 2019
6. Andrews, S., Ayotte, R.: Fi: smart coding for smart contracts. https://fi-code.com. Accessed 12 Dec 2019
7. Bernardo, B., Cauderlier, R., Hu, Z., Pesin, B., Tesson, J.: Mi-Cho-Coq, a framework for certifying Tezos Smart Contracts. In: Proceedings of the First Workshop on Formal Methods for Blockchains, FMBC 2019 (2019). (to be published). https://arxiv.org/abs/1909.08671
8. Bhargavan, K., et al.: Formal verification of smart contracts: short paper. In: PLAS 2016, pp. 91–96. ACM, New York (2016). https://doi.org/10.1145/2993600.2993611
9. Chapman, J., Kireev, R., Nester, C., Wadler, P.: System F in Agda, for fun and profit. In: Hutton, G. (ed.) MPC 2019. LNCS, vol. 11825, pp. 255–297. Springer, Cham (2019). https://doi.org/10.1007/978-3-030-33636-3_10
10. Duhamel, G., Rognier, B., Sturb, P.Y., Edukera: Archetype: a Tezos smart contract development solution dedicated to contract quality insurance. https://docs.archetype-lang.org. Accessed 12 Dec 2019

11. Grishchenko, I., Maffei, M., Schneidewind, C.: A semantic framework for the security analysis of ethereum smart contracts. In: Bauer, L., Küsters, R. (eds.) POST 2018. LNCS, vol. 10804, pp. 243–269. Springer, Cham (2018). https://doi.org/10.1007/978-3-319-89722-6_10

12. Hildenbrandt, E., et al.: KEVM: a complete semantics of the ethereum virtual machine. In: 2018 IEEE 31st Computer Security Foundations Symposium, pp. 204–217. IEEE (2018)

13. DaiLambda, Inc.: SCaml: it's not a scam. https://www.dailambda.jp/blog/2019-12-07-scaml/. Accessed 12 Dec 2019

14. Peyton Jones, M., Gkoumas, V., Kireev, R., MacKenzie, K., Nester, C., Wadler, P.: Unraveling recursion: compiling an IR with recursion to system F. In: Hutton, G. (ed.) MPC 2019. LNCS, vol. 11825, pp. 414–443. Springer, Cham (2019). https://doi.org/10.1007/978-3-030-33636-3_15

15. Labs, C.: Juvix: a more elegant language for a more civilized age. https://github.com/cryptiumlabs/juvix. Accessed 12 Dec 2019

16. Maurel, F., Arena, S.C.: SmartPy. https://smartpy.io. Accessed 12 Dec 2019

17. Nomadic Labs: Mi-Cho-Coq public repository. https://gitlab.com/nomadic-labs/mi-cho-coq

18. Sergey, I., Kumar, A., Hobor, A.: Scilla: a smart contract intermediate-level language. CoRR abs/1801.00687 (2018). http://arxiv.org/abs/1801.00687

19. Sergey, I., Nagaraj, V., Johannsen, J., Kumar, A., Trunov, A., Hao, K.C.G.: Safer smart contract programming with Scilla. In: PACMPL 3(OOPSLA), pp. 185:1–185:30 (2019). https://doi.org/10.1145/3360611

20. Sewell, P., Nardelli, F.Z., Owens, S.: Ott. https://github.com/ott-lang/ott

21. Verification, R.: A K semantics of Tezos' Michelson language. https://github.com/runtimeverification/michelson-semantics. Accessed 12 Dec 2019

A Formally Verified Static Analysis Framework for Compositional Contracts

Fritz Henglein[1,2]([⊠]), Christian Kjær Larsen[1], and Agata Murawska[1,2]

[1] University of Copenhagen, Copenhagen, Denmark
{henglein,c.kjaer,agata}@di.ku.dk
[2] Deon Digital, Copenhagen, Denmark

Abstract. A (commercial or financial) contract is a mutual agreement to exchange resources such as money, goods and services amongst multiple parties. It expresses which actions may, must and must not be performed by its parties at which time, location and under which other conditions.

We present a general framework for statically analyzing *digital contracts*, formal specifications of contracts, expressed in *Contract Specification Language* (CSL). Semantically, a CSL contract classifies traces of events into compliant (complete and successful) and noncompliant (incomplete or manifestly breached) ones.

Our analysis framework is based on compositional abstract interpretation, which soundly approximates the set of traces a contract denotes by an abstract value in a lattice. The framework is parameterized by a lattice and an interpretation of contract primitives and combinators, satisfying certain requirements. It treats recursion by unrestricted unfolding. Employing Schmidt's natural semantics approach, we interpret our inference system coinductively to account for infinite derivation trees, and prove their abstract interpretation sound.

Finally, we show some example applications: participation analysis (who is possibly involved in a transfer to whom; who does definitely participate in a contract) and fairness analysis (bounds on how much is gained by each participant under any compliant execution of the contract).

The semantics of CSL, the abstract interpretation framework and its correctness theorem, and the example analyses as instances of the abstract interpretation framework have all been mechanized in the Coq proof assistant.

1 Introduction

Rising interest in distributed ledger technology has spawned increased development of *smart contract languages*, specification and programming languages for expressing and managing the execution state of a multi-party contract.

© Springer Nature Switzerland AG 2020
M. Bernhard et al. (Eds.): FC 2020 Workshops, LNCS 12063, pp. 599–619, 2020.
https://doi.org/10.1007/978-3-030-54455-3_42

1.1   Digital Contracts, Control and Settlement

Smart contract languages are often full-fledged, Turing-complete, expressive programming languages that combine—and conflate—the *contract* (a "passive" object like to a protocol or rulebook, corresponding to a paper contract), its *control* (validating actions by the contract parties; performing actions on behalf of contract parties such as receiving escrow payments; soliciting and reacting to other relevant events such as stock prices in derivatives contracts) and the *settlement* (validation and effecting) of resource transfers. They are thus hard to analyze both in principle and in practice.

In contrast to this, *Contract Specification Language* [4], used by Deon Digital [14] for specifying contracts in a finance, insurance and other domains, is a relatively simple, CSP-like domain-specific language with deliberately few constructs for composing contracts from subcontracts. CSL is a *digital contract* language with its own, independent semantics; it specifies only contracts, not their control nor their settlement.

We find it advantageous to keep contracts, control and settlement logically and architecturally separated under the motto *smart contract = contract + control + settlement*, analogous to Kowalski's *algorithm = logic + control* [25]. It facilitates having the same contract managed by a choice of contract managers: with or without escrow [18], with different collateral requirements [15], different or changing regulatory reporting requirements, etc.; and employing existing resource managers, notably the banking system, without intermediation (tokenization) [17,19].

Keeping contracts and contract managers separate supports portability, analysis, adaptive control.[1] In particular, digital contracts can be *analyzed* without having to analyze the full programming language(s) in which their management and resource transfers are coded.

1.2   Contributions

We claim the following novel contributions:

- We provide a semantic framework for digital contracts and a novel abstract interpretation framework for soundly analyzing contracts written in the contract specification language CSL, including support for specifying contracts using general recursion.
- We provide illustrative analyses that represent important properties of a contract: Who is transferring resources to whom? Who may be involved (participate) in the contract? Who is definitely expected to participate – have they signed up to the contract? Is the contract always roughly fair (e.g. under a mark-to-market valuation of all resources exchanged) under *any* valid execution?

---

[1] If desirable; "code is law" by contract parties fixing the association of a specific immutable contract manager is a *possibility*, not a *necessity* in this framework.

– We specify containment semantics, the abstract interpretation framework of
  CSL and formally verify the soundness of the general framework, as well as
  the correctness of presented example analyses, in the Coq proof assistant.

Our approach is based on CSL's containment semantics, which is formulated as
a proof of compliance for a *complete* event trace. Intuitively, this is like asking
only at the very end whether the events occurred constitute a valid, complete
execution. In practice, CSL contracts are *monitored* online, processing one event
at a time. Here, we exploit the powerful meta-theoretic property that the monitoring semantics and the containment semantics are equivalent. If we consider
the monitoring semantics as the primary semantics, the containment semantics
crucially provides a (co)induction principle for compositional analysis of contracts. It facilitates a powerful, but also deceptively simple way of formulating
abstract interpretations and proving their soundness.

1.3 Paper Organization

The remainder of the paper is organized as follows. In Sect. 2 we present a couple
of examples of contracts in CSL and discuss the analyses we would like to perform
on them. This informal presentation of CSL is followed by a proper introduction
in Sect. 3. We then present our general analysis framework and examples of
concrete analyses of participation and fairness in Sect. 4. Details regarding the
complete Coq mechanization[2] of the presented theory follow in Sect. 5. Section 6
concludes with related work and discussion of future work.

2 Preview

We begin by looking at a few multi-party contracts and the types of analyses we
might be interested in applying to them.

The first example is a sales contract, where we use a trusted third party
(escrow manager) to make sure that a seller of an item delivers it before receiving
the payment. Here we first expect a payment from the buyer to the escrow. Then
we have a choice of either delivering the bike and getting the money from the
escrow manager before the deadline, or returning the money after the deadline.
In CSL this can be written in the following, slightly simplified way:

```
letrec sale[trusted, seller, buyer, goods, payment, deadline] =
  Transfer(buyer, trusted, payment, _).
    (Transfer(seller, buyer, goods, T | T < deadline).
    Transfer(trusted, seller, payment, T' | True).Success
  + Transfer(trusted, buyer, payment, T | T > deadline).Success)

  in sale("3rd", "shop", "alice", 1 bike, 1000 EUR, 2019-09-01)
```

---

[2] Available at https://ayertienna.github.io/csl_formalization_wtsc20.zip.

In this multiparty contract we are interested in the possible resource flows between the involved parties. For instance, we want to check that the trusted third party never receives money from the seller, and is only handling resources from the buyer. We call this *participation analysis*, and the result of it is a relation between pairs of agents. For the escrow sale contract this relation is $R_p = \{(3rd \rightarrow shop), (shop \rightarrow alice), (alice \rightarrow 3rd), (3rd \rightarrow alice)\}$.

We might also be interested in checking how much each agent can gain (or lose) by participating in the contract. *Fairness analysis* infers lower and upper bounds on the utility of participating in the contract for each participant. As an input to the analysis, we provide a valuation function mapping a unit of a resource type to a real number representing its value in some base currency, for instance: $V = \{bike \mapsto 900, EUR \mapsto 1\}$. Looking at the contract, there are two possible outcomes. If the shop does not deliver the bike, neither the shop nor Alice have any gain or loss. If the shop delivers the bike, it gains 100 and Alice loses 100 because of the difference between value and purchase price. The result of the analysis we would like to obtain is $R_q = \{(3rd, [0, 0]), (shop, [0, 100]), (alice, [-100, 0])\}$.

The `sale` contract is fairly simple to analyze, since it does not contain any recursion or transfers with complicated acceptance conditions. However, things can quickly get harder, for instance if we look at this loan contract:

```
letrec repay[amount, interest, payments, from, to] =
    Transfer(from, to, R, _ | R = amount * payments + interest).Success
  + Transfer(from, to, R, _ | payments > 1 ∧ R = amount + interest).
    repay(amount, interest, payments - 1, from, to)

    in Transfer("bob", "alice", 1200 EUR, _) .
       repay(100 EUR, 10 EUR, 12, "alice", "bob")
```

The participation analysis is still easy, returning $R_p = \{(bob \rightarrow alice), (alice \rightarrow bob)\}$. Analyzing the fairness is a bit more tricky, but it is still possible to infer that in this case, $R_q = \{(alice, [-120, -10]), (bob, [10, 120])\}$. Now let us combine `sale` with `repay` in the following way:

```
letrec sale[trusted, seller, buyer, item, payment, deadline] = ...
       repay[amount, interest, payments, from, to] = ...
in sale("3rd", "shop", "bob", 1 bike, 1000 EUR, 2019-09-01);
   (sale("3rd", "bob", "alice", 1 bike, 1 EUR, 2019-09-08)
   || repay(100 EUR, 5 EUR, 10, "alice", "bob"))
```

It may not be immediately obvious, but this is an extremely unfair contract, since the second `sale` contract (or both of them) may be canceled, and yet `alice` is obliged to pay back the 1000 EUR (with interest!). In this case, the potential gains and losses of the contract participants are much greater:

$$R_q = \{(shop, [0, 100]), (3rd, [0, 0]), (alice, [-1050, -6]), (bob, [-94, 1050])\}.$$

These examples show that while contracts are compositional, their properties might not be. Indeed, cleverly combining two relatively fair contracts results in a contract where one of the parties can cheat the other. Our goal in this paper is to make it relatively easy to build analyses like the ones above.

3 Contract Specification Language

We now give a formal introduction to CSL, a domain-specific language for compositional contract specification. We note that the presentation of the language is limited to features required for the contract analysis introduced in the next section. For a more detailed overview, see Andersen et al. [4].

3.1 Syntax

CSL is used to describe possible interactions between *agents* exchanging *resources*. It supports *contract templates*, i.e. (potentially mutually recursive) contracts, which may further depend on a vector of formal parameters. A contract can therefore depend on both expression variables and contract template variables. We denote the context containing the former as Δ, and the latter as Γ. The basic syntax for contracts is given by the following grammar:

$$c ::= \mathsf{Success} \mid \mathsf{Failure} \mid c_1 + c_2 \mid c_1 \parallel c_2 \mid c_1; c_2 \mid$$
$$\quad \mathsf{Transfer}(A_1, A_2, R, T \mid P).c \mid f(a)$$
$$D ::= \{f_i[X_i] = c_i\}_i$$
$$r ::= \mathsf{letrec}\ D\ \mathsf{in}\ c$$

The first two constructs represent finished contracts: Success denotes the successfully completed contract, whereas Failure indicates an unfulfillable contract or a manifest contract breach. The following three are contract combinators: an alternative of executing contract c_1 or c_2 is expressed as $c_1 + c_2$; if the goal is to execute two contracts in parallel, $c_1 \parallel c_2$ is used; and finally, $c_1; c_2$ represents sequential composition of contracts. Next, $\mathsf{Transfer}(A_1, A_2, R, T \mid P).c$ is a *resource transfer* between two agents, the most basic form of resource exchange, indicating that agent A_1 is obliged to send resource R to agent A_2 at some time T such that the predicate[3] P is true; the contract then continues as c. Here A_1, A_2, R and T are binding occurrences of variables, whose scope is both P and c. The variables are bound when the contract is matched against a concrete event $e = \mathsf{transfer}(a_1, a_2, r, t)$. We use concrete values in place of binders to indicate equality constraints, e.g. $\mathsf{Transfer}(\mathsf{alice}, \mathsf{bob}, R, T \mid P).c$ is short-hand for $\mathsf{Transfer}(A, B, R, T \mid P \wedge A = \mathsf{alice} \wedge B = \mathsf{bob}).c$. $f(a)$ is an instantiation of a contract template named f with a vector of concrete arguments a. Contract templates are collected in an environment $D = \{f_i[X_i] = c_i\}_i$, where each c_i is a contract depending on formal arguments vector X_i. Upon instantiation, these arguments become concrete values from the expression language. Lastly, contract c using a collection of contract templates D is written as $\mathsf{letrec}\ D\ \mathsf{in}\ c$.

---

[3] "Predicate" in the sense of a formula denoting a Boolean-valued function.

$$\Gamma; \Delta \vdash \mathsf{Success} : \mathsf{Contract} \qquad\qquad \Gamma; \Delta \vdash \mathsf{Failure} : \mathsf{Contract}$$

$$\frac{(\Gamma; \Delta \vdash c_i : \mathsf{Contract})_{i=1,2} \quad \mathsf{op} \in \{+, \|, ;\}}{\Gamma; \Delta \vdash c_1 \ \mathsf{op} \ c_2 : \mathsf{Contract}} \qquad \frac{f : \Delta' \to \mathsf{Contract} \in \Gamma \quad \Delta \vdash a : \Delta'}{\Gamma; \Delta \vdash f(a) : \mathsf{Contract}}$$

$$\frac{(\Delta' = \Delta, A_1 : \mathsf{Agent}, A_2 : \mathsf{Agent}, R : \mathsf{Resource}, T : \mathsf{Time})}{\Gamma; \Delta' \vdash c : \mathsf{Contract} \qquad\qquad \Delta' \vdash P : \mathsf{Boolean}}{\Gamma; \Delta \vdash \mathsf{Transfer}(A_1, A_2, R, T \mid P).c : \mathsf{Contract}}$$

$$\frac{(\Gamma; \Delta'_i \vdash c_i : \mathsf{Contract})_i \qquad \Gamma = \{f_i : \Delta'_i \to \mathsf{Contract}\}_i}{\vdash \{f_i[\boldsymbol{X_i}] = c_i\}_i : \Gamma}$$

$$\frac{\vdash D : \Gamma \qquad \Gamma; \cdot \vdash c : \mathsf{Contract}}{\vdash \mathsf{letrec} \ D \ \mathsf{in} \ c : \mathsf{Contract}}$$

Fig. 1. Well-formedness of contracts

Figure 1 presents a simple type system ensuring well-formedness of contracts. It relies on a typed expression language with a typing judgment of the form $\Delta \vdash a : \tau$ (e.g. $\Delta' \vdash P$: Boolean), which can be generalized to vectors of expressions: $\Delta \vdash \boldsymbol{a} : \Delta'$. In the remainder of this paper, we assume all contracts are well-formed.

Events and Traces. The execution of the interactions specified in a contract takes the form of a sequence of *events*, which are external to the specification. We typically refer to this event sequence as a *trace*. Since CSL has only one type of basic interaction between agents – specified as $\mathsf{Transfer}(A_1, A_2, R, T \mid P).c$ – we accordingly have one type of events that can occur in a trace: $e ::= \mathsf{transfer}(a_1, a_2, r, t)$. A $\mathsf{transfer}(a_1, a_2, r, t)$ event indicates that a concrete agent a_1 has sent resource r to agent a_2 at a time t. A trace s is then a finite sequence of these events in the order in which they occurred. The language can be extended to support user-defined business events [2].

Expression Language. CSL is parametric in the choice of the expression language; however, types Boolean, Agent, Resource and Time need to be present as those are used to decide whether an event $e = \mathsf{transfer}(a_1, a_2, r, t)$ is accepted by contract $\mathsf{Transfer}(A_1, A_2, R, T \mid P).c$. This is done by checking the value of expression P under assignment $\{A_1 \mapsto a_1, A_2 \mapsto a_2, R \mapsto r, T \mapsto t\}$. As the value of an expression may also depend on expression variables listed in context Δ, we need a concrete environment δ corresponding to it. We denote a mapping of expression a to a concrete value as $Q[\![a]\!]^{\delta}$. For convenience, we write $\delta \models P$ if $Q[\![P]\!]^{\delta} = \mathsf{true}$ and $\delta \not\models P$ if $Q[\![P]\!]^{\delta} = \mathsf{false}$.

3.2   Contract Satisfaction

A CSL contract specifies the expected behaviour of participating parties. Above we have provided some intuitions for accepting a single event by matching it against a Transfer contract. Here we make these intuitions more formal, and generalize accepting a single event to a trace satisfying a contract. The complete rules of the contract satisfaction relation for traces are presented in Fig. 2.

$$\frac{}{\delta \vdash_D \epsilon : \mathsf{Success}} \qquad \frac{\delta \vdash_D s : c_1}{\delta \vdash_D s : c_1 + c_2} \qquad \frac{\delta \vdash_D s : c_2}{\delta \vdash_D s : c_1 + c_2}$$

$$\frac{\delta \vdash_D s_1 : c_1 \quad \delta \vdash_D s_2 : c_2 \quad (s_1, s_2) \rightsquigarrow s}{\delta \vdash_D s : c_1 \parallel c_2} \qquad \frac{\delta \vdash_D s_1 : c_1 \quad \delta \vdash_D s_2 : c_2}{\delta \vdash_D s_1 \mathbin{+\mkern-10mu+} s_2 : c_1 ; c_2}$$

$$\frac{Q[\![P]\!]^{\delta'} = \mathsf{true} \quad \delta' \vdash_D s : c \quad (\delta' = \delta, \{A_1 \mapsto a_1, A_2 \mapsto a_2, R \mapsto r, T \mapsto t\})}{\delta \vdash_D \mathsf{transfer}(a_1, a_2, r, t)\, s : \mathsf{Transfer}(A_1, A_2, R, T \mid P).c}$$

$$\frac{\boldsymbol{X} \mapsto \boldsymbol{v} \vdash_D s : c \quad f(\boldsymbol{X}) = c \in D \quad \boldsymbol{v} = Q[\![\boldsymbol{a}]\!]^{\delta}}{\delta \vdash_D s : f(\boldsymbol{a})}$$

Fig. 2. Contract satisfaction

An empty trace (ϵ) satisfies a Success contract, matching the intuition that Success denotes a completed contract. To satisfy a contract offering an alternative $c_1 + c_2$, the trace must satisfy one of its components, c_1 or c_2, expressed in the next two rules. To satisfy a parallel composition of contracts $c_1 \parallel c_2$, trace s must be decomposed into s_1 and s_2, satisfying, respectively, c_1 and c_2. This decomposition may be an arbitrary interleaving, denoted by $(s_1, s_2) \rightsquigarrow s$. By contrast, in sequential composition $c_1 ; c_2$ we require that trace s is cut into two, $s = s_1 \mathbin{+\mkern-10mu+} s_2$, as c_1 must be satisfied before anything happens in c_2. Matching an event $\mathsf{transfer}(a_1, a_2, r, t)$ against contract $\mathsf{Transfer}(A_1, A_2, R, T \mid P).c$ is the crucial case of contract satisfaction. Concrete values a_1, a_2, r and t are provided for formal arguments A_1, A_2, R and T, respectively, which extend the existing concrete environment δ. In this extended environment, we check that the expression P evaluates to true and that the remainder of the trace, s, satisfies contract c. Finally, for a trace to satisfy a contract template instantiation, we must change the concrete environment δ to be the evaluation of arguments $\boldsymbol{a}$ passed to the template f. We then check the definition of template f, and verify that indeed, trace s satisfies that contract.

4 Static Analysis

In this section we define a general framework for analysis of compositional contracts, and discuss requirements on its components that will guarantee the soundness of resulting analyses. We follow by providing some concrete instances: possible and definite participation in a contract and fairness analysis. For more details, see Larsen [26].

4.1   General Analysis Framework

CSL as a language can be decomposed into two components: contracts and predicates. The former are a fixed, predefined set of operations that describe interactions between participants. The latter provide a basis for accepting or rejecting an event submitted by a participant. Naturally, analysis of compositional contracts specified in CSL will, correspondingly, consist of two parts.

The overall objective of static analysis is to infer properties of a program (here: contract) without the need to "run" it on all inputs. This typically involves keeping track of how the abstract environment changes throughout execution. In CSL, the list of contracts is static; there are no contract variables. However, the expression environment is affected by both incoming events, which introduce new binders and restrictions on values; as well as contract template calls, which alter the local environment. The expression analysis is used to make these changes and restrictions explicit.

In this section, we specify requirements on both predicate and contract analysis that guarantee the soundness of the analysis results with respect to the contract satisfaction relation (containment) defined in Sect. 3.2.

Predicate Analysis. To capture bindings we require an abstract environment with abstract values $M : Var \to A$, together with an abstraction function $\alpha : \mathcal{D} \to A$ from concrete to abstract values. We often choose A to be the power-set lattice of values, in which case $\alpha(v) = \{v\}$. For two abstract environments m_1, m_2 we write $m_1 \sqsubseteq m_2$ iff $\forall x. m_1(x) \sqsubseteq m_2(x)$.

Whether to accept or reject an incoming event is determined by the predicate P in $\mathsf{Transfer}(A, B, R, T \mid P).c$. With a concrete environment δ, we can simply check whether $\delta \models P$ holds. Working with abstract values, we want to extract the restrictions on variables that make P evaluate to true, and use them to refine the abstract environment. We describe this transformation as a function $[\![P]\!]^\sharp : M \to M_\perp$. As the type suggests, this analysis also has the choice of returning $\perp$ to signal unsatisfiability, making the analysis much more precise if we can determine that a $\mathsf{Transfer}$ will never accept any events. We also require an abstract expression semantics for evaluating arguments to contract templates $[\![a]\!]^\sharp_m : A$, which in most cases is a simple lookup in m.

$$\delta \sim m := \forall x \in Var.\alpha(\delta(x)) \sqsubseteq m(x) \tag{1}$$

$$\delta \sim m \wedge \delta \models P \to \delta \sim [\![P]\!]^\sharp(m) \tag{2}$$

$$\delta \sim m \wedge [\![P]\!]^\sharp(m) = \perp \to \delta \not\models P \tag{3}$$

$$m_1 \sqsubseteq m_2' \wedge [\![P]\!]^\sharp(m_1) = m_2 \neq \perp \wedge [\![P]\!]^\sharp(m_1') = m_2' \to m_2 \sqsubseteq m_2' \tag{4}$$

$$m \sqsubseteq m' \wedge [\![P]\!]^\sharp(m') = \perp \to [\![P]\!]^\sharp(m) = \perp \tag{5}$$

Fig. 3. Constraints for predicate analysis

The properties that we require of a predicate analysis and abstract environment are gathered on Fig. 3. They include relating abstract and concrete environment, as specified in Eq. 1, which we abbreviate $\delta \sim m$. When the abstract and concrete environments are related, we expect the abstract one to preserve the overapproximation when the predicate is satisfiable, as expressed by Eq. 2. Similarly, we expect that if the predicate analysis signals unsatisfiability, then the predicate is indeed not satisfied, as given by Eq. 3. Predicate analysis transformation $[\![P]\!]^\sharp$ should in general be monotone and failure-preserving, as specified by Eqs. 4 and 5. Similar requirements regarding over-approximation and monotonicity preservation can be stated for the $[\![a]\!]^\sharp$ function.

Depending on the choice of expression language, predicate analysis may get costly and complicated. It is therefore important to ensure that an "identity analysis", which performs no refinements, is an allowed instance we can use as the analysis of last resort. Most implementations will also rely on some form of unification for analysis of equality predicates, as in practice we often specify e.g. "the sender of the first event is the same, as the receiver of the second one".

Abstract Collecting Semantics. To define an abstract collecting semantics for contract analysis, we begin with a complete lattice $(L, \sqsubseteq, \sqcup, \sqcap, \bot, \top)$ describing properties of traces. We also need a representation function $\beta : Tr \to L$ mapping traces to the best properties describing them. We will use this representation function to later relate the abstract constraints to the trace satisfaction relation shown in Fig. 2. Our goal is to define an analysis $[\![c]\!]^\sharp_m \in L$ describing all possible traces. In other words, the following is our approximation of soundness:

$$\forall s \in Tr, (\delta \vdash^D s : c) \wedge \delta \sim m \Rightarrow \beta(s) \sqsubseteq [\![c]\!]^\sharp_m \tag{6}$$

Since we want the analysis to be compositional, we need combination functions for $+$, $;$ and $\parallel$, which can only combine the results for subcontracts, $C_+, C_;, C_\parallel : L \times L \to L$. Further, to analyze contract $\mathsf{Transfer}(A_1, A_2, R, T \mid P).c$ we must combine the result for c with the result of analyzing P given the bound variables: $C_{\mathsf{Transfer}} : L \times M \times Var^4 \to L$. This time, the combinator might depend on the newly introduced bound variables, the result of the subcontract and the predicate analysis. We also require a designated lattice element $L_{\mathsf{Success}} \in L$ for the analysis of the successful contract.

The generic abstract collecting semantics for CSL can be seen on Fig. 4. The analysis for both $C_;$ and $C_\parallel$ are left unspecified, however for C_+ we have no choice but to use the $\sqcup$ operator of the underlying lattice. We note that as we explicitly distinguish between the predicate analysis returning $\bot$ or a concrete value, we require that analysis to be decidable. There are some further restrictions on the relationship between β and the abstract collecting semantics:

$$\beta(\langle\rangle) \sqsubseteq L_{\mathsf{Success}}$$

$$\beta(t_1) \sqsubseteq \ell_1 \wedge \beta(t_2) \sqsubseteq \ell_2 \rightarrow \beta(t_1 +\!\!\!+ t_2) \sqsubseteq C_;(\ell_1, \ell_2)$$

$$\beta(t_1) \sqsubseteq \ell_1 \wedge \beta(t_2) \sqsubseteq \ell_2 \wedge (t_1, t_2) \rightsquigarrow t \rightarrow \beta(t) \sqsubseteq C_{\parallel}(\ell_1, \ell_2)$$

$$\delta[A_1 \mapsto a_1, A_2 \mapsto a_2, R \mapsto r, T \mapsto t] \sim m \wedge \beta(s) \sqsubseteq \ell \rightarrow$$
$$\beta(\mathsf{transfer}(a_1, a_2, r, t)\, s) \sqsubseteq C_{\mathsf{Transfer}}(\ell, m, A_1, A_2, R, T)$$

$\boxed{D, m \triangleright c : \ell}$ 　　　　　　Contract specification c has abstract trace ℓ

$$\dfrac{}{D, m \triangleright \mathsf{Success} : L_{\mathsf{Success}}} \qquad \dfrac{}{D, m \triangleright \mathsf{Failure} : \bot}$$

$$\dfrac{D, m \triangleright c_1 : \ell_1 \quad D \triangleright c_2 : \ell_2}{D, m \triangleright c_1 \parallel c_2 : C_{\parallel}(\ell_1, \ell_2)} \qquad \dfrac{D, m \triangleright c_1 : \ell_1 \quad D \triangleright c_2 : \ell_2}{D, m \triangleright c_1 ; c_2 : C_;(\ell_1, \ell_2)}$$

$$\dfrac{D, m \triangleright c_1 : \ell_1 \quad D \triangleright c_2 : \ell_2}{D, m \triangleright c_1 + c_2 : \ell_1 \sqcup \ell_2} \qquad \dfrac{[\![P]\!]^{\sharp} m = \bot}{D, m \triangleright \mathsf{Transfer}(A_1, A_2, R, T \mid P).c : \bot}$$

$$\dfrac{D, m' \triangleright c : \ell \quad m' = [\![P]\!]^{\sharp} m \neq \bot}{D, m \triangleright \mathsf{Transfer}(A_1, A_2, R, T \mid P).c : C_{\mathsf{Transfer}}(\ell, m', A_1, A_2, R, T)}$$

$$\dfrac{m' = [\![(a_1, x_1), \ldots, (a_n, x_n)]\!]^{\sharp} m \quad D, m' \triangleright c : \ell}{D, m \triangleright f(a_1, \ldots, a_n) : \ell} D(f) = (f[x_1, \ldots, x_n] = c)$$

Fig. 4. Abstract collecting semantics

$$\beta(\langle\rangle) \sqsubseteq L_{\mathsf{Success}}$$

$$\beta(t_1) \sqsubseteq \ell_1 \wedge \beta(t_2) \sqsubseteq \ell_2 \rightarrow \beta(t_1 +\!\!\!+ t_2) \sqsubseteq C_;(\ell_1, \ell_2)$$

$$\beta(t_1) \sqsubseteq \ell_1 \wedge \beta(t_2) \sqsubseteq \ell_2 \wedge (t_1, t_2) \rightsquigarrow t \rightarrow \beta(t) \sqsubseteq C_{\parallel}(\ell_1, \ell_2)$$

$$\delta[A_1 \mapsto a_1, A_2 \mapsto a_2, R \mapsto r, T \mapsto t] \sim m \wedge \beta(s) \sqsubseteq \ell \rightarrow$$
$$\beta(\mathsf{transfer}(a_1, a_2, r, t)\, s) \sqsubseteq C_{\mathsf{Transfer}}(\ell, m, A_1, A_2, R, T)$$

Finally, we require all the C_{op}, as well as C_{Transfer} to be monotone. This facilitates using widening techniques for both the environment and trace approximations.

Infinite Abstract Trees. Before we discuss the soundness of our analysis, we have to think about what kind of derivation trees can we encounter when analyzing arbitrary contracts. While it is true that all concrete traces of any contract will be finite, the language still allows recursive contracts to be defined. This results in the possibility of constructing an infinite derivation tree using rules from Fig. 4. To address this, we will now treat the $D, m \triangleright c : \ell$ judgment as coinductive.

Let $\mathcal{U}_A$ be the set of ω-deep, finitely branching trees with nodes labeled by either $D, m \triangleright c : \ell$ or Δ. We follow Schmidt [32] in defining the well-formed abstract semantic trees to be the greatest fixed point of a functorial $\bar{\Phi}$ corresponding to the judgments from Fig. 4. Its least fixed point yields only finite trees; the greatest fixed point includes infinite trees arrived at by infinite unfolding of recursive definitions. We then say that the abstract semantics of the contract specification c in an abstract environment $m \in M$ is a $t \in \mathsf{gfp}(\bar{\Phi})$ such that the root of the tree is a judgment: $root(t) = D, m \rhd c : \ell$ for some $\ell \in L$. Intuitively, abstract semantic trees are built using the rules from the abstract collecting semantics, but can have possibly infinite paths.

Soundness. We can now state that abstract semantic trees soundly predict satisfying traces.

Theorem 1 (Soundness of approximation). *If* $\mathcal{H} :: \delta \vdash_D s : c$, $\delta \sim m$ *and we have a tree* $t \in \mathcal{U}_A$ *with* $root(t) = D, m \rhd c : \ell$ *then* $\beta(s) \sqsubseteq \ell$.

Proof. Structural induction on the derivation of trace satisfaction, $\mathcal{H}$.

We again follow Schmidt [32] in our approach of defining a binary relation on trees, $\preceq_{\mathcal{U}_A} \subseteq \mathcal{U}_A \times \mathcal{U}_A$ as the largest binary relation satisfying:

- $t \preceq_{\mathcal{U}_A} t'$ if $t' = \Delta$.
- $t \preceq_{\mathcal{U}_A} t'$ if $root(t) = D, m \rhd c : \ell$, $root(t') = D, m' \rhd c : \ell'$, $m \sqsubseteq m'$, $\ell \sqsubseteq \ell'$ and for all subtrees i of t there exists a subtree j of t' such that $t_i \preceq_{\mathcal{U}_A} t'_j$.

Informally this is a relation between trees such that if we explore them in the same way, t will be more precise than t'.

Theorem 2 (Soundness of widening). *If* $m \sqsubseteq m'$, t_1, t_2 *with* $root(t_1) = D, m \rhd c : \ell_1$ *and* $root(t_2) = D, m' \rhd c : \ell_2$ *then* $t_1 \preceq_{\mathcal{U}_A} t_2$.

Proof. The relation $\preceq_{\mathcal{U}_A}$ on trees is closed; the remaining cases are by induction on c.

4.2   Example Analyses

We finish this section by showing some example instantiations of the framework. For space-efficiency reasons we omit the statements of required properties, as they are simply concretisations of the properties mentioned in the general framework description, this time with concrete lattices. The proofs of all these properties can be found in the accompanying Coq development.

Potential Participation. We are interested in inferring a relation on the parties transferring resources. The intended meaning of the analysis is that if a pair of agents (a, b) is in the result, there might be a transfer of resources from a to b in some satisfying trace. For this analysis, the abstract environment will only track the agent variables: $L_c = \mathcal{P}(\mathcal{A} \times \mathcal{A})$, $M_c = Var_{\text{agent}} \rightarrow \mathcal{P}(\mathcal{A})$.

The representation function β accumulates all the agents participating in the events of a given trace.

$$\beta(\mathsf{transfer}(a_1, b_1, r_1, t_1), \ldots, \mathsf{transfer}(a_n, b_n, r_n, t_n)) = \{(a_1, b_1), \ldots, (a_n, b_n)\}$$

The correctness of the analysis relies on the fact that β is a homomorphism with respect to append, interleaving and union.

Lemma 1. *If $s_1 + s_2 = s$ or $(s_1, s_2) \rightsquigarrow s$ then $\beta(s) = \beta(s_1) \cup \beta(s_2)$.*

Proof. By proving two inclusions; both by induction on the derivation of $s_1 + s_2 = s$ or $(s_1, s_2) \rightsquigarrow s$, respectively.

The analyses of Failure and Success are simple, since in both cases no one is communicating, so $L_{\mathsf{Success}} = L_{\mathsf{Failure}} = \bot = \emptyset$. For all the contract combinators we just join the results of the subcontracts $C_{\mathsf{op}} = \sqcup$ for op $\in \{+, ;, \|\}$, since in the case of choice we do not know statically which of the subcontracts will be satisfied. For Transfer we take all the possible pairs of values for sender and receiver: $C_{\mathsf{Transfer}}(l, m, a_1, a_2, r, t) = l \cup (m(a_1) \times m(a_2))$. If we assume that the expression language only allows testing agents for equality we can use a simple unification algorithm for the predicate analysis.

Fairness. In this analysis we are interested in estimating the cost of participating in a contract for every agent. This time, the lattice is the total function lattice on the intervals on the real number line augmented with $\pm\infty$. The abstract environment is a mapping from variables to sets of agents or resources.

$$L_c = Var \to \mathcal{I}_{\mathbb{R}}, \quad M_c = Var_{\mathrm{agent}} \cup Var_{\mathrm{resource}} \to \mathcal{A} \cup \mathcal{R}$$

We will also need $V : \mathcal{R} \to \mathbb{R}$, a valuation function that provides the value of one unit of any resource type. We can extend it to sets of resources by joining the resulting singleton intervals:

$$V_L(R) = \bigsqcup \{[V(r), V(r)] \mid r \in R\}.$$

Let $\oplus$ be addition on intervals, extended pointwise to maps. We make an entry with the negative value of the resource for the sender, and an entry with the value of the resource for the receiver.

$$\beta_V'(a_1, a_2, r, t) = \begin{cases} \{a_1 \mapsto [-V(r), -V(r)], a_2 \mapsto [V(r), V(r)]\} & \text{when } a_1 \neq a_2 \\ \{a_1 \mapsto [0, 0]\} & \text{when } a_1 = a_2 \end{cases}$$

The representation function is simply a fold over the trace, parameterized by valuation function V:

$$\beta_V(s) = \mathsf{fold}(\oplus, \{v \mapsto [0, 0] \mid v \in Var\}, \mathsf{map}(\beta_V', s)).$$

In the correctness of fairness analysis we again need a result relating concatenation, interleaving and $\oplus$.

Lemma 2. *If $s_1 +\!\!+ s_2 = s$ or $(s_1, s_2) \rightsquigarrow s$ then for all valuations V, $\beta(s) = \beta_V(s_1) \oplus \beta_V(s_2)$.*

Proof. Induction on the derivation of $s_1 +\!\!+ s_2 = s$ or $(s_1, s_2) \rightsquigarrow s$, respectively.

The analysis of the successful contract maps every agent to the singleton interval of 0, representing that nothing is transferred: $L_{\mathsf{Success}} = \{v \mapsto [0,0] \mid v \in Var\}$. In the case of $+$ we have no other option than to join the intervals to accommodate both alternatives, $C_+ = \sqcup$. For sequential and parallel composition we know that both subcontracts are satisfied, so we can add all the intervals: $C_; = C_\| = \oplus$.

The Transfer analysis has to distinguish between two cases. If there is exactly one sender or one receiver for the event, we can be precise. Otherwise we will have to widen to interval to include $[0,0]$, since we do not know the actual agent:

$$V_{\mathsf{Transfer}}(A, R) = \begin{cases} \{a \mapsto V_L(R)\} & \text{when } A = \{a\} \\ \{a \mapsto [0,0] \sqcup V_L(R) \mid a \in A\} & \text{otherwise} \end{cases}$$

We can then use this to define the analysis of the Transfer:

$$C_{\mathsf{Transfer}}(l, m, a_1, a_2, r, t) =$$
$$l \oplus V_{\mathsf{Transfer}}(m(a_1), -m(r)) \oplus V_{\mathsf{Transfer}}(m(a_2), m(r))$$

Definite Participation. Where in the first example we wanted to know about pairs of agents who *might* participate in the contract, here we want to calculate the set of agents who *definitely* participate as the sender.

Formally, agent a is definitely participating (as a sender) in contract c if for every trace s such that $\delta \vdash_D s : c$, there exist s_1, s_2, b, r, t such that $s = s_1 +\!\!+ \mathsf{transfer}(a, b, r, t)\, s_2$. Similarly to the potential participation example, the abstract environment will only track the agent variables: $L_c = \mathcal{P}(\mathcal{A})$, $M_c = Var_{\mathsf{agent}} \to \mathcal{P}(\mathcal{A})$. Interestingly, the representation function also has to be (almost) identical:

$$\beta(\mathsf{transfer}(a_1, b_1, r_1, t_1), \ldots, \mathsf{transfer}(a_n, b_n, r_n, t_n)) = \{a_1, \ldots, a_n\}$$

This is of course a huge overapproximation, but indeed any agent who is definitely participating in the contract, will be captured by β.

The requirement for C_+ to be the $\sqcup$ of the lattice gives away that, compared to the potential participation analysis, we will have to invert the ordering on the lattice to get the required structure. We can then set $C_;$ and $C_\|$ to be $\cup$ (which is $\sqcap$), and define the L_{Success} as $\emptyset$, or the $\top$ of the lattice.

The analysis for Transfer is, as usual, the most interesting. We only want to include a sender of a transfer in the result, if the predicate identifies them uniquely – in other words, if the abstract value corresponding to the sender is a singleton.

$$C_{\mathsf{Transfer}}(l, m, a_1, a_2, r, t) = \begin{cases} \{a_1\} \cup l & \text{when } m(a_1) \text{ is a singleton} \\ l & \text{otherwise} \end{cases}$$

In this example, the requirements for appends and interleavings are in fact identical as in the potential participation case.

Lemma 3. *If $s_1 \mathbin{+\mkern-8mu+} s_2 = s$ or $(s_1, s_2) \rightsquigarrow s$ then $\beta(s) = \beta(s_1) \cup \beta(s_2)$.*

Proof. By proving two inclusions; both by induction on the derivation of $s_1 \mathbin{+\mkern-8mu+} s_2 = s$ or $(s_1, s_2) \rightsquigarrow s$, respectively.

5   Coq Mechanization

Both the trace semantics of CSL and the abstract collecting semantics have been mechanized in the Coq proof assistant[4]. We have also mechanically verified the argument that the concrete analyses mentioned in the previous section are indeed correct instantiations of the general contract analysis framework. While the specifics of the implementation are best understood by looking at the code, this section provides a general overview of what – and how – has been mechanized. For a more in-depth discussion of the implementation choices, see Larsen [26]

5.1   Mechanized Semantics of CSL

The formalization of CSL uses dependently typed De Bruijn indices in the style of Benton et al. [9].

```
Inductive ty : Set := Agent | Resource | Timestamp | Bool.
Inductive contract (Γ : list (list ty)) (Δ : list ty) : Type
```

To represent a concrete environment δ, we use a heterogeneous list indexed by the corresponding typing environment Δ. As the language of expressions we have picked for the mechanization is extremely simple, we can denote the base types using the corresponding Coq types. To capture contract templates, we again use heterogeneous lists.

```
Definition tyDenote (τ : ty) : Set := (...).
Definition env Δ := hlist tyDenote Δ.
Definition template_env Γ := hlist (contract Γ) Γ.
```

Traces are represented as lists of events of appropriate types (i.e. quadruples of concrete values). The trace satisfaction semantics from Fig. 2 is encoded very naturally as an inductive definition.

```
Inductive event : Set :=
| Event : tyDenote Agent → tyDenote Agent →
          tyDenote Resource → tyDenote Timestamp → event.
Definition trace := list event.
Inductive csat :
    ∀ Γ Δ, env Δ → template_env Γ → trace → contract Γ Δ → Prop
```

---

[4] Coq sources: https://ayertienna.github.io/csl_formalization_wtsc20.zip.

5.2   Generic Analysis Framework

To implement the analysis framework as described in the previous section, we make use of Coq's type classes. We first define a type class describing requirements for predicate and template arguments' analysis.

```
Class PredicateAnalysis (A : ty → Type) '(L : SetLattice A)
```

Next, we define contract analysis relying on the predicate analysis being provided.

```
Class CSLAnalysis (L : Type) (A : ty → Type) '(Lattice L) '(PredicateAnalysis A)
```

Finally, we specify a coinductive type for the analysis, and prove its soundness, corresponding to Theorem 1.

```
CoInductive csl_analysis L A '(CA : CSLAnalysis L A) :
    ∀ Γ Δ, contract Γ Δ → template_env Γ → hlist A Δ → L → Prop := (...)
```

```
Theorem csl_analysis_sound L A '(CA : CSLAnalysis L A) :
    ∀ Γ Δ (D : template_env Γ) (δ : env Δ) (m : hlist A Δ) (c : contract Γ Δ) r t,
        aenv_correct δ m ∧ csl_analysis CA c D m r ∧ csat δ D t c → Incl (β t) r.
```

We also show that the environment widening is sound, corresponding to Theorem 2. This time we are using the inductive version of the CSL analysis type.

```
Inductive csl_analysis L A '(CA : CSLAnalysis L A) :
    ∀ Γ Δ, contract Γ Δ → template_env Γ → hlist A Δ → L → Prop := (...)
Lemma env_widening_sound L A '(CSLAnalysis L A) :
    ∀ Γ Δ (D : template_env Γ) (m m' : hlist A Δ) (c : contract Γ Δ) s s',
        aenv_Incl m m' ∧ ind_csl_analysis c D m s ∧
        ind_csl_analysis c D m' s' → Incl s s'.
```

Concrete Analyses. The provided Coq sources contain three instances of the CSLAnalysis class, corresponding to the examples described in the previous section. Due to space considerations, we only give more details about the potential participation analysis.

One key difference between the definitions on paper and in the definitions in Coq is the formalization of sets. For the predicate analysis we use finite sets to describe analysis results. We use a minor generalization of sets to approximate the power-set domain of values indexed by the base type.

```
Inductive abstract_set τ : Type :=
| FullSet : abstract_set τ
| ActualSet : set (tyDenote τ) → abstract_set τ.
```

For this particular analysis, the abstract domain consists of pairs of agents. As we sometimes might not know anything about one of them, we must distinguish between concrete values and "any value" placeholders.

```
Inductive abstract_value τ : Type :=
| AnyValue : abstract_value τ
| ActualValue : tyDenote τ → abstract_value τ.
Definition abstract_agent_pair := (abstract_value Agent * abstract_value Agent).
```

We can then show that abstract sets form a lattice, and so do abstract values. With those instances at hand, we still need to show all the properties required by the contract analysis type class.

We further provide a mechanization of simple expression analysis, which is aware of the equality constraints between literals and variables. This is sufficient for the participation analysis, as the only operation supported for the `Agent` type is equality testing.

```
Program Instance possible_values_predicate_analysis :
  @PredicateAnalysis _ _ abstract_set_setlattice := (..)
```

Finally, the resulting declaration of `CSLAnalysis` instance can be given:

```
Program Instance participation_possible_values :
  CSLAnalysis aap_set_lattice possible_values_predicate_analysis :=
{
  L__succ := bot; C__par := join; C__seq := join; C__transfer := (..);
  β := β_participation; β__transfer := (..); β__par := (..); β__seq := (..);
  monotone_C__par := (..); monotone_C__seq := (..); monotone_C__transfer := (..)
}.
```

We refer to the source code for more details, including an example of a contract running the obtained analysis.

6 Conclusion

In this paper we have outlined, designed, implemented, verified and mechanized a framework for analysis of CSL contracts, illustrated by a few example analyses. While these example analyses are relatively simple, we find the generality of our abstract interpretation based analysis framework promising enough to capture more complex contract properties, including those with significant legal consequence, e.g. agent obligation in contracts, utility to participants under all executions, recognition of single-sided contracts (i.e. ones where only one of the parties has any obligations remaining), etc. We found that using type classes in the mechanization of our framework makes it relatively easy to experiment with new analyses in a formal setting. Conversely, Coq mechanization interleaved with and driving the framework design has aided in identifying subtleties and tricky technical aspects that might be (and have been [4]) overlooked.

Related Work. There is a rich literature on declarative contract languages going back 30 years [23]. Many of these are *propositional* in nature: they model the control flow and discrete temporal properties, but not the real-time and quantitative aspects—how *much* by *which time*—that are crucial in real-world contracts: Delivery of a bicycle by tomorrow, by the end of the century or without any deadline are crucially different, as is having to pay $5, $500 or $500,000,000 for it.

Harz and Knottenbelt [16] provide a recent overview of contract languages that incorporate quantitative aspects of resource transfers. Within their classification, CSL can be placed in the high-level language tier; it is closest to

DAML [13] and Marlowe [33], which CSL predates by a decade [3,4,24]. CSL is motivated by the seminal works by Peyton Jones and Eber [31] on compositional financial contracts, and by McCarthy [28] on the Resources-Events-Agents (REA) model for economic accounting. It draws on (propositional) process calculus and language theory, but is extended with real-time (deadline) and quantitative resource aspects crucial to real-world contracts. It was originally designed as a component of a DSL-based enterprise systems architecture [2,20], but is presently employed mostly in the financial domain where it is used to not only express payment requirements, but also notifications and other business events in negotiation processes.[5]

Most tools for analyzing smart contracts focus on security properties of Ethereum-style smart contracts. They have identified numerous Ethereum smart contracts that are potentially unsafe in the sense of permitting a (pseudonymous) user, such as a miner, to draw unfair[6] advantage. They typically look for unsafe programming patterns; see e.g. Nikolic, Nikolic, Kolluri, Sergey, Saxena, Hobor [30] and Luu, Chu, Olickel, Saxena, Hobor [27].

An important property is *liquidity*, the guarantee that a smart contract cannot lock up a nonzero balance of Ether or any other user-defined resource it controls [8]. This is a special property of smart contracts that *exclusively* control resources they have issued or received.[7]

CSL specifies digital contracts between the contract parties, independent of any particular third-party contract manager (such as an Ethereum-style smart contract) they may eventually employ for control (execution) [15]. The question of liquidity is inapplicable to a digital contract, but can be posed of a contract manager. For example, a contract manager that performs an escrow function and is guaranteed to be abortable and in such case pays back all escrow amounts, guarantees that *all* digital contracts managed by it are liquid. Likewise, a contract manager that only *monitors* payments by contract parties to each other without receiving or disbursing any payments itself trivially guarantees liquidity.

Chatterjee, Goharshady and Velner [11] present a language for expressing multiparty *games* as state machines with a fixed number of rounds of concurrent moves by all parties. They analyze them game-theoretically, that is under the assumption that each party employs an optimal strategy (also called policy) that maximizes their utility (gains). In this setting, a game is considered fair if the expected pay-off for no party is substantially higher than the others' *assuming* each party acts optimally for themselves. This notion of fairness is different than our example analysis, where we stipulate that *all* valid and complete executions

---

[5] See www.deondigital.com.

[6] Unfair in the sense of providing unexpected gains or losses to participants. Note that under the adage of "code is law" an unfair contract is still a contract that cannot be changed: it is what it is.

[7] The pattern of pseudonymous parties collateralizing participation in a contract by depositing money with a trusted third party is common and practically unavoidable: The parties being pseudonymous, they could just walk away once they owe more than they are owed. This may explain why each Ethereum-style smart contract is "born" with an associated Ether account.

of a contract be fair, also those where a party acts suboptimally, e.g. when overlooking a deadline, failing to make a move or just making a bad move because they don't know any better. A contract that is fair in our strong sense typically stipulates that resource exchanges be fair and be atomically executed (possibly using an escrow manager) or permit only "bad" moves that are outside the control of the contract partners (e.g. the price of a stock falling after it has been purchased).

Bahr, Berthold, Elsman [7] have pioneered mechanized formalization of contract language semantics, property checking and static analysis. They design and formalize denotational and operational semantics of a multi-party extension of the seminal Peyton Jones/Eber financial contract language [31], including a static check for *causality* and static computation of a contract's *horizon*. Causality guarantees that a contractually required payment cannot depend on a future observation. A contract's horizon is its maximal life time. More recently, Annenkov and Elsman have extended this framework to certifiably correctly compile contracts to a payout language and extract stochastic simulation code in Futhark [21] for high-performance execution on GPUs [5]. They not only *mechanize* the semantics and analysis of the financial contract language in Coq, they automatically extract certifiably correct code from their constructive Coq proofs.

At the intersection of Ethereum-style smart contracts and mechanized semantics and verification, Bhargavan *et al.* [10] have embedded Solidity and EVM in F* and use the dependent type system of F*, which employs powerful SMT solving, to detect unsafe programming patterns such as not checking the return value of send-messages. Chen, Park, and Roşu have verified core properties of some important smart contracts in Ethereum [12] using the K framework to formalize the semantics of EVM [22]. Amani, Bégel, Bortin and Staples formalize EVM and design a program logic for expressing properties of EVM code in Isabelle/HOL [1]. Annenkov, Nielsen, Spitters [6,29] formalize functional programming languages for expressing smart contracts and prove in Coq that a multiparty smart contract for decentralized voting on and adopting proposals satisfies its high-level (partial) specification.

We believe our work is unique in providing a mechanized, formally verified *framework* for user-definable static analyses of arbitrary (CSL-specifiable) contracts, not only specific analyses or verification of specific (smart) contracts.

Future Work. Directions for future investigation include finding more examples of properties to be verified using the proposed general technique, including analysis of temporal properties. One interesting case, briefly mentioned before, is the relational analysis of relative gains of contract participants: instead of estimating intervals of gains and losses for each participant independently, we would relate gains of one party relative to those of others. This would allow us to perform a more sophisticated fairness analysis.

We recognize that the style of analysis presented here has its limitations. While we can define an analysis of a universally-quantified property (definite participation can be one example), the approximation we get might not always be satisfactory. It might therefore be worth investigating a more direct approach, defining properties for whole sets of traces. Another limitation worth addressing in future developments is the inability to reason about failing traces. While we can quite often work around this caveat by using dual statements, we again risk loosing precision.

An orthogonal line of work is to get the existing analysis incorporated into Deon Digital's [14] contract specification language, a more expressive variant of CSL allowing, among other things, for user-defined events beyond a simple Transfer.

Acknowledgements. We would like to thank the anonymous referees for their critical and helpful comments.

This work has been facilitated by financial support from Deon Digital and Innovation Fund Denmark for the project *Formal verification for formal contracts* under contract number 7092-00003B.

References

1. Amani, S., Bégel, M., Bortin, M., Staples, M.: Towards verifying Ethereum smart contract bytecode in Isabelle/HOL. In: Proceedings of the 7th ACM SIGPLAN International Conference on Certified Programs and Proofs, pp. 66–77. ACM (2018)
2. Andersen, J., Bahr, P., Henglein, F., Hvitved, T.: Domain-specific languages for enterprise systems. In: Margaria, T., Steffen, B. (eds.) ISoLA 2014. LNCS, vol. 8802, pp. 73–95. Springer, Heidelberg (2014). https://doi.org/10.1007/978-3-662-45234-9_6
3. Andersen, J., Elsborg, E., Henglein, F., Simonsen, J.G., Stefansen, C.: Compositional specification of commercial contracts. In: ISoLA (Preliminary Proceedings), 30 October 2004, pp. 103–110 (2004)
4. Andersen, J., Elsborg, E., Henglein, F., Simonsen, J.G., Stefansen, C.: Compositional specification of commercial contracts. STTT **8**(6), 485–516 (2006). https://doi.org/10.1007/s10009-006-0010-1
5. Annenkov, D., Elsman, M.: Certified compilation of financial contracts. In: Proceedings of the 20th International Symposium on Principles and Practice of Declarative Programming, PPDP 2018, pp. 5:1–5:13. ACM, New York (2018)
6. Annenkov, D., Nielsen, J.B., Spitters, B.: Towards a smart contract verification framework in Coq. In: Proceedings of the 9th ACM SIGPLAN International Conference on Certified Proofs and Programs (CPP) (2020)
7. Bahr, P., Berthold, J., Elsman, M.: Certified symbolic management of financial multi-party contracts. In: Proceedings of the ACM International Conference on Functional Programming (ICFP), August 2015. SIGPLAN Not. **50**(9), 315–327
8. Bartoletti, M., Zunino, R.: Verifying liquidity of bitcoin contracts. Cryptology ePrint Archive, Report 2018/1125 (2018). https://eprint.iacr.org/2018/1125
9. Benton, N., Hur, C.-K., Kennedy, A.J., McBride, C.: Strongly typed term representations in Coq. J. Autom. Reason. **49**(2), 141–159 (2012). https://doi.org/10.1007/s10817-011-9219-0

10. Bhargavan, K., et al.: Formal verification of smart contracts. In: Proceedings of the 2016 ACM Workshop on Programming Languages and Analysis for Security-PLAS 2016, pp. 91–96 (2016)

11. Chatterjee, K., Goharshady, A.K., Velner, Y.: Quantitative analysis of smart contracts. CoRR, abs/1801.03367 (2018)

12. Chen, X., Park, D., Roşu, G.: A language-independent approach to smart contract verification. In: Margaria, T., Steffen, B. (eds.) ISoLA 2018. LNCS, vol. 11247, pp. 405–413. Springer, Cham (2018). https://doi.org/10.1007/978-3-030-03427-6_30

13. DAML: Digital Asset Modelling Language. https://daml.com/

14. Deon Digital: CSL Language Guide. https://deondigital.com/docs/v0.39.0/

15. Egelund-Müller, B., Elsman, M., Henglein, F., Ross, O.: Automated execution of financial contracts on blockchains. Bus. Inf. Syst. Eng. 59(6), 457–467 (2017). https://doi.org/10.1007/s12599-017-0507-z

16. Harz, D., Knottenbelt, W.J.: Towards safer smart contracts: a survey of languages and verification methods. CoRR, abs/1809.09805 (2018)

17. Henglein, F.: Smart digital contracts: algebraic foundations for resource accounting. Oregon Programming Languages Summer School (OPLSS), Smart Digital Contracts, Lecture 2, June 2019

18. Henglein, F.: Smart digital contracts: contract specification and life-cycle management. Oregon Programming Languages Summer School (OPLSS), Smart Digital Contracts, Lecture 3, June 2019

19. Henglein, F.: Smart digital contracts: introduction. Oregon Programming Languages Summer School (OPLSS), Smart Digital Contracts, Lecture 1, June 2019

20. Henglein, F., Larsen, K.F., Simonsen, J.G., Stefansen, C.: POETS: process-oriented event-driven transaction systems. J. Log. Algebraic Program. 78(5), 381–401 (2009)

21. Henriksen, T., Serup, N., Elsman, M., Henglein, F., Oancea, C.: Futhark: purely functional GPU-programming with nested parallelism and in-place array updates. In: Proceedings of the ACM SIGPLAN Conference on Programming Language Design and Implementation (PLDI), Barcelona, Spain, June 2017, pp. 556–571. ACM (2017). HIPEAC Best Paper Award

22. Hildenbrandt, E., et al.: KEVM: a complete semantics of the ethereum virtual machine. In: Proceedings of the 31st IEEE Computer Security Foundations Symposium (CSF) (2018)

23. Hvitved, T.: A survey of formal languages for contracts. In: Fourth Workshop on Formal Languages and Analysis of Contract-Oriented Software (FLACOS 2010), pp. 29–32 (2010)

24. Hvitved, T., Klaedtke, F., Zălinescu, E.: A trace-based model for multiparty contracts. J. Log. Algebraic Program. 81(2), 72–98 (2012)

25. Kowalski, R.: Algorithm = logic + control. Commun. ACM 22(7), 424–436 (1979)

26. Larsen, C.K.: Declarative contracts. Mechanized semantics and analysis. Master's thesis, University of Copenhagen, Denmark (2019). https://ckjaer.dk/files/thesis.pdf

27. Luu, L., Chu, D.-H., Olickel, H., Saxena, P., Hobor, A.: Making smart contracts smarter. In: Proceedings of the 2016 ACM SIGSAC Conference on Computer and Communications Security, CCS 2016, pp. 254–269. ACM, New York (2016)

28. McCarthy, W.E.: The REA accounting model: a generalized framework for accounting systems in a shared data environment. Account. Rev. LVII(3), 554–578 (1982)

29. Nielsen, J.B., Spitters, B.: Smart contract interactions in Coq. arXiv preprint arXiv:1911.04732 (2019)

30. Nikolic, I., Kolluri, A., Sergey, I., Saxena, P., Hobor, A.: Finding the greedy, prodigal, and suicidal contracts at scale. arXiv:1802.06038v1 [cs.CR], arXiv, February 2018
31. Peyton Jones, S., Eber, J.-M., Seward, J.: Composing contracts: an adventure in financial engineering (functional pearl). SIGPLAN Not. **35**(9), 280–292 (2000)
32. Schmidt, D.A.: Natural-semantics-based abstract interpretation (preliminary version). In: Mycroft, A. (ed.) SAS 1995. LNCS, vol. 983, pp. 1–18. Springer, Heidelberg (1995). https://doi.org/10.1007/3-540-60360-3_28
33. Lamela Seijas, P., Thompson, S.: Marlowe: financial contracts on blockchain. In: Margaria, T., Steffen, B. (eds.) ISoLA 2018. LNCS, vol. 11247, pp. 356–375. Springer, Cham (2018). https://doi.org/10.1007/978-3-030-03427-6_27

Author Index

Printed in the United States
By Bookmasters